DENTAL BIOMATERIALS

(Principles and Applications)

Zohaib Khurshid
Zeeshan Sheikh

©

Paramount Books (Pvt.) Limited

Karachi | Lahore | Islamabad | Faisalabad | Peshawar | Abbottabad | Hyderabad

Dental Biomaterials

by

Zohaib Khurshid

Zeeshan Sheikh

Medical knowledge is constantly changing. As new information becomes available, changes in treatment, procedures, equipment and the use of drugs become necessary. The editors, contributors and the publishers have, as far as it is possible, taken care to ensure that the information given in this text is accurate and up-to-date. However, readers are strongly advised to confirm that the information, especially with regard to drug usage, complies with the latest legislation and standards of practice.

Second Edition 2014

Paramount Books (Pvt.) Limited

152/O, Block-2, P.E.C.H.S., Karachi-75400, Pakistan
Tel: 34310030, Fax: 34553772, E-mail: paramount@cyber.net.pk
Website: www.paramountbooks.com.pk

ISBN: 978-969-494-960-4
Printed in Pakistan.

Dedicated to

My Grandfather Dr. Munawar Alvi
My Parents
And
Altamash Institute of Dental Medicine

CONTENTS

PREFACE

Dentists will be authorized and legalized end-users of dental materials, both as students and after graduation. During undergraduate studies, it is essential that dental materials should be taught so as to enhance understanding of their properties and clinical uses. There are still a few challenges in this respect; not all the dental schools have dental biomaterials science an independent status in the curriculum. In too many cases the facilitation is provided by colleagues lacking commitment. Clinical procedures of operative dentistry may be thoroughly taught but little attention is paid to the actual material properties. It may remain unexplained what is then so special regarding certain materials that they are more often used clinically. What does actually happen during setting of say restorative filling materials and luting cements? We never should overlook the significance of adhesion, its applications and understanding in contemporary dentistry.

In the retail market we have a plethora of dental textbooks with varying contents and perspectives. All of them certainly serve well today. For a dental educator one of the problems is selecting the most appropriate book to serve in dental facilitation. Should it cover all basic sciences behind? Hardly. Would it need delve into the physio-chemical theories? I doubt - as we may leave such aspects for post-graduate levels. Would we then need some fresh faces to contribute for a totally new textbook in dental biomaterials? I believe a justified answer is: yes, this is needed.

I was both surprised and pleased when Lecturer Dr Zohaib Khursid Sultan (of Fatima Jinnah Dental College, Karachi, Pakistan) contacted me. For those who don't know, he has already earned a feather to his cap by having published a dental textbook "Dental Biomaterials – Principles and Applications", 1st edition, in 2010. He invited me to contribute a chapter on dental silver amalgam to his textbook "Dental Biomaterials – Principles and Applications"- 2nd edition. This kind invitation I accepted with great content. In addition, the two editors of this book, Dr. Zohaib and Dr. Zeeshan Sheikh, have invited a team of contributors representing a dynamic, expanding generation of tomorrow's dentists from Pakistan, Canada, Saudi-Arabia and UK. This said, we could see and conclude from the table of contents of this book that it provides the undergraduate readers with sufficient basics of dental biomaterials.

After being introduced to dental materials and dental biomaterials, readers of "Dental Biomaterials – Principles and Applications" may gain a fresh insight of biomaterials in implant dentistry, endodontics, nanomaterials in dentistry, dental silver amalgam, resin composites, dental cements and bone replacement materials. Procedures at dental laboratories and clinics are sufficiently covered as well as dental polymeric, metallic and ceramic materials.

I feel privileged to write this preface to the book Dr. Zohaib Khurshid and Dr. Zeeshan Sheikh have successfully edited. The outcome of a laborious team of dental professionals and experts has now materialized. Let me conclude by saying that Dr. Zohaib and Dr. Zeeshan are to be congratulated with their contributing team for this cornerstone outcome in dental education and modern learning. I am convinced that you, the reader, will agree with me, and I am confident that this book will find wide use not only in Asia but globally.

October 17, 2013, Hong Kong, PR China

Dr. Jukka Pekka MATINLINNA 馬裕祺 博士

Assoc. Professor in Dental Materials Science

Visiting Professor, King Saud University, College of Applied Medical Sciences, Riyadh, Saudi-Arabia

Visiting Professor, Universitas Gadjah Mada, Faculty of Dentistry, Yogyakarta, Indonesia

The University of Hong Kong

Faculty of Dentistry

Dental Materials Science

HONG KONG

ACKNOWLEDGEMENT

The authors express their thanks to the following individuals for their contributions:

To our professors and mentors, who imparted their knowledge and wisdom, enabling us to undertake this project of publishing a book. To the contributing authors who provided us with their expertise and chapters. Their acceptance of our suggestions and editing has been very much appreciated. The dental students, who appreciated the first edition of this book and encouraged us to move forward and strive to make the second edition better, we thank them for their ongoing cooperation and dedication to this project in the midst of their busy schedules. We thank all of the above for their ongoing cooperation and dedication to this project in the midst of their busy schedules. And lastly, to the team at Paramount publications.

EDITORS

Dr Zohaib Khurshid
B.D.S, C-Implant, C-Nano-Tech
Lecturer in Dental Biomaterials
Altamash Institute of Dental Sciences
MPhil Student Biomaterials
University of Birmingham
UK

Dr. Mohammad Zeeshan Azam Sheikh
BDS, Dip.DH, MSc, PhD (candidate)
Associate Professor. Department of Material Sciences and Preclinical Dentistry
Associate Professor. Department of Oral Anatomy
Altamash Institute of Dental Medicine, Karachi, Pakistan
PhD (candidate).
Faculty of Dentistry,
McGill University
Canada

CO-EDITORS

Dr. Sana Shahab
B.D.S, C-Implant
Former Lecturer in Dental Physiology Department
Fatima Jinnah Dental College
MSc (candidate) Dental Biomaterials
University of Sheffield
UK

Dr. Mustafa Naseem
B.D.S, MDPH University of Sheffield
Assistant Professor
Department of Community Dentistry
Dr. Ziauddin Dental College
Karachi
Pakistan

ADVISORS

Prof. Dr. Muhammad Altamash
President/Principal
Altamash Institute of Dental Medicine
Karachi, Pakistan

Prof. Dr Ashraf Ali Meo
Chairman of Materials Department
NED University of Engineering & Technology,
Karachi Pakistan

Prof. Waleed Rida Murshid
Dean of College of Dentistry,
Taibah University
Al-Madinah Al-Munawarrah,
Kingdom of Saudi Arabia

Dr. Khalid bin Hidayatullah Alsamdani
Assistant Professor and Head of Restorative Dentistry
College of Dentistry, Taibah University
Al-Madinah Al-Munawarrah,
Kingdom of Saudi Arabia

Dr Giath Gazal
Assistant Professor and Head of Oral and Maxillofacial Surgery
College of Dentistry, Taibah University
Al-Madinah Al-Munawarrah,
Kingdom of Saudi Arabia

Dr Wamiq Musheer Fareed
Senior Lecturer Oral and Maxillofacial Surgery
College of Dentistry, Taibah University
Al-Madinah Al-Munawarrah,
Kingdom of Saudi Arabia

Dr. Muhammad Adeel Mudasser
Senior Registrar
Orthodontics Department
Jinnah Medical & Dental College
Karachi, Pakistan

Dr. Muhammad Sohail Zafar
PhD; MSc; BSc; BDS
Assistant Professor (Dental Biomaterials)
College of Dentistry, Taibah University
Al-Madinah Al-Munawarrah,
Kingdom of Saudi Arabia

CONTRIBUTORS

Dr. Jukka Pekka Matinlinna
Assoc. Professor Dental Materials Science
The University of Hong Kong,
Faculty of Dentistry,
Hong Kong SAR, PR China
Undergraduate Program Director
Postgraduate Program Director
Docent, Adjunct Professor, PD (Helsinki, Finland) in Biomaterials Science
Docent, Adjunct Professor,
PD (Turku, Finland) Dental Biomaterials
Docent, Adjunct Professor, PD (Turku, Finland) Biomaterials Chemistry (School of Chemistry)
Visiting Professor, King Saud University, College of Applied Medical Sciences, Riyadh, Saudi-Arabia
Visiting Professor, Universitas Gadjah Mada, Faculty of Dentistry,
Yogyakarta, Indonesia

Eng. Faaz Butt
Lecturer, Materials & Metallurgy
NED University, Karachi
Pakistan

Dr. Shariq Najeeb
BDS, MSc Dental Biomaterials (Student)
University Sheffield
UK

Dr. Samina Khan
BDS, MSc Advanced General Dentistry (Student)
University of Birmingham
UK

Dr. Fahad Siddique
BDS, MSc Oral Health sciences (Student)
University of McGill
Canada

Dr. Adeel Mudasser
BDS, FCPS-I (Orthodontics)
Senior Registrar Orthodontics Department
Jinnah Medical and Dental College
Karachi
Pakistan

Dr. Vesna Miletic
Assistant Professor
Department of Restorative Odontology and Endodontic
School of Dental Medicine
University of Belgrade.
Post-doctoral research at the University of Edinburgh and KU Leuven (Belgium).

Dr. Muhammad Sohail Zafar
PhD; MSc; BSc; BDS
Assistant Professor (Dental Biomaterials) College of Dentistry,
Taibah University
Al-Madinah Al-Munawarrah
Kingdom of Saudi Arabia

Dr. Ahad Shahid Ahmed
BDS, MSc (candidate)
Department of Dentistry, Jewish General Hospital
Faculty of Dentistry, McGill University
Montreal, QC,
Canada

Chapter

2

CHARACTERIZATION OF BIOMATERIALS IN RELATION TO DENTISTRY

Eng. Faaz Butt & Dr. Zohaib

INTRODUCTION

- Dental biomaterials are subjected to a very hostile environment, in which pH, salivary flow and mechanical loading fluctuate constantly and often rapidly. These challenges require substantial research and development to provide products for the clinician. Much of this is possible through the application of fundamental concepts of material sciences.
- The understanding of properties of polymer ceramics, and metal is crucial to their selection and design for dental restorations. It is important to know the comparative values of properties of different restorative material; it is also essential to know quality of the supporting and investing hard and soft tissue.
- The material properties are illustrated in (Fig. 2.1.)

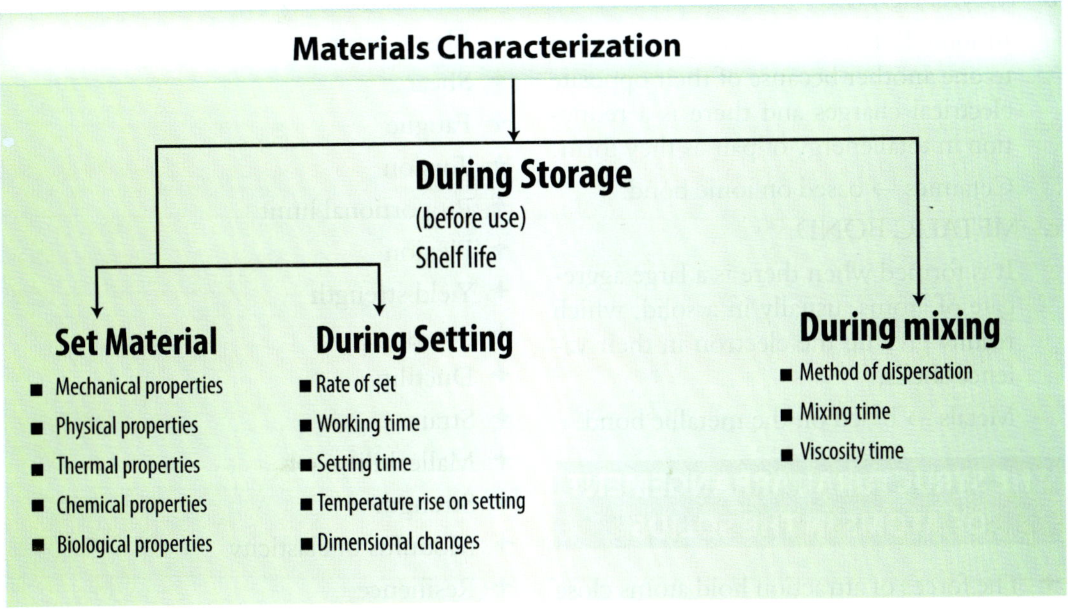

Fig: 2.1. Description of Mechanical Properties.

ATOMIC BUILDING BLOCKS

- All materials are built up from atoms and molecules, so it is not surprising that there is a close relationship between the atomic basis of a material and its properties.
- Important in this context are nature of the atoms and the ways in which they are arranged.
- When two atoms are bought together they may link to form a molecule with the bonding called primary bond.

TYPES OF PRIMARY BOND

There are three types of primary bonds:

a. COVALENT BOND:

The covalent bond is the simplest and strongest bond. It forms when atoms share their electrons so that each electron shell achieves an inert gas structure.

Molecular solids → based on the covalent and secondary bonds, including an important group of

materials known as polymer.

b. IONIC BOND:

In ionic bonding two ions are attracted to one another because of their opposite electrical charges and there is a reduction in total energy of pair as they form.

Ceramics → based on ionic bond.

c. METALIC BOND:

It is formed when there is a large aggregate of atoms, usually in a solid, which readily give up the electron in their valence shells.

Metals → based on the metallic bond.

THE STRUCTURAL ARRANGEMENT OF ATOMS IN THE SOLIDS

- The forces of attraction hold atoms close together, the mutual repulsion of nuclei means that equilibrium spacing is attracted at which these forces balance.
- An external force is needed to move the atoms close together or further apart. This inter atomic spacing is the configuration of minimum energy, and in order to achieve this there is a tendency for the atoms to adopt a regular close-packed arrangement.
- When atoms are arranged like this the material is said to be crystalline.
- Any solid in which there is no symmetry of the atoms is said to be amorphous.

PHYSICAL PROPERTIES

- Co-efficient of thermal expansion
- Thermal conductivity/diffusivity
- Wettability
- Adhesion
- Optical properties

MECHANICAL PROPERTIES

- Compression
- Hardness
- Tension
- Elastic limit
- Shear
- Fatigue
- Torsion
- Proportional limit
- Flexion
- Yield strength
- Stress
- Ductility
- Strain
- Malleability
- Strength
- Modulus of elasticity
- Resilience
- Viscoelasticity

CHEMICAL PROPERTIES

- Solubility and erosion
- Leaching
- Galvanic Pain
- Corrosion
- Sorption
- Tarnish

BIOLOGICAL PROPERTIES

- Non – irritant
- Non – toxic
- Non – carcinogenic
- Non – allergic
- Not harm the pulp when used as filling materials

MECHANICAL PROPERTIES

1. STRESS

- Internal force between the body which tends to protect the body from the outside force.
- The force per unit area in a body which resists an external force.
- Classified according to direction:
  a. Compressive Stress – a force under a load that tends to shorten or flatten the body.
  b. Tensile – force that can resist elongation or stretching of body.
  c. Shear – force that can resist a twisting motion: sliding of one portion of a body over another.
  d. Complex – combination of compressive, tensile and shear.

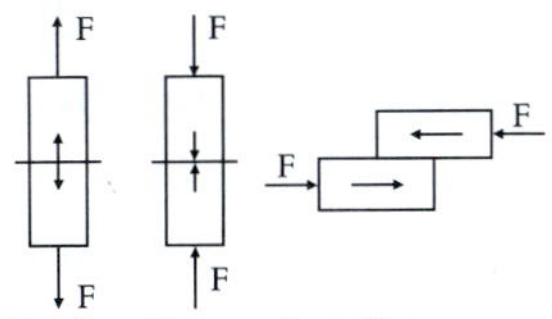

Fig: 2.2. Illustrtion showing different directions of forces.

2. STRAIN

- The applications of an external force to a body or test specimen result in a change in dimension of that body.
- The numerical value of stain is given by the expression:

  $$\text{Strain} = \frac{\text{Change in length}}{\text{Original length}}$$

- It is a measure of the fractional change in length caused by the applied force.
- It is a dimension less quantity.
- It may be elastic or plastic or a combination of both.

a. Elastic Strain

deformation that is recovered upon removal of an externally applied force.

b. Plastic Strain

deformation that is not recoverable when the externally applied force is removed.

3. ELASTIC LIMIT

- The greatest stress to which a material can be subjected to such that it will return to its original dimension when the force are released.

4. FLEXIBILITY

- Ability of the material to be twisted or contoured in any desired form without breaking.

5. RESILIENCE/SPRINGINGNESS

- Amount of energy absorbed by a structure when it is stressed not to exceed its proportional limit.

6. STRENGTH

- It is the maximal stress required to fracture a structure.

- It has three types;

a. Tensile strength
b. Compressive strength
c. Shear strength

7. TOUGHNESS

- Being difficult to break.
- Energy required to fracturing a material.

8. BRITTLENESS

- A material which fractures immediately after its proportional limit is crossed is known as a brittle material.

9. DUCTILITY

- The ability of a material to withstand permanent deformation under a tensile load without rupture.

10. MALLEABILITY

- The ability of a material to be hammered or pressed to thin sheets without undergoing fracture.

11. HARDNESS

- Resistance to penetration when indented by a hard substance.
- There are numerous factors which influence the hardness of a material such as strength, proportional limit, ductility, malleability. Etc.
- There are many surface hardness tests. The tests more frequently used are:
  a. Brinell hardness number (BHN).
  b. Rockwell Hardness Number (RHN).
  c. Vickers Hardness Test (VHT).
  d. Knoop Hardness Test (KHT). (Fig: 2.3)

Fig: 2.3. Microhardness Testing Machine.

CHEMICAL PROPERTIES

INTRODUCTION

- The longevity of dental materials depends very highly on the chemical properties. The material should:
  - Not corrode
  - Not dissolve
  - Not leach out
  - Not erode

1. SOLUBILITY

"Is simply a measurement of the extent to which it will dissolve in a given fluid, for example water or saliva".

2. EROSION

"Is a process which combines the chemical process of dissolution with a mild mechanical action".

Material Sciences

"Damaged produced by the impingement of particles on an object".

Dentistry

"The destruction of natural hard tissues by acids (either occurring naturally or present in food/drinks) and mild mechanical actions.

3. LEACHING OF CONSTITUENTS

"Constituents of the materials may be lost into the oral fluids by a diffusion process commonly referred to as Leaching".

- **Consequences**
  - Change in material properties
  - leaching of toxic & irritants
- **Mechanisim o f Leaching**
  - *By Ion exchange* → there is a good chance that fluoride ions will be replaced by another anion (e.g. hydroxyl) and the integrity of the materials is maintained.
  - *By washout* → Is likely to be accompanied by gradual degradation.

4. DEGRADATION OF POLYMER

A. Water Absorption

- Represents the amount of water absorbed on the surface and absorbed into the body of material during its fabrication or when restoration is in service.
- Example acrylic denture absorbs water at a high degree
  - Warpage
  - Dimensional changes

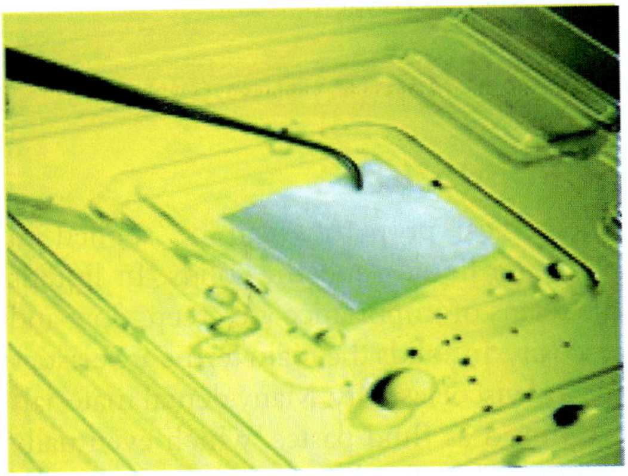

Fig: 2.4. Showing Polymer Membrane.

B. Bond Rupture

- The degradation of polymer by the breakdown of covalent bond is known as *Scission.*
- Bond rupture can be due to:
  - Radiation
  - Heat
  - Chemical attack
- There are situations in which the breakdown of the polymer can work to our advantage.(e.g. Biodegradable polymer such as Suture and Periodontal Membranes). (Fig 2.4)

5. DEGRADATION OF CERAMIC

- Ceramic is very resistant to electrochemical corrosion but is still susceptible to chemical corrosion.
- For example, glass is made from SiO2 and Na_2O (soda) will rapidly dissolve in water and CaO (lime) is added to reduce its susceptibility to dissolution.
- Chemical interaction between the ceramic and the environment at the crack tip can have a profound effect on the rate of crack growth.
- Water or water at a crack tip can react with the Si-O-Si bond at the tip of the crack in a silica-based glass, forming hydroxides and this process is known as ***Static Fatigue***.

6. DEGRADATION OF METALS

- By two processes:
  - Corrosion
  - Tarnish

A. CORROSION

- Defined as a *"chemical or electrochemical process in which solid is attacked by an environmental agent resulting in partial or complete disintegration (loss of e) of metal".*

- Metals undergo electro/chemical reaction forming corrosion products.
- High noble alloys are chemically stable, so do not undergo corrosion.
- May lead to passivation.
- Gold resists chemical attacks. Makes the material weak
- May seal margins. Zinc can be used to minimize corrosion.

TYPES OF CORROSION

- GALVANIC CORROSION
- PITTING CORROSION
- STRESS CORROSION

I. Static Corrosion

"It is the degradation due to mechanical stress and a corrosive environment exhibited by cracking".

II. Pitting Corrosion

"Localized corrosion on surface of iron which was protected by oxide layer. In presence of Cl the layer breaks and allows corrosion of underlying metal".

III. Galvanism

- It is the accelerated attack on metal when electrochemically dissimilar metals are in electric contact within a liquid.
- The two dissimilar metals with differing electrode potentials come in contact in presence of saliva that acts as the electrolyte.
- A passage of current passes through the pulp and pain is felt by the patient.
- May occur between amalgam and gold.
- Anode is the site of oxidation and positive ions are formed
- Cathode is the site of reduction reaction where consumption of ions occurs.

CONSEQUENCES OF CORROSION

- Pain due to flow of the galvanic current.
- Metallic taste due to release of ions
- Detoriation of appearance and its mechanical properties.
- Formation of corrosive products.

METHOD TO REDUCE CORROSION

- Homogeneous distribution of metal atoms in the alloy decreases the tendency for corrosion to occur.
- Coating iron with tin, because tin is stable and it protects the metal.
- To eliminate galvanic shock coat the metallic restoration with varnish. This layer acts as an insulator.

B. TARNISH

- Tarnish is a process by *which a metal surface is dulled or discolored due to a formation of oxide layer on the surface (due to oxidation)*
- It is the product of chemical reactions between metals and non-metals such as oxygen.

RHEOLOGICAL PROPERTIES

INTRODUCTION

Rheological properties can be applied in both, the liquids and the solids. In liquids the terms of importance are creep, flow and viscosity. In solids the main terms are elasticity and viscoelasticity. Many dental materials are mixed as fluid pastes, which eventually solidify. The mixed pastes are adapted to the required shape. The setting of that material involves a change in viscosity. ***Rheology*** is *the* *science of the study of flow and deformation of the matter".*

RHEOLOGICAL PROPERTIES

- Viscosity
- Creep
- Flow
- Viscoelasticity
- Elasticity
- Thixotrophy

1. VISCOSITY

"Is resistance to flow"

- Therefore, a liquid with a high viscosity is thick and has a high resistance to flow and a liquid with a low viscosity is thin and has a low resistance to flow.
- Viscosity is caused by the internal frictional forces in the liquid and is measured as shear stress divided by shear strain rate.
- Units of measurement are centipoises.

a. Shear Rate

"Is a function of flow rate".

b. Shear Stress

"It is a pressure required for flow"

Examples

- Dental materials like cements and impression materials change from liquid to solid i0n the mouth.
- Gypsum products used in making models and casts transform from slurry material to solid.
- Waxes and resins are super-cooled liquids.

Viscosity of Liquids Depend on

- Nature of the substance
- Temperature
- Pressure (higher pressure causes viscosity to decrease)

2. FLOW

- Flow is a large amount of deformation produced more rapidly under a smaller force.
- The best example of flow is of wax.

3. ELASTICITY

- Elasticity is a property of a material to come back to its original position after the removal of applied force without any amount of permanent dimensional changes.
- When a material undergoes full elastic recovery after the removal of applied force is known as its elasticity.

4. VISCOELASTICIY

- When the recovery takes place slowly, or a degree of permanent deformation remains.
- Or when stress is removed from a body and it comes back slowly into its original shape with a slight deformation.

5. CREEP

- Slow deformation under constant stress is Creep.
- It is a time dependant plastic strain of a material under a static or constant load.
- The amount of creep depends on the materials, temperature, load and the time till which the load is applied.
- Creep is a degree of small deformation under a large stress over a long time period.

- Creep may lead to deformation of dental restorations.
- Creep may also lead to an unacceptable fit of a partial denture. (Fig: 2.5)

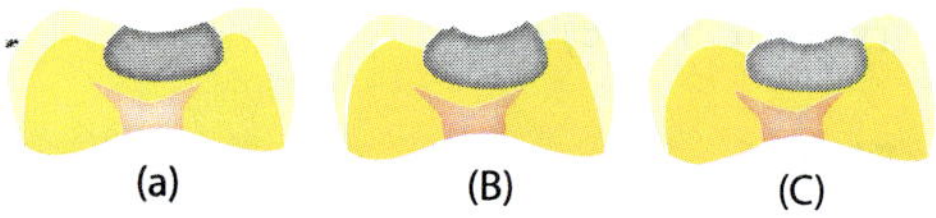

Fig: 2.5. Showing plastic deformation of dental amalgam.

6. THIXOTROPY

- It is defined as "Any fluid shows a time-dependent change in viscosity".
- Thixotropic materials become liquid and less viscous under repeated application of pressure.
- *Example* is some impression materials (Gels and hydrocolloids).Material does not flow out of the tray till it is placed over teeth and pressure is applied.

TYPES OF FLUIDS & PASTE

- There are three types of fluid.

A. Newtonian (ideal) Liquids

- These are the liquids with a constant viscosity regardless of shear rate.
- *Examples* include water and newly mixed zinc phosphate cement.

B. Pseudo plastic (shear-thinning) Liquids

- Show a decrease in viscosity with an increase in shear rate.
- *Examples* include the polycarboxylate cements and non-water mixed glass ionomer cements.

C. Dilatants (shear-thickening) Liquids

- Show an increase in viscosity with an increase in shear rate.
- *Examples* include Traditional (conventional) resin composites.

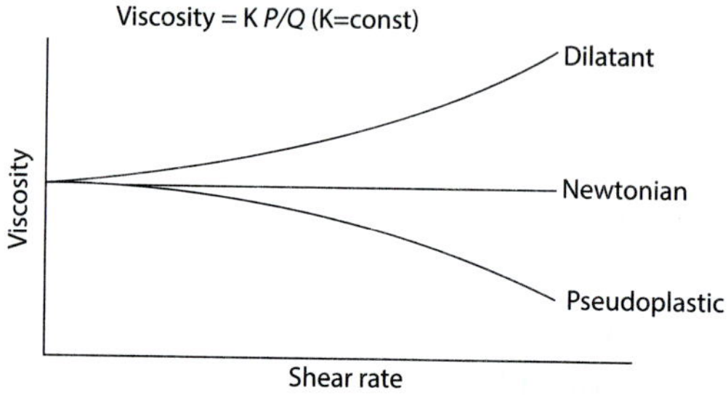

Materials with

Low viscosity---low pressure and high flow.

High viscosity----high pressure and small rate of flow.

CLINICAL APPLICATIONS OF RHEOLOGY

- The aqueous and non-aqueous elastomeric impression materials, being viscoelastic, should be removed from the mouth with a snap to minimize permanent deformation.
- Ideally, we want cements and light-body (syringe) impression materials to be Pseudoplastic so that with increasing shear strain rate, they exhibit a decrease in viscosity.

BIOLOGICAL PROPERTIES OF DENTAL MATERIALS

Should be harmless to the pulp and the soft tissues.

- No toxic substance that can be absorbed into the circulatory system to cause toxic response.
- Free of sensitivity agents to cause an allergic response.
- No carcinogenic potential.

REFERENCES

1. Kenneth Anusavice (2012), Phillips' *Science of Dental Materials, (12th Edition,)* Saunder
2. Ronald Sakaguchi & John M.Power(2011), *Craig's Restorative Dental Materials, (13th Edition,)* Mosby
3. Richard Van Noort (2007), *Introduction to Dental Materials*, (3rd ed,) Mosby Ltd., China
4. B W Darvell (2009), *Materials science for Dentistry (9th edition)*,Woodhead Publishing Limited, UK.
5. John M. Power & John C.wataha(2012), *Dental Materials Properties and Manipulation, (10th Edition,) Elsevier*, India
6. Smith, William F. Hashemi, Javad (2006), *Foundations of Materials Science and Engineering* (4th ed.), McGraw-Hill, ISBN 0-07-295358-6
7. Richard Curtis & Timothy Watson(2008), *Dental Biomaterials Imaging, Testing and Modelling*, Woodhead Publishing in Materials, North America
8. Gottfried Schmalz & Dorthe Arenholt-bindslev(2009), *Biocompatibility of Dental Materials*, Springer, Germany

Chapter 3

GYPSUM PRODUCTS IN DENTISTRY

Dr. Mustafa

INTRODUCTION

Gypsum is a mineral mined in various parts of the world and is also produced as a byproduct of flue gas desulfurization in some of the coal-fired electric power plants. It is white powdery mineral with the chemical name calcium sulphate dihydrate ($CaSO_4.2H_2O$). Its products used in dentistry are based on calcium sulphate hemihydrates ($CaSO_4. H_2O$). Various crystalline forms of gypsum such as selenite and alabaster exist in nature. (Fig: 3.1)

Fig: 3.1. Showing crystal form of gypsum.

Dental plaster, dental stone, high-strength dental stone and casting investment constitute gypsum products. They are *supplied as* hemihydrates powder that is produced by heating ground gypsum particles. When mixed with water the mixture reverts back to gypsum.

A mixture of plaster (gypsum product), lime and water is used in joining the stone blocks of ancient Egypt's pyramids. Gypsum and gypsum products are used today for many applications including building construction, soil conditioning, food additives, pharmaceutical uses, medical devices and dental applications. Main uses in dentistry include casts on models, dies and investments.

DENTAL CAST

It is dimensionally accurate positive replica of the teeth and the surrounding oral structures made by producing impression [negative replica] with a durable hard material. (Fig: 3.2)

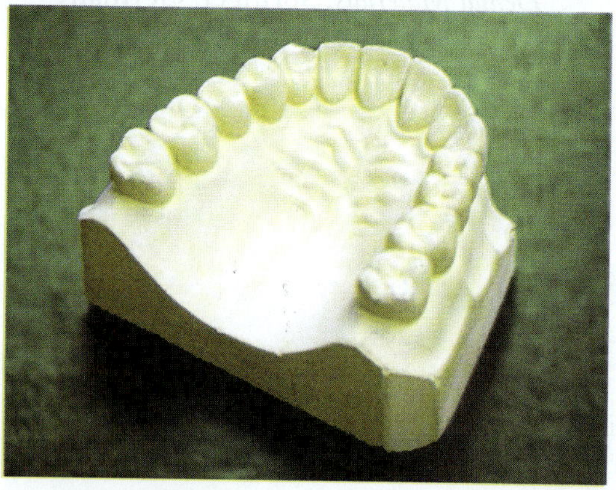

Fig: 3.2. Dental cast.

REQUIREMENTS OF DENTAL CAST MATERIAL

a. Should have good dimensional accuracy.
b. Should have adequate mechanical properties.
c. Should have good dimensional stability after setting.
d. Should be fluid at the time of pouring so that it gives fine details.
e. Should be compatible with all the materials with which it comes in contact.
f. Should give good color contrast.
g. Should not be expensive.
h. Should be easy to manipulate.

CLASSIFICATION OF DENTAL GYPSUM

Type 1	Dental Plaster	impression
Type 2	Dental Plaster	model
Type 3	Dental Stone	die, model
Type 4	Dental Stone	die,high strength, low expansion
Type 5	Dental Stone	die, high strength, and high expansion.

COMPOSITION

On heating during manufacturing process, gypsum loses 1.5 moles water of crystallization out of 2 moles and is construed into the hemihydrates form of $CaSO_4$.

Gypsum → Gypsum product + water

$$2CaSO_4.2H_2O \rightarrow (CaSO_4)_2.H_2O + 3H_2O$$

Calcium sulphate dihydrate | Calcium sulphate hemihydrate

Application of gypsum product in density involves the reverses of the above reaction.

$$(CaSO_4)_2.H_2O + 3H_2O \rightarrow 2CaSO_4.2H_2O$$

BASIC REACTION IN MATERIAL SCIENCES

Gypsum products are all manufactured by the dehydration of the dihydrate using various processes but they all have common underline chemistry.

1. DEHYDRATION

When gypsum is heated, dehydration of the dihydrate occurs in two distinct stages. The fairly rapid loss of three quarters of water of crystallization at about 130°C results in the formation of hemihydrates. Further complete dehydration occurs at higher temperatures resulting in the formation of anhydrites. The orthorhombic form is obtained by heating above 200°C. It is so slow in reacting with water that it is known as dead burnt plaster (it does not form a usual setting mixture with water).

$$CaSO4.2H2O \xrightarrow{110\text{-}130\ ^{\circ}C} (CaSO_4)2.H_2O \xrightarrow{130\text{-}200\ ^{\circ}C} CaSO_4 \xrightarrow{200\text{-}1000\ ^{\circ}C} CaSO_4$$

gypsum | Cacium sulfate hemihydrates alpha/beta | Hexagonal anhydrite | Orthorhombic anhydrite

2. REHYDRATION

When the dehydration product reacts with water it gives the same reaction product (dihydrate) but the rates are considerably different. Rehydration involves a simple mechanism in which the hemihydrate readily dissolves in water at low temperature, but the solution becomes supersaturated with respect to dihydrate before it is saturated with hemihydrate. As a result dihydrate may commence to precipitate from the solution by the formation of the needle-like crystals. This continuous precipitation then prevents the solution from becoming saturated with hemihydrate, which therefore continue to dissolve. The process continues untill all the hemihydratyes are consumed.

MANUFACTURING OF GYPSUM PRODUCTS

The process of heating gypsum for manufacturing plaster is called calcination (see Fig. 3.3).

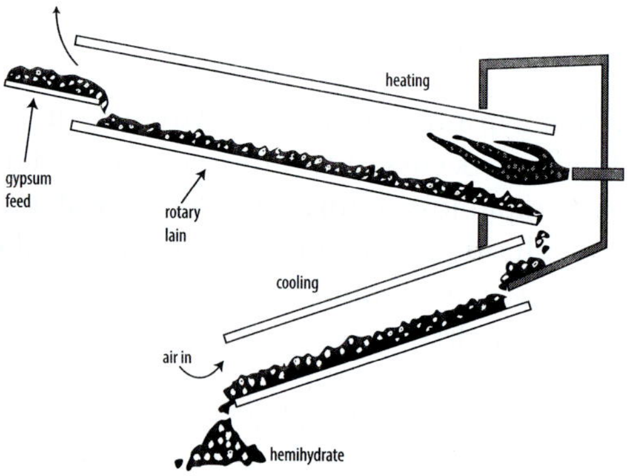

Fig: 3.3 The outline design of rotary kiln for the production of Calcium Sulphate Hemihdrate plaster of paris.

The amount of mixing water required for a given fluidity varies with the nature of hemihydrate powder. The particles of plaster are very porous, large and irregular. Due to this irregularity in shape the particles do not pack together very well and requires high gauging water. Whereas dental stone require less guaging water as the particles are more regular and very smooth.

COMPARISON BETWEEN DENTAL PLASTER AND DENTAL STONE

DENTAL PLASTER
✦ Type I, II.
✦ Calcined Ca-sulphate hemihydrates.
✦ Produced by dry calcinations.
✦ Hemihydrate particles are large.
✦ Particles are irregular in shape and size.
✦ Plaster particles are porous.
✦ They are weaker in strength.
✦ Require more water for mixing.
✦ Poor packing ability.
✦ High surface free energy.
✦ Crystal habit that of hemihydrates.
✦ Low apparent density.
✦ Use as modeling and impression material.
DENTAL STONE
✦ Type III, IV and V.
✦ Autoclaved Ca-sulphate hemihydrates.
✦ Produced by wet calcinations.
✦ Hemihydrate particles are small.
✦ Particles are regular in shape and size.
✦ Plaster particles are virtually non porous.
✦ They are stronger in strength.
✦ Require less water for mixing.
✦ Better packing ability.
✦ Low surface free energy.
✦ Crystal habit that of hexagonal.
✦ High apparent density.
✦ Use as model and die material.

DEHYDRATION BY HEAT OR OTHER	FORMULATION			
Mineral	→	Plaster	→	Model plaster (lab plaster) Gypsum
Hydrocal	→	Dental stone		
Densite	→	High-strength dental stone		

SETTING OF GYPSUM PRODUCT

- The reaction between gypsum product and water produces solid gypsum, and the heat evolved in the exothermic reaction is equal to the heat used for calcination.
- The set material never attain 100% conversion unless they are exposed to high humidity for a long time.
- Unreacted hemihydrates remain in the material.
- There are three theories of gypsum setting:

1. COLLOIDAL THEORY

- It proposes that when powder is mixed with water the hemihydrates enter into colloidal state thorough sol-gel mechanisms.
- In the solution state, hemihydrates particles are hydrated to form dihydrate, thereby entering into the active state.
- As the measured amount of water is consumed, the mass is converted into the solid gel.

2. HYDRATION THEORY

This theory suggests that rehydrated plaster particles unite through hydrogen bonding with sulphate group to form the set material.

3. DISSOLUTION PRECIPITATION THEORY

a. This is the most widely accepted theory by Louis Chatelier in 1885. This theory is based on dissolution of plaster and instant recrystallization of gypsum, followed by interlocking of the crystals to form the set product.

b. This reaction is possible because the solubility of hemihydrates in water is four times greater than that of dihydrate near room temperature. The setting reaction occurs as follows;

- When the hemihydrate is mixed with water, a suspension is formed that is fluid and workable.
- The hemihydrates dissolve until a saturated solution of Ca_2 and SO_4 is formed.
- This saturated hemihydrates solution is supersaturated with respect to the solubility of dihydrate; precipitation of dihydrate occurs.
- As the dihydrate precipitates, hemihydrate continues to dissolve. They process as either new crystals are formed or further growth occurs on the crystals already present until no further dihydrate can precipitate out of solution.

$(CaSO_4)_2.H_2O + 3H_2O \rightarrow$

Calcium sulphate calcium sulphate

$2CaSO_4.2H_2O$ + Unreacted $(CaSO_4)_2.H_2O$ + heat

Hemihydrates

dihydrate

Depending on the methods of calcinations different forms of hemihydrates are formed. These include:

a. Dental plaster or beta hemihydrate.
b. Dental stone or alpha hemihydrates/hydrocal.
c. Improved stone or high strength stone/densite.

$$CaSo_4.\ 2H_2O \xrightarrow{\textbf{heat}} CaSo_4.\ ½\,H_2O$$

100 – 130°C (B-hemihydrates)

A. PLASTER OF PARIS (β-Hemihydrates)

1. Gypsum is ground and heated in an open kettle at a temperature of 100 to 130°C.

2. A crystalline form of hemihydrates is formed known as β hemihydrates.
3. It has very poor crystalline properties because of the lack of the medium through which the ions could diffuse to form good crystals.
4. The particles are irregular in shape and are porous.
5. Water / powder ratio is 0.5 i.e. 50/100 requires more gauging water.

Fig: 3.4 Hemihydrate (Plaster of Paris).

B. DENTAL STONE (α Hemihydrates)

1. Gypsum is calcined under steam pressure in an autoclave at a temperature of 120 to 130°C at 17 lbs/sq. inch for 5 to 7 hours. The resultant product is known as dental stone or α hemihydrates, also known as artificial stone or hydrocal.
2. The particles are more uniform, prismatic in shape and dense. (Fig: 3.5)
3. Requires much less gauging water, thus the product obtained is much stronger and harder than beta-hemihydrates.

Fig: 3.5. Dental Stone (Fine Particles).

C. HIGH STRENGTH STONE/DENSITE

1. Densite is the densest of the raw materials.
2. It is produced by boiling gypsum in a 30% solution of $CaCl_2$ after which the chloride is washed away with hot water and the material is ground to the desired fineness.
3. Type 4 and type 5 high-strength dental stones are manufactured with high density raw material.
4. The hemihydrates crystals are produced which are least porous than other types.

MANIPULATION OF DENTAL GYPSUM & ITS SETTING CHARACTERISTICS

STEPS OF MANIPULATION

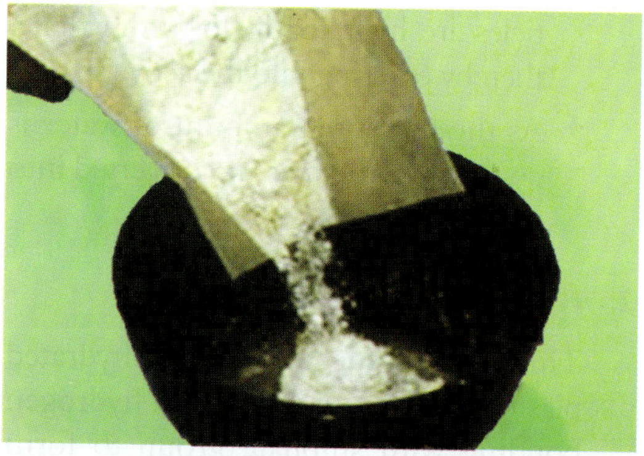

Fig: 3.6. Step 1: Water/Powder Ratio.

Fig: 3.6. Step 2: Trapping for air bubbles removal.

Fig: 3.6. Step 3: Mixing.

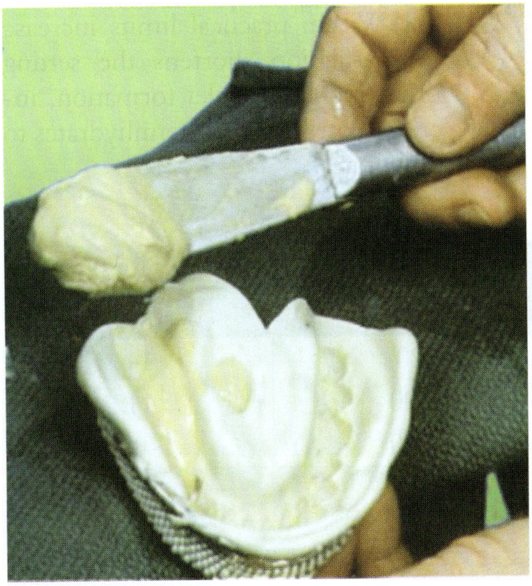

Fig: 3.6. Step 4: Pouring in Impression.

a. The "water powder ratio" is very important because it affects setting, strength and setting expansion.

b. The main differences among plaster, stone and high strength stone are the size, shape and porosity of the calcium sulphate hemihydrates crystals.

c. These differences influence the amount of excess water required for workable mixing.

d. Increasing the water powder ratio produces thinner mixture that takes longer time to set.

e. When a gypsum product is mixed with a lower w/p ratio the mixed mass is thicker and more difficult to manipulate. In this case the set material is usually stronger.

f. W/P ratio also affects the setting expansion.

g. Thicker mix → ↑ Expansion.

Table 3.1 shows ISO standardized water powder ratio.

MATERIAL	WATER	POWDER	W/P RATIO
Amount	(ml)	(g)	(ml/g)
Plaster of Paris	50-60	100	0.55
Dental Stone	20-35	100	0.30

4. SOLUBILITY

The setting reaction of water with calcium sulphate hemihydrates to form calcium sulphate dihydrate is caused by the difference in solubility between these two components. Calcium sulphate dihydrate is less soluble than hemihydrates form. When hemihydrates dissolve in water, the dihydrate having low solubility is supersaturated and precipitates out of solution from point of nucleation in the form of needle like crystals.

Table: 3.2: Solubility of calcium sulphate hemihydrates and calcium sulphate dihydrate.

TEMPERATURE (°C)	CALCIUM SULPHATE HEMIHYDRATES (G/100 G WATER)	CALCIUM SULPHATE DIHYDRATE (G/100 G WATER)
20	0.90	0.200
25	0.80	0.205
30	0.72	0.209
40	0.61	0.210
50	0.50	0.205
100	0.17	0.170

1. VOLUMETRIC CONTRACTION

- Theoretically calcium sulphate hemihydrates should contract volumetrically during setting process but the experiments have determined that all gypsum products expand linearly during setting.
- When 145.15g of calcium sulphate hemihydrates react with 27.02g of water, the result is 172.17g of calcium sulphate dihydrate.
- The volume of calcium sulphate hemihydrates is added to the volume of water and the sum of the volume will be about 7% less than the volume of calcium sulphate dihydrate. About 0.2%- 0.4% linear expansion is obtained.
- The contraction of gypsum is not visible and when the volumetric contraction is measured by a dilatometer, it is determined to be about 7%.
- These materials are porous when set because of the expansion of the outer dimension caused by the simultaneous true volumetric contraction of calcium sulphate dehydrate.

2. EFFECT OF SPATULATION

- The mixing process is known as *spatulation*. It is definite on setting time and setting expansion of the material. Within practical limits increase in spatulation shortens the setting time (increase nuclei formation, increase conversion of hemihydrates to dihydrate).

Table: 3.3. Effect of spatulation on setting time.

MATERIAL	W/ RATIO (ML/G)	SPATULATION TIME	SETTING TIME (MIN)
Model plaster	0.50	20	14
	0.50	100	11
	0.50	200	8
Dental stone	0.30	20	10
	0.30	100	8

3. EFFECT OF HUMIDITY

- When the relative humidity increases to 70% and above, moisture in the air can cause some conversion of hemihydrates to dihydrates. Dihydrate crystals can accelerate reaction by providing more nuclei for crystallization; the initial result is acceleration of setting. Further contamination by moisture can retard setting of gypsum.

4. EFFECT OF COLLOIDAL SYSTEM AND pH

- Colloidal system such as agar and alginate retard setting of gypsum product which can be overcome by adding accelerator.
- These colloids do not retard setting by altering the solubility ratio of hemihydrates and dihydrate, rather they get absorbed on the nucleation site thus interfering in the hydration reaction.
- Liquids with low pH such as saliva, retard the setting reaction.
- Liquids with high pH accelerate the setting.

5. EFFECT OF TEMPERATURE

- The temperature of water used for mixing, as well as the temperature of the environment has an effect on the setting of gypsum product. The temperature has two main effects
  - i. Firstly, increasing the temperature alters the solubilities of calcium sulphate hemihydrates and calcium dihydrate; this affects the rate of reaction. The ratio of the solubilities of hemihydrates and dihydrate at 20°C is 4.5. As the temperature increases, solubility decreases until the ratio becomes 1 at 100°C. Setting is increased with low solubility which results in slow reaction.
  - ii. Second effect is the change in ion mobility with temperature. As temperature increases, the mobility of calcium and sulphate ions also increases, which tends to increase the rate of reaction and setting time.
- Increasing the temperature from 20°C to 30°C, cause the solubility ratio to decrease from 4.5 to 3.4 which should retard the reaction. At the same time, the mobility of the ions increases, which should accelerate the setting reaction.

Table: 3.4: Effect of temperature on setting.

TEMPERATURE (°C)	SOLUBILITY RATIO OF CALCIUM SULPHATE HEMIHYDRATES AND DIHYDRATE.
20	4.5
25	3.90
30	3.0
40	2.90
50	2.43
100	1

Table. 3.5. Summary of effect of Manipulative Variable on Properties of Gypsum Products.

MANIPULATIVE VARIABLES	SETTING TIME	CONSISTENCY	SETTING EXPANSION	STRENGTH
Increase W/P ratio	Increase	Increase	Decrease	Decrease
Increase rate of spatulation	Decrease	Decrease	Increase	No effect
Increase temperature of mixing water from 23C to 30C	Decrease	Decrease	Increase	No effect

TEST FOR FLUIDITY OF DENTAL GYPSUM

The fluidity of dental gypsum products is normally measured by one of the two methods outlined in the ISO standards.

1. SLUM TEST

- For type 1 and 2 slum test is recommended. In this test, known volume of a mixed material is allowed to slum on to the glass plate at a time indicated by the manufacturer as the pouring time (2 – 3 min for most material).

2. CORE PENETRATION TEST

- The fluidity of type 3, 4 and 5 is determined by core penetration test. The depth of penetration of a core falling under a load for 15 seconds into a known material is measured 3 mints after starting to mix powder and water.

SETTING TEST OF GYPSUM PRODUCTS

The setting characteristics of gypsum products have traditionally been measured in terms of their ability to resist penetration by needle.

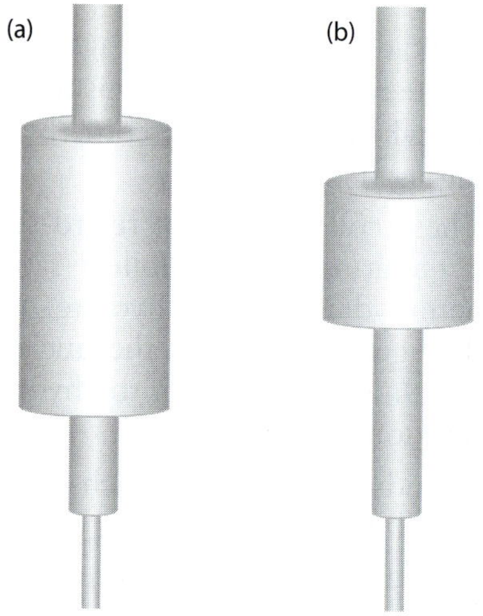

Fig: 3.7. Indentors used to assess setting characteristics of gypsum products.

Sometimes reffered as Gillmore needle.

Ability to support needle (a) indicates initial set.

Ability to support needle (b) indicates final set.

- The heavier needle has a smaller tip diameter than the lighter one and applies greater pressure to the surface of material under test. (Fig 3.7)
- The initial setting time is defined as the time taken for the material to develop sufficient strength such that it is able to support the lighter needle. The time at which the material is able to support the heavier needle, indicates the time between the initial and

final setting time and is indicative of the fact that the model or die is hard enough to be used.

- The ISO specification for dental gypsum products requires the use of Vicat needle for judging setting time. This system has built-in dial gauge allowing depth of penetration to be measured. But the most common is Gillmore needle test.

3. GILLMORE NEEDLE TEST

a. The Gillmore needle test is frequently used as quick and easy way of testing setting time, particularly for gypsum products.

b. This device applies a fixed stress on a small circular area of the flattened surface of the setting material, using a flat-ended cylinder indenter; it may be viewed as another kind of hardness test.

c. Unlike the hardness rest, Gillmore needle can only indicate when the penetration resistance strength has exceeded a certain value. It cannot indicate where the reaction has complete or how far it is to go.

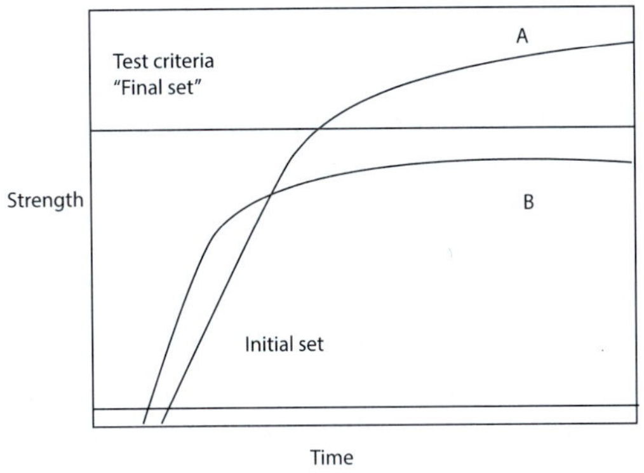

Fig:3.8. Gillmore needle test.

d. Supposing, the indentation hardness test can be determined for a material, we might have curves like in (Fig: 3.8).

e. Curve A shows a material for which a "final setting time" can be determined using a Gillmore needle.

f. Curve B on the other hand, shows a material which never set according to the same criterion simply because its strength is insufficient to withstand test stress, even though it may have more or less completed reaction well before A.

SETTING TIMES

1. INITIAL SETTING TIME

a. Is also known as working time. In initial setting, viscosity of the plaster increases and flow decreases.

b. At this stage solubility is about 0.8% at room temperature.

c. At this stage small portions of the hemihydrates crystals are converted into dihydrates and then the reaction proceeds and more crystals are converted into dihydrate crystals.

2. FINAL SETTING TIME

- It is that time at which the material can be separated from the impression without distortion or fracture at this time chemical reaction is over.

Setting Characteristics Can Be Affected By

a. Un-converted dihydrates.
b. Age of the material. (Shelf life)
c. Storage condition.
d. Presence of anhydrates.

- Setting reaction is exothermic in nature and temperature is around 30°C. During setting there may be a small expansion due to outward thrust of growing crystals.
- The magnitude of hygroscopic expansion however varies from one type of gypsum material to another.

Plaster	0.2% - 0.3%
Dental stone	0.08% - 0.1%
High strength stone	0.01% - 0.08%

CONTROL OF SETTING TIME

There are three mechanisms to control setting time of gypsum.

1. SOLUBILITY OF HEMIHYDRATES

If the solubility of hemihydrates is increased, super saturation of dihydrate is achieved faster, which accelerates the rate of dihydrate crystal deposition.

2. NUMBER OF NUCLEI OF CRYSTALLIZATION

Nucleation is the first step at which Ca and SO_4 in solution start to assemble in cluster on the nanometer scale, becoming stable under operating condition. The cluster form nuclei. The greater the nuclei more will be the crystallization and sooner the mass will become harder

3. RATE OF CRYSTAL GROWTH

Increasing or decreasing the rate of crystal growth will accelerate or retard the setting time. There are two sources of controlling setting time of gypsum.

- By manufacturers
- By operators

A. By Manufacturers

- High concentration of nucleating agent
- (Unconverted $CaSO_4$ Dihydrates) → more rapid Crystallization
- Accelerators are used to increase the rate of reaction so that setting time is reduced, e.g. potassium sulphates.
- Retarders are used to decrease the setting time e.g. borax **[$Na_2 B_4 0_7 H_2O$].**

B. By Operators

- Temperature; Little Effect

  ↑ Temperatures →accelerates the solution process but retards

  Crystallization
- W/P Ratio: ↑ W/P → Retards setting
- Mixing time: M/T → Accelerates setting

PHENOMENON OF DILATANCY

When a powder is allowed to settle under gravity, each particle tends to fit as closely as possible into the space, particularly if vibrated. Most powders are irregular in shape therefore if the particles are to be rotated, the distance between their centres and that on an adjacent contacting particles must increase to allow rotation to continue. When powder is stirred, all particles will tend to rotate to some extent from their well-packed position (Fig. 3.9). If they move away from each other the bulk volume of the powder must increase, and therefore so must the gauging volume. This is called Dilatancy. Dilatant mixture are easily recognized because they become harder when stirred faster.

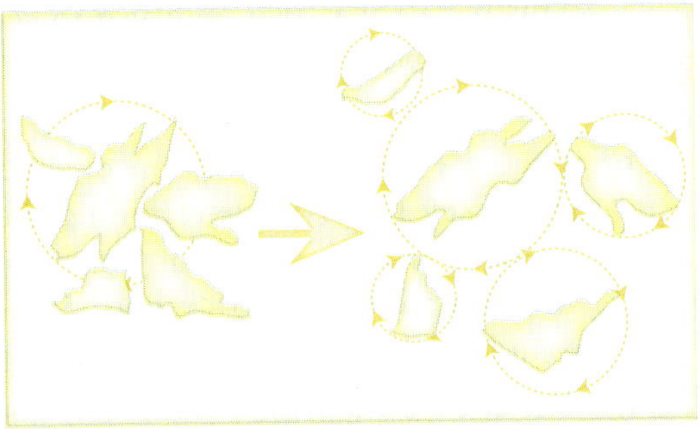

Fig: 3.9. The tumbling of of particles during stirring requires sufficient space. If this is not present initially, the bulk must expand it. Each particle has an associated swept volume.

MODIFIERS

The setting reaction is dependent on the relative solubilites of the hemihydrates and dihydrates but modifiers are the substances that Affect the setting by accelerating or retarding the setting reaction.

1. POTASSIUM SULPHATE

a. Potassium sulphate (K_2SO_4) reacts with water and hemihydrates to produce 'syngenite' [$K_2(CaSO4)_2.H_2O$].

b. This compound crystallizes very rapidly, and encourages the growth of more crystals.

c. This has the effect of reducing the overall expansion and accelerating setting reaction.

d. When present as a 2% solution in water it will reduce the setting time from approximately 10 to 4 minutes.

2. SODIUM SULPHATE

a. When the sulphate concentration is increased the dissolution of hemihydrates will be inhibited.

b. Its solubility products will then be attained by dissolution of less hemihydrates.

c. If during the reaction the solubility product of sodium sulphate is exceeded, sodium sulphate decahydrate will precipitate and may block the dissolution of hemihydrates; depending on the amount of water present. There is optimum concentration of sodium sulphate for accelerating effect.

3. ' SALT EFFECT

a. Salt provide additional site for crystal formation. The higher density of crystals limits the growth of crystals.

b. The increasing sites for nucleation will increase the rate of setting of material; the hemihydrates will dissolve more rapidly and increase the rate of reaction.

c. If the salt is in high concentration it will deposit onto the surface of crystal and prevent further growth, this will reduce the rate of reaction.

d. For example, the overall setting rate goes maximum with the addition of salt.

4. BORAX

a. The addition borax ($Na_2B_4O_7.H_2O$) is important because it counteracts the increased rate of setting in inclusion of above additives.

b. It is the retarder of the setting process.

c. The addition of borax leads to the formation of calcium tartaborate, which deposits on the dihydrate crystals and prevent further growth.

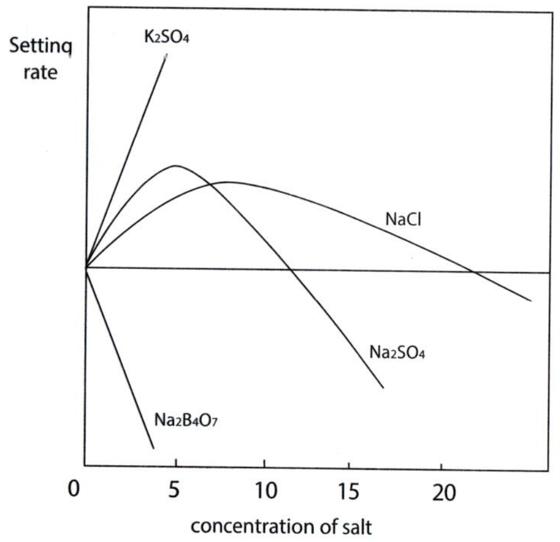

Fig: 3.10. Effect of various added salts on setting rate

DEFECTS OF GYPSUM PRODUCTS

1. POROSITY

a. Excess water is always required to produce useable slurry; this excess must be left at the end of reaction.

b. The set gypsum product has both solid and liquid phase present.

c. The expansion will have drawn either air or more water (if this was provided for hygroscopic expansion) into the structure; neither air nor water has any strength.

d. The strength of set mass depends strongly, roughly or inversely on the volume fraction of pores and become zero when volume fraction is less than unity.

e. This is the critical porosity when the structure is incapable of supporting itself, either the skeleton that is left is too weak to carry its own weight or the structural elements, as they grow do not make contact to create such a skeleton.

f. This behavior is also observed in cements, investments, amalgam and porcelain.

g. The excess volume fraction of fluid is the key factor in determining the strength of this type of material, which represents zero strength phases in final structure.

h. The effect is the same weather it is water after evaporation, air or a mixture of both, permeating the whole body.

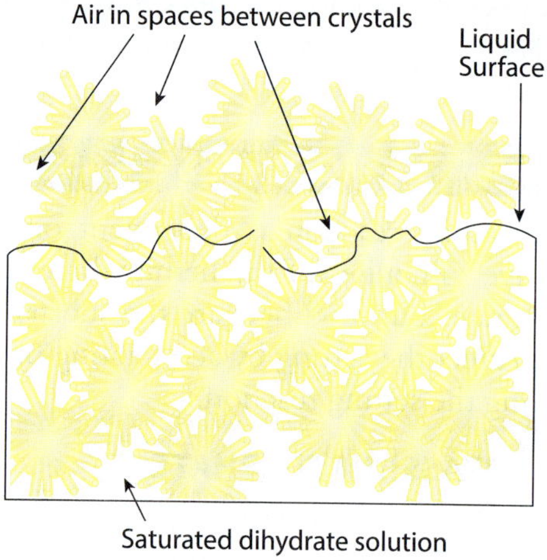

Fig: 3.11. The spaces between dehydrate crystals may be filled by air or liquid neither has any strength.

2. BUBBLES

a. A source of porosity that is air bubbles is introduced during mixing.

b. If the mixing is done by hand, air bubbles are readily incorporated which results in presence of air bubbles in final structure and reduces the strength.

c. The size of bubbles will be greater than the space between dihydrate crystals (Fig 3.12) and by reference of Griffth Criterion, it lowers the strength rapidly than would be expected.

d. That is why the mixing under vacuum and casting with vibration (to allow bubbles to escape) are the preferred and recommended techniques.

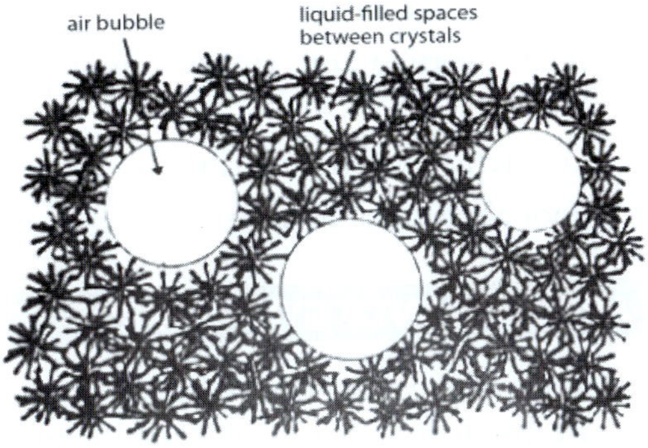

Fig: 3.12. There are two kinds of porosity: small scale distributed porosity between dehydrate crystals and large, discrete air bubbles.

OTHER PHENOMENA

1. CRYSTAL GROWTH EXPANSION

a. Gypsum material always shows expansion on setting, 0.2%-0.6% (linear). The growing crystal, in radiating areas called spherulites, centered on some site of nucleation, must make contact with their neighbor and exert a minute force on each other as they grow. These contacts should be geometrically perfect, so that there will be many sites at which a new atom could be fitted but some of these will not have space because of an adjacent surface. There is a thermodynamic driving force which tends to squeeze the atom into space that is now under slight compression. The effect of the contact point is to generate a force, but it is only detectable when reaction has proceeded sufficiently far from the growing crystals to contact their neighbour throughout the mass, this is called crystal growth pressure.

b. As long as the growing crystals of dihydrate are not in contact the mixture will remain fluid and flow under gravity. The net volume of the reactants and reaction product continue to decrease as the setting reaction proceed, water is being consumed and occupies less and less space. The expansion and contraction must be controlled if accuracy is to be achieved.

2. HYGROSCOPIC EXPANSION

a. The expansion due to outward thrust of the growing crystals is hygroscopic expansion.

b. The effect of the contraction force associated with loss of gloss may be overcome by adding extra water, either by immersing the setting mixture in water or by adding few drops to the surface, thus allowing water and not the air to be drawn into the space created by the decrease in volume of the reactants.

c. The liquid surface does not then enter the pores, the tension due to meniscus curvature is not generated and the expansion by crystal growth is uninhibited, this results in double expansion. This phenomenon is referred to as *hygroscopic expansion*.

d. This is purely physical in origin.

3. THERMAL EXPANSION

a. This expansion occurs at the same time when the temperature is rising.

b. The majority of the expansion is not primarily thermal but due to the crystal growth pressure and necessarily can only start after a certain amount of reaction has already occurred and the growing crystals have become large to come into contact with other dihydrate, the walls of the container or solids.

c. This can be seen by the fact that the temperature starts to rise (because the reaction is exothermic) before the expansion is noticed.

PROPERTIES OF SET MATERIAL

The strength of gypsum material is directly related to the density of mass because high strength stone is mixed with the least amount of water so it gives stronger set material.

a. The strength of gypsum depend on:
   - Porosity of the set material.
   - Time for which the material is allowed to dry after setting.

b. Model plaster, being the least dense, is the weakest of the gypsum.

c. Gypsum is very brittle material.

d. Transverse strength is very low, that's why it is more fragile.

e. Good dimensional stability.

f. Set material is slightly soluble in water. Solubility increases with rise in temperature.

ADVANTAGES

a. Inexpensive.

b. Easy to use.

c. Good accuracy.

d. Reproduce the fine details from the impression.

e. Good dimensional stability.

f. Good color contrast.

DISADVANTAGES

a. Mechanical properties are not good.

b. Chances of fracture.

c. Poor surface detail.

d. Poor wetting of rubber impression material.

e. Low tensile strength, brittle.

f. Poor abrasion resistance.

APPLICATION OF GYPSUM PRODUCT

a. Materials that are derived from gypsum are used in a variety of dental applications. They include:
   - Models and dies
   - Impression materials.
   - Moulds
   - Refractory investment

b. Gypsum products are used for the production of study models for oral and maxillofacial structures and for the dental laboratory operation in production of dental prostheses.

c. They are also used to form models and cast on which wax dental prostheses and restoration are constructed.

d. When gypsum product is mixed with refractory filler like silica, it become more heat resistant and can be used to form moulds for the casting of molten metal in anatomic form for dental restoration.

e. Impression plaster is used to make impression of edentulous patient while dental stone is used to make die.

f. As a binder with silica in gold alloy casting investment, soldering investment and investment for low melting point Ni/Cr alloy.

INFECTION CONTROL

There is always a risk of cross infection to dental office personnel by micro-organism, including hepatitis B and HIV, via dental impressions. Model, casts and die should be disinfected with a spray of iodophor according to manufacturer's instruction or by immersion in 1: 10 dilution of a 5 % sodium hypochlorite solution for 30 minutes. After disinfection, model should be examined for its surface details and damages. Ethylene oxide is best for complete sterilization of model. Disinfection of impression is recommended over that of the model because it is easier, cheap, more effective and limits the introduction of contaminated items into the laboratory area.

REFERENCES

1. Cornelius Klein and Cornelius S. Hurlbut, Jr., 1985,Manual of Mineralogy, John Wiley, (20th ed.), pp. 352–353,ISBN 0-471-80580-7
2. N.B. Singh (2007), "Calcium sulphate hemihydrate hydration leading to gypsum crystallization", *Progress in Crystal Growth and Characterization of Materials*, vol. 53, no. 1, pp. 57–77.
3. M.R. Christoffersen, J. Christoffersen & M.P.C. Weijnen, G.M. Van Rosmalen (1982), "Crystal growth of calcium sulphate dihydrate at low supersaturation", *Journal of Crystal Growth*, vol. 58, no. 3, pp. 585–595.
4. Jen-Chang Yang, Hong-Da Wu & Naichia Teng, Dian-yu Ji, Sheng-yang Lee (2012), "Novel attempts for the synthesis of calcium sulfate hydrates in calcium chloride solutions under atmospheric conditions", *Ceramics International*, vol. 38, no. 1, pp. 381–387.
5. Kenneth Anusavice (2012), *Phillips' Science of Dental Materials, 12th Edition,* Saunder.
6. Ronald Sakaguchi & John M.Power(2011), *Craig's Restorative Dental Materials, 13th Edition,* Mosby
7. Richard Van Noort (2007), *Introduction to Dental Materials,* 3rd ed, Mosby Ltd., China
8. B W Darvell (2009), *Materials Science for Dentistry (9th edition),*Woodhead Publishing Limited, UK.
9. John M. Power & John C.wataha(2012), *DENTAL MATERIALS Properties and Manipulation, (10th Edition),* ELSEVIER, India.

Chapter 4

DENTAL WAXES

Dr. Fahad Siddiqui

INTRODUCTION

Dental waxes primarily consist of two or more components which may either be natural or synthetic waxes, resins, oils, fats and pigments. Appropriate blending of components is done to achieve desirable properties of the material for a specific application.

Waxes are thermoplastic materials which allow them to be mouldable above a specific temperature and to be transformed into a solid state, when cooled. In other words, waxes remain solid around room temperature, but melt without decomposing, to form mobile liquids. This thermoplastic property makes them handy for a range of applications in dentistry. Dental waxes have poor mechanical properties, but due to their thermoplastic nature they are commonly used to form wax patterns for dental appliances (e.g. dentures) before casting. Waxes are used in pattern formation of inlays, crowns, pontics and partial and complete dentures.

In dentistry, waxes usually serve the purpose of wax pattern construction. They may however aid in other procedures as well e.g., at the bite registration stage of complete denture fabrication and to record impression of edentulous areas.

CLASSIFICATION

Waxes can be classified in two ways:

1. ACCORDING TO DENTAL USE

PATTERN WAXES
Inlay wax
Casting wax
Modelling wax

PROCESSING WAXES
Sticky wax
Carding Wax
Boxing wax

BITE REGISTRATION WAXES
Bite registration wax
Connective wax
----

2. ACCORDING TO SOURCES

SOURCES

- **Natural**
  - **Mineral**: Paraffin wax, Micro crystalline, Montan wax
  - **Animal**: Bees wax, Spermaceti wax
  - **Plant**: Carnauba wax, Candelilla wax, Japan wax
- **Synthetic**
  - Polyethylene Wax

WAX PATTERN

Wax patterns are formed on a stone model, die or on a prepared cavity in the mouth during fabrication of dental appliances. These patterns determine the final shape and size of the appliance or restoration being casted through a technique known as the *lost-wax technique*. In lost-wax technique, the wax is burned out or 'lost', leaving behind a space (mould) which is then replaced by polymer or alloy depending on the appliance under production, e.g. complete denture or a metal crown.

To carry out the lost-wax technique, waxes must exhibit few desirable characteristics as listed below:

1. Conforming to the exact contour of appliance that is being constructed.
2. Not being a subject to dimensional changes during the process.
3. Not leaving behind residues.

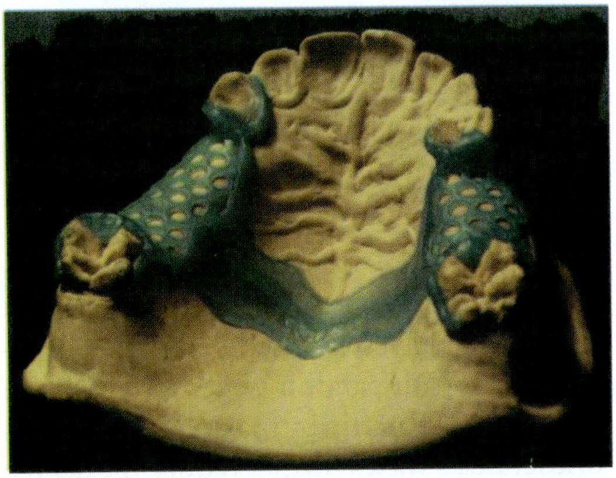

Fig: 4.1. Wax pattern for Removable Partial denture.

Wax patterns are fabricated in a number of ways, as listed below:

1. ***Direct technique:*** Given that the wax pattern is carved or produced within the tooth, it is called the direct technique.
2. ***Indirect technique:*** Technique involving the wax pattern being carved on a model is known as the indirect technique.
3. ***Indirect-direct technique:*** In cases where the pattern is constructed through an indirect technique followed by final adjustments within the patient's mouth before the next step of casting is known as the indirect-direct technique.

METHODS OF WAX PATTERN CONSTRUCTION

A. Dipping

The purpose of this method is to develop a thin, uniform and well-adapted layer of wax onto the die. The procedure is known as such because it is completed by literally "dipping" the die into molten wax. The use of this method is limited in dentistry and is employed specifically in cases where mass production of wax patterns is required.

B. Addition Method

In this method, bulk of the wax pattern is carved on to the die. This procedure is carried out by melting the wax, and then dropping this melted wax onto the die. The liquid wax is then carved to form the desired wax pattern. Although this technique is used frequently in dentistry but it has a disadvantage of making the wax pattern vulnerable to distortion. Distortion may be a consequence of the subsequent strain that is accumulated during multiple additions of wax layers.

C. Molten press method

This method is completed by adding molten wax and applying pressure with fingers simultaneously. Molten press method assures that the wax is adapted closely and free of irregularities.

D. Injection method

In this method, molten wax is injected through a heated metallic syringe into a mould. Injection method is used for wax patterns that require precise and accurate dimensions.

Even though there are different methods of wax pattern construction, it should be noted that regardless of the methods used, the wax pattern must be adapted as accurately as possible. This is because the casting procedures that follow are expected to be less accurate than the wax pattern. Therefore, it is of paramount importance to carve an accurate wax pattern along with minimizing the risks of distortion.

COMPOSITION

Waxes as discussed earlier are a blend of thermoplastic materials, which can be softened by heating and reverted to their solid states when cooled. The prime components of waxes are derived from mineral, animal or vegetable origin.

1. MINERAL

Paraffin wax is obtained from petroleum by dewaxing light lubricating oil stocks. It is colourless and odourless wax. Paraffin consists of a mixture of solid straight-chain hydrocarbons. The softening temperature for paraffin ranges within 37-55 C, whereas the melting temperature ranges within 48-70 C. Furthermore, it is worthy to note that paraffin waxes are brittle at room temperature.

Fig: 4.2. Paraffin Wax.

Microcrystalline waxes are a type of wax produced by 'de-oiling' petroleum as part of the petroleum refining process. Microcrystalline waxes have a melting temperature range of 65-90 C, and when paraffin is added to these waxes, the melting temperature is raised however softening temperature is lowered. Due to these alterations in melting and softening temperatures, paraffin becomes less brittle when added to microcrystalline waxes in contrast to when used alone. Microcrystalline waxes (Fig: 4.3) are normally darker, more viscous, denser, tackier and more elastic than paraffin waxes. They also have a higher molecular weight and melting point.

Fig: 4.3. Microcrystalline Wax.

2. ANIMAL

Bee's waxes are derived from the honeycombs. They consist of natural, partially crystalline polyesters. Bee's waxes are often mixed with paraffin waxes to enrich the properties of paraffin by making the latter less brittle. Bee's waxes further reduce the degree to which paraffin waxes flow under stress at temperatures just below their melting point.

Fig: 4.4. Bee's wax.

3. VEGETABLE

Carnauba waxes are extracted from trees and plants. Vegetable waxes are very hard and thick natured waxes with a high melting temperature that ranges around 180-185 C. Carnauba waxes are added to paraffin to reduce the flow at mouth as it alters the softening temperature.

PROPERTIES

The properties of dental waxes are largely characterised by their *melting* and *softening* temperatures; the latter is closely related to solid-solid transition temperature. *Co-efficient of thermal expansion* is another important property as it defines the accuracy of waxes. For instance, inlay waxes tend to have a high co-efficient of thermal expansion and are therefore not appropriate to be used in the direct technique of wax pattern construction. This is because there is a high amount of expansion and contraction by each degree of temperature change from mouth to room temperature. *Dimensional stability* is predominantly reliant on the stresses that are accumulated in the course of contraction once the wax has been moulded. Mechanical properties of waxes to be considered are its *brittleness* and *flow* within its working temperature range. We will now discuss these properties in overt details.

THERMAL PROPERTIES

Dental waxes have a crystalline structure and are characterised by a definite melting temperature. When waxes are heated, an endothermic peak occurs just below the melting point. This endothermic peak reflects the 'solid-solid transition' state of waxes, which is suggestive of a change in the crystalline structure. At this temperature, the crystalline structures of waxes are converted from a solid brittle state to a rather soft and mouldable state. Because of this softening which takes place at this temperature, solid-solid transition temperature is sometimes also stated as the *softening temperature*. For the direct technique of pattern formation, softening temperature must be just above the mouth temperature. This is to warrant that when the material is being placed in the patient's mouth, it is in a mouldable state. Manufacturers can control the melting and softening temperature of waxes by blending various mixtures of natural and synthetic waxes.

Waxes are poor thermal conductors and therefore require sufficient time for thorough softening of the material before moulding can be attempted. Once the waxes are moulded, they are allowed to cool down. However, due to high values of coefficient of thermal expansion, waxes may undergo significant contraction during the process of cooling. The low thermal conductivity coupled with high coefficient of thermal expansion can often result in the solidification of the outer surfaces of waxes well before the core of the material. This phenomenon may lead to the reduction of thermal contraction and development of internal stresses. Relief of these internal stresses may result in dimensional changes. To avoid such detrimental circumstances, thorough softening for an adequate time above solid-solid transition temperature must be ensured.

Methods of Softening Wax

1. Using Bunsen burner.
2. Using Warm Water.
3. Using Infra-red Lamp.
4. Using Wax Annealer; an ideal method.

MECHANICAL PROPERTIES

One of the most important mechanical properties of waxes includes its *flow* value. In ideal situation waxes must flow substantially at moulding temperature, but should exhibit none or only minor flow at mouth and/or room temperatures in order to avoid distortion.

Flow value of wax is the prime factor which defines its mouldability. In other words, the material's capability to record details is reliant on how much the material can flow at 'moulding temperature'. For direct techniques, the moulding temperature is just above mouth temperature, whereas for indirect techniques, it is just above the room temperature. Due to the importance of flow, it is essential to test the material prior to use. Flow is measured by applying specific load to a cylindrical specimen at a given temperature and measuring the extent of compression of the material. The ANSI/ADA Specification No. 4 has set certain standards for the flow of waxes about a specific temperature. For instance, according to this specification Type 1 inlay waxes at 37 C are allowed only a 1% flow. This value varies according to the types of waxes.

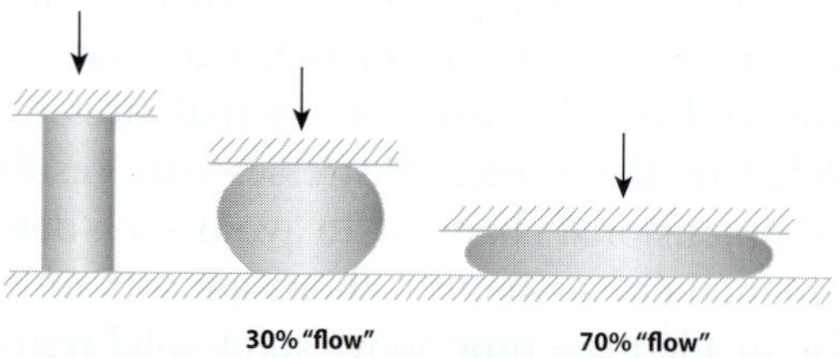

Fig: 4.5. ADA4 specification for testing wax flow.

Distortion has to be avoided at all times or it may result in unwanted circumstances, particularly at the stage of wax pattern removal either from the mouth or die. Distortion may be a result of thermal contraction, which eventually may lead to development, and then relief of internal stresses as discussed before. Contraction stresses may also be relieved as a result of other factors such as: trapped air, moulding, carving, removal and storage conditions (time and temperature) allowing for distortion to take place.

The *brittleness* of waxes may also be controlled to an extent by the manufacturers through modifying the blend of waxes in order to produce desirable properties for the intended application. For instance, in the fabrication of dentures, the wax denture base may have to be removed from the cast several times and therefore waxes used for this procedure requires to be less brittle and exhibit toughness. In other situations, brittleness may be preferred e.g., inlay waxes are required to brittle so that they fracture when removed from an undercut area because this helps in locating undercuts in cavity. That can then be adjusted by the dentists.

APPLICATIONS IN DENTISTRY

The most common application of waxes in dentistry is their use as impression materials and modelling and inlay waxes which are used for the construction of wax pattern. Modelling and inlay waxes are also known as *pattern waxes*. We will now discuss these applications in detail.

1. DENTURE MODELLING WAXES

Modelling waxes essentially consist of paraffin and beeswax with a melting point that ranges 49-58 C. These waxes are usually supplied in *sheet form*. In fabrication of dentures modelling waxes play a critical role.

Modelling waxes are used to construct a wax rim. The wax rim could either be adapted on the model itself or otherwise on a denture base. Wax rim after adaptation is placed into patient's mouth for 'bite-registration' in order to ensure a detailed record of the occlusal relationship. After the occlusal details have been noted, teeth set-up is completed by mounting artificial teeth on the wax rim. After the occlusal relationship has been recorded, and teeth set-up has been done, the wax rim is then inserted in the patient's mouth at the *try-in* stage of denture construction. (Fig: 4.6)

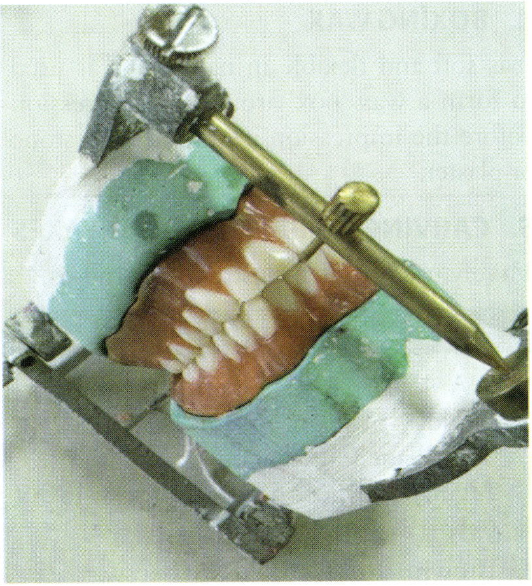

Fig: 4.6. Try-in Stage of Complete denture.

To perform the above mentioned procedures, waxes must exhibit a few desirable properties. A major property that is essential in waxes at this stage is their *toughness.* Waxes are required to be tough so that they are not distorted at the registration stage and the try-in stage. Modelling waxes must also have a softening temperature which is above mouth temperature to avoid distortion at these two stages.

There are three types of waxes used for the above mentioned purposes: 1) Soft wax (Type 1), Hard wax (Type 2) and Extra hard (Type 3). They are classified into these types based on the differences in their softening temperatures. Type 1 waxes are made in a way that they remain hard at room temperature but soften at mouth temperature. They are mainly used in building contours and veneers. Type 2 waxes are used in mild climates, whereas Type 3 is used in warmer climates. Type 2 and 3 both are used in the construction of wax patterns. Although these two types of modelling waxes are relatively hard, care must be taken during construction of wax pattern. This is because there is a risk that they might become a subject to softening and subsequent distortion if kept in mouth for too long. Therefore it is important to take precautions at the bite-registration and try-in stages. Furthermore, waxes usually have high coefficient of thermal expansion and hence could be a subject to dimensional changes.

Temporary denture bases are at risk of distortion unless precautions are taken during their construction. Alternatively, other materials and/or techniques could be applied. For instance, in construction of temporary denture bases, it is recommended that shellac (wax-like resin) be used due to its better stability at mouth temperature.

2. INLAY WAXES

Inlay waxes are primarily a combination of natural and/or synthetic waxes. Natural waxes maybe hydrocarbons of paraffin and microcrystalline waxes. Other natural origin waxes could include carnauba wax, candelilla wax and resins. Synthetic waxes are usually a product of *chemical synthesis* between different natural waxes. Inlay waxes are supplied either in stick or cone form.

Inlay waxes are principally used for wax patterns in both direct and indirect techniques. Although inlay waxes can be used for direct technique (intra-oral) but their use is limited to relatively simple procedures such as in carving wax patterns for casts and posts for anterior teeth. The inlay waxes are classified as: Soft (Type 1) and Hard (Type 2). This classification is based on the differences in the *flow* characteristic of these materials and hence serves for different purposes. Type 1 (Soft) is usually used in indirect technique of wax pattern construction for inlays, pontics and crowns. Type 2 materials on the other hand are suitable to be used in direct technique of wax patterns for uses in the construction of inlays and crowns.

Fig: 4.7. Inlay wax pattern for crown construction.

In the construction of *direct wax patterns*, inlay wax is softened and then inserted into the tooth cavity with an appropriate pressure until the wax cools. Care must be taken to avoid patient discomfort which could occur in case of excessive pressure. Softening of wax must take place just above mouth temperature but care must be taken not to raise the temperature to an extent that excessive thermal contraction takes place. To avoid dimensional changes due to stress relief, the wax pattern must be invested as early as possible. Ideally, the material should be hard at mouth temperature and must fracture if the cavity has undesirable undercuts so that the undercut areas could be located.

As for the construction of *indirect wax patterns* which are produced on a model, the procedure is almost similar to that in the direct technique. However, the wax may soften at a relatively lower temperature than that in direct technique but attention must be given to use a wax that does not soften at room temperature. This is because there is a high risk that the wax may flow rather than remain softened slightly above room temperature. Inlay waxes for indirect techniques are softened with dry heat or by heating over a flame.

3. STICKY WAX

It is sticky when melted, and exhibits brittleness when cooled down. It is commonly used to temporary hold components of prostheses together as well as in repair for wax patterns.

4. BOXING WAX

It is soft and flexible in nature and is used to form a wax 'box' around an impression before the impression is poured with stone or plaster.

5. CARVING & PRESENTATION WAXES

Merely used for demonstration purposes.

REFERENCES

1. E A. Baker (1982) Chemistry and morphology of plant epicuticular waxes. In The Plant Cuticle. Ed. DF Cutler, KL Alvin, CE Price. Academic Press. ISBN 0-12-199920-3
2. Brown, R, H. (1981) Beeswax (2nd edition) Bee Books New and Old, Burrow Bridge, Somerset UK. ISBN 0-905652-15-0
3. B.W. Darvell (2009) Materials Science for Dentistry, (9th) Ed., Woodhead Publishing, Cambridge, UK.
4. K.J. Anusavice, K. J. (2003) Philips' Science of Dental Materials, (11th Ed.) (Elsevier).
5. McCabe, J. F. & Walls, A. W.G. (2008), Applied Dental Materials, 9th Ed.,Blackwell Publishing Ltd, Oxford, UK.

Chapter 5

INVESTMENT AND REFRACTORY DIES

Dr. Mustafa & Dr. Sana Shahab

INTRODUCTION

- After the production of wax pattern (either direct or indirect methods). The wax pattern is embedded in an investment material.
- When the investment sets hard, the wax and sprue are removed by softening and or burning with an alloy or ceramic using a casting technique.

Types of Wax Pattern

For Acrylic Dentures;

- Wax pattern, in which the teeth have been setup, is embedded in a two-part mould, made up of Plaster of Paris or Dental Stones or mixture of the two contained in a two – part mould, metal container which is known as 'Flask'.

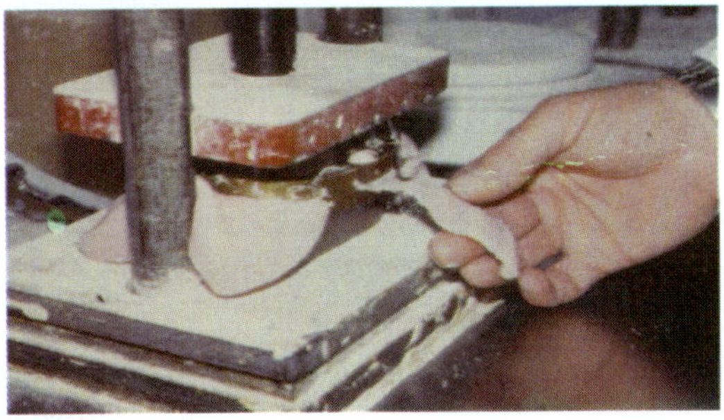

Fig: 5.1. Showing Flash of Acrylic.

The wax is removed by boiling H2O leaving the teeth embedded in the set gypsum.

- The space of wax is subsequently filled with the polymeric denture base material e.g. Acrylic Resin Material.

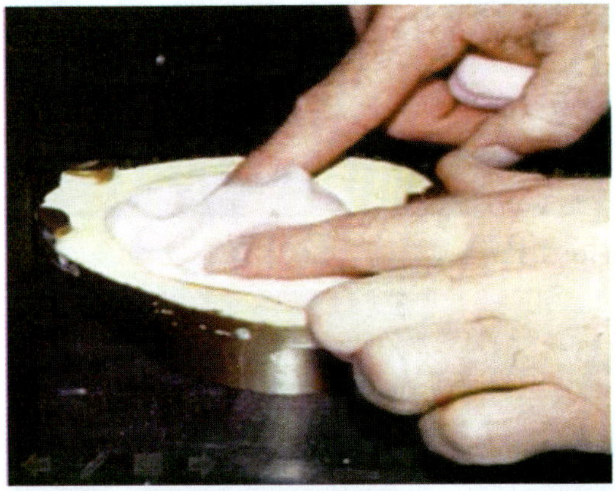

Fig: 5.2 Showing packing of Acrylic.

For Casting Metals and Alloys;

- Wax pattern of an inlay or other casts restoration is embedded in a Heat-Resistant investment material, which is capable of setting to a hard mass.
- The wax is removed from such mould usually by burning out or Lost Wax-Technique, then the space of wax is replaced by Molten Alloy.

DENTAL INVESTMENT MATERIAL

- It is a ceramic based material which is suitable for forming a mould into which a metal or alloy is appropriately cast. Reason for reinforcing ceramic is to produce material which withstands high temperature associated with the casting procedure and not to chemically react with cast metal. The procedure for forming the mould is described as "investing".

Fig: 5.3.a

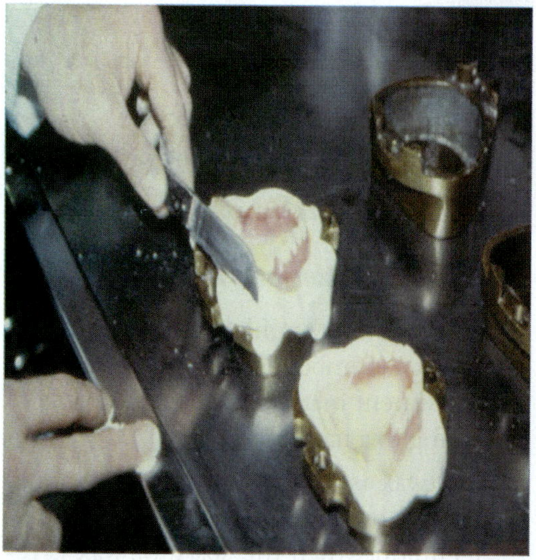

Fig: 5.3.b. Showing Investment Procedure.

Requirements of Investment Material

a. The mould must expand to compensate for the casting shrinkage, or cooling of the alloy.
b. The powder should have fine particle size to give a smooth surface on the casting.
c. The investment should be easily manipulated.
d. It should have a suitable setting time.
e. The material should have a smooth consistency when mixed.
f. The investment material should be capable of reproducing the shape, size and detail of wax pattern.
g. The investment material should with stand high temperature e.g. from 900 C to 1500 C.
h. Investment material should retain its integrity at the casting temperatures.
i. Should not crack or decompose.

REFRACTORY DIE MATERIALS

- These are used for making dies on which ceramic restorations are constructed.
- A pre requisite of the refractory die material is an ability to retain their structural integrity at temperature used to fire ceramics.

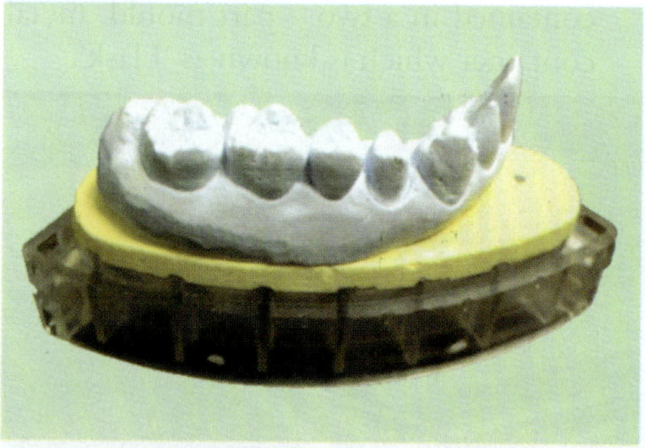

Fig: 5.4. Showing Die Material.

Available Materials

- Investment materials consist of a mixture of a refractory material, normally silica and a binder, which binds the refractory particles together.
- The nature of the binder characterizes the material into three groups.
- They are referred to as:
  a. Gypsum Bonded investment.
  b. Silica Bonded investment.
  c. Phosphate Bonded investment.

GYPSUM BONDED MATERIALS

COMPOSITION

INGREDIENT	%	FUNCTION
Silica	60 – 65%	Acts as a refractory material. Provides mould expansion by the setting expansion.
Calcium Sulphate Hemihydrate	30 – 35%	Act as a binder. Provide sufficient Strength to the mould. To contribute to the mould expansion by setting expansion.
Graphite Powder	Traces	Used as reducing agent. Provides a non-oxidizing atmosphere in the mould.
Boric Acid	5%	It offers the physical Properties like setting time and setting expansion.

Role of Silica

a. It imparts refractory properties to the investment.
b. Silica is responsible for producing expansion which is necessary to compensate for the casting shrinkage.
c. The expansion is accomplished by a combination of simple thermal expansion coupled with a crystalline inversion which results in a significant expansion.

Role of Binder(Calcium Sulphate Hemihydrate)

a. It holds the other ingredients together.
b. It provides rigidity to the investment.
c. It is primarily responsible for both normal setting and hygroscopic expansion.

Role of Boric acid

a. It is included in the formulation to assist in elimination of the contraction caused by the binder.
b. It is also added to strengthen the hardened investment.

Role of Graphite

Graphite particles are added to prevent oxidation of gold castings by creating a reducing atmosphere within the heated mould chamber

MANIPULATION

- Mix measured quality of powder and water using a flexible rubber bowl and spatula on in a vacuum investment mixing machine.
- Correct proportioning of W/P ratio [30: 100] is necessary.
- Before investing the wax pattern, it is cleaned to remove any oil or grease.
- The casting ring is usually lined with a wet asbestos strip – This does two things:

a. It facilitates mould expansion.

b. It minimizes hygroscopic expansion.

- Setting time is about 8 – 10 minutes.

PROPERTIES

- Easy to manipulate → smooth consistency.
- Setting time of these materials can be easily controlled, as for stone and dental plaster.
- The total expansion of the mould is generally sufficient to compensate for the shrinkage on cooling of gold alloys (about 1.5% by volume).
- The investments containing finer particles of silicon and CaSo4 – H2O give smoother surfaces on the finished casting.
- The set investment is porous, as is set gypsum this help to prevent backpressure, porosity in castings.
- The strength is sufficient to stand with the forces of the molten alloys.

CLASSIFICATION

- On the basis of expansion.
- Three types of gypsum bonded investment can be identified as follows;

TYPE I	Thermal expansion, for casting inlays and crowns.
TYPE II	Hygroscopic expansion, for casting inlays and crowns.
TYPE III	For casting complete and partial dentures.

USES

- For casting of inlays and crowns.
- For casting complete and partial dentures.
- As a soldering investment.

SILICA BONDED INVESTMENT

SUPPLY

- This investment is supplied with two bottles of special liquid to be mixed with the investments.
- One bottle contains diluted water – soluble silicate solution such as sodium silicate.
- The other bottle usually contains directed acid solution such as a solution of hydrochloric acid.

COMPOSITION

POWDER
Particles of silica glass
Magnesium.
LIQUID
Ethyl silicate.
Water
Alcohol
Colloidal silica and acid.

SETTING REACTION

Hydrolysis

A slow hydrolysis of ethyl silicate occurs producing a sol of silicic acid with the liberation of ethyl alcohol as a by-product.

$$(C_2H_5O)4Si + 4H_2O \rightarrow Si(OH)_4 + 4C_2H_5OH$$

Gelation

- The silicic acid sol forms silica gel on mixing with quartz or cristobalite powder under alkaline conditions.
- The necessary pH is achieved by presence of magnesium oxide in the powder.
- There is a slight shrinkage at this stage.

Drying

- On heating, considerable shrinkage occurs and there is loss of alcohol and water having a mould made of silica particles tightly packed together.

PROPERTIES

Dimensional Changes

- There is a large amount of thermal expansion, due to the very large percentage of silica in the final material.
- This expansion is usually sufficient to compensate;
  a. The setting shrinkage of the investment material.
  b. The casting shrinkage of the alloy.

Porosity

- The particles of the set material are packed so closely together that the porosity is negligible.
- Air spaces or vents must be left in the investment to permit escape of air from the mould.

USES

- They are an alternative to the phosphate-bonded investment, for high temperature casting.
- Used in the casting of base metal alloy partial dentures.

PHOSPHATE BONDED INVESTMENT

COMPOSITION

Powder

- Refractory Silica.
- Binder Magnesium Oxide.

Liquid

- Water or colloidal Silica solution.

SETTING REACTION

- On mixing with water or a colloidal Silica solution, a reaction between the phosphate and oxide occurs to form magnesium ammonium phosphate.

$NH_4.\ H_2\ PO_4 + MgO + 5H_2O \rightarrow Mg.\ NH_4\ PO_4.6H_2O.$

- The crystals of magnesium ammonium phosphate bind the silica particles together to form the set investment mould.
- Use of colloidal solution of silica instead of water for mixing with the powder has the dual effect of increasing the setting expansion and strengthening the set material.
- On heating the investment prior to casting, mould enlargement occurs by both thermal expansion and inversion of the silica.
- At higher temperature renaming phosphate reacts with silica forming complex silica phosphates.
- It causes a significant increase in the strength of the material at the casting temperature.

TYPES

Type 1: For inlays, crowns and other fixed restorations.

Type 2: For partial dentures and other last, removable restoration.

PROPERTIES OF INVESTMENT MATERIALS

Thermal Stability

- It should retain its integrity at high casting temperature. Gypsum bonded decomposes above 1200 C.

- Phosphate and silica bonded are good at high temperatures.

Porosity

- Silica-bonded is porosity's free as compared to other two materials.
- So there are 100% chances of back pressure (internal pressure) which can be overcome by making vents in the investment material.

Compensating Expansion

- Investment material should compensate the casting shrinkage e.g. Gold alloys 1.4%, Ni/Cr 2.0%, Co/Cr 2.3%.

FACTORS AFFECTING THE STRENGTH OF INVESTMENT

a. *Water/powder ratio*: With more water employed in mixing, the compressive strength reduces

b. Heating the investment to 700°C may increase or decrease the strength as much as 65%, depending on the composition. The greatest reduction in strength on heating is found in investments containing sodium chloride.

c. After the investment cools to room temperature, its strength decreases considerably, because of fine cracks that form during cooling

APPLICATION OF VARIOUS INVESTMENT MATERIALS

INVESTMENTS	PRIMARY USE
Dental plaster or stone Gypsum Bonded Silica Bonded	Mould for Acrylic denture Mould for gold casting alloys Mould for base metal
Phosphate Bonded	Mould for base metal and Gold casting alloys Mould for cast ceramics Refractory and die for ceramic Build ups

Chapter

6

APPLICATION OF METALS AND ALLOYS IN DENTISTRY

Eng. Faaz Butt, Dr. Zohaib & Dr. Adeel

CRYSTAL STRUCTURE OF METALS & ALLOYS

INTRODUCTION

Metals are defined as "An opaque lustrous chemical substance which is a good conductor of heat and electricity and when polished is a good reflector of light". They are used not only as restorative materials but also as tools and in orthopedic surgeries.

They can be base metals or noble/inert metals.In dentistry most frequently used metals are:

1. NOBEL METALS

This group of metals consists of mainly anticorrosive metals. They are highly inert since they cannot form oxide layer. In case of gold the layer of oxide which forms is highly unstable.

Gold	Au	IB
Silver/Argentums	Ag	IB
Platinum Group metals	Pt	VIIIB

2. BASE METALS

Base metals are usually used with combination of other metals. These metals are prone to oxide formation which does not make them suitable for dental applications. Once oxide layer is formed these metals lose their integrity and become dangerous for dental applications. To increase their anticorrosion behaviour they are used in combinations.

e.g. Iron(Fe), Copper(Cu) etc.

CLASSIFICATION OF METALS

In existing elements found in periodic table; 70% are metals. They are classified in various types i.e. Alkali, alkaline earth metals, transition and rare earth metals.

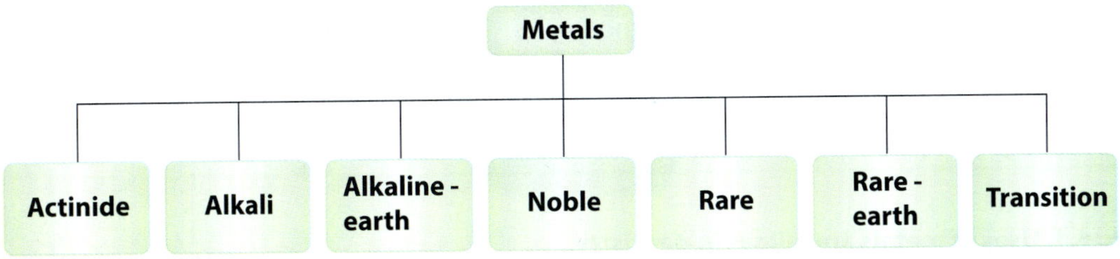

1. ACCORDING TO THEIR COMPOSITION

***Pure metals*:** Metals composed of only one metallic element. For example: gold, silver, iron, copper etc.

***Metal alloys*:** An alloy is a homogeneous combination of two or more metals. For example: bronze, brass, steel, etc

2. ACCORDING TO THEIR IRON CONTENT

Ferrous: These are iron (the pure metal) or alloys that contain iron (steel and castiron).

Non ferrous: These are pure metals which aren't iron (e.g. copper) or metal alloys that don't contain iron e.g. bronze, copper, aluminium, lead, Zinc, tin, brass, titanium, chrome, silver, gold.

3. ACCORDING TO THEIR DENSITY

Ultra light: Density less than 2 g/cm3. *For example*, magnesium.

Light: Density between 2 and 5 g/cm3. Aluminium and titanium are light.

Heavy: Density superior to g/cm3. All the other metals are heavy: steel, copper, gold, zinc, tin.

APPLICATION OF METALS IN DENTISTRY

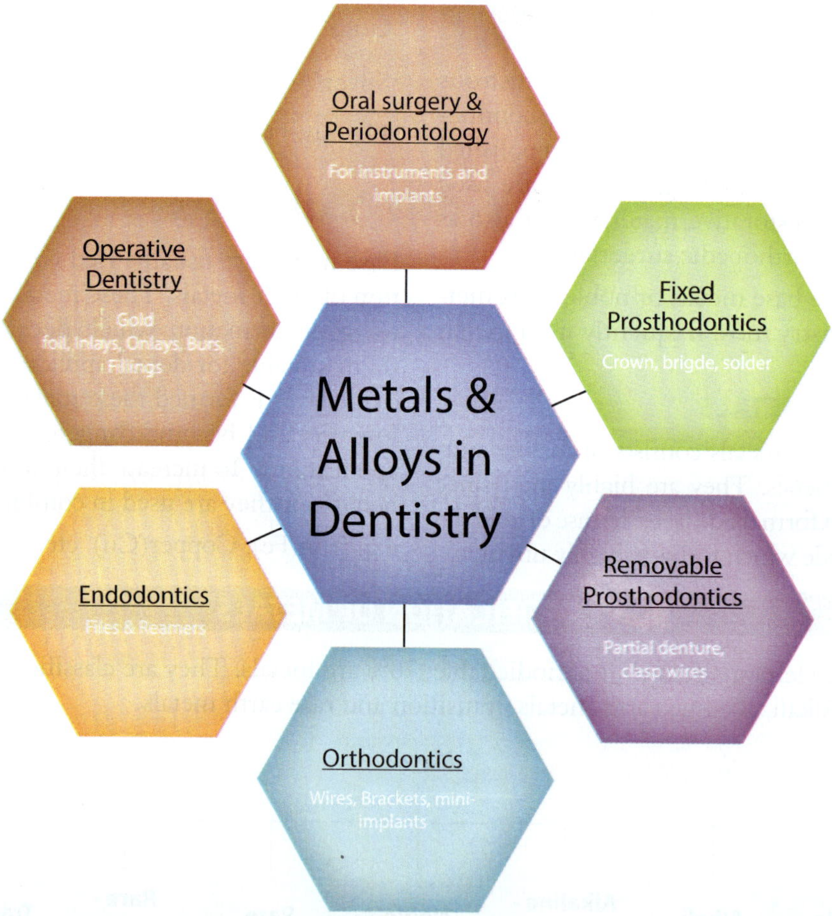

Fig: 6.1. Uses of metals and alloys in dentistry.

ATOMIC STRUCTURE OF METALS

Metals at atomic level exist as crystalline arrays /arrangements that extend and are repeated in 3 dimensions. Metals microscopically comprise the following components;

a. Nuclei + Core of electrons = atoms
b. Grains and Grain boundaries =Polycrystalline Materials
c. Without grains=Single Crystal Materials

The nuclei and the core of electron form the atomic center and the ionizable electrons float among the atomic positions. Due to this arrangement metals have no net charge since the atomic centers are neutralized. The mobility of the valence electrons is responsible for the conduction of heat and electricity. *GRAINS* are collection of randomly oriented crystals (orderly arranged atoms) making up the metal. When molten metal cools the solidification process starts from the nuclei and the crystals grow as dendrites (3d structures) from these sites. Crystal growth continues till all the material has solidified and all the dendrites are in contact. Each of these crystals is called ***grain*** and the area between these crystals is called ***grain boundary.*** (Fig: 6.2)

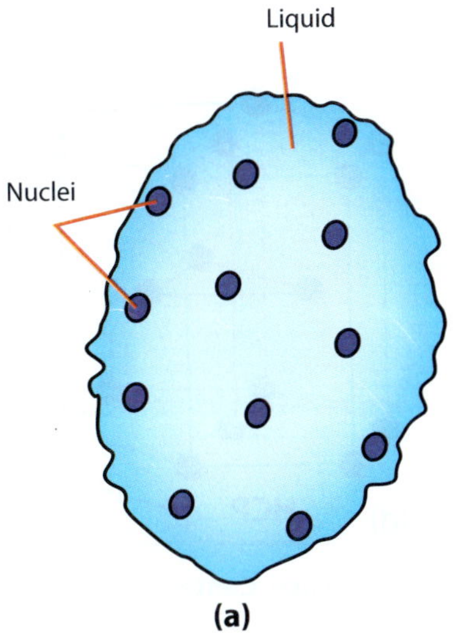

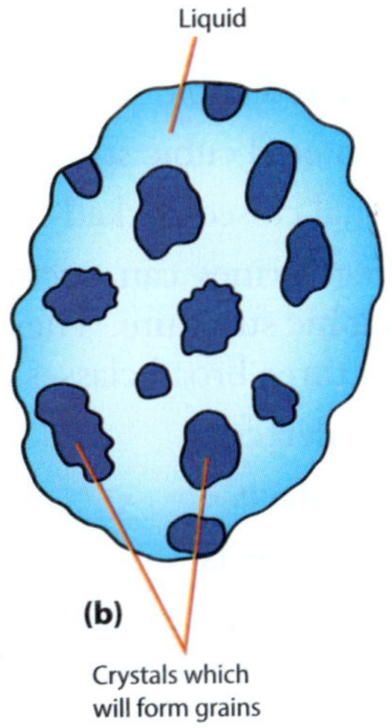

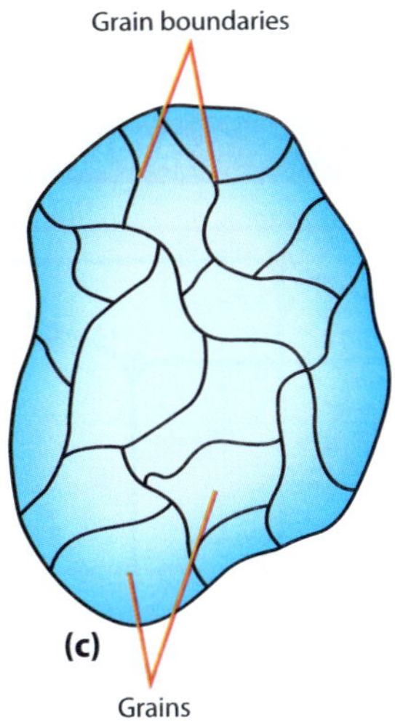

Fig: 6.2. Showing Solidification of metal. (a) (b) and (c).

There are metals which do not possess grains. There manufacturing process involves various complexities. They are weaker than their polycrystalline counterparts. These metals are prepared by very slow cooling of melt.

CRYSTALLOGRAPHIC FORM OF METALS

The atoms in the crystal can then be arranged in different crystallographic forms. (Fig: 6.3) Most common of them are:

a. Cubic structure

b. Face centered cubic structure

c. Body centered cubic structure

d. Hexagonal closed packed structure

Defects/irregularities can occur within the crystallographic structure. These defects are classified in three broad classes.

a. Point defects

b. Line defects

c. Planar defects

Point defects are limites to various sites with in lattice. It happen when there is an atom displaced by other kind of atom. For example if in gold lattice (FCC) one position of gold is replaced by an iron atom.

Line defects comprises dislocations which are units of atomic arrays that are not complete. It can move within the lattice under high stress. This dislocation moves till it reaches a grain boundary. The plane along which the defect moves is called *slip plane* and the stress needed to cause the movement is called *yield stress.*

Planar defects include grain boundaries which are natural barriers to the movement of dislocations.If the applied stress is greater than the yield stress then the metal will be permanently deformed due to the movement of the dislocations. The concentration of grain boundary increases as the grain size decreases. Metals with finer grain structure will be harder and will have a high value of yield stress.

IMPERFECTION IN CRYSTAL STRUCTURE

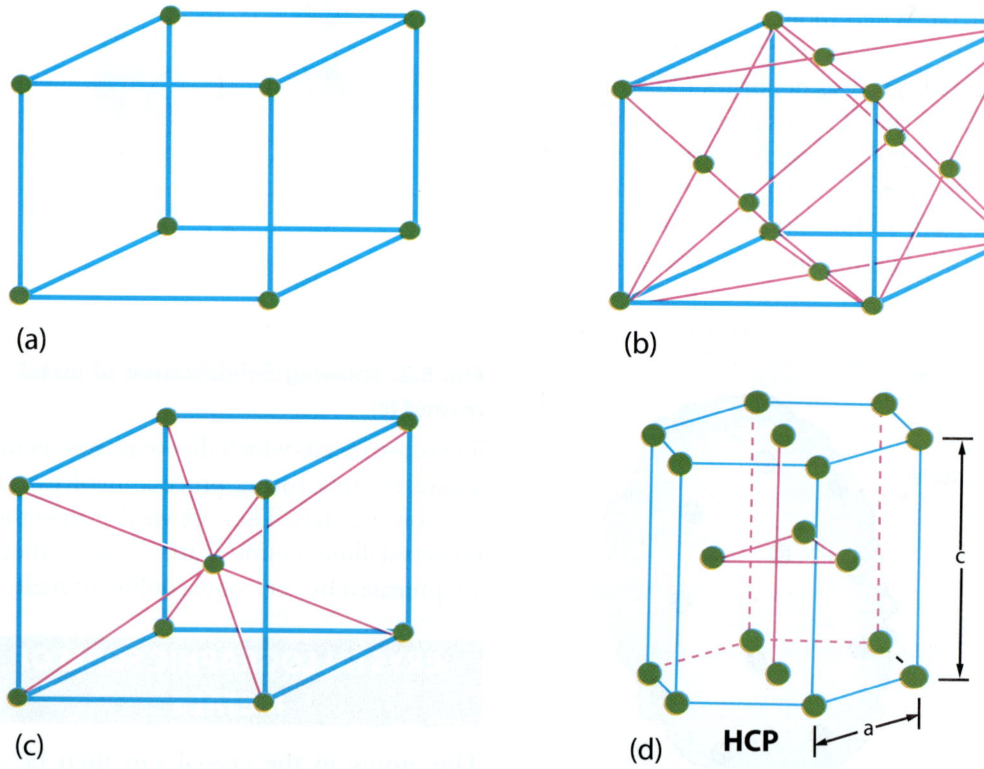

Fig: 6.3. Showing differnt crystal arrangement A. Cubic, B. Face Centered Cubic C. Body centered Cubic D. Hexagonal closed Packed.

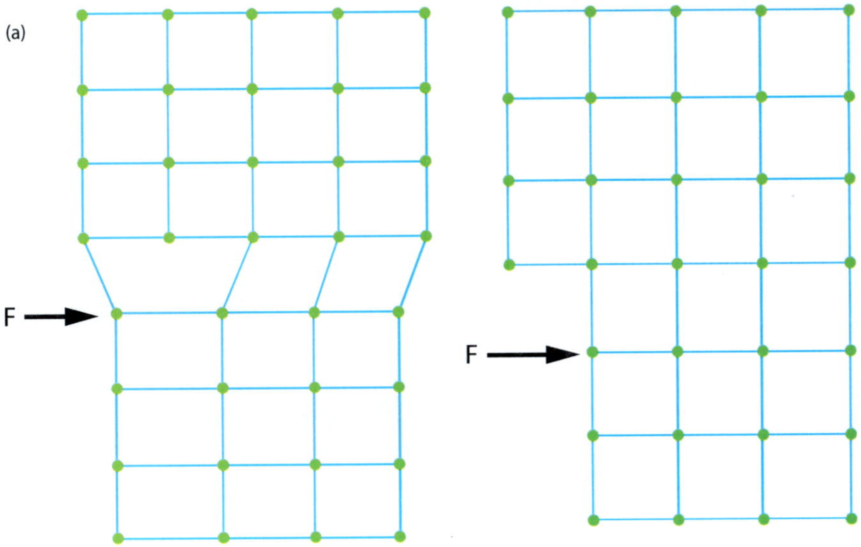

Fig: 6.4. Planer defects.

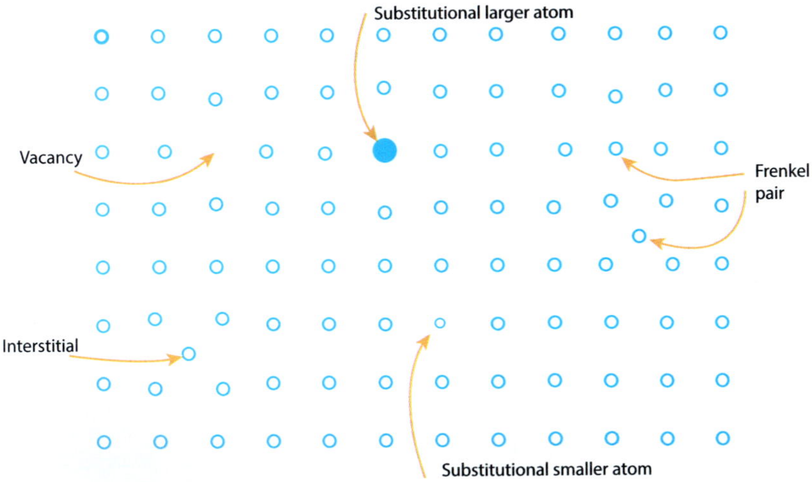

Fig: 6.5. Showing Point defects.

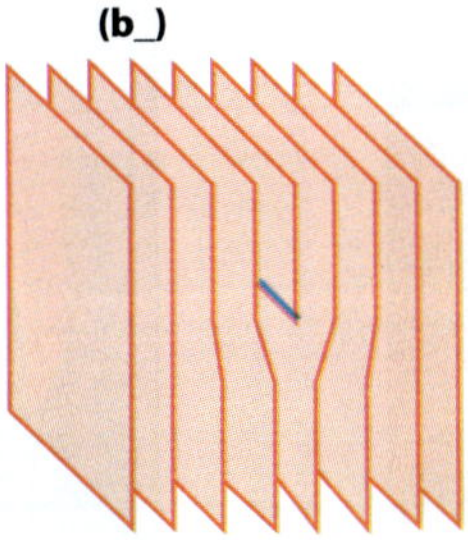

Fig: 6.6. Showing Line defects.

PROPERTIES OF METAL

1. PHYSICAL PROPERTIES

- They have high thermal and electrical conductivity.
- Ability to be deformed under tensile and compressive forces.
- They are opaque shiny and lustrous. Due to the free electrons that do not transmit light waves
- They have high density. This is due to the presence of the tightly packed crystal lattice.

2. CHEMICAL PROPERTIES

- They form cations through the loss of electrons that react with oxygen resulting in corrosion.
- Plating metals can decrease corrosion.

3. MECHANICAL PROPERTIES

- They are ductile and malleable.
- They can be deformed plastically due to the application of stress and change in temperature.

DUCTILITY

- The ability of a metal to plastically deform without breaking or fracturing.
- The ability of a material to be bent or stretched without undergoing fracture.

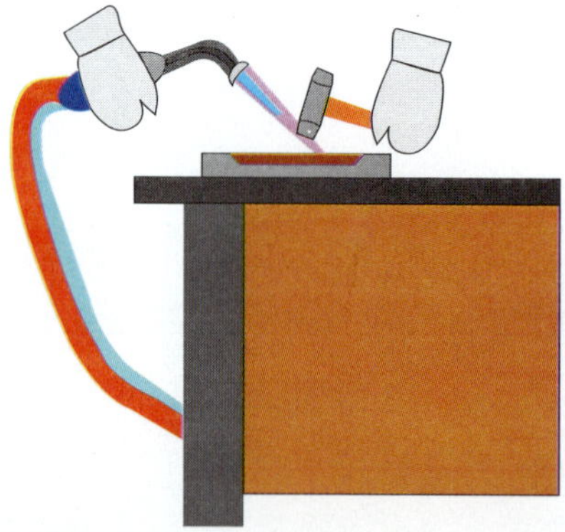

Fig: 6.7. Illustration showing working on material.

MALLEABILITY

- The ability of a material to be hammered or pressed to thin sheets without undergoing fracture.

Fig: 6.8. Illustration showing hammering of a material.

SHAPING OF METALS & ALLOYS

There are three ways for shaping metals and alloys;

- Casting
- Cold working
- Amalgamation

1. CASTING

"It is a procedure in which molten metal is poured in mould"

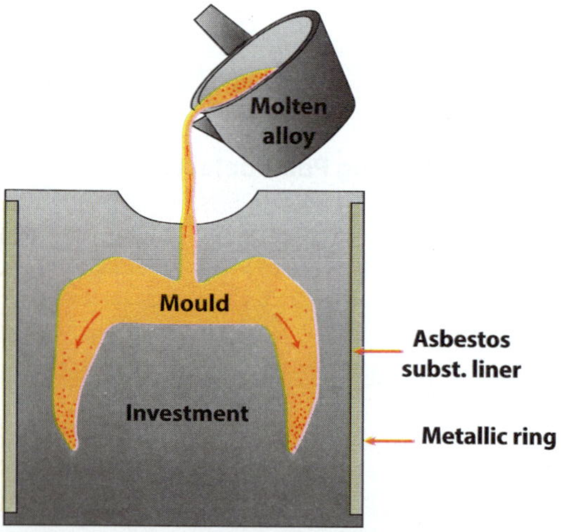

Fig: 6.9. Casting Procedure.

2. COLD WORKING

It is defined as the plastic deformation of metals below the recrystallization temperature. In most cases of manufacturing, such cold forming is done at room temperature. Sometimes, however, the working may be done at elevated temperatures that will provide increased ductility and reduced strength, but will be below the recrystallization temperature.

Movement of dislocations along the slip planes within the crystal structure due to high shear stress results in plastic deformation. Since these movements/deformations are occurring at low temperatures and at stresses greater than the yield stress, it is referred to as cold working. Dislocations may collect and prevent further plastic deformation since no atomic planes can slip over each other and hence the strength of the metal increases.

Effects of cold working

- Change in the metals microstructure with increased concentration of dislocations at the grain boundaries.
- Changes in grain shape .They are not equiaxed rather they acquire a fibrous grain structure.

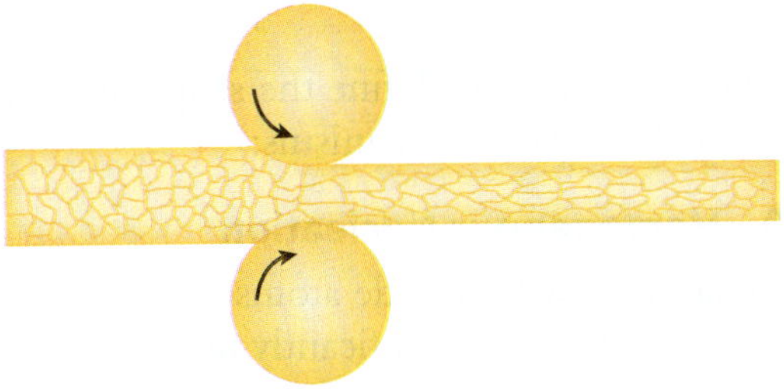

Cold work being rolled
into copper alloy strip.

Fig: 6.10. Showing grain shape change during cold working.

- The material becomes harder and stronger and has a high value of yield stress.
- The properties of ductility and malleability are decreased.
- Formation of internal stresses within the metal.
- It is also referred to as ***work hardening.***
- Strength of the material may fall as the working temperature is elevated.
- As the dislocations collect the strength of the material increases.
- Cold working beyond the limit of ductility and malleability results in a fracture of the material.

Temperature below which work hardening is possible is called as ***recrystallization temperature***.

- If cold worked metal with a fibrous grain structure is heated above recrystallization temperature, the atoms will come back to its equiaxed position and become softer.
- The material will have high value of ductility and lower value of yield stress.
- Recrystallization temperature can be called as ***softening temperature*** for metals.
- This temperature can have adverse effect on the mechanical properties of metal.
- If the material is maintained above recrystallization temperature for sufficient period of time diffusion of atoms may occur across grain boundary resulting in grain growth.
- This may affect the properties hence should be avoided.
- Cold working can cause the formation of internal stresses in the metal. Once these stresses are relieved it may lead to distortion of the object.
- These internal stresses can be avoided or eliminated by using low temperature heat treatment ***stress relief annealing***.
- Annealing is done at temperatures below recrystallization temperature.

APPLICATION IN DENTISTRY;

- Formation of wires used as clasps.
- Bending of wires or clasps during fabrication and alteration of appliances.
- Base plates of dentures.

ADVANTAGES
No heat required
Better surface finish
Superior dimensional structure
Better reproducibility
Contamination problem is minimized
DISADVANTAGES
Greater force required
Heavy machinery required for it
Metal is less ductile
Metal surface must be clean
Undesirable residual stresses may be produced

3. AMALGAMATION

It is defined as the process of combining or uniting multiple entities into one form. In dentistry, amalgam is an alloy of mercury with various metals used for dental fillings. It commonly consists of mercury, silver, tin, copper, and other trace metals. Dental amalgams were first documented in a Tang Dynasty medical text written by Su Kung in 659, and appeared in Germany in 1528. In the 1800s, amalgam became the dental restorative material of choice due to its low cost, ease of application, strength, and durability.

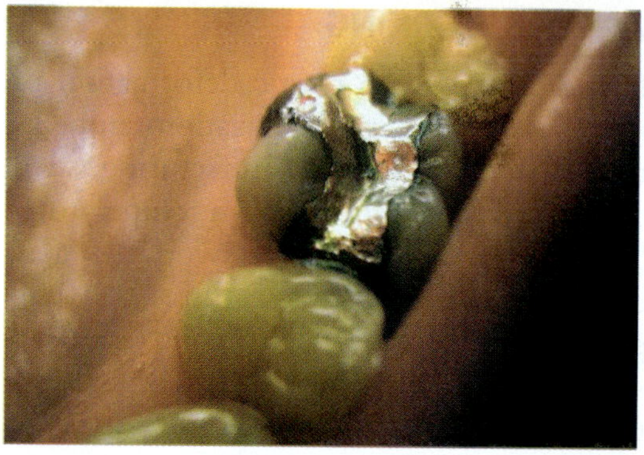

Fig: 6.11. Showing amalgam filling in molar tooth.

SOLIDIFICATION OF METALS

Freezing or **solidification** is a phase transition in which a liquid turns into a solid when its temperature is lowered below its point. Solidification is a comprehensive process of transformation of the melt of an alloy into a solid piece of the alloy, involving crystallization of the liquid phase, segregation of impurities and alloying elements, liberation of the gases dissolved in the melt, shrinkage cavities and porosity formation. Metals are melted to produce finished and semi-finished parts.

TWO STEPS OF SOLIDIFICATION

Nucleation: Formation of stable nuclei.

Growth of nuclei: Formation of grain structure.

Thermal gradients define the shape of each grain. Two main mechanisms:

A. Homogenous Nucleation

Metal itself will provide atoms to form nuclei. Metal, when significantly undercooled, has several slow moving atoms which bond each other to form nuclei. Cluster of atoms below *critical size* is called embryo. If the cluster of atoms reaches critical size, they grow into crystals. Else get dissolved. Cluster of atoms that are greater than critical size are called nucleus.

B. Heterogeneous nucleation

Nucleation occurs in a liquid on the surfaces of structural material, insoluble impurities and other structural material that lower. These structures, called *nucleating agents*, lower the free energy required to form stable nucleus.

Nucleating agents also lower the critical size. Smaller amount of undercooling is required for solidification. Used excessively in industries.

COOLING CURVES

A **cooling curve** represents the change of phase of matter, typically from a gas to a solid or a liquid to a solid.

Below illustration is an example of a cooling curve used in castings. As the metal changes its state from liquid to solid, the latent heat of fusion entrapped between atoms. Then changes occur, heat energy released and causes the falling temperature of a cooling metal. Temperature of liquid metal is raised and remains at that temperature until it solidifies. This is known as arrest. Above the arrest, metal is in liquid state and temperature at which first solid occurs is known as *Liquidus*. Below the arrest the metal is in solid state and the temperature at which the last solidifies is known as *Solidus*.

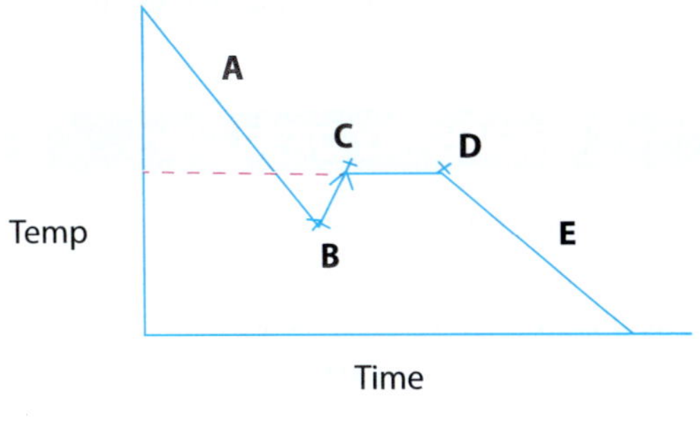

Fig: 6.12. Cooling pattern of pure metal showing (A) Liquid, (B) Supercooling, (C) Beginning of solidification or Liquidus, (D) End of Solidification or Solidus, and (E) Solid.

CORING

During solidification the composition of grains may not be uniform. This causes the exterior of the material to harden faster than the interior. Coring causes the centres of the grains to retain more of the higher melting temperature element. In this case, the dendrite arms formed from the exterior have a different composition than the alloy in the inner regions, resulting in a local compositional difference. Thus, introduction of non-Homogenous structure as the solid solution alloy solidifies is known as Coring.

GRAIN STRUCTURE

When metals solidify, represent following structures

- Equiaxed grain structure
- Fine grain
- Coarse grain
- Refined grain structure

1. EQUIAXED GRAIN STRUCTURE

- After crystallization, grain have same dimension in each direction, measured from central nucleus.
- They are not perfectly spherical or cubic.

2. FINE GRAIN STRUCTURE

- Is achieved by QUENCHING.
- Many nuclei of crystallization.
- Large number of small grains.
- Generally harder and have higher value of yield stress.

3. REFINED GRAIN STRUCTURE

- Few nuclei of crystallization.
- Larger grain size.
- Normally fine grain structure achieved by seeding the molten materials with an additive metals which forms nuclei of crystallization.
- Achieved by slow cooling.

QUENCHING

Is defining as "a procedure in which rapid cooling of molten metal's or alloys following casting".

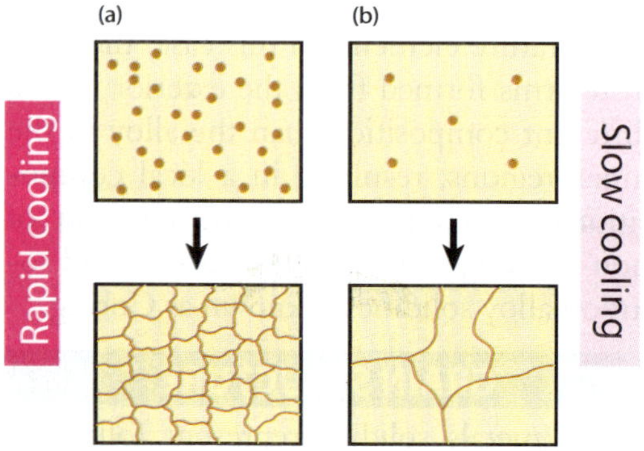

Fig: 6.13. Showing grain Changes, due to different cooling melteod A. Rapid Cooling B. Slow cooling.

Rapid cooling, as by immersion in oil or water, of a metal object from the high temperature at which it has been shaped. This usually is undertaken to maintain mechanical properties associated with a crystalline structure or phase distribution that would be lost upon slow cooling. The technique is commonly applied to steel objects, to which it imparts hardness. On the other hand, copper objects that have become hardened by hammering or other deformation at ordinary temperatures can be restored to the malleable state by heating and quenching.

ANNEALING

In case of annealing the material is heated upto some temperature near solid liquid line of phase diagram. In case of steel, temperature is raised to austenite region. There the metals are soaked for some time depending on size of metal and then furnace cooled. This kind of slow cooling provides the time for grain growth and avoids presence of stress within materials. The annealed metal is soft, ductile and at the same time tough with sufficient strength.

NORMALISING

In this treatment the temperature of metal is raised to processing temperature. Then the material is cooled in air this provides intermediate strength and ductility with specific grain growth depending on the composition of metal/alloy.

STRESS RELIEVING TREATMENTS

Electro polishing	Surface irregulaties produced. Remove by polishing.
Annealing	Controlled heating & cooling process designed to produce desired properties in a metal. To stabilize & increase machinability
Alloy Ageing	Lower temp treatment approx 100 C for 1 hour. Remove internal stress produce during cutting. Increase storage life.

CHEMISTRY OF ALLOYS

Alloy is a metallic material formed by the intimate blending of two more metals. Some time a non – metal may be added.

OR

Alloy is a combination of two or more metals which are generally, mutually soluble in the liquid condition.

METHOD OF ALLOYING OR ALLOYAGE

The processes of making alloys Are;

1. By melting together the base metal and the alloying element, mixing them thoroughly, and allowing the mixture to cool and solidify – this is a common method.
2. Sintering or by powder metallurgy – Metals are powdered, mixed and pressed to the desired shape and then heated but not melted till the powders unite to form a solid mass.

AIMS OF ALLOYING

a. To lower the melting point.
b. To increase hardness and strength.
c. To increase fluidity of liquid metal.
d. To increase resistance to tarnish and corrosion.
e. To change the microscopic structure of the metal.
f. To change the colour of the metal.
g. To make casting or working on the metal easy.

CLASSIFICATION OF ALLOYS

It can be classified on the following basis:

1. ON THE BASIS OF NOBILITY

Alloys with noble metals		Alloys with noble metals
Gold-based Au+Pd+Pt ≥75% (most gold)	Low-gold Au+Pd+Pt 25-75%	Cobalt-chromium (Co-Cr)
Palladium-based Au+Pd+Pt ≥75% (most palladium)	Silver-based alloys (Ag-Pd)	Titanium (Ti)
"Precious" (at least 75% noble metals)	"Semi-precious" (25-75% noble metals)	"Non-precious" (base metals)

Noble metals: Gold (Au), Palladium (Pd) Platinum (Pt)
Silver (Ag) is not a noble metal

2. ON THE BASIS OF NUMBER OF METALS

1. **Binary Alloy**

   Mixtures of two metals are termed binary alloys.

2. **Ternary Alloy**
   - Mixtures of three metals are termed ternary alloys.

3. **Quaternary Alloys**
   - Mixture of four metals are termed quaternary alloy.

3. ON THE BASIS OF MISCIBILITY (SOLUBILITY)

a. **Solid Solution**
   - These are the alloys in which two ingredient metals are soluble in each other both in liquid state as well as in solid state for example gold and copper alloys.

b. **Eutectic Mixture**
   - The ingredient metals are soluble in each other; in liquid state, but separate out (precipitate) as different layers in solid state.
   - For example: Silver and Copper alloys.

c. **Intermetallic Compound**
   - Partial solubility by chemical reaction.
   - For example: Silver and tin alloy.

d. **Peritectic Alloy**
   - They are the alloys involving phase reactions and transformations upon solidification because of partial solubility of constituent metals.
   - For example: - Ag and Sn.

4. ON THE BASIS OF DENTAL USE

a. **Casting Alloys**
   - Dental casting gold alloys.
   - Silver Palladium.
   - Nickel Chromium. (Ni / Cr)
   - Cobalt Chromium. (Co / Cr)

b. **Wrought Alloys**
   - Stainless steel.
   - Cobalt Chromium Nickel. (Co / Cr / Ni)
   - Titanium Alloys.
   - Gold.

c. **Alloys for Porcelain Bonding**
   - High Gold.
   - Medium Gold.
   - Silver Palladium. (Ni / Cr)

d. **Alloys for Implant**
   - Titanium.
   - Hydroxyl Apatite – Coated titanium.

e. **Alloy for Filling Of Restorative Purposes**
   - Amalgam.
   - Pure gold filling.

PHASE DIAGRAMS

Alloys can consist of different phases depending upon composition and temperature. Phase diagram is a graphical way of representing relationship between phases.

These diagrams give information about particular phase being present at specific temperature.

SOLID SOLUTIONS

Easy way to understand phase diagram is to consider a binary system of element or two system element. For instance steel which is an alloy of iron and carbon. The Fe-C phase diagram is shown in the following diagram.

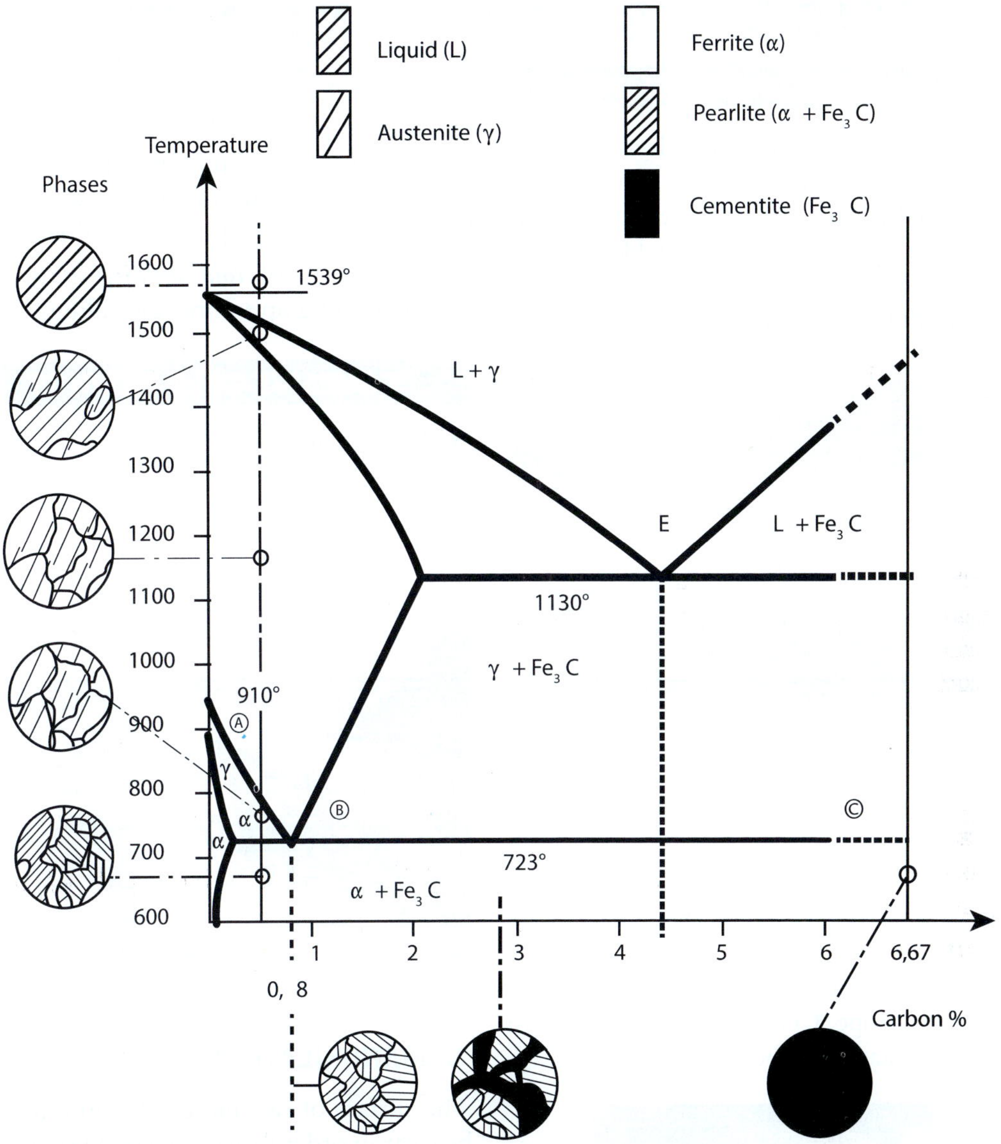

Fig: 6.14. Showing iron carbon phase diagram.

Iron carbon diagram gives relationship between different phases of steel alloy as a function of temperature. The phase's morphology is dependent upon the composition or in particular the amount of carbon in iron. At very lower percentages of carbon only single phase " ferrite" is present at room temperature but at this point if we raise the temperature beyond 900^{0}C then phase transformation takes place and results in austenite. Moving onwards at x-axis at higher percentage of carbon; greater then 0.8% the phase will change to pearlite which is a lamellar mixture of ferrite (white) and cementite (black line). In (Fig: 6.14) iron carbon phase diagram gives the relation between different phases that may be present at any given temperature.

GOLD & NOBLE ALLOYS IN DENTISTRY

INTRODUCTION

Gold is very malleable, ductile and can be readily cold worked. This characteristic is utilized in the restoration of teeth using pure gold fillings. Alloys of gold are commonly used for cast restorations. It's an historical filling material.

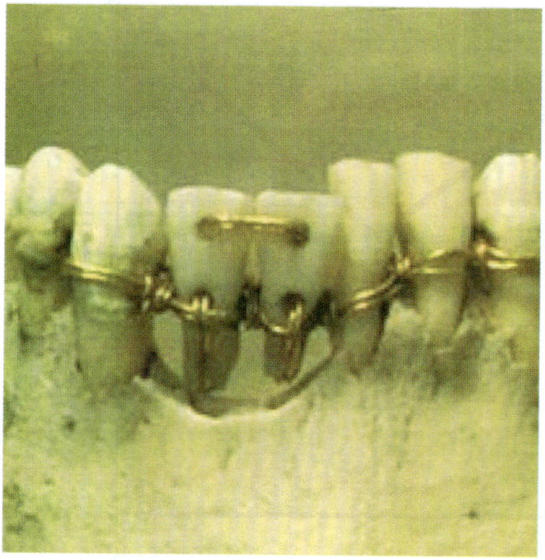

Fig: 6.15. Showing loose teeth were held together with gold wire.

In certain regions of the world, especially in Eastern Europe, Central Asia gold teeth are worn as a status symbol of wealth.

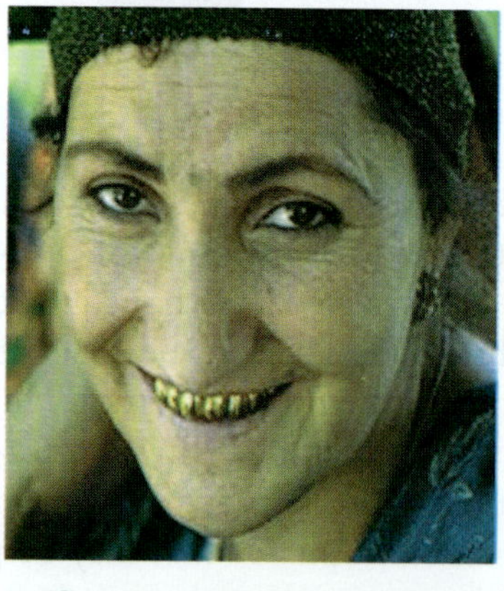

Fig: 6.16. Showing lady with gold crown.

PURE GOLD FILLINGS

When two pieces of pure gold are pressed together, metallic bonds are formed at their point of contact and the gold is welded together, without the application of heat.

This property of ***cold welding*** *is* utilized when building up a pure gold filling.

COHESIVE GOLD FILLINGS

- Manipulation
- Degassing
- Compaction

Fig: 6.17. Showing gold foil.

1. MANIPULATION

The surface of two pieces of gold foil must be clear in order to achieve good bond.

2. DEGASSING

Before packing gold foil into a cavity it should be heated in an electric furnace or gas flame at temperature. 250 C – 350 C.

The purpose of heating is to remove absorbed gases, particularly O2 from the metal surface, in order to improve the weld ability or contact between foils.

3. COMPACTION

After degassing clean and decontaminated piece is packed into the cavity. Each piece is condensed or compacted by a number of methods.

- A plugger and hand mallet.
- A pneumatic vibratory condenser.
- An electrically driven condenser.

The force of compaction should be applied to the surface of the foil.

Properties

- It is perfectly corrosion resistant.
- Does not rely on a relatively soluble cement lute for retention.
- No gingival irritation.
- Less marginal leakage.

TRADITIONAL CASTING GOLD ALLOYS

Pure gold is a soft and ductile metal and it's not involved in casting restoration and appliances. Dental casting gold are alloyed with copper, silver, platinum, nickle and zinc. Alloying gold with these metals not only improves its physical and mechanical properties and also reduces its cost.

TYPES	USES
Type 1, low strength	For castings subject to very slight stress, E.g. inlays.
Type 2, medium strength	For castings subject to moderate stress. e.g. inlays and onlays.
Type 3, high strength	For castings subject to high stress, e.g. onlays, thin cast backings, pontics, full-crowns and saddles.
Type 4, extra high strength	For castings subject to very high stress and thin in cross section, e.g. saddles, bars, clasps, crowns, bridges and partial denture frameworks.

MECHANICAL PROPERTIES OF CASTING GOLD ALLOYS

Type	Hardness	Proportional limit	Strength	Ductility	Corrosion resistance
1					
2	|	|	|	|	|
3	Increases	Increases	Increases	Decreases	Decreases
4	↓	↓	↓	↓	↓

COMPOSITION

Type	Au (%)	Ag (%)	Cu (%)	Pt/Pd (%)	Zn (%)
1 (low strength)	85	11	3	-	1
2 (medium strength)	75	12	10	2	1
3 (high strength)	70	14	10	5	1
4 (extra high strength)	65	9	15	10	1

IDEAL REQUIREMENT OF DENTAL CASTING ALLOYS

a. It should be bio compatible.
b. It should have good corrosion and tarnish resistance.
c. It should not be very hard because it causes difficulty in polishing.
d. It should have adequate mechanical properties.
e. It should have high density and good flow when molten.
f. It should be inexpensive.

FUNCTIONS OF EACH INGREDIENT METAL IN CASTING ALLOY

1. GOLD

- It provides tarnish and corrosion resistance and has a desirable appearance.
- Also provides ductility and malleability.

2. SILVER

- It provides hardness and strength.
- It whitens the alloy thus over comes the reddening effect of copper.

3. COPPER

- It is the principal hardener.
- It reduces the melting point and density of gold and it gives the alloy a reddish color.

4. PLATINUM / PALLADIUM

- It increases strength and corrosion resistance.
- It also increases melting point and has a whitening effect on the alloy.
- It helps to reduce the grain size.

5. ZINC

- It acts as a scavenger for oxygen without zinc the silver in the alloys causes absorption of oxygen during melting.
- It makes the alloy more castable.

LOW GOLD CONTENT ALLOY

Also known as "economical gold". The low gold alloys were developed as a result of increase in gold prices. These alloys were not only less expensive, but also had good tarnish and corrosion resistance. Their properties are comparable to Type 3 and Type 4 gold alloys.

SILVER – PALLADIUM ALLOY

These alloys were introduced as a alternative to gold alloys. It is predominantly silver in composition and palladium (at least 25%) is added to provide nobility and resistance to tarnish. They may or may not contain copper and gold.

COMPOSITION

- Ag → 70 to 75%
- Pd → 25%

PROPERTIES

- They have lower ductility and corrosion resistance.
- They also have a significantly lower density than gold alloy. This may affect its cast ability.

NOBEL ALLOYS FOR METAL – BONDED CERAMIC RESTORATION

Alloys of precious metals are commonly used for the fabrication of metal – bonded Ceramic restorations.

IDEAL REQUIREMENTS

- They should be thermal stability durable.
- They should bond to the ceramic.
- They should be compatible with the ceramic.
- They act as support for the ceramic.

SOLDERING & BRAZING IN NOBLE METALS

INTRODUCTION

In dentistry, it may be necessary to connect metal components together permanently. Examples include assembling wrought alloy clasps to a cast Co-Cr-Mo denture base or connecting the pontic to the abutments of a bridge.

The main techniques of metal joining are:

a. Soldering (Brazing)

b. Welding

Some larger restorations / appliances produced from cast alloys produced in two more parts which are then joined together by soldering or brazing. In dentistry the terms soldering and brazing are used interchangeably.

BRAZING

"An alloy suitable for use as a filler material in operations in which dental alloy(s) parts are joined to form a dental restoration" ISO Standardized.

By definition, the term **soldering** (or soft-soldering) applies where the intermediary alloy melts below 450°C and **brazing** (or hard-soldering, sometimes silver-soldering) where this temperature is above 450°C.

Practically, the difference is that soldering is carried out where significant mechanical strength is not required in the joint whereas brazing uses an Ag-Cu solder to obtain considerable strength.

IDEAL REQUIREMENTS FOR SOLDERING AND BRAZING

- It should be capable of forming a *strong corrosion resistant joint* b/w the two components being joined without changing their structure or properties.
- There should be no visible signs of corrosion when a brazed joint is *soaked in a solution of lactic acid* and *sodium chloride* for 7 *days*.
- In order that the components being joined do not suffer from recrystallization, grain growth or distortion during the brazing procedure it is important that the brazing material has a *flow temperature which is well below the melting point* of the alloys being joined.

FLOW TEMPERATURE

"As the lowest temperature at which the filler material is fluid enough to flow into the gap and to wet the surface of the metallic parts".

Procedure Issues

- Solders are susceptible to oxidation during the melting procedure and the resulting oxides can weaken the soldered joint.
- So, for this reason we can add **Fluxes**, in order to protect the alloy surface from oxidation during soldering e.g. Fluoride Salt and Borax.

TECHNIQUES OF SOLDERING

Where high precision is not required, the components may be FREEHAND SOLDERED. This involves holding the components in contact over the heat source by hand, after the flux and solder have been applied. The complete assembly is heated until the solder flows

- Where greater accuracy is required, **JIG SOLDERING** may be employed and a small jig used to hold the components in more accurate registration before heating
- For precision soldering, such as the

joining of the components of a bridge, the pontic and abutments are first placed on the master cast and assembled with sticky wax (which is kept clear of the surfaces to be soldered). The temporarily assembled structure in then invested in dental investment - **INVESTMENT SOLDERING** - and the investment allowed to set.

Fig: 6.18. Showing Soldering Procedure.

FUNCTIONS OF SOLDERS

The solders must melt below that of liquefaction of the alloy to be soldered.

1. Solders must wet the alloy to be soldered and they should have low viscosity so thay can flow freely.
2. The corrosion resistance must be controlled since the soldering material is metal and it would be in contact with another metal. This provides the formation of galvanic cell and electrons may flow from one side to another which would result in deterioration of metals i.e. corrosion.
3. Corrosion can be prevented by suitable control over composition.

WELDING

"The joining of metals by melting the relevant surfaces together (with or without a filler metal)". The technique of SPOT WELDING may be used for the joining of stainless steel components, in certain circumstances. The spot-welding device consists of two copper electrodes between which the components to be joined are placed. The components are held in contact under pressure and a large current is passed across the electrodes and through the components for a brief period. If the electrical conductivity of these components is relatively low, the heat generated is sufficient to melt the metal at the point of contact. Other alloys which are suitable for spot welding include Co-Cr-Mo and Ni-Cr but the technique cannot be applied to the gold alloys.

BASE METAL CASTING ALLOYS

INTRODUCTION

Base metal alloys contain no gold, silver, and platinum or palladium. The two most commonly used base metal alloys in dentistry are:

- Nickel – chromium (Ni / Cr)
- Cobalt – chromium (Co / Cr)

- But electrical induction method is to be favoured because it is carried out under more controlled condition.
- When using oxyacetylene flames the ratio of oxygen to acetylene must be carefully controlled otherwise;
  - Too much oxygen may cause oxidation of the alloy.

COMPOSITION OF BASE METAL ALLOYS

Table: 6.1. Cobalt-Chromium Alloys.

INGREDIENT	PERCENTAGE	FUNCTION
Cobalt	35 – 65 %	Imparts hardness, Strength and rigidity to the alloy. It has a high melting point.
Chromium	20 – 35 %	Its passivating effect ensures Corrosion res star ce. It reduces the melting point. It also acts in solid solution Hardening.
Molybdenum	4 – 8 %	It is affecting hardness. It reduces ductility to a lesser extent than tungsten. It refines grain structure.
Nickel	0.20 %	It decreases strength, hardness modulus of elasticity and fusion temperature. It increases ductility of the alloys. Thus, control of carbon content in alloys is important.

Table: 6.2. Nickle Chromium Alloys.

INGREDIENT	PERCENTAGE	FUNCTION
Nickel	75 %	Same as in cobalt – chromium Alloys.
Chromium	20 %	Same as in cobalt – chromium Alloys.
Molybdenum	4 – 8 %	Same as in cobalt – chromium Alloys.
Beryllium	2 – 4 %	Same as in cobalt – chromium Alloys.

MANIPULATION OF BASE METAL CASTING ALLOYS

The fusion temperatures of the Ni/Cr and Co/Cr alloys varies with composition but are generally in the range 1200-1500 °C.

- Melting of base metal alloys by acetylene – oxygen flame or an electrical induction furnace.
  - An excess of acetylene produces an increase in the metal carbide content leading to embitterment.
- Investment mould for base metal alloys must be capable of maintaining their integrity at high casting temperature used.
- For investment; silica – bonded and phosphate bonded materials are favoured.
- The density values of base metal alloys

are approximately half those of the casting gold alloys.

- For this reason the thrust developed during casting may be somewhat lower, with the possibility that the casting may not adequately fill the mould.
- Casting machines used for base metal alloys must therefore be capable of producing extra thrust, which over comes this deficiency.
- The greatest expense involved in producing a Co / Cr dental casting is in the time required for trimming and polishing.
- Finer investment can be used to give a smooth surface requiring less finishing.
- The Co/Cr is very hard and difficult to polish – After casting, it is usual to sandblast.
- The metal to remove any surface roughness or adherent investment material as well as the green layer of oxide which coats the surface after casting. Electrolytic polishing may then be carried out.
- The process of electro polishing is not used for Ni/Cr alloy castings.
- Ni/Cr is normally used for crown and bridgework and it is necessary to maintain the accuracy.
- This accuracy may be lost during polishing procedures and care is required to avoid such problems.

COMPARISON WITH CASTING GOLD ALLOYS

The two groups of base metal alloys offer alternatives to the casting gold alloys at potentially considerable saving in cast. Following table gives comparison with casting gold alloys.

Table: 6.3. Comparison between base metal alloys.

PROPERTIES (UNIT)	Co/Cr	Ni/Cr
Density (g cm – 3)	8	8
Fusion Temperature	As high as	as high as
1500	C1350 C	
Casting shrinkage (%)	2.3	2.0
Tensile strength (Mpa)	850	600
Proportional limit (Mpa)	700	500
Modulus of elasticity (Gpa)	220	220
Hardness (Vickers)	420	300
Ductility (% elongation)	3	3 – 30

Table: 6.4. Comparative properties of Co/Cr alloys and type 4 casting gold alloys for partial dentures.

PROPERTY (UNITS)	Co/Cr	TYPE 4 GOLD ALLOY	COMMENTS
Density (g cm^{-3})	8	15	More difficult to produce defect-free casting for Co/Cr alloys but denture frameworks are lighter
Fusion temperature	As high as 1500°C	Normally lower than 1000°C	Co/Cr alloys require electical induction furnace or oxyacetylene equipment Cannot use gypsum-bonded investments for Co/Cr alloys
Casting shrinkage (%)	2.3	1.4	Mostly compensated for correct choice of investment
Tensile strength (MPa)	850	750	Both acceptable
Proportional limit (MPa)	700	500	Both acceptable; car resist stresses without deformation
Modulus of elasticity (GPa)	220	100	Co/Cr more rigid for equivalent thickness; advantage for connectors; disadvantage for clasps
Hardness (Vickers)	420	250	Co/Cr more difficult to polish but retains polish during service
Ductility (% elongation)	3	15 (as cast) 8 (hardened)	Co/Cr clasps may fracture if adjustments are attempted

Table: 6.5. Comparative properties of Ni/Cr alloys and type 3 casting gold alloys for cast restorations.

PROPERTY (UNITS)	Ni/Cr	TYPE 3 GOLD ALLOY	COMMENTS
Density (g cm^{-3})	8	15	More difficult to produce-free casting for Ni/Cr alloys
Fusion temperature	As high as 1350°C 2.0	Normally lower than 1000°C	Ni/Cr alloys require electical induction furnace or oxyacetylene equipment
Casting shrinkage (%)	2.0	1.4	Mostly compensated for by correct choice of investment
Tensile strength (MPa)	600	540	Both adequate for the applications being considered

Proportional limit (MPa)	500	290	Both high enough to prevent distortion for applications being considered; note that values are lower than for partial denture alloys (Table 6.5)
Modulus of elasticity (GPa)	220	8.5	Higher modulus of Ni/Cr is an advantage for lager restorations, e.g. bridges and for porcelain-bonded restorations
Hardness (Vickers)	300	150	Ni/Cr more diffcult to polish retains polish during service
Ductility (% elongation)	3-30	20	Relatively large values suggest that burnishing is possible; however, large proportional limit values suggest high forces would be required

CAST PARTIAL DENTURE ALLOYS

The two major components of cast partial denture frame works are:

- Connectors
- Clasps

CONNECTORS

"In fixed dental prosthodontics, the portion of a fixed dental prosthesis that unites the retainer(s) and pontics(s)". (GPT). (Fig: 6.19)

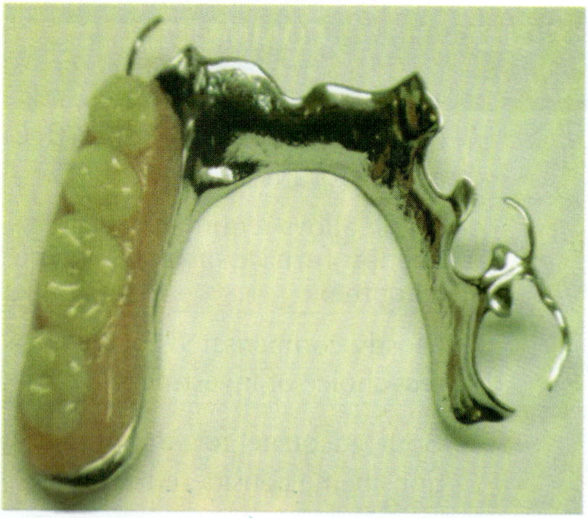

Fig: 6.19. Showing Cast Partial denture.

1. IDEAL REQUIREMENT

a. It should be rigid.

b. It should have high value of modulus of elasticity.

c. It should not be permanently deformed by the action of mechanical stresses.

2. AVAILABLE MATERIAL

- The Co/Cr alloys most closely meet these requirements.
- In addition, the lower density of the Co/Cr means that dentures constructed from material are lighter, the more so if the connectors are of thinner section.

CLASPS

"The component of the clasp assembly that engages a portion of the tooth surface and either enters an undercut for retention or remains entirely above the height of contour to act as a reciprocating element. Generally it is used to stabilize and retain a removable dental prosthesis". (GPT)

1. IDEAL REQUIREMENT

a. It should have high value of proportional limit in order to prevent deformation.

b. A lower value of modulus of elasticity is required and it enables the clasp to increased flexibility.

c. The alloy used to construct clasps should ideally be ductile so that adjustments can be made to clasps without fracturing.

2. AVAILABLE MATERIAL

- The gold alloys most closely match the requirements for clasp since they have adequately high proportional limits, lower value of modulus of elasticity the Co/Cr alloys and greater ductility.

NOTE

There has been an increased use of Ni/Cr alloys for partial denture frame work casting. This is due to the relative ease of finishing and polishing compared with Co/Cr as consequences of the lower hardness value.

BASE METAL ALLOYS FOR PROCELAIN BONDING

MAIN REQUIREMENTS

a. It should be of higher melting point than porcelain.

b. It should be similar co-efficient of thermal expansion to porcelain.

c. Does not cause discoloration of the porcelain.

d. It should have high modulus of elasticity to avoid fracture of porcelain.

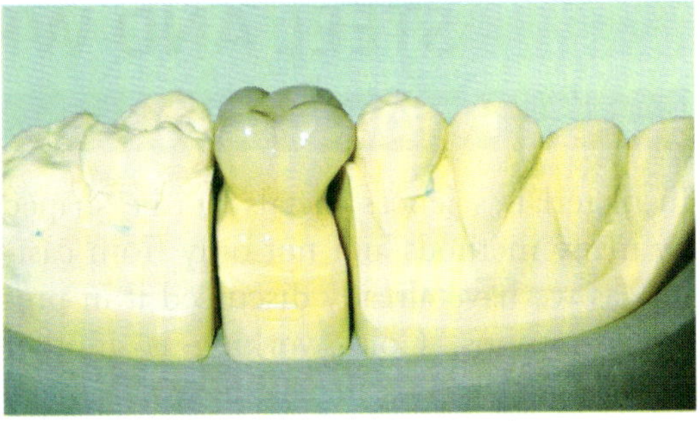

Fig: 6.20. Showing Porcelain crown.

AVAILABLE MATERIAL

- Nickel / Chromium
- Cobalt / Chromium formulation

BIOCOMATIBILITY OF BASE METAL ALLOYS

Base metal casting alloys contain some components which should be regarded as either toxic or known to cause allergic reactions in some people viz.

BERYLLIUM

- It is known as animal carcinogen and possesses a potential threat to dental personal who inhale metal dust during polishing or grinding procedures.

NICKLE

- Nickel causes allergy like contact dermatitis than all other metals. combined and that relatively small nickel concentrations can be problematical.

STEEL AND WROUGHT ALLOYS

INTRODUCTION

In materials sciences metals can be shaped by many methods and not only from casting, as we have already discussed it in previous sections. Cold working is another method for shaping metals, in which metal is hammered, rolled, drawn or bent into the desired shape at temperature well below the recrystallization temperature of the metal, often at room temperature. Thus, metals or alloys which have been cold worked into any desired shape are known as Wrought Alloys.

Example of The use of Wrought Alloys

In dentistry wrought alloys are used for making instruments, burs, wires and occasionally denture bases.

COMMON WROUGHT ALLOYS

- Steel.
- Stainless steel.

STEEL

Steel is an alloy of iron and carbon. The carbon content is less than 2% because greater quantities of carbon produce a very brittle alloy, which is unsuitable for cold working.

STRUCTURES

According to temperature and concentration of carbon, steel is able to adopt a variety of structures. Above 723 °C an interstitial solid solution of carbon in a face, centred cubic iron matrix is formed and is termed as Austenite.

When Austenite is unstable below 723 °C (the critical temperature) the face centred cubic iron matrix breaks down to form two phases:

1st Phase

It consists of a very dilute solid solution of carbon in iron (up to 0.02 % C) and is called ferrite. It is a softer and more ductile.

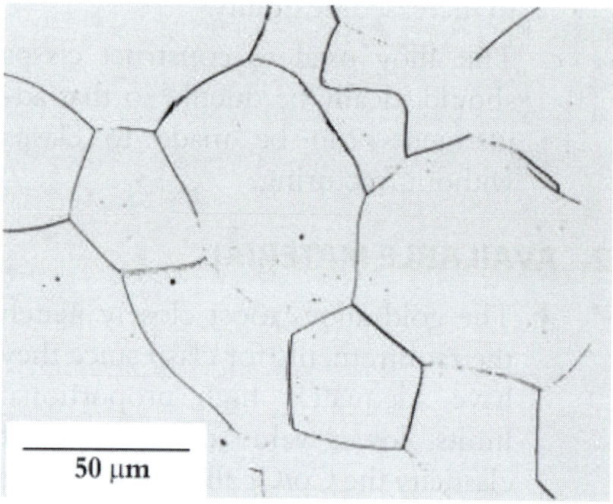

2nd Phase

It is a specific compound of iron and carbon with formula Fe3C2 called Cementite. It is a very hard and brittle material. The mixture of Ferrite and Cementite is termed Pearlite.

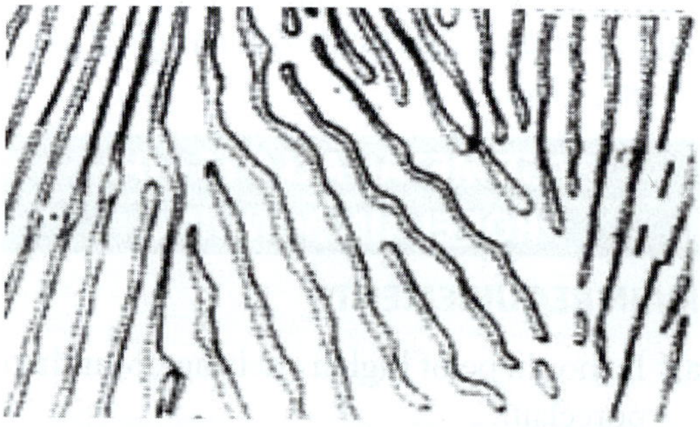

EUTECTIC METALS

Eutectic refers to the behaviour of an alloy of two mutually insoluble metals during crystallization. Eutectic alloys are an alloy containing 0.8% carbon.

HYPER-EUTECTIC ALLOYS

Alloys with greater concentrations of carbon are called Hypereutectoid alloys. The

Hyper-eutectoid alloys contain relatively greater amounts of Cementite and is commonly used to produce cutting instrument such as burs.

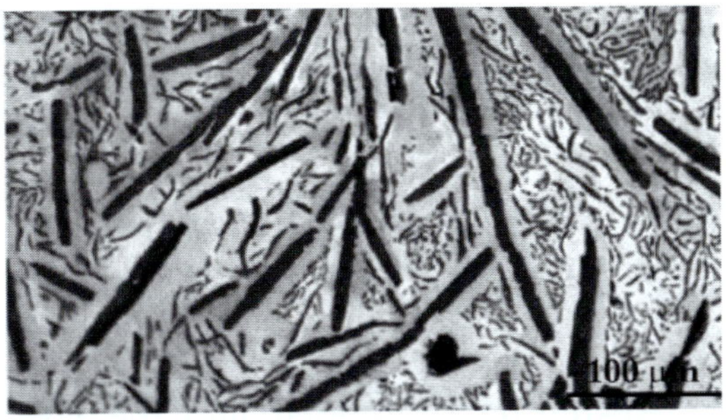

HYPO-EUTECTIC ALLOYS

Alloys with smaller carbon content are called Hypo eutectoid alloys. The Hypo-eutectoid alloys contain greater amount of Ferrite and is used for the construction of non-cutting instruments such as forceps.

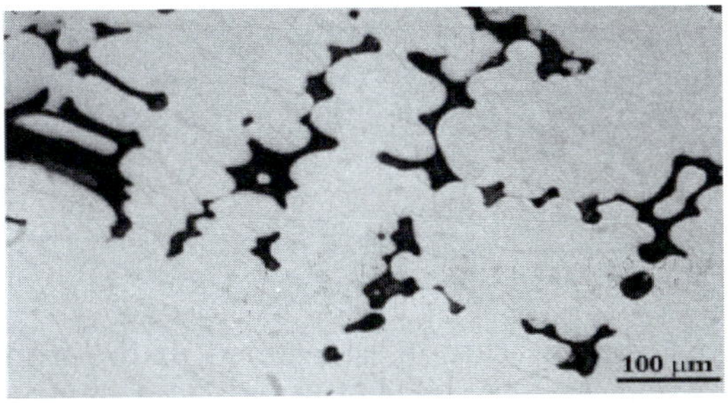

reduction in hardness is usually accompanied by an increase in ductility, thereby decreasing the brittleness of the metal. Tempering is usually performed after quenching, which is rapid cooling of the metal to put it in its hardest state. Tempering is accomplished by controlled heating of the quenched workpiece to a temperature below its "lower critical temperature". This is also called the lower transformation temperature or lower arrest (A_1) temperature; the temperature at which the crystalline phases of the alloy, called Ferrite and Cementite, begin combining to form a single-phase solid solution referred to as Austenite. Heating above this temperature is avoided, so as not to destroy the very-hard, quenched microstructure, called *Martensite*.

The degree of conversion depends on the tempering temperature and the tempering time.

The process of heat treatment and tempering is illustrated in Fig. 6.18.

PROPERTY	HYPER-EUTECTOID	HYPO-EUTECTOID
Hardness	Hard	Soft
Crystal Structure	Cementite	Ferrite
Ductility	Brittle	Ductile
Applications	Cutting instrument e.g. Burs	Non-cutting instrument e.g. Forceps

TEMPERING CYCLE/HEAT TREATMENT OF STEEL

Tempering is a heat treatment technique applied to Ferrous alloys, such as steel or cast iron, to accomplish greater toughness by decreasing the hardness of the alloy. The

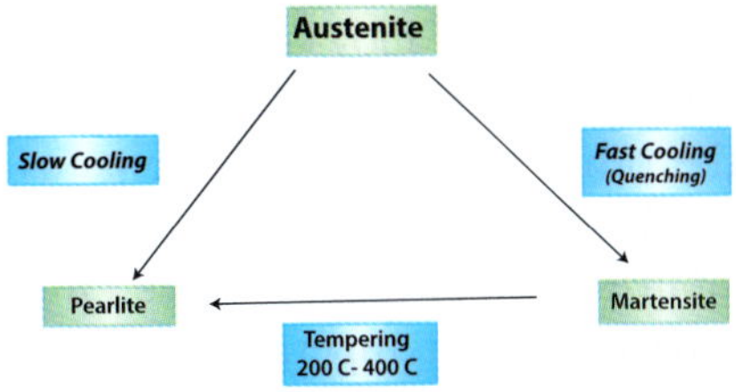

Fig: 6.18. Illustration of tempering cycle.

AUSTENITE

Austenite is a metallic, non-magnetic solid solution of carbon and iron that exists in steel above the critical temperature of 1333°F (723°C). Its face-centred cubic (FCC) structure allows it to hold a high proportion of carbon in solution. As it cools, this structure either breaks down into a mixture of **Ferrite** and **Cementite** (usually in the structural forms pearlite or bainite), or undergoes a slight lattice distortion known as **martensitic transformation**.

The rate of cooling determines the relative proportions of these materials and therefore the mechanical properties (e.g. hardness, tensile strength) of the steel. Quenching (to induce martensitic transformation), followed by tempering (to break down some martensite and retained austenite), is the most common heat treatment for high-performance steels. The addition of certain other metals, such as manganese and nickel, can stabilize the austenitic structure, facilitating heat-treatment of low-alloy steels. In the extreme case of austenitic stainless steel, much higher alloy content makes this structure stable even at room temperature. On the other hand, such elements as silicon, molybdenum, and chromium tend to de-stabilize austenite, raising the eutectoid temperature (the temperature where two phases, Ferrite and Cementite, become a single phase, Austenite).

Austenite can contain far more carbon than Ferrite, between 0.8% at 1333°F (723°C) and 2.08% at 2098°F (1148°C). Thus, above the critical temperature, all of the carbon contained in Ferrite and Cementite (for a steel of 0.8% C) is dissolved in the austenite.

MARTENSITE

Martensite is a body-centered tetragonal form of iron in which some carbon is dissolved. Martensite forms during quenching, when the face centered cubic lattice of **Austenite** is distorted into the body centered tetragonal structure without the loss of its contained carbon atoms into **Cementite** and **Ferrite**.

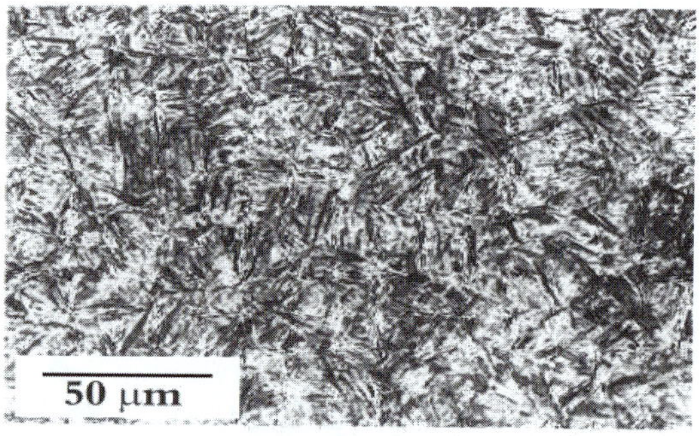

Instead, the carbon is retained in the iron crystal structure, which is stretched slightly so that it is no longer cubic. Martensite is more or less Ferrite supersaturated with carbon. Compare the grain size in the micrograph with **tempered Martensite**.

PEARLITE

Pearlite is a lamellar structure consisting of alternating bands of **Ferrite** and **Cementite**. Pearlite exists in equilibrium in carbon steels at normal temperatures.

ADVANTAGE AND DISADVANTAGE

The ability to be hardened by heat treatment is one of the major *advantages* of steel. It has also a *disadvantage* of its susceptibility to corrosion.

STAINLESS STEEL

Steel is an alloy of iron and carbon but addition of chromium produces a passive surface oxide layer, which gives stainless steel. Nickel is also present in many stainless steels and it contributes towards corrosion resistance and helps to strengthen the alloy.

High oxidation resistance in air at ambient temperature is normally achieved with additions of more than 12% (by weight) chromium. The chromium forms a layer of chromium (III) oxide (Cr2O3) when exposed to oxygen. The layer is too thin to be visible, meaning the metal stays shiny. It is, however, impervious to water and air, protecting the metal beneath. Also, when the surface is scratched this layer quickly reforms. This phenomenon is called passivation by materials scientists, and is seen in other metals, such as aluminium.

When stainless steel parts such as nuts and bolts are forced together, the oxide layer can be scraped off causing the parts to weld together. When disassembled, the welded material may be torn and pitted, an effect that is known as *galling*.

CLASSIFIED BY THEIR CRYSTALLINE STRUCTURE

1. AUSTENITIC STAINLESS STEELS

comprise over 70% of total stainless steel production. They contain a maximum of 0.15% carbon a minimum of 16% chromium and sufficient nickel and/or manganese to retain an austenitic structure at all temperatures from the cryogenic region to the melting point of the alloy. A typical composition is 18% chromium and 8% nickel, commonly known as *18/8 stainless*. Super austenitic stainless steels such as alloy AL-6XN exhibit great resistance to chloride pitting crevice corrosion and stress-corrosion cracking.

2. FERRITIC STAINLESS STEELS

are highly corrosion resistant, but far less durable than austenitic grades and cannot be hardened by heat treatment. They contain between 10.5% and 27% chromium and very little nickel, if any. Most recipes include molybdenum; some, aluminium or titanium. Common ferritic grades include 18Cr-2Mo, 26Cr-1Mo, 29Cr-4Mo, and 29Cr-4Mo-2Ni.

3. MARTENSITIC STAINLESS STEELS

are not as corrosion resistant as the other two classes, but are extremely strong and tough as well as highly machinable, and can be hardened by heat treatment. They contain 11.5 to 18% chromium and significant amounts of carbon. Some grades include additional alloying elements in small quantities.

18 / 8 STAINLESS STEEL

One of the most commonly used stainless steels contain 18 % chromium and 8 % nickel and is termed as 18 / 8 stainless steel.

1. AUSTENITIC STAINLESS STEEL

18 / 8 stainless steel has a critical temperature below the point at which atomic movements are possible and sometimes referred to as Austenitic stainless steel.

Used for non – cutting instruments, wires and occasionally as denture bases.

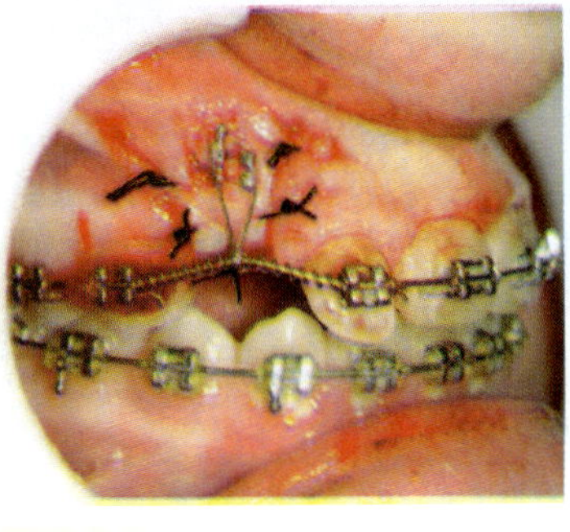

2. MARTENSITIC STAINLESS STEEL

When smaller quantities of chromium and nickel are incorporated into steel it is possible to produce an alloy, which has adequate corrosion resistance, but it can be hardened by heat treatment. This alloy is capable of forming a martensitic structure and referred to as martensitic stainless steel. Used to construct cutting instruments and probes.

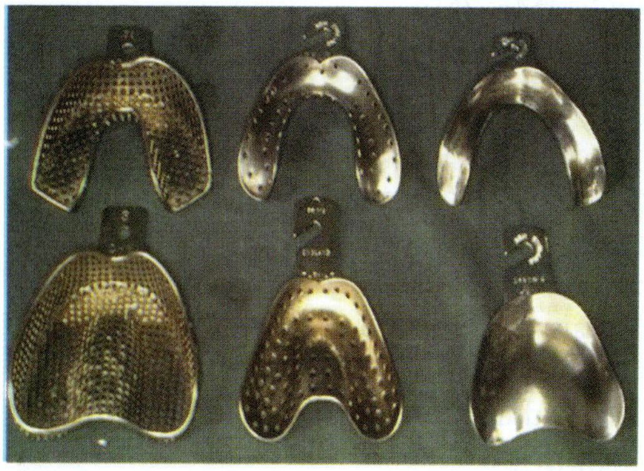

STAINLESS STEEL DENTURE BASES

Stainless steel denture bases are formed from very thin pressed / rolled sheets of wrought stainless steel. A thin sheet of 18 / 8 stainless steel (approximately 0.2 mm thick) is pressed between an alloy or epoxy resin die and counter die. The method of applying the pressure required for swaging may vary.

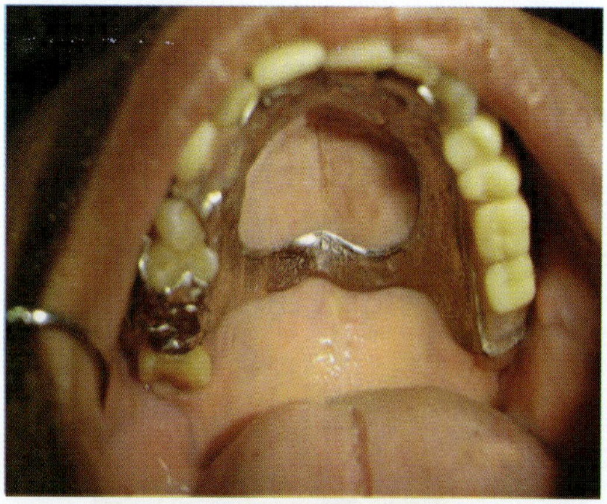

PROPERTIES

a. It has high values of modulus of elasticity and proportional limit.
b. It is fracture resistant.
c. It has good thermal conductivity.
d. Such dentures are not heavy, because of the thinness of the material and the fact that the density of steel is not high compared to some other metallic materials.

ADVANTAGES

Stainless steel denture bases conduct heat rapidly through the thin metallic sheet, thus ensuring that the patient retains a normal reflex reaction to hot and cold stimuli.

DISADVANTAGES

The main disadvantages are the lack of surface detail on the swaged plate and perhaps more significantly the involved technique required for swaging attaching retention tags by welding and processing of the acrylic parts of the denture.

WIRES

Wires are normally produced by drawing an ingot of alloy through dies of gradually decreasing cross – section to produce a circular, ovoid or square section are wire in which the grain structure is highly fibrous in nature.

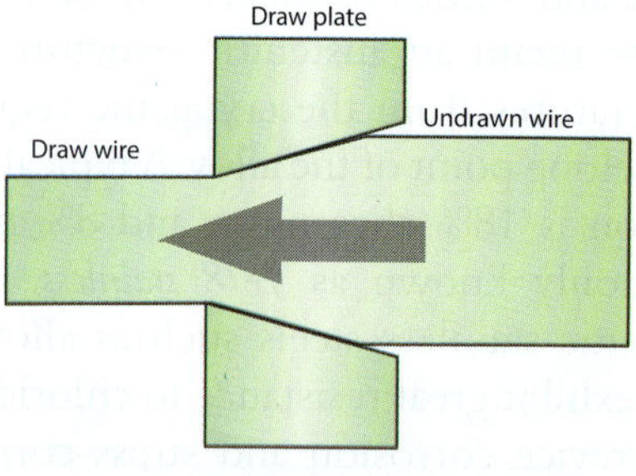

3. IDEAL REQUIREMENTS

a. It should have springiness.
b. It should be stiff.
c. It should be good corrosion resistant in order that it can withstand attack from oral fluids.
d. It should possess sufficient ductility to resist fracture during Its bending procedure.
e. It should be capable of being easily joined either by soldering or by welding, without impairing the mechanical properties of the wire or reducing the corrosion resistance.

Table: 6.6. Summary of properties of commonly used wires.

MATERIAL	STIFFNESS	SPRINGBACK ABILITY	DUCTILITY	EASE OF SOLDERING OR WELDING
Stainless steel	High	Good	Adequate	Reasonable
Gold alloy	Medium	Adequate	Adequate	Easy to solder
Co/Cr alloy	High	Adequate following heat treatment	Good in soft state	Difficult
Ni/Ti alloy	Low	Excellent	Poor	Difficult
β-To	Medium	Good	Adequate	Joined by welding

REFERENCES

1. Degarmo, E. Paul; Black, J T. Kohser, Ronald A. (2003), Materials and Processes in Manufacturing (9th ed.), Wiley, ISBN 0-471-65653-4.
2. Smith, William F. Hashemi, Javad (2006), Foundations of Materials Science and Engineering (4th ed.), McGraw-Hill, ISBN 0-07-295358-6.
3. Powers John M. Wataha John C.(2013), Dental Materials: Properties and Manipulation (10th ed.), Elsevier, ISBN 978-0-323-07836-8
4. Noort, Richard Van. (2007), Introduction to dental materials (3rd ed.), Elsevier, ISBN 978 0 7234 34047
5. William D. Callister, Jr., David G. Rethwisch (2009), Materials Science and Engineering (8th ed.), John Wiley & Sons Canada, Limited, ISBN 9780470556733
6. John F.mccabe & Angus W.g Walls(2008), *Applied Dental Materials,* Blackwell Publisher, Hong Kong
7. Beddoes, J. and Bibby, M.J. Principles of Metal Manufacturing Processes. Elsevier Butterworth-Heinemann, 1999. ISBN 0-340-73162-1

Chapter

7

CASTING PROCEDURE FOR DENTAL ALLOYS

Dr. Adeel & Dr. Mustafa

CASTING

Casting is the process by which a wax pattern of a restoration is converted to a replicate in a dental alloy. (Fig: 7.1) The casting process is used to make dental restorations such as inlays, onlays, crowns, bridges and removable partial dentures. (Fig: 7.2)

In dentistry all casting is done using same form or adaptation of the lost wax technique. The lost wax technique has been used for centuries but its use in dentistry was not common until 1907 when W.H. Taggart introduced his technique with the casting machine.

The process consists of surrounding the wax pattern with a mold made of heat resistant investment material, eliminating the wax by heating and then introducing molten metal into the mold through a channel called sprue. In dentistry the resulting casting must be an accurate reproduction of the wax pattern in both surface details and overall dimension. Small variation in investing or casting can significantly affect the quality of the final restoration. Successful castings depend on attention to detail and consistency of technique. An understanding of the exact influence of each variable in the technique is important so rational decisions can be made to modify the technique as needed for a given procedure.

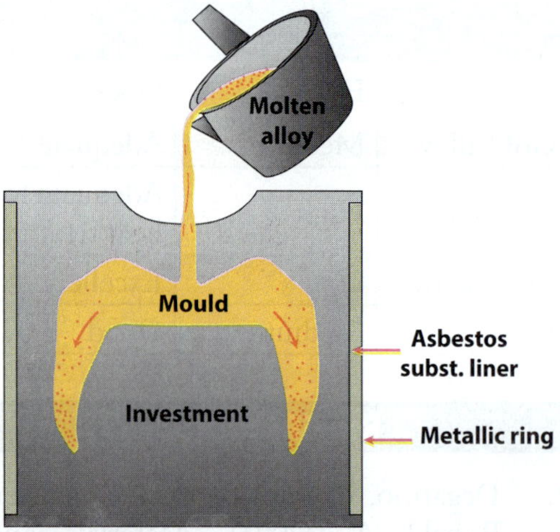

Fig: 7.1. Illustration showing the procedure of Casting.

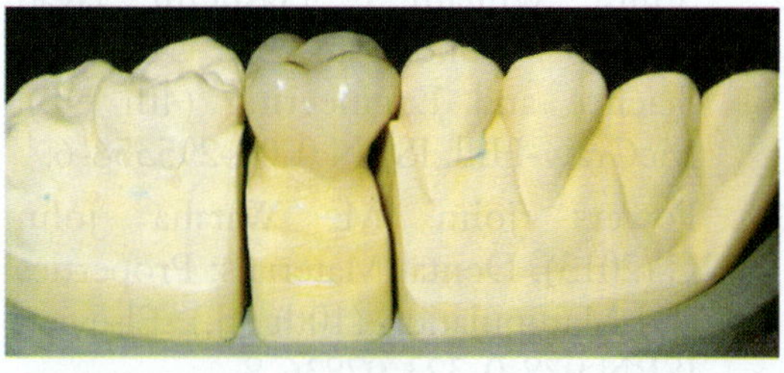

Fig: 7.2. Porcelain fused to metal crown.

STEPS IN MAKING A CAST RESTORATION

Following are the Steps of Making Metal Crown.

- Tooth / teeth preparation.
- Impression.
- Model pouring.
- Wax pattern fabrication.
- Attachment of sprue former.
- Ring liner placement.
- Investing.
- Burn out or wax elimination.
- Casting.
- Recovery.
- Pickling.
- Polishing

DETAIL OF STEPS

1. TOOTH / TEETH PREPARATION

- Prepare a tooth or teeth to receive a cast restoration. (Fig: 7.3)

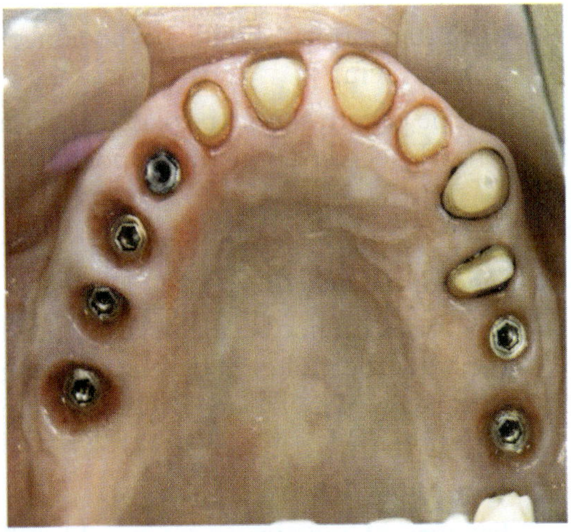

Fig: 7.3. Clinical picture showing upper arch in which crown cutting is done in anterior teeth.

2. IMPRESSION

- After crown cutting next stage is to take an accurate impression of the prepared tooth. (Fig: 7.4)
- Available materials are;
  - Alginate
  - Elastomers

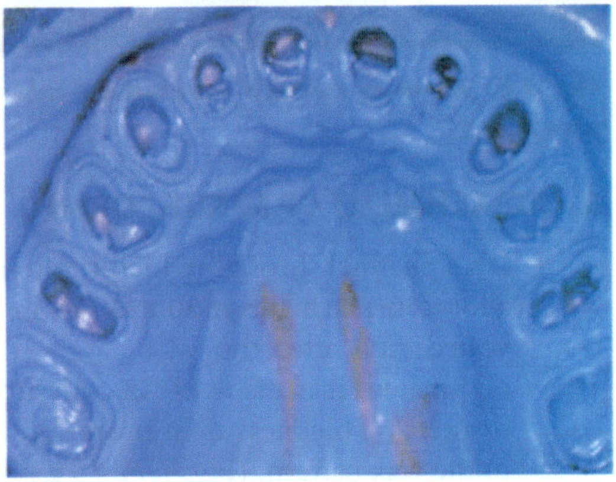

Fig: 7.4. Showing elastomeric impression.

3. DIE PREPARATION

- A die prepared from die stone or the impression is electro formed. (Fig: 7.5).
- A die spacer is coated or painted over the die, which provides space for the luting cement.

Fig: 7.5. Showing dies preparation from impression.

4. WAX PATTERN

- Make a wax pattern from type 2 in-lay casting wax, with all precaution to avoid distortion. (Fig: 7.6).

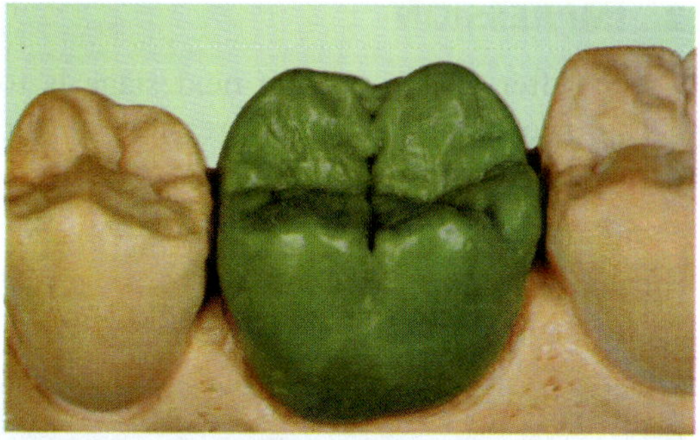

Fig: 7.6. Showing pattern making by Inlay wax type 2.

5. ATTACHMENT OF SPRUE FORMER

- It's a channel through which molten alloy can reach the mould in an invested ring after the wax has been eliminated. It is made of wax, plastic or metal. Thickness is in proportion to the wax pattern. (Fig: 7.7)

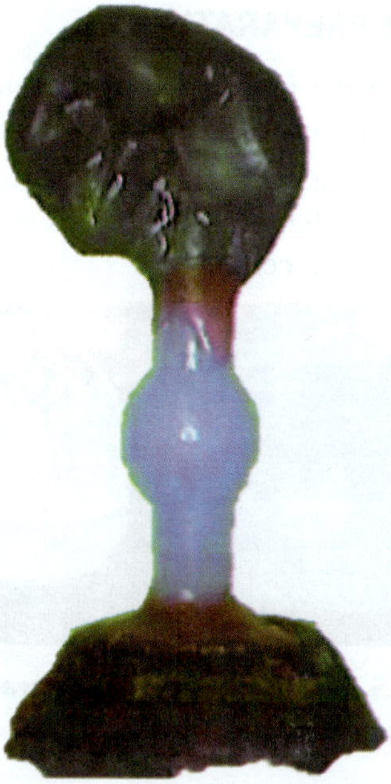

Fig: 7.7. Showing sprue attachment with pattern.

Function of sprue

a. To form amount for the wax pattern.
b. To form a channel for the ingress of molten alloys during casting.
c. To compensate for alloy shrinkage during solidification.
d. To create a channel for elimination of wax during burnout.

Sprue Former Direction

a. The Sprue former should be directed away from any thin or delicate parts of pattern.
b. It should not be attached at a right angle to a broad flat surface. Sprueing should be done at a 45-degree angle to the proximal wall.

Sprue Former Length

a. The length of the Sprue former depends on the length of the casting ring.
b. Length of the Sprue former should be such that it keeps the wax pattern about 6 to 8 mm away from the casting ring.
c. Sprue former should be no longer than 2 cm.
d. The pattern should be placed as close to the center of the ring as possible.

Significance

- ***Short Sprue Length***

  The gases cannot be adequately vented to permit the molten alloy to fill the ring completely leading to Back Pressure Porosity.

- ***Long Sprue Length***

  Fracture of investment, as mould will not withstand the impact force of the entering molten alloy.

Sprue Former Diameter/Gauge

a. Sprue Former should be thicker than the pattern to which it is attached.

b. Since the thin sections solidify and contract first, they will draw molten metal from thicker sections.

c. Diameter 8(3mm), 10(2.5mm), 12(2mm) gauge.

d. Sprue acts as an ideal reservoir for these sections. (Fig: 7.8).

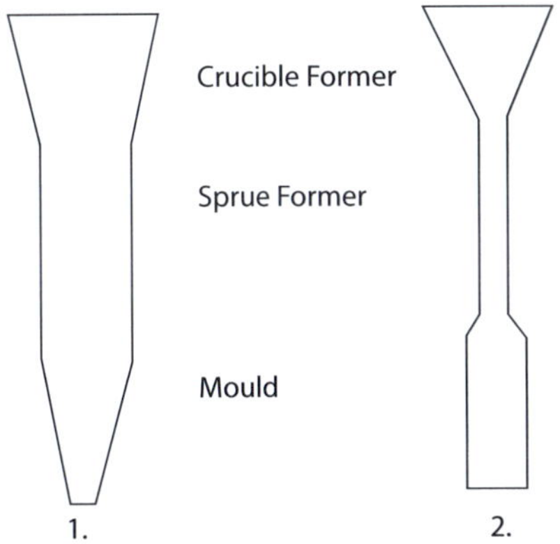

Fig: 7.8. The Crucible, Sprue and the Mould should be considered as being a wedge – shape (1) Correct (2) Incorrect.

Available Materials

a. Metallic

b. Wax

c. Plastic

6. RING LINER PLACEMENT

- A ring liner is placed on the inner side of the casting ring. It should be short at one end. (Fig: 7.10).

Function

a. Allows for mould expansion.

b. When the ring is transferred from the furnace to the casting machines, it reduces loss of heat as it is a thermal insulator.

c. Permits easy separation of the investment from the ring after the casting is over.

Types

There are two types of ring liner

A. Asbestos Ring Liner

- Traditional material for lining casting rings until it was learned that it posed a potential health risk to dental laboratory technicians.
- Asbestos fiber bundles were found to produce hazardous-size respirable particles capable of causing lung disease.(Fig: 7.9).

Fig: 7.9. Asbestos liner (SEM magnification x 500).

B. Non-asbestos Ring Liners

- Ceramic (aluminum silicate).
- Cellulose (paper).
- Ceramic-cellulose combination.

Fig: 7.10. Arrow indicates casting ring-liner.

Purpose of Casting Ring Liner

a. Ring liner is the most commonly

used technique to provide investment expansion.

b. To ensure uniform expansion, liner is cut to fit the inside diameter of the casting ring with no overlap.

c. Thickness of the liner should not be less than approximately 1mm.

d. Place the liner somewhat short of the ends of the ring, 3mm, tends to produce a more uniform expansion, therefore less chance for distortion of the wax pattern & mould.

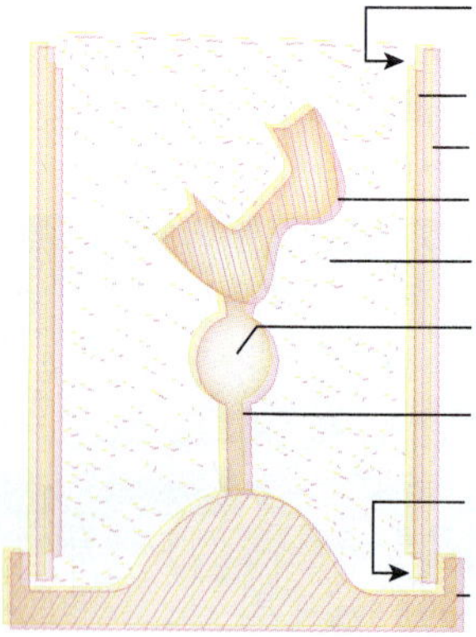

Fig: 7.11. Ring liner short of the ends of the ring about 3mm.

7. INVESTING

- Apply wetting agent on the wax pattern. Seat the casting ring into the crucible former taking care that there is uniform space around the wax pattern. The pattern should be located near the center of the ring.
- Mix the investment as per the recommended W / P ratio and vibrate. Take some investment on the brush and apply on the wax pattern pushing it forwards from an edge to the deeper parts of the pattern to avoid air bubbles.
- The ring is reseated on the crucible former and placed on the vibrator and gradually filled with the remaining investment mix. Allow it to set for 1 hour.

Fig: 7.12. Investment material being poured after vacuum mixing.

8. BURNOUT OR WAX ELIMINATION

- The purpose of burnout is the wax elimination of wax from the mould cavity and achieving thermal expansion.
- Separate the crucible from the ring. If metallic sprier former is used, it should be removed before burnout. Plastic sprier requires double burnout.
- For burnout the ring is heated gradually to 400 °C in 20 minutes and maintains it for 30 minutes. In the next 30 minutes, raise the temperature to 700 C and maintain it for 30 minutes.
- Invested ring is placed in a room temperature furnace.
- Phosphate-bonded investments-temperature range----700 to 870 °C
- Temperature rate of rise for the burnout furnace is 10 °C / min.

9. CASTING

After Burn-out wax next step is to flow melted alloy.

CASTING MACHINES

- **Air pressure casting machines**

  Alloy is melted in situ in crucible hollow of the ring, followed by applied air pressure on the melt.

- **Centrifugal casting machine**

  Alloy is melted in a crucible, and forced in to mould by centrifugal force.

- **Electrical Resistance/ Induction melting machine**

  Alloy is melted electrically by a resistance or induction furnace, and then cast into mould centrifugally.

A. Centrifugal Machines

- A variety of centrifugal machines is available.
- It is spring driven or motor driven. Alloy is fused by electric resistance or induction furnace or on a refractory tray by a blowtorch. (Fig: 7.13).
- The main advantage of centrifugal machines is the simplicity of design and operation with the opportunity to cast both large and small casting on the same machine.

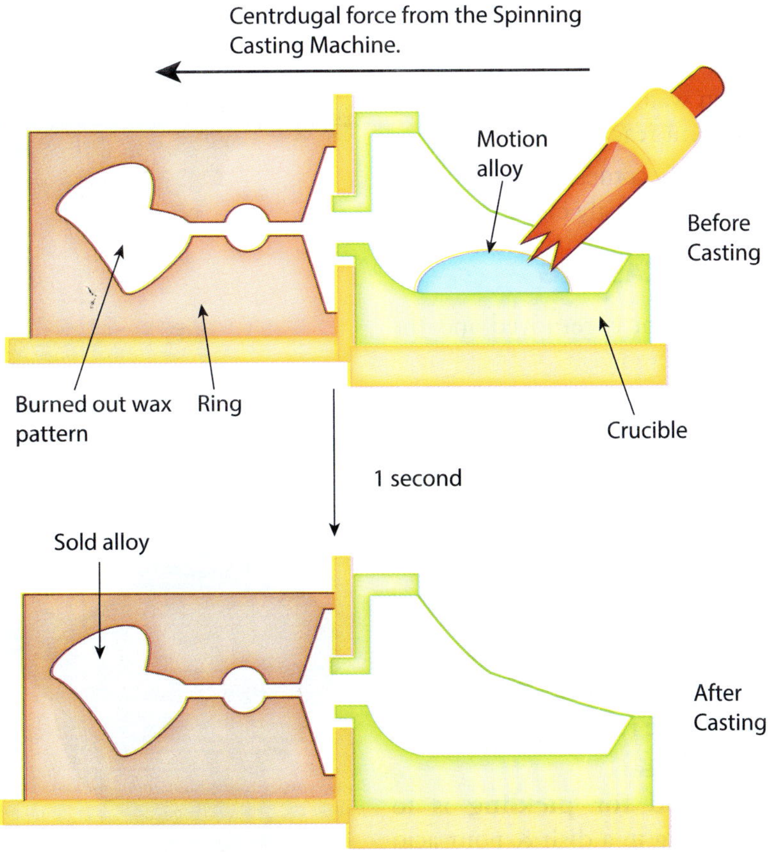

Fig: 7.13. Illustration showing centrifugal machine cross-section before casting and after casting.

B. Air Pressure Machine

- In air pressure type of machine, either compressed air or gases like carbon dioxide or nitrogen can be used to force the molten metal into the mould. This type of machine is satisfactory for making small castings.

10. QUENCHING (For Gold Alloys)

- Consider the gold crown & bridge alloys.
- After casting has been completed, ring is removed & quenched in water.

Advantages

1. Noble metal is left in an annealed condition for burnishing & polishing. When water contacts hot investment, violent reaction ensues.
2. Investment becomes soft, granular & casting is more easily cleaned.

11. RECOVERY OF CASTING

- The investment is removed and the casting recovered.

12. SAND BLASTING

- The casting is held in a sandblasting machine to clean the investment from its surface.

13. PICKLING

- Surface of the casting appears dark with oxides and tarnish. Such a surface film can be removed by a process called **Pickling**.
- **Best method for pickling** is to place a casting in a dish & pour acid over it.
- Heat the acid but do not boil it.
  - i. Hydrochloric acid
  - ii. Sulphuric acid
  - iii. Ultrasonic devices
- Gold and palladium based metal ceramic alloys and base metals, these alloys are not generally pickled.

14. POLISHING

- Minimum polishing is required if all the procedure from the ware pattern to casting are followed meticulously.

LABORATORY STEPS OF DENTAL CASTING

Fig: 7.14. Step 1: Making of wax pattern.

Fig: 7.14. Step 2: Sprue Attachment.

Fig: 7.14. Step 3: Pattern Attachment to crucible.

Fig: 7.14. Step 4: Wax burn-out and casting stage.

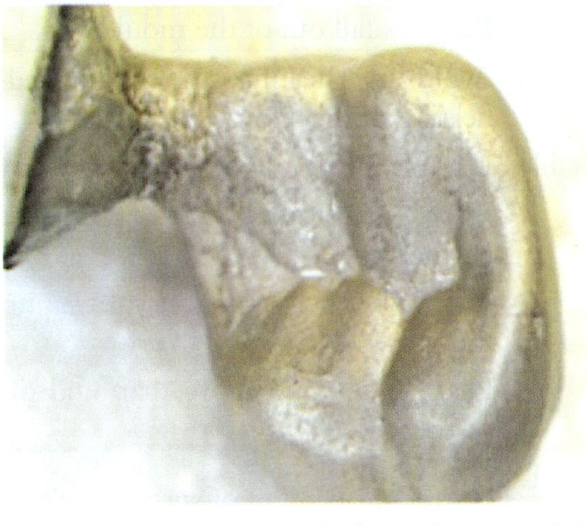

Fig: 7.14. Step 5: Removal of Cast from mould.

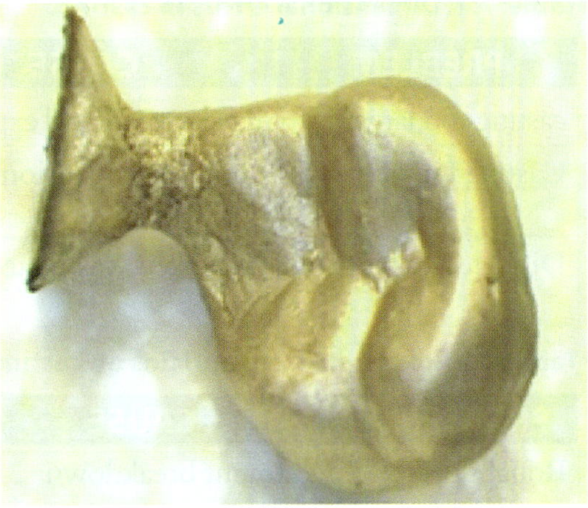

Fig: 7.14. Step 6: Cleaning of Cast.

Fig: 7.14. Step 7: Polishing of Gold Crown.

DEFECTS IN CASTING

- If proper procedure is not followed, the casting may have some defects.
- The casting in such a case may not fit or may have poor esthetic and mechanical properties.

Table: 7.1. Dimensional errors in casting.

PREBLEM	CAUSE	METHOD AVOIDING FAULT
casting too large	Excessive mould expension	Use correct temperature.
Casting too large	Too little expansion	Use correct type of investment material.
Distorted casting	Distorted wax pattern	Heat the mould sufficiently, Correct handling of wax.

Table: 7.2. Rough surfaces and fins on casting.

PROBLEM	CAUSE	METHOD AVOIDING FAULT
Rough surface	Investment breakdown Air bubbles on wax pettern Week surface of investment	Avoid overheating mould and allow correct use of wetting agent or correct vacuum investing technique. Avoid use of too high water/powder ratio of investment. Avoid dilution of the investment material from evaporation of too much wetting agent. Avoid too rapid heating of investment.
Fins on casting	Cracking of investment material.	

Table: 7.3. Porosity.

PROBLEM	CAUSE	METHOD AVOIDING FAULT
Irregular Voids	Shringkage on cooling of alloy	Use sprues of correct thickness. Place sprues at bulkiest section of the pattern. Reservoir sufficiently near the pattern to be effective.
Irregular Voids	Inclusion of particles of investment material	Heat mould upside down so that Particles fall out of the mould.
Spherical voids	Occluded gases in the molten alloy	Avoid overheating and prolonged heating of the alloy.
Rounded margins; reglar large voids	Back-pressre effect; air unable to escape from mould	Use sufficient casting force. Use investment of adequate permeability. Avoid presence of residue of wax in mould. Place Pattern no more than end of casting ring.
Porosity	Turbulent flow of molten alloy into mould	Correct placement of sprues.

REFERENCES

1. Ralph W. Phillips (1991), Skinner's Science of Dental Materials, (2nd ed.), Saunders.
2. W. Patrick Naylor (2009), Introduction to Metal-Ceramic Technology, (2nd ed.), Quintessence Pub.
3. Richard W. Blakeslee, Robert P. Renner & Alexander Shiu(1980), Dental Technology: Theory and Practice, Mosby.
4. E.C. Combe (1986), Notes on Dental Materials, (5th ed.), Churchill Livingstone.
5. Kenneth Anusavice (2012), Phillips' Science of Dental Materials, (12th ed.), Saunder.
6. Ronald Sakaguchi & John M.power(2011), Craig's Restorative Dental Materials, (13th ed.), Mosby
7. Richard Van Noort (2007), Introduction to Dental Materials, (3rd ed.), Mosby Ltd., China
8. B W Darvell (2009), Materials science for Dentistry (9th ed.),Woodhead Publishing Limited, UK.
9. John M. Power & John C.wataha(2012), DENTAL MATERIALS Properties and Manipulation, (10th ed.), ELSEVIER, India.

Chapter

8

DENTAL IMPLANTS AND THEIR SURFACE MODIFICATIONS

Dr. Shariq Najeeb & Dr. Jukka Matinlinna

INTRODUCTION

A dental implant is a metallic prosthesis that functions as a root for supporting artificial teeth to replace missing or lost dentition. Over one million dental implants are placed every year. An implant is in direct contact with the alveolar bone. The idea of placing 'prostheses' such as shells into the jaw bone dates back to the ancient Mayan civilization; archeological excavation sites have led to the discovery of human jaw bone with tooth-shaped shells embedded in it. The concept of modern implantology was discovered rather accidentally by P. I. Brånemark. While conducting research on bone regeneration around titanium chambers inserted in rabit femurs, he noticed that after several months he was unable to remove them. He later developed an implant system which could be used to support dental prostheses. The requirements of dental implants are: biocompatibility, stability, acceptable function and ease of manufacture. Prior to the introduction of the Brånemark implant system, sub-periosteal implants were used. Sub-periosteal consisted of a cobalt-chromium framework resting over the bone under the oral mucosa. This design is now outdated and has been replaced by osseointegrated dental implants. Another older type of implant is the blade-vent implant. In these implants, one end of the implant (the blade) is inserted into the bone whilst the other end projects through the mucosa into the oral cavity. These implants carry a very high risk of infection and, ultimately, implant failure.

OSSEOINTEGRATION

When any biomaterial is inserted into the living tissue, almost immediately, it is covered by cell adhesion proteins. Surface characteristics such as wettability and charges affect the quality of absorption of these proteins onto the implant. Cells then interact with these proteins to adhere to the implant surface. Similarly in bone tissue, osteoblasts, the bone forming cells, are laid down onto the implant surface and consequently, there is a direct bone-implant interface formed. This interface is known as Osseointegration. If there is a loose connective tissue formed instead of a bone-implant interface, the implant fails. Osseointegration is the main factor that dictates the success of dental implants. According to Brånemark, Osseointegration depends on the quality of the bone, surface morphology of the implant, the implant material, surgical technique employed to place the implant and the design of the implant. This chapter will discuss about the biomaterial aspects of dental implants – the materials used to make them and the different surface and design modifications that are employed to make implants more osseoinductive.

CLINICAL ASPECTS

Placing an implant consists of two phases: 1) Surgical and 2) Prosthetic. In the surgical phase, a water-cooled drill is used to produce a preparation in the bone after a flap has been raised. The water-cooled drill ensures that the bone is not damaged due to the heat produced due to drilling. The procedure should be carried in aseptic conditions to prevent any ingress of bacteria. Following this, an implant is placed into the prepared area and a healing screw or an abutment is placed on to the implant. After the tissues have healed, an impression is taken and a prosthesis is constructed and placed on to the implant. Immediate loading has become more common in recent times. This involves placement of an implant immediately in to an extraction site.

1. IMPLANT MATERIALS

Modern implants are mostly made of Titanium Ti. Titanium is a transition metal and it is commercially available in different grades according to the composition and the mechanical and physical properties. Modern dental implants are either made from grade 4 commercially pure titanium (grade 4 cpTi) or a grade 5 titanium alloy (Ti6Al4V). Grade 5 titanium alloys have higher yield strength and better fatigue properties than grade 4 titanium. A major advantage of using titanium and its alloy as an implant material is its excellent corrosion resistance. This is because of a formation of an extremely inert and very compact and thin oxide layer on the surface. The oxide layer does not affect the physical and mechanical properties of the implant and it shields the inner layers of the metal lattice against corrosion. The disadvantage of using titanium is its very high modulus of elasticity. Natural teeth are actually made of a composite of dentine and enamel. Dentine provides a relatively flexible layer of tissues beneath the hard enamel and makes the tooth less brittle by reducing the modulus of elasticity. Meanwhile, the periodontal ligaments act as 'shock-absorbers' (much like a bumper of a car!) against excessive occlusal forces. When an implant replaces a tooth, this composite nature of the natural hard tissues is lost which can be potentially harmful to the bone and the natural teeth. Furthermore, any gap between the bone and the implant can lead to ingress of microorganisms into the periodontal tissues and ultimately cause peri-implantitis. There have also been cases of titanium hypersensitivity. Another disadvantage of using titanium implants is the grey colour which can show through the prosthesis and the gingival margins. This is particularly problematic in the anterior region.

Due to the above described disadvantages of titanium research is being conducted to find alternatives. PEEK (polyetheretherketone) and zirconia (zirconium dioxide, ZrO2) have been suggested as alternatives. However, titanium still has a substantially high clinical success-rate and has been a mainstay in dental implantology for over 30 years.

Zirconia is ceramics and it is being considered as an alternative to titanium as full dental implants because it has an added advantage of being white (tooth-coloured after coloring) while having adequate mechanical properties and extremely biocompatibility (no adverse reactions reported). Surface modification of zirconia implants is considerably more challenging than for titanium implants as ceramic materials are brittle of their nature. Although there is a limited amount of data available for 5-year survival rate for zirconia implants, further clinical trials probably will make the prospect of zirconia as an implant material clearer in the future. Recently, titanium-zirconium alloy (TiZr) implants have been introduced commercially. These implants have the advantage of having higher mechanical properties even in smaller diameters and a higher bone-implant contact when compared to titanium implants.

PEEK is another material that has the potential to replace titanium. It can be reinforced by other materials such as carbon. However, more research and clinical trials need to be carried out before the material can be used more widely.

2. SURFACE TREATMENT OF DENTAL IMPLANTS

Before Ti and Ti-alloy implants are inserted into the bone, their surfaces have to be modified. This is done because of two reasons: 1) to make the implants more biocompatible with the bone and 2) to make the implants osseoconductive (i.e. to stimulate bone formation). Surface modification of implants increases the rate of Osseointegration so as to minimize the marginal leakage of contaminants and bacteria into the bone-implant interface so that the primary stability can be achieved as rapidly as possible and to curtail the chances of peri-implantitis.

There have been many methods suggested to modify the surface of Ti and Ti-alloy implants. These include increasing the hydrophilicity, roughening the surface of implants, thermal plasma spraying of particles, introducing biomimetic and osteoconductive coatings on implants and incorporation of growth factors and drugs on the surfaces.

Surface wettability and charge

Living tissues have a very high water content. To ensure maximum interaction with the proteins and tissues, a surface must be hydrophilic. Some studies have advocated that hydrophilic sand-blasted, large grit and acid-etched (SLA) implants produce a higher bone-to-implant contact (BIC) than regular implants. However, other studies have suggested that hydrophilicity has no effect on the BIC. Hydrophilicity of dental implants can also be increased by treating the SLA surfaces with nitrogen and isotonic sodium chloride.

Surface roughness

Implant surfaces can be roughened on three levels: macro, micro and nano. Macro level surface roughness involves introducing roughness of more than 10 (μm). Implant geometry and a threaded screw design can used to produce surface roughness at a macroscopic level. Increasing the surface area of the implant produces are a higher mechanical inter-locking between implant and bone. However, increasing the surface roughness at the macro level also increases the chances of leakage at the bone-implant interface and peri-implantitis.

Micro-level roughness introduces porosities in the range of 1-10 (μm). Ideally, the pits must be approximately 1.5 (μm) in depth and 4 (μm) in diameter. A rough, short implant is indicated for ridges with insufficient bone quantity or anatomical restrictions. Many studies have suggested that such implants require a higher amount of force to be removed than smooth implants.

A. Plasma-spraying

Plasma-spraying involves projecting particles on to the implant surfaces through a high-temperature plasma torch. The molted particles strike the implant and they condense to form a rough film. There are two materials that can be plasma-sprayed onto the implant surfaces: titanium and calcium hydroxyapatite (Ca-HA).

Titanium, when plasma-sprayed on to an implant, produces an average roughness of around 7 (μm). Studies have shown that using titanium plasma spraying (TPS) increases the tensile strength at the bone-implant interface. A disadvantage of using TPS is the possibility of dislodging of the titanium particles into the adjacent tissues and their migration to major organs such as liver and spleen. Clinical studies suggest that there is no significant difference between SLA and TPS and implant surfaces. However, a preclinical study has suggested the superiority of hydroxyapatite plasma sprayed implants when compared to TPS implants.

Hydroxyapatite (HA) particles can also be plasma sprayed on to implant surfaces. A film with thickness ranging from a few micrometers to a few millimeters is produced after it is which is grit/sand-blasted to roughen the surface of the film. The biggest advantage of using hydroxyapatite film is its ability to increase the saturation of body fluids over the implant surface. A layer of biological hydroxyapatite is deposited over the surface. The biological HA layer contains proteins and can serve as a matrix for attachment of osteoblasts that can lay down bone over the implant surface.

HA coatings exist in different phases over the implant surfaces. These phases include tricalcium phosphates, tetracalcium phosphates and amorphous calcium phosphates. These phases can separate from each other and can lead to delamination of HA particles. Hence, a major disadvantage of using HA as a surface modification is the possibility of implant failure due to the breakdown of the HA-implant interface. Furthermore, it is very difficult to coat small implants having a complex design with HA. Due to these reasons, HA-coated implants have been discouraged to be used in dentistry.

B. Grit-blasting

Implant surfaces can also be roughened by a grit-blasting. The surface is blasted with hard ceramic particles at high velocity using compressed air. Alumina (Al_2O_3), titanium dioxide (TiO_2) and calcium phosphate particles can grit-blasted on to implant surfaces. A disadvantage of using alumina as a grit-blasting material is the possibility of the particles being embedded in to the implant surface. These particles are very difficult to be removed and can be released into the surrounding tissues causing loss of Osseointegration.

Titanium oxide particles with average size of 25 μm can produce roughness ranging 1-2 μm. Microimplants coated with titanium dioxide have shown better BIC, marginal bone levels and 10-year success rates than conventional machine implants in humans. Alumina and titanium have both been shown to increase the biomechanical fixation of dental implants although on a cellular they do not seem to have much effect.

Grit-blasting with calcium phosphates produces implants with a clean, uniformly textured and a pure surface. Any calcium phosphate particles remaining can get easily resorbed by the tissues and are osseoconductive. Studies show that calcium phosphates produce a similar BIC when compared to grit-blasting with alumina and titanium dioxide.

C. Acid etching

Strong, corrosive mineral acids such as HCl, H_2SO_4, HNO_3 and HF can be used to roughen implant surfaces. They produce microscopic pits that improve the mechanical interlocking of bone with the implant surface. Dual-acid etching involves the immersion of dental implants in a mixture of concentrated HCl and H_2SO_4 at 100°C. Clinical success rates of dual-acid etched implants have been seen to exceed 3 years. The etched surface provides a larger surface area for the attachment of fibrin and osteogenic cells. The dual acid-etched surfaces are more wettable and hence hydrophilic which is thought to promote Osseointegration.

Immersing implants in concentrated fluoride solutions also produces etched surfaces. Titanium reacts with fluoride ions to form titanium tetrafluoride, TiF_4. Thus, the fluoride is incorporated into the etched titanium surface. TiF_4 is bioactive and has a favorable osteogenic effect on the surrounding bone. Studies have shown that this chemical treatment can increase the osteoblastic activity by stimulating the differentiation of progenitor cells into osteoblasts.

Acid etching has some drawbacks. The process has been shown to make implant surfaces brittle by the formation of microcracks that ultimately lead to a diminished fatigue-resistance due to the absorption of hydrogen from the surrounding tissues. This embrittlement of titanium implants due to hydrogen absorption is known as *hydrogen embrittlement*.

D. Anodization

Strong acids can also be used to produce roughness at the nano and micro by anodization. The Ti-based implants are immersed in a solution of a strong acid at high voltages which thickens oxide layer in some areas of the titanium surface and dissolves the oxide layer in other areas. This leads to creation of micro and nano porosities on the implant surface. The process produces a roughened *and* a modified surface which can increase the micromechanical. Addition of magnesium, calcium, sulfur and phosphorous have been shown to increase the removal force of dental implants.

Biomimetic calcium phosphate coatings

As discussed before, plasma-spraying of HA on the implant surface can have drawbacks. The biggest disadvantage is the failure of the implant-HA due to the instability brought about by the high temperatures involved plasma-spraying. To overcome this, calcium phosphates can be mineralized onto the implant surface. This is similar to the natural process of bone mineralization. Two methods can be employed to produce biomimetic Ca-P coatings: electrolysis and immersion in simulated body fluid (SBF). Electrolysis uses the implant as the cathode and a platinum anode. They are both immersed in a solution of Ca-P and the phosphates are deposited on the implant.

Ca-P coatings can be also deposited by immersion of the implants in buffered SBF containing calcium phosphates in varying concentrations. They are then immersed in an alkaline solution to produce titanium hydroxyl ions on the implant surface. The Ca-P ions then can interact with these ions to form coatings on the implant surface.

Incorporation of growth factors and drugs on the surfaces

The surfaces of dental implants can be made osseoconductive by incorporating various growth factors and drugs on to them. Growth factors that can be used to produce such surfaces include transformin growth factor (TGF), bone morphogenic proteins (BMPs) and insulin like growth factors. Some drugs such as bisphosphonates and antibiotics such as amoxicillin can also be used as coatings. Bisphosphonates have test in human subjects with positive effect on marginal bone quantity. Collagen fibers can also be combine with HA and then coated on dental implants to be used as biomimetic implant coatings.

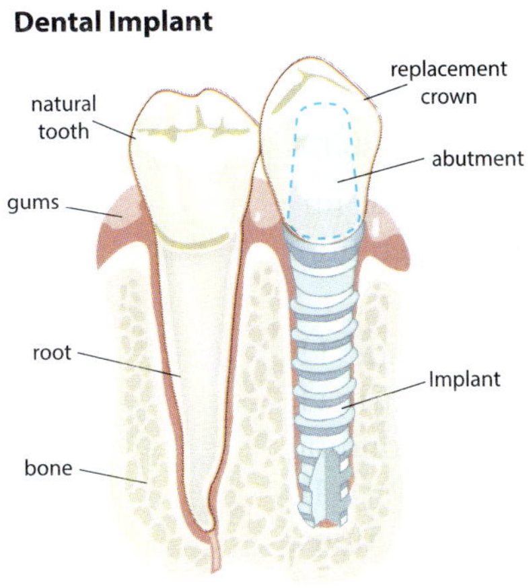

Fig: 8.1.A. Comparison between a dental implant (right) and a natural tooth (left).

Fig: 8.1.B. Macro surface features of a titanium implant.

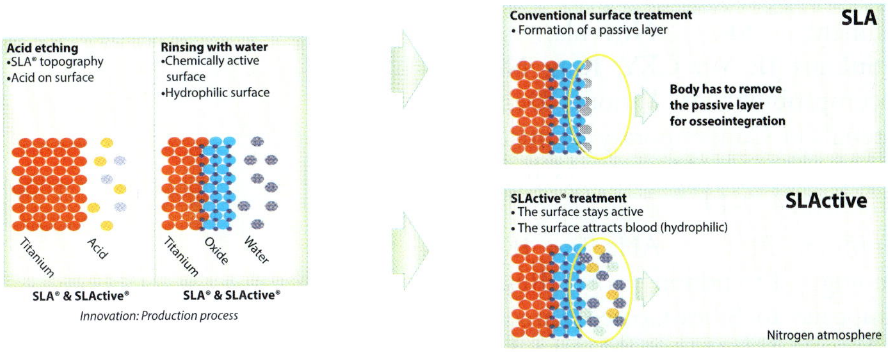

Fig: 8.1.C. Schematic diagram of a SLA and a SLActive surface modified implant (Straumann).

REFERENCES

1. *Albrektsson* et al. Osseointegrated titanium implants. Acta orthop. scand. 1981.
2. *Le Gu´ehennec* et al. Surface treatments of titanium dental implants for rapid osseointegration. Dental Materials. 2007.
3. *Ellingsen* et al. Advances in dental implant materials and tissue regeneration. Periodontology 2000. 2006.
4. Aboushelib MN, Mirmohamadi H, Matinlinna JP, Kukk E, Ounsi H, Salameh Z. Innovations in bonding to zirconia based materials. Part II: Focusing on chemical interactions. Dent Mater 2009; 25: 989-993.
5. Guo CY, Tang ATH, Matinlinna JP. Insights into Surface Treatment Methods of Titanium Dental Implants. J Adhes Sci Technol 2012; 26: 189-205.
6. Mallineni SK, Nuvvula, S, Matinlinna JP, Yiu CKY, King NM. Biocompatibility of Various Dental Materials of Contemporary Dentistry: a Narrative Insight. J Investigat Clinical Dent 2013; 4: 9-19.
7. Choi AH, Ben-Nissan B, Matinlinna JP, Conway RC. Current perspectives: Calcium Phosphate Nanocoatings and Nanocomposite Coatings in Dentistry, J Dent Res 2013; 92(10): 853-859.
8. Mallineni SK, Nuvvula, S, Matinlinna JP, Yiu CKY, King NM. Biocompatibility of Various Dental Materials of Contemporary Dentistry: a Narrative Insight. J Investigat Clinical Dent 2013; 4: 9-19
9. Matinlinna JP, Choi AH, Tsoi JKH. Bonding Promotion of Resin-Composite to Silica-Coated Zirconia Implant Surface using a Novel Silane System. Clin Oral Implants Res 2013; 24: 290-296.
10. Matinlinna JP, Tsoi JKH, de Vries J, Busscher HJ. Characterization of Novel Silane Systems on Titanium Implant Surfaces. Clin Oral Implants Res 2013; 24: 688-697.

Chapter 9

APPLICATION OF POLYMER TECHNOLOGY IN DENTISTRY

Dr. Zohaib & Dr. Sana Shahab

INTRODUCTION

Polymer science or macromolecular science is a subfield of materials science concerned with polymers, primarily synthetic polymers. The field of polymer science comprises three main sub-disciplines;

Polymer chemistry or macromolecular chemistry which deals with the chemical synthesis and chemical properties of polymers or macromolecules.

1. Polymer Physics is concerned with the bulk properties of polymer materials and engineering applications.
2. Polymer Characterization is concerned with the analysis of chemical structure and morphology and the determination of physical properties in relation to compositional and structural parameters.
3. Polymers (poly = many, mer = unit) are made by linking small molecules (mers) through *primary covalent* bonding in the main molecular chain backbone with C, N, O, Si, etc. Polymers have a major role in most areas of dentistry.

Now a days, Synthetic polymers have been widely used in both restorative and prosthetic dentistry for over five decades, and used in medical disposable supplies, dental materials, implants, dressings, bleaching tray, extracorporeal devices, encapsulants, polymeric drug delivery systems, tissue engineering scaffold, and brackets in orthodontic treatment.

Applications for acrylic polymers based on functional methacrylate, include dentures, restorative materials, relining and repair material, soft liners, bonding agents, temporary crown and bridges. Elastomeric materials such as silicones, polysulphides and alginates are used for recording impressions of the hard and soft oral tissues, which are then utilized for constructing appliances outside the mouth. Water-soluble polymers are used in adhesive dental cements. Polymer composites an important part of restorative dentistry, at present is the material with the widest range of indications and is vital to modern dentistry.

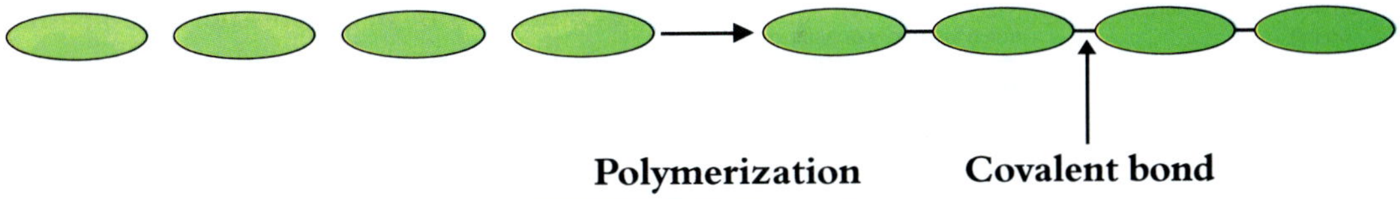

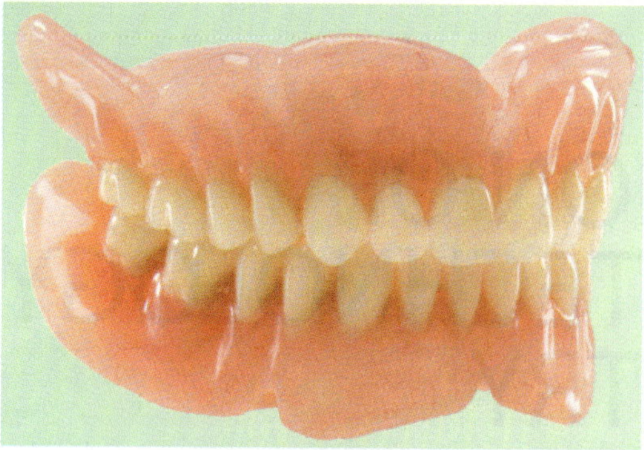

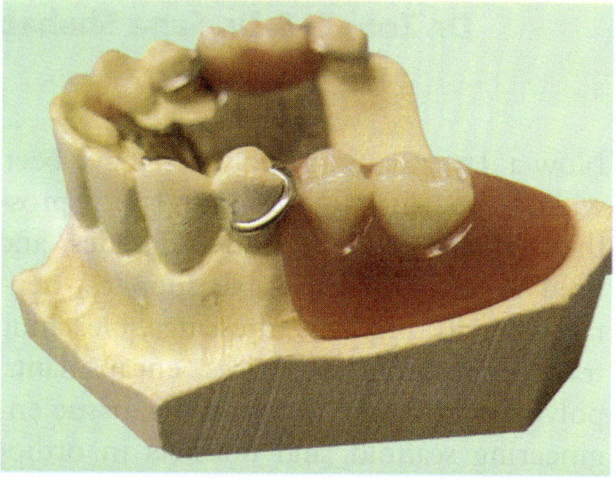

TYPES OF POLYMER

✦ ON THE BASIS OF SPECIES OF MONOMER
  a. Homopolymer
  b. Heteropolymer

✦ ON THE BASIS OF FABRICATION
  a. Thermoplastic Polymer
  b. Thermosetting Polymer

CLASSIFICATION OF POLYMERS

POLYMERS

- THERMOPLASTIC POLYMERS
  They can be softened.
  On heating and rehardned on cooling.
- THERMOSETTING RESINS
  They are condensation Polymers
  Which are partly polymerized berore moulding to produce a viscous liquid.

TOPOLOGY OF POLYMER CHAIN

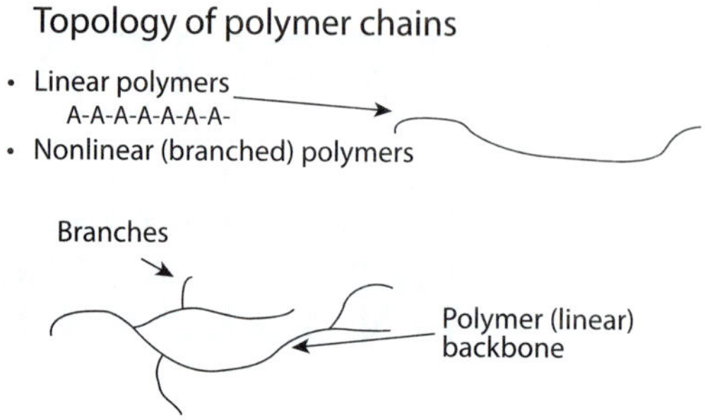

SOURCES OF POLYMER

NATURAL SOURCES	SYNTHETICS SOURCES
Agar	PVC (Poly vinyl Chloride
Cellulose	Polyethylene
Proteins	
Naturalrubber	
Collagen	
Silk	

POLYMERIZATION

The process by which monomers are converted into polymers is called polymerization.

Monomers (Liquid/Gases) —POLYMERIZATION (Addition/Condensation)→ Polymers (Crystalline)

Soft → Rigid

CHEMISTRY OF POLYMERIZATION

"All monomer have double bond in common, which is opened up to allow the monomer to bond to a neighboring monomer. This process of preparing polymers from monomer is called Polymerization".

The conversion of monomers molecules into polymers may proceed by either an;

✦ Addition Reaction.

✦ Condensation Reaction.

ADDITION POLYMERIZATION

a. Addition reaction simply involves the joining together of two molecules to form a third, larger molecule. The polymerization reaction of acrylic resins, called addition polymerization, is very common in dental materials.

b. Acrylic resins and composite materials, such as restorative materials, cements, sealants, and adhesives, all set via addition polymerization

c. Addition polymerization involves the addition of a reactive species with a monomer to form a larger reactive species, which is capable of further addition with monomer.

d. The reaction may be visualized as follows;

$$R^{\star} \quad + M \rightarrow R - M^{\star}$$

$$R - M^{\star} + M \rightarrow R - M - M^{\star}$$

$$R - M - M^{\star} + \rightarrow R - M - M^{\star} \text{ etc.}$$

e. The initial reactive species is represented by $R^{\star}$ and the monomer molecules by M –

f. Above examples explain how monomer molecules are added during each stage of the polymerization reaction and eventually a long chain molecule is produced.

g. Addition reaction may be ionic in nature or it may by a free radical, depend supon the reactive species.

h. The free radicals are produced by reactive agents called initiators.

i. Initiators are basically molecules, which contain one relatively weak bond, which is able to undergo decomposition to form two reactive species each carrying an unpaired electron.

j. The decomposition of initiator may be accomplished either by heating or by reaction with chemical activator.

DIFFERENT INTIATORS		DIFFERENT ACTIVATORS
	FOR CHEMICAL CURE	
BENZOYL PEROXIDASE	→	N, N-DIMETHYL-P-TOLUIDINE
	FOR LIGHT CURE	
Benzoic methyl ether	→	Radiation sensitive
Ketones (Camphroquinone)	→	Ultra violet radiation

k. The polymerization processes follow a well-documented pattern, which consists of four main stages.

1. *Activation*

An initiator molecule can become activated (change into a free radical) by heat, light, or a chemical reaction. As a result of the various activation methods, materials are classified as ***heat-activated*** (also known as heat-cure), ***chemically activated*** (also known as cold-cure or chemical-cure), or ***photo activated*** (also known as photo-cure or light-cure).

HEAT ACTIVATED
✦ Heat-activated acrylic resins typically use benzoyl peroxide (BPO) as the initiator. Heat is the activator.
✦ When heated to 60°C, BPO breaks down into CO2 and free radical molecules.
✦ Heat-activated acrylic resins come from the manufacturer as a powder/liquid system.
✦ The powder and liquid are mixed to form a dough for moulding into the desired shape, but the polymerization reaction does not start until the material is heated, typically in a hot water bath.
✦ Most complete and partial dentures use heat-activated acrylic resins for the denture base.

CHEMICALLY ACTIVATED
✦ Chemically activated acrylic resins also commonly use BPO as the initiator.
✦ Activators used in dental polymers belong to a group of chemicals called tertiary amines.
✦ Chemically activated materials are typically a powder and a liquid that are mixed together to start the polymerization process.
✦ Chemically activated acrylic resins are used to make temporary crowns, custom impressions trays, orthodontic retainers, and many other dental devices.

2. *Initiation*

The polymerization reaction is initiated when the radical, formed on activation, reacts with a monomer molecule. Initiation reaction is an addition reaction producing other active free radicals, which are capable of further reaction.

3. *Propagation*

The free radicals can react with other molecules of monomer, thus the reaction proceeds, leading to formation of a polymer chain. It is the growth or lengthening of the chain. The free radical of the "initiated chain" reacts with a monomer, and the chain is one monomer longer. The process is similar to initiation. Propagation involves adding the second, third, fourth, and later monomers to the growing chain until that chain is hundreds or even thousands of monomers long. Polymerization continues as long as monomers are available to react with the free radicals at the end of the growing chain.

Polymerization reactions result in a long chain of monomers. Such addition polymerization reactions are also called *chain-lengthening reactions*.

$R + M \rightarrow R\text{-}M$

$R - M + M \rightarrow R - M - M$ and so on.

4. *Termination*

This occurs when two free radicals react to form a stable molecule. Polymerization is possible until the supply of monomer molecule is exhausted. These reactions produce dead polymer chains, which are not capable of further additions. Other reactions, which may cause termination of polymerization, are due to presence of impurity, solvent.

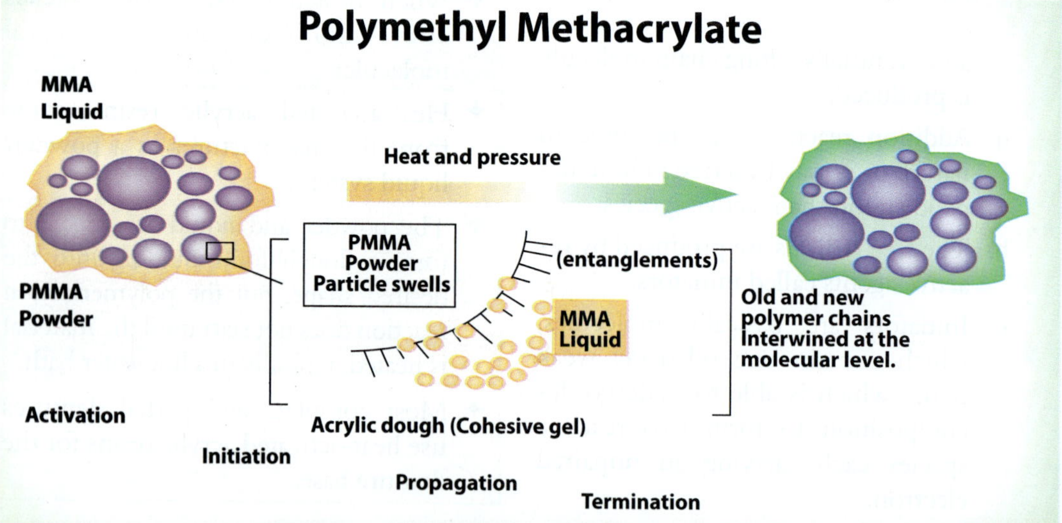

CONDENSATION POLYMERIZATION

This is the chemical reaction that joins together the building blocks of biologic polymers. Biologic polymers (proteins) are important components of the tissues of the body. In a typical condensation reaction, a hydrogen atom and a hydroxyl group (OH) are taken from the monomers and are combined to form water (H2O). Reaction byproducts other than water are produced by other condensation polymerization reactions, but water is the most common byproduct. The name "condensation" polymerization is based on the production of water.

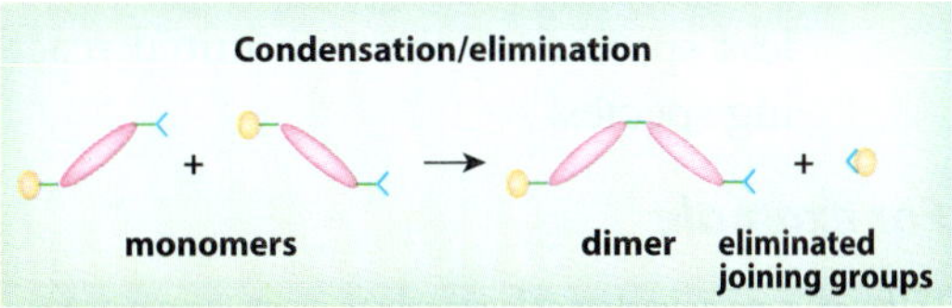

For example

An esterification reaction in which an organic acid and an alcohol react together to form an ester with the evolution of water.

USES OF CONDENSATION POLYMERIZATION

1. Production of Nylon 6, 6.
2. Production of Nylon 6.
3. The synthesis of poly di-methysiloxane (silicon rubber).

CHANGES DURING POLYMERIZATION

1. Phase changes
   - From liquid to solid
2. Temperature changes
   - Exothermic reaction
3. Dimensional changes
   - Results in net contraction or shrinkage

FACTORS AFFECTING THE POLYMER PROPERTIES

Factors, which have an important influence on the properties of the resulting polymer, are:

- Molecular weight.
- Degree of chain branching or cross linking.

1. MOLECULAR WEIGHT AND COMPOSITION

- The molecular weight and its distribution have a great effect on the properties of a polymer since its rigidity is primarily due to the immobilization or entanglement of the chains.
- By increasing the molecular weight the polymer chains become longer and less mobile and a more rigid material results as shown in (Fig: 9.1).
- Equally important is that all chains should be equal in length since if there are short chains they will act as plasticizers.
- Another obvious way of changing properties is to change the chemical composition of the backbone or side chains. Substituting the backbone carbon of a polyethylene with divalent oxygen or sulpher will decrease the melting and glass transition temperatures and the chain becomes more flexible.
- On the other hand if the backbone chains can be made more rigid then a stiffer polymer will result.

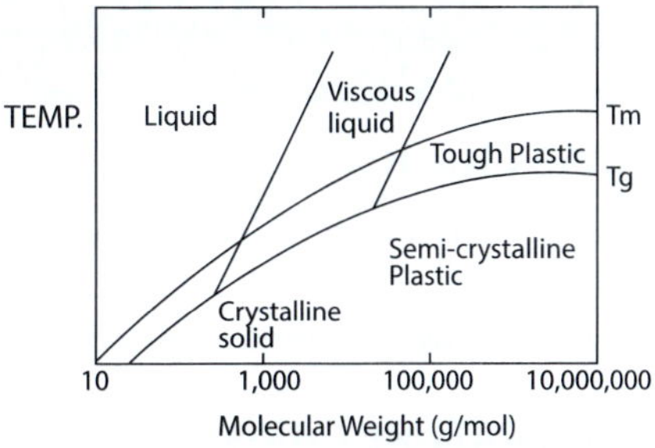

Fig: 9.1. Approximate relations among molecular weight, Tg, Tm, and polymer properties.

2. DEGREE OF CHAIN BRANCHING OR CROSS-LINKING

Cross linking or chain branching lowers the melting temperature.This is due to the interference of the cross-linking which causes decreased mobility of the chains, resulting in further retardation of the crystallization rate. In fact, a large degree of cross-linking can prevent crystallization completely. However, when the cross-linking density increases for a rubber, the material becomes harder and the glass transition temperature also increases.

FUNCTION OF CROSS-LINKING AGENT
1. The cross-linking molecules reduces the likelihood of small surface cracks which occur in the denture when it is allowed to dry. These small cracks are called craze cracks and are produced by stresses created during the drying
2. They reduce the solubility and water absorption of the polymer
3. Increases thermal resistance (dentures are easily finished, grinded and polished without melting).
4. Too much of cross-linking agent will produce brittle materials

PHYSICAL CHANGES OCCURING DURING POLYMERIZATION

1. PHASE CHANGES

During polymerization, as the average molecule weight increases and chain enlargement occurs, and viscosity begins to increase.

2. TEMPERATURE CHANGES

a. Polymerization reaction is usually exothermic in nature and causes a marked increase in temperature of the polymerizing material.

b. Another occurrence on some materials is that elevated temperature during polymerization causes vaporization of some un-converted monomer producing spherical voids, known as gaseous porosity in the set material.

3. DIMENSIONAL CHANGES

a. Each addition or condensation reaction which takes place during polymerization result in a small contraction.

b. Since the resulting species occupies less space than the two initial reacting species.

For example

When methylmethacrylate is converted to polymethyl methacrylate, a volumetric shrinkage of about 21% occurs (acrylic resin material).

POLYMER BOND RUPTURE

"The degradation of polymer by the breakdown of Covalent bond due to Radiation, chemical attack or heat called as Scission".

Result As

- Properties depend on the molecular weight of the chain.
- Reducing the Mw result in Loss of Mechanical Properties.

STRUCTURE AND PROPERTIES OF POLYMER

Factors, which control the structure and therefore, the properties of polymers include:

1. The molecular structure of the repeating units including the use of copolymers.

2. The molecular weight or chain length.
3. The degree of chains branching.
4. The presence of cross – linking and the cross – link density.
5. The presence of plasticizers of fillers.

DISCRIPTION OF STRUCTURE & PROPERTIES

1. PHYSICAL STRUCTURE

a. Polymers exist as;
   i. Fibers of nylon.
   ii. Amorphous polymer e.g. methyl methacrylate.
   iii. Crystalline polymer e.g. polyethylene.
   iv. Elastomers or rubber e.g. silicones.

b. Rubber and amorphous polymer are the most relevant to dental polymers.

c. Two basic properties which characterize polymers are glass transition temperature (Tg) and melting temperature (TM).
   i. Tg and Tm both have different values in crystalline polymers.
   ii. The glass transition temperature (Tg) is the temperature at which molecular motions become such that whole chains are able to move.
   iii. It is like softening temperature and can be estimated mechanically by noting the temperature at which a sudden change in elastic modulus occurs.
   iv. Behavior of amorphous polymers below their glass transition temperatures generally behave as rigid solid and above the glass transition temperature they may behave as viscous liquid, flexible solids or rubbers.

2. EFFECTS OF MOLECULAR WEIGHT

- Polymerization is a random process, some chains grow faster than other-some are terminated before others.
- Thus not all chains have same length so they do not have some molecular weight.
- Polymer of high molecular weight → Greater molecular enlargement, great rigidity more strength and high values of Tg and melting temperature.
- Polymer of low molecular weight → Opposite to high molecular weight polymers.

3. EFFECTS OF CROSS LINKING

a. Small Degree of cross-linking limits the amount of movement of polymer chains. When the material is stressed causes deformation.

b. Polymers with high degree of cross-linking cause high TG, harder, more brittle and more resistant to the action of solvents.

4. EFFECTS OF ADDING PLASTICIZERS

a. Plasticizers are the liquids which are able to penetrate between the randomly oriented chains of a polymer-As a result the units or molecules are further apart and the forces between them are less.

b. Addition of plasticizers can cause:
   i. Soft material
   ii. Flexible by lowering its Tg
   iii. Rubbery

5. EFFECTS OF CO-POLYMERS

a. Polymer chains which contain two or more different types of monomeric units can be prepared are termed as Co-polymer.

b. Co-polymerization is done for special application.

METHODS OF FABRICATING POLYMERS

Some polymers are produced in powder form and fabricated at a later stage by softening and moulding. Techniques for moulding include:

- Injection moulding
- Vacuum forming
- Blow moulding

In dentistry, use of injection moulding technique is getting importance. Below picture showing how polymer is injected in a mould for making Partial denture as well as complete denture. (Fig: 9.2)

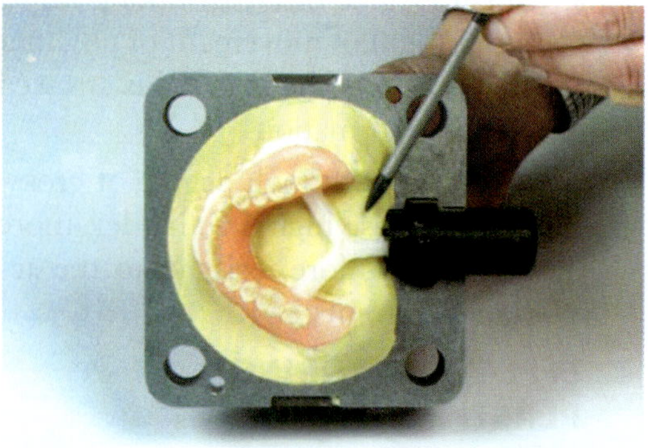

Fig: 9.2. Injection moulding technique.

ADVANTAGES AND DISADVANTAGES OF INJECTION MOULDING TECHNIQUE

Advantages

1. These polymers have high impact resistance.
2. They do not contain MMA monomer, so they may be used for patients who are allergic to Methylmeth Acyrlate.

Disadvantages

1. The equipment for processing these polymers is more expensive.
2. The craze resistance of these materials is lower than conventional acrylics.
3. Difficulties associated with attachment of teeth to the denture base.

DENTURE BASE POLYMERS

INTRODUCTION

Denture base is that part of the denture, which rests on the soft tissues and so, does not include the artificial teeth. In 1940 Vulcanite was the most widely used denture base polymer but it is a highly cross linked natural rubber which was difficult to pigment and tend to become unhygienic due to the uptake of saliva.

That's why, now a days acrylic resin is used universally for denture base construction.

Fig: 9.3 (A). Vulcanite Material.

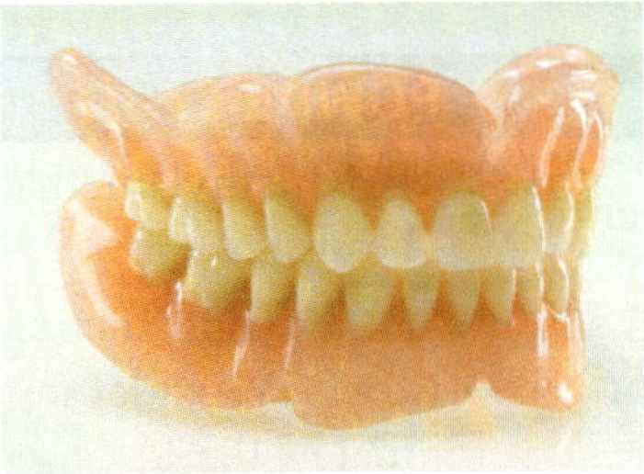

Fig: 9.3 (B). Acrylic Material.

REQUIREMENTS OF DENTURE BASE POLYMERS

1. PHYSICAL PROPERTIES

a. Should be capable of matching the appearance of the natural oral soft tissues.

b. Should have high value of glass transition temperature (Tg) to prevent softening and distortion during use.

c. Should have good dimensional stability in order that the shape of the denture does not change over a period of time.

d. Should have a low value of specific gravity in order that denture should be as light as possible.

e. Should have high value of thermal conductivity which would enable the denture wearer to maintain a healthy oral mucosa and to retain a normal reaction to hot and cold stimuli.

f. Should be radio opaque.

2. MECHANICAL PROPERTIES

a. Should be rigid.

b. Should have high value of modulus of elasticity.

c. Should have high value of elastic limit.

d. Should have sufficient flexural strength to resist fracture.

e. Should have an adequate fatigue life and high value of fatigue limit.

f. Should have adequate impact strength.

g. Should have sufficient abrasion resistance.

3. CHEMICAL PROPERTIES

a. Should be chemically inert.

b. Should be in soluble in oral fluid.

c. Should not absorb water or saliva.

4. BIOLOGICAL PROPERTIES

a. Should not be harmful to the technician.

b. Should be hygienic does not allow growth of bacteria and fungi.

5. MISCELLANEOUS PROPERTIES

a. Should be inexpensive.
b. Should have long shelf life.
c. Should have easy to manipulate and fabricate.
d. Should be repaired easily.

ACRYLIC DENTURE BASE MATERIALS

1. INTRODUCTION

The acrylic resins are derivatives of ethylene and contain a vinyl group in their structural formula.

- 95% of the complete dentures made today use one of the acrylic resins.
- Acrylic resins are now the material of choice because
  a. They have the required aesthetics quality
  b. They are inexpensive
  c. They ae easy to process
  d. They have low density
  e. They have sufficient mechanical properties
- Their disadvantages are :
  a. Barely have adequate strength
  b. Is susceptible to distortion
  c. Have a low thermal conductivity
  d. Is radiolucent

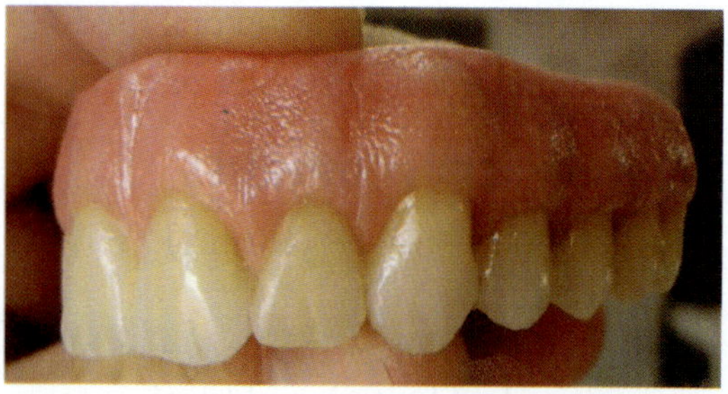

2. CLASSIFICATION

Based on the method used for its activation;

TYPE	CLASS	DESCRIPTION
1	2	Heat – processing polymers, powder and liquid
	2	Heat processed (Plastic Cake)
2	1	Auto polymerize polymer, powder and liquid.
	1	Auto polymerizes polymers. powder and liquid pour type resins.
3	–	Thermoplastic blank or powder
4	–	Light – activated material
5	–	Microwave – cured material

3. SUPPLY AS

These are available as powder and liquid.

4. COMPOSITION

POWDER		
Polymer	→	Polymethyl methacrylate beads.
Initiator	→	A peroxide such as benzoyl Peroxide (approximately 0.5%)
Pigments	→	Salts of cadmium or iron or Organic dyes.
LIQUID		
Monomer	→	Methyl methacrylate
Cross – Linking Agent	→	Ethylene glycodimethacrylate (approximately 10%)
Inhibitor	→	hydroquinone
Activator	→	N. N – dimethyl – p – toluidine (Approx. 10%)

PROPERTIES OF MMA

- Melting point – 48°C
- Bonding point – 100.3°C
- Density -0.945g/ml
- Heat of polymerization (exothermic reaction)- 54.kJ/mol
- Coloruless liquid
- Immiscible with but miscible with organic solvents
- Irritant
- Flammable

PROPERTIES OF POLYMETHYL METHACRYLATE

- Transparency and high clarity
- Density 1.2g/cm^3 (causes polymerization)
- Polymeriztion shrinkage – 6% by vol%
- Polymerization shrinkage -0.2-0.5% (linear)
- Compression strength 90-100MPa
- Tensile strength -55 MPa
- Very rigid – elastic modulus above 2.4GPa
- Water absorption up to app. 1.0 wt.%
- Hardness – 15 – 18KHN
- Temperature glass transition Tg=105 – 120°C
- Wear resistance – fair
- Fatigue resistance – good
- Soluble in organic solvents (MMA, acetone, toluene, etc)

HEAT CURING MATERIALS

Mixing

a. The mixing of powder and liquid to form dough which is packed into a gypsum mould for curing.

b. The powder / liquid ratio is 2.5:1 and it's important to control the 'workability' of the mix as well as the dimensional change on setting.

DRAWBACKS OF USING INAPPROPRIATE POWDER/LIQUID
If the powder/liquid ratio is too high:
1. The mix becomes 'dry' , unmanageable and weak.
2. The mixture will not flow when placed under pressure in the gypsum mould.
3. It may produce a granular effect on the denture surface, which is normally referred to as granular porosity.
If too much monomer is added:
1. It will produce excessive polymerization shrinkage.
2. A loss of quality of fit to the denture bearing surface.
3. Porosity may occur.
4. Additional time will be required to reach packing consistency.

c. It undergoes volumetric polymerization shrinkage of 5 to 6% and it is reduced by using a mix with a high powder liquid ratio.

d. Powder is added in liquid while mixing so that each powder particle is wetted by monomer.

e. The mixture is then stirred and allowed to stand and a lid is placed on the mixing vessel.

f. Immediately after mixing, a material undergoes to following stages:

Sandy → Sticky → Doughy → Rubbery → Hard

Powder and Liquid.

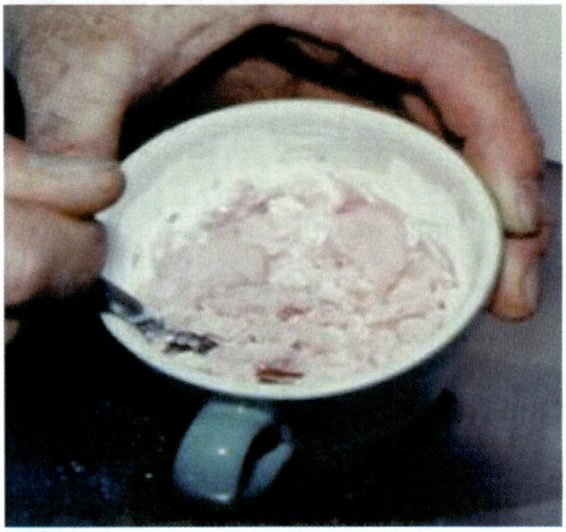

Mixing.

Sticky.

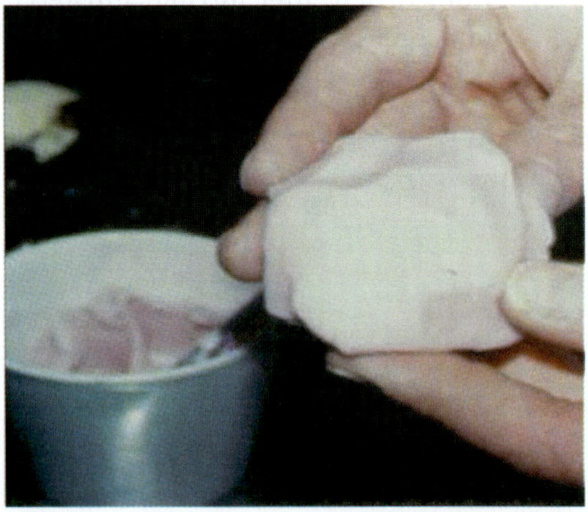

Dough.

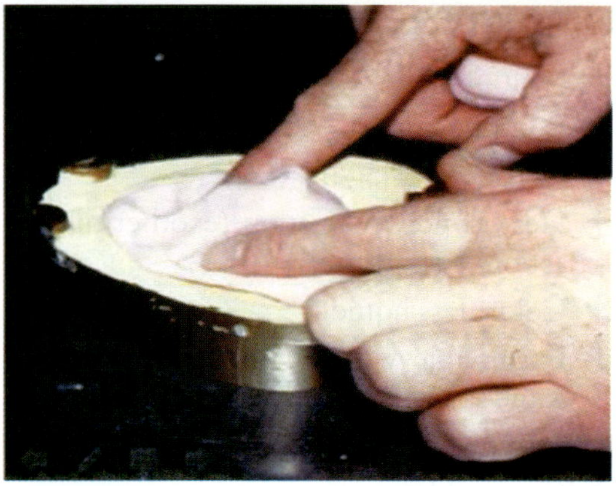

Packing.

g. Doughing time is short.

h. Working time is long.

i. Dough is packed into the two part gypsum mould and trial closure is done and it causes excess material to form a "Flash" at the point where the two halves of the flask meet.

j. The flask is then opened and "flash" is removed then closed again under pressure using threaded bench press.

k. The applied pressure ensures that dough flows into every part of the mould, reduction in the polymerization shrinkage and prevents formation of Raised Bite.

Fig: 9.4. Acrylic mixing cup for mixing.

CURING

a. After filling the mould with dough, the next stage is to polymerize the monomer to produce the final processed.

b. Curing is carried out by placing the clamped flask in either a water bath or an air oven.

c. During curing attention should be paid to certain facts;

   1. Benzoyl peroxide initiator begins to decompose rapidly to form free radicals above 65 C.
   2. The polymerization reaction is highly exothermic.
   3. The boiling point of the monomer is 100.3C.
   4. It is important to get a high degree of conversion from monomer to polymer and production of high molecular weight polymer is required to produce a material with good mechanical properties.

I. Fast cycle

- Place flask in cold water and allow it to boil ifor 1 hour.
- Let it boil for 1 hour and then cool down slowly.

II. Slow cycle

- Cure at 70°c for 7 hours followed by 3 hours at 100°c .
- A slow cycle is better with larger amounts of material.
- Generally, slow cures result in better dimensional accuracy.

III. Rapid Heating

- More residual monomer.
- Reduced toughness.
- Heat builds up from exothermic reaction.
- Porosity.
  a. Loss of strength
  b. Bad esthetics (opaque and cloudy color)

IV. Microwave Curing

- Uses a microwave.
- Flasks are non-metallic.
- Reduced time.

COMPARISION

HEAT CURED RESIN	SELF CURED RESIN
Thermal energy is the activator.	Uses chemical activator.
Porosity of material is less.	Porosity is greater.
Show lesser distortion.	Show greater distortion.
Less initial deformation.	More initial deformation.
Less creep and quicker recovery.	Increased creep and slow recovery.
Color stability is good.	Poor color stability.
Difficult to deflask.	Easy to deflask.
Commonly used as denture base material and for artificial teeth.	Very useful as repair and re-lining of dentures.

PROPERTIES

1. PHYSICAL PROPERTIES

a. Its appearance is adequate.

b. They are available in variety of shades and opacities and can be veined or unveined.

c. The value of Tg may vary from one product to another depending on the molecular weight and residual monomer.

   i. For heat cure → 105 C

   ii. For cold cure → 90 C

   iii. For light activated → higher than conventional acrylic.

d. Have low values of specific gravity (approximately 1.2 $g.cm^{-3}$) because they are composed to "light" atom e.g. carbon, hydrogen and oxygen.

e. They are radiolucent because of ethane; O atoms are poor x-ray absorbers.

2. MECHANICAL PROPERTIES

a. Compared with alloys, it is soft, weak and flexible material.

b. It provides the denture base sufficient thickness, rigidity and strength.

c. The transverse strength of acrylic is adequate to resist masticatory loads.

d. It has poor impact strength.

e. Crazing may sometimes appear on the surface of on acrylic denture.

f. This is a series of surface cracks, which may have a weakening effect on the base.

g. Its hardness is 20 VHN.

3. CHEMICAL AND BIOLOGICAL PROPERTIES

a. Acrylic resin slowly absorbs water and saliva.

b. Due to absorption of water dimensional change occurs but they are insignificant.

c. Associated with water absorption is the ability of certain organisms to colonize the fitting surface of an acrylic denture and cause denture stomatitis.

d. Allergic reactions occur due to MMA monomer.

4. DENTURE RADIOLUCENCY

a. Problems when accidents displace fractured segments

   - Lungs
   - Skull
   - stomach

b. Salts and fillers reduce esthetics, strength

c. Organometallics are toxic

   - Bromine containing organics lack heat stability, must be added in quantities that plasticize the denture, causing creep and water sorption.

Table: 9.1. Mechanical properties of acrylic resin (a comparison with certain alloys).

	MODULUS OF ELASTICITY (GPA)	TENSILE STRENGTH (MPA)	HARDNESS (VHN)
Acrylic resin	2.5	85	20
Co/Cr	220	850	420
Stainless steel	220	1000	400

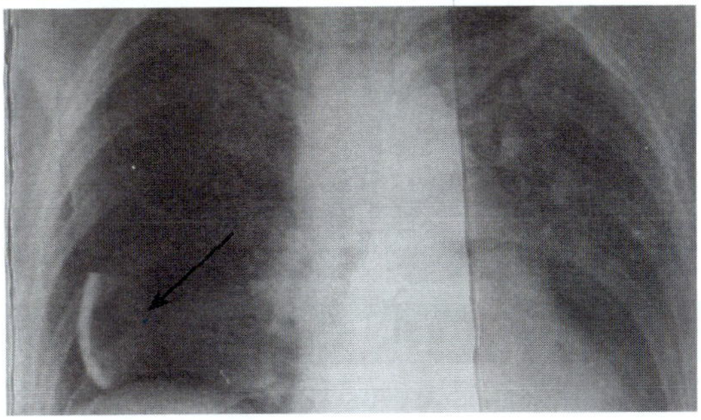

Fig: 9.5. Broken piece of denture (left side) shown in chest x-ray.

5. POROSITES

There are three types of porosities:

A. Granular Porosity

a. It happens when;
   - Higher powder liquid ratio results in a dry mix.
   - A dry mix is unmanageable and the mixture will not flow under pressure.
   - Insufficient monomer to bind all polymers beads together.
   - Loss of monomer during setting.

b. It is characterized by a blotch, opaque surface.

B. Gaseous Porosity

a. If the temperature of dough is raised above the boiling point of monomer i.e. 100.3-degree centigrade the monomer will boil.

b. Produce spherical voids in the hottest part of the curing dough.

C. Contractile Porosity

- Occurs due to use of insufficient dough to create an excess in the mould or the application of insufficient pressure during curing can lead to porosity voids dispersed throughout the whole mass of the denture base.

AUTO POLYMERIZING MATERIALS

INTRODUCTION

a. It is also called self-cure resin materials.

b. Mixing is same as heat cure materials.

c. Increase in viscosity occurs due to a combination of physical and chemical changes occurring in the mix.

d. It reaches dough stage quickly and decreases working time.

e. They have inferior mechanical properties and high residual monomer content.

f. It is used for repairing and re-lining of denture.

MODIFIED ACRYLIC MATERIALS

INTRODUCTION

In modified acrylic materials attempts have been made to improve impact strength, fatigue resistance or rapidity.

REINFORCED BY

a. Elastomers are incorporated to improve impact strength.

b. Carbon fibers inserts are used to improve fatigue resistance and flexural strength.

c. Bromine containing additives are use to increase radiopacity.

ALTERNATIVE POLYMERS

- The major alternatives to acrylic polymers or modified acrylic are:
  - Polycarbonates
  - Vinyl polymers
- Used inpatients who are allergic to acrylic and when greater impact strength is required. They are processed by injection moulding technique.

DENTURE LINING MATERIALS

INTRODUCTION

It is the addition of new denture base material to the fitting surface of the existing ill fitting old denture. These materials may be of hard or soft type. The hard denture liners are the heat cure or cold cure acrylic resin denture base materials.

USES

a. To improve the fit of existing material.
b. Soft materials are used, which act as a cushion to enable traumatized tissue to heat.
c. Patents that are unable to tolerate a hard denture base should be provided with a permanent soft cushion.

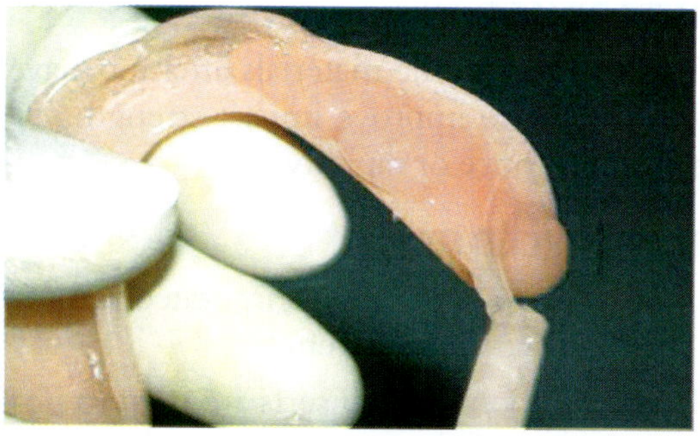

Fig: 9.6. Application of Lining Material.

IDEAL REQUIREMENTS

a. Should be odorless, tasteless.
b. Should be non-toxic, non-irritant.
c. Should be soft and resistant to abrasion.
d. Should be esthetically acceptable.
e. Should have good shelf life.
f. Should be simple to manipulate.
g. Should be good bond between lining and denture base.
h. Should be easy to clean.

CLASSIFICATION

DENTURE LINING MATERIAL
- Hard Reline Material
- Tissue Conditioner
- Soft Lining Material

HARD RELINE MATERIALS

These materials are used to provide a chair side reline to the denture. The method should be distinguished from laboratory Relining and Rebasing Techniques that involve replacing most of the denture base resin with fresh, heat cured polymer.

MODE OF SUPPLY

- These are supplied as powder and liquid, which are mixed together.

TYPES

- Type I
- Type II

The main difference between the two types is that the liquid in the type I material contains *methyl methacrylate monomer* and the liquid of the type II material contain *butyl methacrylate monomer.*

COMPOSITION

Type I

POWDER
Polymer beads (Polymethyl Methacrylate)
Initiator (Benzoyl Peroxide)
Pigments Probably Inorganic salt
LIQUID
Monomer (Methyl Methacrylate)
Plasticizer (Di-n-butyl p thalate)
Chemical activator (Tertiary A0mine)

Type II

POWDER
Polymer Beads (Polymethyl Methacrylate)
Initiator (Benzoyl Peroxide)
Pigments Probably Inorganic salt
LIQUID
Monomer (Butyl Methacrylate Tertiary Amine)

MANIPULATION

a. The normal procedure is to relieve the fitting surface of the denture by grinding away some of the hard acrylic denture base.

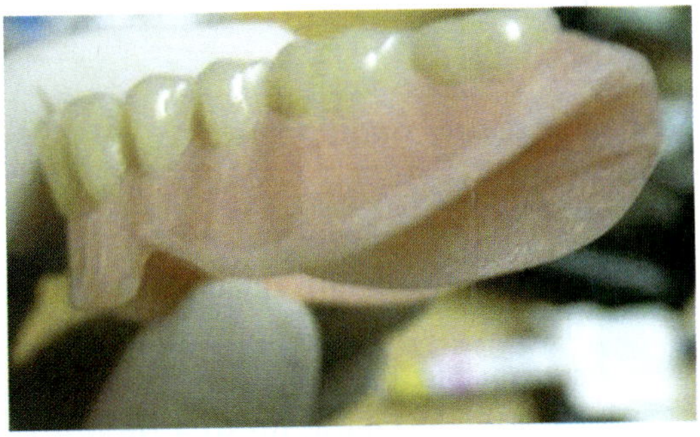

Fig: 9.7. Border of denture is trimmed for rebasing.

b. The powder and liquid of the hard reline material are then mixed in the recommended proportions to give a fluid mix of material.

c. Then apply to the fitting surface of denture.

d. Ask the patient to close his mouth.

e. Wait till rubbery stage and then remove it from the patient mouth.

f. And allow it to set. Setting may be accelerated by placing denture in warm water.

g. The relined denture is normally ready for trimming and polishing within 30 minutes.

PROPERTIES

a. Type I is irritant because it contains methylcethacrylate monomer and type II is containing butyl methacrylate monomer which is known to be a far less irritant substance than methylmethacrylate.

b. Both type I and II materials have low values of glass transition temperature (Tg). The reasons for this are the presence of plasticizer in type I materials and the use of higher methacrylate (ethyl and butyl) in the type II materials.

c. They are dimensionally instable.

d. The reline materials are often porous due to air inclusion during mixing of the powder and liquid – Such porous surface will be more likely to become contaminated with oral debris and be colonized by micro-organisms including Candida Albicans.

TISSUE CONDITIONERS

INTRODUCTION

Tissue conditioners are soft denture liners, which may be applied to the fitting surface of a denture.

REQUIREMENTS

a. Should have an adequate cushioning affect on the underlying soft tissues.

b. Should be resilient in order that masticatory loads are absorbed without causing permanent deformation of the lining.

c. Should be elastic.

COMPOSITION

POWDER
Polymer Beads (Polymethyl Methacrylate)

LIQUID
Solvent Ethyl alcohoe
Plasticizer Butyl phthalyl butyl glycolate

MANIPULATION

a. Tissue conditioners are used in chair-side techniques.

b. Apply mixed material to the fitting surface of denture; thickness of tissue conditioners should be adequate.

PROPERTIES

a. They are initially very soft and visco-elastic.

b. They lack a well – defined elastic behavior and it makes the measurement of rigidity difficult.

c. Tissue conditioners should be replaced with fresh material every 2 – 3 days until the tissues have healed.

d. They are non-irritants due to the absence of acrylic monomers from the liquid component.

APPLICATIONS

a. They are used to provide a temporary cushion, which prevents masticatory loads from being transferred to underlying hard and soft tissues.

b. They are often applied to the dentures of patients who have undergone surgery. This reduces pain and helps prevent traumatization of the wound.

c. Can be used to fill the gap between the denture base and the socket at the time of insertion of the immediate denture.

d. Also used as functional impression materials.

SOFT LINING MATERIALS

There are two types of soft lining material available in the market:

- Temporary soft lining materials.
- Permanent soft lining materials.

1. TEMPORARY SOFT LINING MATERIALS

Introduction

These materials are very similar to the tissue conditioners.

Mode of Supply

Supplied as powder and liquid.

Composition

Similar as tissue conditioners.

Properties

a. The materials are not as soft as the tissue conditioners immediately after setting but they retain their softness for longer, taking up to a month or two to harden.

b. They are visco elastic in nature.

c. It gives a cushioning effect under dynamic conditions of loading.

d. It is possible to soak such dentures over night in dilute sodium hypochlorite to help to prevent infection risk.

Uses

a. Used in place of tissue conditioners in cases where it is not practicable to replace the conditioners every 2 – 3 days.

b. Used as a means of temporarily improving the fit of an ill – fitting denture until such a time as a new denture can be constructed.

c. Used as a diagnostic aid to ascertain whether the patient would benefit from a permanent soft lining.

A. Stage 1.

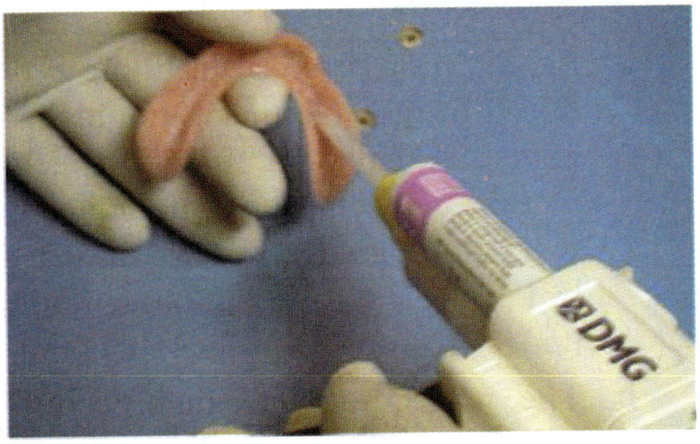

B. Stage 2.

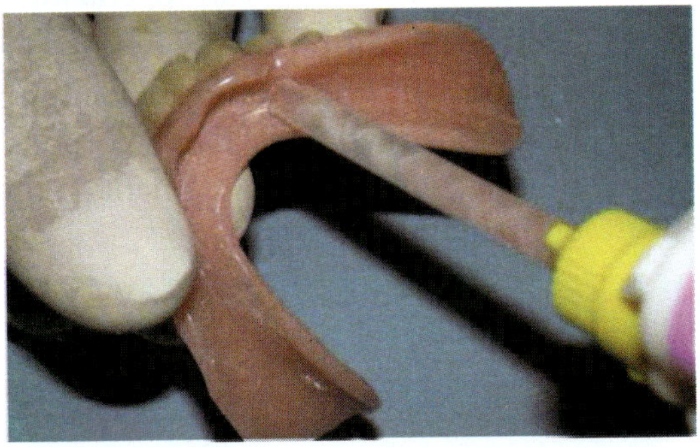

C. Stage 3.

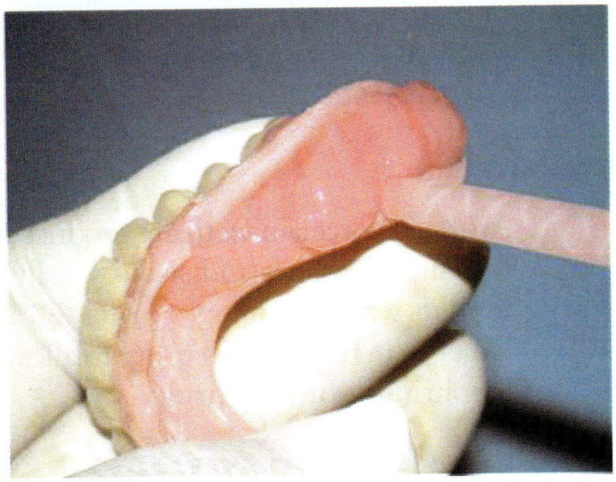

Fig: 9.8. Clinical Stages of Application of Soft Lining Material.

2. PERMANENT SOFT LINING MATERIALS

Introduction

Permanent soft lining materials are most commonly used for patients who cannot tolerate a hard base. This problem generally arises if the patient has an irregular mandibular alveolar ridge covered by a thin and relatively non-resilient mucosa.

Requirements

a. Should be permanently soft.
b. There should be no distortion.
c. Should have good adherence.
d. Should be non-toxic and non-irritant.
e. Should be anti bacterial/fungal.

AVAILABLE MATERIALS

✦ The types of materials, which are available for, use as permanent soft lining are as follows:

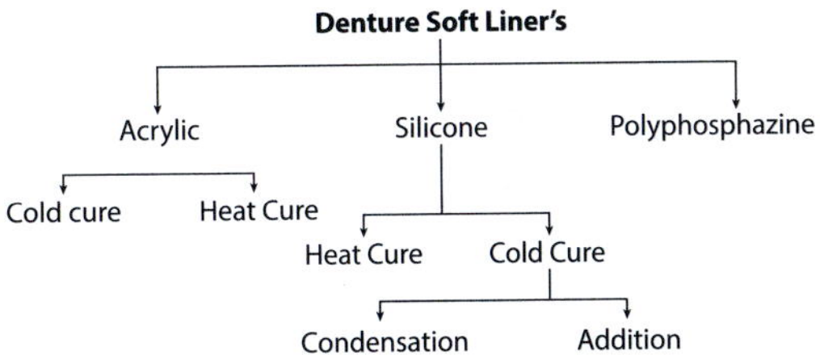

ARTIFICIAL TEETH

INTRODUCTION

The main components of a denture are the artificial teeth.

AVAILABLE MATERIALS

The two materials which are commonly used for the production of artificial teeth are:

- Acrylic resins
- Porcelain

IDEAL REQUIREMENTS

a. The most important requirements of artificial teeth is good appearance.

b. The artificial teeth should be indistinguishable from natural teeth in shape, colour and translucency.

c. There should be good attachment between the artificial teeth and the denture base.

d. The introduction of artificial into the base should not adversely affect base material. That is the artificial tooth and base material should be compatible.

e. The artificial teeth should be of low density in order that they do not increase the weight of the denture.

f. The artificial teeth should be strong and tough in order to resist fracture.

g. They should be hard enough to resist abrasive forces in the mouth and during cleaning but should allow grinding with a dental bur so that adjustments to the occlusion can be made by the dentist at the chair-side.

METHOD OF MANUFACTURING ARTIFICIAL TEETH BY DIFFERENT MATERIALS

Methods of manufacturing artificial teeth by different materials are as follows:

By Acrylic Resins

a. Acrylic resin artificial teeth are produced in reusable metal moulds using either the dough moulding technique, or by injection moulding in which the acrylic powder is softened by beating and forced into the mould under pressure.

b. The resins used are highly cross-linked in order to produce artificial teeth, which are resistant to crazing.

c. The main difference between the material and those used for denture base construction is the incorporation of tooth-colored pigments rather than pink ones.

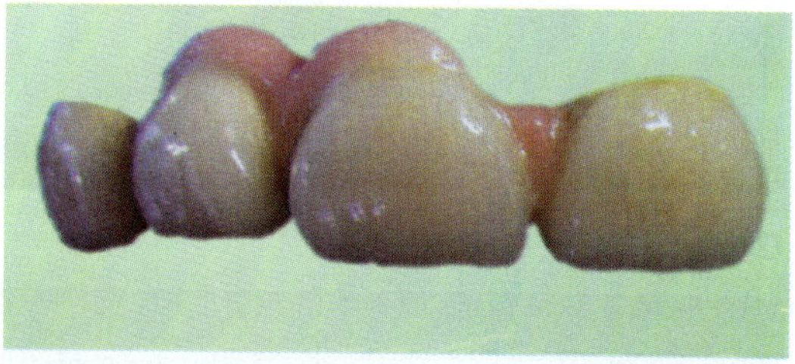

Fig: 9.9. Acrylic teeth.

By Porcelain

a. Artificial porcelain teeth are produced to standard shapes and sizes by using moulds which are approximately 30% larger than required, in order to allow for shrinkage during firing.

b. Small holes or metal pins are incorporated in the base of the porcelain teeth during their production. These are used to give mechanical attachment to the denture base.

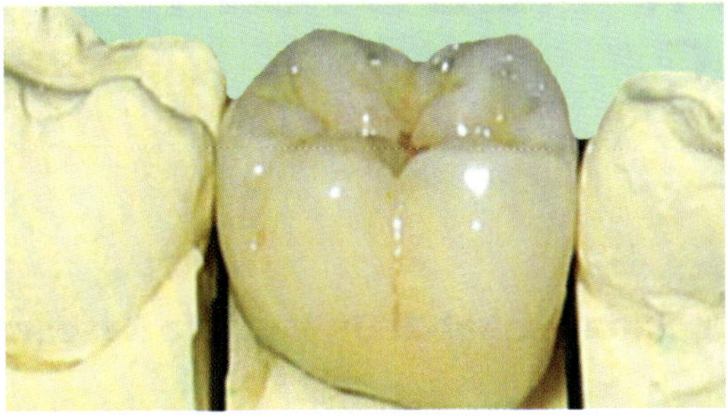

Fig: 9.10. Porcelain used to Metal Crown.

REFERENCES

1. Painter, Paul C.; Coleman, Michael M. (1997). *Fundamentals of Polymer science: an Introductory Text*. Lancaster, Pa.: Technomic Pub. Co. p. 1. ISBN 1-56676-559-5.
2. McCrum, N. G.; Buckley, C. P.; Bucknall, C. B. (1997). *Principles of Polymer engineering*. Oxford; New York: Oxford University Press. p. 1. ISBN 0-19-856526-7.
3. Kenneth Anusavice (2012), *Phillips' Science of Dental Materials, (12th Edition.)*, Saunders.
4. John M. Power & John C.wataha (2012), *DENTAL MATERIALS Properties and Manipulation (10th Edition)*, ELSEVIER, India.
5. John McCabe & Angus W.G. Walls (2008), *Applied Dental Materials*, Blackwell Publisher, Hong Kong.

PROPERTIES OF ACRYLIC VS PORCELAIN

PROPERTIES	ACRYLIC RESIN	PORCELAIN
Abrasion resistance	Low	High
Staining	Easily stain	Does not stain
Clicking sound	Absent	Present
Case of fabrication	Easily	Difficult
Adjustability	Easily	Difficult
Bonding	Chemical	Mechanical
Trauma to denture bearing arch	Less	More
Shiny	Less	More
Density	Less dense	More dense
Hardness (VHN)	20	500
Modules of elasticity (Gpa)	25	80
Co-efficient of thermal expansion (ppm C1)	80	70
Expensive	Less	More
Disadvantage	Discolouration	Chipping

Chapter 10

DENTAL IMPRESSION MATERIALS

Dr. Sana Shahab & Dr. Mustafa Naseem

INTRODUCTION

Those materials that are used to take impression of teeth and surrounding structures of oral cavity for making accurate prosthesis of the patient.

How do we use impression material?

A. Examine the patient

With the help of impression tray select the size of the tray, and check the patient whether it is edentulous/dentulous.

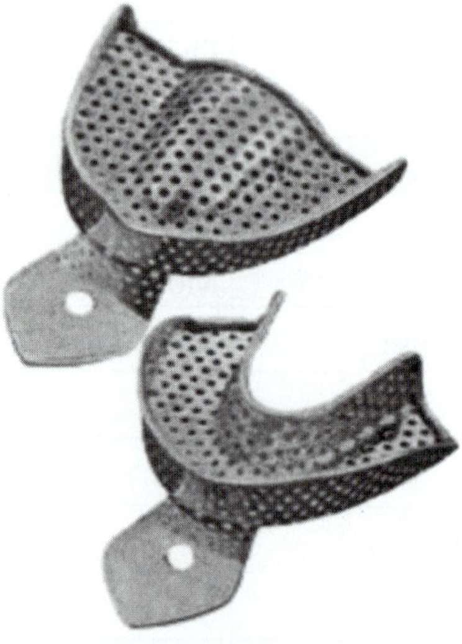

Fig: 10.1. Metalic stock trays.

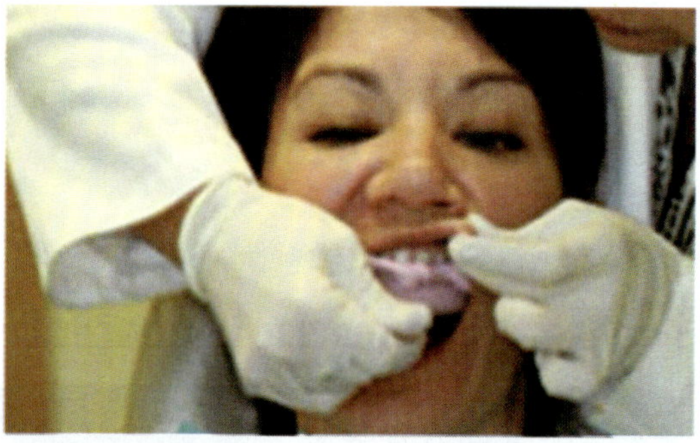

Fig: 10.2. Checking impression tray size in Patients mouth.

B. Load of material in tray

Select the material which type of it would be used to taking such impression.

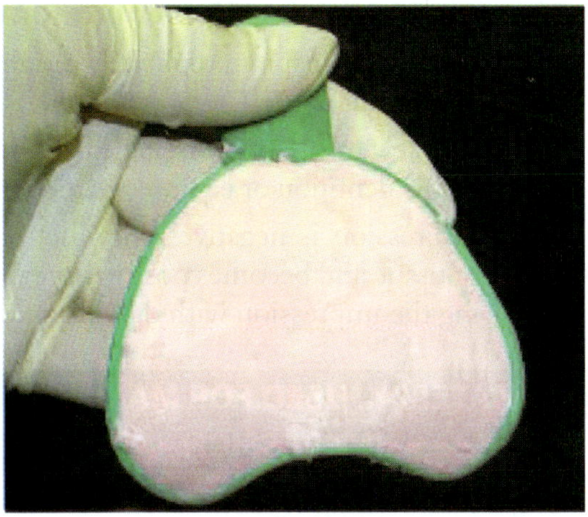

Fig 10.3. Impression materials loaded In tray.

C. Take impression

The material should be fluid enough when it is inserted in the oral cavity to adapt with the oral tissues.

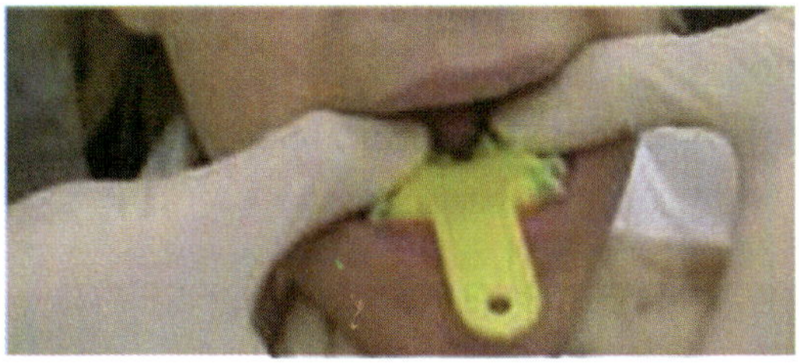

Fig: 10.4. Taking Impression.

D. Pour model

The model is poured with dental stone plaster. For examination of oral tissues or for making prosthesis e.g. Partial denture or crown or bridge.

Fig: 10.5. Set Impression material, after it is removed from mouth ready for pouring model.

Fig: 10.6. Mixing dental stone/plaster.

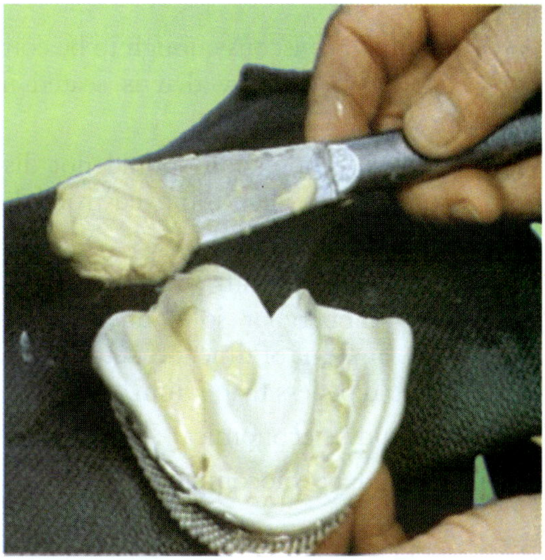

Fig: 10.7. Pouring of dental Impression with dental plaster/stone.

IMPRESSION

It is a negative record of tissue of mouth. It is used to register or produce the form and relationship of teeth and surrounding tissue. The negative reproduction of tissue given by the impression material is filled up with dental stone and other model materials to get a positive cast.

DIE

The positive reproduction of single tooth is described as die.

CAST/MODEL

When several teeth or a whole arch is reproduced, it is called a cast or model.

REQUIREMENTs OF IDEAL IMPRESSION MATERIAL

a. Should have pleasant taste, odour , colour and esthetics
b. Should not contain any toxic or irritating ingredients.
c. Should have adequate shelf life for adequate storage and distribution.
d. Should be fluid enough to adapt with oral tissue.
e. Should be viscous enough to be contained in the tray that is seated in mouth.
f. The set impression should not distort or tear when removed from the mouth.
g. While in mouth they transform into rubbery or solid in a reasonable amount of time. i.e. setting time should be less than 7 min.
h. Should be economical
i. Should be biocompatible with oral tissues.

OBJECTIVES OF IMPRESSION MATERIAL

Used to make an accurate replica or mould of hard/soft tissue.

a. The area may vary from single tooth to whole dentition or edentulous model.
b. Impression is negative reproduction of tissue and becomes positive by filling the impression with dental stone.

MATERIAL USED FOR MAKING IMPRESSION

a. Elastic Impression material
b. Inelastic Impression material
c. Hydrocolloids

CLASSIFICATION

- According to mode of setting
- According to dental use
- According to chemical property
- According to viscosity

A. ACCORDING TO MODE OF SETTING

BY CHEMICAL REACTION
✦ Impression plaster
✦ Zinc oxide Eugenol
✦ Alginate
✦ Poly ether
✦ Polysulfide
✦ Silicans

BY TEMPERATURE
✦ Impression compound
✦ Impression waxes
✦ Agar

B. ACCORDING TO DENTAL USE

EDENTULOUS
Impression plaster
Impression compound
Zinc oxide Eugenol
Impression wax

DENTULOUS
Alginate
Agar
Poly sulfide
Poly ether
Silicon rubber

C. ACCORDING TO CHEMICAL PROPERTIES

a. **Before setting**

MUCOSTATIC (VISCOUS)
Impression plaster
Zinc oxude Eugenol
Impression waxes
Alginate
Agar

MUCOCOMPRESSIVE (LESS VISCOUS)
Impression compound
Putty Elastomer

b. **After setting**

ELASTIC
a. **Synthetic Elastomer**
Polysulfide
Silicons
Poly ether
b. **Hydrocolloids**
Alginate
Agar

NON ELASTIC
Impression Plaster
Impression compound
Zinc oxide Eugenol
Impression wax

D. ACCORDING TO VISCOSITY:-

HIGH VISCOSITY
Impression compound
Putty Elastomer

MEDIUM VISCOSITY
Regular elastomers

LOW VISCOSITY
Impression plaster
Impression paste
Hydrocolloids a. Reversible b. Irreversible

Viscosity of different Impression material

MATERIAL	VISCOSITY (PAS)
Impression compound	4000
Impression plaster	60
Zinc oxide/eugenol paste	60
Alginate	50
Light-bodied elastomer	30
'Putty' elastomer	800

CLINICAL CONSIDERATION

A. Choice Of Impression Material

The fundamental choice for impression material is between rigid and elastomeric product.

1. ***Rigid Material***

- Used where undercuts are not present.
- Impression fractures during removal.
- Can be used in complete denture patients.
- Can also be used for edentulous arch.

2. ***Impression Tray***

- Used as rigid containers carrying the impression material into the mouth, for maintaining it in position during setting or hardening and supporting it during removal from mouth and when pouring the cast.

B. Types of Impression Trays

Stock Tray (may be metallic or non metallic)	Custom made Trays (Special Tray)

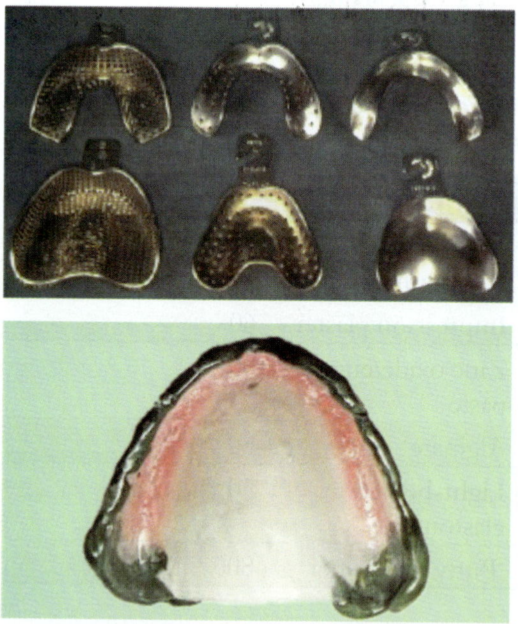

Fig: 10.8. Stock trays (Metalic).

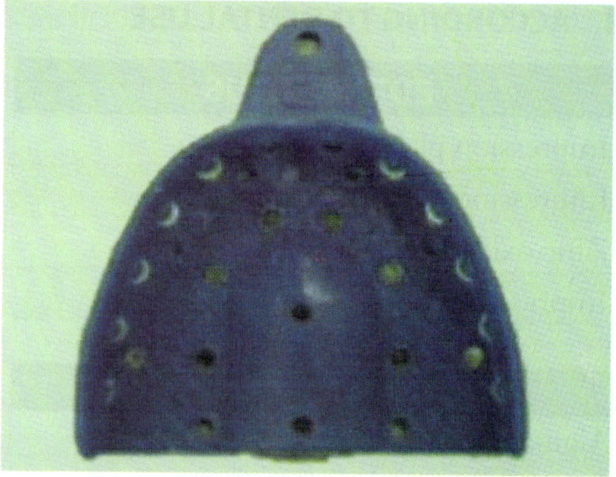

Fig: 10.9. Custom made (Special) Trays.

TISSUE MANAGEMENT

a. While taking impression it is important to record the surface of teeth as well as the relationship between the teeth and soft tissue surrounding them.
b. With fixed prosthodontics (crown/ bridge work) the preparation of teeth commonly extends up to or beneath the gingival margin.
c. It is necessary, therefore to displace the gingival tissues away from the preparation prior to syringing in light bodied material around tooth.
d. This displacement of gingival tissue can be achieved by:
    i. Retraction cord with hemostatic agent or plain
    ii. Electrosurgical unit
    iii. Soft tissue laser

IMPRESSION TECHNIQUE

a. The specific technique used for each material will vary from product to product.
b. To obtain greatest accuracy the teeth need to be clean and dry.

c. Salivary contamination is usually prevented by using a combination of cotton rolls and absorbent pads "Dry Gaurds".
d. The impression needs to be placed in the mouth whilst the impression material is fluid and left in the mouth until it is set fully.
e. After removing the impression from the mouth it is necessary to check that the surface of teeth is accurately represented in the impression or not.
f. Impression material, which extends beyond the tray will be unsupported and should be trimmed back to the extent of the of impression trays.
g. If this is not done, there may be problem with distortion extent of the model produced by weight of model making (commonly dental plaster or dental stone).

DISINFECTIVE OF IMPRESSION OR CROSS INFECTION CONTROL

a. It is important that impressions are disinfected prior to their being sent to the laboratory for the manufacture of model/prosthesis/appliances, to protect the laboratory staff from the transmission of infection from patient.
b. Impression should be rinsed in water immediately on removal from the patient's mouth to remove any obvious sign of saliva, blood and debris. Disinfection of the impression should be carried out before model is cast or the impression is sent to an outside laboratory.
c. Synthetic Elastomer including Condensation Silicones, Addition Silicones and Polysulfide can be disinfected with all EPA- registered disinfectants without the loss of surface quality or accuracy if disinfection time is short. The impression should be immersed for the time specified for each disinfectant. After disinfection, the impression should be removed, rinsed and poured with gypsum product as soon as possible.
d. The method for disinfecting hydrocolloid impressions recommended by the Centers for disease control and prevention is to use house hold bleach (1-10 dilution) iodophors or synthetic phenols as disinfectant. Spray with disinfectant and place in a seal plastic bag for manufacture's recommended time.
e. The method for disinfecting impression compound and Zinc Oxide Eugenol is 2% alkaline glutaraldehyde solution; the impression should be immersed in this solution for some time, rinsed and poured immediately.

NON ELASTIC IMPRESSION MATERIAL

INTRODUCTION

Non-inelastic impressions are those materials that exhibit an insignificant amount of elastic deformation when subjected to tensile stresses. They tend to fracture without exhibiting any plastic deformation if the stress from applied forces exceeds. Four main types of products form the group of impression materials classified as non-elastic materials, which are as follows.

a. Impression plaster.
b. Impression compound.
c. Impression waxes.
d. Zinc oxide / Eugenol impression pastes.

They are classified together for convenience rather than for reasons of similarity in composition or properties. A factor that links the materials is their inability to accurately record undercuts.

IMPRESSION PLASTER

Impression plaster is similar in composition to the dental plaster used to construct models and dies.

Fig: 10.10. Impression Plaster.

COMPOSITION

WATER / POWDER RATIO

60 ml: 10 gram (0.60 W/p Ratio)

MANIPULATION

- Powder is mixed with water at a powder / water ratio of 0.6% in a rubber bowl with a spatula 50 – 60 gm of plaster in 100 ml of water.
- Powder water ratio is higher than normally used for producing plaster to achieve mucostatic material.
- Freshly mixed plaster is too fluid and is normally used in a special tray constructed using 1 – 1.5 mm spacer.

β-Calcium Sulphate Hemihydrates as a main ingredient	
Anti – expansion agents	→ Accelerator -----Potassium Sulphate 4% → Retarders --------Borax 0.4-1%
Pigments	→ Alizarin Red 0.04%
Starch	→ Soluble plaster – due to swelling of starch when boiling water is poured over it and helps in removal of impression from cast.
NaCl	→ Shortens setting reaction/ expands setting reaction

- The tray may be constructed from acrylic resins or shellac.
- Another technique is to record the plaster impression as a wash in a preliminary compound impression.
- The technique for insertion of the impression into the mouth involves "pudding" the impression into place.
- With plaster the tray is gently moved from side to side and antero posteriorly to best take advantage of the handling characteristic of the material, particularly its fluidity.
- Before casting a plaster model in a plaster impression, the impression must be coated with a separating agent, otherwise separation is impossible.
- The mixed impression material is initially very fluid and is capable of recording soft tissues in the uncompressed.
- The hemihydrate particles are capable o absorbing moisture from the surface of the oral soft tissues and allowing very intimate contact between the impression material and the tissues.
- The water – absorbing nature of these materials often causes patients to complain about a very dry sensation after having impression recorded.

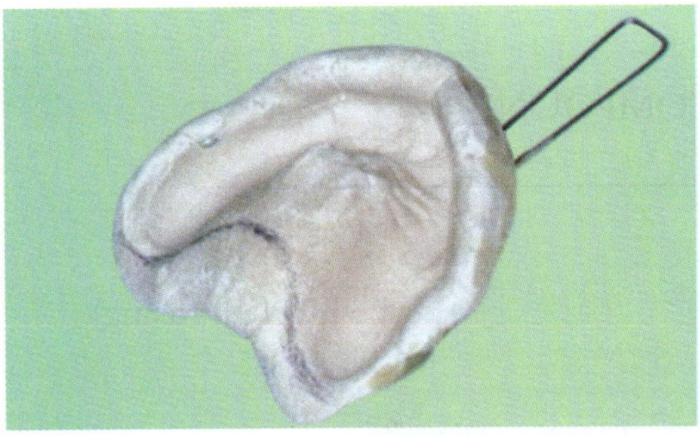

Fig: 10.11. Impression of edentulus patient with impression plaster.

- Disinfection of a plaster impression can be achieved with a 10 – minute soak in sodium hypochlorite solution.

PROPERTIES

A. Brittleness

Impression plaster is very brittle after setting.

B. Strength

Much lower strength so that fracture can occur easily if the material engages an undercut.

C. Setting Expansion

Its expansion is actually equivalent to that observed for a low expansion die stone.

D. Setting Time

More rapid setting in order to avoid inconvenience or discomfort to both the patient and dentist.

E. Biocompatibility

Nontoxic and un-pleasant.

F. Cost

It is economical or cheap.

USES

- For impression taking of complete denture.
- For flabby ridge impression.
- For bite registration.

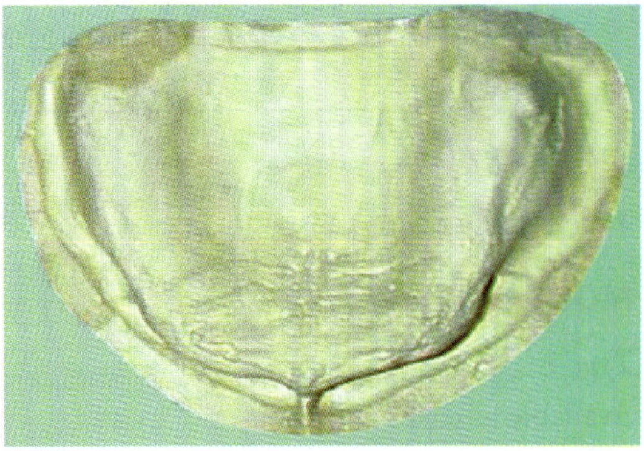

Fig: 10.12. Impression poured with impression plaster.

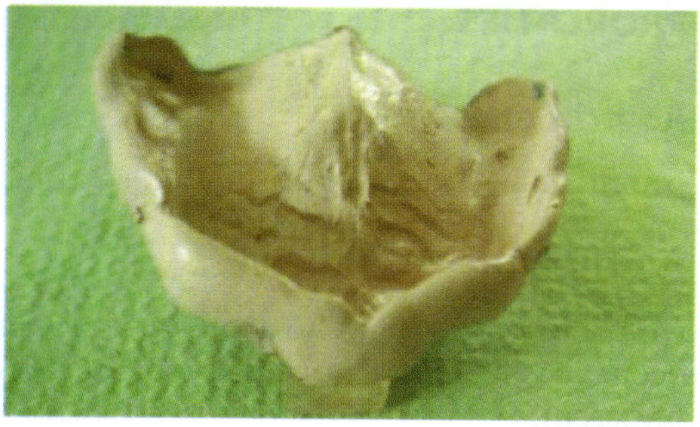

Fig: 10.13. Impression compound used for impression of Edenlutous arch.

IMPRESSION COMPOUND OR COMPONENT

- It is a rigid, reversible impression material that sets by physical changes.
- It is also a thermoplastic material i-e soften on heating and harden on cooling.

PROPERTIES

A. Viscosity

- Most viscous of the impression material.
- Two advantage of high viscosity;
  - a. Give fine detail.
  - b. Characterizes compound as a Mucocompression impression material.

VISCOSITY VALUES FOR SOME IMPRESSION MATERIALS:

Impression compound	4000
Imression plaster	60
Zinc oxide/eugenol paste	60
Alginate	50
Light-bodied elastomer	30
'Putty' elastomer	800

7. COMPOSITION

COMPONENT	EXAMPLE	FUNCTION
Thermoplastic material (47%)	Natural or synthetic resins and waxes	Characterises the softening temperature
Faller (50%)	Talc	Gives 'body' by increasing viscosity of the softened material; reduces thermal contraction
Lubricant (3%)	Stearic acid	Improves flow properties

CLASSIFICATION

IMPRESSION COMPOUND

Type I (Low fusing)

Type II (High fusing)

MODE OF SUPPLY

Type 1

Available as cakes and sticks.

Type 2

Available as sheets and cones.

B. Elastic / Rigidity

Compound is fairly Rigid after setting and has a poor elastic property.

Fig: 10.14. Periphries taken with stick component.

C. Thermal Expansion

- They have a large value of coefficient of thermal expansion and undergo considerable shrinkage on removal from the mouth.
- For the most accurate result the model should be poured as soon as possible.

D. Flow

- Flow of the impression material could be advantageous as well as harmful.
- Flow is desirable once the material has been softened during this period when it presses the tissue, it should flow into all the details of the tissue.
- Greater the flow, more accurate the impression.
- Once the compound hardens, it should have minimum flow, otherwise it will get distorted.

FLOW	AT 37°C	AT 45°C
Type I	20%or less	
Type II	2% or less	between 70 and 85%

E. Distortion

Since the release of strains is unavoidable, the safest procedure to prevent distortion is to pour the cast immediately or at least with in the first hour.

MANIPULATION

Sheets and Cakes form

- When a large amount of compound is softened as for complete denture impressions, a thermostatically controlled water bath at 50 – 60 C is used.
- Then compound is kneaded to suitable shape and placed in a non-perforated warm, dry tray and seated in position.

Kneading: - The manipulation of the impression compound with fingers when it is softened in a water bath is called Kneading.

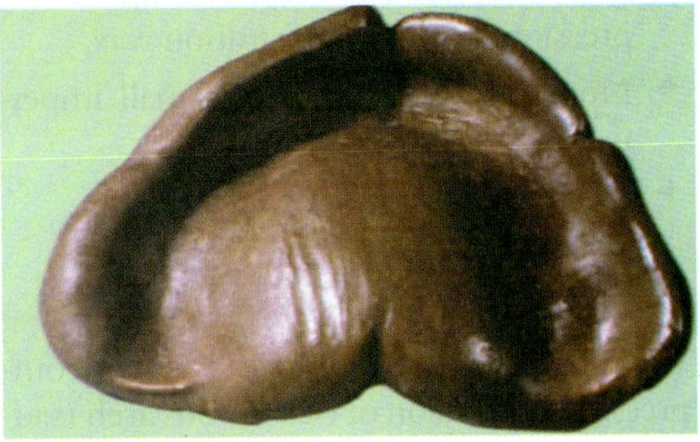

Fig: 10.15. Impression of dental compound.

Low fusing or green stick

- It is softened by holding it at some distance above the flame.
- It is warmed carefully by rotating to avoid over heating the outside portion.

USES

- For making preliminary impressions of complete dentures.
- For individual tooth impression (copper ring technique).
- Peripheral tracing or border moulding.
- To make a special tray.

IMPRESSION WAXES

They are thermoplastic materials which flow readily at mouth temperature and are relatively soft even at room temperature.

COMPOSITION

It is a mixture of low melting paraffin wax and Bee's wax in a ratio of about 3:1. This composition ensures a very high degree of flow at mouth temperature.

MANIPULATION

They are applied with a brush in small quantities to fill in areas of impressions in which in-sufficient material has been used or in which air blow or crease has caused a defect.

USES

- It is rarely used to record complete impression. i.e. Bite registration wax.
- Normally used to correct small imperfection on other impressions.
- Also used in Applegate technique.

APPLEGATE TECHNIQUE

Waxes are used to produce a muco-compressive impression of edentulous arch (saddle) partial denture, so called as Applegate technique.

ZINC OXIDE / EUGENOL IMPRESSION PASTE

INTRODUCTION

The mixture of zinc oxide / eugenol has a wide application in dentistry;

1. Impression material for edentulous patients.
2. Corrective impression.
3. Bite registration paste.
4. Temporary filling – sedative.
5. Cementing and insulating medium.
6. Root canal-filling material.
7. Surgical pack in periodontal surgical procedure.

SUPPLIED AS

- Normally supplied as two pastes, which are mixed together on a paper pad or glass slab.
- One of the tubes as the catalyst paste and the other the base.

CLASSIFICATION

- Zinc oxide / Eugenol impression paste produces a rigid impression with a high degree of accuracy and good reproduction of surface detail.
- Depending upon hardness according to ADA specification it is classified as;
  - i. Type I or (hard)
  - ii. Type II or (soft)

COMPOSITION

	COMPONENT	FUNCTION
Paste 1	Zinc Oxide	Reactive ingredient, which takes part in setting reaction.
	Olive Oil, Linseed	inert component used to form
	Oil	paste with zinc oxide.
	Zinc acetate	To accelerate setting
	Water (trace)	To accelerate setting
Paste 2	Eugenol (Oil of Cloves)	Reactive ingredient, which takes part in setting.
	Kaolin, talc or Equivalent	Inert filler used to form a paste with eugenol.

SETTING REACTION

- On mixing the two pastes, a reaction between zinc oxide and eugenol begins.
- The setting reaction is a typical acid base reaction to form a chelate.
- The reaction is also known as CHELATION and the product is called ZINC EUGENOLATE.
- 2 C10 H12 O2 + ZnO → Zn (C10 H11 O2) 2 + H2O.
- The zinc eugenolate formed is a matrix surrounding free zinc oxide particles.
- The chelate thought to form as an amorphous gel that tends to crystallize imparting increased strength to set mass.
- Formation of the crystalline zinc eugenolate is greatly enhanced when the setting reaction is accelerated by zinc acetate di-hydrate which is more soluble than Zn (OH)2 and can supply zinc ions more rapidly.
- An acetic acid is a more active accelerator for the setting reaction than water. It increases the speed for formation of the zinc hydroxide.
- The free eugenol content of the set cement is probably very low.

Fig: 10.16. Mixing Paster of Zinc Oxide Eugenol.

PROPERTIES

1. Sufficiently fluid and gives fine details.
2. No or little dimensional changes.
3. Non elastic that's why cannot be used in undercut areas.
4. Compatible with model material. The paste can be removed from stone by softening it in water at 60 C.
5. No toxic and unpleasant taste.
6. The setting time is reduced in the presence of water and under high temperature.
7. Defects on the surface of the impression can be corrected using an impression wax..

ELASTIC IMPRESSION MATERIAL HYDROCOLLOIDS

INTRODUCTION

Hydrocolloid impression materials used in dentistry are based on colloidal suspensions of polysaccharides in water.

COLLOIDAL SUSPENSION

It is characterized by the fact that it behaves neither as a solution, in which the solute is dissolved in the solvent, nor as a true suspension in which a heterogeneous structure exists with solid particles being suspended in a liquid.

For example

- Solution of sugar in water.
- The sugar molecules are solute and are dispersed uniformly in the water (solvent).
- There is a mutual attraction between sugar and water molecules.

HYDROCOLLOID

- When the fluid medium of the colloid is water, it is normally referred to as a Hydrocolloid.
- Dental Hydrocolloid impression materials exist in two forms:

1. IN THE SOL FORM:

They are fluid with low viscosity and there is a random arrangement of the polysaccharide chains.

2. IN THE GEL FORM:

The materials are more viscous and may develop elastic properties if the long polysaccharide chains become aligned.

- Gel formation is induced by cooling the sol.
- The formation of gel and development of elastic properties through alignment for polysaccharide chains.
- The chain become aligned and is mutually attracted by Vander Walls forces.
- Inter molecular hydrogen bonds may be formed between adjacent chains, enhancing the elasticity of the gel.
- On reheating the gel, these bonds are readily destroyed and the material reverts to the solution form. These materials are called Reversible Hydrocolloids. (Agar)
- As we already discussed that gel formation involves the production of strong intermolecular cross – links between polysaccharide chains.
- If materials do not require cooling in order to encourage gel formation and once formed the gel does not readily revert to the sol form. That materials are the irreversible Hydrocolloids. (Alginates)

AGAR

- Agar Hydrocolloids was the first successful elastic impression material to be used in dentistry.
- It is an organic hydrophilic, polysaccharide extracted from certain types of seaweeds.

SUPPLIED AS

Gel in a flexible, tooth paste – like tube or syringe.

COMPOSITION

COMPONENT	WEIGHT %	FUNCTION
Agar	13 – 17%	it provides the dispensed phase of the sol and the continuous fibril structure of the gel.
Borates	0.2 – 0.5%	strengthens the gel by providing inter molecular attraction.
Sulphates (K2SO4)	0 – 2%	Gypsum hardener to counteract the retarding effect of borax.
Wax	0.5 – 1%	Filler.
Water	about 85%	Forms dispersion medium.

MANIPULATION

- Reversible Hydrocolloids are normally conditioned prior to use, using a specially designed conditioning bath.
- This consists of three compartments each containing water.

A. Boiling container / liquefaction section

- The tube or syringe of gel is first placed in the 100 C bath. (Atleast 10 – 45 minutes).
- This rapidly converts the gel to sol and the contents of the tube become very fluid.

B. Storage container

- The tube is then transferred to the 65 C bath where it is stored until required for use.
- This temperature is high enough to maintain the material in the sol form.
- At this stage material should be uniformly softened and mixed.

C. Tempering container

- A few minutes before the impression is recorded; the contents are cooled to 45 C.
- If the material is maintained at this temperature for long, it slowly begins to revert to the gel form.
- There a temperature hysteresis effect occurs.

Hysteresis is basically “a physical phenomenon in which a material such as reversible hydrocolloids passes from a solid to a gel state at one temperature and a gel to a solid at another temperature”.

- For solving this problem we use water – cooled impression trays.
- It is a metal stock tray with a narrow – bore metal tube attached to the outer surface.
- The tube is connected to a cold water supply and the circulating water reduces the temperature of the tray.
- The coolest areas of the sol are converted to gel more rapidly than that in contact with the oral tissues.
- This arrangement is advantageous. If

slight movement of the impression tray takes place during setting, the material adjacent to the oral tissues can flow to compensate, thus reducing in accuracies.

- Removal from the mouth is accomplished with a snapping action.
- The reversible hydrocolloids are very susceptible to water uptake and loss (syneresis and imbibition).
- The model should be poured within 30 minutes of the impression being recorded.
- It is not possible to use a hydrocolloid impression to make metal coated or epoxy resin dies.

CLASSIFICATION

On the basis of consistency;

AGAR

- Type I — High consistency
- Type II — Medium consistency
- Type III — Low consistency

PROPERTIES

- Elastic, mucostatic, viscoelastic impression material.
- The set material can be withdrawn over undercut areas.
- Adhesion with tray is poor.
- Models should be set up imbed.
- Non toxic and non – irritant.
- Poor tear resistance.
- Adequate shelf life.
- We can re-use the material after sterilization (by sodium hypochlorite).

USES

It can be used for making impression of;

- Complete dental arch.
- Partial dental arch.
- Crown
- Bridge work.

This material is widely used as Laboratory duplicating materials.

ALGINATE

INTRODUCTION

- The word alginate comes from the term "Algin" which is a peculiar mucous extract yielded by certain brow seaweed.
- It is irreversible hydrocolloids.

Fig: 10.17. Alginate.

MODE OF SUPPLY

- It is supplied as a powder that is packed.
- In bulk or in sockets
- In pre-weighed individual containers.

COMPOSITION

MATERIAL	AMOUNT (%)	FUNCTION
Sodium or potassium	11 – 16	Main reactive ingredient, Salt of Alginic acid forms sol with water and becomes cross-linked to form gel.
CaSO.2HO (GYPSUM)	11 – 17	Source of Ca+ ions which causes cross-link of the Alginate chains.
NaPO	1 – 3	Used to control the Working time.
Inert filler such as:	65 – 75	Gives "body" and enables Diatomaceous earth easy manipulation. Reaction indicator (present gives colour change In some products) when setting is complete.

MANIPULATION

Fig: 10.18. Mixing of alginate using rubber bowl and spatula.

- For mixing, we need;
  - i. A clean flexible plastic bowl.
  - ii. A clean wide bladed, reasonably stiff metal spatula.
- The proper W: P ratio as specified by the manufacturer should be used.
- The mixing is started with a stirring a motion to wet the powder with water.
- Once the powder has been moistened, rapid spatulation against the side of the bowl is done.
- A vigorous figure of eight motion is used with the mix being swiped or stropped against the sides of the rubber mixing bowl.
- This helps to;
  - i. Remove most of the air bubbles.
  - ii. Wipe dissolved alginate from the surface of the yet undissolved alginate thereby promoting complete dissolution.
  - iii. When material gain 'creamy' consistency, stopped spatulation and loaded the tray.
- A perforated tray is used so that the material is forced out slightly through the holes in the tray during loading, there by locking itself mechanically into the tray.

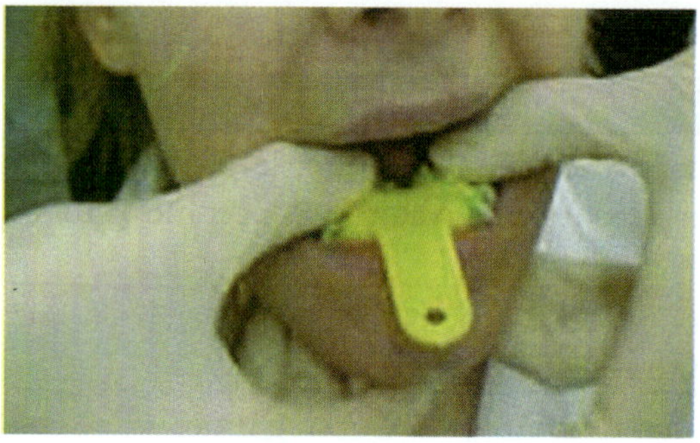

Fig: 10.19. Taking Alginate impression.

- Otherwise an adhesive such as molten sticky wax can be applied to the tray.
- After removal from the mouth, the impression should be;
  - Washed with cold water to remove saliva.
  - Covered with a damp napkin to prevent syneresis.
  - Cast should be poured as soon as possible, preferably not more than 15 minutes after taking the impression.
  - The irreversible hydrocolloids may be by 10 – min immersion in, or spraying of, some antimicrobial agent such as sodium hypochlorite or glutaraldehyde without significant dimensional changes.

Fig: 10.20. Set Alginate impression.

SETTING REACTION

- On mixing, an Alginate sol is formed.
  - Ca reacts with Na-Alginate to form gel.
  - Na2PO4 reacts with Ca and increase working time.
- Sodium Alginate readily reacts with calcium ions derived from the dissolved gypsum to form calcium alginate.
- The replacement of nonviolent sodium with divalent calcium results in the cross linking of the alginate chains and the conversion of the material from the sol to gel form.
- As setting reaction proceeds, and the degree of cross-linking increases, the gel develops elastic properties.

PROPERTIES

- It is an elastic, mucostatic and pseudo plastic.
- It is sufficiently fluid to record fine details.
- It can be withdrawn over undercuts without tearing.
- Not dimensionally stable on storage, because of evaporation.
- Compatible with model materials.
- Non-toxic, non-irritant, pleasant taste and odour.
- Adhesion to the tray is poor.

USES

- For making preliminary impressions for complete dentures.
- For making impressions for orthodontic and study models.

ADVANTAGES

- Inexpensive.
- Easy to use.

- Hydrophilic.
  - Displace moisture, blood, fluids.
- Stock trays.

DISADVANTAGE

- Tears easily.
- Dimensionally unstable;
  - immediate pour
  - single cast
- Lower detail reproduction;
  - unacceptable for fixed pros
- High permanent deformation.
- Difficult to disinfect.

MODIFIED ALGINATES

MODIFIED BY

- Alginate is modified by incorporation of silicone polymers.

MODE OF SUPPLY

- Two pates which are mixed together.

SETTING CHARACTERISTICS

- The setting characteristics of the modified alginate materials are similar to those of the conventional products.

PROPERTIES

- They show marginally better fine – detail reproduction and tear resistance but have poor dimensional stability.

USES

- Same as conventional products.

ELASTOMERIC IMPRESSION MATERIALS

CAUSE OF INVENTION

To main problems faced while using hydrocolloids are:

- Poor tear resistance
- Poor dimensional stability.

These drawbacks have been overcome by the invention of synthetic elastomers.

TYPES OF ELASTOMERS

There are four types of elastomers in general use:

- Poly sulphides.
- Silicon rubbers (condensation curing type).
- Silicon rubbers (addition curing type).
- Poly ether.

POLY-SULPHIDES

SUPPLIED AS

- Two paste system
  - i. Base
  - ii. Catalyst
- Two viscosities (low and high).
- One paste is normally labeled BASE PASTE whilst the other is labeled CATATYST PASTE.
- The liquid polysulphide pre-polymer in the base paste can be represented by the formula:

$HS(C_2H_4\text{-}OCH_2\text{-}OC_2H_4\ SS)23$
$C_2H_4\text{-}OCH_2\text{-}OC_2H_4\text{-}SH$

Although the actual structure is known to is slightly more complex than groups shown in the structural formula.

- The viscosity of the paste is governed by the quantity of filler incorporated by the manufacturer.

COMPOSITION

	COMPONENT	FUNCTION
BASE PASTE Polymerized linked to form	Polysulphides pre-polymer with terminal and pendent thiol (SH) groups Plasticizer di-n-butyl phthalate. Inner filler-possibly chalk or titanium dioxide.	This is further and cross rubber. To control viscosity. To give "BODY" control viscosity and modify physical properties.
CATALYST PASTE	Lead dioxide or other alternatives oxidizing agent sulphur Inner oil-normally paraffinic type or din-butyl phthalate.	To react with thiol group causing setting. Involved in setting reaction. To form a paste with Pb 2 and sulpher.

CHARACTERSTICS OF PASTES

Base Paste

The base paste is normally white, due to the filler and has an unpleasant odour caused by the high concentration of thiol groups.

Catalyst paste

The color of the catalyst paste is governed by the nature of the oxidizing agent used; materials containing lead dioxide are normally dark brown.

Difference between pastes

- The color contrast between the two pastes is an aid to efficient mixing which is continued until a homogenous color, with no streaks is achieved.
- An adhesive is used to promote adherent in between the impression material and tray.

GRADES OF PASTE

- Light bodied
- Medium bodied
- Heavy bodied having increased filler content and viscosity values.

SETTING REACTION

- On mixing the two pastes, terminal and pendant thiol groups of pre-polymer chains undergo a reaction with lead dioxide.
- The reaction is of the condensation polymerization type, since one molecule of water is produced as a by-product of each reaction stage.
- As chain reaction proceeds, the viscosity increases.
- When the degree of cross linking reaches a certain level, the material develops elastic properties.

PROPERTIES

- The polysulphide elastomers have very good tear resistance. They can withstand about 700% tensile strain before tearing.
- They are considered as viscoelastic and recover only slowly and not completely after being compressed or stretched.
- The better dimensional stability of the heavy-bodied material is due to the fact that they contain a lower concentration of reactive groups and therefore produce fewer byproducts.
- The heavy bodied materials are potentially more accurate since they exhibit less setting and thermal contraction then high viscosity, means that they are unable to record the same level of fine detail as the more fluid light bodied materials.
- Setting commences immediately on mixing of two pastes and is characterized by the gradual increase of viscosity and a rather slow development of elasticity.

ADVANTAGES OF POLYSULPHIDES

- Reasonable tear strength and good elastic properties.
- Moderately hydrophilic and hence can work well in the presence of some moisture.
- Commonly used for crown and bridge impressions.

DISADVANTAGES

- The use of lead compounds in polysulphides materials has been questioned because of the known toxic effects of lead. It is unlikely that the lead contained in these products is able to exert a harmful effect as the material in the patient's mouth for only a few minutes and is hydrophobic reducing the chances of "washing out" of lead compounds by saliva.

- There have been some limited reports of allergic responses to these materials from people with an allergy to latex product.
- It is expensive.

CLINICAL TECHNIQUES

- These materials are most commonly used in two viscosities high, and low and must be used in a special tray.
- The clinical technique usually adopted for polysulphides is a "ONE STAGE PROCEDURE".
- Freshly mixed low viscosity material is loaded into an impression syringe and high viscosity material is loaded into the special tray.
- The light bodied material is injected around those teeth on which cavities have been cut or crown cores prepared.
- The tray containing heavy-body material is then seated in such a way that the two materials can set simultaneously.
- The bulk of the impression is recorded in heavy-body material assuring optimum accuracy and dimensional stability.
- The thin layer of the impression adjacent to the oral tissue is recorded in light bodied material assuring optimum fine detail reproduction.
- The cast should be poured 24 hours of mixing if possible.

SURFACE QUALITY AND REPRODUCTION

a. Model plaster poured against alginate.
b. Dental stone poured against the same alginate
c. The same dental stone poured against polysulfide. It should be emphasized that another alginate with the same plaster and stone could yield opposite results.(fig)

A

B

C

Fig:10.21 Showing surface details alginate vs. polysulfide.

CLINICAL USES

They are used for crown and bridge work.

SILICONE RUBBERS (CONDENSATION CURING)

SUPPLIED AS

- These materials may be supplied as:
- Two pastes.
- As paste and liquid.

MANIPULATION

Proportioning of the paste/liquid materials is done by mixing together a color contrast between the pastes that enables the operator to see when proper mixing has been achieved.

GRADES OF PASTE

- Light bodied
- Regular bodied
- Heavy bodied
- Putty materials it is a paste of very high viscosity and it denotes an important difference between the silicon's and polysulphides.

SETTING REACTING

- On mixing the two components, paste and liquid, a setting reaction begins in which terminal hydroxyl groups, of prepolymer chains react with the cross-linking agents under the influence of the catalyst.
- Each molecule of cross-linking agent may potentially react with up to four prepolymer chains causing extensive cross-linking.
- Each reaction stage also produces one molecule of ethyl alcohol as a bi-product.
- Cross-linking produces and increases in viscosity and the rapid development of elastic properties.

	COMPONENT	FUNCTION
Paste	Hydroxylterminated poly-di-methly siloxane (liquid silicone prepolymer) inert filler such as silica	Undergoes cross -linking to form rubber Gives "BODY" controls viscosity and modifiies physical properties
Liquid	Alkyl silicate such as tetra ethyl silicate join compound such as di buty tin Dilaurate	Acts as cross- Linking agent Acts. Asreaction catalyst

PROPERTIES

- The silicon impression materials are very hydrophobic and are readily repelled by water and saliva. If a dry field is not secured "BLOW HOLES" are likely to occur in the impression as the material will fail to drive away the residual moisture.
- The setting reaction of silicon material tend to be more favourable than that of the polysulphides as setting reactions are generally shorter and elasticity develops later.
- The silicon has elastic properties which mostly approach the idea of complete and instantaneous recovery following stretching or compression.
- In the case of silicon an additional, very high viscosity or putty paste exists which has even lower setting and thermal contraction values than the conventional heavy bodied materials, it also has better dimensional stability.
- Dimensional changes of regular bodied condensation silicon silicones are slightly greater than those of regular bodied of polysulphides but are smaller compared to changes that occur with alginate.
- Silicon elastomers may be considered essentially non-toxic, despite the fact that they contain heavy metal catalyst.
- The liquid component of liquid/paste materials may be hazardous if not handled carefully accidental splash may cause irritation and blistering of eyes.

ADVANTAGES

- Better elastic properties.
- Clean, pleasant.
- Stock tray
  - putty-wash
- Good working and setting time.

DISADVANTAGES

- Poor dimensional stability
  - high shrinkage
    - Polymerization.
    - Evaporation of ethanol.
- pour immediately
  - Within 30 minutes.
- Hydrophobic
  - Poor wettability.

SILLICON RUBBER (ADDITIONAL CURING TYPE)

SUPPLIED AS

They are supplied as two pastes.

SETTING REACTION

- On mixing the two pastes and a platinum catalyzed addition reaction occurs causing cross-linking between the two types of siloxane prepolymer.
- The reaction does not involve production of byproducts although it has been reported that these materials occasionally involve hydrogen.
- Cross linking produces an increase in the viscosity coupled with the development of elastic properties.

PROPERTIES

- They have adequate setting characteristics and tear resistance coupled with nearly ideal elasticity.
- The combined use of putty light bodied materials enable accurate impression to be recorded.
- Silicon elastomers are inherently hydrophobic in nature, a characteristic which can cause imperfection in impression if the area to be recorded cannot be thoroughly dried.

- The mixed silicon material is repelled by moisture and this can result in "blow holes" in the impressions.

CLINICAL APPLICATIONS

The addition cured materials are preferred on basis of their greater dimensional stability.

Light bodied materials

Used to record accurate surface details on prepared tooth surface through medium viscosity, commonly used as a mono phase material during either crown and bridge work or dentine manufacture.

Heavy-bodied materials

Used to support light body in stock trays for crown and bridge impressions, two pastes which are now available in soft and hard formats.

Putty material (Wash impression)

Wash impression can be performed as a one stage procedure during which both viscosities of material are produced simultaneously.

The clinician then syringes the light bodied material around the preparation/teeth whilst an assistant places the heavier material into a stock tray.

The loaded tray is then inserted into the mouth and the two viscosities blend together and set.

Advantages

- Highly accurate.
- High dimensional stability;
- Pour up to one week
- Stock or custom trays.
- Multiple casts.
- Easy to mix.
- Pleasant odor.

DISADVANTAGES

- Expensive.
- Sulfur inhibits set
- Latex gloves.
- Ferric and Al sulfate retraction solution.
- Short working time.
- Lower tear strength.
- Possible hydrogen gas release;
  a. bubbles on die
  b. palladium added to absorb

POLYEHTERS

SUPPLIED AS

These materials are normally supplied as two paste system:

- Base paste
- Catalyst paste

COMPOSITION

	COMPONENT	FUNCTION
Base Paste (Large Tube)	Amine-Terminated pre/polymer Inert filler-silica	Becomes cross-linked to form rubber To give "BODY" and control viscosity and physical properties To aid mixing
	Plasticizer e.g. PHTHALATE	
Catalyst paste	Ester derivative of aromatic sulphocin Aid inert filler-silica Plaslicizer	Intiates cross-linking To form paste To aid mixing

CLINICAL APPLICATION

These are used for crown and bridge work.

ADVANTAGES

- Highly accurate.
- Good dimensional stability.
- Stock or dual-arch trays.
- Good surface detail.
- Pour within one week;
- Kept dry
- Multiple casts.
- Good wettability.

DISADVANTAGE

- Expensive.
- Short working time.
- Rigid
- difficult to remove from undercuts
- Bitter taste.
- Low tear strength.
- Absorbs water;
- Changes dimension

HANDLING PROPERTIES

	Agar	Alginate	Polysulfide	Condensation Silicone	Addition Silicone	Polyether
Preparation	Boil temper store	Powder water	2 pastes	2 pastes or paste/liquid	2pastes	2pastes
Ease of use	Technique sensitive	Good	Fair	Fair	Excellent	Good
Patient Reaction	Thermal shock	Pleasant, clean	Unpleasant, stains	Pleasant, clean	pleasant	Unpleasant clean
Ease of removal	Very easy	Very easy	Easy	Moderate	Moderate	Moderate to difficult
Disinfection	Poor	Poor	Fair	Fair	Excellent	Fair
Working Time (min)	7-15	2.5	5-7	3	2-4.5	2.5
Setting Time (min)	5	3.5	8-12	6-8	3-7	4.5
Stability	1 hour 100%RH	Immediate pour	1hour	immediate pour	1week	1week kept dry
Wettability and Castability	Excellent	Excellent	Fair	Fair	Fair to good	Good
Cost	Low	Very low	Low	Moderate	High to very high	Very high

PROPERTIES						
	Agar	**Alginate**	**Polysulphide**	**Condensation Silicone**	**Addition Silicone**	**Polyether**
Elastic Recovery (%)	98.8	97.3	94.5-99.6	98.2-99.6	99-99.9	98.3-99.0
Flexibility (%)	11	12	8.5-20.0	3.5-7.8	1.3-5.6	1.9-3.3
Flow (%)	--	--	0.4-1.9	<0.10	<0.05	<0.05
Shrinkage 24 hours (%)	Extreme	Extreme	0.4-0.5	0.2-1.0	0.01-0.2	0.2-0.3
Tear Strength (g/cm)	700	380-700	2240-7410	2280-4370	1640-5260	1700-4800

Comparison of Properties

- Working time
  - longest to shortest
  - agar > polysulphide > silicones > alginate = polyether
- Setting time
  - shortest to longest
  - alginate < polyether < agar < silicones < polysulphide
- Stiffness
  - most to least
  - polyether > addition silicone > condensation silicone > polysulphide = hydrocolloids
- Tear strength
  - greatest to least
  - polysulphide > addition silicone > polyether > condensation silicone >> hydrocolloids.
- Cost
  - lowest to highest
  - alginate < agar = polysulphide <condensation silicone < addition silicone < polyether
- Dimensional stability
  - best to worst
  - addition silicone > polyether > polysulphide > condensation silicone > hydrocolloid
- Wettability
  - best to worst
  - hydrocolloids > polyether > hydrophilic addition silicone > polysulphide > hydrophobic addition silicone = condensation silicone
- Castability
  - best to worst
  - hydrocolloids > hydrophilic addition silicone > polyether > polysulphide > hydrophobic addition silicone = condensation silicone.

Chapter 11

CERAMIC PRODUCTS IN DENTISTRY

Dr. Zohaib & Dr. Sana Shahab

INTRODUCTION

Ceramics is driven from Greek wovd "KERAMOS" meaning burnt stuff but it is related to material produced by firing or burning. The first ceramics fabricated by man were earthenware pots used for domestic purpose. This material is opaque, relatively weak and porous and would be unsuitable for dental applications. Silica and feldspar was added to improve translucency and strength required for dental application and was given the name of PORCELAIN also known as Conventional or feldsphatic porcelain. Dentistry has turned to porcelain for the production of artificial teeth, crowns, bridges and veneers.

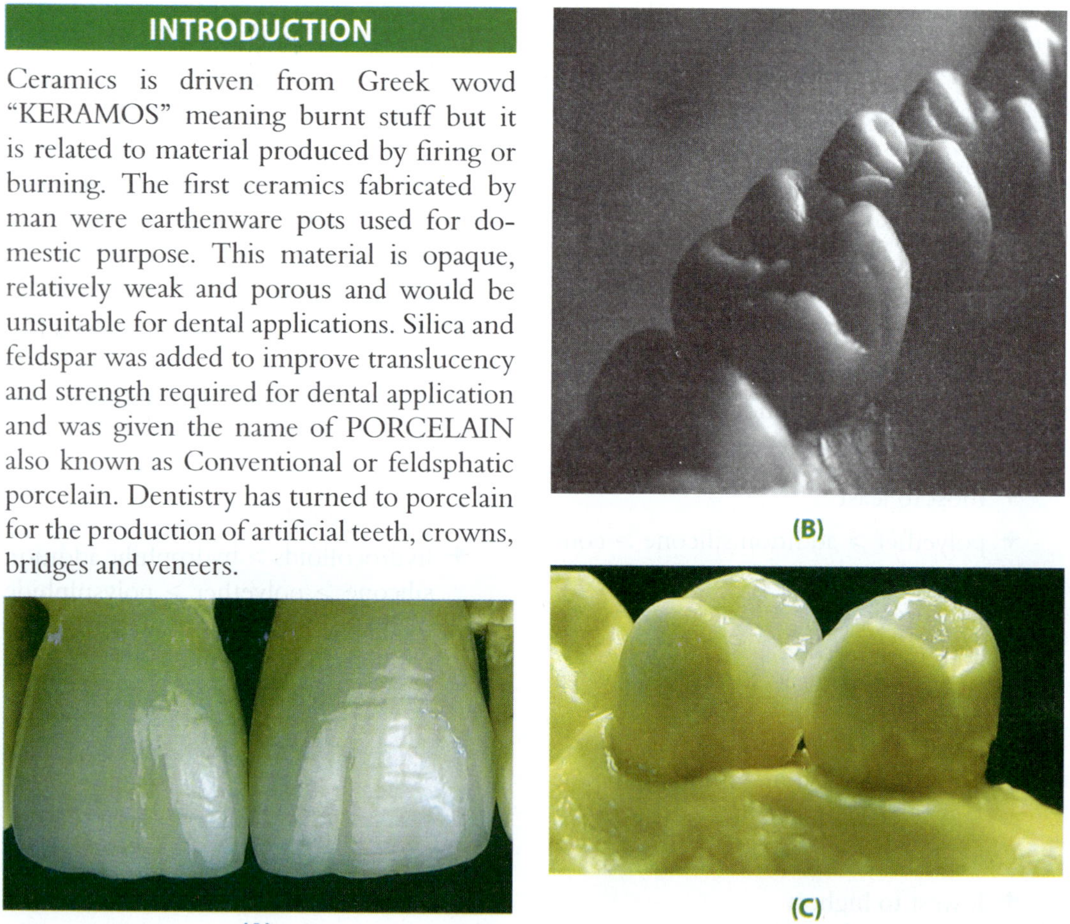

(A)

(B)

(C)

Fig: 11.1. A few applications of ceramic in dentistry. (a) Veneers, (b) All-ceramic Crown, (c) Indirect Inlays.

CLASSIFICATION OF DENTAL PORCELAIN

Dental porcelain can be classified as follow:

1. ACCORDING TO FIRING TEMPERATURE

- High fusing -1300C.
- Medium fusing - 1100-1300C.
- Low fusing – 850C.
- Ultra low fusing – less than 850C.

2. ACCORDING TO TYPES

- Feldsphatic porcelain.
- Aluminous porcelain.
- Cast glass ceramic.
- Lucite reinforced.
- Glass infiltrate.

3. ACCORDING TO PROCESSING METHOD

- Sintered porcelain.
- Cast porcelain.
- Machined porcelain.

4. ACCORDING TO THE RESTORATION USE

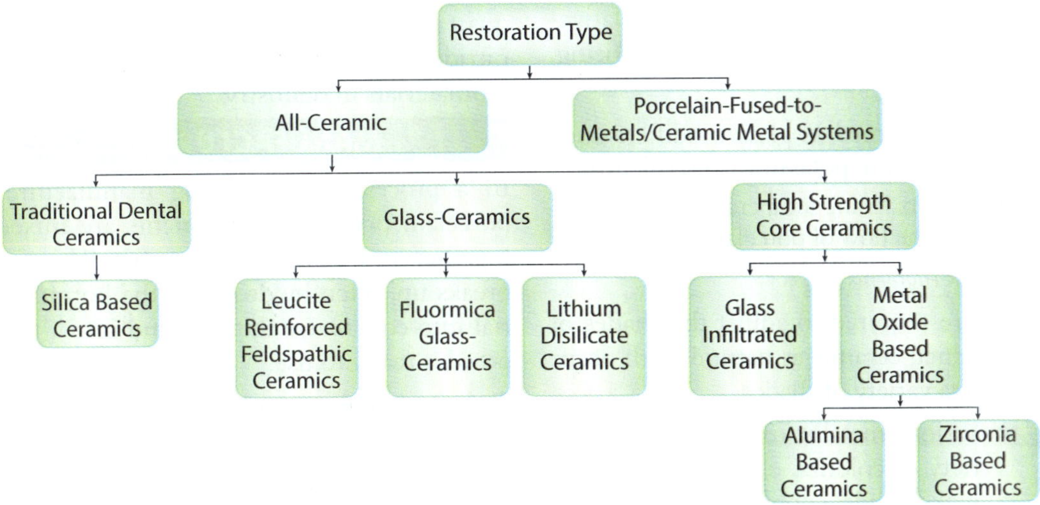

MODE OF SUPPLY

Porcelain is supplied as kit containing:

1. Fine ceramic powders in different shades;
   - Enamel.
   - Denture.
   - Core/opaquer.

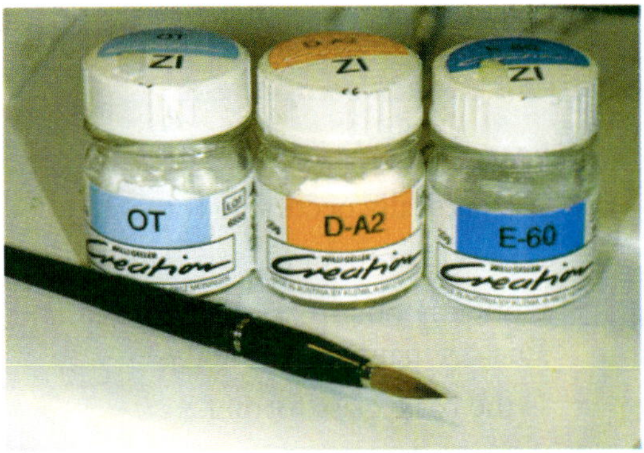

Fig: 11.2. Fine ceramic powders bottles.

2. Special liquid/distilled water.
3. Stains or colour modifiers.
4. Glaze.

COMPOSITION

- Feldspar
- Kaolin
- Quartz Alumna
- Alkalis
- Colour Pigments
- Opacifiers

Functions of each component

a. *Feldspar*

- Is a naturally occurring mineral.
- Basic constituent of porcelain.
- Contains potash, soda, alumina and silica as main components.
- Is the basic glass former.
- Acts as a binder.

b. *Kaolin*

- Is white day like material i-e hydrated alumino silicate.
- Gives opacity to the mass and may act as a binder too.

c. *Quartz*

- Quartz is a form of silica.
- Acts as a refractory skeleton providing strength and hardness to porcelain during firing. It remains relatively unchanged during and after firing.

d. *Alkalis*

- Also termed as glass modifiers such as sodium, potassium and calcium.
- Lowers fusing temperature and increasees the flow of porcelain during firing.

e. *Colour Pigments*

- Are required to adjust the shades of dental ceramic as natural teeth occur in a variety of shades.
- Various metallic oxides provide a variety of colours. e.g. titanium oxide, nickel oxide, copper oxide etc.

f. *Opacifiers*

- Are added to increase the opacity ignored to stimulate natural teeth.
- Oxides of tin, zirconium and titanium are commonly used as Opacifiers.

Table 11.1 Percentage of each component.

MATERIALS	CLAY	SILICA	BINDER	GLASS
Decorative Porcelain	50	25	25	0
High Fusing	4	15	80	0
Low Fusing	0	25	60	15

STRUCTURE OF PORCELAIN

Ceramics are basically compounds of metallic and non-metallic elements consisting of oxides, nitrides, carbides, and silicates. Typical silicates are made up of Si-tetrahedrons,SiO_4^{4+}. The structural alignment of ceramics is in the form of crystalline solid or glasses. Ceramics used in dentistry predominantly contain non-metallic and metallic elements and are mostly based on silicon that is usually found in the form of silica (silicon dioxide), SiO2, due to silicon's high affinity for oxygen. When silica occurs as a crystalline material, it can be in the form of quartz, cristobalite, and tridymite. Silica in dental ceramics is usually in the form of quartz. Because of the black appearance of nitrides and carbides, they are not used as biomaterials in dentistry.

MANUFACTURING

In a process called fitting manufactures porcelain powders, components are mixed together and fused to form a frit. This frit breaks up, often by dropping the hot material into cold water then ground into a fine powder ready to use.

Today's dental ceramic restorations may be fabricated by traditional stacking and sintering, but also by infusion, pressing, or machining.

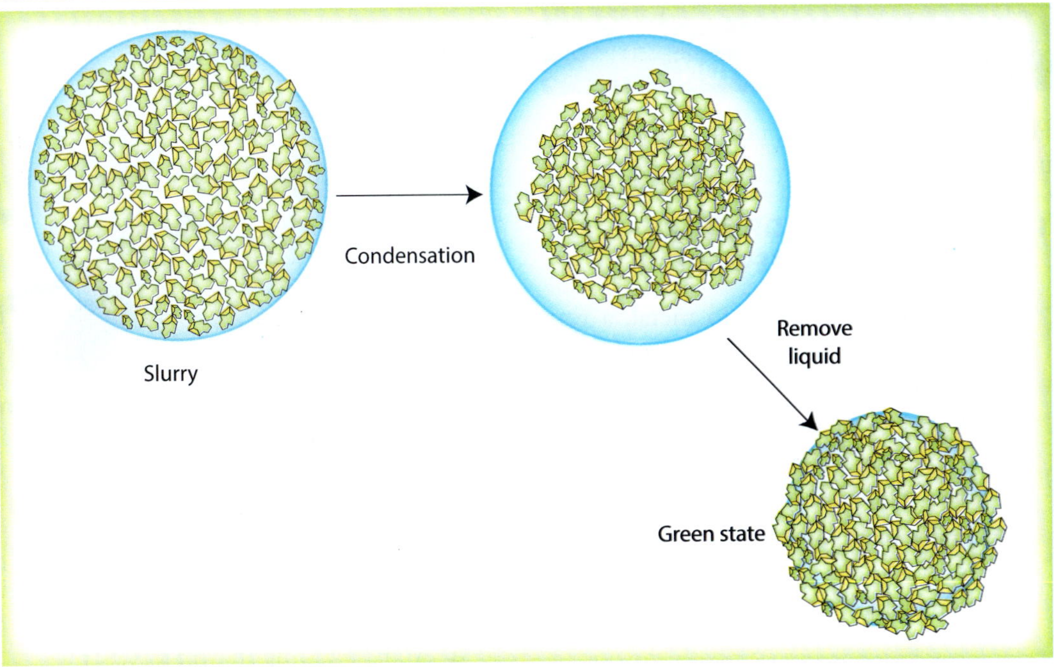

A. Green State.

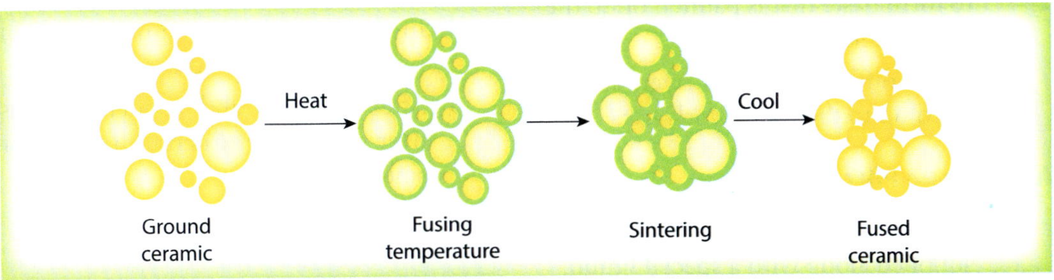

B. Fused Ceramic.

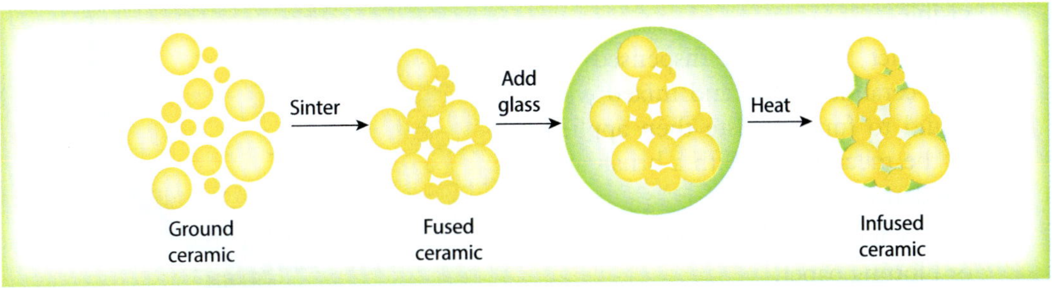

C. Infused Ceramic.

Fig: 11.3. Illustrstion showing diffrent state of Cereamic (A) Green State, (B) Fused Ceramic, (C) Infused Ceramic.

MANIPULATION AND TECHNICAL CONSIDERATION

Porcelain manipulation consists of following steps;

1. CONSTRUCTION OF METAL COPING OR FRAMEWORK

- For porcelain fused to metal, a wax pattern of intended restoration is constructed and cast in metal.
- A variety of metals are used for the framework, like Nobel metals alloys, base metals alloys and titanium too.
- Framework of platinum foil coping is swaged on to the die made for all porcelain crowns.

2. PORCELAIN APPLICATION

- Porcelain powder mixes with water to form paste that is painted on to the framework with a brush.
- Three different types of layers are applied on to the framework are;

A. Opaque Porcelain

- It is a dense yellowish white powder supplied along with a special liquid.
- It is used to cover the metal framework and prevents it from being visible.
- Opaquer powder is dispensed on to a ceramic palette and mixed with liquid to form a paste then applied to the metal frame with a brush and condensed.
- Excess liquid is blotted with a tissue or blotting paper.
- Opaquer is built up and is placed in porcelain furnace and fired.

Fig: 11.4. Metal framework for porcelain built-up by opaque layer.

B. Denture And Enamel Porcelain

- The dentine powder [pink powder] is mixed with water or the liquid supplied.
- A glass spatula should be used.
- The bulk of the tooth is built up with dentine.
- In the incisal area enamel porcelain (white powder) is added.
- After built up and condensation is over and it is returned to furnace for sintering.

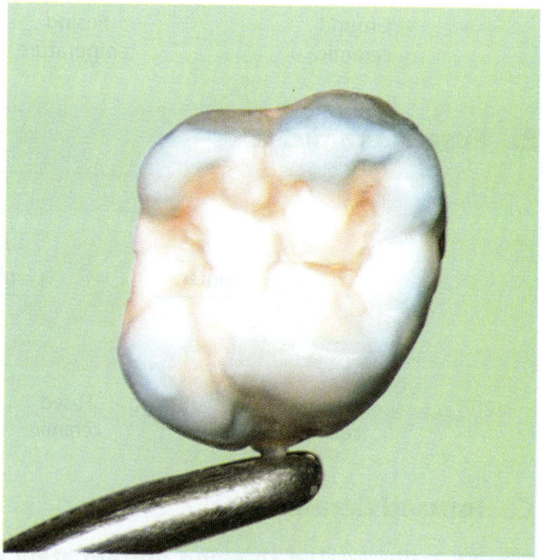

(A)

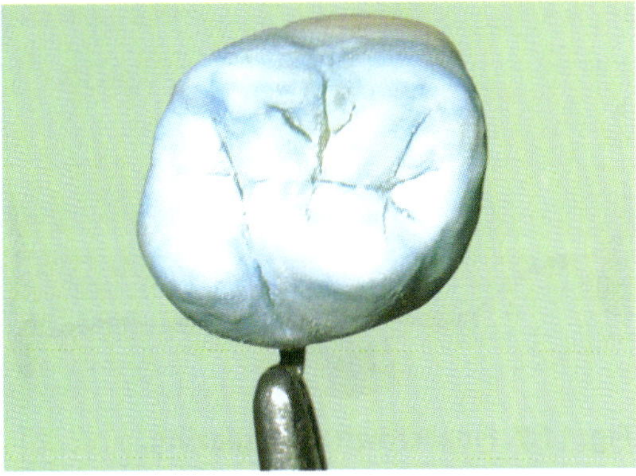

(B)

Fig: 11.5. Showing different shades of porcelain.(a) Dentine , (b) Enamel.

C. Gingival And Transparent Porcelain

- Enamel of natural teeth appears transparent usually seen at the incise edges thus transparent porcelain may be applied while cervical portions of teeth are darker where cervical porcelain is applied.

D. Surface Staining, Characterization And Effects

- Staining and characterization helps and make the restoration look natural and helps it to blend with the adjacent teeth.
- Stained powders are mixed with liquid and applied with the brush.

3. COMPACTION OR CONDENSATION

- The process of packing the powder particle together and removing excess water is known as condensation.
- Proper condensation packs the particles together thus minimizing the porosity and reducing firings shrinkage.
  - Vibration.
  - Spatulation.
  - Dry powder.

4. FIRING

- The process of sintering and fusing the condensation mass is known as firing.
- The powder particles fuse together making the restoration dense and strong.
- It is done in a porcelain furnace.

5. PORCELAIN FURNACE

- Firming is carried out in a porcelain furnace.
- Modern furnaces may be computer controlled and may have built in program to control the firing cycle.
- Programs can be altered by operator too.

Fig: 11.6. Porcelain Furnace.

6. FIRING CYCLE

The entire of preheating firing, subjecting to increased pressure, holding and cooling is known as a firing cycle.

A. Pre-heating

- It is done as the condense mass should not be placed in the hot furnace directly.
- It can cause rapid formation of steam that may break up the mass.
- It is done for five minutes.

B. Vaccum firing

- It is done by creating a vaccum during porcelain firing that helps reduce the porosity in ceramic.
- Vaccum is later released that increases the pressure in the furnace which further reduces the size of any residual bubbles that have not been eliminated by vaccum.

C. Cooling

- Cooling of fired porcelain from firming temperature to room temperature is well controlled.
- Rapid cooling can cause the porcelain to crack or it can reduce stress, which may weaken porcelain.

7. GLAZING

- Glazing is a process by which the restoration is given a smooth, glossy surface.
- *Objectives of glazing.*
  - i. Enhances Esthetics
  - ii. Enhances Hygiene
  - iii. Improves Strength
  - iv. Reduces the wear of opposing teeth

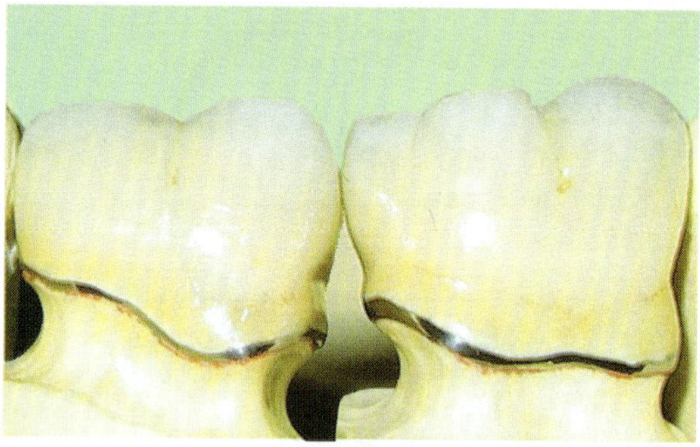

Fig: 11.7. Final crown after glazing.

PROPERTIES

1. STRENGTH

- Porcelain has good strength but is brittle and tends to fracture.

2. WEAR RESISTANCE

- More resistance to wear than natural teeth.

3. THERMAL PROPERTIES

- It has low thermal conductivity and coelticiency of thermal expansion is close to that of natural teeth.

4. DIMENSIONAL STABILITY

- Fired porcelain is dimensionally stable.

5. CHEMICAL STABILITY

- Is insoluble and impermeable to oral fluids.

6. ESTHETIC PROPERTIES

- It has excellent esthetic quality and colour stability.

7. BIOCOMPATIBILITY

- Excellent compatibility with oral tissues.

ALUMINA INSERTS AND ALUMINOUS PORCELAIN

- The major disadvantage of porcelain is brittleness.
- Powdered alumina may be added to porcelain in order to achieve a significant strengthening.
- Alumina particles act as crack stoppers preventing the propagation of crack through the body of porcelain.
- Alumina content is about 40%.
- It has good mechanical properties and is used to construct the inner core of porcelain crown.
- Flexural strength values are typically 110 MPa while 80 MPa for unreinforced porcelain.

INJECTION MOULDED GLASS CERAMIC

- It is a unique way of fabrication.
- It is a pre-cerammed glass ceramic having a high concentration of leucite crystals blends it with resins to form cylindrical blocks.
- Using a wax pattern a mould is prepared in which a resin ceramic block is heated at 180C and is injected under high pressure.
- Firing is carried out in a special furnace using controlled temperature up to 1300C.
- Layered porcelain is backed over the surface of the coping to produce the finish crown.

CAD - CAM CERAMICS

- CAD – CAM stands for computer aided design – computer aided manufacture.
- This is a Hi-tech approach to provide patients with durable tooth coloured restorations.
- Prepared tooth surface is scanned into the computer.
- Signals from computer operate the milling machine, which fabricate the restoration.
- One advantage of this technique is that the ceramic manufacturing process including forming and heat-treating are under the control of the manufacture.
- Cementation of CAD-CAM restorations normally involves the use of dual cured composite cements.

Fig: 11.8. Chair-side CAD/CAM system for all-ceramic restorations fabrication.

CAST GLASS CERAMICS

- Porcelain having properties closer to glass.
- Crown is made by centrifugal casting technique.
- Creaming process is unique to this porcelain.
- Crown pattern is first constructed in wax and is invested in a phosphate-bonded investment.
- After burning out wax the glass is melted out and cast into the mould in a centrifugal casting machine at 1300 C.
- The glass restoration is then heat-treated at 1075 C for 10 Hr – a process termed as *Ceraming* by which glass is strengthened.
- It reduces the transparency of glass making it more opaque and less glass like.
- Then ceramic restoration is built with dentine and animal porcelain condensed and fired to complete the restoration.

PORCELAIN VENEERS

- Porcelain veneers offer a means of improving the appearance of stained or discolored teeth.
- The veneer consists of a thin shell like structure which is ideally fabricated in such a way that it can be closely adapted to the prepared.
- Most authorities do advise the removal of about 0.5 mm of labial enamel.
- The veneers are normally 0.5 – 0.8mm thick.
- Constructing may be from feldspathic porcelain, glass ceramic, pressed ceramic or CAD – CAM technique and are bonded to the tooth enamel using a composite resin luting agents.
- The bonding is achieved by etching the enamel with a phosphoric acid solution or gel.
- The fitting surface of the veneer is etched with a solution of hydro floric acid, then dried and treated with a saline coupling agent to aid bonding to the composite resin.

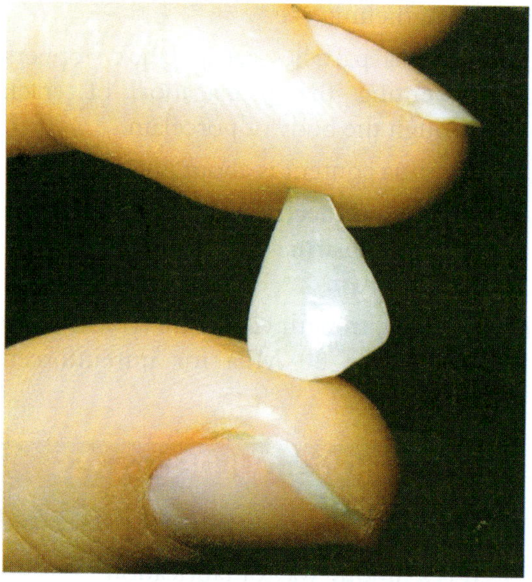

Fig: 11.9. Porcelain veneer.

PORCELAIN FUSED TO METAL

INTRODUCTION

- Porcelain fused to metal restoration involves a marrying of the good mechanical properties of cast dental alloys with the excellent esthetic properties of porcelain.
- Feldspathic porcelains used for PFM work normally contain significant amounts of Leucite.
- The Leucite increases the coefficient of thermal expansion of the porcelain to a value which is closer to that for the metal.
- The presence of Leucite also helps to strengthen the ceramic.

REQUIREMENTS OF THE ALLOYS

1. They should be capable of withstanding procession firing without melting or suffering creep.
2. The alloy should be sufficiently rigid to support a very brittle porcelain veneer otherwise fracture of the veneer is inevitable.
3. The alloy should be capable of forming a bond with the porcelain veneer.
4. The alloy should have a value of coefficiency of thermal expansion.

ALLOYS FOR PORCELAIN BONDING

There are four types of alloy currently available or porcelain bonding.

a. High – gold alloys.
b. Low – gold alloys.
c. Silver – palladium alloys.
d. Nickel – chromium alloys.

TOOTH PREPARATION FOR PFM RESTORATION

- During tooth preparation it is necessary to allow about 1.5 mm in thickness for metal coping (O.3 O.5mm).
- The porcelain veneers (1.0 mm) to achieve optimal aesthetes.

CAPILLARY TECHNOLOGY

- The capillary technology or cap-tek system is an alternative means of producing porcelain metal restoration.
- The metal substructure is produced in two stages:

First Stage

- A wax strip loaded with powdered, high palladium content metal is adapted to the cast.
- This is fired in order to burn off the wax and sinter the metal, forming a three – dimensional capillary network.

Second Stage

- Wax strip, heavily loaded with almost pure gold (97% pure), is applied to the surface of the sintered layer and cheering a second firing, the wax is again burnt off and the molten gold infiltrates the capillary network to form a metal substructure with composite structure.
- The bonding between the metal and porcelain is achieved through mechanical.

BONDED PLATINIUM FOIL

This technique involves laying down two platinum foils on the working die as opposed to normal single foil.

Surface of the Outer Foil

- Is then tin-plated and the porcelain crown constructed and fired on top of the tin-plated surface.
- Porcelain bonds to the layer of tin oxide on the tin-plated surface.

Inner Platinum Foil

- Is removed prior to cementation of the crown whilst one platinum foil remains bonded to inner surface of the crown.

Advantage

- This foil helps to prevent crack formation on the inner surface.

Table: 11.2. Differences between metal-ceramic and all ceramic crown.

METAL-CERAMIC CROWN	ALL-CERAMIC
Less esthetic	More esthetic
Special equipment not required	Special equipment required
Placement of margins in anterior region should be sub-gingival	Margin should be supragingival
Predictability is high	Predictability is low
Not expensive	Expensive

Fig: 11.10. Cross section of All-ceram crown and PFM-crown.

REFERENCES

1. Van Noort R (2007) Introduction to dental materials, (3rd edn.) Elsevier, Philadelphia
2. Hämmerle C, Sailer I, Thoma A, Hälg G, Suter A, Ramel C (2008) Dental ceramics: Essential aspects for clinical practice. Quintessence, Surrey.
3. John F.mccabe & Angus W.g Walls(2008), Applied Dental Materials, Blackwell Publisher, Hong Kong
4. Smith, William F.; Hashemi, Javad (2006), *Foundations of Materials Science and Engineering* (4th ed.), McGraw-Hill, ISBN 0-07-295358-6.
5. Stephen Chu, & Irfan Ahmad, (2005), "*A Historical Perspective of Synthetic Ceramic And Traditional Feldspathic Porcelain*", *Practical Procedures & Aesthetic Dentistry*, vol. 17, no. pp. 593-598.
6. Gary Willie Ho, & Jukka Pekka Matinlinna (2011), "Insights on Ceramics as Dental Materials. Part I: Ceramic Material Types in Dentistry", , vol. 3, no. pp. 109-115.

Chapter 12

DENTAL AMALGAM

Dr. Jukka Matinlinna

INTRODUCTION

Some *dental materials* are used to restore diseased (caries, secondary caries), traumatized (incl. wear) or lost teeth, or neighboring tooth structures (and tissues), and rehabilitate biting functions.

Dental materials can be classified as restorative materials, preventive materials and auxiliary materials. On the other hand, any material that is used for the above described purpose may be regarded as a biomaterial.

IDEALLY RESTORATIVE DENTAL MATERIALS SHOULD BE

- Inert.
- Biocompatible.
- Non-irritant.
- Non-cytotoxic.
- Not carcinogenic or mutagenic.
- Not appreciably soluble in oral fluids.
- Dimensionally stable.
- Possessing adequate biomechanical properties.
- Acceptable to patients.
- Cleansable.
- Indistinguishable from natural tissue.
- Long lasting when a permanent restoration done.
- Induce fast healing process (if relevant).
- Possessing adhesion to tooth tissues (if relevant).
- Osteoconductive and capable of osseointegration (if relevant).

Examples

Restorative dental materials can be classified as (a) direct and (b) indirect materials.

Direct restorative materials, such as resin-based composites (resin composites, filled resins), dental silver amalgam and glass ionomer cements (GIC), are used directly inside the oral cavity in a plastic form which will then set to restore the function of teeth.

Provisional (temporary) dental materials are used for a limited planned period of time, usually a few days or a few weeks. It may be necessary for the dentist to decide the definitive treatment, such as in the case of very deep cavities. In such a case the application of zinc oxide (ZnO) eugenol cement (ZOE) as *a temporary filling material* may be used. Also, a prepared tooth may need to be covered with *an acrylic temporary crown* before the definitive crown is prepared by the dental laboratory.

DENTAL SILVER AMALGAM

An *amalgam* is an alloy that contains mercury (Hg) as one of its constituents. Mercury is a liquid metal at room temperature.

Dental silver amalgam has been the most commonly used *direct restorative filling material* having served for more than 160 years. It is a permanent restorative material mainly used to restore cavities of decayed permanent posterior teeth. It is has been a very effective and economical restorative material over a long time. Its challenges may be related to its appearance and while some have expressed doubts about its safety, there are no substantiated problems. One of the current aspects in the discussion is whether resin composite type restorative materials can replace amalgam.

Dental silver amalgam has many advantages: low cost and high durability; it is believed to be a completely safe restorative material. On the other hand, while *lichen planus* is reported to be associated with its presence, this still lacks verification.

Dental silver amalgam consists essentially of a mixture of a silver-tin (Ag-Sn) alloy and mercury. The alloy also contains copper (Cu), but may also contain other elements such as palladium (Pd) and zinc (Zn). These are intended to improve clinical performance and handling characteristics. Nowadays amalgam is available in the market as *pre-dosed capsules* that contain both components.

Amalgam is by material type a *composite* material. NB: in general, a composite material is defined as a combination of two (or more) materials designed to give more desirable properties, and may be designed to replicate naturally occurring materials. Dental amalgam is *weak in tension*, due to the low tensile strength of the reaction products, and the presence of porosity. Crack initiation takes place in shear and is internal. If an amalgam restoration is of poor quality, due to the presence of porosity, it can be mainly attributed to improper handling procedures.

In general, the setting reaction of amalgam involves dimensional changes (Figure: 12.1). During the early stage of setting contraction occurs. Then, during the later stage of setting the pressure caused by growing crystal leads to expansion.

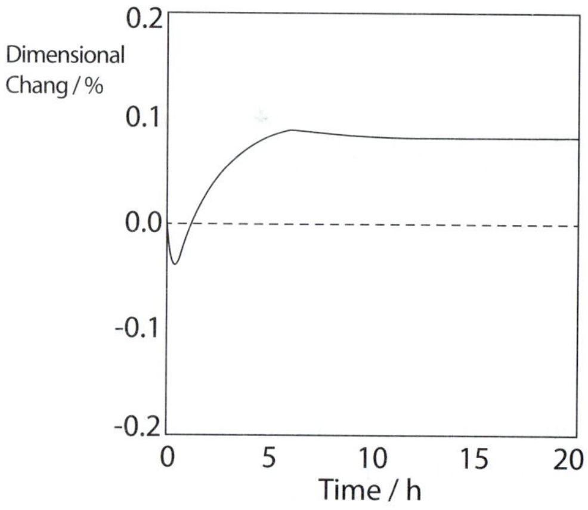

Fig: 12.1. Typical dimensional change curve for a setting dental silver amalgam (reproduced with permission from B. W. Darvell, Materials science for dentistry 9th edition, Woodhead Publishing Limited: www.woodheadpublishing.com).

MIXING

During mixing (also wrongly called trituration or amalgamation), in which the alloy powder and mercury are vigorously shaken together, often with an included object called a pestle (Figure: 12.2), the alloy particles are wetted by and then dissolve in the mercury to produce the amalgam paste which is a then used to restore a prepared and lined cavity. Mixing time affects dimensional changes (Figure: 12.3).

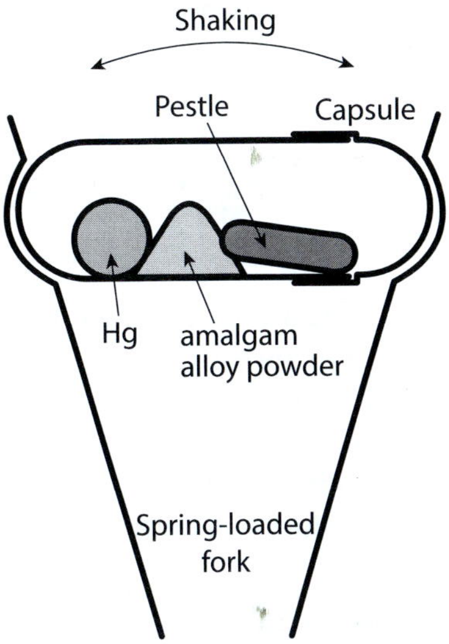

Fig: 12.2. During trituration of amalgam capsules strong shaking is generated, a pestle inside the capsule mixes the mercury and amalgam alloy powder (reproduced with permission from B. W. Darvell, Materials science for dentistry 9th edition, Woodhead Publishing Limited: www.woodheadpublishing.com).

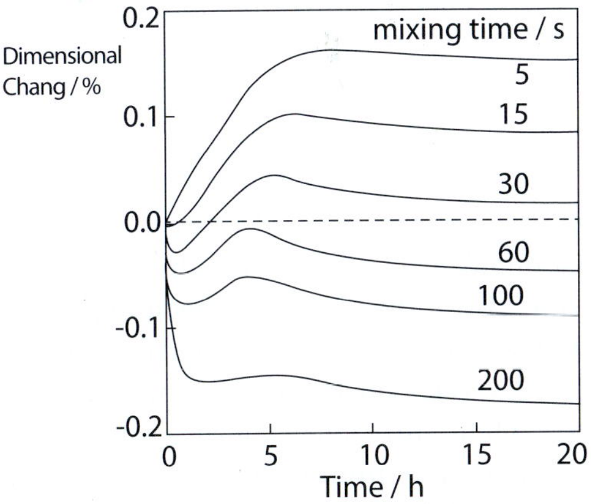

Fig: 12.3. Dimensional changes: dimensional change as a function of time after mixing in hours when mixing time varies between 5 to 200 s (reproduced with permission from B. W. Darvell, Materials science for dentistry 9th edition, Woodhead Publishing Limited: www.woodheadpublishing.com).

The setting reaction then involves the precipitation of various intermetallic substances (phases), but it is intended that a proportion of the original alloy particles remain in order to confer strength on the set amalgam

The strength of an amalgam (of a given brand and type) is dependent mainly upon the mixing and manipulation. The following factors affect the mechanical strength:

a. The speed of amalgam handling before it sets.

b. The mixing time.

c. The pressure used in packing.

The amount of mercury needed to wet all particles and occupy the space between the particles ranges from 40 - 60% mercury by weight.

A cervical amalgam restoration may be subject to masticatory forces and fail (Fig: 12.4).

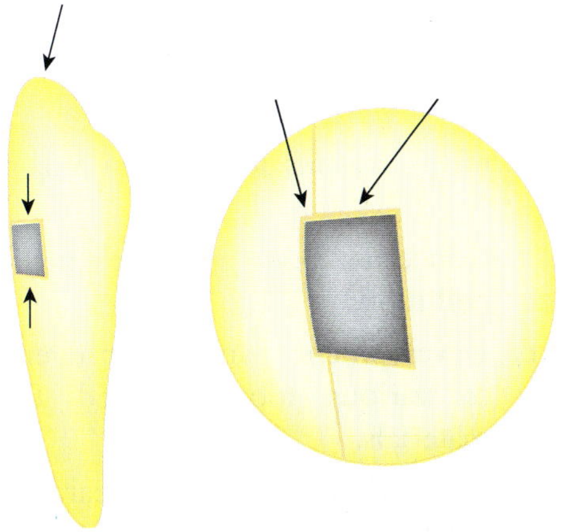

Fig: 12.4. An amalgam filling may extrude by deflection under heavy masticatory forces and over time (reproduced with permission from B. W. Darvell, Materials science for dentistry 9th edition, Woodhead Publishing Limited: www.woodheadpublishing.com).

COMPOSITION

The dental silver amalgam alloy powders may be: a) lathe-cut, b) spherical, or c) admixed

Lathe-cut powder: the particles are irregular and splinter-like in shape and they are formed by shaving off and grinding a ribbon from an ingot of the alloy. The resultant particles are sieved to get the proper powder particle size.

Spherical powder: also called atomized powder, is made by forcing the molten alloy through a small orifice with inert gas under high pressure, which 'atomizes' the liquid. The droplets solidify into near-spherical particles.

Admixed powder: a mixture of two alloys; usually lathe-cut and spherical particles, in order to achieve different properties than can be achieved with a single alloy.

USE OF AMALGAM

The use of amalgam is expected to decrease, at least in western world countries. It has been already banned in some Scandinavian countries for environmental reasons (waste disposal).

Some of the reasons to abandon amalgam are:

a. Concerns about environmental Hg pollution.
b. Development and improvement of various tooth-coloured filling materials.
c. The dark, unattractive appearance of old amalgam.

Even so, when cavities need to be filled the preparation of a cavity for an amalgam-filling inevitably may mean substantial *loss of sound tooth-substance.* This is due to the mechanical retention needed ("key"). Clinically it is noteworthy that preparing molar teeth with amalgam may include the risk for gap formation if the matrix band is over tightened (Fig: 12.5).

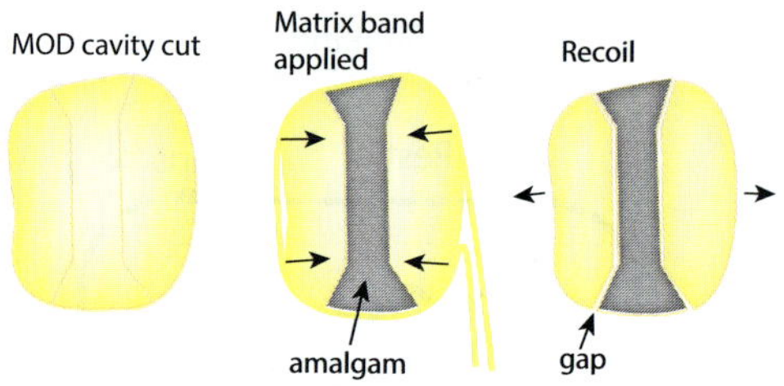

Fig: 12.5. A mesio-occlusal-distal (MOD) cut in a molar: gap formation may take place (reproduced with permission from B. W. Darvell, Materials science for dentistry 9th edition, Woodhead Publishing Limited: www.woodheadpublishing.com).

MERCURY

Mercury (Hg, *hydrargyrum*, "liquid silver") is obtained by roasting *cinnabar* mineral (HgS). It is volatile at room temperature and its melting point is -38.9 °C. It is a heavy, silvery-white, dense metal. Mercury as such is a poor conductor of heat.

Elemental (free) Hg may be converted to soluble inorganic compounds. These may be methylated in aquatic systems by microorganisms and this leads to the formation of *methylmercury*. Methylmercury may easily enter the food-chain and accumulate in the tissues of large predatory fish.

Methylmercury is readily absorbed by the gastrointestinal tract. Methylmercury exposure in adults has also been linked to increased risk of cardiovascular diseases. Mercury released from amalgam fillings is toxic when sufficient exposure occurs. On the other hand, minimal safe levels have not been established and, in general, mercury exposure appears to be very low.

WORKING SAFETY

It has been observed that the Hg body burden of dental personnel is normally higher than in the general population. Data available dealing with urine and blood mercury is considered relevant because they reflect actual exposure. It has been reported that the mean urine Hg levels in dental teams range between 3 - 22 μg/L, when the normal range is 1 - 5 μg/L. On the other hand, most dental chair-side team personnel do not touch amalgam during mixing and placement

The increased body burden is attributed to dental personnel mixing and applying dental amalgam and *removing amalgam restorations*.

LOW-COPPER AND HIGH-COPPER AMALGAM

In the early so-called *low-copper amalgams*, the amalgamation reaction produced a tin-mercury phase as a product which is also known as gamma-2 (γ_2). The complete reaction of *high-copper amalgams* produces no or very little γ_2. This has an effect on increasing corrosion resistance and decreasing marginal creep in class II cavities.

AMALGAM SETTING REACTIONS

A conventional (low copper) amalgam sets as:

$$Ag_3Sn\ (\gamma) + Hg \rightarrow Ag_2Hg_3\ (\gamma_1) + Sn_{7\text{-}8}Hg\ (\gamma_2) + Ag_3Sn\ (\gamma) \qquad (1)$$

In this reaction, Hg is a limiting reactant. The set amalgam theoretically has no free Hg. A small amount of Cu is included in the alloy (up to 6%) to increase the strength and hardness of the set amalgam.

Up to 2% of Zn may be added to scavenge the oxygen and sulpher content in amalgam, although hardly any remains in the final material. In principle, Zn can react with water in saliva (only if mixed in – which never happens under rubber dam) and may induce pores in the matrix:

$$Zn + 2\,H_2O \rightarrow Zn(OH)_2 + H_2 \qquad (2)$$

In one case of an admixed alloy, eutectic Ag-Cu particles are included:

$$Sn_{7\text{-}8}Hg\ (\gamma_2) + Ag\text{-}Cu \rightarrow Cu_6Sn_5\ (\eta') + Ag_2Hg_3\ (\gamma_1) \qquad (3)$$

The compound Ag-Cu is actually a two-phase alloy. The Cu_6Sn_5 (phase η') is less corrodable, and the crystals may inhibit slip in the γ_1 *i.e.* Ag_2Hg_3 grains by acting to interrupt that slip under load. This may reduce the creep of the high-copper amalgam.

A Cu-based unicompositional amalgam alloy is one composed of Ag-Sn-Cu reacts (4) with Hg:

$$Ag_3Sn\ (\gamma)\text{-}Cu_3Sn\ (\varepsilon) + Hg \rightarrow Ag_2Hg_3\ (\gamma_1) + Cu_6Sn_5\ (\eta') + Ag_3Sn\ (\gamma)\text{-}Cu_3Sn\ (\varepsilon) \qquad (4)$$

Initially, the Hg would react with γ-phase Ag_3Sn, and then forms γ_1 and γ_2 solid species. Next, solid Cu_3Sn would react with γ_2 *i.e.* $Sn_{7\text{-}8}Hg$:

$$Sn_{7\text{-}8}Hg\ (\gamma_2) + Cu_3Sn\ (\varepsilon) \rightarrow Cu_6Sn_5\ (\eta') + Hg \qquad (5)$$

This is a very slow process and the product Hg would then immediately react with remaining γ-phase Ag_3Sn. The higher the copper content (>25%), the lower would be the amount of Ag, thus the amalgam type may have a higher risk of free mercury remaining after setting.

Many restorative materials that are used in dentistry set through a chemical reaction. Dental silver amalgam is relatively slow to set. As can be judged by dimensional changes at 37 °C, its setting has not stopped at 150 h. On the other hand, its tensile strength has been shown to increase at least 100 h and even to 7 days in one instance at least. Amalgam's strength may vary: its compressive strength is heavily compromised if the amalgam contains pores due to improper condensation (Fig: 12.6).

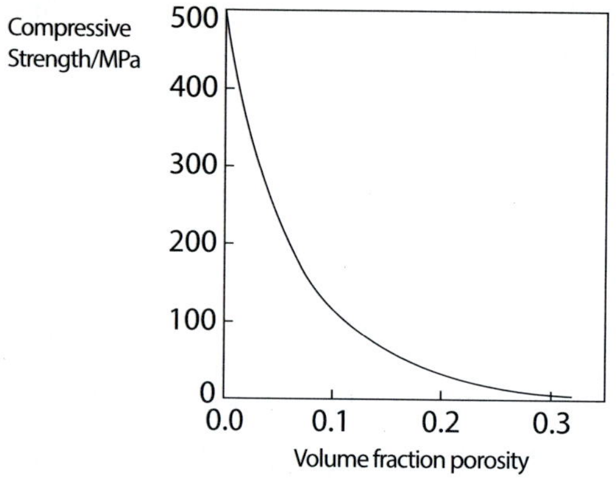

Fig: 12.6. Amalgam's compressive strength as a function of volume fraction porosity (Hg content is constant) (reproduced with permission from B. W. Darvell, Materials science for dentistry 9th edition, Woodhead Publishing Limited: www.woodheadpublishing.com).

As indicated above, dental silver amalgam is a polyphase metallic material, and the electrode potential differences between the various phases are substantial. *Galvanic corrosion* of the most electropositive phase, γ_{2}-Sn-Hg, is thus guaranteed. In principle, amalgam restorations are thereby self-sealing in a relatively short time. However, if the crevice is large, this cannot occur and recurrent caries may develop. Over time, amalgam corrosion products may seal the tooth-restoration interface thereby preventing bacterial leakage. Marginal sealing is, however, not guaranteed (Fig: 12.7).

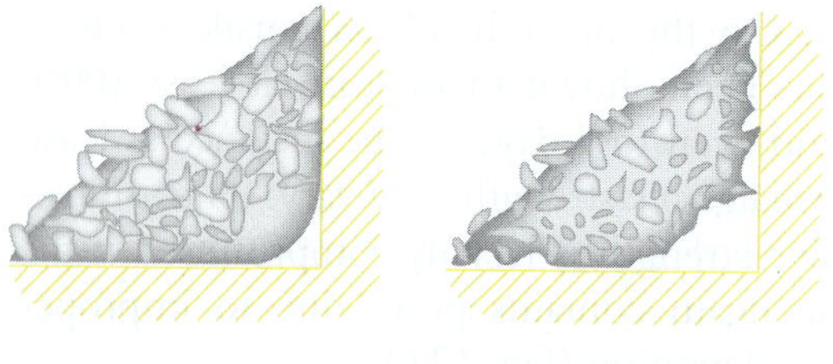

Fig: 12.7. Silver dental amalgam in tooth cavity: due to surface tension and shrinkage. of Hg, marginal seal may be compromised ((reproduced with permission from B. W. Darvell, Materials science for dentistry 9th edition, Woodhead Publishing Limited: www.woodheadpublishing.com).

REPORTED ADVANTAGES OF AMALGAM

- Good long-term clinical performance.
- Ease of manipulation by dentist.
- One-appointment placement.
- Long-lasting if placed under ideal conditions
- Minimal placement time compared with other restorative materials.
- Often can be repaired.
- Economical.
- Durable.
- Least technique sensitivity of all restorative materials.
- Applicability to a broad range of clinical situations.
- Newer formulations have greater long-term resistance to surface corrosion.
- Corrosion products seal the tooth-restoration interface and prevent bacterial leakage.

REPORTED DISADVANTAGES OF AMALGAM

- Some destruction of sound tooth tissue to gain retention.
- Marginal breakdown occurs.
- Poor appearance.
- Local allergic potential and possible predisposition to oral diseases.
- Concern about possible mercury toxicity and environmental issues.
- Oral galvanism potential.

ACKNOWLEDGEMENTS

Professor Brian W. Darvell (The University of Kuwait) is warmly acknowledged for providing the illustrations.

REFERENCES

1. A. Mustafa and J.P. Matinlinna (2014) Materials in Dentistry, In: *Handbook of Oral Biomaterials* (Ed. J.P. Matinlinna), Chapter 3, Pan Stanford, Singapore, ISBN 978-981-4463-12-6 *(in press)*
2. B.W. Darvell (2009) Materials Science for Dentistry, (9th Ed.), Woodhead Publishing, Cambridge, UK.
3. K.J. Anusavice, K. J. (2003) *Philips' Science of Dental Materials*, (11th Ed.) (Elsevier).
4. The FDI World Dental Federation and the World Health Organization (1997) A consensus statement. *www.fdiworldental.org*
5. American Dental Association (2009) Council on Scientific Affairs, April 2009. *www.ada.org*
6. B.W. Darvell (2012) Development of strength in silver amalgam, *Dental Materials* 28; e207-e217.
7. B.W. Darvell (2012) Effects of corrosion on the strength of dental silver amalgam, *Dental Materials* 28; e160-e167.
8. Mallineni SK, Nuvvula, S, Matinlinna JP, Yiu CKY, King NM. Biocompatibility of Various Dental Materials of Contemporary Dentistry: A Narrative Insight. J Investigat Clinical Dent 2013; 4: 9-19

Chapter 13

DENTAL COMPOSITE CHEMISTRY AND ITS USES

Dr. Zohaib & Dr. Samina Khan

INTRODUCTION

With the advancement in polymer science, new resin reinforced by means of fillers has been developed. In general, the properties of these composite resins are superior to those of conventional unfilled resins like acrylic resin. Historically, silicate cements were developed first as esthetic material followed by acrylic resins, and then by composite resins.

ACRYLIC RESINS

INTRODUCTION

That type of unfilled direct resins have been largely replaced by the composite resins. Discussion on it is necessary to understand the chemistry and properties of the newer resin systems.

MODE OF SUPPLY

They are supplied as powder and liquid.

COMPOSITION

POWDER

Polymethyl methacrylate Benzoyl peroxide (initiator) Colour pigments.

LIQUID

Methlymethacrylate monomer N, N-dimeltyl-P-toluidine (activator)

ADVANTAGES

a. Less prone to erode.
b. It has low solubility.
c. It is less acidic.
d. It is less brittle.
e. It has good thermal insulator.
f. It has good appearance.

DISADVANTAGES

a. Level of residual methyl methacrylate monomer, which is irritant.
b. Material undergoes setting contraction (6% by volume) and it can produce marginal gap.
c. It has low value of modulus of elasticity and it indicates that acrylic resin is a far more flexible than either enamel or dentine.
d. It has low compressive strength and hardness value and this value reflects that it has poor durability.

Current Status

This material is still in use for temporary crown and bridge costruction.

COMPOSITE

In materials sciences it is defined as a product, which consists of at least two distinct phases normally formed by blending together components having different structures and properties. Composite is made by combining two or more dissimilar material in such a way that the resultant material has a property superior to any of its parental ones.

Typical engineered composite materials include:

a. Composite building materials such as cement, concrete.
b. Reinforced plastics such as fiber-reinforced polymer.
c. Metal Composites.
d. Ceramic Composites (composite ceramic and metal matrices).

The resulting material will have properties superior or intermediate to those of the individual components. Example of natural composite materials is tooth enamel and dentine.

In dentistry, combination of resin such as Bis-GMA and its analogs with filler matrix used as restorative materials and adhesive purpose. The composition of resin-based dental composites has evolved significantly since the materials were first introduced to dentistry more than 50 years ago (Fig: 13.1).

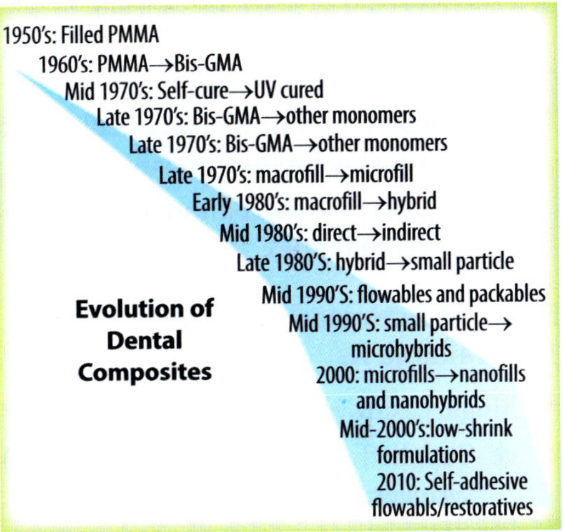

Fig: 13.1. A perspective on the evolution of dental composites.

Within each type of composite, the materials are further distinguished by the characteristics of their reinforcing fillers, and in particular their size (Fig. 13. 2).

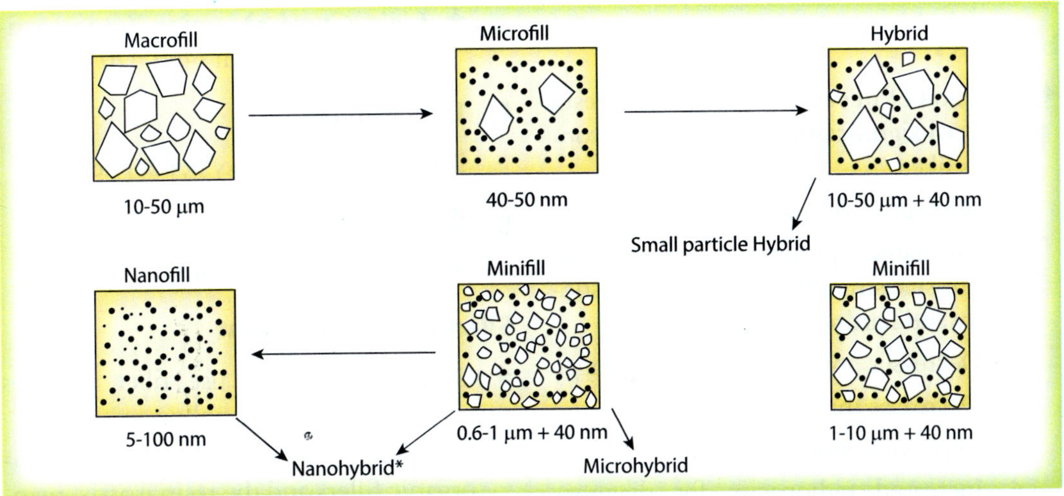

Fig: 13.2. The chronological development of the state of the art of dental composite formulations based on filler particle modifications.

MODE OF SUPPLY

A. Chemically Activated Composite Resin Are Available As

- Two Paste Systems
  - Base and catalyst paste supplied in small jars or syringes.
- Powder-Liquid Systems
  - Powder (in organic phase plus the initiator) is supplied in jars.
  - Liquid (Bis-GMA diluted with monomer) in bottles.

B. Light Activated Composite Resin Is Available As

- Single paste system
  - Supplied in light-light (Dark) syringes.

COMPOSITION

Important Constituents

a. Resins

- Bis GMA or urethane diacrylate + dilvent monomer-TEGDMA.

b. Fillers

- Addition of filler particles in to the resin material significantly improves its properties like;
  1. Added to strengthen the material.
  2. Mechanical properties such as compressive strength, modulus of elasticity and hardness
  3. Decreases polymerization shrinkage.
  4. Decreases thermal expansion.
  5. Improved optical properties.
  6. Increased radiopacity for diagnostic purposes (by the introduction of barium and strontium).

Minor Constituents

a. Principal

Bis-phenol-A and glycidyl methacrylate or Bowens resin – (high molecular weight monomer).

b. Diluent

(Low-molecular weight) monomer.

a. Mono-functional e.g. methylmethacrylate
b. Difunctional e.g. ethylene glycol dimethacrylate

c. Polymerization Inhibitor

Responsible for discoloration e.g. hydroquinone.

d. Silane Coupling Agents

Causes Bond between particles and fillers.

e. Initiator / Activator Components

- ***Chemical Cured*** → Benzoyl peroxide initiator tertiary amine activator e.g. N-N-dimethyl-P-toluidine.
- ***Light Cured*** → amine-Ketone activated by blue light (460-470 nm).

f. U-V Stablizer

2-hydroxy 4 methoxy benzophenone.

g. Colour Pigments

- to match tooth colour.

Silane Coupling Agent

- Dental composites use filler particles coated with silane coupling agents.
- To provide a good bond between the inorganic fillers and the resin matrix, manufacturers treat the surface of the filler with silane.

- It has groups that react with the inorganic filler and other groups that react with the organic matrix.

CLASSIFICATION

On the following basis;

A. According To Willems

Willems et al is based on a number of parameters such as Young's module, the percentage (by volume) of inorganic filler, the size of the main particles, surface roughness and compressive stress.

COMPOSITE TYPE	FILLER
Densified composites Midway-filled Ultrafine Fine Compact-filled>60% by volume Ultrafine Fine	< 60% by volume Particles < 3 µm Particles > 3 µm < 60% by volume Particles < 3 µm Particles > 3 µm
Microfine compoites ✦ Hemogeneous ✦ Hemogeneous	Average particle size = 0.04 µm
Miscellaneous compoites	Blends densified and microfine composites
Traditional Composites	Equivalent to what are termed macrofill composites in other classifications
Fibre-reinforced composites	Industrial-use composites

B. According To Particle Size

I. Macrofilled/Conventional Composite

- Barium/Strontium glass – 2.5-5 um in size
- Filler = 78 – 80%

Properties

- It has good mechanical properties.
- Hard to polish.
- It requires coupling agent.

II. Microfilled Composite

- Colloidal silica particles – 0.04 um in size
- Filler = 30-60%

Properties

- Not strong as macrofill.
- It has high % of resin matrix.
- It is highly polishable.
- Good esthetic for anterior teeth.

III. Hybrid Composites

- It is a mixture of both conventional and microfill particles.
- Using filler loading of about 75% conventional size (1-50 um) and 8% submicron size. (0.04 um average).

Properties

- It has good strength and can be polished to a smooth surface.

IV. Nano-Composite

- Improved Hybrid Composites.
- Continue to maximize the amount of filler present by controlling the particle size and distribution to improve the clinical performance.
- The average particle size has decreased and nano-sized particles have been added.
- The results are slight improvements in strength and polymerization shrinkage.
- Particles size varies from 40 nm to 0.7 nm.
- Nanoparticle filled composites

exhibit outstanding esthetics, are easy to polish and possess an enhanced wear resistance.

C. According to Method of Polymerization

ISO standard classification for resin based restorative material (Depends upon the application).

Type 1

- Restoration of cavities involving occlusal surfaces.

Type 2

- All other polymer based filling and restorative materials.
- The standard further sub divides the material into 3 classes.

Class 1

- Comprises self-curing materials whose setting is activated by mixing and initiator and an activator.

Class 2

- Materials are those whose setting is affected by application of energy from an external source such as blue light or heat.
- These materials are further sub divided as follows.

Class 2 Group 1

- Materials whose use requires the energy to be applied intra-orally.

Class 2 Group 2

- Materials whose method of use required the energy to be applied extra orally.
- It is designed for the production of composite inlays and onlays.

Class 3

- They are dual-cure which have a self curing chemical mechanism but are also cured by the application of external energy.

SPECIAL USE COMPOSITE MATERIALS

1. FLOWABLE COMPOSITES

- Flow into the cavity preparation because of their lower viscosity (low filler content), Weaker, less abrasion-resistant material results.
- Uses include restoration of Class V cavities, margin repairs, pit and fissure sealants, as a base for Class I, II and III restorations.

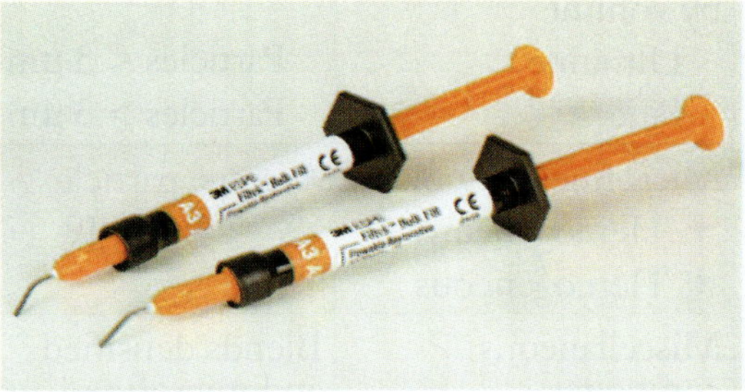

Fig: 13.3. Flowable composite syringe.

2. PACKABLE COMPOSITES

They have a filler particle feature that inhibits the filler particles from sliding by one another "thicker, stiffer feel" results, makes placement of the material into the cavity preparation easier, and has potential to achieve tight contact points.

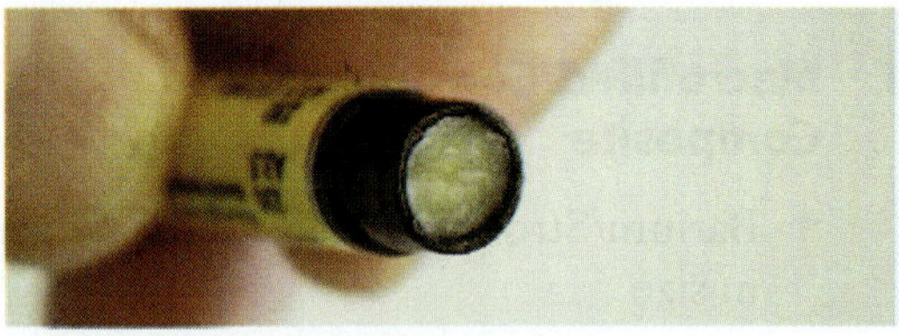

Fig: 13.4. Packable composite.

PROPERTIES OF COMPOSITES

1. SETTING CHARACTERISTICS

A. Chemical Activated Materials

- Setting commences immediately after mixing the two components (paste and paste or paste and liquid etc).
- The rate of set is uniform throughout the bulk of the material causing a gradual increase in viscosity at room temperature.
- The materials have a limited working time and must be inserted into the prepared cavity before they become unmanageable.
- The standard requires that the working time (timed from start of mixing) should be at least 90 seconds.

B. For Light Activated Materials

- A minimal increase in viscosity takes place before the material is exposed to the activating light source.
- Longer working time.
- The ability to set rapidly after exposure to a light source is termed command setting.
- Activation is first achieved in the surface layers of the materials where the light intensity is greater.
- High viscosity and darker shades materials retard the diffusion of active free radicals.
- Depth of cure decreases as the distance from the material increases.

2. LIGHT ACTIVATING UNITS

- The purpose of the light activation unit is to deliver high intensity radiation of the correct wavelength to the surface of the material in order to activate polymerization.
- The critical wavelength used by the vast majority of units and materials is 470 nm, which corresponds to the blue region of the visible spectrum.
- Two approaches have been used to deliver this blue light on the mouth.

A. Light Source

- Light sources include halogen lights, plasma arc lights, argon lasers, and light-emitting diodes.
- Because the working time of light-cure materials is determined by the user, they are widely popular.

B. Light Activation Units

- **QTH** most widely used.
- The light source is usually a quartz-halogen bulb. Light is transmitted to the hose tip by a fiberoptic bundle.

Plasma Arc Lamps

- Use xenon bulb
- High Power output
- Require very efficient cooling systems
- Shorter curing time
- Greater depth of cure

Lasers

- Increased efficiency
- Collimated beam
- Shorter curing time
- Heat production is minimized

Light Emitting Diodes (LED)

- Semiconductor that emits light
- Requires low current

- Portable, Rechargeable units
- Emit virtually no heat

C. Factors Affecting Cure

I. Equipment

- Bulb frosting or degradation
- Light reflector degradation
- Optical filter degradation
- Fibre-optic bundle breakage
- Light-guide fracture
- Tip contamination by resin buildup
- Line voltage inconsistencies
- Sterilization problems
- Infection control barriers

II. Procedural

- Light tip direction
- Access to restoration
- DISTANCE from surface
- Size of tip
- Tip movement
- TIME of exposure

III. Restorative Factors

- Restoration thickness
- Cavity design
- Filler - amount and size
- Restoration shade
- Monomer ratios

3. SETTING CONTRACTION

- The setting contraction of composite resin is considerably smaller than that observed for un-filled acrylic resins.
- Two factors contribute to this reduction.

Firstly

- The use of layer monomer and co monomer molecules effectively reduce concentration of reactive groups in a given volume of material.

Secondly

- Additions of fillers which take no part in the setting reaction further reduce the concentration of reactive methacrylate groups.
- The setting contraction depends on the number of addition reaction which take place during polymerization and is therefore much smaller for composite materials values of around 1.5-3.0 volumetric contraction are typical as opposed to 6% for acrylics.
- The setting contraction varies from one type of composite to another;
  1. Products with higher filler loading undergo less shrinkage.
  2. Heavily filled hybrid materials exhibit the lowest shrinkage values.
  3. Micro filled materials have lower shrinkage values than would be expected from their low filler contents.

Table: 13.1. Differences between visible light and UV light-cured system.

PROPERTY	VISIBLE LIGHT-CURED	UV LIGHT-CURED
Curing time	20-40 seconds	1 minute
Depth of curing	Greater	Less
Transmission through enamel	More	Less
Intensity of light over a period of time	Remains same	Fall rapidly
Working range	400-500nm	360-400nm

- Shrinkage can compromise marginal seal and rupture adhesive bonds created at the tooth restorative interface.
- Layering techniques, particularly applicable to use with light activated material, can be used to limit the damaging effects of shrinkage.
- The total volumetric contraction which occurs depends upon;
    1. The bulk of material used.
    2. On cavity size.
    3. Clinical technique.
- The ability of a resin based filling material to compensate for shrinkage by flow depends on the cavity configuration.
- When there is a small ratio of contact surface area to free surface area flow occurs readily over the free area in order to minimize the stress at the interface.
- When there is little free surface area of material, little flow can occur and a larger stress at the interface results.
- The ratio of bonded free area can therefore be used to predict interfacial stress caused by shrinkage the ratio has become known as the *C-factor or configuration factor.*

4. THERMAL PROPERTIES

- Depend upon inorganic filler content.
- > Filler content < co-efficient of thermal expansion.
- Thermal diffusivity close to dentine.
- It is a good thermal insulator.
- Co-efficient of thermal expansion is four times that of tooth.
- Co-efficient of thermal expansion of Micro filled > hybrid.

5. MECHANICAL PROPERTIES

- The mechanical properties of composite materials depend upon
    - Filler content
    - Type of filler
    - Efficiency of the filler resin coupling process
    - Degree of porosity in the set material
- Compressive strength, tensile strength, flexural strength, modulus of elasticity is greater in hybrid material than conventional and micro filled.

Table: 13.2. Comparisons of mechanical properties of different dental composites.

PROPERTY	TRADITIONAL	MICROFILLED	SMALL PARTICLE	HYBRID
Compressive strength (MPa)	250-300	250-300	350-400	300-350
Tensile strength (MPa)	50-65	30-50	75-90	70-90
Elastic Modulus (GPa)	8-15	3-6	15-20	7-12
Coefficient of Thermal expansion (10^{-6} / °C)	25-35	50-60	19-26	3040
KNOOP HARDNESS	55	5-30	5060	50-60

6. SURFACE CHARACTERISTICS

- Surface hardness, roughness and abrasion resistance are properties which are mainly controlled by the filler content and particle size.
- The surface of a composite material is initially very smooth and glossy due to contact with a matrix strip during setting.
- The surface layer is initially richer in resin than the bulk of the material and few, if any, filler particles are exposed at the surface.
- Surface roughness may be caused by:
  - i. Abrasive forces exerted on materials during service, e.g. from food stuffs, denitrifies etc.
  - ii. During contouring and polishing.
- A smooth surface can be restored to a roughened composite by using a "GLAZING AGENT"- These consist of resins which are identical to composites except that they do not contain filler particles. The glaze is applied to the surface of composite and sets to form a smooth surface layer of about 100 um thickness. The material is very soft, however, and is soon abraded, revealing the composite surface again.

7. APPEARANCE

- Composite materials, when freshly placed, offer an excellent match with surrounding tooth substance.

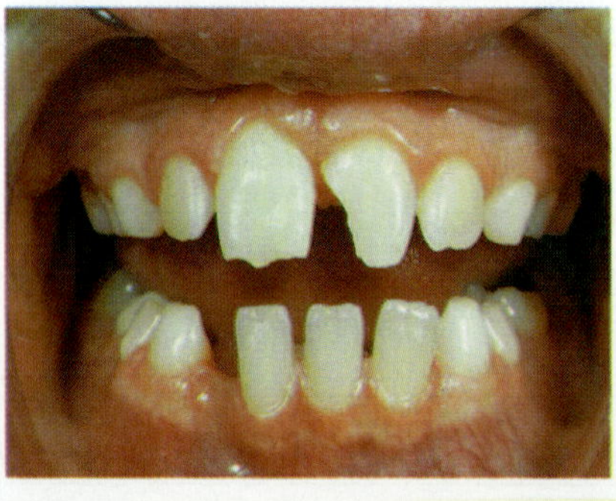

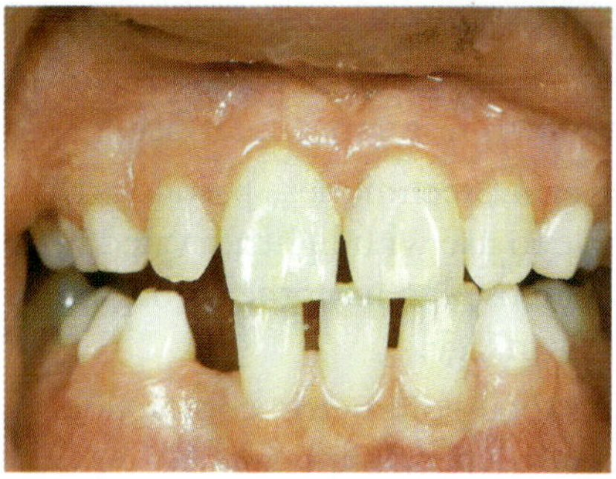

Fig: 13.5. clinical picture representing appearance of composite with natural structure.

- The availability of a variety of shades, combined with a degree of translucency imparted by the filler, enables the dentist to achieve a very pleasing result.
- Polishing reduces the glass, however, and abrasion may further increase surface roughness.
- The surface may eventually become stained due to deposition of coloured foodstuffs or to tobacco tars.
- The micro filled products are capable of maintaining a smoother surface than either the conventional or hybrid materials.

8. CAVITY LININGS

- Although monomers employed in composite materials may be considered potentially harmful to the pulp, they are generally strongly bound in a highly cross linked network following setting.
- It is normal practice to line cavities prior to placement of composite restoration.
- The material of choice is morally CALCIUM HYDROXIDE product.
- No need of lining if cavity is sealed to micro leakage.

9. ADHESION

- Composites do not inherently form a durable bond with tooth substance.
- Retention of the material is generally achieved by using undercut cavities. (Use a technique of Acid Etching).

CLINICAL HANDLING NOTES FOR COMPOSITES

1. CAVITY DESIGN AND BONDING TO ENAMEL

- The ability of composites to form a durable seal to both enamel and dentine has allowed modification to cavity design to both minimize the destruction of otherwise sound enamel and dentine and to maximize the performance of these restorations.
- Access through enamel should be sufficient to permit removal of underlying decayed dentine.
- Composite resins exhibit good flow characteristics in their pre-polymerized form. Cavities should be designed to use this property with rounded internal line angles and smooth flowing contours.
- Traditional cavity design has included the removal of deep tortuous fissures adjacent to areas of decay as these were regarded as being at high risk from carious attack. This is not required when using a composite as these areas can be prepared and then sealed using a compatible fissure sealant system to achieve EXTENSION FOR PREVENTION.
- Cavities designed for tooth coloured restoration rely heavily on their bonding to enamel and/or dentine to achieve retention and resistance to displacement.
- Once any unsupported enamel has been removed, the cavity margins need to be designed to minimize the bond strength that can be achieved with either enamel or dentine.
- Attachment of composites to enamel is achieved primarily by etching the enamel surface with acid.

Etching Enamel Surface With Acid

- This etching process results in preferential dissolution of either the enamel prism cores or the prism boundaries producing a micro porous enamel surface with high surface energy.
- The pattern and quality of etching depend on
  1. The acid used.
  2. The orientation of the enamel prisms in relation to the cavity margin.
- Classically enamel is etched with between 30% and 37% phosphoric acid, although more recently a wider variety of acids have been used including 10% phosphoric, citric and maleic.
- The etching time is specific to a given acid and hence manufacturer recommendations should be followed with care.
- Unfortunately the production of a 90° cavo-surface angle giving well-supported enamel margins will result in prism being exposed for etching parallel to their long axis.
- Production of cavo surface angle of the order of 120° will help to overcome this problem by exposing etch pattern, although it is not as easy to finish a tooth coloured restoration accurately to an oblique margin.
- Attachment to the etched surface is established using:

1. An unfilled resin (the resin, which forms the basis of the composite).
2. A dentine bonding agent (DBA).

2. THE BONDING OF COMPOSITES TO DENTINE

- In order to achieve bonding the surface of the dentine needs to be demineralized using an acid. This results in removal of the smear layer (a layer of loosely attached cutting debris from surface preparation) and then demineralization of the dentine, exposing collagen.
- Care is required in handling this prepared surface to achieve reliable bonding.
- After surface treatment dentine bonding agent (DBA) is applied onto the dentine surface.

3. MATERIAL PLACEMENT

- There are two considerations to be taken into account when placing composites in a cavity.
    - i. Maximizing quality of care.
    - ii. Minimizing the adverse effects of polymerization shrinkage on tooth.
- All currently available composites shrink on setting by between 1.5 and 3% by volume (depending on filler type and loading).

In summary;

a. Chemically activated resins shrink towards their center and will cure in bulk.
b. Visible light cured resins shrink towards the curing light and can only be cured in thin section.

4. MINIMIZING QUALITY OF CURE

- It is necessary to place visible light cure (VLC) resins in increments of not more than 2mm in depth to ensure adequate cure using currently available curing units.

5. CURE DEPTH

- The 2-mm cure depth is dependent upon;
    - i. Colour and translucency of the resin.
    - ii. The distance, the light is away from the surface of the composite and whether or not the curing is being performed through another tissue (e.g. enamel or dentine).

6. INCREMENTAL DEPTH

- Should be reduced for dark shades, where the light tip has to be some distance from the resin or when cure is being attempted through tooth tissue.

7. MINIMIZING THE ADVERSE EFFECTS OF POLYMERIZATION SHRINKAGE

- The adverse effects of polymerization shrinkage include distortion of the tooth and failure to establish a marginal seal, both of which can result in postoperative sensitivity.

Table: 13.3. Factors that influence the composite resin polymerisation process.

FACTORS	CLINICAL REPERCUSSIONS
Curing time	It depends on resin shade, light intensity, resin thickness, curing through tooth structure and composite filling.
Shade of resin	Darker composite shades cure more slowly and less deeply than lighter shades (60 seconds at a maximum depth of 0.5 mm).
Temperature	Composite at room temperature cure more completely and rapidly.
Thickness of resin	Optimum thickness is l-2 mm.
Type of filler	Microfine composites are more difficult to cure than heavily loaded composites.
Distance between light and resin	Optimum distance < l mm, with the light positioned 90 degrees from the Composite surface.
Light source quality	Wavelength between 400 to 500 nm. A power density about 600 mW/cmf is required to ensure that 400 mW/cm; reaches the first increment of composite in a posterior box.
Polymerisation shrinkage	Depends on the amount of organic phase.

A. Incremental Placement Techniques

- There have been two techniques for incremental curing described.
  - i. Herring bone method
  - ii. Lateral filling method
- Both techniques minimize the wall to wall effects of shrinkage, (See below).

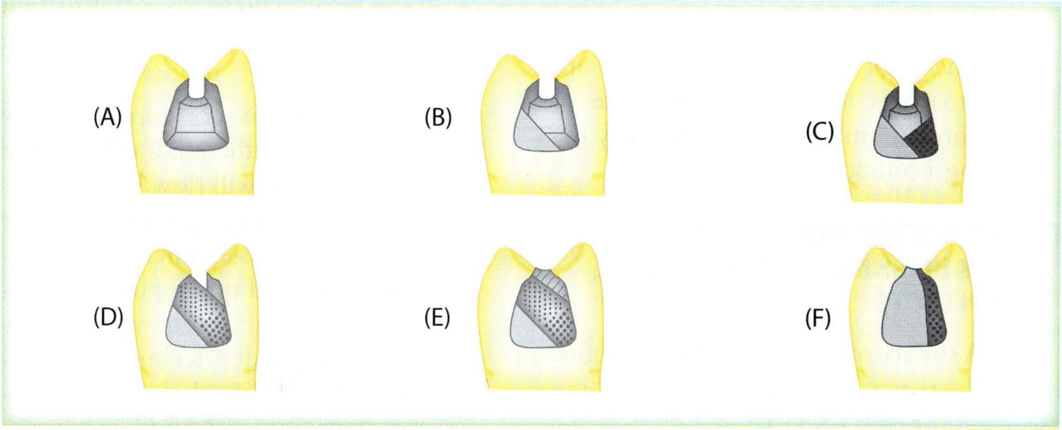

Fig: 13.6. Composites should be introduced into large cavities in increments to maximize quality of cure and help to reduce polymerisation stress . On completion of the cavity (a) composite is placed in the cavity in diagonal increments, producing a herringbone effect (b-e) to restore the defect an alternative approach is a lateral incremental filling technique (f).

B. Directional Curing Techniques

- VLC material start to cure at the surface closest to the curing light and then shrink towards the light. This can be used to help establish and maintain a marginal seal.
- At the base of a box, curing can be initiated by using a light transmitting wedge to cure the increment closest to the cervical margins first.
- Curing of the remainder of the increment will then be undertaken from the occlusal aspect.

C. Increasing The Effective Filler Loading

- One of the principal methods of reducing polymerization shrinkage in composites is to increase the relative proportion of filler to resin.
- It is, however, possible to increase effective filler loading by;
  - i. Incorporating either a pre-polymerized piece of composite into the restoration.
  - ii. Using commercially available quartz inserts to achieve the same effect.
- The logical extension of this approach is to make a composite or porcelain inlay and lute the inlay using a composite luting agent.

8. MATRIX TECHNIQUES AND THE ESTABLISHMENT OF PROXIMAL CONTACTS

- A surface of matrix has three benefits.
  - i. It helps to guide the formation of a peripheral profile of the restoration.
  - ii. It isolates the resin from the atmosphere which helps to minimize the effect of air inhibition of cure the resin at the surface and the layer of material immediately adjacent to the matrix is resin-rich.
  - iii. Produces a high gloss surface giving optimal appearance on placement.
- Two materials are used to produce clear flexible matrix structures for use with composites.
  - Cellulose Acetate
  - Polyester film (Mylar ® or Melinex ®)
- Matrix for proximal cavities on anterior teeth should be placed between teeth after the enamel has been prepared for bonding but before the DBA or unfilled resin is applied to the prepared tooth tissues.
- Matrix technique for proximal cavities on posterior teeth involve placing a band around the tooth with some form of lightening mechanism. If a tooth only has one proximal box and the opposite surface is intact, forming a good contact with a adjacent tooth, it can be difficult to pass a transparent band through such a contact as the matrix material is relatively fragile.
- If the matrix is not applied before the DBA/resin there is a risk that the unfilled resins will flow between adjacent teeth, linking them together and making subsequent matrix placement difficult if not impossible. This approach applies even when an incremental buildup techniques is being used even though the matrix does not come into use until the increments begin to restore the peripheral contour of the tooth.

9. FINISHING AND POLISHING

- If surface finishing is required, this is probably best achieved by;
  - i. Contouring the material with a diamond stone or tungsten carbide bur.
  - ii. Polishing with a composite finishing system comprising mildly abrasive pastes and discs.

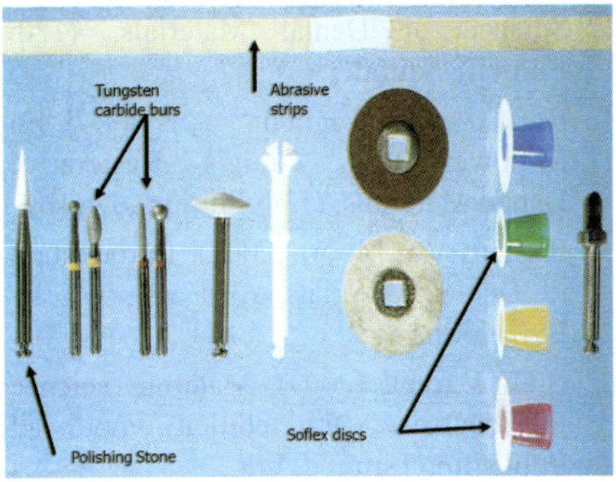

Fig: 13.7. Avaliable materials for finishing and polishing of dental composite.

- Surface glaze are supplied with some materials; these are essentially unfilled polymers. Though a glaze can give a smooth surface initially, it is unlikely that its benefit will last long.
- TWO CRITICAL FACTORS for Finishing and Polishing;
  - Abrasive size
  - Filler particle size

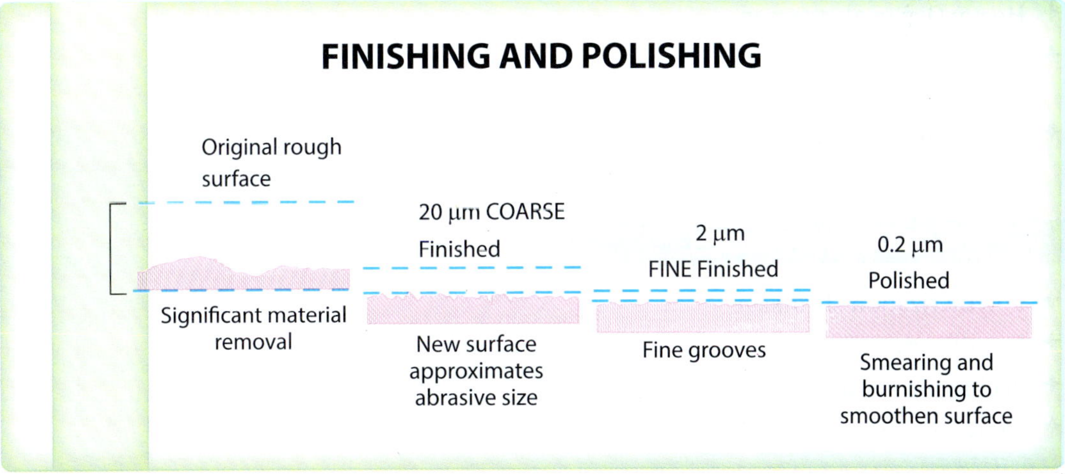

Fig: 13.8. Illustration showing different surface characteristics after polishing.

APPLICATIONS OF COMPOSITES

- Class I, II, III, IV, V and VI restorations
- Foundations or core buildups
- Sealants and Preventive resin restorations
- Esthetic enhancement procedures Veneers, diastema closure.
- Composite Inlays for certain cavities

ADVANTAGES

- Aesthetics
- Conservative tooth structure removal
- Less complex tooth preparation
- Insulation
- Bonding Advantages
  - Decreased microleakage, recurrent caries, postoperative sensitivity.
  - Increased retention and increased strength of remaining tooth structure.

CONTRAINDICATIONS

- Isolation
- Heavy Occlusal stresses
- When all occlusal contacts are on composite
- Restorations that extend onto root surface

DISADVANTAGES

- Polymerization shrinkage
- Possible greater wear
- Technique sensitive
- More expensive

REFERENCES

1. Willems G, Lambrechts P, Braem M, Celis JP, Vanherle G. A classification of dental composites according to their morphological and mechanical characteristics. Dent Mater 1992;8:310-9.
2. Chen M-H. Update on dental nanocomposites. J Dent Res 2010;89:549–60.
3. Kenneth Anusavice (2012), Phillips' Science of Dental Materials, (12th Edition), Saunder.
4. Ronald Sakaguchi & John M.power(2011), Craig's Restorative Dental Materials, (13th Edition), Mosby
5. Richard Van Noort (2007), Introduction to Dental Materials, (3rd ed), Mosby Ltd., China
6. B W Darvell (2009), Materials science for dentistry (9th edition),Woodhead Publishing Limited, UK.
7. John M. Power & John C.Wataha(2012), DENTAL MATERIALS Properties and Manipulation, (10th Edition), ELSEVIER, India.

Chapter 14

GLASS IONOMER CEMENTS AND THEIR MODIFICATIONS

Dr. Zohaib, Dr. Mustafa & Dr. Sana Shahab

INTRODUCTION

Glass ionomer restorative materials are the hybrids of the silicate and polycarboxylate cements. It consists of interpenetrating network of inorganic and organic components forming a matrix in which particles of unreacted glass are embedded.

Polycarboxylate were developed several years earlier and were the first dental cements for which an inherent adhesion to tooth substance could be demonstrated. In late 1960s Glass-ionomer became available as a result of the pioneering studies of Alan Wilson and Brian Kent at the Laboratory of the Government Chemist, London. Commercial dental cements of this type were launched in 1975, though these had very inferior properties compared with the materials available today.

When zinc oxide of the polycarboxylate material was replaced by a reactive ion leachable glass similar to that used previously in silicate cements a storage, less soluble and more translucent cement could be produced.

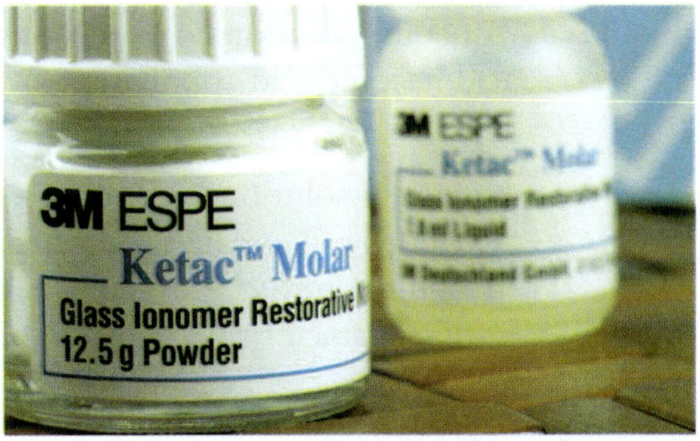

Fig: 14.1. GIC restorative material.

CLASSIFICATION

Types and their uses:

Type I – For luting cast restorations and orthodontic bands.

Type II (A) – Aesthetics restorative cements, used for class III and class V cavities.

Type II (B) – Reinforced restorative material, mainly used for core build up.

1. Miracle mix – GIC powder + Ag amalgam alloy powder.
2. Class cermet – GIC powder + pure Au/ Ag (mostly Ag), also known as ketac silver.

Type III – Lining cement, base.

Type IV – Visible light activated liners/bases.

Type V - Glass ionomer for stabilization and protection.

Type VI - ART in anterior teeth.

Type VII – High viscous/ condensable glass ionomers, ART for posterior teeth.

COMPOSITION OF GLASS IONOMER CEMENTS

POWDER/LIQUID MATERIAL	
Powder	Sodium aluminosilicate glass with about 20% CAF and other minor additives
Liquid	Aqueous solutions of acrylic acid/itaconic acid copolymer **OR** Aqueous solution of maleic acid polymer and tartaric acid in some products to control setting characteristic.
POWDER/WATER MATERIAL	
Powder	Glass (as above) + vacuum dried poly acid (acrylic, maleic or copolymer).
Liquid	Manufacturers supply dropper bottles, which the operator fills with water **OR** The manufacturer supplies a dilute aqueous solution of tartaric acid.

SUPPLIED AS

- Powder and liquid
- Powder mixed with water
- Encapsulated form

SETTING REACTION

The setting reaction of conventional glass ionomer cement is acid (liquid) - base (powder) reaction leading to the formation of polycarboxylate salts that comprise the cement matrix.

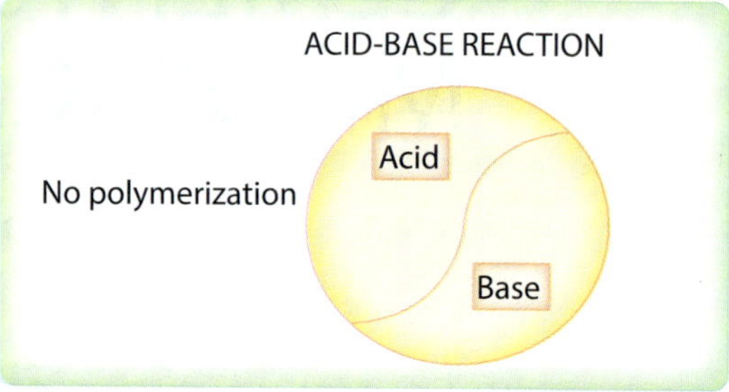

Fig: 14.2. Illustration showing GIC is set by acid/base reaction.

The reaction occurs in three distinct stages:

- Dissolution
- Gelation
- Final maturation stage

1. DISSOLUTION STAGE

It is characterized by the dissolution of polyacids. The carboxylic acid dissociates to form negatively charged carboxylate anions, $RCOO^{-}$, and positively charged protons, H^{+}. the positively charged protons, H^{+}, then attack the surface of the glass filling body, causing disintegration of the glass structure and release of the cement-forming metal ions, Al^{3+} and Ca^{2+}

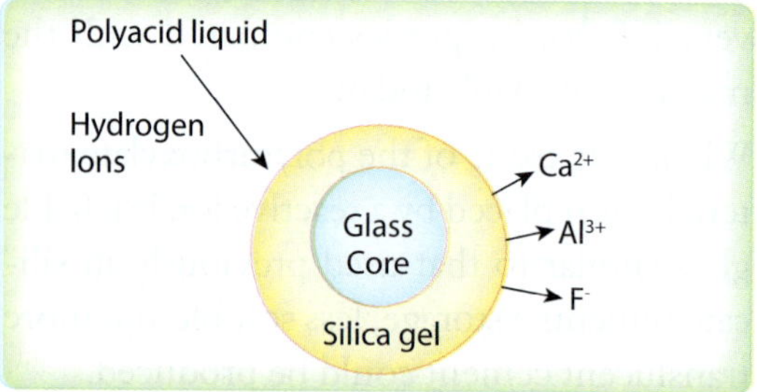

Fig: 14.3. Various stages of setting reaction - Dissolution.

2. GELATION STAGE

It is characterized by the reaction of Ca^{2+} ions with polyacid chains to form calcium polyacrylate. Calcium ions are the main active ion species at this stage. These ions are present in aqueous solution, which means that they are quite susceptible to the attack of aqueous solutions (i.e., being washed out).

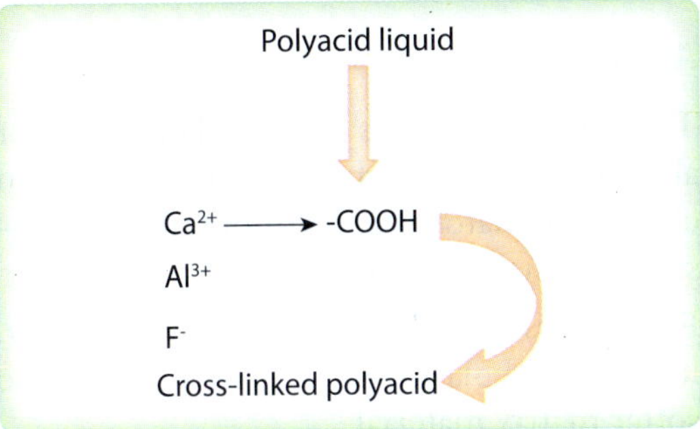

Fig: 14.4. Various stages of setting reaction Gelation stage.

This is the reason why glass ionomer cements have to be protected from moisture during this phase. However, the opposite effect, i.e. drying out, is no less determental, which can be easily explained as the reaction requires an aqueous medium to proceed. The process of hydration is severely impaired or prevented in the absence of water, which limits the supply of ions needed for the setting reaction.

3. FINAL MATURATION STAGE

During the final maturation stage, the Al3+ ions are increasingly deposited in the matrix, leading to a three–dimensional, highly cross-linked calcium aluminum carboxylate gel. Later this gel undergoes hydration which increases its strength.

Sodium and fluoride do not participate in the cross-linking of the cements. Some of the sodium ions may replace the hydrogen ions of carboxylic group, whereas the rest combine with the fluoride to form the sodium fluoride uniformly dispersed in the set mass, which provides the anticariogenic property to the cement.

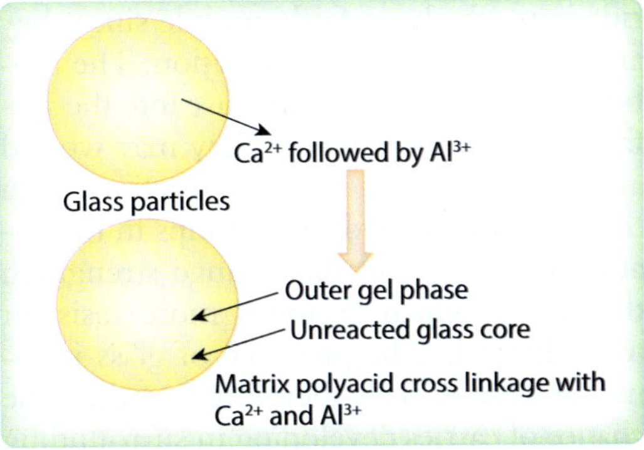

Fig: 14.5. Schematic representation of reaction of aluminosilicate glass particles with aqueous polyacid solutions.

PROPERTIES

Effect of moisture during GIC setting

The setting reaction is rather protracted despite a fairly rapid initial hardening. The material must be protected from the moisture contamination during first hour; otherwise strength and solubility are adversely affected.

Hence it is necessary to varnish the surface of the filling immediately after initial hardening.

Adherence of the dentine surface

One of the important properties of the material is their ability to adhere to both enamel and dentine, although the precise mechanism of bending is still somewhat unclear.

Thermal diffusivity

The thermal diffusivity value for glass ionomer cement is close to that of dentine. Hence the material has an adequate thermal insulating effect on the pulp and helps to protect it from trauma.

Fluoride release

The matrix phase of set glass ionomer cement contains significant amount of fluoride ions which are fairly mobile since they are not involved in salt formation. The mobile fluoride ions readily diffuse into the surface of the cement where they may wound away with saliva or undergo reactions with the surrounding hydroxyl groups in the apatite structures and this change strengthen the apatite which becomes more resistant to acid attack. The presence of glass ionomer cement is likely therefore to reduce the chance of carries developing in surrounding tooth substance.

Fluoride absorption

Not only can the matrix phase of the cement gradually release the fluoride but it can also absorb the fluoride ions released by the tooth pastes and mouth washes.

Coefficient of thermal expansion

Value of coefficiency of thermal expansion for glass ionomer cements (13-16 ppm C-1) quite closely match to the value recorded for tooth substance (8-11 ppm C-1). This during adhesion to enamel and dentine helps to prevent inversion of pulp by micro leakage.

Compressive strength

The glass ionomers are selectively brittle, having a flexural strength on 15 to 20 MPa (CF 70 MPa for composites), and cannot be considered suitable as general filling materials for permanent teeth.

Acid erosion

Glass ionomer, like close relatives the silicates, are susceptible to acid erosion.

This is an inherent property to materials which are effectively inorganic to salts formed by an acid base reaction.

Factors which affect the rate of erosion

Factors which affect the rate of erosion include the pH of eroding medium (e.g. saliva plaque and drinks) and the maturity of the cement at the time it contacts the acid.

To reduce the risk of acid erosion it is essential that cements are protected with warmish or resin during setting.

Abrasion

The glass ionomers have relatively poor abrasive resistance which results not only in change of anatomical form but also in considerable surface roughness.

Roughness may also be caused by polishing, leaving hard glass core protruding from the softer matrix material.

Appearance

In terms of appearance, glass ionomer offer a responsible match for the natural tooth particularly to dentine, although most authorities agree that a better match is achieved with resin matrix composite.

The translucency of restorative cements is achieved through the presence of unreacted glass, which is able to transmit light.

Radiolucency

Then conventional glass ionomer restorative cements lack radio opacity and cannot readily be detected using radiographic techniques.

The incorporation of metals of greater atomic numbers either in metallic form (e.g. silver) or oxide (e.g. barium oxide) can be used to impart radio opacity and a significant loss of translucency and colour match. This may not be capable of many restorative applications but may be perfectly acceptable for applications in which the appearance of cement is of little consequence e.g.

cavity lining or core build up. There is one commercially available restorative material which exhibits some radio opacity.

Biocompatibility

Glass ionomer have acceptable biocompatibility despite their acidic nature.

However, the cements based on poly acids have traditionally been considered less harmful than those based on phosphoric acid, dueto two reasons:

First, the acids used are weaker than phosphoric acid.

Second, the poly acid chains are large and immobile, their mobility being further restricted by their affinity for calcium ions in the tooth to which the material is applied.

Pupal studies indicate that glass ionomer cements cause a mild inflammatory response which is normally resolved within 30 days.

ADVANTAGES AND DISADVANTAGES OF GIC

Advantages

Glass ionomer became more popular during late 80s because of the following reasons:

1. Higher survivorship rate, compared to zinc phosphate cement
2. Their fluoride release potential
3. They are self-adhesive to both enamel and dentin
4. No heat is produced during setting
5. Biocompatibility in host environment
6. Excellent marginal seal-no shrinkage

Disadvantages

1. Initial sensitivity of glass ionomer to moisture and dehydration
2. Slow development of strength
3. Short working time and no command set
4. Low fracture toughness
5. Low wear resistance

APPLICATION AND CLINICAL HANDLING NOTES

USE OF GIC

A. Root surface caries

They are used to restore the loss of root structure from tooth as a consequence of tooth decay or cervical abrasion cavity. Both of these lesions tend to occur close to the cervical margin of the tooth.

Root caries tends to spread laterally across the tooth surface and centrally towards the pulp. Once it has been removed the resultant cavity tends to be broad and shallow.

B. Abrasion cavities

Abrasion cavities were once thought to be the product of overzealous tooth brushing possibly in association with the use of an abrasive dentifrice. It is now recognized that both dietary factors and functional leading of teeth (causing teeth to bend) can be cofactors in their etiology.

The morphology of such lesions is variable, some are relatively dish shaped and shallower while the other are more v-shaped and tend to be deeper.

In both cases the tooth surface is likely to be caries free and highly burnished. The material can be used in these cavities.

C. Class-III cavities

The use of glass ionomers for restoring the class-III cavities has been advocated.

The early materials are far from ideal,

being more adequate than either silicates or composites.

D. Cavities in deciduous teeth

Glass ionomer cements are gaining wide acceptance as filling material for deciduous teeth, often being used in preference to amalgam in deciduous molars.

E. Class- I and class-II in permanent teeth

Some new restorative techniques offer alternative to traditional class-I and class-II cavities in posterior teeth in adults.

F. Others

- The cementation of cast alloy and porce lain restorations
- Cementation of orthodontic bands
- Bonding of brackets with GIC has an advantage of avoiding acid etching, therefore elimination of mineral loss that occurs during debonding with adhesive resins
- As cavity liners or base materials under composite and amalgam
- As an esthetic restorative material for class III and class V (erosion lesions) preparation
- As pit and fissure sealant
- As a core build up material
- Temporary anterior and posterior restoration

G. Application of GIC outside dentistry

Outside dentistry, glass-ionomers have begun to find use that exploits their good biocompatibility. These include artificial ear ossicles and bone-substitute plates for craniofacial reconstruction. Experimental studies have reported other uses outside clinical dentistry, including orthopedics and ENT surgery (for fixation of cochlear implants and for sealing defects in the skull). These are thus well-established biomaterials, which have every prospect of becoming more important in a variety of surgical applications in the years ahead.

Cavity Preparation

It is like a tunnel with its origin either from occlusal surfaces a short distance from the buccal aspect. The tunnel leads into the area of carious dentine which is removed using rotary instruments. Glass ionomer cement is than inserted into the cavity with an appropriate matrix.

Available Material And Technique

A variety of agents have been used for this purpose, including citric acid.

However, the most effective agent seems to be 10% - 15% poly (acrylic) acid. This is applied to the tooth surface for 30 seconds than washed off and the tooth is dried, but not desiccated, to achieve a receptive surface for bonding.

Matrix Techniques

Generally the glass ionomer cements are used to restore the proximal cavities on anterior teeth and defects on the root surfaces, weather the product of wear or decay.

Procedure

The matrix is adapted to the tooth surface at the completion of cavity preparation.

It is then removed and placed on a side. The dentine is prepared for bonding and a slightly access material is placed in the cavity.

The matrix is then placed again making sure that its gingival portion is not resting on the cervical floor of the cavity, but lies outside the tooth surface.

These relatively rigid metal foils are very good for insertion into the gingival area and help to restore the area properly but care must be taken that they are not caught on the gingival floor of the cavity.

The matrix should be left undisturbed until the material sets properly and then it can be removed carefully using sharp probe or excavator. Matrix technique, for tunnel preparation requires a thin metal strip to be passed between the teeth and then adapted to the contour of the tooth using wedge.

Finishing and Polishing

Glass ionomer cements are water based hence they are highly susceptible to either desiccation or excessive moisture contamination during the early phase of their setting reaction. They achieve a clinical set part through the chemical process of cement formation.

Maturation continues for at least an hour and with some materials up to 24 hours, the surface of the cement should be protected during that time period. A variety of materials has been suggested for moisture protection, from cocoa butter, copal and resin varnish to unfilled methacrylate based resins. This latter group is by far the most effective at delaying water flow into and out of the cement.

The unfilled resin should be applied to the surface of the cements as soon as matrix is removed. Any finishing that is required removes this protective layer.

GLASS IONOMER CEMENT MODIFICATIONS & THEIR APPLICATIONS

INTRODUCTION

Since these early materials, a number of modifications have become available. They are:

1. The use of alternative polymers, such as acrylic/maleic acid, as the polyacid component.
2. The use of dried polymer powders blended with the glass, and activated by the addition of water.
3. The development of cermet-containing cements, in which the filler consists of a cermet (i.e. a ceramic-metal hybrid, in this case being calcium fluoro alumino silicate glass fused to silver) rather than a pure glass. These materials are used in situations where radiopacity is required, and for core build-up under crowns.
4. Metal-reinforced cements, where a metal, such as Silver-tin alloy or stainless steel, is added to an otherwise conventional glass-ionomer in an attempt to reinforce the set cement

Resin-modified cements, in which the conventional Acid-base components are complemented with monomers and initiators capable of undergoing photochemical polymerization.

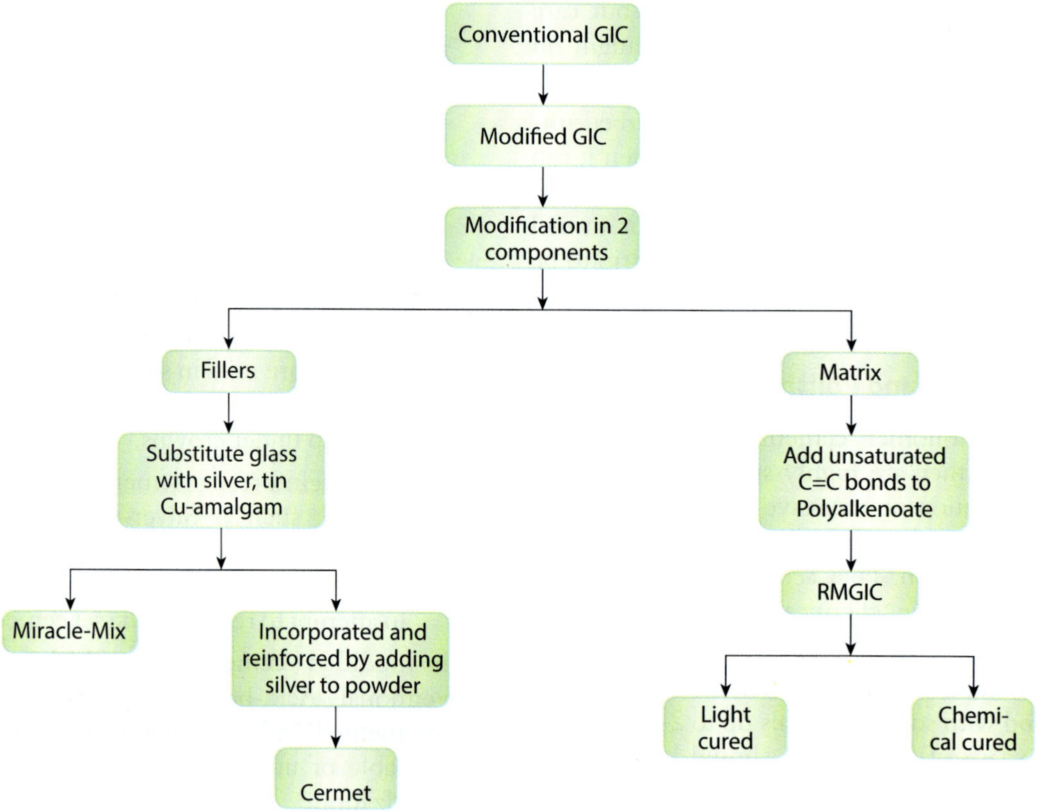

RESIN-MODIFIED GLASS IONOMERS AND RELATED MATERIALS

INTRODUCTION

The previous chapters have considered two of the most important groups of tooth coloured restoration materials.

- Composites.
- Glass ionomers.

Both of the products have advantages and disadvantages, which are summarized in following table. The properties of these materials dictate that no single material from either group is suitable for all applications on the part of the dentist, which takes account of the limitations of the products. It was recognized that if it were possible to combine the characteristics of the two types of product, it may be possible to advantageous properties of both materials. Whilst at the same time over coming some of the disadvantages. Early attempts at producing hybrid products involved blending together components of commercially available glass ionomer and composite materials to produce a material which, though no viable as a clinically usable product, demonstrated the possibility of combining two apparently dissimilar materials.

Table: 14.1. Summary of the advantage and disadvantages of composites and glass ionomer cements.

MATERIAL	ADVANTAGES	DISADVANTAGES
Composite	Strong tough	No inherent adhesion
	Insoluble	Shrinkage
	Radiopaque	No fluoride release
	Quick setting	
Glass ionomer	Inherent adhesion	Brittle
	Little shrinkage	Soluble
	Fluoride release	Not Radiopaque
	Biocompatible	Wear
		Water sensitive
		Slow setting

COMPOSITION & CLASSIFICATION

- An attempt has been made to further sub-divide products in these categories:
  - Modified composites
  - Resin modified glass ionomers.

MODIFIED COMPOSITES

INTRODUCTION

- These products are essentially resin-matrix composites in which the usual inert filler has been replaced by an ion-leachable alumino silicate glass in order to encourage fluoride release.

SETTING CHARACTERISTICS

- No-acid base reaction takes place during the setting of these materials.
- Setting in through free radial polymerization of methacrylate group (often light activated).
- In some materials the resin, in addition to the normal dimethacrylate components also contains acidic (normally alkenoic) groups in order to generate the possibility of an acid base reaction with the glass components.
- These products are often referred to as Acid modified composites.
- The term composer has also been used to describe these products.
- The primary setting reaction is still through polymerization of methacrylate groups in the resin component.
- Following setting through polymerization it is thought that some acid base reaction can occur as the resin takes up water and the acid groups become ionized.
- This process may enable the surface of the glass particles to react in order to liberate fluoride.

MODE OF SUPPLY

- Supplied as pre-mixed in small single close syringes.

Table: 14.2. Summary of the nature of the available materials.

MATERIAL	NUMBER REQUIRED	COMPONENTS MIXING	ACTIVE INGREDIENTS
Modified composites	1 or 2	2 components-yes	Fluoroalumino silicate glass.
		1 component-no	Methacrylate resin (acid
		(Components)	modified).
			Activators/initiators/stablizers
Resin-modified glass	2 or 3	Yes	Fluo or alumin osilicate glass
			Methacrylate polyacid
			Hydroxyethyl methacrylate
			(HEMA)
			Water
			Activators/initiatiors/stablizer

RESIN MODIFIED GLASS IONOMERS

INTRODUCTION

- These products are truly based on a hybrid of the two parent groups of materials.
- In their simplest form they consist of a powder and liquid which require mixing prior to activation of polymerization (often by light activation).

COMPOSITION

Powder	✦ Ion-Leachable glass
	✦ Initiator for light curing
	✦ Initiator for chemical curing
Liquid	a. Methacrylate Resin ✦ It enables setting to occur by polymerization.
	b. Polyacid ✦ It reacts with the ion-Leachable glass to bring about setting by an acid base Mechanism.
	c. Hydroxyethyl Methacrylate (Hema) ✦ A hydrophilic methacrylate which enables both the resin and acid components to coexist in aqueous solution, the HEMA also takes part in the polymerization reaction.
	d. WATER ✦ Which is an essential component required to allow ionization of the acid component so that the acid base reaction can occur.

SETTING REACTION

- When the powder and liquid components of the cement are mixed together the acid base reaction can begin immediately, as the acid groups are able to react with the glass in the presence of water.
- Polymerization takes over as the primary setting reaction as soon as sufficient free radicals become available to initiate the reaction.
- For light activated products this corresponds to the time at which light irradiation occurs.
- The light source used to activate polymerization is of the same type as that used for light activated composites.
- Polymerization involves the pendant methacrylate groups of the modified resin along with any free HEMA present in the liquid components.

NOTE

The glass components of both modified composites and resin modified glass ionomers have been modified in most materials in order to incorporate a heavy metal (e.g. Strontium) which imparts radiopacity.

SETTING CHARACTERISTICS

- The resin modified glass ionomers used for restoration applications are all light activated. Many do not possesses the long working time associated with light activated composites.
- There are three possible explanations for this behavior.

First

The acid base reaction proceeds immediately after mixing and before exposure to activating light.

Second

Many materials contain chemically activated polymerization to proceed before exposure to activating light.

Third

- Some materials are very sensitive to ambient visible light.
- In order to achieve acceptable results with these products it is best to carry out placement and shaping as soon as possible after mixing.
- The setting reaction in all cases is highly EXOTHERMIC and a temperature size of 10 C above ambient can be readily produced in a medium sized cavity.

PROPERTIES

1. PHYSICAL PROPERTIES

- The differences in properties of conventional GIC and resin modified GIC are due to lesser amount of water and carboxylic acid in the liquid.
- There is reduction in translucency of resin modified material due to the differences in the refractive index between the powder and set matrix.

2. STRENGTH

- Tensile strength of resin modified GICs is higher than conventional GIC due to greater plastic deformation that takes place before fracture occurs.

3. ADHESION

- They are used primarily as lines and bases. They have higher bound strength to composite.

CLINICAL HANDLING NOTES

- The handling characteristics and clinical techniques used for these materials are different to those for the conventional. GICs not the least because they become hard, as a consequence of the visible light activated reaction, well before the acid base reaction is complete.
- Matrix techniques are similar to those used for composites with transparent cellulose acetate or polyester strips on proximal surfaces.
- These materials are not as susceptible to desiccation as the chemically setting types and consequently surface finishing can be undertaken immediately after placement.

CERMETS

INTRODUCTION

- Cermets are essentially metal reinforced, glass ionomer cements (GIC).
- The metal used in the commercially available material is silver, although many other metals such as tin, gold, titanium and palladium have been tried.
- The cements powder is manufactured by mixing and then petting under pressure a mealier of glass and metal powder.
- The pellets are fused at around 800°C, then ground to fine powder
- The powder particles consist of regions of metal firmly bended to the glass

SETTING REACTION

- The setting reaction for cement material is identical to that for other glass ionomers,
- Because of presence of metallic phases within the materials they are gray in colour and therefore unsuitable for use as aesthetic restoration
- The presence of silver also imparts a degree of radiopacity to cermet materials which is not present in conventional glass ionomers
- The materials appear to have a greater value or compressive strength and fatigue limit than conventional glass ionomers. The flexural strength and resistance to abrasive wear appear to no better than values recorded for conventional glass ionomers.
- The Cermets based on silver have much lower fluoride release rate than equivalent conventional glass ionomers.

REFERENCES

1. Kenneth Anusavice (2012), Phillips' Science of Dental Materials, (12th ed.), Saunder.
2. Ronald Sakaguchi & John M.power(2011), Craig's Restorative Dental Materials, (13th ed.), Mosby
3. Richard Van Noort (2007), Introduction to Dental Materials, (3rd ed.), Mosby Ltd., China
4. B W Darvell (2009), Materials science for dentistry (9th ed.),Woodhead Publishing Limited, UK.
5. John M. Power & John C.wataha(2012),DENTAL MATERIALS Properties and Manipulation, (10th ed.), ELSEVIER, India
6. Gottfried Schmalz & Dorthe Arenholt-bindslev(2009), Biocompatibility of Dental Materials, Springer, Germany.

Chapter 15

DENTAL ADHESIVE SYSTEMS

Dr. Vesna Miletic

INTRODUCTION

Dental adhesive systems form an intermediate layer between the tooth and restoration, effectively bonding a resin-based restorative material or cement and hard dental tissues i.e enamel and dentine. Dental adhesives are based on a blend of resin monomers, mostly methacrylates and dimethacrylates. Adhesion to enamel and dentine is primarily based on "micro-mechanical interlocking" through superficial demineralisation of enamel and dentine followed by adhesive infiltration into the demineralised tissue though certain monomers are able to chemically bond to hydroxyapatite. This inter-phase formed by adhesive resin and tooth tissue is called the "hybrid layer". On the other side, the adhesive forms covalent bonds with monomers in resin-based composite or cement. Similarly to resin-based composites, adhesives also harden through the process of polymerization, which may be light or chemically-initiated. Most contemporary adhesives belong to the light-cured rather than chemically-cured materials. Some adhesives contain both photo-initiators and chemically curing initiators and are referred to as "dual-cured adhesives".

Dental adhesives are often referred to as "dentine bonding agents" or "dentine adhesives". This terminology most likely originates from the scientific focus being on dentine bonding which remains to be a challenge as opposed to enamel bonding, which proves to be reliable and durable following phosphoric acid etching and adhesive application. Since the adhesives are applied to enamel as well as to dentine, the term "dental adhesive system" or "dental adhesive" is more appropriate.

COMPOSITION

Dental adhesives consist of resin monomers, solvents, initiators, stabilizers and may contain fillers. There are three categories of resin monomers: functional, cross-linking and intermediary monomers. Functional monomers contain at least one acidic group, -COOH or $-H_2PO_3$. Their primary role is interaction with Ca ions from hydroxyapatite that leads to demineralisation. Functional monomers are also responsible for enhanced wetting and promoting adhesion into the substrate. Polymerizable methacrylate groups (C=C) allow functional monomers to become part of polymer chains. The so-called spacer groups between the methacrylate and acidic groups affect properties such as acidity, hydrophilicity, hydrolytical stability. Among the most common functional monomers are HEMA, 4-META, 10-MDP, Phenyl-P*.

Cross-linking monomers are mostly dimethacrylates, such as BisGMA, UDMA, TEGDMA and BisEMA**, which contain two polymerizable methacrylate groups (C=C). During polymerization, these monomers form cross-linked polymers which are responsible for mechanical properties of the adhesive. Cross-linking monomers are well solvated in organic solvents, ethanol and acetone, and only limitedly in water due to their hydrophobic nature. Cross-linking monomers are often used in conjunction to optimize monomer to polymer conversion rate, viscosity and flexibility.

Intermediary monomers, such as PENTA, PMGDM and Pyro-EMA*** phosphate, contain at least one acidic group and multiple polymerizable methacrylate groups. Acidic groups provide etching ability and multiple methacrylate groups contribute to cross-linkage.

Solvents are used to dissolve resin monomers and modulate properties such as viscosity and hydrophilicity which affect bonding to a hydrophilic substrate such as dentine. Improved wetting promotes adhesion through resin infiltration into the substrate and re-expansion of collagen fibrils following acid etching. This ultimately results in stronger bond to dentine. The most commonly used solvents in dental adhesives are ethanol, acetone and water. Water is also responsible for ionization of acidic functional monomers in self-etch adhesives that do not require the use of phosphoric acid for separate etching of enamel and dentine.

Initiators in dental adhesives are the same as those in resin-based composites and may be classified as photo-initiators or chemical initiators. The former are excited by blue light to produce free radicals required to start the polymerization reaction. The latter are chemical compounds whose admixture sets off the initiation reaction resulting in the formation of free radicals which then propagate polymerization. The most commonly used photo-initiator system is *camphorquinone* and *tertiary amine* which serves as a hydrogen donor exciting camphorquinone following light activation. Among other photo-initiators are phenyl-propanedione and monoacylphosphine oxide (Lucirin TPO). An important requirement of photo-initiators is that their absorption spectrum should match the emission spectrum of light-curing units. This is the case for camphorquinone which absorbs around 460 nm and corresponds practically to all light-curing units. In the case of camphorquinone/tertiary amine system, monomer to polymer conversion is dependent on the adhesive composition and total energy delivered to the adhesive by the light source and not the type of light source itself.

Alternative photo-initiators, phenyl-propanedione and Lucirin TPO, absorb around 400 nm which corresponds to halogen light-curing units but falls outside the emission

---

✦ HEMA - 2-hydroxyethyl methacrylate; 4-META - 4-methacryloyloxyethyl trimellitate anhydride; 10-MDP - 10- methacryloyloxydecyl dihydrogenphosphate; Phenyl-P - 2-(methacryloyloxyethyl)phenyl hydrogenphosphate

✦ BisGMA - bisphenol A diglycidyl methacrylate; UDMA - urethane dimethacrylate; TEGDMA - triethyleneglycol dimethacrylate; BisEMA - ethoxylated bisphenol A glycol dimethacrylate

✦ PENTA - dipentaerythritol pentaacrylate monophosphate; PMGDM - pyromellitic glycerol dimethacrylate; Pyro-EMA - tetramethacryloyloxyethyl pyrophosphate

spectra of most monowave LED units, which contain a single emission peak narrower than that of halogen units. More recent polywave LED light-curing units contain two emission peaks, one around 460 nm to match the absorption of camphorquinone and the other around 400 nm to match phenyl-propanedione, Lucirin TPO and similar alternative photo-initiators (Fig: 15.1). It has been shown that Lucirin TPO can be used instead of the camphorquinone/tertiary amine system in dental adhesives when cured with these compatible light sources.

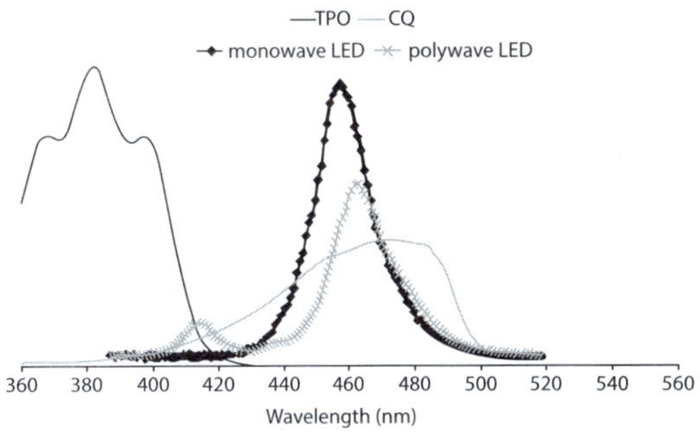

Fig: 15.1. Absorption spectra of photo-initiators camphorquinone and Lucirin TPO and emission spectra of a monowave and a polywave LED light-curing unit. There is no overlapping of the Lucirin TPO and monowave LED unit spectra. The additional peak around 410 nm in the spectrum of the polywave LED unit overlaps with the spectrum of Lucirin TPO.

Chemical initiators are used in separate systems and once mixed initiate the formation of free radicals and further polymerization reaction. The most frequent chemical initiators are benzoyl-peroxide with a tertiary amine coinitiator and tri-n-butyl borane which does not require a coinitiator. Both benzoyl-peroxide and tri-n-butyl borane are instable in water and are not suitable for water-containing adhesives.

Stabilizers or inhibitors are antioxidants added in minute quantities to prevent spontaneous formation of free radicals and further polymerization of dental adhesives. The most commonly used are butylated hydroxytoluene and monomethyl ether hydroquinone. These small quantities of stabilizers are negligible once light-induced or chemically-induced polymerization starts.

Fillers are used to improve mechanical properties and film thickness especially in acetone containing adhesives. Fillers are various forms of silicon-dioxide used in quantities much smaller than those in resin-based composites in order to maintain lower viscosity. Inter-fibrilar spaces among collagen fibrils in the demineralized dentine are believed to be of nano size. Only filler particles of the corresponding size may allow their penetration into the collagen network.

CLASSIFICATION

For many years, dental adhesives were classified according to generations. Besides being non-informative, there is an underlying implication of such classification that a more recent generation is better than previous ones. Numerous studies have shown *e.g.* bond strengths of 7th generation adhesives are inferior to those of 4th generation adhesives.

Current classification is based on adhesives composition and the number of application steps (Fig: 15.2).

- three-step etch-and-rinse adhesives;
- two-step etch-and-rinse adhesives;
- two-step self-etch adhesives;
- one-step self-etch adhesives

Fig: 15.2. Classification of dental adhesive systems.

Etch-and-rinse adhesives (also referred to as "total-etch" adhesives) are used with an acid, most commonly 35-37% phosphoric acid, which is applied first to enamel and dentine. Upon etching and rinsing away the acid, primer and bond are applied as separate steps (three-step etch-and-rinse) or as one solution (two-step etch-and-rinse). Phosphoric acid demineralises enamel and dentine, exposes collagen network and opens dentinal tubules (Fig: 15.3). Primer is used to enhance monomer infiltration into the etched substrate, re-expand collagen fibrils and bridge the hydrophilic dentine and hydrophobic adhesive resin present in the overlying bond.

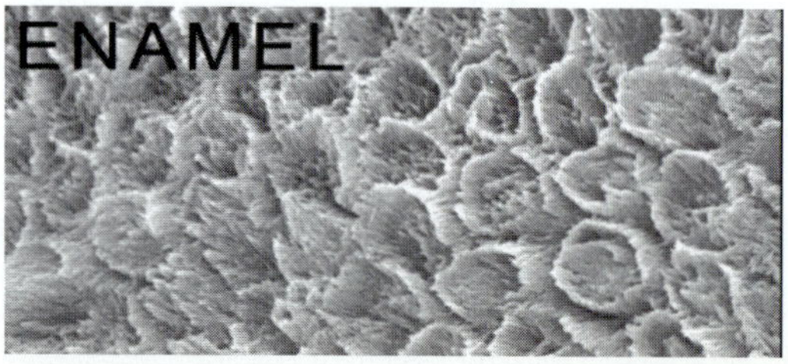

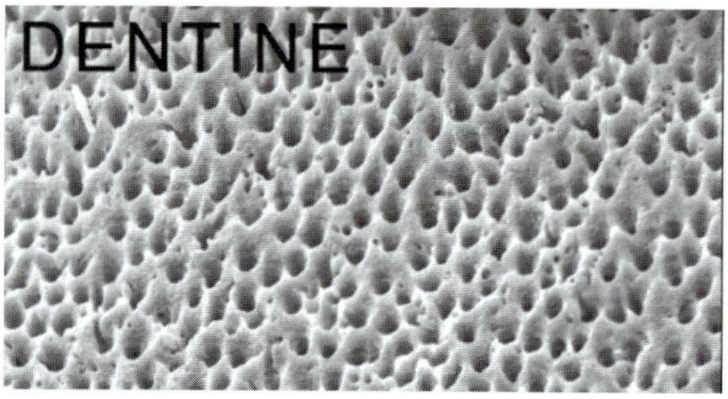

Fig: 15.3. Enamel and dentine etched with phosphoric acid.

Self-etch adhesives contain acidic monomers able to demineralise enamel and dentine without the prior use of phosphoric acid. In two-step self-etch adhesives, a self-etching primer is applied as a separate, non-rinsing step followed by the application of a bonding agent. In one-step self-etch adhesives, all ingredients are mixed in one bottle and applied as a single step. Self-etch adhesives differ in pH due to differences in the acidity of self-etching monomers which affects the etching depth in the dental substrate. Based on pH values, self-etch adhesives are classified as "strong" ($pH < 1$), "intermediately strong" (pH 1-2), "mild" ($pH \sim 2$) and "ultra-mild" ($pH > 2.5$).

The aforementioned classification is more informative than "generations" as it is clear how many steps are involved in the clinical procedure. Furthermore, information regarding the composition is clearer, e.g. it is evident whether an adhesive system is based on phosphoric acid etching or self-etching monomers.

APPLICATION PROTOCOLS

There are two main application protocols for contemporary dental adhesive systems – (1) etch-and-rinse or total-etch and (2) self-etch protocol. The following are the most common recommendations. Manufacturers' instructions should be followed in any particular case.

1. ETCH-AND-RINSE PROTOCOL

a. Application of the 34-37% phosphoric acid in the form of gel to enamel at cavity margins;

b. After 15 s, the gel is applied to dentine of the entire cavity and left in place for 15 s. In this way, enamel is etched for 30 s and dentine for 15 s. Although etching times may vary in different systems, most commonly recommended etching times are 15-30 s for enamel and 10-15 s for dentine;

c. The gel is then rinsed with air-water spray for 5-15 s depending on the manufacturer's recommendation;

d. The cavity is then dried using oil- and water-free compressed air. This phase is critical since it is important to thoroughly dry enamel but overdrying dentine ("dry bonding") results in the collapse of collagen fibrils and significant reduction of resin-dentine bond strengths. Therefore, "wet bonding" procedure is recommended although no manufacturer states clearly how this should be achieved for their particular adhesive. It is often stated to use mild air spray, a foam pellet or other suitable absorbent in order to achieve a glossy wet surface of dentine. It is clear that the drying phase presents the greatest risk of failure in this application protocol, because of the vague explanation and the unknown effect of drying in vivo;

i. *In three-step etch-and-rinse adhesives,* the primer is applied as a separate step by brushing or rubbing the entire etched cavity usually for about 5-15 s. Either one or two coats may be recommended. The intention with the separate priming step is to completely replace the water in inter-fibrillar spaces of the exposed collagen network by infiltration of hydrophilic monomers such as HEMA. The primer may also re-expand the collapsed collagen network. The primer is dried for 5-15 seconds until there is no movement of the material in the cavity. This allows the layer to become thinner and enhances solvent removal, although more than half of the solvent is likely to remain *in situ*.

The adhesive bond is applied over the primed surface of the cavity by brushing or rubbing usually for about 5-15 seconds. After drying for about 5 seconds which creates a thinner layer and prevents pooling in the cavity, the adhesive system is light-cured for 10-20 seconds depending on the light source and the curing distance. If the light-curing unit operates at an intensity less than 700 mW/cm^2 or the distance between the light-tip and the cavity surface is 10 mm or more, light curing should be done for 20 seconds. Polymerization of the adhesive bond on top of the primer creates a chemical bond between the two and allows a three-dimensional cross-linkage to be formed by dimethacrylate monomers such as BisGMA, UDMA and TEGDMA.

ii. In two-step etch-and-rinse adhesives, the primer-bond mixture provided in one bottle is applied as a single step by brushing or rubbing the entire cavity for about 10-20 seconds. Agitated motion is sometimes recommended. The adhesive is then dried for about 5 seconds similarly to the aforementioned three-step adhesives, and then light-cured for 10-20 seconds. (Fig: 15.4).

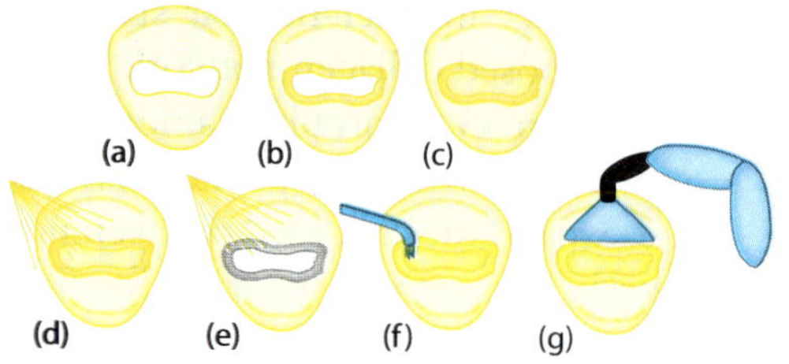

Fig: 15.4. General application protocol for two-step etch-and-rinse adhesives. (A) Prepared cavity; (B) Phosphoric acid on cavity margins - enamel; (C) Phosphoric acid in entire cavity - dentine; (D) Rinsing with water jet spray; (E) Drying with compressed air; (F) Application of adhesive to the entire cavity; (G) Light curing.

2. SELF-ETCH PROTOCOL

a. No acid etching is involved.

b.

i. *In two-step self-etch adhesives*, self-etching primer is applied to the entire cavity. The application itself may be recommended to last for a certain period, e.g. 20 seconds or it may be recommended to leave the primer in place for this time before air drying. This time is required for self-etching monomers to dissolve hydroxyapatite from surface and subsurface parts of enamel and dentine. Hydroxyapatite may be removed entirely or partially from these few microns, partially meaning that some hydroxyapatite crystals are left in situ. This process is dependent on the acidic capacity (pH) of the self-etching primer.

The primer is dried to a thin, immobile layer with oil- and water-free compressed air for a few seconds, usually with moderate air pressure;

Bonding agent is then applied over the primed surface and air-dried;

The adhesive system is light-cured for 10-20 s depending on the light source and curing distance. If the light-curing unit operates at intensity less than 700 mW/cm^2 or the distance between the light-tip and the cavity surface is 10 mm or more, light curing should be done for 20 s (Fig: 15.5). *In the case of Filtek Silorane, the primer and bonding agent are cured separately.*

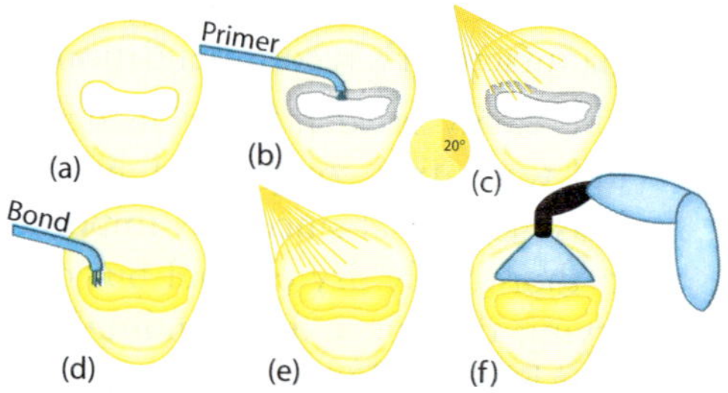

Fig: 15.5. General application protocol for two-step self-etch adhesives. (A) Prepared cavity; (B) Application of primer to the entire cavity - enamel and dentine; (C) Air-drying of primer; (D) Application of bond to the entire cavity - enamel and dentine; (D) Air-drying of bond; (F) Light curing.

ii. *In one-step self-etch adhesives,* one drop of adhesive is dispensed into a dispensing well and applied using an applicator brush to the entire cavity. Some adhesives have components separated in two bottles or uni-dose tips in which case these are mixed before application. The application itself may be recommended to last for e.g. 20 seconds or it may be recommended to leave the adhesive in place, undisturbed for this time prior to air-drying. One or two coats may be recommended.

During this time, etching of enamel and dentine and infiltration of the adhesive resin occur simultaneously.

The adhesive is dried for few seconds using gentle to maximum air-pressure, depending on manufacturers' instructions, to form a thin layer with no visible movement of the adhesive and to avoid pooling in the cavity corners;

The adhesive is light-cured for 10-20 seconds depending on the light source and curing distance.

3. SELECTIVE-ETCH PROTOCOL

This protocol is based on the advantages of both the etch-and-rinse and self-etch protocols. Essentially, enamel is etched with phosphoric acid and self-etch adhesive is applied to the entire cavity i.e. the acid-etched enamel and non-etched dentine. Both two-step and one-step self-etch adhesives may be applied using the selective-etch protocol.

a. 34-37% phosphoric acid in the form of gel is applied to enamel at cavity margins and left to react for 10-15 s, according to manufacturer's instructions;
b. the gel is rinsed with air-water spray and the cavity is gently air-dried (but not over-dried) with air or cotton-pellets;
c. self-etch adhesive is applied to the entire cavity according to the self-etch protocol;
d. The adhesive is light-cured for 10-20 s depending on the light source and curing distance (Fig: 15.6).

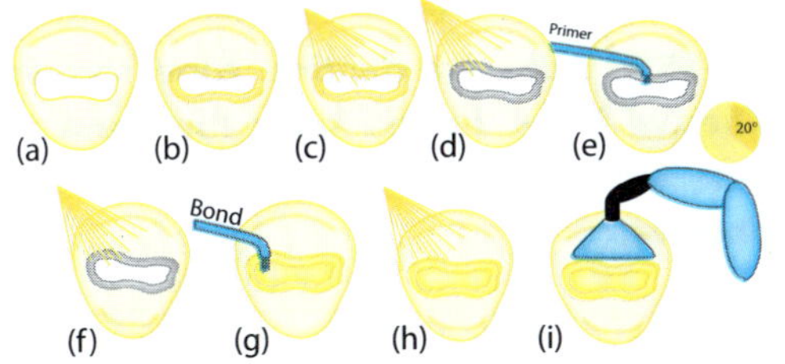

Fig: 15.6. General selective-etch protocol for two-step self-etch adhesives. (A) Prepared cavity; (B) Phosphoric acid on cavity margins - enamel; (C) Rinsing with water jet spray; (D) Drying with compressed air; (E) Application of primer to the entire cavity - enamel and dentine; (F) Air-drying of primer; (G) Application of bond to the entire cavity - enamel and dentine; (H) Air-drying of bond; (I) Light curing.

ADHESIVE INTERACTION WITH ENAMEL AND DENTINE

Etching tooth tissues with phosphoric acid or acidic monomers involves removal of the smear layer as well as mineral component, hydroxyapatite, from the surface and subsurface of enamel and dentine. Following acid etching or simultaneously with etching by acidic monomers, adhesive resin penetrates into the etched prisms and inter-prismatic spaces of enamel or exposed collagen network, partially demineralised dentine and open dentinal tubules. Light-curing of the adhesive results in the formation of an adhesive-enamel and adhesive-dentine zone consisting of two or three microscopically distinctive parts:

Adhesive Layer - is formed purely by adhesive resin and varies in thickness from a few microns to several tens of microns;

Hybrid Layer - consists of adhesive resin and encapsulated enamel prisms or collagen fibrils and partially demineralised hydroxyapatite crystals in dentine and varies in thickness from less than half a micron in ultra-mild to about 8 microns in etch-and-rinse adhesives. In general, etch-and-rinse adhesives form the thickest and one-step self-etch adhesives the thinnest hybrid layers. This layer is also known as the "inter-diffusion zone". The hybrid layer in dentine is considered by Pashley et al. "a unique form of tissue engineering" created *in situ* with collagen fibrils and inter-fibrillar spaces serving as a natural scaffold with 1000 times smaller porosities compared to most artificial scaffolds.

Resin Tags – formed in dentinal tubules, may be up to a few hundred microns long. Resin tags of etch-and-rinse adhesive are conically shaped and may form lateral branches (Fig: 15.7). whereas those of self-etch adhesives appear as rod-like structures of uniform thickness and fewer if any lateral branches (Fig: 15.8). Such characteristic appearance of resin tags is a consequence of stronger etching by phosphoric acid which removes hydroxyapatite to a greater extent than weaker acidic monomers in self-etch adhesives from the orifice and immediate inner zones of dentinal tubules and open lateral canals between them, which are subsequently filled by adhesive resin.

The primary mechanism involved in adhesive bonding to enamel and dentine is the mechanical inter-locking within the hybrid layer. Another mechanism is the chemical bonding of some acidic functional monomers with Ca ions from hydroxyapatite according to the "adhesion-decalcification (AD) concept" proposed by Yoshida et al. According to the AD-concept, phosphoric acids and acidic groups from self-etching monomers ionically bond with hydroxyapatite Ca ions to form Ca salts. Whether this ionic bond will remain stable or will debond depends on the hydrolytic stability of the formed Ca salt. In the former case, only limited decalcification occurs whereas in the latter case surface is decalcified to a much greater extent of several microns with the exposure of collagen fibrils. An example of the acidic functional monomer capable of forming a stable ionic bond with Ca ions from enamel and dentine is 10-methacryloyloxydecyl dihydrogen phosphate (10-MDP). On the other hand, phosphoric acid interacts with enamel and dentine hydroxyapatite by forming an unstable bond which quickly debonds removing the superficial Ca ions and leaving the typical etched pattern.

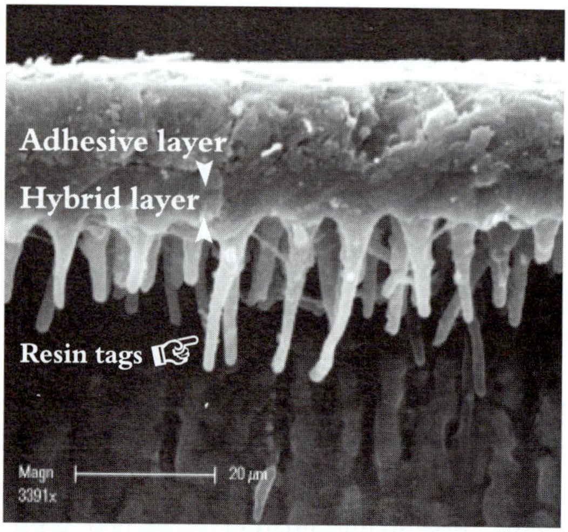

Fig: 15.7. Adhesive-dentine zone showing adhesive layer, hybrid layer (between the white arrows) and resin tags of an etch-and-rinse adhesive.

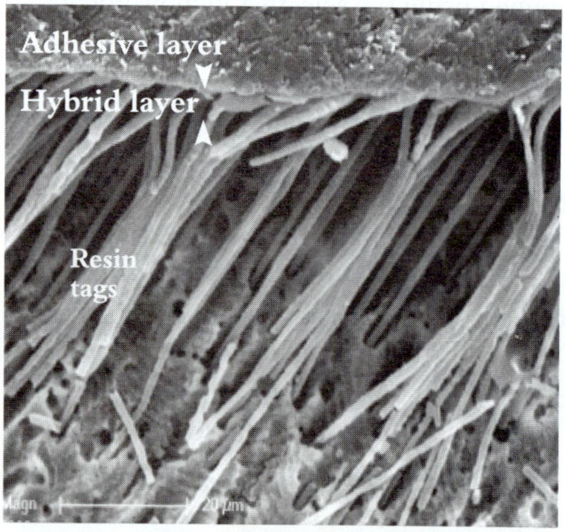

Fig: 15.8. Adhesive-dentine zone showing adhesive layer, hybrid layer (between the white arrows) and resin tags of a self-etch adhesive.

1. ENAMEL BONDING

Enamel bonding is considered reliable in contemporary clinical practice. This is attributed to the absence of collagen and negligible amount of water compared to dentine. Studies have shown superior bond strengths of etch-and-rinse adhesives to enamel compared to dentine. Regarding bond strength values, self-etch adhesives have not shown such a distinctive trend towards superior bonding to enamel than dentine. Some adhesives produce higher bond strength to enamel whereas the substrate has no effect on bond strength values for others. Marginal integrity assessment through dye penetration tests have also confirmed that adhesives are more capable of sealing enamel than dentine. Enamel-adhesive interface is associated with less leakage and often is found to be leakage-free.

Etch-and-rinse adhesives produce higher bond strengths to enamel compared to self-etch adhesives. These are associated with more profound etching of enamel with phosphoric acid compared to acidic monomers contained in self-etching primers or one-step self-etch adhesives. Following deeper removal of enamel hydroxyapatite, subsequent adhesive infiltration of the etched surface results in the formation of thicker hybrid layer by etch-and-rinse adhesives. It has been suggested that enamel bonding with etch-and-rinse adhesives is reliable in the long term and is considered important for maintaining the adhesive-dentine bond.

Self-etch adhesives have shown greater variability regarding bond strengths and the durability of enamel-adhesive bond compared to etch-and-rinse adhesives. Generally, two-step self-etch adhesives produce higher enamel bond strengths than one-step self-etch adhesives. In line with lower bond strength, the mode of failure is predominantly adhesive at the adhesive-enamel interface compared to more mixed failures involving parts of composite resin or the substrate observed for two-step self-etch adhesives. Self-etch adhesives bond to the substrate through the smear layer modification, dissociation or dissolution. Their bonding strategy is based on the ability of the acidic monomers to interact with hydroxyapatite. The acidity as well as the stability of ionic bonding to Ca from hydroxyapatite influence the ability of acidic monomers to create the etched pattern within enamel (as well as dentine) favourable for strong and durable bond. Self-etch adhesives produce significantly higher bond strengths to ground than unground enamel. The absence of the regular micro-retentive surface can be observed in ultrastructural studies using electron microscopy techniques. Inferior bonding to unground enamel is associated with the inability of acidic monomers to create such effective demineralization and retentive surface as phosphoric acid. Superficial aprismatic layer in unground or uncut enamel acts as a barrier to the adhesive infiltration. Removal of this layer by grinding with silicone-carbide paper or diamond bur enables deeper adhesive penetration, especially in bur-cut enamel. Subsequent polymerization of adhesive resin provides firm micro-mechanical interlocking required for durable seal. It is, therefore, recommended to roughen uncut enamel prior to the application of self-etch adhesives in the clinical practice.

Another strategy to improve enamel bonding of self-etch adhesives, particularly one-step systems, is to apply phosphoric acid etching prior to adhesive application. It has been shown that this approach leads to significantly higher bond strengths compared to the use of self-etch adhesives alone. Ultrastructural investigation using transmission electron microscopy revealed a characteristic retentive pattern with distinctive macro- and micro-tags. On the other hand, etching dentine with phosphoric acid prior to the application of self-etch adhesives does not improve bonding efficiency to dentine. Similar or lower immediate bond strength to dentine was reported for the total-etch compared to the self-etch protocol. "Therefore, extending one- and two-step self-etch adhesives to multi-mode systems involving only enamel etching with phosphoric acid has become the so-called "selective etch" approach.

2. DENTINE BONDING

Bonding to dentine is considered more clinically challenging and unpredictable than enamel bonding for both etch-and-rinse and self-etch adhesives. The presence of collagen and water are the main factors associated with inferior bonding efficiency to dentine than enamel.

Hybrid layer is considered the weakest link of the tooth-restoration bond. Fractures at the adhesive-dentine interface, or 'adhesive' failures, occur predominantly in the hybrid layer (Fig: 15.9).

There are numerous in vitro studies on immediate and long-term bond strength of adhesives to dentine. Since there is a great variation in methodological approaches, it is often difficult, if not impossible, to compare studies from different research groups. Even more than a decade ago, Leloup et al. expressed their concern regarding the lack of standardized methodology for bond strength testing in an extensive meta-analysis of the then available literature. They reported discrepancies in bond strength values for the same products among different research groups as well as large standard deviations.

Leloup et al. classified factors that affect dentine bonding into four groups: (1) dentine substrate, (2) adhesive and composite, (3) storage conditions and (4) testing conditions. Origin and type of teeth, simulated pulpal pressure, type of adhesive and composite, storage solution and type of test all significantly influenced bond strength values. Conversely, occlusal versus non-occlusal dentine location and thermocycling did not affect bond strength. Higher mean

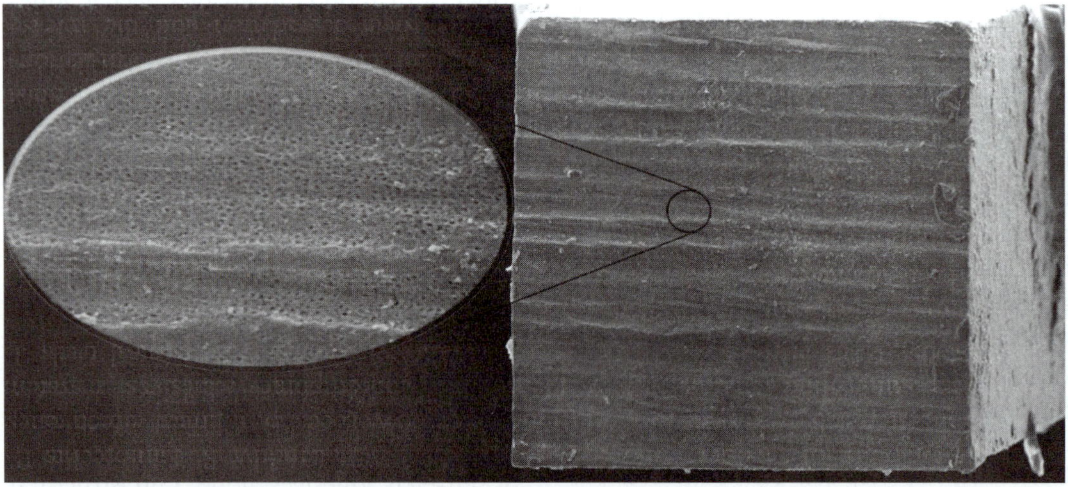

Fig: 15.9. 'Adhesive' fracture/failure of the adhesive-dentine bond. Scratches across the surface originate from sample preparation with a diamond bur. Zoomed part shows open dentinal tubules indicating that the fracture occurred within and at the bottom of the hybrid layer.

bond strength values were reported for etch-and-rinse adhesives compared to previous systems which only modified or dissolved the smear layer. Furthermore, a positive correlation was established between bond strength and cohesive failures meaning that higher bond strength values were associated with greater occurrence of cohesive failures within the substrate or composite resin.

The latest meta-analysis of the parameters involved in dentine bonding was published in 2012 by De Munck et al. Not only did the authors cover the most recent studies including contemporary adhesive systems, they created 'artificial neural networks' as a computational tool to predict the outcome of tests e.g. bond strength values of adhesive systems. Two most important factors involved in dentine bonding identified by the artificial neural networks were 'research group' and 'adhesive'. The least important factors seem to be 'storage time', thermo-cycling' and 'adhesive age'. It is likely that 'research group' has such a great importance on bond strength testing because it encompasses several other factors such as testing conditions (type of test, crosshead speed) and substrate (origin, storage time and temperature, sectioning, preparation, pulpal pressure) which were singled out in the previous meta-analysis by Leloup et al.

The highest immediate bond strength to dentine with values exceeding 40 MPa has been reported for three-step etch-and-rinse and two-step self-etch adhesives. Their simplified counterparts, two-step etch-and-rinse and especially one-step self-etch adhesives have shown substantially lower bonding efficiency. One-step self-etch adhesives consistently produced the lowest mean bond strength values of about 20 MPa. Following artificial aging i.e. at least six months of water storage, two-step self-etch adhesives have had the most resistant dentine bonding whereas all other adhesive classes appeared prone to degradation processes that lowered bond strength. Among the adhesive brands, Optibond FL (3-step etch-and-rinse; Kerr) and Clearfil SE Bond (2-step self-etch; Kuraray) have shown the highest strength values and most resistant dentine bonding. It is interesting to notice that although self-adhesive composites are not adhesives *per se*, they are sometimes classified as 0-step self-etch adhesives. More importantly, these materials have shown inferior dentine bonding than one-step self-etch adhesives, mean bond strength of around 10 MPa and great variability of the obtained values.

The results of numerous in vitro studies indicating inferior dentine (and enamel) bonding of one-step self-etch adhesives are corroborated with clinical data. A meta-analysis by Peumans et al. comprised 85 clinical studies reporting on clinical bonding effectiveness of dental adhesives in non-carious class V lesions. The pool of data shows that the mean annual failure rate of three-step etch-and-rinse and two-step self-etch adhesives is below 5%. Their simplified counterparts have shown less reliable clinical effectiveness expressed as higher annual failure rates. In particular, inferior clinical performance has been associated with one-step self-etch adhesives whose mean value is about 8% but standard deviation varies greatly (11.3%).

It is clear that simplifying clinical procedure and reducing the number of application steps for dental adhesives reduces the risk of manipulation mistakes by clinicians. This is probably the single most important driving force for manufacturers to keep one-step self-etch adhesives on the market in spite of the clear evidence of their substandard performance both in vitro and in vivo. Dentists should be aware of the advantages and disadvantages of all adhesive classes in order to make a proper selection for their everyday practice. Careful procedure and meticulous attention to detail should be followed in case of multiple-step application which ensures the best and long-lasting results.

DEGRADATION OF ADHESIVE-TOOTH BOND

Adhesive-tooth bonds, particularly the one with dentine, degrade over time compromising the clinical performance of a restoration. Numerous in vitro studies have shown reduced bond strengths of most adhesives after several months to several years of aging. Generally speaking, water degradation is more important for the loss of bonding effectiveness than thermal cycling.

Although adhesive-enamel bond is more resistant to degradation than adhesive-dentine bond, theoretically the same degradation processes may occur as in composite resins. Oral fluids, mainly water, enzymes and bacterial by-products are involved in various degradation processes.

Two main mechanisms of water degradation are hydrolysis and plasticization although oxidation of pendant C=C double bond in the polymer was also reported. Hydrolysis occurs in resin-based materials due to the presence of ester groups –COO that link the methacrylate group $CH_2=CH_2$ with the rest of the monomer molecule. Plasticization occurs due to water penetration into the matrix and subsequent expansion of intermolecular spaces. This expansion results in reduced frictional forces between polymer chains and the so-called *'swelling'* of polymer chains.

Salivary enzymes, for example cholesterol esterase, have shown the potential to hydrolyze ester bonds within the polymer. However, the required levels of these enzymes for degradation of adhesive-enamel bond are still unknown.

DEGRADATION OF ADHESIVE-DENTINE BOND

There are additional processes involved in the degradation of adhesive-dentine bond due to the presence of intricate collagen network in the substrate. Pashley et al. reported on the potential of host-derived enzymes matrix metalloproteinase (MMPs) to degrade collagen, incompletely infiltrated and encapsulated by adhesive resin.

MMPs belong to the group of endogenous dentine proteases. Among these, MMP-2, -3, -8, -9 and -20, activated upon dentine etching with phosphoric acid are thought to slowly break down exposed insoluble collagen fibrils to smaller soluble fragments called *gelatin peptides*. Further dissolution of gelatin peptides lead to the discontinuity within the hybrid layer and loss of retention. Non-encapsulated collagen fibrils are localized in the bottom parts of the hybrid layer. Exposure of non-encapsulated collagen fibrils occurs due to deeper dentine demineralization by acid etching than subsequent adhesive infiltration as reported by Santini and Miletic. This discrepancy was found to be virtually non-existing in the case of self-etch adhesives. Another contributing factor is that monomer to polymer conversion is compromised within the hybrid layer, most likely due to the presence of water and residual solvent. Degree of conversion values are significantly lower in the hybrid layer than in the adhesive layer resulting in a pool of leachable monomers. Also, outward fluid movement from dentinal tubules towards the hybrid layer is thought to prevent resin infiltration and encapsulation of exposed collagen fibrils.

MMPs have been identified and visualized using zymography within the hybrid layer of etch-and-rinse adhesives as well as inside dentinal tubules. Most recent study by Mazzoni et al. has shown that self-etch adhesives are also capable of activating MMPs in dentine, albeit to a lesser extent than etch-and-rinse adhesives.

Cysteine cathepsins have been identified in dentine as another group of endogenous enzymes with the potential to degrade collagen fibrils. Cathepsins originating from the pulp are also active in carious lesions, especially in deep and active lesions. The mechanism of collagen degradation by cysteine cathepsins is the cleavage or severing collagen triple helix or telopeptide extensions. The role of these enzymes in the degradation of adhesive-dentine bond is not yet fully investigated.

Potential strategies to eliminate the adverse effects of MMPs and cathepsins are still in the laboratory phase. These strategies include but are not limited to (1) inhibition using specific (galardin) or non-specific inhibitors (chlorhexidine); (2) inactivation with cross-linking agents (glutaraldehyde, proanthocyanidins, carbodiimide) and (3) chelation with metal ions (Ca, Zn). The listed agents may be used to treat dentine directly or may be added to dentine conditioners and primers. However, future research will shed more light into their potential use and effectiveness in clinical conditions.

REFERENCES

1. Nakabayashi N, Kojima K, Masuhara E. The promotion of adhesion by the infiltration of monomers into tooth substrates. J Biomed Mater Res 1982;16:265-273.
2. Yoshihara K, Yoshida Y, Hayakawa S, Nagaoka N, Irie M, Ogawa T, Van Landuyt KL, Osaka A, Suzuki K, Minagi S, Van Meerbeek B. Nanolayering of phosphoric acid ester monomer on enamel and dentin. Acta Biomater 2011;7:3187-3195.
3. Nakabayashi N, Pashley DH. Hybridization of dental hard tissues. Tokyo: Quintessence Publishing Co, Ltd; 1998.
4. Peutzfeldt A. Resin composites in dentistry: the monomer systems. Eur J Oral Sci 1997;105:97-116.
5. Gwinnett AJ, Kanca JA, 3rd. Micromorphology of the bonded dentin interface and its relationship to bond strength. Am J Dent 1992;5:73-77.
6. Moszner N, Salz U, Zimmermann J. Chemical aspects of self-etching enamel-dentin adhesives: A systematic review. Dent Mater 2005;21:895-910.
7. Santini A. Current status of visible light activation units and the curing of light-activated resin-based composite materials. Dent Update 2010;37:214-216, 218-220, 223-227.
8. Miletic V, Santini A. Micro-raman assessment of the ratio of carbon-carbon double bonds of two adhesive systems cured with LED or halogen light-curing units. J Adhes Dent 2010;12:461-467.
9. Arikawa H, Takahashi H, Kanie T, Ban S. Effect of various visible light photoinitiators on the polymerization and color of light-activated resins. Dent Mater J 2009;28:454-460.
10. Miletic V, Santini A. Micro-Raman spectroscopic analysis of the degree of conversion of composite resins containing different initiators cured by polywave or monowave LED units. J Dent 2012;40:106-113.
11. Ilie N, Hickel R. Can CQ be completely replaced by alternative initiators in dental adhesives? Dent Mater J 2008;27:221-228.
12. Van Meerbeek B, Dhem A, Goret-Nicaise M, Braem M, Lambrechts P,

VanHerle G. Comparative SEM and TEM examination of the ultrastructure of the resin-dentin interdiffusion zone. J Dent Res 1993;72:495-501.

13. Kugel G, Ferrari M. The science of bonding: from first to sixth generation. J Am Dent Assoc 2000;131 Suppl:20S-25S.
14. De Munck J, Van Landuyt K, Peumans M, Poitevin A, Lambrechts P, Braem M, Van Meerbeek B. A critical review of the durability of adhesion to tooth tissue: methods and results. J Dent Res 2005;84:118-132.
15. Van Meerbeek B, Yoshihara K, Yoshida Y, Mine A, De Munck J, Van Landuyt KL. State of the art of self-etch adhesives. Dent Mater 2011;27:17-28.
16. Yiu CK, Pashley EL, Hiraishi N, King NM, Goracci C, Ferrari M, Carvalho RM, Pashley DH, Tay FR. Solvent and water retention in dental adhesive blends after evaporation. Biomaterials 2005;26:6863-6872.
17. Santini A, Miletic V. Comparison of the hybrid layer formed by Silorane adhesive, one-step self-etch and etch and rinse systems using confocal micro-Raman spectroscopy and SEM. J Dent 2008;36:683-691.
18. Santini A, Milia E, Miletic V. A review of SEM and TEM studies on the hybridisation of dentine. In: Méndez-Vilas A, editor. Microscopy: Science, Technology, Applications and Education. Spain; Formatex; 2010. p. 256-268.
19. Pashley DH, Tay FR, Breschi L, Tjaderhane L, Carvalho RM, Carrilho M, Tezvergil-Mutluay A. State of the art etch-and-rinse adhesives. Dent Mater 2011;27:1-16.
20. Miletic V. Micro-Raman spectroscopic studies on the adhesive-dentine interface and the degree of conversion of dental adhesives [Ph.D. thesis]. Edinburgh: The University of Edinburgh; 2010.
21. Yoshida Y, Van Meerbeek B, Nakayama Y, Yoshioka M, Snauwaert J, Abe Y, Lambrechts P, Vanherle G, Okazaki M. Adhesion to and decalcification of hydroxyapatite by carboxylic acids. J Dent Res 2001;80:1565-1569.
22. Goracci C, Sadek FT, Monticelli F, Cardoso PE, Ferrari M. Microtensile bond strength of self-etching adhesives to enamel and dentin. J Adhes Dent 2004;6:313-318.
23. Yazici AR, Celik C, Ozgunaltay G, Dayangac B. Bond strength of different adhesive systems to dental hard tissues. Oper Dent 2007;32:166-172.
24. Santini A, Ivanovic V, Ibbetson R, Milia E. Influence of cavity configuration on microleakage around Class V restorations bonded with seven self-etching adhesives. J Esthet Restor Dent 2004;16:128-135; discussion 136.
25. Rosales-Leal JI. Microleakage of Class V composite restorations placed with etch-and-rinse and self-etching adhesives before and after thermocycling. J Adhes Dent 2007;9 Suppl 2:255-259.
26. De Munck J, Van Meerbeek B, Satoshi I, Vargas M, Yoshida Y, Armstrong S, Lambrechts P, Vanherle G. Microtensile bond strengths of one- and two-step self-etch adhesives to bur-cut enamel and dentin. Am J Dent 2003;16:414-420.
27. Abdalla AI, Feilzer AJ. Four-year water degradation of a total-etch and two self-etching adhesives bonded to dentin. J Dent 2008;36:611-617.
28. Reis A, Moura K, Pellizzaro A, Dal-Bianco

K, de Andrade AM, Loguercio AD. Durability of enamel bonding using one-step self-etch systems on ground and unground enamel. Oper Dent 2009;34:181-191.

29. Gregoire G, Ahmed Y. Evaluation of the enamel etching capacity of six contemporary self-etching adhesives. J Dent 2007;35:388-397.

30. Moura SK, Pelizzaro A, Dal Bianco K, de Goes MF, Loguercio AD, Reis A, Grande RH. Does the acidity of self-etching primers affect bond strength and surface morphology of enamel? J Adhes Dent 2006;8:75-83.

31. Mine A, De Munck J, Vivan Cardoso M, Van Landuyt KL, Poitevin A, Kuboki T, Yoshida Y, Suzuki K, Van Meerbeek B. Enamel-smear compromises bonding by mild self-etch adhesives. J Dent Res 2010;89:1505-1509.

32. Van Landuyt KL, Peumans M, De Munck J, Lambrechts P, Van Meerbeek B. Extension of a one-step self-etch adhesive into a multi-step adhesive. Dent Mater 2006;22:533-544.

33. Hanabusa M, Mine A, Kuboki T, Momoi Y, Van Ende A, Van Meerbeek B, De Munck J. Bonding effectiveness of a new 'multi-mode' adhesive to enamel and dentine. J Dent 2012;40:475-484.

34. Leloup G, D'Hoore W, Bouter D, Degrange M, Vreven J. Meta-analytical review of factors involved in dentin adherence. J Dent Res 2001;80:1605-1614.

35. De Munck J, Mine A, Poitevin A, Van Ende A, Cardoso MV, Van Landuyt KL, Peumans M, Van Meerbeek B. Meta-analytical review of parameters involved in dentin bonding. J Dent Res 2012;91:351-357.

36. Peumans M, Kanumilli P, De Munck J, Van Landuyt K, Lambrechts P, Van Meerbeek B. Clinical effectiveness of contemporary adhesives: a systematic review of current clinical trials. Dent Mater 2005;21:864-881.

37. Hashimoto M, Ohno H, Kaga M, Endo K, Sano H, Oguchi H. In vivo degradation of resin-dentin bonds in humans over 1 to 3 years. J Dent Res 2000;79:1385-1391.

38. Santerre J, Shajii L, Leung BW. Relation of dental composite formulations to their degradation and the release of hydrolyzed polymeric-resin-derived products. Crit Rev Oral Biol Med 2001;12:136-151.

39. Finer Y, Santerre JP. The influence of resin chemistry on a dental composite's biodegradation. J Biomed Mater Res A 2004;69:233-246.

40. Oysaed H, Ruyter IE, Sjovik Kleven IJ. Release of formaldehyde from dental composites. J Dent Res 1988;67:1289-1294.

41. Pashley DH, Tay FR, Yiu C, Hashimoto M, Breschi L, Carvalho RM, Ito S. Collagen degradation by host-derived enzymes during aging. J Dent Res 2004;83:216-221.

42. Santini A, Miletic V. Quantitative micro-Raman assessment of dentine demineralization, adhesive penetration, and degree of conversion of three dentine bonding systems. Eur J Oral Sci 2008;116:177-183.

43. Miletic V, Santini A, Trkulja I. Quantification of monomer elution and carbon-carbon double bonds in dental adhesive systems using HPLC and micro-Raman spectroscopy. J Dent 2009;37:177-184.

44. Hashimoto M, Ito S, Tay FR, Svizero

NR, Sano H, Kaga M, Pashley DH. Fluid movement across the resin-dentin interface during and after bonding. J Dent Res 2004;83:843-848.

45. Mazzoni A, Nascimento FD, Carrilho M, Tersariol I, Papa V, Tjaderhane L, Di Lenarda R, Tay FR, Pashley DH, Breschi L. MMP activity in the hybrid layer detected with in situ zymography. J Dent Res 2012;91:467-472.

46. Mazzoni A, Scaffa P, Carrilho M, Tjaderhane L, Di Lenarda R, Polimeni A, Tezvergil-Mutluay A, Tay FR, Pashley DH, Breschi L. Effects of etch-and-rinse and self-etch adhesives on dentin MMP-2 and MMP-9. J Dent Res 2013;92:82-86.

47. Tersariol IL, Geraldeli S, Minciotti CL, Nascimento FD, Paakkonen V, Martins MT, Carrilho MR, Pashley DH, Tay FR, Salo T, Tjaderhane L. Cysteine cathepsins in human dentin-pulp complex. J Endod 2010;36:475-481.

48. Nascimento FD, Minciotti CL, Geraldeli S, Carrilho MR, Pashley DH, Tay FR, Nader HB, Salo T, Tjaderhane L, Tersariol IL. Cysteine cathepsins in human carious dentin. J Dent Res 2011;90:506-511.

49. Kirschke H, Kembhavi AA, Bohley P, Barrett AJ. Action of rat liver cathepsin L on collagen and other substrates. Biochem J 1982;201:367-372.

50. Brömme D, Okamoto K, Wang BB, Biroc S. Human cathepsin O2, a matrix protein-degrading cysteine protease expressed in osteoclasts. Functional expression of human cathepsin O2 in Spodoptera frugiperda and characterization of the enzyme. J Biol Chem 1996;271:2126-2132.

Chapter 16

DENTAL CEMENTS

Dr. Sana Shahab & Dr. Zohaib

INTRODUCTION

Cements are defined as a *material that produces a mechanical interlocking effect on hardening*. In dentistry, cements are defined as a *Substance that hardens to act as a base, liner filling materials and luting or adhesive to build prostheses to tooth structure or to each other*.

Dental cements are used for a variety of dental applications e.g. use as luting agents, pulp-protecting agents or cavity-lining material. Dental cements are hard, brittle materials formed by mixing powder and liquid together. They are either resin cements or acid-base cements.

As these materials used in a very sensitive environment so they must fulfill basic requirement which are as follows, discussed under particular category.

LINING MATERIALS

Certain filling materials are not suitable for placing directly into a freshly prepared cavity. In such circumstances, a layer of cavity lining material is placed in the **occlusal floor** of the cavity, and on the **pulpal axial** dentine wall for class II cavities, prior to placement of the filling.

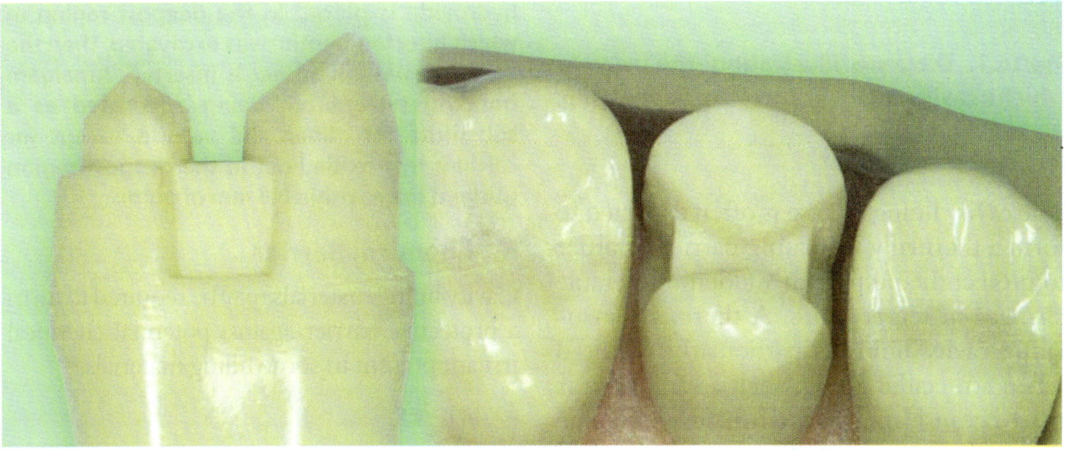

A. Axial Wall. **B. Occlusal View.**

REQUIREMENTS

Depend on the

a. Depth of the cavity.

b. Thickness of residual dentine.

c. Type of filling material.

PURPOSE OF LINNING OR BASE

a. To acts as a barrier between the filling material and the dentine which, by virtue of the dentinal tubules, has direct access to the sensitive pulp.

b. To provide sufficient mechanical strength to resist disruption during the placement of filling.

c. To provide a firm, rigid base this will adequately support the filling above it.

d. To provide a thermal, chemical and electrical barrier.(see Fig: 16.1)

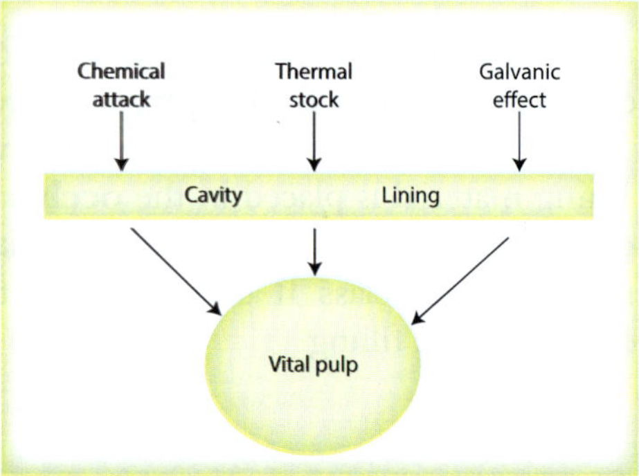

Fig:16.1. Diagram illustrating the way in which a cavity lining protects the dental pulp.

A. Thermal Barrier

The cavity lining or base is often expected to form a thermally insulating barrier in order to protect the pulp from sudden intolerable changes in temperature. A thermally insulating cavity lining is particularly required when a metallic filling, such as amalgam is used because the thermal diffusivity value for amalgam is about 40 times greater than that for dentine.

I. In Deep Cavities

- Having only a thin residual layer of dentine, and there is a danger of "thermal shock" to the pulp when the patient takes hot or cold.
- A layer of insulating cavity lining material of sufficient thickness helps to prevent this.

II. In Shallow Cavities

- There is a relatively thick layer of residual dentine; it becomes less important to use a lining with thermal insulating properties.
- In such shallow cavities, the base and walls of the cavity can be lined with a *varnish*.

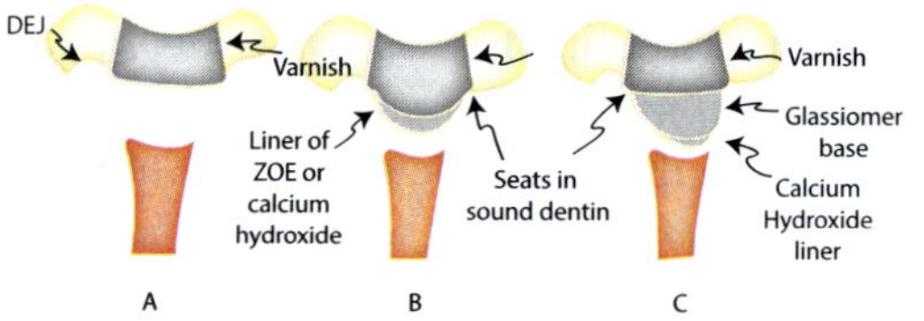

Fig: 16.2 Schematic exaples of use of liners and bases for amalgam restorations. A, For shallow amalgam tooth preparations, varnish or sealer is applied to walls of preparation before insertion. B, For moderate-depth tooth preparations, liners may be placed for thermal protection and pulpal medication. (Note seats in sound dentin for amalgamrestoration.) C, In very deep perparation, light- cured calcium hydroxide is placed in the deepest region in which infected dentin was excavated, then the base of glass- ionomer is inserted. Amalgam bonding system are being advocated as a substitute for liner and varnish except for calcium hydroxide liner in the deepest region (judged to be within 0.5 mm of pulp).

B. Chemical Barrier

Cavity lining materials may be required to form a protective barrier against potential chemical irritant present in some filling materials.

Examples

- Phosphoric acid in silicate filing material and Acrylic monomer.

C. Electrical Barrier

To protect the pulp from galvanic pain due to the presence of dissimilar metals placed adjacent or opposing to each other. Varnish (polystyrene resin) is most commonly used. Most of the lining materials used are either water based or contain polar organometallic compounds, because they are not ideal electrical insulators.

D. Strength and Flow

It should have sufficient working time so that it can easily place in the cavity having sufficient flow. It should have rapid setting once placed in the cavity so that it can achieved maximum strength before filing is placed over it.

E. Radiopacity

Cavity linings should, ideally, be radio opaque in order that the dentist can observe them on radiographs, thereby aiding the diagnosis of caries around the filling. A radio lucent lining material may hinder the early detection of such lesions.

Examples

- Zinc phosphate cements.
- Zinc oxide/eugenol.
- Ca (OH)2
- Orthro-ethoxy benzoic acid.

LUTING MATERIALS

Many dental appliances and restoration are constructed outside the patient's mouth and then fixed into place using a cement luting material.

Examples

a. Fixing of porcelain and metal crowns.
b. Bridges
c. Inlays
d. Metal posts

IDEAL REQUIREMENTS

a. It should be non-toxic and non-irritant.
b. It should be capable of bending.
c. It should have suitable mechanical property.
d. It should be insoluble.
e. It should have low viscosity.
f. It should have good insulator of both electrical and thermal stimulations.

Available Materials

a. Zinc phosphate.
b. Glass ionomer cement.
c. Polymer luting agents.

ENDODONTIC CEMENTS

These cements are used to seal the root canal prior to insertion of gutta percha during root canal treatment.

IDEAL REQUIREMENTS

a. It should resist dissolution.
b. It should produce good seal in root canal treatment.
c. It should be radio opaque.
d. Its setting characteristic should be compatible with warm, moist environment of the root canal.
e. It should be bio-compatible.

Example

- Non-Setting Ca (OH)2

ORTHODONTIC CEMENTS

These cements are especially in orthodontics for attaching bands and brackets.

IDEAL REQUIREMENTS

a. It should securely place the bands and bracket.

b. It should easily remove after treatment.

c. It should have low viscosity.

d. It should have adequate setting time.

e. It should be biocompatible.

CLASSIFICATION OF CEMENTS

1. ON THE BASIS OF DIFFERENT ACIDS.

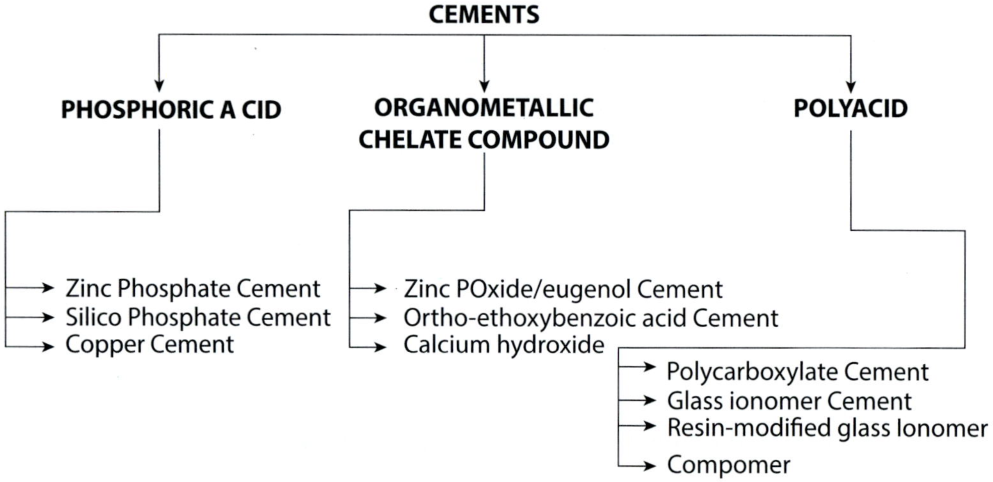

2. ON THE BASIS OF DIFFERENT COMPOUNDS

WATER-BASED ACID-BASE CEMENTS	NON-AQUEOUS ACID-BASE CEMENTS	RESIN-BASED
Zinc Phosphate (Zn3(PO4)2)	Zinc Oxide Eugenol	Acrylate Resin Cements
Zinc Polyacrylate (Polycarboxylate)	Non- Eugenol Zinc Oxide	Methacrylate Resin Cements
Glass Ionomer Cements (GIC)	---------	Self-adhesive resin cements which contain silicate
These contain metal oxide or silicate fillers embedded in a salt matrix	These contain metal oxide fillers embedded in a metal salt matrix	Fillers in an organic resin matrix

COMPARISON BETWEEN DIFFEFRENT CEMENTS

1. COMPRESSIVE STRENGTH (MPa).

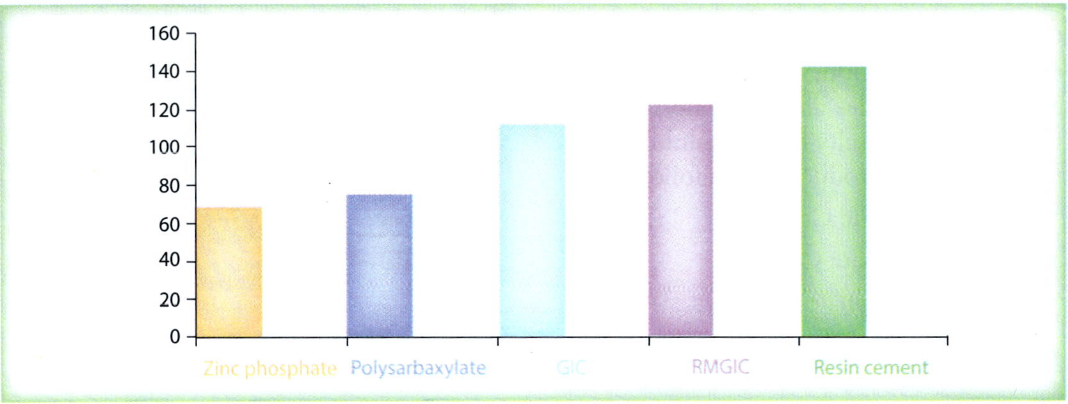

2. BOND STRENGTH (MPa).

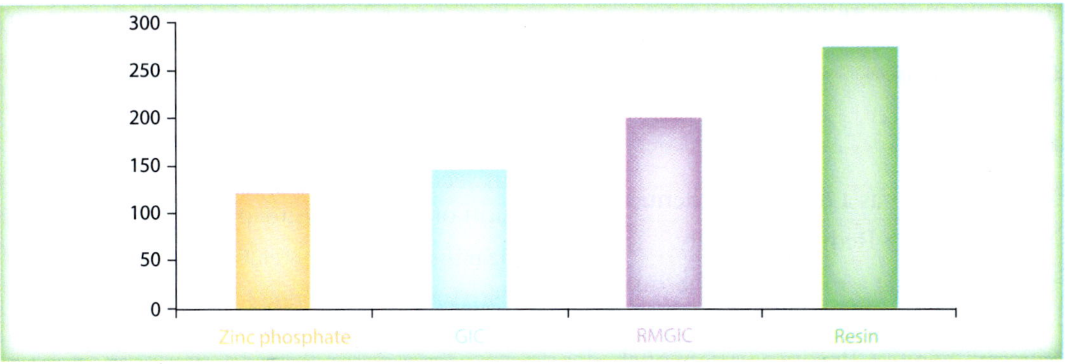

3. FILM THICKNESS (µm).

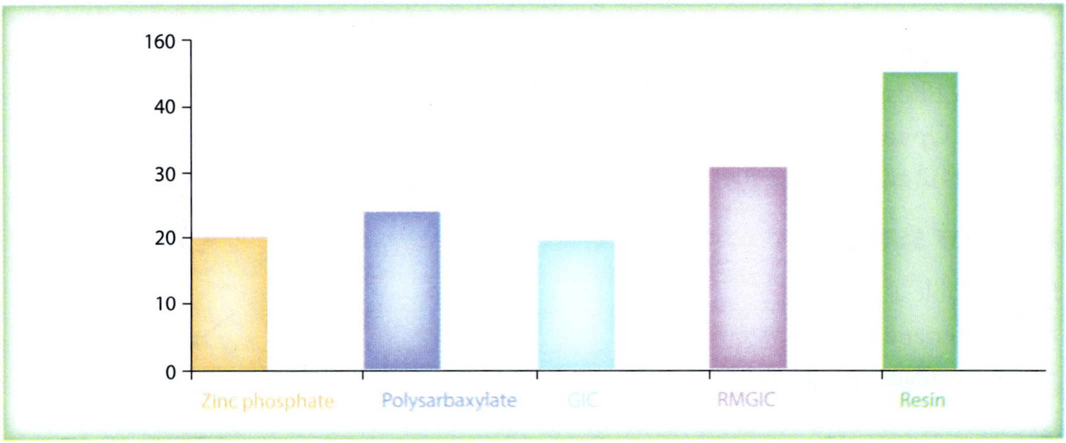

CEMENTS BASED ON PHOSPHORIC ACID

INTRODUCTION

One group of widely used cements based on the vigorous reaction, which occurs between certain basic oxides and phosphoric acid to form phosphate salts of low solubility. The names of these products are as follows;

- Zinc Phosphate Cements.
- Silico Phosphate Cements.
- Copper Phosphate Cements.

ZINC PHOSPHATE CEMENTS

It is material, which is widely used as lining cement under direct restoration and as a luting. Cement for indirect restoration.

COMPOSITION

Powder

ZnO (90%) → as a main ingredient.

MgO (10%) → Reduce reactivity.

Bismuth Oxide → Improve the quality of set material.

Silicon Oxide → Produce variety of shades

Fluoride → Reduces carries.

Liquid

Aqueous solution : 50%-60% Concentrations of Phosphoric Acid

Al PO4 : Up to 10% act as the buffer

Zn3 (PO4)2 and stabilize the pH

MODE OF SUPPLY

It is available as;

- Powder and Liquid system
- Encapsulated products

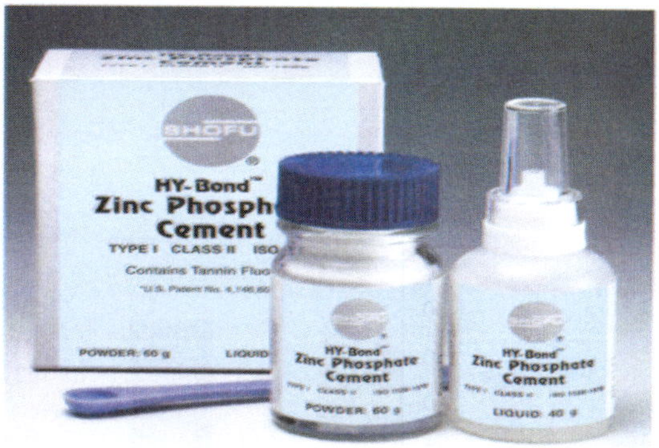

SETTING REACTION

On mixing the powder and liquid together, following two phases occurs:

1st Phase

First super facial layer of ZnO dissolve by the acid salts in the formation of acid Zinc phosphate.

2nd Phase

In second phase of setting there is a formation of hydrated Zinc phosphate.

3ZnO + 2H3 PO4 + H2O → Zn3 (PO4)4H2O.

Final mass is hydrated Zinc phosphate that is virtually insoluble and crystallizes to form a phosphate matrix that bind together the central un reacted portion of the Zinc Oxide.

Reaction is rapid and exothermic in nature.

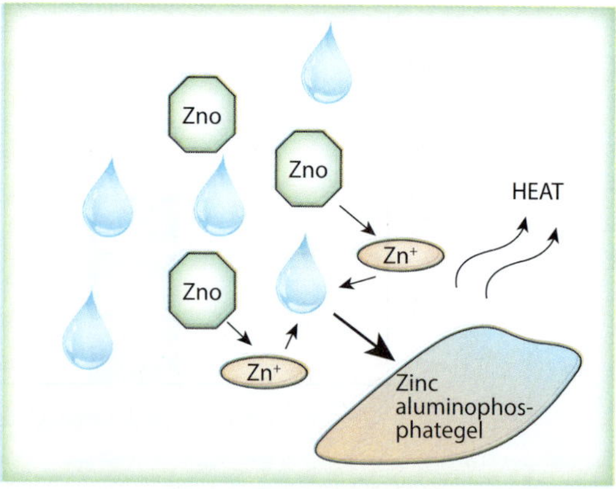

MANIPULATIVE VARIABLES

The powder / liquid ratio depends on the application.

For Cavity Lining

Putty like consistency having a powder / Liquid ratio of about 3.5:1 is used.

For Luting

A more fluid mix, with lower powder / liquid ratio, is employed to ensure flow of the cement during seating of the restoration.

Remember

If lowering the powder / liquid ratio produces a weaker, more soluble and more irritant material.

- Luting cement 80 Mpa [Due to difference
- Lining cement 140 Mpa of powder / liquid ratio]

B. Setting Time and Working Time

- ✦ Sufficient working and setting time.
- ✦ *Depends upon;*
  - Amount of powder used.
  - Manipulative variable.
  - Composition of liquid.

C. Film Thickness

- ✦ Controlled by;
  - ✦ Powder / liquid ratio
  - ✦ Particle size of powder

EFFECTS OF MANIPULATION ON SOME PROPERTIES

MANIPULATIVE VARIABLE	PROPERTIES				
	Copressive strength	Film thickness	Solubility	Initial addity	Setting time
Decreased powder/ liquid ratio	↓	↓	↑		
Increase rate of powder incorporation	↓	↑	↑		↓
Increase mixing temperature	↓	↑	↑		↓
Water contamination	↓	↑	↑		↓

PROPERTIES

A. Strength

- ✦ Stronger lining material than calcium hydroxide Ca (OH)2.
- ✦ Strength depends on manipulative variable.
- ✦ Compressive strength after 24 hours for

- ✦ Ideal cement thickness is 25-micron meter.

D. Solubility

- ✦ According to ADA specification, it shows relatively low solubility – of about 0.06% wt.
- ✦ Erode slowly in mouth by the action of dissolution and abrasion.

Controlled by;

- Amount of powder.
- Water content.

Effects;

- Loss of restoration.
- Caries formation.

E. Retention

- Not adhesive to restoration or tooth preparation.
- Achieved by flowing of cement in small undercuts present on the fitting surface of restoration and on tooth preparation.
- Also depends on correct convergence of axial walls.
- Ideal taper 10° (5° on each side).

F. Dimensional Changes

- Contract to small amount on setting but negligible.

G. Pulpal Reaction

- Zinc phosphate has low pH. (acidic)
- Inflammatory response in pulp.

Depend on;

- Depth of cavity.
- Amount of residual dentine.

Controlled by;

- Sub-lining.
- Fluoride.

H. Thermal Reaction

- Good thermal and insulating properties when used under metallic restoration.

I. Appearance

- Set material is Opaque due to high concentration on of un-reacted ZnO.
- Affect the esthetic if used for cementation under porcelain jacket crown.
- Avoid by placing margin with in gingival cervice.

USES

- As a lining material under amalgam filling.
- As a luting cement in non – vital tooth.

SILICOPHOSPHATE CEMENTS

These cements are basically hybrids of Zinc phosphate and silicate material. Their properties mimicking silicates. It has a property of releasing fluoride because of aluminosilicate glass particle.

MODE OF SUPPLY

They are supplied as powder and liquid.

COMPOSITION

Powder

- Zinc Oxide
- Alumina silicate glass.

Liquid

- Aqueous solution of phosphoric acid
- Zinc and aluminum phosphates.

CLASSIFICATION AND APPLICATIONS

TYPES	APPLICATIONS
Type I	For the cementation of fixed restorations and orthodontic bands, luting cements for porcelain crows where their extra translucency at the margins is considered an advantage.
Type II	As a temporary posterior filling material.
Type III	As a dual purpose materials for cementing and temporary filling.

SETTING REACTION

Produces a matrix of zinc and aluminum phosphates enclosing un reacted cores of zinc oxide and glass particles.

PROPERTIES

- These cements are stronger and less soluble than other phosphate cements.
- It contain significant amount of fluoride hence provide anti cariogenic effect.
- Material sets very fast so it should be mixed quickly.

ADVANTAGES
Silicophosphate cements have good strength, toughness and abrassion resistance properties.
Considerable flouride release.
Considerable translucency.
Lower solubility and better bonding.
DISADVANTAGES
Low initial pH
Manipulation is more critical than with zinc phosphate cements.
Since the film thickness is appreciably greater than that of zinc phosphate cement, it is not recommended for luting precision castings
It may cause pulpal sensitivity of long duration

USES

- As die material in some cases.
- For filling in deciduous teeth and temporary restoration in permanent teeth.

COPPER CEMENTS

These materials are closely related to the Zinc-Phosphate cements.

MODE OF SUPPLY

They are supplied as powder and liquid.

COMPOSITION

Powder

- Zinc oxide
- Black copper oxide

Liquid

- Aqueous solution of phosphoric Acid.

SETTING REACTION

Is similar to that for Zinc phosphate materials.

PROPERTIES

- Appearance is black.
- Bacterial effect.
- Not durable.
- Filling material in primary teeth where complete removal of caries is impossible.

USES

- For cementation of orthodontic appliances.
- For cementation of cast silver cap splints that are used occasionally during the management of facial fracture.

CEMENTS BASED ON POLYACID

INTRODUCTION

Two types of cement based on polyacids are in common use for both luting and cavity lining application.

1st Product

The first products to be developed were the polycarboxylate cements-which rely on the reaction between zinc oxide and a polyacids.

2nd Product

The second groups of products are described as glass ionomer as polyalkenoate cements.

SETTING REACTION

The setting reaction takes place between a polyacid molecule and cations released from an ion-leachable glass.

POLYCARBOXYLATE CEMENTS

INTRODUCTION

Poly carboxylate cement was the first cement system developed with a potential for adhesion to tooth structure.

MODE OF SUPPLY

Available as;

- Powder and liquid in bottles.
- Powder which is mixed with water (water settable cements).
- Pre-capsulated powder/liquid system.

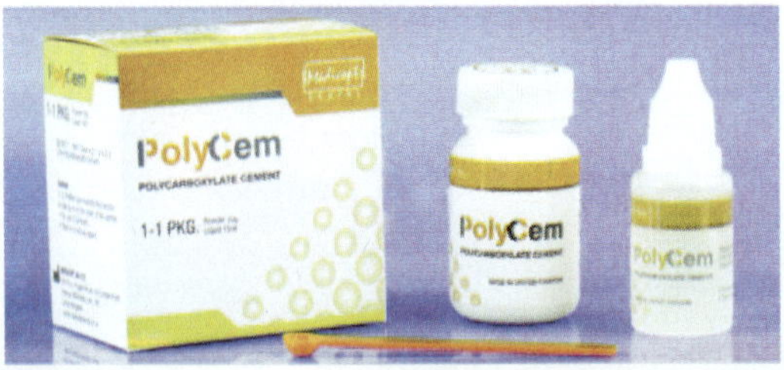

COMPOSITION

Powder

- Zinc oxide.
- Magnesium oxide.

Liquid

- Aqueous solution of polycarboxylic acid 40%
- Concentration.

SETTING REACTION

- On mixing the powder with water, the polyacrylic acid dissolves and starts to react with zinc oxide.
- Zinc oxides behaves as a basic oxide and undergoes in acid-base reaction with acid groups in the polyacids to form a reaction product which consists of cores of unreacted zinc oxide bound together by a salt matrix in which polyacrylic acid chains are cross linked through divalent zinc ions.
- Its setting time is about 7 to 9 minutes.

PROPERTIES

A. Comprehensive Strength

- Poly carboxylate cement is inferior to zinc phosphate cement but similar to ortho-ethoxy benzoic acid cement.
- Comprehensive strength is about 80 Mpa.

B. Solubility

- Laboratory tests show that the solubility values for polycarboxylate cements are greater than those for zinc phosphate, silicon phosphate and glass ionomer materials.
- Despite this apparent disadvantage, the

materials are widely used for luting without appearing to display an-unduly high failure rate.

C. Adhesion

- The material forms strong bond with stainless steel as well as with enamel and dentine.
- But only a weal bond with gold and no perceptible bond with porcelain.

D. Biocompatibility

- These cements have very little irritant effect on the pulp because;
- Polyacrylic acid is a weaker acid than phosphoric acid.
- Penetration of polyacrylic acid into the dentinal tubules is less because of its higher molecular weight and larger size.

E. Optical properties

- They are very opaque due to large quantities of unreacted zinc oxide.

F. Thermal properties:-

- Poly carboxylate cements are good thermal insulates.

USES

- Used as luting cements for attaching;
  - Crowns
  - Bridges
  - Inlays
- Also used as cavity base materials.

GLASS IONOMER CEMENTS

INTRODUCTION

- That's cavity lining and luting aments are of broadly similar composition with glass ionomer restorative materials.
- One difference is that the luting and cavity lining cements contain glass of smaller particle size to allow the formation of a thinner film thickness during luting.

MODE OF SUPPLY

- Available as;
  - Powder and liquid.
  - Powder and water.

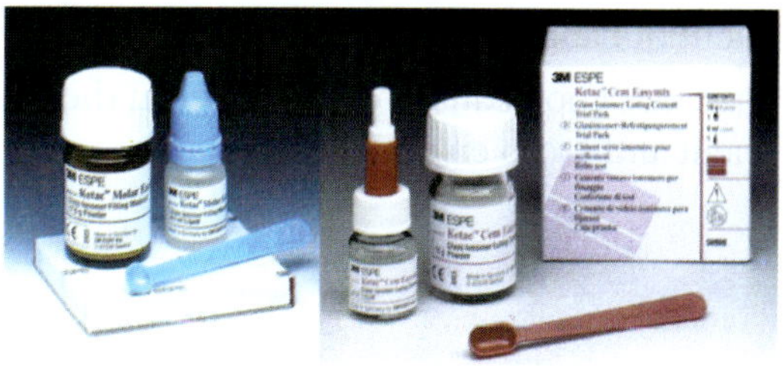

PROPERTIES

A. Comprehensive Strength

- The set materials are stronger than the poly carboxylate product having a compressive strength value of about 130 Mpa.
- The materials can withstand amalgam condensation and are occasionally used as cavity lining for amalgam restorations.

B. Optical Properties

- It contains radio-opacifying agents like barium salts or metallic silver.

C. Solubility

- They are less soluble than polycarboxylate, and most of the other cement products.
- Solubility of the cements is slow and maintained release of fluoride which may help to protect adjacent tooth substance from attack by the acids of plaque.

D. Biocompatibility

- The pulpal response may be classified as mild.
- The pulpal reaction is greater than zinc oxide eugenol but less than zinc phosphate cement.

USES

Widely used in orthodontics for the attachment of bands.

Provides good adhesive seal between the cement and tooth enamel.

CEMENTS BASED ON ORGANOMETALIC CHELATE COMPOUND

INTRODUCTION

- Many types of cement used in dentistry can be characterized by setting reaction, which involves the formation of chelate compounds between zinc ions and ortho-disubstituted aromatic compounds.
- Three types of aromatic compounds are commonly used;
    1. Zinc oxide / eugenol cements.
    2. Ortho-ethoxy benzoic acid (EBA) cements.
    3. Calcium hydroxide cements, in which the aromatic ligands are silicylates.

ZINC OXIDE / EUGENOL CEMENTS

INTRODUCTION

These cements based on organomatallic chelate compound. Some products also contain hydrogenated resin or polystyrene and are known as Resin-rein forced zinc oxide / eugenol cements.

MODE OF SUPPLY

Supplied in two forms.

1. Powder and liquid.
2. Two paste system.

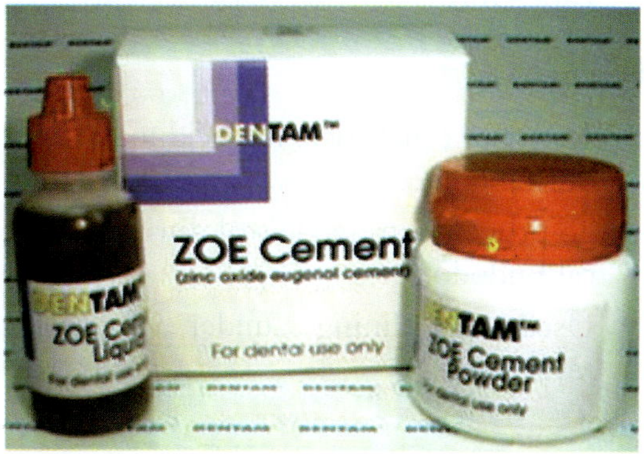

CLASSIFICATION OF ZINC OXIDE-EUGENOL CEMENT

Type 1 – Temporary luting cement

Type 2 – Permanent luting cement

Type 3 – Temporary restorative material

Type 4 – Intermediate restorative material

COMPOSITION

	FUNCTION	COMPONENTS
Powder	Zinc oxide Zinc acetate (1-5%)	Primary reactive ingredient Accelerator
Liquid	Eugenol Olive oil (5-15%)	Primary reactive ingredient To control viscosity

SETTING REACTION

- Setting reaction involves chelation of two eugenol molecules with one zinc ion to form zinc eugenolate.
- This reaction proceeds very slowly in the absence of moisture.

PROPERTIES

A. Setting Characteristics

- Ideal in nature.
- Having adequate working time followed by rapid setting after placing in cavity.
- Rapid setting is due to residual moisture in cavity and higher temperature of mouth.

B. Strength

- Lower compressive strength than zinc phosphate cements.

20 Mpa (un-reinforced material)

40 Mpa (reinforced material)

- The nature of the setting reaction is such that the materials develop their strength rapidly.
- The reinforced materials in particular are unlikely to flow or fracture during amalgam condensation, providing correct technique is used.

C. Solubility

- High solubility due to which eugenol is leached out.
- Hydrolysis of zinc eugenolate and disintegration of cement occur when eugenol is replaced by H2O.
- Not suitable for luting purpose except on temporary basis.

D. Pulpal Reaction

- Unconsumed eugenol is able to leach from set material and this substance has been to be irritant under certain condition.
- It appears to have an obtundant effect on the pulp.

E. Thermal Properties

- Effective thermal barrier under metallic restoration.

ADVANTAGES
Reasonable resistence to marginal penetration.
They have good sealing ability.
They have an obtundant effect on the pulp tissues.

DISADVANTAGES
Low strength.
Low abrassion resistance.
High solubility and disintegration in oral fluids.

USES

- As a lining or sub lining material under amalgam restoration.
- As a temporary luting cement.
- As a temporary filling material.

ZINC OXIDE / EUGENOL ROOT CANAL PASTES

INTRODUCTION

These pastes used alone or in combination with gutta percha or silver points. They are modification form of zinc oxide / Eugenol lining material.

COMPOSITION

A part from normal composition of zinc oxide / eugenol cement they contain;

- Barium Sulphate.
- Bismuth trioxide.
- Water absorbing compounds.
- Anti-inflammatory drugs.
- Para – formaldehyde. (Disinfectant)

USES

- As a root canal paste in deciduous teeth during pulpectomy.
- To provide retrograde seal during surgical Endodontic.
- Used as lining under amalgam restoration.

ORTHO – ETHOXY BENZOIC ACID [EBA] CEMENTS

INTRODUCTION

These cements are based on organometallic chelate compounds.

6. MODE OF SUPPLY

- Powder and liquid.

COMPOSITION

	COMPONENTS	FUNCTION
Powder	Zinc oxide (60%) Quartz (35%) Hydrogenated Resin (5%)	Primary reactive ingredient Reinforcing agents.
Liquid	O – Ethoxy benzoic acid Eugenol	Reactive ingredient

SETTING REACTION

There is a formation of chelate compound with zinc ions to form zinc o – ethoxy benzoate.

PROPERTIES

- Settings characteristic are similar to zinc oxide / eugenol and are similarly affected by moisture.
- The set material is stronger than the reinforced zinc oxide / eugenol product due to the high powder / liquid ratio and the presence of fillers.
- Low solubility due to greater resistance of ortho-ethoxy benzoate to hydrolysis.
- Good thermal and insulating properties.

ADVANTAGES
They are easy to manipulate.
Long working time.
Good flow characteristics.
Strength and film thickness can be comparable to those of zinc phosphate cements.

DISADVANTAGES
Critical proportioning.
Hydrolytic breakdown in oral fluids.
Liability to plastic deformation.
Poor retention than zinc phosphate cements.

USES

- As a lining material under amalgam restoration.
- As a luting cement.

CALCIUM HYDROXIDE CEMENTS

INTRODUCTION

Calcium hydroxide is an odorless white powder that is very slightly soluble in water and insoluble in alcohol. They are reactively weak cements.

MODE OF SUPPLY

Available as:

- Two paste system containing base and catalyst pastes in collapsible tubes.
- Light cured system.

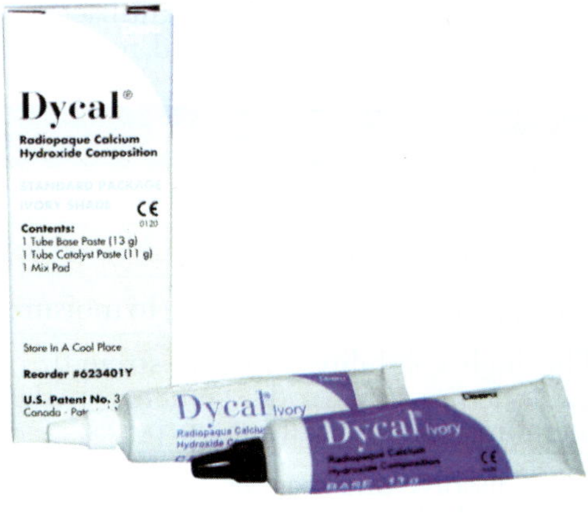

COMPOSITION

COMPONENT		FUNCTION
PASTE 1	Calcium hydroxide (50%) Zinc oxide (10%) Zinc stearate (0.5%) Ethyl toleline Sulphon amide (39.5%)	Primary reactive ingredient. Accelerator Oil compound. act as carrier.
PASTE 2	Glycol Salicylate (40%) Titanium dioxide Calcium Sulphate Calcium Tungstate	Primary reactive ingredient. inert filler, Pigments and radio pacifiers.

SETTING REACTION

- On mixing two pastes glycol salicylate reacts with zinc oxide and calcium hydroxide to form chalet compounds.
- Sulphon amide acts a carrier and has no therapeutic effect.
- Some cement contain paraffin oil instead of sulphonamide. (Hydrophobic release CaOH)
- This may have an adverse effect on the antibacterial properties of the cement.

ADVANTAGES
Easy manipulation.
Rapid hardening in thin layers.
Good sealing characteristics
Beneficial effects on carious dentin and exposed pulps.
Non-irritant to tissues with antibacterial action and Stimulation of hard reparative dentin formation.

DISADVANTAGES
Low strength even when fully set.
Exhibit plastic deformation.
They are weakened by exposure to moisure.
The high solubility and low strength of the calcium hydroxide cements makes them unsuitable for luting purposes.
They dissolve under acidic conditions and marginal leakage occurs.

PROPERTIES

A. Setting Characteristic

- Initial mixed material has low viscosity and setting proceed slowly.
- Moisture affects the rate of setting.
- Light activated material set hard as soon as it expose to light.
- Disadvantage with light activated material is exothermic nature of reaction.

B. Strength

- Set material is weak with compressive strength of 20 Mpa.
- Light activated materials are brittle materials as compared to two paste systems under amalgam filling.

C. Solubility

- Highly soluble in aqueous medium.
- Calcium hydroxide leaches out generating an alkaline medium.

D. Secondary dentine formation

- The material also initiate calcification and formation of secondary dentine layer to the base of the cavity.
- This calcification process is due to irritant of pulp tissues by cement, which intern activate TGF beta (growth factor) which act on odontoblast to start forming dentine at pulpal floor.

Working time	1-2 min
Setting time	2-3 min
Compressive strength	6-20 MPa (depending upon time period)
Tensile strength	1-2 MPa
Solubility	High
pH	11-12

USES

- Pulp capping agent.
- A pexification.
- A pexogenesis.
- Root canal sealer.
- As a lining or sub-lining materials.

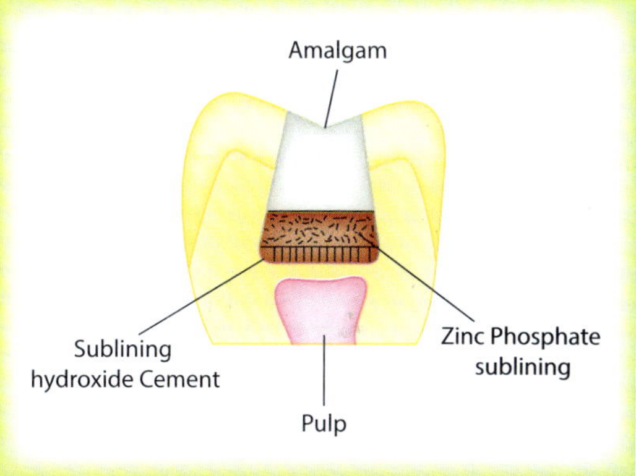

Fig: 16.3. Use of Calcuim hydroxide cement as a sublining benath a zine phosphate cement lining.

REFERENCES

1. "Dental Cements" *Definition of dental cement*. The Free Dictionary by Farlex. 2007. Retrieved 2008-08-11.
2. Theodore Roberson, Harald O. Heymann & Edward J. Swift(2006),*Sturdevant's Art and Science of Operative Dentistry,* (5th ed), Mosby
3. James B. Summit, J. Williams Robins & Thomas J. Hilton,richard S. Schwartz(2006), *Fundamentals of Operative Dentistry: A Contemporary Approach,* Quintessence Publishing, USA.
4. Theodore P. Croll, & John W. Nicholson (2002), "Glass ionomer cements in pediatric dentistry: review of the literature", *Peadiatric Dentistry*, vol. 24, no. pp. 423-429.
5. Ebru Sümer & Yalçın Değer (2011), "Contemporary Permanent Luting Agents Used in Dentistry: A Literature", *International Journal of Restorative Dentistry*, vol. 1, no. pp. 26-31.
6. Cornelis H. Pameijer (2011), "A Review of Luting Agents", *International Journal of Dentistry*, vol., no. pp. 7.
7. Kenneth Anusavice (2012), *Phillips' Science of Dental Materials, (12th Edition),* Saunder.
8. Ronald Sakaguchi & John M.power(2011), *Craig's Restorative Dental Materials, (13th Edition),* Mosby
9. Li ZC, White SN. Mechanical properties of dental luting cements. J Prosthet Dent 1999;81(5):597-609
10. White SN, Yu Z. Film thickness of new adhesive luting agents. J Prosthet Dent 1992;67(6):782-90
11. Ergin S, Gemalmaz D. Retentive properties of five luting cements on base and noble metal copings. J Prosthet Dent 2002;885:491-9Li ZC, White SN. Mechanical properties of dental luting cements. J Prosthet Dent 1999;81(5):597-609
12. White SN, Yu Z. Film thickness of new adhesive luting agents. J Prosthet Dent 1992;67(6):782-90
13. Ergin S, Gemalmaz D. Retentive properties of five luting cements on base and noble metal copings. J Prosthet Dent 2002;885:491-97

Chapter

17

BIOMATERIALS USED IN ENDODONTICS AND THEIR APPLICATIONS

Dr. Mai S. Ali, Dr. Mohamed-Nur Abdallah, Dr. Mo'ath Q. Momani, Dr. Mohammed B. Saeed, Dr. M. Shoaib H. Siddiqui & Dr. Zeeshan Sheikh

INTRODUCTION

Endodontics is a division of clinical dentistry related to the study of biology, morphology, physiology, aetiology and diagnosis of pathology, and treatment of dental pulp and periradicular tissues. The aim of endodontics (surgical and/or non-surgical) includes, the differential diagnosis and management and treatment of oral pain from pulpal and/or periradicular origin; vital pulp therapy procedures (paedodontics and adult endodontics); non-surgical treatment of root canal systems and their filling (obturation); surgical removal of diseased tissues resulting from pulpal pathology; repair procedures related to the removed tissues and iatrogenic defects; management of trauma to teeth (such as replantation of avulsed teeth and root fracture) hemi-sections, root-end resections, and root amputation root-end fillings; bleaching of discoloured teeth (internal bleaching); retreatment of previously endodontically treated teeth; and treatment with posts and cores for coronal restorations.

The success of non-surgical endodontic treatments is highly dependent on the access cavity preparation. In order to obtain a straight line access to the canal system, the clinician should have a thorough knowledge of the anatomy of the tooth being treated and have available the correct armamentaria. Following adequate access, proper cleaning and shaping of the root canals is required which is achieved by chemo-mechanical debridement. The mechanical preparation provides the space for the disinfectants and irrigants to perform their action on the microorganisms and biofilms adhering to the root canal walls. Moreover, intra-canal medicaments can be applied within the canal whenever the clinician finds their use effective in eliminating any residual bacteria. It is imperative to have a high quality obturation of the root canal system. By entombing any remaining bacteria inside the canals and achieving a fluid tight seal we can prevent bacterial contamination of the periradicular tissues. The long-term prognosis also depends on the quality and integrity of the coronal seal, i.e. post-core-permanent restoration. Therefore, it is crucial to prevent the ingress of oral fluids (microleakage), or at least keep it to a minimum, by placing the most suitable restorative and endodontic materials.

Endodontic materials and instruments can be broadly categorized as those utilized to maintain pulp vitality and those used in pulp canal therapy for disinfection of the pulp space (irrigants and intra-canal medicaments) and root canal filling (solid materials and sealers). Current endodontic materials and instruments include those that have been thoroughly tested by scientific investigation, clinical usage, and time, as well as others that are the result of new knowledge in the field of dental materials. Knowing the particular qualities of materials can aid the clinician in choosing those that are appropriate for a given situation.

MATERIALS USED IN VITAL PULP THERAPY

The purpose of vital pulp therapy is to treat reversible pulpal injury and maintain pulp vitality and function in both primary and permanent teeth. Pulp vitality is extremely crucial for tooth viability as it provides nutrition and serves as a biosensor for any pathogenic stimuli. Reversible pulpal injury can be either due to caries, trauma or iatrogenic reasons. Vital pulp therapy includes two treatment approaches according to the depth of the cavity (Fig.17.1): (1) indirect pulp capping in cases of deep dentinal cavities without exposing the tooth pulp; and (2) direct pulp capping or pulpotomy in cases where the pulp is exposed.

Among the most commonly used pulp capping agents in dentistry are:

- Zinc oxide eugenol
- Calcium hydroxide $Ca(OH)_2$
- Glass ionomer
- Corticosteroids and antibiotics
- Polycarboxylate cement
- Bonding agents
- CPC (Calcium phosphate cement)
- Bone morphologic proteins (BMPs)
- Mineral trioxide aggregate (MTA)
- Biodentine

Ideal properties of pulp capping materials are summarized in Table 17.1; however, none of the currently available materials satisfies them all. This chapter will focus on MTA and Biodentine, since they have many uses in the field of Endodontics.

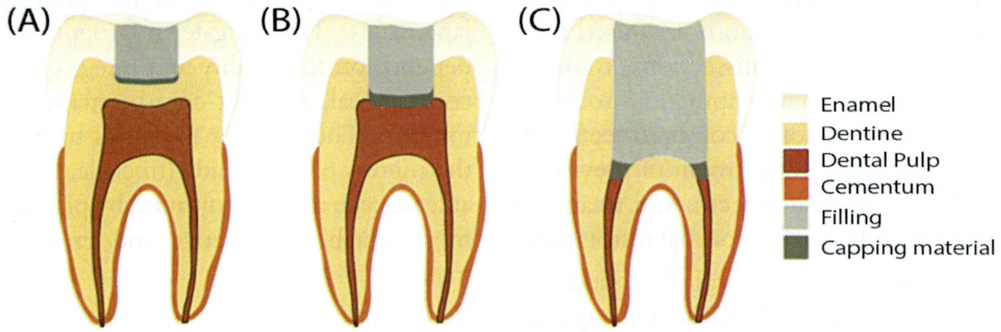

Fig: 17.1. Vital pulp therapy. (a) Indirect pulp capping; (b) Direct pulp capping and (c) pulpotomy.

Table: 17.1. Properties of an ideal pulp-capping material.

✦ Biocompatible
✦ Ensures a lasting seal of cavity margins, preferably via a molecular bond with dentine
✦ Has a bacteriostatic action or at least does not promote bacterial growth
✦ Induces the formation of hard tissue
✦ Stable
✦ Should not be soluble
✦ Should not be absorbable
✦ Should not be sensitive to moisture
✦ Easy to handle and manipulate
✦ Radiopaque

MINERAL TRIOXIDE AGGREGATE (MTA)

MTA was first introduced by Mahmoud Torabinejad and first reported in the literature in 1993. It is essentially a fine hydrophilic powder available as single use sachets of 1 gram (Table:17.2) and sometimes premeasured water sachets are provided for ease of use. It is a calcium-oxide based material, basically similar to Portland cement although MTA contains bismuth oxide to improve its radiopacity.

Table: 17.2. General components of MTA powder.

✦ Tricalciumsilicate ✦ Dicalcium silicate ✦ Tricalciumaluminate ✦ Bismuth Oxide (opacifier) ✦ Calcium carbonate	✦ Trace amounts of calcium oxide, free magnesium oxide, potassium and sodium sulfate compounds. ✦ Might contain insoluble residues (e.g. free crystalline silica)

Moreover, MTA particles are more uniform and smaller in size compared to Portland cement particles.

Table: 17.3. Differences between gray and white MTA.

PROPERTY	GRAY MTA	WHITE MTA
Particle Size	Larger (8 times)	Smaller, finer and more homogenous
Iron/magnesium/aluminium content	Higher (contributes to the gray colour)	Lower
pH value	Lower	Higher
Hydroxyapatite crystal formation	More cystals formed and contains less silica and phosphorus	Less crystals formed and contains more silica and phosphorus
Solubility	Lower	Higher
Compressive strength	Higher	Lower

Two types of MTA are currently available: gray and white MTA.

Their difference in colour is mainly due to lesser content of aluminium, magnesium and iron oxides in the white MTA. (Table: 17.3) summarizes the differences between the two types of MTA.

MTA is usually prepared by mixing 3 parts of powder with 1 part of water. This hydration process leads to the formation of a poorly crystallized porous gel of the hydrated forms of the components with some calcium hydroxide. This mixing process should not last more than 4 minutes otherwise it may result in dehydration of the mix. The physical and biological properties of this colloidal gel mixture vary according to several factors: powder-to-liquid ratio, mixing method, pressure during condensation, humidity, type of storage media, pH of the environment.

Some of the appreciable properties of MTA include: its good sealing ability and marginal adaptation, good biocompatibility, good compressive strength and excellent long term prognosis. In addition, it shows no signs of solubility when mixed properly and has a good pulp response and stimulates tissue regeneration. Some claim that MTA has an antimicrobial effect; however, Torabinejad et al reported that MTA only have some effect on five types of facultative bacterial (S.mitis, S.mutans, S.salivarius, Lactobacillus and S.epidermidis) but no effect against the anaerobes.

All these properties make MTA one of the most versatile materials with many clinical applications. Some of these clinical applications are:

- As a root-end filling.
- As a pulp capping material or pulpotomy (vital pulp therapy).
- As a pulp capping agent in vital teeth with open apex to promote root formation (apexogenesis)
- As an apical plug in teeth with necrotic pulp and open apex (apexification).
- As root canal sealer.
- To repair lateral and furcation root perforations).
- As a root canal obturation material (MTA monoblock).

Despite its many advantage, MTA has some drawbacks such as:

- It may discolour the tooth.
- Long setting time.
- Difficult to handle.
- Currently, there is no solvent available for MTA and it is difficult to be removed which may make retreatment a challenge.
- Relatively expensive.
- Presence of toxic elements in the material composition (arsenic).

BIODENTINE (SEPTODONT, SAINT-MAUR-DES-FOSSES,FRANCE)

Biodentine is a newer calcium silicate material (Table: 17.4 summarizes its properties); its powder contains tricalcium silicate, dicalcium silicate, calcium carbonate and zirconium dioxide as a radiopacifier. The liquid is made of calcium chloride in an aqueous solution and an admixture of modified polycarboxylate. Calcium chloride is used as a setting accelerator and water reducing agent while polycarboxylate is used as a super plasticising agent. A single dose of liquid is dropped in a disposable cap containing the powder and then mixed with an amalgamator for 30 seconds. Like other tricalcium materials, Biodentine is characterized by the release of calcium hydroxide when it comes in contact with tissue fluids forms hydroxyapatite. This material is reported to induce pulp cell differentiation and biomineralization in vitro, suggesting its ability to stimulate reparative dentinogenesis after direct pulp capping and therefore can be considered as a good dentine substitute. Moreover, Biodentine was developed to overcome the drawbacks of MTA such as discoloration, long setting time, high cost and poor handling properties. Biodentine can be indicated for the same endodontic uses as MTA.

Table: 17.4. Properties of Biodentine.

✦ Good sealing ability.
✦ High compressive strength.
✦ Short setting time.
✦ Biocompatible.
✦ Bioactive: it can form hydroxyapatite after immersion in a phosphate solution.
✦ Induces biomineralization.
✦ Resistance to dislodgement when used as a repair material and irrigants do not influence its resistance.
✦ Color stability.

MATERIALS USED AS ROOT CANAL IRRIGANTS

Removal of pulpal tissue, microbes and dentine shavings from the canal is achieved via mechanical preparation and chemical irrigation. Root canal irrigation plays an important role in disinfection of the root canal system and is critical for success. According to Zehnder (2006), an ideal irrigant should have all the properties listed in (Table: 17.5), yet none of the available ones combine all those characteristics. Therefore, clinicians usually use the one that has the most important properties or a combination of different irrigants to complete each other's action. (Table: 17.6) summarizes the properties and effects of different irrigants.

Table: 17.5. Ideal properties of a root canal irrigant.

✦ Broad antimicrobial spectrum.
✦ High efficacy against anaerobic and facultative microorganisms organized in the biofilm.
✦ Able to dissolve necrotic pulp tissue remnants.
✦ Able to inactivate endotoxins.
✦ Able to prevent the formation of a smear layer during instrumentation or to dissolve it once formed
✦ Systemically, nontoxic, nonantigenic, and noncarcinogenic if it comes in contact with vital tissues.
✦ Noncaustic to periodontal tissues.
✦ Little potential to cause an anaphylactic reaction.
✦ Has low surface tension.
✦ Does not stain tooth structures.
✦ Has no adverse effects on the sealing ability of filling materials.
✦ Relatively inexpensive.

Table: 17.6. Properties and effects of different irrigants.

IRRIGANT	ANTIBACTERIAL EFFECT	DISSOLUTION OF TISSUES	SMEAR LAYER REMOVAL	CONCENTRATION
NaOCl	Effective antibacterial agent by breaking down proteins into amino acids	Dissolves necrotic tissue at low concentrations At high concentration it dissolves both vital and necrotic tissues	Removes the organic part of smear layer	Varies 0.5%-6.25%
EDTA	Limited antibacterial effect	No dissolution capacity	Removes inorganic part of smear layer	17%
CHX	Effective antibacterial agent against gram positive and gram negative, and yeasts	No dissolution capacity	No smear layer removal	2%
MTAD	Antibacterial effect due to doxycycline	No dissolution capacity	Removes smear layer through doxycycline and citric acid	
CITRIC ACID	No antibacterial effect	No dissolution capacity	Removes smear layer	10%-50%
H_2O_2	Antibacterial effect	No dissolution capacity	None	3%-5%
IKI	Antibacterial effect	No dissolution capacity	None	2%-5%

SODIUM HYPOCHLORITE (NaOCl)

Sodium hypochlorite (NaOCl) is the most commonly used irrigant worldwide. It is an alkaline, hypertonic solution. In water, NaOCl ionizes to produce sodium ion (Na^+) and hypochlorite ion (OCl^-) which establishes equilibrium with hypochlorous acid HOCl according to the following equation:

$$NaOCl + H_2O \leftrightarrow NaOH + HOCl \leftrightarrow Na^+ + OH^{-+} H^+ + OCl^-$$

Between pH 4-7, chlorine exists predominately in the form of hypochlorous acid. Hypochlorous acid is more bactericidal than hypochlorite ion which predominates at pH above 9. NaOCl is distinguished by its ability to dissolve both vital and necrotic pulp tissues; however, it is more efficient at dissolving necrotic tissue. It has an excellent antibacterial action by breaking down proteins into amino acids and dissolving the organic part of the smear layer and biofilms. It acts as a lubricant and flushes away all the debris packed inside the canal. Probably, two of its most important characteristics are that it is readily available and inexpensive.

NaOCl also has some disadvantages. Prolonged irrigation using NaOCl will affect the flexural strength of dentin. Moreover, sodium hypochlorite accident is one of the complications that may encounter the clinician. To avoid this complication, the use of specially designed irrigation needles is recommended which should not be wedged in the canal and should be inserted loosely. Allergic reactions are rare, but if present then Iodine potassium iodide would be the irrigant of choice.

NaOCl is available in different concentrations varying from 0.5% to 6.25%. With lower concentrations, it can dissolve necrotic tissues only, while in higher concentrations it dissolves both vital and necrotic tissue but it is more toxic. To avoid the negative impact of sodium hypochlorite toxicity, we can increase the effectiveness of a low concentration through different ways:

- Increase the volume of low concentration NaOCl
- Increase the temperature of low-concentration NaOCl (e.g. a 0.5% NaOCl solution heated to approximately 60°C will have the effects equivalent to 5.25% NaOCl with decreased toxicity)
- Ultrasonic activation of NaOCl to create cavitational effects. Preferably after the canal preparation.
- Adding a detergent to the NaOCl solution to decrease surface tension which will promote penetration of NaOCl into the tubules and hence have a wider effect in eliminating bacteria.

ETHYLENEDIAMINE TETRA-ACETIC ACID (EDTA)

It is a polyaminocarboxylic acid (Fig:17.2), colourless and water soluble. EDTA works on direct exposure for extended periods of time by extracting bacterial surface proteins by combining with metal ions from the cell envelope which can eventually lead to cell death. It also sequesters di- and tri-cationic metal ions such as Ca^{2+} and Fe^{3+}, those metal ions bound to EDTA remain in solution but with diminished reactivity.

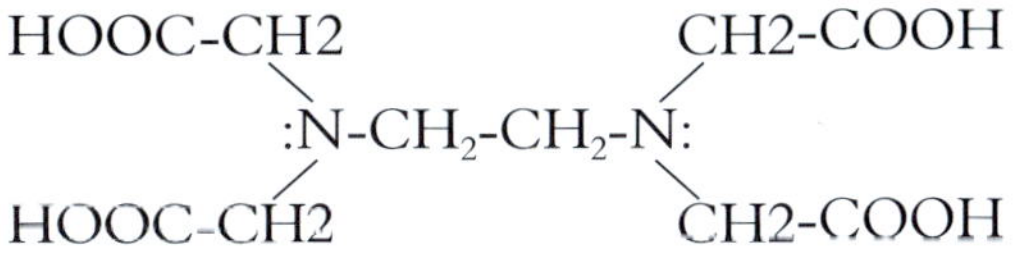

Fig: 17.2. Chemical structure of polyaminocarboxylic acid.

It is a known chelator that reacts with the calcium ions in dentine and forms soluble calcium chelates. One of its major uses is EDTA is to open an occluded, very fine canal since it is capable of decalcifying to a depth of 20–30 μm in 5 min.. EDTA is used in a concentration of 17%, it has limited antiseptic activity. However since it removes the inorganic part of smear layers and biofilms, it contributes to the antibacterial activity when used synergistically with NaOCl.

EDTA retains its ability to form calcium-complexes when mixed with NaOCl. EDTA causes NaOCl to lose its tissue-dissolving capacity, with virtually no free chlorine detected in combinations. This suggests that EDTA and NaOCl should be used separately and with copious amounts of NaOCl administered to wash out remnants of the EDTA. Therefore, EDTA is preferably used at the end of a procedure to remove the smear layer.

CHLORHEXIDINE (CHX)

Chlorhexidine (CHX) is a broad spectrum antimicrobial agent and has been widely used as a disinfectant for a long time. It belongs to polybiguanide antibacterial family, consisting of two symmetric four-chlorophenyl rings and two biguanide groups connected by a central hexamethylene chain (Fig: 17.3). CHX is a positively charged hydrophobic and lipophilic molecule that interacts with phospholipids and lipopolysaccharides on the cell membrane of bacteria and enters the cell through some type of active or passive transport mechanism.

2% CHX has better antibacterial efficacy than 0.12%. High concentrations are bactericidal since it damages the cell membrane which causes precipitation of the cytoplasm. While low concentrations are bacteriostatic, low molecular weight substances like potassium and phosphorus will leak out without the cell being irreversibly damaged.

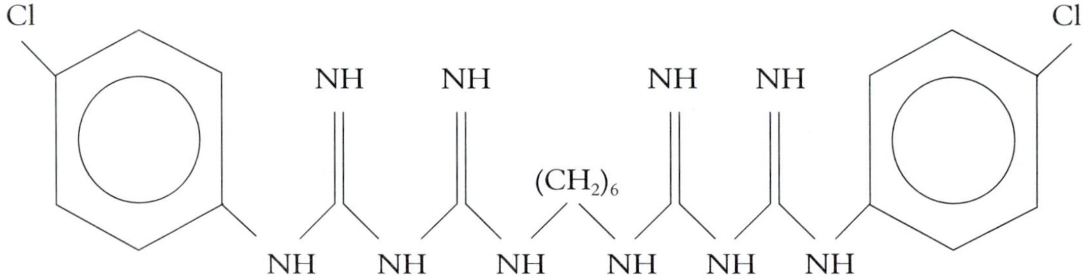

Fig: 17.3. Chemical structure of polybiguanide family.

CHX is distinguished by its antimicrobial effect and substantivity. It is cationic with positive charge which interacts with the negatively charged phosphate groups of bacteria's cell wall, this disrupts the microorganism's permeability altering its equilibrium and making CHX antimicrobial. Unlike sodium hypochlorite, CHX lacks the bad smell, periapical reaction if extruded outside the apex, and bleaching spots on patient's clothes, yet it does not have NaOCl property of dissolving tissues. Hence, although NaOCl and CHX have comparable antibacterial effects, NaOCl dissolving capacity makes it superior.

CHX is effective against both gram-positive and gram-negative bacteria as well as yeasts, although its activity against Gram-negative bacteria is not as good as against Gram-positive bacteria. CHX is available as gel, liquid, or controlled-release devices. Some studies reported that CHX gel is better than liquid. However, the mode of application is not the important factor in the effect of CHX; its concentration is the pivotal one.

Substantivity is considered as a unique characteristic for CHX. Due to its cationic nature, it can be absorbed by anionic substrates such as the oral mucosa, and adsorbed on hydroxyapatite and teeth. Substantivity prolongs the antimicrobial effect of CHX. For that reason, when CHX is used as an irrigant and intracanal medicament it delays coronal recontamination. Furthermore, CHX improves the resin-dentin bond stability due to its broad spectrum matrix metalloproteinase inhibitory effect.

When CHX and NaOCl interact, they form PCA para-Chloroaniline which is a neutral toxic insoluble precipitate. It forms due to dicationic acid (CHX) and base (NaOCl) reaction. PCA causes colour change (brownish-reddish). This precipitate may interfere with the seal of obturation and cause cyanosis due to methemoglobin formation. Moreover, it has also been shown to be cytotoxic in rats and possibly carcinogenic in humans. (Table: 17.7) shows interactions between different irrigants.

Table: 17.7. Possible interactions between different irrigants.

INTERACTIONS	SODIUM HYPOCHLORITE	EDTA	CHLORHEXIDINE
SODIUM HYPOCHLORITE		EDTA retains its calcium-complexing ability when mixed with NaOCl A bubbling effect reflects the chemical reaction but has no effect on cleansing.	PCA a precipitate that causes color change (brownish-reddish) and may interfere with the seal of obturation.
EDTA	NaOCl loses its tissue-dissolving capacity, with virtually no free chlorine detected in combinations. A bubbling effect reflects the chemical rxn but has no effect on cleansing.		White precipitate that involves the formation of salt rather than undergoing a chemical reaction.
CHLORHEXIDINE	PCA a precipitate that causes color change (brownish-reddish) and may interfere with the seal of obturation.	White precipitate that involves the formation of salt rather than undergoing a chemical reaction.	

MTAD

MTAD is a mixture of a tetracycline (3% doxycycline hyclate), an acid (4.25% citric acid) and a detergent (0.5% polysorbate-80 (Tween 80)) (Table: 17.8). It is the first irrigant produced that is capable of removing both the smear layer and disinfecting the root canal system. It is mixed as a liquid and powder and recommended as a final rinse for 5 minutes.

Table: 17.8. Composition of MTAD and function of its different components.

DOXYCYCLINE	CITRIC ACID	TWEEN 80
✦ Isomer of tetracycline. ✦ Broad spectrum antibiotic. ✦ Bacteriostatic by inhibition of protein synthesis. ✦ In high concentrations it is bactericidal. ✦ Has an effect in smear layer removal.	✦ Smear layer removal. ✦ Addition of NaOCl is important to remove organic part of smear layer	✦ Main action is lowering surface tension. ✦ May increase antibacterial effect: a. Directly by affecting the bacterial cell membrane. b. Indirectly through facilitating the penetration of MTAD into dentin ✦ It may decrease antibacterial effect: a. By being a nutrient to some bacteria b. By inactivating CHX and iodine effect if CHX and IKI were used as irrigants.

The whole mixture may have synergistic effect on the disruption of the bacterial cell wall and on the cytoplasmic membrane. MTAD components impart its mode of action which includes:

- ✦ Lowering the surface tension through Tween 80 which allows the irrigant to penetrate the dentinal tubules and inaccessible areas.
- ✦ Smear layer Removal through doxycycline and citric acid.
- ✦ Antibacterial Efficacy due to doxycycline.

CITRIC ACID

It is an organic acid and a chelator used in concentrations between 10%-50%. It is more potent as a chelator than EDTA at similar concentrations and has high efficiency in removing the smear layer and detaching bacterial biofilms adhering to root canals. Although EDTA is a weak antibacterial but it is stronger than citric acid in bacterial growth inhibition.

TETRACLEAN

It is similar to MTAD, but they differ in the concentration of antibiotics and kind of detergent used. In MTAD, doxycycline has the concentration of 150mg/5ml while the concentration of doxycycline in Tetraclean is 50 mg/5ml. The detergent of MTAD detergent is Tween 80 while polypropylene Glycol is the one used in Tetraclean.

HYDROGEN PEROXIDE

H_2O_2 is a clear and colourless liquid. It is used widely as a disinfectant; however it has a poor popularity among endodontists. It produces hydroxyl-free radicals (HO^-) that attack microbial components such as proteins and DNA. It comes in concentrations ranging from 3% - 5%. It is active against bacteria, viruses and yeasts. However, some bacteria produce catalase or superoxide dismutase which can provide them partial protection against H_2O_2. It is not recommended to be used a routine irrigant.

IODINE POTASSIUM IODIDE (IKI)

It consists of 2% iodine (I) in 4% potassium iodide (KI) and it is a halogen releasing agent. IKI is used as an irrigant due to its excellent antibacterial effect and low cytotoxicity. It is an oxidizing agent which reacts with free sulfhydryl groups of bacterial enzymes, cleaving disulfide bonds. In the rare cases where there is hypersensitivity to NaOCl and CHX, IKI is the ideal irrigant due its low cytotoxicity. Nevertheless, there are more allergy concerns linked to IKI compared to NaOCl and CHX. IKI also stains dentin which is one of its major the shortcomings.

INTRACANAL MEDICAMENTS

It has been a trend among clinicians to use intracanal medicaments if root canal treatment could not be completed in one visit. According to Athanassiadis (2007) (Table: 17. 9), intracanal medicaments are necessary adjuncts to inhibit bacterial regrowth between appointments due to surviving bacteria and leaky temporary restorations. There are various materials that can be used as intracanal medicaments to enhance the antimicrobial effect of our cleaning procedures. (Table: 17.10)

Table: 17.9. Some of the newer available irrigants.

IRRIGANT	DESCRIPTION
Smear Clear (SybronEndo)	✦ Clear. ✦ Odorless. ✦ Water soluble solution. ✦ Water + 17% EDTA + salts + a cationic surfactant (cetrimide) + anionic surfactant.
Hydroxyethlidene Bisphosphonate (HEBP)	✦ Little interference with NaOCl. ✦ Alternative to citric acid and EDTA. ✦ Prevents bone resorption. ✦ Used systematically in patients suffering osteoporosis and Paget's disease. ✦ Needs to be studied with further investigations.
QMix	✦ Contains EDTA, CHX, and a detergent ✦ Ready-use ✦ Used as a final rinse after NaOCl ✦ It lowers surface tension, removes smear layer and has an antibacterial effect.

Table: 17.10. Rationale of intra-canal medicaments use.

✦ To eliminate or destroy any remaining viable bacteria in the root canal system that have not been destroyed by the chemomechanical preparation process (i.e., instrumentation and irrigation).
✦ To reduce periradicular inflammation and hence reduce pain.
✦ To help eliminate apical exudate if it is present.
✦ To prevent or arrest inflammatory root resorption if it is present.
✦ To prevent re-infection of the root canal system by acting as both a chemical and a physical barrier if the temporary or interim restoration breaks down.

PHENOL COMPOUNDS

Several phenolic preparations have been used for disinfecting root canals such as phenol, camphorated phenol, paramonochlorophenol, thymol, cresol and camphorated parachlorophenol. Applying those compounds through cotton pellets or paper points allows its vaporization. Those vapours come in direct contact with microorganisms once they penetrate the root canal system. Refer to (Table: 17.11) for phenol's description.

Table: 17.11. Description of phenol.

✦ Carbolic acid C_6H_5OH.
✦ Nonspecific protoplasm poison.
✦ Concentration of 1% to 2% gives an optimal antimicrobial effect. Increasing the concentration to almost 30% lowers and shortens its effect.

Derivatives of phenol are known to be more antiseptic and toxic than phenol itself. Moreover, camphorated preparations are less toxic because camphoration slows the release of toxins to the surrounding tissues. However, the antimicrobial effect accompanied with those compounds does not balance the cytotoxicity caused by them. For that reason, their use has been decreased significantly.

FORMALDEHYDE

Formaldehyde preparations are widely used despite its known mutagenic effect and cytotoxicity. Formaldehyde is a volatile material that produces antimicrobial vapours when applied in cotton pellet, nevertheless, its use as an antimicrobial medicament is not justified due to its toxicity and it should not be used anymore.

Examples of formaldehyde preparations are:

- Formocresol : formaldehyde component is between 19% and 37%
- Tricresol formalin: formaldehyde component is 90% and contains 10% tricresol.

HALOGENS

When halogens are used as an intracanal medicament they come in the form of chloramine-T, an N-chloro tosylamide sodium salt. Iodine Potassium Iodide (IKI) is used as both an irrigant and intracanal medicament. 2% iodine in 4% potassium iodide dissolved in 94 ml of distilled water. It releases antimicrobial vapours which can disinfect dentin in 5 minutes and has low toxicity, however, it can stain dentin and is considered a severe allergen.

CALCIUM HYDROXIDE

Calcium Hydroxide has a special importance in dentistry. It has been used extensively as an intracanal medicament since Hermann introduced it in 1920. It is a slurry of $Ca(OH)_2$ in a water base. It can be mixed with water or saline and should have a thick consistency in order to carry as many as possible of $Ca(OH)_2$ particles. Chemically, calcium hydroxide is classified as a strong base with a high pH (approximately 12.5–12.8). Calcium hydroxide high pH kills bacteria by direct contact; hence it should fill the entire length of the canal homogenously in order to exert its maximum biological effect. This can be achieved using Lentulo spirals.

Fig: 17.4. summarizes the physical and chemical effect of $Ca(OH)_2$. In general, Calcium Hydroxide biological properties is exerted through the ionic dissociation of Ca^{2+} and OH^- ions, this contributes to a high pH which makes $Ca(OH)_2$ antimicrobial. It also has the ability to inactivate and hydrolyse bacterial lipopolysaccharides (LPS) especially in necrotic cases. Promoting hard tissue formation is yet another significant action exerted by $Ca(OH)_2$. However, $Ca(OH)_2$ has some limitations such as the rate of diffusion of hydroxyl ions is slowed due to the inherent buffering capacity of the dentine.

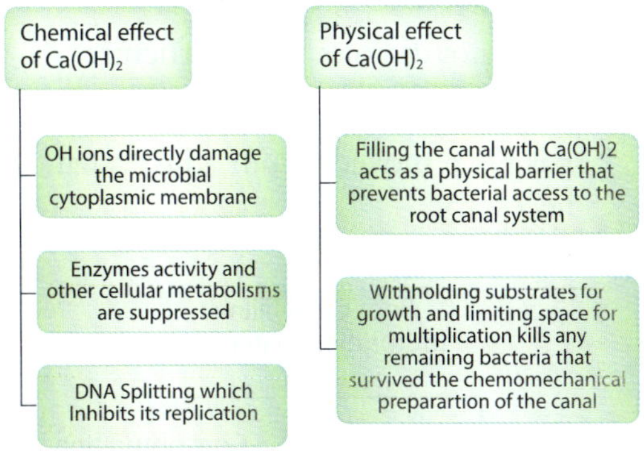

Fig: 17.4. Physical and chemical effects of $Ca(OH)_2$.

There is controversy regarding the use of calcium hydroxide, since it was shown that it does not reduce the number of bacteria significantly when used as an inter-appointment medicament. Moreover, 20% to 45% residue is left on the canal walls even after irrigating with NaOCl or EDTA; this residue will affect the sealing ability of zinc oxide eugenol sealers.

CHLORHEXIDINE

Refer to chlorhexidine in Irrigants section for more details. Chlorhexidine in a concentration of 2% is used as an irrigant and intracanal medicament. One of its important properties is its substantive antimicrobial activity that prevents bacterial colonization for prolonged periods of time once it comes in contact with root dentin. It is present in different modes of application, liquid, gel, or controlled-release device and all those modes have the same efficacy.

Care should be taken not to combine the use of sodium hypochlorite and chlorhexidine. An acid-base reaction, CHX is a dicationic acid which makes it a proton-donor while NaOCl is alkaline that accepts protons from CHX. The result of this proton exchange is the formation of an insoluble precipitate called para-chloroaniline (PCA) which is toxic, results in discoloration and affects the sealing of obturation materials.

LEDERMIX

When patients are experiencing severe endodontic pain, Ledermix (Lederle Pharmaceuticals, Wolfratshausen, Germany) can be used as an initial medicament so that the patient would be symptom-free in subsequent visits. Schroeder developed this material as a combination of antibiotic/corticosteroids paste.

Ledermix paste is a non-setting, water-soluble paste material with a combination of a tetracycline antibiotic, demeclocycline HCl (at a concentration of 3.2%), and a corticosteroid, triamcinolone acetonide (concentration 1%), in a polyethylene glycol base.

Controversy regarding products containing corticosteroids is present due to concern regarding its release to the body's circulation.

TRIPLE ANTIBIOTICS PASTES

This medicament is composed of three antibiotics in one paste which are metronidazole, ciprofloxacin, and minocycline. It is found to be effective at eradicating bacteria, although there are concerns related to its use, such as tooth discoloration from minocycline and bacterial resistance. In addition, this combination has been used clinically in regenerative endodontics where complete root formation was observed in young permanent teeth despite the presence of an open apex with a periapical radiolucency and a draining buccal sinus tract.

BIOACTIVE GLASS

Bioactive glass consists of SiO_2–Na_2O-CaO–P_2O_5 system. Its antimicrobial mechanism of action is still not fully understood.

ROOT CANAL OBTURATION MATERIALS

Throughout the history of endodontics many materials were used as root filling materials from tin foil, cotton pellets, plaster of Paris to not even filling the root canal and leaving it empty. Grossman (1987) outlined the properties of an ideal obturation material and provided criteria that can help clinicians identify the best obturation material as it is detailed in (Table: 17.12.).

After effective chemomechanical debridement, the disinfected root canal should be sealed in order to prevent reinfection. Obturation should block the canal:

- Apically to block the exit of surviving microorganisms to the periradicular tissue.
- Coronally to prevent reinfection of the pulp space from the oral cavity
- Throughout the canal to seal the openings of accessory and lateral canals.

Obturation involves the use of two kinds of materials (Fig: 17.5); one is the core obturation material in the solid form (e.g. gutta-percha and resilon) and another semisolid cementing medium (i.e. sealers).

Table: 17.12. Properties of an ideal obturation material.

✦ Easily manipulated and provides ample working time
✦ Dimensionally stable with no shrinkage once inserted
✦ Seals the canal laterally and apically, conforming to its complex internal anatomy
✦ Nonirritating to the periapical tissues
✦ Impervious to moisture and nonporous
✦ Unaffected by tissue fluids-no corrosion or oxidization
✦ Inhibits bacterial growth
✦ Radiopaque and easily discernible on radiographs
✦ Does not discolor tooth structure
✦ Sterile
✦ Easily removed from the canal if necessary

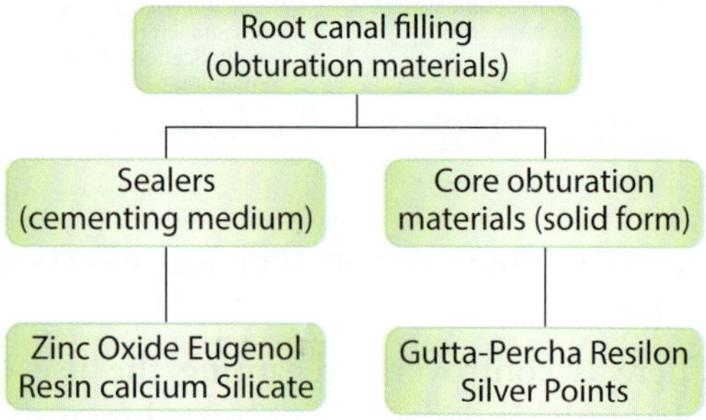

Fig: 17.5. Diagrammatic illustration of the root canal fillings.

1. CORE OBTURATION MATERIALS

A. Silver Cones

Jasper introduced silver cones in 1933 claiming they are as successful as gutta-percha. Silver Points are rigid and have the same diameter and taper as the instruments used to shape the canal, this made them easily placed and allowed a more predictable length control. Although silver points followed most of the properties Grossman identified yet it had a major disadvantage that is it inability to fill the canal and seal it apically and laterally because silver points lacked adaptability and plasticity. Table: 17.13 lists the main advantage and disadvantage of Silver Points.

Since silver points couldn't seal the canal perfectly and left too much space to be filled with sealers this lead to leakage. This leakage caused corrosion of silver points and formation of silver salts. Those corrosion products are cytotoxic. With those major disadvantages of silver points their use nowadays is considered as below the standard of care.

Table: 17.13. Advantages and disadvantages of Silver Points

ADVANTAGES OF SILVER POINTS
✦ Rigid
✦ Have the same taper and diameter as the files used to shape the canal.
✦ Easily placed inside the canal
✦ More predictable length control

DISADVANTAGES OF SILVER POINTS
✦ Non adaptable and unable to fill canal irregularities and this permits leakage
✦ It corrodes when in contact with tissue fluids or saliva.
✦ The cytotoxic corrosion by-products impair periapical healing.
✦ Difficult to remove if retreatment is indicated

B. Gutta-Percha

Gutta-Percha is now considered as the most widely used obturation material. Gutta-percha is derived from various species of rubber trees from Malaysia, Borneo, Indonesia, and South America, mainly Brazil. It is the *trans* isomer of 1,4-polyisoprene (rubber) and it exists in two crystalline forms (α and β). The α-phase gutta-percha has superior thermoplastic properties. This characteristic is utilised in heat-softened gutta-percha obturation techniques (Thermafil and Obtura) and is now considered the gold standard. Natural rubber is the *cis* isomer of 1,4-polyisoprene, the different isomers have different alignment of CH_2 group along the double bond (Fig: 17.6). They are on opposite sides in the *trans* isomer (gutta-percha) while In the *cis* form (natural rubber), they are on the same side. The elasticity of natural rubber comes from its configuration where one chain is allowed to move past another, while the *trans* form of gutta-percha makes it more linear which crystallizes more readily, this makes gutta-percha more brittle, less elastic and harder.

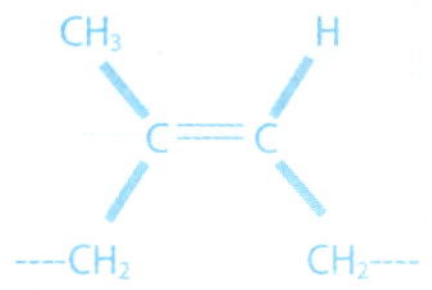

Natural Rubber (cis 1,4 polyisoprene)
CH_2 groups are on the same side of the double bond. This stereo-chemical configuration allows mobility of one chain over another and gives natural rubber its elasticity.

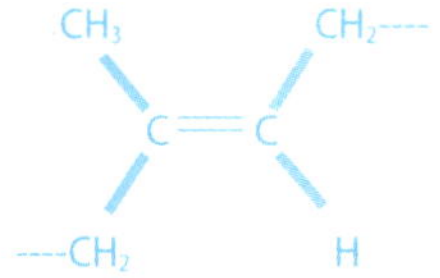

Gutta-prercha (trans 1,4 polyisoprene)
CH_2 groups are on opposits sides of double bond. This stereo-chemical configuration makes gutta-percha more linear, harder and more brittle.

Fig: 17.6. *Cis and tran* isomers of 1,4-polyisoprene (natural rubber and gutta-percha).

According to Friedman (1975), ironically, Gutta-percha is not the main constituent of these obturation points and it contains zinc oxide as a filler, wax and resins as plasticizers and radio-opacifiers heavy metals such as barium sulfate (Table. 17.14).

Table: 17.14. Composition of Gutta-Percha Points.

59-76%	Zinc Oxide
18-22%	Gutta-Percha
1-18%	Heavy metals salts
1-4%	Wax or resin

Gutta-percha does not fulfil all the properties identified by Grossman (1987) but it satisfies most of them. However, unlike silver points, its main disadvantage is that it lacks rigidity. Other disadvantages include its inability to seal without a sealer. Table: 17.15 summarizes the advantages and disadvantages of gutta-percha.

Table: 17.15. Advantage and disadvantages of gutta-percha points.

ADVANTAGES OF GUTTA-PERCHA
✦ Plasticity
✦ Ease of manipulation
✦ Minimal toxicity(inert)
✦ Radiopaque
✦ Can be removed with heat or solvents
✦ Adapts with compaction to canal irregularities
DISADVANTAGES OF GUTTA-PERCHA
✦ Lack of adhesion to dentin
✦ Shrinkage on cooling(1%-2%)
✦ Elasticity (rebounds, pulls away)
✦ Oxidizes to air and light and becomes more brittle

Gutta-Percha is available in standardized ISO (International Standards Organization) sizes. Initially it came in the standard 0.02 taper but with the introduction of newer shaping instruments with larger tapers, Gutta-percha points are manufactured to match those instruments. Gutta-Percha can be sterilized by 5.25% NaOCl for one minute then rinsed in ethyl alcohol to remove crystallized NaOCl which if not removed would impair the obturation seal. It is important to note that it can not be heat-sterilized. Gutta-Percha oxidizes to air and light and becomes brittle, consequently storage in a cool dry place like refrigerators is imperative. It can be softened by chloroform, halothane and in a less degree by turpentine and xylene.

A. Resilon

Resilon is a polyurethane thermoplastic root canal filling material. It is used with certain sealers such as Epiphany, RealSeal, Resinate.

The introduction of this material aimed to achieve what is called "monoblock" where the resilon sealer (epiphany) bonds to both the etched canal wall and the resilon cone, but whether this can be truly achieved is still controversial. Moreover, the use of this bonding resin does not strengthen the tooth.

Resilon consists of:

- Methacrylate resin (difunctional) BisGMA
- Bioactive Glass
- Radiopaque fillers (bismuth oxychloride and barium sulfate) makes up 65% of its content.

It is similar to Gutta-Percha in having the same ISO sizes and shapes; it can also be softened with heat and chloroform and used with any obturation technique (lateral condensation, thermoplasticized, carrier-based). Its seal is comparable to Gutta-Percha. Resilon is nontoxic, no mutagenic, and biocompatible. It is also compatible to be used with cores and posts that are resin placed.

The Resilon system consists of a primer, a sealer, and synthetic polymer points or pellets. Preparatory steps are needed to use this material, such as using a Self-Etch Primer. This primer consists of sulfonic acid-terminated functional monomer, 2-hydroxyethyl methacrylate HEMA, water, polymerization initiator. The primer is applied (2-3 drops) with pipette or syringe or a paper point. It is essential to know that sodium hypochlorite affects the bond of the primer so it is mandatory to use EDTA as a final rinse before rinsing the canal with sterile water, saline, or chlorhexidine.

ROOT CANAL SEALERS (Cementing medium)

Since root filling materials do not bond to the dentinal wall of root canal, sealers are essential to seal the space between the two surfaces and fill the voids and irregularities in the root canal anatomy during obturation.

In 1982, Grossman outlined the properties of an ideal sealer (Table: 17.16).

Table: 17.16. Properties of an ideal root canal sealer.

✦ Exhibits tackiness when mixed to provide good adhesion between it and the canal wall when set.
✦ Can establish a hermetic seal.
✦ Radiopaque.
✦ Made of a very fine powder, so that it can mix easily with liquid.
✦ Exhibits a slow set.
✦ Does not undergo shrinkage on setting.
✦ Does not stain the tooth structure.
✦ Bacteriostatic, or at least does not encourage bacterial growth.
✦ Insoluble in tissue fluids.
✦ Tissue tolerant; that is, nonirritating to periradicular tissue.
✦ Soluble in a common solvent if it is necessary to remove the root canal filling.

Different kinds of sealers are present, each with their advantages and disadvantage but no current sealer satisfies all the characteristics needed. Those types are:

ZINC OXIDE EUGENOL SEALERS

It is the most commonly used sealer so far. There are various product brands that have zinc oxide eugenol as the main ingredient and eugenol as the liquid used for mixing. These products only differ in the other components added to the sealer.

The earliest formula of zinc oxide eugenol was Rickert's formula. It satisfied most of Grossman's properties except that it caused staining to tooth tissues due to silver particles. Pulp Canal Sealer (SybronEndo) followed Rickert's formula but it had a very rapid setting time, this was modified in Pulp Canal Sealer EWT (extended working time) which was marketed as having a 6 hours working time. Those two brands were used extensively by clinicians in thermoplastic warm vertical obturation.

Grossman modified Rickert's formula by removing the silver particles to make a non-staining sealer such as Proscol (Procosol, Inc., Philadelphia, PA) and Roth's Sealer (Roth's Pharmacy, Chicago, 11). Grossman Formula in Proscol contained zinc oxide, hydrogenated staybelite resin, bismuth subcarbonate and barium sulfate. Roth has the same formula with the substitution of bismuth subnitrate for bismuth subcarbonate.

Wach's sealer (Balas Dental, Chicago,IL) powder contains zinc oxide, bismuth subnitrate, bismuth sub iodide, magnesium oxide, and calcium phosphate, while the liquid consists of oil of cloves,eucalyptol, Canada balsam, and beechwood creosote. Canada balsam is what makes this sealer different than other sealers when used in lateral compaction due its tacky property that softens the gutta-percha into a more homogeneous mass.

Unlike the previous powder/liquid formulas, a catalyst/base sealer named Tubliseal is another brand that is known to be easily mixed with a two paste system in two separate tubes. The paste contains zinc oxide-base, barium sulfate for radiopacity, and mineral oil, cornstarch, and lecithin. The catalyst tube has polypale resin, eugenol, and thymol iodide. Tubliseal has the disadvantage of having a rapid setting time and that is modified in Tubliseal EWT.

Zinc Oxide Eugenol sealers are distinguished with having the ability of adding materials to its constituents to enhance its properties. Paraformaldehyde was added for antimicrobial and mummifying effects but it is not acceptable anymore due to its circulation to other body parts. Corticosteroids can suppress inflammatory reactions. Canada Balsam can be added for a more sticky and tacky properties that would improve the sealer's adhesion to dentin. Rosins (colophony) which are derived from conifers, were initially added for better adhesive properties but it was later on found that resins acids which form 90% of rosins work similarly to quaternary ammonium compounds in increasing the cell membrane permeability of affected cells. Although this might be cytotoxic, yet the addition of resin acids to zinc oxide may be beneficial.

CALCIUM HYDROXIDE SEALERS

This sealer was introduced to take advantage of calcium hydroxide antibacterial and hard tissue formation properties. SealApex, CRCS, Apexit all have in common having calcium hydroxide as one of the main ingredients. (Fig: 17.17)

Table: 17.17. Composition of different Calcium Hydroxide $Ca(OH)_2$ sealers.

TYPE OF $Ca(OH)_2$ SEALER	INGREDIENTS
Sealapex	Base: Zinc oxide, calcium hydroxide,butyl benzene, sulfonamide, and zinc stearate. Catalyst: Barium sulfate and titanium dioxide for radiopacity, a proprietary resin, isobutyl salicylate, and aerocil R792.
CRCS	Powder: Calcium hydroxide, Zinc oxide, Bismuth dioxide and Barium sulfate. Liquid: Eugenol and Eucalyptol.
Apexit	Base: Calcium hydroxide, zinc oxide, calcium oxide , silicon dioxide, zinc stearate, hydrogenized colophony , tricalcium phosphate and polydimethylsiloxane Activator: Trimethyl hexanedioldiasalicylate, bismuth carbonate basic, bismuth oxide, silicon dioxide, 1,3-butanedioldisalicylate, hydrogenized colophony, tricalcium phosphate, zinc stearate,

NON-EUGENOL SEALERS

Those sealers are derived from periodontal dressings. Eugenol was removed due to its irritating effect. Nogenol (GC America, Inc., Alsip, IL) is the brand for this type of sealers. It is a catalyst/base sealer with a base of zinc oxide, barium sulfate, bismuth oxychloride, and vegetable oil and the catalyst containing Hydrogenated rosin, methyl abietate, lauric acid, chlorothymol, and salicylic acid.

GLASS IONOMER SEALERS

Due to Glass Ionomer dentin binding ability Ketac-Endo (3M, Minneapolis, MN) was manufactured. Activ GP (Brasseler USA, Savannah, GA) is gutta-percha impregnated with glass-ionomer and it needs a glass ionomer sealer.

RESIN SEALERS

These sealers are either epoxy-resin sealers like AH-26 and AH-plus or Urethane Methacrylate resin sealers like EndoRez and Epiphany. AH-26 (Dentsply International Maillfer) is a bisphenol epoxy resin sealer that uses hexamethylenetetramine (methenamine) for polymerization.The methenamine releases some formaldehyde as it sets, and this is the major disadvantage of using this sealer. Staining and extending working time are other disadvantages. Besides its adhesion advantage, AH-26 has increased radiopacity, low solubility, slight shrinkage, and tissue compatibility. AH-plus (Dentsply International) is a modification of AH-26 without formaldehyde release. It also has lower solubility, more radiopaque and shorter setting time compared to AH-26.

Epiphany (Pentron Clinical Technologies) or Real Seal (Sybron Endo) contain urethane dimethacrylate (UDMA), Poly-(ethylene glycol) dimethacrylates (PEGDMA), ethoxylated bisphenol A-dimethacrylate (EBPADMA), Bisphenol-A-glycidyldimethacrylate (BisGMA) resins and are used with Resilon. Epiphany needs 25 minutes to set; consequently it is essential light cure the coronal surface for 40 seconds to achieve coronal seal since complete set takes longer time. EndoRez (Ultradent, South Jordon, UT) is a hydrophilic UDMA resin sealer that reportedly has good canal wetting and flow into dentinal tubules.

OTHERS

Other types of sealers include: silicone-based sealers, chloropercha, bioceramic sealers (Calcium Silicate Sealers) and sealers containing formaldehyde. For more details about these sealers refer to Table: 17.18. which summarizes some of the sealers in endodontics.

Table: 17.18. Root canal sealers.

	DESCRIPTION	ADVANTAGES	DISADVANTAGES	EXAMPLES
ZINC OXIDE EUGENOL CEMENT SEALER	✦ Most commonly used sealer. ✦ Modification of the regular ZOE. ✦ The mixing vehicle is mostly eugenol. ✦ Powder contains ZnO that has been finely sifted to enhance the flow. ✦ Setting process is a chemical reaction with physical embedding of ZnO in a matrix of zinc eugenolate. ✦ Free Eugenol always remains in the mass as irritant.	✦ Absorbed if extruded into periradicular tissue. ✦ Antimicrobial effect through ZnO or additives such as rosin and canad Balsam or corticosteroids.	✦ Shrinks on setting. ✦ stains the tooth . (Roth's Sealer was developed to be as a non-staining ZOE sealer).	✦ Pulp Canal Sealer (SybronEndo) ✦ Pulp Canal Sealer EWT ✦ Proscol (Procosol, Inc., Philadelphia, PA) ✦ Roth (Roth's Pharmacy, Chicago, 11) ✦ Tubliseal (Sybron Endo/ Kerr) ✦ Wach's Sealer Balas Dental, Chicago,IL)
CALCIUM HYDROXIDE SEALERS	✦ It was developed for two main reasons : 1. Antimicrobial effect 2. Osteogenic-Cementogenic potential ✦ However, these two effects were not demonstrated.		✦ Needs to be soluble in order to leach out the hydroxyl group responsible for its activity but sealers should not exhibit solubility. ✦ Poor cohesive strength ✦ Poor dentin adhesion	✦ Calciobiotic Root Canal Sealer (CRCS) (Coltene Whaledent, Altstatten, Switzerland) ✦ Sealapex (Sybron Endo) ✦ Apexit(Ivoclar Vivadent)

NON-EUGENOL SEALERS	✦ Developed from periodontal dressings	✦ No irritating effect of eugenol		✦ Nogenol (GCAmerica, Alsip, IL)
GLASS LONOMER SEALERS	✦ Developed to take advantage of their bond to dentin, fluoride release, antimicrobial activity, and biocompatibility.	✦ Dentin binding ✦ Minimal tissue irritation. ✦ Low toxicity.	✦ Solubility concern ✦ Inadequate bonding with gutta-percha ✦ Minimal antibacterial effect	✦ Ketac-Endo (3M ESPE, Minneapolis, MN) ✦ ActivGP (Brassier USA, Savannak, GA) which is a gutta-percha cone impregnated with GI coating.
RESIN	✦ Introduced because it provides good adhesion ✦ AH-26 and AH-plus are epoxy-resins . While Epiphany is a dual curable dental resin composed of BisGMA, ethoxylated BisGMA, UDMA, hydrophilic difunctional methacrylates and fillers.	✦ Good adhesion ability. ✦ Does not contain eugenol		✦ AH-26 (Dentsply International Maillfer) ✦ AH-Plus (Dentsply International) ✦ Epiphany (Pentran Clinical Technologies) ✦ EndaREZ (Ultradent Products, South Jordan, UT) Diaket (3M ESPE)
SILICONE-BASED SEALERS	✦ Two materials are available: 1. RoekoSeal (Langenau, Germany): which is a polyvinyl siloxane or polydimethyl siloxane root canal sealer 2. Gutta Flow (Cuyahoga Falls, OH): i. Cold, flowable, self-curing obturation material for root canals that combines gutta-percha and polydimethylsiloxane sealer (RoekoSeal) into one injectable system. ii. Fills canal irregularities. iii. Inject the material in the canal and then place a single master cone. iv. Working time is 15 minutes and cures in 25-30 minutes.			

CHLOROPERCHA	✦ White gutta-percha (Alba) chloroform ✦ Not used anymore	✦ The addition of chloroform allows the gutta-percha cone to fit better in the canal.	✦ No adhesive ability. ✦ Toxicity of chloroform	
BIOCERAMICS (CALCIUM SILICATE) SEALERS	✦ Composed of zirconium oxide and calcium silicates.	✦ Hydrophilic ✦ Sets by utilizing moisture ✦ No shrinkage on setting ✦ Antimicrobial effect-during setting ✦ Biocompatible	✦ Hardens on setting which may make retreatment difficult if required.	✦ iRootSP or Endosequence BC Sealer (Innovative BioCeramix Inc., Vancouver, Canada) ✦ MTA Fillapex (Angelus) ✦ Tech Biosealer Endo (TB E, Isasan, Rovello Porro, Italy)
SEALERS CONTAINING FORMALDEHYDE	✦ Absolutely contraindicated		✦ Toxic ✦ Overextension causes irreversible neurotoxicity dysesthesia	✦ Endomethasone (Septodont, Paris, France) ✦ Rieber's paste (Amubarut; Wera Karl, Biesingen, Germany) ✦ N2 (Indrag-Ag,sa, Losone, Switzerland) ✦ SPAD

ROOT-END FILLING MATERIALS:

Apical Surgery is an indispensible part of endodontics, since certain cases require root end resection (apicoectomy) to reach a favourable outcome. Many materials have been used to fill the root end after resection, but none of them verify all the requirements of an ideal root end filling. Chong &Pitt Ford (2005) summarized the requirements of an ideal root-end filling material as shown in (Table: 17.19).

Table: 17.19. Requirements of an ideal root-and filling material.

✦ Should adhere or bond to tooth tissue and "seal" the root end three dimensionally.
✦ Should not promote, and preferably inhibit, the growth of pathogenic microorganisms
✦ Dimensionally stable and unaffected by moisture in either the set or unset state.
✦ Well tolerated by periradicular tissues with no inflammatory reactions.
✦ Stimulates the regeneration of normal periodontium.
✦ Non-toxic both locally and systemically.
✦ Should not corrode or be electrochemically active
✦ Should not stain the tooth or the periradicular tissues
✦ Easily distinguishable on radiographs
✦ Has a long shelf life
✦ Easy to handle

AMALGAM

It is radio-opaque and manipulated easily. Yet its biocompatibility is poor and associated with inflammation.

EBA (SUPER ETHOXY-BENZOIC ACID)

EBA is a zinc-oxide eugenol that is liquid-modified to decrease the amount of the free eugenol and subsequently decrease the toxicity. Super EBA has much better physical properties than ZOE such as high compressive strength and better tensile strength. Reports showed a good healing response to super EBA with minimal chronic inflammation at the root apex and less apical leakage. Refer to Table: 17.20 for the composition of EBA.

Table: 17.20. Super Ethoxy-Benzoic Acid (EBA).

POWDER
✦ Zinc-oxide 60 % (primary reactive agent)
✦ Quartz 35% (reinforcing agent)
✦ Hydrogenated resin 5% (reinforcing agent)
LIQUID
✦ Eugenol 65% (primary reactive ingredient)
✦ Ortho-Ethoxybenzoic acid 35% (primary reactive ingredient) - added to modify the physical properties and control the setting time.

INTERMEDIATE RESTORATIVE MATERIAL (IRM)

It is a variant of ZOE that has the polymethylmethacrylate added to it, in order to enhance its physical properties (Table: 17.21). The reaction is a chelation reaction between zinc and eugenol. The set material is viscous with a higher sealing ability and apical leakage resistance compared to the basic ZOE. It is well-tolerated by the periapical tissue but without hard tissue regenerative capabilities.

Table:17.21. Intermediate Restorative Material (IRM).

POWDER
✦ 75% zinc oxide (primary reactive ingredient)
✦ 20-25% poly-metha resin (reinforcing strength)
LIQUID
✦ 99% eugenol (reactive ingredient)
✦ 1% acetic acid

DENTINE-BONDED RESIN COMPOSITE (RETROPLAST):

Retroplast is a composite resin used in combination with GLUMA®, a dentinal bonding agent has been developed as a root-end filling (Table: 17.22). It is a two - paste system that forms a dual cure composite when mixed that sets in a polymerization reaction. It is a promising material regarding hard tissue generation and healing of periapical tissue

Table: 17.22. Retroplast.

PASTE A
✦ Bis-GMA/TEGDIVIA 1:1
✦ Benzoyl peroxide N,N-di (hydroxyethyl)-p-toluidine
✦ BHT
PASTE B
✦ Resin ytterbium trifluoride aerosil ferric oxide
GLUMA®: Specifically-designed dentine bonding agent to condition the root-end surface in conjugation with EDTA.

RESIN – IONOMER MATERIALS

These materials are resin - ionomer suspension combining the advantages of composite and glass-ionomer. Geristore is paste-paste formulation; it is a hydrophilic bis-GMA with a long term fluoride release activated by light for 40 seconds. In addition to that, it is a self- adhesive material with no need for an agent to adhere it to the tooth structure.

POST AND CORE SYSTEMS

Endodontic treatment often involves extensive removal of tooth tissues which weakens the tooth and makes it less resistance to occlusal stresses. The most commonly used methods for reinforcing endodontically treated teeth are usually pin-retained cores or post and core systems. Post and core is a dental procedure that involves restoring the lost tooth structure and rebuilding the tooth morphology in order to provide the required support for future restoration, such as a crown or bridges. It consists of two parts: a post that fits in to the root canal and a core portion that project above the gum. The goal of this procedure is to provide the sufficient structure under the final restoration which can be either a crown or a bridge so it can withstand occlusal forces and function normally. The properties of the ideal post and core system are mentioned in (Table: 17.23).

Table: 17.23. Properties of an ideal post and core system.

✦ Should have satisfactory physical properties such as modulus of elasticity, compressive strength, and coefficient of thermal expansion that are close to dentine.
✦ The post is able to transfer stresses to the remaining tooth structure without created high stresses that might fracture the tooth.
✦ The core is able to transfer stresses from the final restoration to the post and tooth.
✦ Provides maximum retention with minimal removal of tooth tissue.
✦ Good biocompatibility and should not be corrosive.
✦ Aesthetically compatible with the final restoration.
✦ Can be retrieved in cases of retreatments or failures.

POSTS

There are two main categories of posts: cast (custom-made) or prefabricated. (Table: 17.24). In the case of the cast post, the post and core material are cast as a single unit.

Recently, many dentists prefer using the prefabricated posts because the procedure usually needs one appointment, cheaper and simpler. Although, the cast post and core system is more complex and take two appointments to finish, some clinicians prefer to use as the post and core acts as a single unit and can be casted with a ferrule effect that supports the tooth against wedging forces and prevents tooth fracture.

CAST POST AND CORE SYSTEM (CUSTOM MADE)

Cast post and core system was the standard for many years and is still used by some clinicians. They may also be indicated in small teeth with minimal tooth structure available. Cast gold alloy (type III or IV), post and core have been used for decades as a foundation restoration to support the final restoration in endodontically treated teeth. Cast gold alloys (type III or IV) are inert materials with a modulus of elasticity, stiffness, and coefficient of thermal expansion similar to those of enamel. It has good compressive strength that can withstand normal occlusal forces. Their major disadvantage, however, is aesthetics, since the metal shows through the newer all-ceramic restorations.

The second type of material that have been used in this system are base metal alloys (cobalt, chrome, nickel titanium). These alloys have better corrosive resistance, with high strength and modulus of elasticity and are relatively cheap. However, these alloys have high hardness and are difficult to adjust.

PREFABRICATED POSTS

Three types of prefabricated posts are currently available: metal posts, fibre-reinforced resin posts and ceramic posts.

METAL POSTS

Metal prefabricated posts are made from different alloys such stainless steel, titanium, platimium-gold-palladoim (Pt-Au-Pd or PGP), cobalt chrome (Co-Cr) or nickel chromium (Ni-Cr). Compared to cast posts, these metal posts have more suitable physical properties as they have a high modulus of elasticity and are, essentially, more rigid.

FIBRE- REINFORCED RESIN POSTS

Currently, there are two types present: carbon fibre-reinforced and glass fiber-reinforced posts. These posts have the potential to bond to the remaining tooth structure, thus, it is claimed that they provide stronger support to the remaining tooth structure than the metal posts. Moreover, flexural modulus of elasticity of fiber-reinforced posts is close to that of dentin which helps in decreasing the incidence of root fracture. They have significantly lower stiffness and strength compared to metal and ceramic cast posts. Like metal cast posts, the carbon type presents as aesthetic problem.

CERAMIC POSTS

These posts can be developed as ceramic composites, woven fiber posts (e.g. polyethylene) and high-strength ceramic posts (zirconia). Ceramics posts are biocompatible with high flexural strength and excellent aesthetic properties. However, it has rather poor bonding capability. This type of post is relatively new, and still required long-term clinical investigations.

Table: 17.24. Summary of some of the types of posts and their advantages and disadvantages.

TYPE OF POST	TYPE OF MATERIAL	ADVANTAGES	DISADVANTAGES
CUSTOM-MADE	Cast gold alloys (type III or IV)	✦ Inert material ✦ Good compressive strength	✦ Poor aesthetics ✦ High cost ✦ Requires atleast two clinical visits
	Base metal alloys	✦ Higher corrosive resistance than gold alloys. ✦ Lower cost than gold alloys.	✦ Poor aesthetics ✦ High hardness and difficult to adjust ✦ Requires atleast two clinical visits
PREFABRICATED	Metal posts	✦ High modulus of elasticity ✦ can often be retrieved in cases or retreatment or failure	✦ Some concerns about nickel sensitivity and metal allergies ✦ Corrosive material
	Fibre reinforced polymer post	✦ Flexural modulus close to that of dentin ✦ Minimal wedging effect within the root canal ✦ Requires less dentin removal ✦ No metal allergies or corrosion ✦ Good aesthetic properties ✦ Bonds to most resin cements and resin-based composite core materials	✦ Weaker physical strength and stiffness compared to metal and ceramic posts ✦ Poor aesthetics of the carbon fibre posts.
	Ceramic	✦ Excellent aesthetics ✦ Good biocompatibility ✦ High flexural strength and fracture toughness.	✦ Poor bonding to dentin ✦ Require removal of more tooth structure ✦ Difficult to retrieve in cases of retreatment or failure.

CORE BUILD-UP MATERIALS

A core material can be either directly or indirectly constructed; it also can be made of metallic, resinous or ceramic materials. In case of endodontically treated teeth, cores are either casted as one unit along with the custom- made post (indirect method), or they are build-up directly on a prefabricated post placed in the root canal. Table: 17.25 summarizes the advantages and disadvantages of the most commonly used materials for direct core build-up materials in endodontically treated teeth.

Table: 17.25. Advantages and disadvantages of some of the materials used as direct core build up materials.

MATERIAL	ADVANTAGES	DISADVANTAGES
AMALGAM	✦ Good physical and mechanical properties. ✦ Can be placed in high-stress areas. ✦ Good physical and mechanical properties. ✦ Conversation of tooth structure.	✦ If tooth loss is extensive, it requires the addition of pins or other technique to provide retention and resistance to rotation. ✦ Requires a minimal coronal tooth structure available. ✦ Long setting time. ✦ Poor aesthetics.
GLASS-IONOMER -	✦ Good in situations of minimal tooth structure is lost. ✦ Conversation of tooth structure	✦ Lack adequate strength as a buildup material. ✦ Difficult to condense.
COMPOSITE RESIN	✦ Good aesthetics. ✦ Good retention to the post and the remaining tooth structure. ✦ High tensile strength. ✦ Short setting time. ✦ Conversation of tooth structure.	✦ Polymerization shrinkage. ✦ Plastic deformation due to water absorption. ✦ Poor Adhesion to dentin especially on the pulpal floor. ✦ Technique sensitive (requires isolation from oral fluids). ✦ Composite is not a good with minimal remaining coronal tooth structure. ✦ Requires an additional adhesive system.

SUMMARY

The principles of endodontic instrumentation and therapy are well-established. Thorough cleaning of the canal system to render it as free as possible of pulpal tissue, bacterial presence and by-products, followed by complete obturation to prevent apical or coronal leakage creates an environment that promotes periradicular healing. The philosophy of achieving a hermetic seal of the root apex has been abandoned in favour of development of a fluid tight antibacterial seal as a requirement for modern root canal sealers. The continuum of research and development of materials and instruments will drive the continued development of new materials for endodontic therapy.

REFERENCES

1. Abbott, P. V. (1992). Sytemic release of corticosteroids following intra-dental use. International Endodontic Journal, 25(4), 189-191. doi: 10.1111/j.1365-2591.1992.tb00748.x
2. Abbott, P. V., Heithersay, G. S., & Hume, W. R. (1988). Release and diffusion through human tooth roots in vitro of corticosteroid and tetracycline trace molecules from Ledermix® paste. Dental Traumatology, 4(2), 55-62. doi: 10.1111/j.1600-9657.1988.tb00295.x
3. Abbott, P. V., Hume, W. R., & Heithersay, G. S. (1989). Barriers to diffusion of Ledermix paste in radicular dentine. Endod Dent Traumatol, 5(2), 98-104.
4. Al-Omiri, M. K., Mahmoud, A. A., Rayyan, M. R., & Abu-Hammad, O. (2010). Fracture Resistance of Teeth Restored with Post-retained Restorations: An Overview. Journal of Endodontics, 36(9), 1439-1449. doi: 10.1016/j.joen.2010.06.005
5. Alhadainy, H. A., & Himel, V. T. (1993). Evaluation of the sealing ability if amalgam, cavit, and glassionomer cement in the repair of furcation perforations. Oral Surgery Oral Medicine Oral Pathology Oral Radiology and Endodontics, 75(3), 362-366. doi: 10.1016/0030-4220(93)90152-t
6. Alkhatib, Z. Z., Baum, R. H., Morse, D. R., Yesilsoy, C., Bhambhani, S., & Furst, M. L. (1990). The antimicrobial effect of various endodontic sealers. Oral Surgery Oral Medicine Oral Pathology Oral Radiology and Endodontics, 70(6), 784-790. doi: 10.1016/0030-4220(90)90022-k
7. Ambard, A. J., & Mueninghoff, L. (2006). Calcium phosphate cement: review of mechanical and biological properties. Journal of prosthodontics : official journal of the American College of Prosthodontists, 15(5), 321-328. doi: 10.1111/j.1532-849X.2006.00129.x
8. Asmussen, E., Peutzfeldt, A., & Heitmann, T. (1999). Stiffness, elastic limit, and strength of newer types of endodontic posts. Journal of Dentistry, 27(4), 275-278. doi: 10.1016/s0300-5712(98)00066-9
9. Athanassiadis, B., Abbott, P. V., & Walsh, L. J. (2007). The use of calcium hydroxide, antibiotics and biocides as antimicrobial medicaments in endodontics. Australian Dental Journal, 52(1), S64-S82. doi: 10.1111/j.1834-7819.2007.tb00527.x
10. Augsburger, R. A., & Peters, D. D. (1990). Radiographic evaluation of extruded obturation materials. Journal of Endodontics, 16(10), 492-497.
11. Babich, H., Wurzburger, B. J., Rubin, Y. L., Sinensky, M. C., & Blau, L. (1995). An in-vitro study of the cytotoxicity of chlorhexidine digluconate to human gingival cells. Cell Biology and Toxicology, 11(2), 79-88. doi: 10.1007/bf00767493
12. Balkenhol, M., Woestmann, B., Rein, C., & Ferger, P. (2007). Survival time of cast post and cores: A 10-year retrospective study. Journal of Dentistry, 35(1), 50-58. doi: 10.1016/j.jdent.2006.04.004
13. Barbosa, S. V., Burkard, D. H., & Spangberg, L. S. W. (1994). Xytotoxic effects of gutta-percha solvents. Journal of Endodontics, 20(1), 6-8. doi: 10.1016/s0099-2399(06)80018-x
14. Basrani, B., Santos, J. M., Tjaderhane, L., Grad, H., Gorduysus, O., Huang, J. F., . . . Friedman, S. (2002). Substantive

antimicrobial activity in chlorhexidine-treated human root dentin. Oral Surgery Oral Medicine Oral Pathology Oral Radiology and Endodontics, 94(2), 240-245. doi: 10.1067/moe.2002.124002

15. Basrani, B. R., Manek, S., Sodhi, R. N., Fillery, E., & Manzur, A. (2007). Interaction between sodium hypochlorite and chlorhexidine gluconate. J Endod, 33(8), 966-969.

16. Bateman, G., Ricketts, D. N. J., & Saunders, W. P. (2003). Fibre-based post systems: A review. British Dental Journal, 195(1), 43-48. doi: 10.1038/sj.bdj.4810278

17. Baumgartner, G., Zehnder, M., & Paque, F. (2007). Enterococcus faecalis type strain leakage through root canals filled with Gutta-Percha/AH plus or Resilon/Epiphany. [Comparative Study

18. Randomized Controlled Trial]. J Endod, 33(1), 45-47.

19. Beltes, P., Koulaouzidou, E., Kotoula, V., & Kortsaris, A. H. (1995). In-vitro evaluation of the cytotoxicity of calcium hydrooxide-based root-canal sealers. Endodontics & Dental Traumatology, 11(5), 245-249.

20. Bergman, B., Lundquist, P., Sjogren, U., & Sundquist, G. (1989). Restorative and endodontic results after treatment with cast post and cores. Journal of Prosthetic Dentistry, 61(1), 10-15. doi: 10.1016/0022-3913(89)90099-1

21. Blomlof, L., Lindskog, S., & Hammarstrom, L. (1988). Influence of pulpal treatments on cemm and tissue-reacitions in the marginal periodontium. Journal of Periodontology, 59(9), 577-583.

22. Bodrumlu, E., Muglali, M., Sumer, M., & Guvenc, T. (2008). The response of subcutaneous connective tissue to a new endodontic filling material. Journal of Biomedical Materials Research Part B-Applied Biomaterials, 84B(2), 463-467. doi: 10.1002/jbm.b.30892

23. Bouillaguet, S., Shaw, L., Barthelemy, J., Krejci, I., & Wataha, J. C. (2008). Long-term sealing ability of Pulp Canal Sealer, AH-Plus, GuttaFlow and Epiphany. International Endodontic Journal, 41(3), 219-226. doi: 10.1111/j.1365-2591.2007.01343.x

24. Bozeman, T. B., Lemon, R. R., & Eleazer, P. D. (2006). Elemental analysis of crystal precipitate from gray and white MTA. Journal of Endodontics, 32(5), 425-428. doi: 10.1016/j.joen.2005.08.009

25. Brady, J. M., & del Rio, C. E. (1975). Corrosion of endodontic silver cones in humans: A scanning electron microscope and X-ray microprobe study. Journal of Endodontics, 1(6), 205-210. doi: 10.1016/s0099-2399(75)80198-1

26. Bystrom, A., & Sundqvist, G. (1985). The antibacterial action of sodium-hypochlorite and EDTA in 60 cases of endodontic therapy. International Endodontic Journal, 18(1), 35-40. doi: 10.1111/j.1365-2591.1985.tb00416.x

27. Camilleri, J., Montesin, F. E., Brady, K., Sweeney, R., Curtis, R. V., & Ford, T. R. P. (2005). The constitution of mineral trioxide aggregate. Dental Materials, 21(4), 297-303. doi: 10.1016/j.dental.2004.05.010

28. Caputo, A. A., & Standlee, J. P. (1976). Pins and posts – why, when and how. Dental clinics of North America, 20(2), 299-311.

29. Cattani-Lorente, M. A., Godin, C.,

& Meyer, J. M. (1993). Early strength of glass ionomer cements. Dental Materials, 9(1), 57-62. doi: http://dx.doi.org/10.1016/0109-5641(93)90107-2

30. Chan, R. W., & Bryant, R. W. (1982). Post-core foundations for endodontically treated posterior teeth. Journal of Prosthetic Dentistry, 48(4), 401-406. doi: 10.1016/0022-3913(82)90074-9
31. Cheung, W. (2005). A review of the management of endodontically treated teeth. Post, core and the final restoration. [Review]. J Am Dent Assoc, 136(5), 611-619.
32. Chieruzzi, M., Pagano, S., Pennacchi, M., Lombardo, G., D'Errico, P., & Kenny, J. M. (2012). Compressive and flexural behaviour of fibre reinforced endodontic posts. Journal of Dentistry, 40(11), 968-978. doi: 10.1016/j.jdent.2012.08.003
33. Chong, B. S., Owadally, I. D., Ford, T. R. P., & Wilson, R. F. (1994). ANTIBACTERIAL ACTIVITY OF POTENTIAL RETROGRADE ROOT FILLING MATERIALS. Endodontics & Dental Traumatology, 10(2), 66-70.
34. Chong, B. S., & Pitt Ford, T. R. (2005). Root-end filling materials: rationale and tissue response. Endodontic Topics, 11(1), 114-130. doi: 10.1111/j.1601-1546.2005.00164.x
35. Christensen, G. J. (1996). When to use fillers, build-ups or posts and cores. Journal of the American Dental Association, 127(9), 1397-1398.
36. Christensen, G. J. (2000). Building up tooth preparations for full crowns--2000. [Comparative Study]. J Am Dent Assoc, 131(4), 505-506.
37. Chutich, M. J., Kaminski, E. J., Miller, D. A., & Lautenschlager, E. P. (1998). Risk assessment of the toxicity of solvents of gutta-percha used in endodontic retreatment. [Research Support, Non-U S Gov't]. J Endod, 24(4), 213-216.
38. Combe, E. C., Shaglouf, A. M., Watts, D. C., & Wilson, N. H. (1999). Mechanical properties of direct core build-up materials. [Comparative Study]. Dent Mater, 15(3), 158-165.
39. De-Deus, G., Namen, F., Galan, J., Jr., & Zehnder, M. (2008). Soft chelating irrigation protocol optimizes bonding quality of Resilon/Epiphany root fillings. Journal of Endodontics, 34(6), 703-705. doi: 10.1016/j.joen.2008.02.024
40. De Santis, R., Prisco, D., Apicella, A., Ambrosio, L., Rengo, S., & Nicolais, L. (2000). Carbon fiber post adhesion to resin luting cement in the restoration of endodontically treated teeth. Journal of Materials Science-Materials in Medicine, 11(4), 201-206.
41. Desai, S., & Chandler, N. (2009). Calcium Hydroxide-Based Root Canal Sealers: A Review. Journal of Endodontics, 35(4), 475-480. doi: 10.1016/j.joen.2008.11.026
42. Dorn, S. O., & Gartner, A. H. (1990). Retrograde filling materials – aretrospective success-failure study of amalgam, EBA, and IRM. Journal of Endodontics, 16(8), 391-393. doi: 10.1016/s0099-2399(06)81912-6
43. Ehrich, D. G., Brian, J. D., & Walker, W. A. (1993). Sodium –hypochlorite accident – inadvertent injection into the maxillary sinus. Journal of Endodontics, 19(4), 180-182. doi: 10.1016/s0099-2399(06)80684-9
44. El-Kalla, I. H., & Garcia-Godoy, F. (1999). Mechanical properties of compomer

restorative materials. Operative Dentistry, 24(1), 2-8.

45. Enkel, B., Dupas, C., Armengol, V., Adou, J. A., Bosco, J., Daculsi, G., . . . Weiss, P. (2008). Bioactive materials in endodontics. Expert Review of Medical Devices, 5(4), 475-494. doi: 10.1586/17434440.5.4.475

46. Estrela, C., Estrela, C. R. A., Barbin, E. L., Spano, J. C. E., Marchesan, M. A., & Pecora, J. D. (2002). Mechanism of action of sodium hypochlorite. Brazilian dental journal, 13(2), 113-117. doi: 10.1590/s0103-64402002000200007

47. Ford, T. R. P., Andreasen, J. O., Dorn, S. O., & Kariyawasam, S. P. (1995). Effect of super-eBA as a root end filling on healing after replantation. Journal of Endodontics, 21(1), 13-15. doi: 10.1016/s0099-2399(06)80550-9

48. Ford, T. R. P., & Roberts, G. J. (1990). Tissue-response to glass ionomer retrograde root fillings. International Endodontic Journal, 23(5), 233-238. doi: 10.1111/j.1365-2591.1990.tb00854.x

49. Friedman, C. M., Sandrik, J. L., Heuer, M. A., & Rapp, G. W. (1975). Composition and mechanical-properties of gutta-percha endodontic points. Journal of Dental Research, 54(5), 921-925. doi: 10.1177/00220345750540052901

50. Friedman, S. (1991). Retrograde approaches in endodontic therapy. Endodontics & Dental Traumatology, 7(3), 97-107.

51. Friedman, S., Lost, C., Zarrabian, M., & Trope, M. (1995). Evaluation of success and failure after endodontic therapy using a glass-ionomer cement sealer. Journal of Endodontics, 21(7), 384-390. doi: 10.1016/s0099-2399(06)80976-3

52. Gatewood, R. S. (2007). Endodontic materials. [Review]. Dent Clin North Am, 51(3), 695-712.

53. Geurtsen, W. (2000). Biocompatibility of resin-modified filling materials. Critical Reviews in Oral Biology & Medicine, 11(3), 333-355.

54. Giardino, L., Ambu, E., Becce, C., Rimondini, L., & Morra, M. (2006). Surface tension comparison of four common root canal irrigants and two new irrigants containing antibiotic. Journal of Endodontics, 32(11), 1091-1093. doi: 10.1016/j.joen.2006.05.008

55. Giardino, L., Ambu, E., Savoldi, E., Rimondini, R., Cassanelli, C., & Debbia, E. A. (2007). Comparative evaluation of antimicrobial efficacy of sodium hypochlorite, MTAD, and tetraclean against Enterococcus faecalis biofilm. Journal of Endodontics, 33(7), 852-855. doi: 10.1016/j.joen.2007.02.012

56. Glazer, B. (2000). Restoration of endodontically treated teeth with carbon fibre posts--a prospective study. Journal (Canadian Dental Association), 66(11), 613-618.

57. Gomes, B., Sato, E., Ferraz, C. C. R., Teixeira, F. B., Zaia, A. A., & Souza-Filho, F. J. (2003). Evaluation of time required for recontamination of coronally sealed canals medicated with calcium hydroxide and chlorhexidine. International Endodontic Journal, 36(9), 604-609. doi: 10.1046/j.1365-2591.2003.00694.x

58. Goodacre, C. J., & Spolnik, K. J. (1994). The prosthodontic management of endodontically treated teeth: a literature review. Part I. Success and failure data, treatment concepts. Journal of prosthodontics : official journal of the

American College of Prosthodontists, 3(4), 243-250. doi: 10.1111/j.1532-849X.1994.tb00162.x

59. Grawehr, M., Sener, B., Waltimo, T., & Zehnder, M. (2003). Interactions of ethylenediamine tetraacetic acid with sodium hypochlorite in aqueous solutions. International Endodontic Journal, 36(6), 411-415. doi: 10.1046/j.1365-2591.2003.00670.x

60. Grossman, I., Abu el Naag, A., & Peled, M. (2003). Root-end filling materials in apicoectomy--a review. Refuʾat ha-peh □eha-shinayim (1993), 20(2), 49-80.

61. Grossman, L. I. (1978). Solubility of root-canal cements. Journal of Dental Research, 57(9-10), 927-927. doi: 10.1177/00220345780570092001

62. Grossman, L. I. (1982). Endodontic Practice (10th ed.). Philadelphia, PA: Lea and Febiger.

63. Grossman, L. I. (1987). Endodontic Practice Lea and Febiger.

64. Grossman, L. I., & Meiman, B. W. (1982). Solution of pulp tissue by chemical agents. Journal of Endodontics, 8, S10-S12. doi: 10.1016/s0099-2399(82)80298-7

65. Hauman, C. H. J., & Love, R. M. (2003a). Biocompatibility of dental materials used in contemporary endodontic therapy: A review. Part 1. Intracanal drugs and substances. International Endodontic Journal, 36(2), 75-85. doi: 10.1046/j.1365-2591.2003.00631.x

66. Hauman, C. H. J., & Love, R. M. (2003b). Biocompatibility of dental materials used in contemporary endodontic therapy: A review. Part 2. Root-canal-filling materials. International Endodontic Journal, 36(3), 147-160. doi: 10.1046/j.1365-2591.2003.00637.x

67. Heling, I., & Chandler, N. P. (1996). The antimicrobial effect within dentinal tubules of four root canal sealers. Journal of Endodontics, 22(5), 257-259. doi: http://dx.doi.org/10.1016/S0099-2399(06)80144-5

68. Holland, R., Otoboni, J. A., de Souza, V., Nery, M. J., Bernabe, P. F. E., & Dezan, E. (2001). Mineral trioxide aggregate repair of lateral root perforations. Journal of Endodontics, 27(4), 281-284. doi: 10.1097/00004770-200104000-00011

69. Hoshino, E., KuriharaAndo, N., Sato, I., Uematsu, H., Sato, M., Kota, K., & Iwaku, M. (1996). In-vitro antibacterial susceptibility of bacteria taken from infected root dentine to a mixture of ciprofloxacin, metronidazole and minocycline. International Endodontic Journal, 29(2), 125-130. doi: 10.1111/j.1365-2591.1996.tb01173.x

70. Huang, F. M., Tai, K. W., Chou, M. Y., & Chang, Y. C. (2002). Cytotoxicity of resin-, zinc oxide-eugenol-, and calcium hydroxide-based root canal sealers on human periodontal ligament cells and permanent V79 cells. Int Endod J, 35(2), 153-158.

71. Kanisavaran, Z. M. (2008). Chlorhexidine gluconate in endodontics: An update review. International Dental Journal, 58(5), 247-257. doi: 10.1922/IDJ_1910Mohamadi11

72. Kawashima, N., Wadachi, R., Suda, H., Yeng, T., & Parashos, P. (2009). Root canal medicaments★. International Dental Journal, 59(1), 5-11. doi: 10.1922/IDJ_2060Kawashima07

73. Kazemi, R. B., Safavi, K. E., & Spangberg, L. S. W. (1993). Dimensional changes of endodontic sealers. Oral Surgery Oral Medicine Oral Pathology Oral Radiology and

Endodontics, 76(6), 766-771. doi: 10.1016/0030-4220(93)90050-e

74. Khashaba, R. M., Lockwood, P. E., Lewis, J. B., Messer, R. L., Chutkan, N. B., & Borke, J. L. (2010). Cytotoxicity, Calcium Release, and pH Changes Generated by Novel Calcium Phosphate Cement Formulations. Journal of Biomedical Materials Research Part B-Applied Biomaterials, 93B(2), 297-303. doi: 10.1002/jbm.b.31494

75. Kleier, D. J., & Averbach, R. E. (1988). Painful dysesthesia of the inferior alveolar nerve following use of a paraformaldehyde-containing root canal sealer. Dental Traumatology, 4(1), 46-48. doi: 10.1111/j.1600-9657.1988.tb00293.x

76. Koch, M. J. (1999). Formaldehyde release from root-canal sealers: influence of method. International Endodontic Journal, 32(1), 10-16. doi: 10.1046/j.1365-2591.1999.00173.x

77. Koulaouzidou, E. A., Margelos, J., Beltes, P., & Kortsaris, A. H. (1999). Cytotoxic effects of different concentrations of neutral and alkaline EDTA solutions used as root canal irrigants. Journal of Endodontics, 25(1), 21-23. doi: 10.1016/s0099-2399(99)80393-8

78. Lambjerg-Hansen, H., & Asmussen, E. (1997). Mechanical properties of endodontic posts. J Oral Rehabil, 24(12), 882-887.

79. Lambjerghansen, H. (1987). VITAL PULPECTOMY AND ROOT FILLING WITH N2 OR ENDOMETHASONE. International Endodontic Journal, 20(4), 194-204. doi: 10.1111/j.1365-2591.1987.tb00613.x

80. Landwerlen, J. R., & Berry, H. H. (1972). The composite resin post and core. The Journal of Prosthetic Dentistry, 28(5), 500-503. doi: http://dx.doi.org/10.1016/0022-3913(72)90061-3

81. Leonardo, M. R., da Silva, L. A. B., Almeida, W. A., & Utrilla, L. S. (1999). Tissue response to an epoxy resin-based root canal sealer. Endodontics & Dental Traumatology, 15(1), 28-32.

82. Leonardo, M. R., da Silva, L. A. B., Tanomaru, M., & da Silva, R. S. (1999). Release of formaldehyde by 4 endodontic sealers. Oral Surgery Oral Medicine Oral Pathology Oral Radiology and Endodontics, 88(2), 221-225. doi: 10.1016/s1079-2104(99)70119-8

83. Losche, G. M. (2000). Restoration of the endodontically treated tooth: Adhesion vs mechanical retention.

84. Lyon, K. F. (2001). Endodontic instruments for root canal therapy. Clinical Techniques in Small Animal Practice, 16(3), 139-150. doi: 10.1053/svms.2001.28166

85. Margelos, J., Eliades, G., Odont, D., Verdelis, C., & Palaghias, G. (1997). Interaction of calcium hydroxide with zinc oxide-eugenol type sealers: A potential clinical problem. Journal of Endodontics, 23(1), 43-48. doi: 10.1016/s0099-2399(97)80206-3

86. McLean, A. (1998). Predictably restoring endodontically treated teeth. Journal (Canadian Dental Association), 64(11), 782-787.

87. Mohammadi, Z., & Abbott, P. V. (2009). The properties and applications of chlorhexidine in endodontics. International Endodontic Journal, 42(4), 288-302. doi: 10.1111/j.1365-2591.2008.01540.x

88. Mohammadi, Z., & Dummer, P. M. H. (2011). Properties and applications of calcium hydroxide in endodontics and dental traumatology. International

Endodontic Journal, 44(8), 697-730. doi: 10.1111/j.1365-2591.2011.01886.x

89. Mollersten, L., Lockowandt, P., & Linden, L. A. (2002). A comparison of strengths of five core and post-and-core systems. Quintessence International, 33(2), 140-149.

90. Morgano, S. M., & Brackett, S. E. (1999). Foundation restorations in fixed prosthodontics: Current knowledge and future needs. Journal of Prosthetic Dentistry, 82(6), 643-657. doi: 10.1016/s0022-3913(99)70005-3

91. Naumann, M., Reich, S., Nothdurft, F. P., Beuer, F., Schirrmeister, J. F., & Dietrich, T. (2008). Survival of glass fiber post restorations over 5 years. American Journal of Dentistry, 21(4), 267-272.

92. Nissan, J., Dmitry, Y., & Assif, D. (2001). The use of reinforced composite resin cement as compensation for reduced post length. Journal of Prosthetic Dentistry, 86(3), 304-308. doi: 10.1067/mpr.2001.114759

93. Nowicka, A., Lipski, M., Parafiniuk, M., Sporniak-Tutak, K., Lichota, D., Kosierkiewicz, A., Buczkowska-Radlinska, J. (2013). Response of Human Dental Pulp Capped with Biodentine and Mineral Trioxide Aggregate. Journal of Endodontics, 39(6), 743-747. doi: 10.1016/j.joen.2013.01.005

94. O'Mahony, A., & Spencer, P. (1999). Core build-up materials and techniques. [Comparative Study

95. Review]. J Ir Dent Assoc, 45(3), 84-90.

96. Oilo, G. (1988). Characterization of glass ionomer filling materials. Dental Materials, 4(3), 129-133. doi: 10.1016/s0109-5641(88)80005-8

97. Oncag, O., Hosgor, M., Hilmioglu, S., Zekioglu, O., Eronat, C., & Burhanoglu, D. (2003). Comparison of antibacterial and toxic effects of various root canal irrigants. [Comparative Study]. Int Endod J, 36(6), 423-432.

98. Orstavik, D. (1988). Antibacterial properties of endodontic materials. International Endodontic Journal, 21(2), 161-169.

99. ØRstavik, D. A. G. (2005). Materials used for root canal obturation: technical, biological and clinical testing. Endodontic Topics, 12(1), 25-38. doi: 10.1111/j.1601-1546.2005.00197.x

100. Pameijer, C. H., & Zmener, O. (2010). Resin materials for root canal obturation. [Review]. Dent Clin North Am, 54(2), 325-344.

101. Paragliola, R., Franco, V., Fabiani, C., Mazzoni, A., Nato, F., Tay, F. R., Grandini, S. (2010). Final Rinse Optimization: Influence of Different Agitation Protocols. Journal of Endodontics, 36(2), 282-285. doi: 10.1016/j.joen.2009.10.004

102. Parirokh, M., & Torabinejad, M. (2010a). Mineral Trioxide Aggregate: A Comprehensive Literature Review-Part I: Chemical, Physical, and Antibacterial Properties. Journal of Endodontics, 36(1), 16-27. doi: 10.1016/j.joen.2009.09.006

103. Parirokh, M., & Torabinejad, M. (2010b). Mineral Trioxide Aggregate: A Comprehensive Literature Review-Part III: Clinical Applications, Drawbacks, and Mechanism of Action. Journal of Endodontics, 36(3), 400-413. doi: 10.1016/j.joen.2009.09.009

104. Peters, O. A. (2004). Current challenges and concepts in the preparation of root canal systems: A review. Journal

of Endodontics, 30(8), 559-567. doi: 10.1097/01.don.0000129039.59003.9d

105. Popescu, I. G., Popescu, M., Man, D., Ciolacu, S., Georgescu, M., Ciurea, T., . . . Ulmeanu, V. (1984). Drug allergy: incidence in terms of age and some drug allergens. Medecine interne, 22(3), 195-202.

106. Purton, D. G., & Love, R. M. (1996). Rigidity and retention of carbon fibre versus stainless steel root canal posts. International Endodontic Journal, 29(4), 262-265. doi: 10.1111/j.1365-2591.1996.tb01379.x

107. Raina, R., Loushine, R. J., Weller, R. N., Tay, F. R., & Pashley, D. H. (2007). Evaluation of the quality of the apical seal in Resilon/Epiphany and Gutta-Percha/AH plus-filled root canals by using a fluid filtration approach. Journal of Endodontics, 33(8), 944-947. doi: 10.1016/j.joen.2007.05.003

108. Rasimick, B. J., Nekich, M., Hladek, M. M., Musikant, B. L., & Deutsch, A. S. (2008). Interaction between Chlorhexidine Digluconate and EDTA. Journal of Endodontics, 34(12), 1521-1523. doi: 10.1016/j.joen.2008.08.039

109. Rud, J., Munksgaard, E. C., Andreasen, J. O., Rud, V., & Asmussen, E. (1991). Retrograde root fillinf with composite and a dentin-bonding agent .1. Endodontics & Dental Traumatology, 7(3), 118-125.

110. Saleh, I. M., Ruyter, I. E., Haapasalo, M., & Orstavik, D. (2002). The effects of dentine pretreatment on the adhesion of root-canal sealers. Int Endod J, 35(10), 859-866.

111. Sarkar, N. K., Caicedo, R., Ritwik, P., Moiseyeva, R., & Kawashima, I. (2005). Physicochemical basis of the biologic properties of mineral trioxide aggregate. Journal of Endodontics, 31(2), 97-100. doi: 10.1097/01.don.0000133155.04468.41

112. Schafer, E., & Zandbiglari, T. (2003). Solubility of root-canal sealers in water and artificial saliva. International Endodontic Journal, 36(10), 660-669. doi: 10.1046/j.1365-2591.2003.00705.x

113. Schilder, H., Goodman, A., & Aldrich, W. (1974a). Thermomechanical properties of gutta-percha.1. Compressibility of gutta-percha. Oral Surgery Oral Medicine Oral Pathology Oral Radiology and Endodontics, 37(6), 946-953. doi: 10.1016/0030-4220(74)90447-2

114. Schilder, H., Goodman, A., & Aldrich, W. (1974b). Thermomechanical properties of gutta-percha .3. Determination of phase-transition temperatures for gutta-percha. Oral Surgery Oral Medicine Oral Pathology Oral Radiology and Endodontics, 38(1), 109-114. doi: 10.1016/0030-4220(74)90321-1

115. Schwartz, R. S., & Robbins, J. W. (2004). Post placement and restoration of endodontically treated teeth: A literature review. Journal of Endodontics, 30(5), 289-301. doi: 10.1097/00004770-200405000-00001

116. Senia, E. S., Marraro, R. V., Mitchell, J. L., Lewis, A. G., & Thomas, L. (1975). Rapid sterilization of gutta-percha cones with 5.25% sodium hypochlorite. Journal of Endodontics, 1(4), 136-140. doi: 10.1016/s0099-2399(75)80098-7

117. Shah, P. M. M., Chong, B. S., Sidhu, S. K., & Ford, T. R. P. (1996). Radiopacity of potential root-end filling materials. Oral Surgery Oral Medicine Oral Pathology Oral Radiology and Endodontics, 81(4), 476-479. doi: 10.1016/s1079-2104(96)80028-x

118. Shipper, G., Orstavik, D., Teixeira, F. B., & Trope, M. (2004). An evaluation of microbial leakage in roots filled with a thermoplastic synthetic polymer-based root canal filling material (Resilon). Journal of Endodontics, 30(5), 342-347. doi: 10.1097/00004770-200405000-00009

119. Short, R. D., Dorn, S. O., & Kuttler, S. (2003). The crystallization of sodium hypochlorite on gutta-percha cones after the rapid-sterilization technique: An SEM study. Journal of Endodontics, 29(10), 670-673. doi: 10.1097/00004770-200310000-00015

120. Sidoli, G. E., King, P. A., & Setchell, D. J. (1997). An in vitro evaluation of a carbon fiber-based post and core system. Journal of Prosthetic Dentistry, 78(1), 5-9. doi: 10.1016/s0022-3913(97)70080-5

121. Siqueira, J. F., Jr., & Lopes, H. P. (1999). Mechanisms of antimicrobial activity of calcium hydroxide: a critical review. [Review]. Int Endod J, 32(5), 361-369.

122. Sokol, D. J. (1984). EFFECTIVE USE OF CURRENT CORE AND POST CONCEPTS. Journal of Prosthetic Dentistry, 52(2), 231-234. doi: 10.1016/0022-3913(84)90101-x

123. Sonat, B., Dalat, D., & Gunhan, O. (1990). PERIAPICAL TISSUE REACTION TO ROOT FILLINGS WITH SEALAPEX. International Endodontic Journal, 23(1), 46-52. doi: 10.1111/j.1365-2591.1990.tb00802.x

124. Spangberg, L. S. W., Barbosa, S. V., & Levigne, G. D. (1993). AH26 relseases formaldehyde. Journal of Endodontics, 19(12), 596-598. doi: 10.1016/s0099-2399(06)80272-4

125. Stewardson, D. A., Shortall, A. C., Marquis, P. M., & Lumley, P. J. (2010). The flexural properties of endodontic post materials. Dental Materials, 26(8), 730-736. doi: 10.1016/j.dental.2010.03.017

126. Tang, G., Samaranayake, L. P., & Yip, H. K. (2004). Molecular evaluation of residual endodontic microorganisms after instrumentation, irrigation and medication with either calcium hydroxide or Septomixine. [Research Support, Non-U S Gov't]. Oral Dis, 10(6), 389-397.

127. Tay, F. R., Loushine, R. J., Weller, R. N., Kimbrough, W. F., Pashley, D. H., Mak, Y. F., Williams, M. C. (2005). Ultrastructural evaluation of the apical seal in roots filled with a polycaprolactone-based root canal filling material. Journal of Endodontics, 31(7), 514-519. doi: 10.1097/01.don.0000152298.81097.b7

128. Tay, F. R., & Pashley, D. H. (2007). Monoblocks in root canals: A hypothetical or a tangible goal. Journal of Endodontics, 33(4), 391-398. doi: 10.1016/j.joen.2006.10.009

129. Tepel, J., Elsawaf, M. D., & Hoppe, W. (1994). Reaction of inflamed periapical tissue to intracanal medicaments and root-canal sealers. Endodontics & Dental Traumatology, 10(5), 233-238.

130. Torabinejad, M., & Ford, T. R. P. (1996). Root end filling materials: A review. Endodontics & Dental Traumatology, 12(4), 161-178.

131. Torabinejad, M., Khademi, A. A., Babagoli, J., Cho, J. B., Ben Johnson, W., Bozhilov, K., Shabahang, S. (2003). A new solution for the removal of the smear layer. Journal of Endodontics, 29(3), 170-175. doi: 10.1097/00004770-200303000-00002

132. Torabinejad, M., & Parirokh, M.

(2010). Mineral Trioxide Aggregate: A Comprehensive Literature Review-Part II: Leakage and Biocompatibility Investigations. Journal of Endodontics, 36(2), 190-202. doi: 10.1016/j.joen.2009.09.010

133. Torabinejad, M., Shabahang, S., Aprecio, R. M., & Kettering, J. D. (2003). The antimicrobial effect of MTAD: An in vitro investigation. Journal of Endodontics, 29(6), 400-403. doi: 10.1097/00004770-200306000-00005

134. Torbjorner, A., & Fransson, B. (2004). A literature review on the prosthetic treatment of structurally compromised teeth. International Journal of Prosthodontics, 17(3), 369-376.

135. Torbjorner, A., Karlsson, S., Syverud, M., & HenstenPettersen, A. (1996). Carbon fiber reinforced root canal posts - Mechanical and cytotoxic properties. European Journal of Oral Sciences, 104(5-6), 605-611. doi: 10.1111/j.1600-0722.1996.tb00149.x

136. Vansan, L. P., Pecora, J. D., Costa, W. F., & Maia Campos, G. (1990). Effects of various irrigating solutions on the cleaning of the root canal with ultrasonic instrumentation. Brazilian dental journal, 1(1), 37-44.

137. Velmurugan, N., & Parameswaran, A. (2004). Custom-made resin post and core. Oper Dent, 29(1), 112-114.

138. Vianna, M. E., Gomes, B., Berber, V. B., Zaia, A. A., Ferraz, C. C. R., & de Souza, F. J. (2004). In vitro evaluation of the antimicrobial activity of chlorhexidine and sodium hypochlorite. Oral Surgery Oral Medicine Oral Pathology Oral Radiology and Endodontics, 97(1), 79-84. doi: 10.1016/s1079-2104(03)00360-3

139. Wachlarowicz, A. J., Joyce, A. P., Roberts, S., & Pashley, D. H. (2007). Effect of endodontic Irrigants on the shear bond strength of epiphany sealer to dentin. Journal of Endodontics, 33(2), 152-155. doi: 10.1016/j.joen.2006.09.011

140. Walivaara, D.-A., Abrahamsson, P., Fogelin, M., & Isaksson, S. (2011). Super-EBA and IRM as root-end fillings in periapical surgery with ultrasonic preparation: a prospective randomized clinical study of 206 consecutive teeth. Oral Surgery Oral Medicine Oral Pathology Oral Radiology and Endodontology, 112(2), 258-263. doi: 10.1016/j.tripleo.2011.01.016

141. Wilkinson, K. L., Beeson, T. J., & Kirkpatrick, T. C. (2007). Fracture resistance of simulated immature teeth filled with resilon, gutta-percha, or composite. J Endod, 33(4), 480-483.

142. Windley, W., Teixeira, F., Levin, L., Sigurdsson, A., & Trope, M. (2005). Disinfection of immature teeth with a triple antibiotic paste. Journal of Endodontics, 31(6), 439-443. doi: 10.1097/01.don.0000148143.80283.ea

143. Yazdi, P. M., Schou, S., Jensen, S. S., Stoltze, K., Kenrad, B., & Sewerin, I. (2007). Dentine-bonded resin composite (Retroplast) for root-end filling: a prospective clinical and radiographic study with a mean follow-up period of 8 years. International Endodontic Journal, 40(7), 493-503. doi: 10.1111/j.1365-2591.2007.01242.x

144. Yoshida, T., Shibata, T., Shinohara, T., Gomyo, S., & Sekine, I. (1995). Clinical evaluation of the efficacy of EDTA solution as an endodontic irrigant. Journal of Endodontics, 21(12), 592-593. doi: 10.1016/s0099-2399(06)81109-x

145. Zakariasen, K. L., Brayton, S. M., &

Collinson, D. M. (1990). Efficient and effective root canal retreatment without chloroform. J Can Dent Assoc, 56(6), 509-512.

146. Zamany, A., Safavi, K., & Spangberg, L. S. W. (2003). The effect of chlorhexidine as an endodontic disinfectant. Oral Surgery Oral Medicine Oral Pathology Oral Radiology and Endodontics, 96(5), 578-581. doi: 10.1016/s1079-2104(03)00168-9

147. Zehnder, M. (2006). Root canal irrigants. [Review]. J Endod, 32(5), 389-398.

148. Zehnder, M., Soderling, E., Salonen, J., & Waltimo, T. (2004). Preliminary evaluation of bioactive glass S53P4 as an endodontic medication in vitro. Journal of Endodontics, 30(4), 220-224. doi: 10.1097/00004770-200404000-00009

149. Zhang, H., Shen, Y., Ruse, N. D., & Haapasalo, M. (2009). Antibacterial Activity of Endodontic Sealers by Modified Direct Contact Test Against Enterococcus faecalis. Journal of Endodontics, 35(7), 1051-1055. doi: 10.1016/j.joen.2009.04.022

150. Zhang, W., Li, Z., & Peng, B. (2009). Assessment of a new root canal sealer's apical sealing ability. Oral Surgery Oral Medicine Oral Pathology Oral Radiology and Endodontology, 107(6), E79-E82. doi: 10.1016/j.tripleo.2009.02.024

151. Zhang, W., Li, Z., & Peng, B. (2010). Ex vivo cytotoxicity of a new calcium silicate-based canal filling material. International Endodontic Journal, 43(9), 769-774. doi: 10.1111/j.1365-2591.2010.01733.x

Chapter 18

NANOMATERIALS IN DENTISTRY

Dr. Sohail Zafar

In recent decades, there has been a significant development in dental biomaterials. The quality of dental services has been improved either by the emergence of new materials with much better properties or by improving the properties of existing materials. The science of nanotechnology has become the most popular area of research currently covering a broad range of applications. This chapter describes the basic concept of nanomaterials, recent innovations in nanomaterials and their applications in dentistry.

Definitions

Nano: Derived from a Greek word meaning dwarf.

Nanometer (nm): In metric system; one billionth of meter (1 nm=10^{-9m}).

Nanomaterials: The materials that have at least one dimension in the scale range of 1-100 nm and demonstrate size dependant characteristic properties.

Nanosciences: The study of nanomaterials for their properties, materials systems and phenomena.

Nanotechnology: The engineering of nanomaterials (at least one dimension at a scale range of 1-100 nm) and miniaturized devices based on nanomaterials.

Nanomedicine: By combining nanosciences and medicine; medical diagnosis, monitoring and treatment at a level of single molecule/molecular assemblies or at a cellular level.

Nanodentistry: The use of nanomaterials and nanotechnology applications for diagnosis, prevention and treatment of oral and dental disease.

Biomimetics: Biomimetics is the science of understanding, how nature has designed, processed and assembled these high performance materials and then applying those principals to make synthetic materials.

INTRODUCTION

Nanotechnology is purposeful engineering on a scale of less than 100 nm to achieve desired properties, functions and performance characteristics. It engages the characterization and control of materials at atomic or molecular level. At nanoscale, the physical, chemical and biological properties differ from the properties at an individual atomic/molecular level and bulk matter. Nanotechnology is one of the most popular areas of current research and has developed in multiple disciplines. There are four main type of materials (Metals, polymers, ceramics and composites) and nanomaterials have been developed in all four categories for practical applications. Due to the unique properties, nanomaterials always remain a focus of interest for biomaterial scientists, so they can achieve results" for medical and dental applications to improve the quality of life. To date, nanomaterials have been developed and are being used practically for a range of medical applications such as drug delivery, gene delivery, imaging tools, molecular diagnostics. (Fig: 18.1) Nanomaterials have also been developed for a range of dental applications, which have been discussed in this chapter.

HISTORICAL BACKGROUND

A long time before the introduction of term "Nanotechnology" the concept was set up by physicist Richard Feynman. He presented the idea entitled *"There's Plenty of Room at the Bottom"* an American Physical Society meeting at the California Institute of Technology in 1959. The transcript of this talk was published in *"Engineering and Science"* later on in 1960. Although Feynman did not apply the term "Nanotechnology or Nanosciences" however described the novel process in which scientist can manipulate materials at atomic or molecular levels. Tokyo Science University Professor Norio Taniguchi used the term nanotechnology for the first time in 1974 to describe the processing and properties of materials at single atom and molecule level. The idea of nanotechnology was further probed in depth and promoted by Dr. K. Eric Drexler and published a book titled *"Engines of Creation-The Coming Era of Nanotechnology"* around late 1980s. In 1991, the publication by Sumio Lijima *"Helical microtubules of graphitic carbon"* introduced the concept of nanotubes and boosted nanomaterials research.

At such a small scale, most of the atoms are surface atoms and impossible to see through a naked eye or even using an ordinary microscopes. The development of scanning microscopes that can be used to see images at atomic or molecular level helped the field of nanotechnology. Scanning tunnelling microscope was developed in 1981. Once scientisits had better equipments with the invention of scanning tunnelling microscopes and atomic force microscope (about 30 years ago) the modern science of nanotechnology was born. An active research is going on to take advantages of nanotechnology and develop materials with enhanced properties and better control over their properties.

NATURE AND NANOMATERIALS

Nature has used nanomaterials widely in natural biomaterials such as bone, teeth, shells, and wood. There is no question about the structure-function relationship and the best performance regarding natural biomaterials.

> *"Nature is a master chemist with incredible talent".*
>
> *"Nature is and will continue to be the best material scientist ever".*

We can learn a lot of lessons from natural materials and following the principles of nature for making these materials. All natural nanomaterials are fabricated under ambient conditions and perform well in the environment. Natural biological materials show many levels of hierarchical structures from the macroscopic to the microscopic length scale with the smallest building blocks being designed with nanometer sized hard insertions implanted into a soft protein matrix.

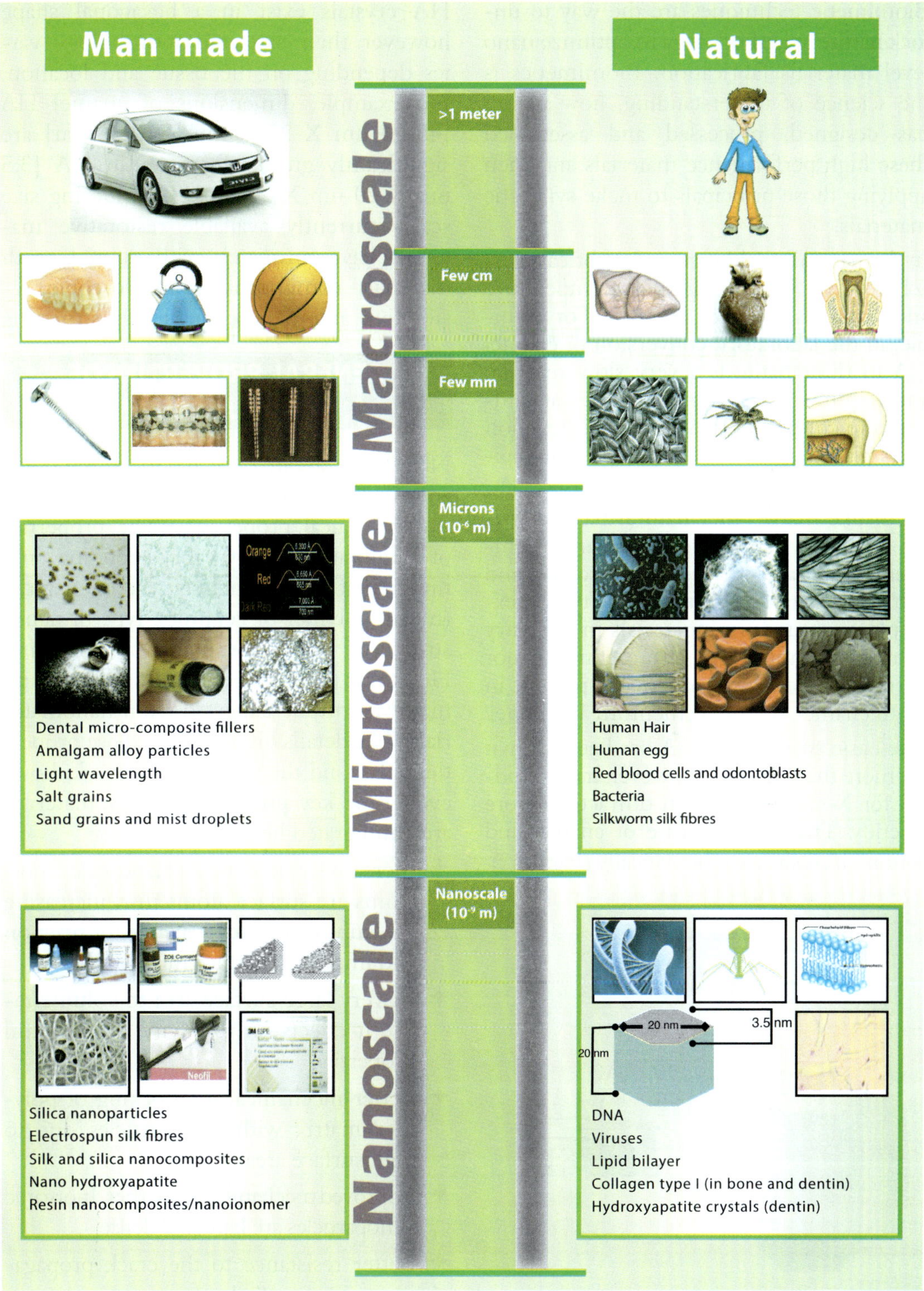

Fig: 18.1. Understanding nanoscale and available examples in natural and synthetic materials.

Biomimetic techniques are the way to unlock nature's methodology to optimize nano level materials fabrication. Biomimetics is the science of understanding, how nature has designed, processed and assembled these high performance materials and then applying those principals to make synthetic materials.

In the natural world nanoscale fabrication is achieved without using high temperature and extremes of pH or pressure. For example, in the laboratory, conversion of enamel HA to fluorapatite is a very slow reaction and requires the presence of CaF_2 at temperature conditions of 900 °C; this reaction takes place by a simple dissolution-precipitation method in natural process.

Teeth like many other natural biomaterials are primarily an inorganic/organic composite material with desirable strength and damage-resistant properties. The typical example of natural nanomaterials in dentistry is hydroxyapatite (HA), representing major portion of inorganic component present in tooth enamel, dentin, cementum and bone.

The basic structure of HA has been known for more than 80 years however, it was studied for X-ray and neutron diffraction more recently. The nanostructure of enamel and dentin HA is shown schematically (Fig: 18.2).

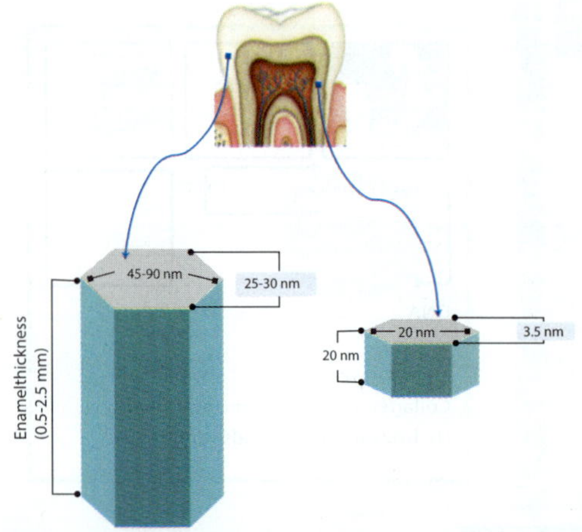

Fig: 18.2. Schematic comparison of enamel and dentin HA nanocrystals.

HA crystals exist in a hexagonal shape however their size and morphology varies depending on the tissue and location. For example, dimensions of enamel HA [45-90 nm X 25-39 nm X 2-3 mm] are significantly greater than dentin HA [3.5 nm X 20 nm X 20 nm]. Considering size scale, currently available restorative materials have mismatch with natural tooth materials compromising macroscopic restorative and nanoscopic tooth structure.

GENERAL PROPERTIES OF NANOMATERIALS

Nanomaterials are expected to exhibit novel and significantly better physical, chemical and biological properties. The properties of nanomaterials may vary depending on a number of factors such as type of material (metal, polymer or ceramic), type of nanostructure, and morphological structure. However, there are certain properties and material attitude expected from nanomaterials. The details discussion of these properties is beyond the scope of this book; however some key properties of nanomaterials are enumerated here:

- Increased reactivity. At nanoscale, most atoms are surface atoms thus increasing the number of sites available for reaction and improved surface functionalities.
- A very large surface area to volume ratio. It effects on reactivity and physical properties.
- Better mechanical interlocking of polymer matrix with nanoparticles due to high surface area.
- Improved mechanical properties. Inorganic nanoparticles are hard and dense.
- Better resistance to the crack propagation under cyclic loads.
- Decrease in grain size. Important for

surface reactions such as catalysis.

- Nanofillers can improve optical properties and more smooth surface finish.
- Nanocomposites have also shown significantly better control over biodegradability.

The details of specific properties are discussed under the subheading of each nanomaterial used in dentistry.

CLASSIFICATIONS

There are different ways for classifying nanomaterials (Table: 18.1). For ease of understanding, nanomaterials are classified on the basis of morphology of basic microscopic unit, materials chemistry and dimensional existence.

Table 18.1 : Classification of nanomaterials.

	CLASSIFICATION	EXAMPLES
A- Based on morphology	Nano clusters	
	Nanofibres	Electrospun polymers/silk
	Nano wire/tubes	Carbon based nanomaterials
	Nanoparticles	Silica, HA, gold, silver
B- Bas on materials chemistry	Carbon based nanomaterials	Fullerenes nanotubes
	Polymer nanomaterials	Electrospun silk nanofibres
	Metallic nanomaterials	Nano-gold and Nano-silver
	Nanoceramics	Silica, titanium oxide and HA nanoparticles
	Nanocomposites	Ceramic/polymer nanocomposites Silica/resin nanocomposites
C- Based on Dimensions	Zero Dimensional	Nanoclusters
	One Dimensional	Nanowires and nanotubes
	Two Dimensional	Nanolayer/films coatings
	Three Dimensional	Tissue engineering scaffolds Polymers and/or composites

CHARACTERIZATION OF NANOMATERIALS

Nanomaterials characterization means use of different techniques and methods to probe materials structure and properties. Regarding nanomaterials characterization, the first question should come in mind is, what kind of information are we looking for and at what resolution? for example;

a. Morphology: nanostructure and architecture.

b. Crystallography: Details of atomic arrangements.

c. Chemical structure: Elements present and chemistry of molecules.

d. Electronic structure: Nature of bonding in atoms.

e. Thermal properties: Reaction to temperature related changes.

f. Mechanical properties: Reaction to external stress and forces applied.

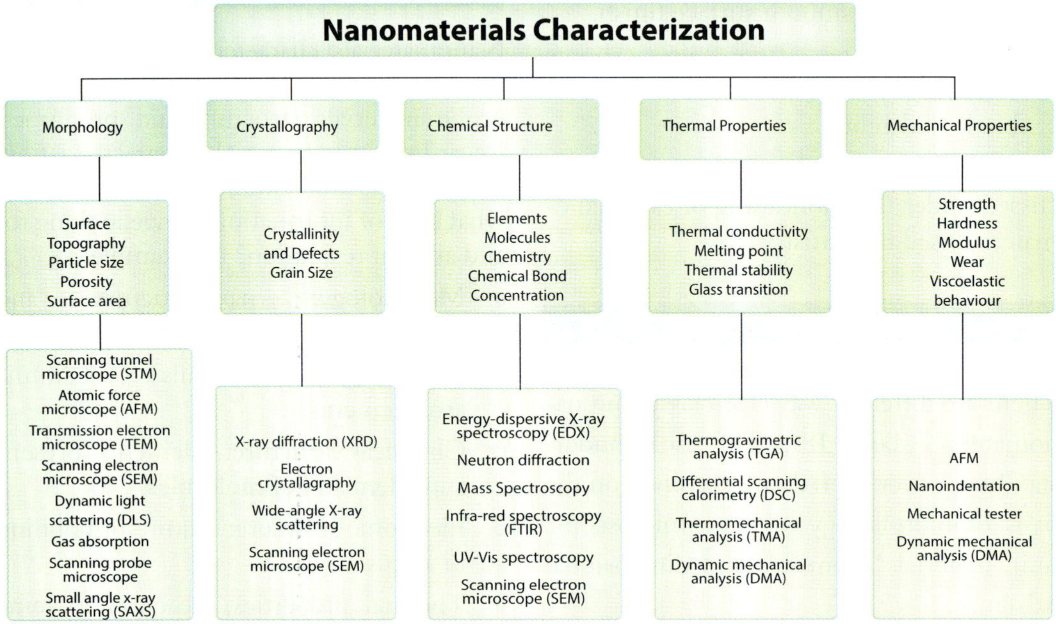

Fig: 18.3. Common techniques used for nanomaterials characterisation.

The data obtained from characterization help to correlate nanostructure, properties and determine the criteria for fabrication. Before using in clinical practice, a detailed characterization and analysis of nanomaterials is required for a complete understanding of materials reaction both *in vitro* and *in vivo.*

WHY DO WE NEED NANO-MATERIALS IN DENTISTRY?

Despite better understanding of the materials chemistry and recent improvements in the physical properties, no material has been found that is ideal for any dental application. For example, there has been a major concern about mercury toxicity from the amalgam restorations for many years. Another major issue is the colour of amalgam for aesthetic considerations and alternative materials are being sought to replace this. The composite restorative materials have promising aesthetics but they are not as good mechanically as amalgams and also are very technique sensitive. Nature has arranged complex biominerals in the best way from the micro to the nano scale and no one can yet combine biological and physical properties to get ideal structures. In addition, no synthetic material can be intelligent enough to respond to external stimuli and react like nature made tissues. The best possible options are;

i. To replace lost dental tissues following the nature's principles (biomimmetic approaches); and producing biomaterials resembling their properties very closely to the replacing materials

ii. Producing synthetic materials matching morphology and properties similar to natural dental tissues

iii. Use of regenerative medicine and tissue engineering technique for replacing lost dental tissue by regenerations.

All these approaches are not possible without the intervention of nanotechnology. For example components required for developing such biomaterials (biomolecules, cells, tissue engineering scaffolds and signal) involves the development of nanomaterials.

Large global market: There is a huge demand and global market for modern dental materials, the dental composite resins developed more recently and gained a huge market of €550 million a year in 2005 all over the world. According to estimates, there is a rapid increase in the use of dental implants; more than 300,000 implanted every year with some patients having more than twelve. There are many other factors that can increase the demand of all biomaterials generally, like more awareness of patients about the biomaterials, better life style, increasing population and life expectancy (average age). For instance, the average life span has increased up to 30 year in USA during the 20th century, and is expected to rise up to hundred years by 2050. Furthermore, a number of centenarians (100 years old) is increasing every year, with an 8.5 % rise per year being observed in Australia. Similarly, there were only 2835 centenarians in Mexico in 1930. This had gone up to 19,000 in 2000 and is expected to increase up to more than 137,000 in 2050.

There is no doubt that the demand of dental biomaterials on a rapid rise and there are no available dental materials having ideal properties for any dental applications. There are plenty of hopes from nanomaterials in terms of either developing new materials or significant improvements in the properties of existing materials. The authors have no hesitation to state that the scope of nanomaterials in dentistry is bright and will be helpful to enhance the quality of life patients.

APPLICATIONS IN DENTISTRY

There is a remarkable research on nanomaterials in recent years that has moved it from theoretical foundation to clinical practice. Currently, there is a wide range of nonomaterial's applications in different subspecialties of dentistry.

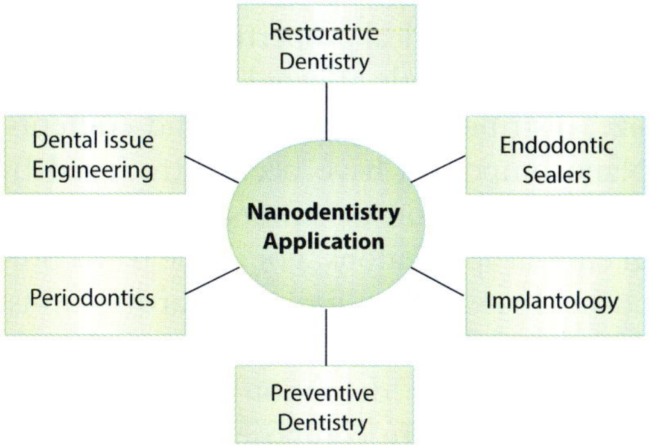

Fig: 18.4. Nanomaterials applications in dentistry.

1. NANOMATERIALS FOR RESTORATIVE DENTISTRY

There are major developments in recent years for restorative materials particularly tooth colored materials. Nano technologies have been applied for the manufacturing of dental composites (Nanocomposites), glass ionomers (Nano-ionomers) and endodontic sealers.

A. Nanocomposites

Since the invention of adhesive dental materials in 1955, resin composites have been used widely and successfully. The nanocomposites were introduced more recently to overcome the shortcomings of conventional resin composites and gain better performance.

There are three main components of dental composites resins; (1) inorganic fillers, (2) polymer matrix and (3) coupling agents. The inorganic filler particles are composed of quartz, glass or silica and comprise a major portion (60-80 Vol %) of dental composites. The classification of resin composites including either it's a microfilled, hybrid or nanocomposites is based on the basic morphology of filler particles. The physical, mechanical and optical properties of resin composites are directly affected by filler particle size, distribution, orientation and contents. Nanocomposites have been introduced by the incorporation of nanoparticles and are in clinical applications. For a true nanocomposites material, the size of all particles must be in the range of 1-100 nm (according to nanotechnology definition). For example nanofills, that are composed of nanoparticles (1-100 nm) and no larger particles are present. The other application of nanotechnology is in nanohybrid composite materials where larger sized particles (0.4-5.0 μ) are also added in to resin matrix alongside nanoparticles.

Key benefits of using nanoparticles in resin composites

The incorporation of nanotechnologies in dental composites has significantly improved their properties;

- Larger surface area and availability of more sites for bonding.
- Nanoparticles size is closer to polymer molecules and result in molecular scale interaction with polymer resin matrix.
- As particle size is smaller than visible light wavelength (400-800 nm) and responsible for higher translucency and aesthetic.
- Better smoothness and gloss finish of restorations.
- Mechanical properties are as good as of microhybrid composites.
- The values of compressive strength (460 MPa), flextural strength (180 MPa) and diametral tensile strength (81 MPa) are higher than any other types of resin composites and glass ionomers.
- Excellent wear resistance; as good as that of natural human enamel in three and five years clinical studies.
- Nano-zirconia particles (5-7 nm) can bring radiopacity without affecting the other properties.

Furthermore, comparing the dimensions of HA present in the natural tooth structure is estimated around 1-10 nm that is significantly smaller than particles size being used for conventional restorative macroscopic materials (0.04-7 μm). This dissimilarity of particle size affects adversely on the bonding of tooth and synthetic materials. By introducing nanotechnologies, this size difference has been reduced remarkably and nanocomposites (nanofillers) have a greater capability of establishing a steady and native interface with natural tooth structures. To summarize, nanofillers resulted in the synthesis of resin composites with improved physical, mechanical and optical properties.

B. Nano glass ionomers (Nanoionomers)

Glass ionomers were introduced by Wilson and Kent in 1970s as dental filling material. There is a wide range of glass ionomers available in the market however their basic chemistry remains the same. Glass ionomers are supplied in powder and liquid form and work on the principle of acid base reaction. The powder is composed of mainly fluoro-alumino-silicate (FAS) glass particles and ions such as strontium, calcium and lanthanum. The liquid is a copolymer of acrylic acid and itaconic acid or maleic acid and supplied as a viscous fluid.

Acid base reaction takes place while powder and liquid are mixed and initial set takes place in 3-4 minutes. Glass ionomers are being used widely because of its excellent properties such as chemical bonding to the tooth structure, biocompatibility and fluoride release. On the other hand, there are a number of shortcomings for this group of materials such as poor aesthetic, prolonged setting reaction, compromised mechanical properties and weaker bond strength. In order to improve the properties and to overcome these shortcomings, an active research is on the way such as addition of cellulose fibers, hydroxylapatite and fluoroapatite and nanotechnologies.

More recently, nanotechnologies have been applied to the resin modified glass ionomers in the form of nanoparticles (nanomers) and nanoclusters in FAS glass. These nanoionomers (Ketac™ nano) have been available for clinical use since 2007. The addition of nanoparticles resulted in the aesthetic improvement of the final restoration and polishablilty. It is important to mention that fluoride release property is not affected by addition of nanoparticles due to the high surface area. In a recent study, the Knoop hardness of Ketac™ nano was observed to be lower (39 KHN) than resin modified (Vitremer) glass ionomers (69.9 KHN). The Knoop hardness of Ketac™ nano (48 KHN) is not fulfilling the American Dental Association (ADA) specifications for restoration hardness; hence cannot be recommended for high stress bearing areas. The manufacturer (3M ESPE) has recommended its use for class I, class III, class V, under the composite and primary teeth.

Another development is the introduction of a new nanomaterial called Equia® System. Inorganic silica nanofillers (40 nm size) were dispersed homogeneously in the polymer matrix. Adding 15 wt % silica nanofillers resulted in good wear resistance and reduction in the initial setting time. Due to better resistance dissolution, disintegration and wear, these materials were observed to maintain polished surface for a longer period of time. There is an enhancement of optical properties and translucency compared to conventional glass ionomers and aesthetic appearance is improved remarkably and claimed as good as of natural teeth.

The effects of additives such as nanoscale hydroxyapatite (HA) and fluoroapatite (FA) on properties of glass ionomers is a hot topic for researchers. Hydroxyapatite crystals are well known for its biocompatibility and have a major contribution in the chemical structure of natural enamel and dentin. The bond strength of resin modified glass ionomers to the tooth structure was measured 0.75 MPa. The bond strength was increased (1.02 MPa) with addition of micro HA (5-10 μm) and where as nano-HA (100-150 nm) further improved the bond strength to 1.91 MPa. This improved strength is probably related to the availability of higher surface area for bonding to tooth structure in case of nano-HA. This high surface area also increase the surface finish and solubility of nano-HA that helps filling the demineralizing micro-pores in the tooth structure. Similarly nano-HA and nano-FA prepared using ethanol based sol-gel method were added to Fuji II glass ionomers. The modified nanofilled glass ionomers exhibited better mechanical properties such as compressive strength, diametral tensile strength and biaxial flexural strength.

Modification of existing glass ionomers using nanomaterials is an active area of current research. A number of other materials such as alumina, alumina/titania, zirconia and yttria stabilized zirconia. There are very high expectations from this ongoing research on nanomaterials in relation to glass ionomers. As a result, It can be hoped that there will be addition of new dental materials in near future or the properties of existing glass ionomers will be improve significantly.

C. EndoSequence BC endodontic Sealer

EndoSequence BC sealer has been developed recently using bioceramic nanotechnologies and composed of calcium silicate, calcium phosphate, calcium hydroxide, zirconia and thickening agent. Nanoparticles used in BC sealer has improved its handling and physical properties. During the hydration reaction in the root canal, nanocomposites structure of calcium silicate and hydroxyapatite is formed. The hydration reaction and setting time is affected by the availability of water and setting time may be prolonged in overly dried canals

Key Benefits

- Available as premixed inject able paste giving benefits of homogeneous mix, convenient to apply and saves time.
- Smaller particle size facilitates delivery of material from 0.012 capillary needle and adopt to irregular dentin surfaces.
- Harden when exposed to moisture present in the root canals; so moisture left in the root canal will not affect the performance of sealer.
- Setting reaction results in the formation of hydroxyapatite; providing bioactivity
- Biocompatible and non cytotoxic.
- Bonding between tooth structure and obturation material.
- High pH (12.8) and excellent antimicrobial properties.

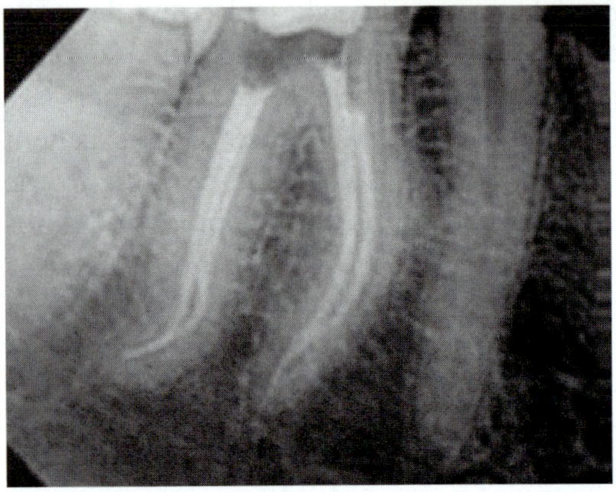

Fig: 18.5. Obturation of lower molar tooth using BC nano Sealer.

- Dimensionally stable; don't shrink or resorb.
- Setting time is 3-4 hours and provide excellent seal.
- Shelf life is two years and can be stored at room temperature.

D. GuttaFlow Sealer

GuttaFlow sealer is one of the latest products introduced for endodontic applications. It is a silicon based sealer with addition of gutta-percha powder and silver nanoparticles. This material is available in the form of uni-dose capsule that can be mixed and injected.

Key Benefits

- Good compatibility and toxicity to tissue is acceptable.
- Excellent sealing of the root canal and better resistance to bacterial penetration.
- No heating required hence no shrinkage and improved sealing capability.
- Working time is 15 minutes and setting time is 30 minutes.
- Dimensionally stable and non soluble after setting.

E. Endodontic sealer modified using antibacterial nanoparticles

For infection point of view, the antibacterial activity of endodontic sealers can be very beneficial. Recently, antibacterial quaternary ammonium polyethyleneimine (QPEI) nanoparticles have been incorporated into existing sealers such as AH plus, Epiphany and Guttaflow. Resin composites containing QPEI nanoparticles resulted in prolonged antibacterial activity without compromising the mechanical properties. In order to obtain similar antibacterial effect in endodontic sealers, 0-2 wt % QPEI nanoparticles were added in to the commercially available sealers.

Key benefits

- Excellent antibacterial; that is expected to last longer when nanoparticles are encapsulated in the matrix.
- 1 wt % addition of QPEI nanoparticles does not cause any cytotoxicity whereas 2 wt % is slightly cytotoxic.
- QPEI nanoparticles are prepolymerised and no byproduct or unwanted products are released.
- QPEI nanoparticles are very stable and no leaching in the surrounding environment.No effect on the biocompatibility of modified sealers.

F. Nano-hydroxyapatite (nano-HA) gutta percha

Nano-hydroxyapatite based endodontic sealer has been developed recently. Nano-HA crystals (40-60 nm) were synthesized using wet chemical method and utilizing calcium hydroxide and phosphoric acid as precursors. This nano sealer is composed of nano HA, bismuth oxide (for radiopacity), hexamethylenetetramine as an activator and bisphenol A diglycidyl ether as liquid.

Key Benefits

- Sealing capabilities are as good as of Epiphany and AH 26 endodontic sealers.
- No adverse affect of heat application used during root filling.

G. Bioactive glass nanomaterials as root canal disinfectant

Bioceramics are well known for excellent biocompatibility and bioactivity. The nano-sized bioactive glass particles prepared in specific composition (58S) have demonstrated antibacterial activity. The bioactive glass (58S, 63S and 72S) have Sio_2-CaO-P_2O_5 system were evaluated for antibacterial activity. The nano-sized particles (20-90 nm) for these bioactive glasses were prepared using sol-gel technique. The optimal concentration of 58s and 63S for antibacterial affect was described at 100 mg/ml. At this concentration (100 mg/ml), antibacterial activity was effective and no bacterial growth was observed on agar plates. The rise in the pH of nano glass materials is also a contributory factor for antibacterial activity. The pH of fresh solution (~7.3); rise up to 8.8 within one day and further rise to more than 9.0 in 5 days. The smaller (nano sized) particle bioactive glasses can result in the enhancement of antibacterial activity by leaching of alkaline species. These bioactive glass nanomaterials are considered to be a good potentials candidate for root canal disinfection applications.

H. Nanomaterials and regenerative endodontic

The applications of nanoscaffold materials for endodontic regeneration are well established. For pulp regeneration, pulp stem cells were purified in the laboratory and grown in sheets on scaffolds. The scaffolds used were composed of nanofibres of biodegradable collagen type I or fibronectin. Self assembling polypeptide hydrogels have been used for pulp tissue regeneration. There is formation of a nanofiber mesh that supported the growing cells. Puramatrix (contain amino acids repeats of alanine, arginine, aspartate) has proven to enhance cell growth. Injectable self assembly collagen I scaffold loaded with exfoliated teeth stem cells resulted in the formation of pulp like tissue and functional odontoblasts. Collagen type I is the most abundant fibrous protein found in the form of nanofibers in Dentin (~80-90 % of organic matrix) and bone. Odontogenic differentiation and mineralization was promoted in the presence of type I collagen scaffolds.

2. NANOMATERIALS FOR PREVENTIVE DENTISTRY

“Prevention is better than cure”. Teeth perform in the dynamic environment of oral cavity where the prevention of tooth decay is very challenging. Due to all advancements and better understanding of oral diseases, the role of preventive dentistry is vital and cannot be denied. Nanomaterials are being used for certain practical applications in preventive dental care such as management of biofilm at tooth surface using nanoapatites and nanomaterials for remineralization of early stage submicron sized enamel lesions.

A. Nanocomposites surface coatings (prevention of biofilm)

The nanocomposites surface coatings were prepared by the incorporation of inorganic nanoparticles in fluoropolymer matrix. These materials play beneficial role by detaching the pellicle and bacterial plaque under the effect of physiological activities in the oral cavity. It has low surface energy that inhibits biofilm attachment to tooth structure and can be used to coat tooth, denture or implant surfaces.

Key benefits

- Modification of tooth surface.
- Easy to clean when used as coating or fissure sealants.
- Wear resistant.
- Biocompatible.
- Low surface energy that helps in the detachment of bacteria and biofilm.
- Can be beneficial in compromised patients such as xerostomia, poor oral hygiene, and high caries rate.

B. Casein phosphopeptide and amorphous calcium phosphate nanocomplexes

Casein phosphopeptide (CPP) and amorphous calcium phosphate (ACP) are nanomaterials having particles of 2.12 nm diameter. These nanomaterials are used effectively for the management of oral biofilm.

Key benefits

- Nanocomplexes are significantly smaller in size than microorganisms; establishing an effective interaction with bacteria in the mouth.
- Bind to the bacterial cell surface and interfere with their adherence with tooth.
- Delays the formation of biofilm.
- Promote remineralization of initial carious lesion and inhibits demineralization.
- Are used in sugar free gums and proven their role in preventing proximal caries.

C. Nanohydroxyl apatite toothpaste

Carbonate hydroxyl apatite nanoparticles (20-100 nm) were used to repair micron sized carious defect in *in vitro* studies. The incorporated nanomaterials repair the carious lesions by depositing hydroxyl apatite in to the demineralized tissues. These tooth pastes contain spheroid or needle like hydroxyl apatite nanoparticles as an active constituent.

Key benefits

- Ease of application as medium of delivery is tooth paste
- Deposition of apatite nanoparticles in the defect
- Remineralization of decaying tissues better than sodium fluoride.

3. NANOMATERIALS FOR PERIODONTICS

Nanomaterials have been used for the cure of periodontal diseases recently showing promising outcome. As a result of ongoing research it is expected to develop more materials for periodontal applications.

A. Nanomaterials drug delivery

A nanomaterials delivery system based on nanoparticles loaded with triclosan has been developed for the cure of periodontal diseases. Poly (D, L-lactide-coglycolide), poly (D, L-lactide) and cellulose phthalate were used to prepare nanoparticles (< 500 nm size). Different batches were loaded using various quantities of triclosan as an active ingredient. This nanomaterial has proven to reduce the inflammation in animal studies. Site specific delivery system such as Arestin is being used for clinical applications where microspheres containing tetracycline are introduced directly into the periodontal pocket. A lot of research is being conducted actively to develop materials for periodontal tissue engineering and promising developments are expected in near future.

4. NANOMATERIALS FOR DENTAL IMPLANTS

The application of dental implant materials is not new; however the modern dental implants become popular after Branemark's novel work on titanium. Dental implants have a high success rate (95 %); failure may be caused by infection, accelerated bone loss or lack of osseointegration. There is no doubt that metallic dental implants have been used successfully for last four decades however there are certain shortcomings in terms of osseointegration and mismatch of mechanical properties of biomaterials and bone. For example, the Young's modulus is almost five times higher than of cortical bone and may cause areas of stress concentration around the implant biomaterials, bone resorption and failure. A plenty of research is being performed for surface modifications of dental implants to overcome these shortcomings. Nanomaterials are proved to improve the mechanical as well as biological properties of titanium.There are very high expectations from nanomaterials research to improve properties and produce new generation of implant materials. A few modifications of implant surface involving nanomaterials are described here.

A. Nanozirconia-alumina materials

These materials are developed using tetragonal zirconia (ZrO_2) nanoparticles and alumina matrix; have improved mechanical properties.

B. Titanium-silica nanocomposites

Silica is well known for its bioactivity for calcified tissue and it promotes the formation of hydroxyapatite. Addition of silica in implant materials enhances the bioactivity by forming Si-OH groups on the surface. Titanium (metal) was added to improve mechanical properties for load bearing applications. These nanocomposites have better hardness and facilitate the tissue and bone growth in to the micro and macro sized pores present in their surface.

C. Calcium phosphorous (Ca-P) nanoparticles

Titanium implant surfaces can be modified using Calcium phosphorous (Ca-P) nanoparticles. Ca-P nanoparticles (crystal size ~ 20 nm) can be deposited on implant surface using sol-gel technique. There is rise in bone growth in CaP modified surfaces compared to the commercially pure titanium and titanium alloys.

D. Hydroxyapatite (HA) nanocrystals

Hydroxyapatite nanocrystals/particles have been used for surface modification of dental implants. HA nanocrystals powder can be prepared using wet chemical process; that can be used to produce either microcrystalline HA (sintering at ~ 1100 for 60 minutes) or nanocrystalline HA (hydrothermal treatment at 200 °C for twenty hours). HA powder can be deposited on to the implant surface at room temperature and result in better adhesion of osteoblasts and more calcium deposition in case of nanocrystalline HA coating compared to traditional HA coating.

5. NANOMATERIALS AND TISSUE ENGINEERING

Tissue engineering is an interdisciplinary field involving multiple disciplines of science and engineering. It has been considered as a part of biomaterials initially, however has developed in to an individual subject on its own because of promising and remarkable developments recently. There are variety of definitions available for tissue engineering in the literature. "Tissue engineering is a science that applies the principles of biology and engineering to develop the functional substitutes for damaged tissues". For any tissue engineering application, it is based on three main components, cell source (mainly stem cells that differentiate into different cell lines), a scaffold (to support and act as carrier for cells) and bioactive molecules or signals (to induce differentiation and tissue formation). There is a wide range of nanotechnology applications in the construction of tissue engineering scaffolds. To construct a scaffold of suitable material and mimicking extracellular matrix to support cell growth, differentiation and functionality is a foremost challenge for researchers. There are different techniques used for constructing nanofibrous polymer scaffolds. Electrospinning is a potential method of fabricating nanomaterials for such applications and is commonly used. (Table: 18.2)

A. Electrospun nanomaterials

Electrospinning can be used for making polymer fibres (from few nanometer diameter to tens of micron); additives such as particles, antimicrobials or enzymes can also be incorporated to get the desired properties in the final materials. Electrospun fibres are collected in the form of porous non-woven mats in three dimensional formats that can provide architecture similar to naturally occurring protein fibrils in the extracellular matrix. Nano-fibres provide high surface area to volume ratio exposing more surface area for cellular interaction, protein absorption and binding sites to cell receptors. The adsorbed proteins can alter their conformation enhancing further exposure of binding sites that is an enormous edge over micro-scale materials available for tissue regeneration. Nano-fibres can facilitate packing of maximum volume fraction by controlling fibres alignment and orientation hence improving the material strength. The desired scaffold properties such as surface morphology, porosity and geometry can also be tailored by varying different electrospinning parameters and can be functionalized for certain applications, for example, bioactive agents for biomedical applications. (Fig: 18.6)

These unique nano-structure features have made electro-spun fibres an excellent candidate for a variety of biomedical applications, e.g. topical or intravenous drug delivery, wound dressings and scaffolding materials for tissue engineering. The discussion of technical parameters affecting electrospinning process is beyond the scope of this book and is not discussed here.

Table: 18.2. Materials electrospun for tissue engineering applications (Examples).

NATURAL POLYMERS	Silk
	Collagen
	Cellulose
SYNTHETIC POLYMERS	Polylactic acid (PLA)
	Polyglycolic acid (PGA)
	Polyethylene glycol (PEG)
NANOCOMPOSITES	Polyvinyl alcohol/gelatin
	Spider Silk-Silica

Fig. 18.6: Scanning electron microscopc picture of electrospun natural silk materials; A and B (Nanofibres as spun), C and D (Sillica condensation in order to prepare nanocomposites).

Tissue engineering is a hot and rapidly growing area of research for regeneration of medical and dental tissues. Nanomaterial scaffolds either electrospun or fabricated by any other technique are being used for a variety of dental tissue regeneration such as dentin, pulp, ligament, bone, neural tissues and tooth.

CONCLUSIVE REMARKS

The application of nanomaterials is the most challenging in the field of medicine and biomedical purposes. This is an area of very active research all around the globe involving a lot of research funding. It can be expected in future that the science of dental materials may change significantly with better understanding and the introduction of new nano-biomaterials.

REFERENSES

1. Paul DR, Robeson LM. Polymer nanotechnology: Nanocomposites. Polymer 2008 7/7;49(15):3187-3204.
2. Broderick M, Neville F, Gibson T, Millner P. Practical nanobiotechnology: Functional nanoparticle production using silaffin R5 peptide. Journal of Biotechnology, 2007 9;131(2, Supplement 1):S11-S11.
3. Hou A, Chen H. Preparation and characterization of silk/silica hybrid biomaterials by sol–gel crosslinking process. Materials Science and Engineering: B 2010 3/15;167(2):124-128.
4. Zhang Y, Lim CT, Ramakrishna S, Huang ZM. Recent development of polymer nanofibers for biomedical and biotechnological applications. J Mater Sci Mater Med 2005;16(10):933-946.
5. Sheeparamatti B, Sheeparamatti R, Kadadevaramath J. Nanotechnology: Inspiration from nature. IETE Tech Rev 2007;24(1):5-8.
6. Gouma P. Nanomaterials for chemical sensors and biotechnology. Singapore; London: World Scientific; 2009.
7. Hieber S, Müller B. Nanodentistry. In: Logothetidis S, editor. : Springer Berlin Heidelberg; 2012. p. 95-107.
8. Mano JF, Reis RL. Some trends on how one can learn from and mimic nature in order to design better biomaterials. Materials Science and Engineering: C 2005 4/28;25(2):93-95.
9. Lieber CM. One-dimensional nanostructures: chemistry, physics & applications. Solid State Commun 1998;107(11):607-616.
10. Sturdevant CM, Roberson TM, Heyman H, Swift EJ. Sturdevant's art & science of operative dentistry. St. Louis, Mo.; London: Mosby; 2001.
11. Moszner N, Klapdohr S. Nanotechnology for dental composites. International Journal of Nanotechnology 2004;1(1):130-156.
12. Sahoo S, Parveen S, Panda J. The present and future of nanotechnology in human health care. Nanomedicine: Nanotechnology, Biology and Medicine 2007;3(1):20-31.
13. Feynman RP. There's plenty of room at the bottom. Engineering and Science 1960;23(5):22-36.
14. Taniguchi N. On the basic concept of 'nano-technology'Proceedings of the International Conference of Production Engineering. Tokyo, Japan: Society of Precision Engineering 1974.
15. Iijima S. Helical microtubules of graphitic carbon. Nature

1991;354(6348):56-58.

16. Hussain F, Hojjati M, Okamoto M, Gorga RE. Review article: polymer-matrix nanocomposites, processing, manufacturing, and application: an overview. J Composite Mater 2006;40(17):1511.
17. Oriakhi C. Nano sandwiches. Chem Br 1998;34(11):59-62.
18. Emsley J. The chemistry of phosphorus : environmental, organic, inorganic, biochemical and spectroscopic aspects. London: Harper & Row; 1976.
19. LeGeros RZ. Calcium phosphates in oral biology and medicine. Basel: Karger; 1991.
20. Low IM, Duraman N, Mahmood U. Mapping the structure, composition and mechanical properties of human teeth. Materials Science and Engineering: C, 2008 3/10;28(2):243-247.
21. Naray-Szabo S. Structure of apatite $(CaF)Ca_4(PO_4)_3$. Z Kristallogr 1930;75:387-398.
22. Kay MI, Young RA, Posner AS. Crystal Structure of Hydroxyapatite. Nature 1964;204(496):1050-&.
23. Jones FH. Teeth and bones: applications of surface science to dental materials and related biomaterials. Surface Science Reports 2001 5;42(3-5):75-205.
24. Fundamentals of operative dentistry : a contemporary approach. 2nd ed. Chicago, Ill. ; London: Quintessence Publishing; 2000.
25. Nanci A. Ten Cate's oral histology : development, structure, and function. (7th ed.) St. Louis, Mo. ; London: Mosby; 2008.
26. Ten Cate AR. Oral histology : development, structure, and function. (4th ed.) St. Louis ; London: Mosby; 1994.
27. Kelsall R, Hamley IW, Geoghegan M. Nanoscale Science and Technology. 2005; .
28. Arcís RW, López-Macipe A, Toledano M, Osorio E, Rodríguez-Clemente R, Murtra J, et al. Mechanical properties of visible light-cured resins reinforced with hydroxyapatite for dental restoration. Dental Materials 2002 1;18(1):49-57.
29. Mota EG, Oshima H, Burnett Jr LH, Pires L, Rosa RS. Evaluation of diametral tensile strength and Knoop microhardness of five nanofilled composites in dentin and enamel shades. Stomatologija 2006;8(3):67-69.
30. Turssi CP, Ferracane JL, Vogel K. Filler features and their effects on wear and degree of conversion of particulate dental resin composites. Biomaterials 2005 8;26(24):4932-4937.
31. Ray SS, Okamoto M. Biodegradable polylactide and Its nanocomposites: opening a new dimension for plastics and composites. Macromolecular Rapid Communications 2003;24(14):815-840.
32. Mohanty A, Drzal L, Misra M. Nano reinforcements of bio-based polymers - The hope and the reality. Abs. The American Chemical Society 2003;225(2):33.
33. Phillips' science of dental materials. 11th ed. St. Louis, Mo. ; Great Britain: Saunders; 2003.
34. Eley BM. The future of dental amalgam: A review of the literature .2. Mercury exposure in dental practice. Br Dent J 1997;182(8):293-297.
35. Eley BM. The future of dental amalgam: A review of the literature .4. Mercury exposure hazards and risk assessment.

Br Dent J 1997;182(10):373-381.

36. Jones DW. A Canadian perspective on the dental amalgam issue. Br Dent J 1998;184(12):581-586.

37. Warfvinge K. Mercury Exposure of a Female Dentist before Pregnancy. Br Dent J 1995;178(4):149-152.

38. Smart ER, Macleod RI, Lawrence CM. Resolution of Lichen-Planus Following Removal of Amalgam Restorations in Patients with Proven Allergy to Mercury Salts - a Pilot-Study. Br Dent J 1995;178(3):108-112.

39. Eley BM. The future of dental amalgam: A review of the literature .7. Possible alternative materials to amalgam For the restoration of posterior teeth. Br Dent J 1997;183(1):11-14.

40. Mclean JW. Alternatives to Amalgam Alloys .1. Br Dent J 1984;157(12):432-433.

41. Yardley RM. Alternatives to Amalgam Alloys .2. Br Dent J 1984;157(12):434-435.

42. Moszner N, Salz U. Recent developments of new components for dental adhesives and composites. Macromolecular Materials and Engineering 2007;292(3):245-271.

43. Biomaterials science : an introduction to materials in medicine. (2nd ed.) Amsterdam ; London: Elsevier Academic Press; 2004.

44. Centers For Disease Control. Ten great public health achievements - United States, 1900-1999. Morb Mortal Weekly Rep 1999;48(12):241-243.

45. Ham-Chande R, Orlando F. Shapes and Limits of Longevity in Mexico. 2005.

46. Richmond RL. The changing face of the Australian population: growth in centenarians. Med J Aust 2008 JUN 16;188(12):720-723.

47. Alberola N, Merle G, Benzarti K. Uniirectional fibre-reinforced polymers: analytical morphology approach and mechanical modelling based on the percolation concept. Polymer 1999;40(2):315-328.

48. Buonocore MG. A Simple Method of Increasing the Adhesion of Acrylic Filling Materials to Enamel Surfaces. Journal of Dental Research 1955 December 1;34(6):849-853.

49. Sakaguchi RL, Powers JM,. Craig's restorative dental materials. Philadelphia, PA: Elsevier/Mosby; 2012.

50. Terry DA. Direct applications of a nanocomposite resin system: Part 1-The evolution of contemporary composite materials. Practical Procedures and Aesthetic Dentistry 2004;16:417-432.

51. Mitra SB, Wu D, Holmes BN. An application of nanotechnology in advanced dental materials. JADA 2003;134(10):1382-1390.

52. Musselman M. Composites make large difference in" small" medical, dental applications. Composites Technology 2003;9(6):24-27.

53. Wilson AD, Kent BE. The glass-ionomer cement, a new translucent dental filling material. Journal of Applied Chemistry and Biotechnology 1971;21(11):313.

54. Ten Cate JM, van Duinen RNB. Hypermineralization of Dentinal Lesions Adjacent to Glass-ionomer Cement Restorations. Journal of Dental Research 1995 June 01;74(6):1266-1271.

55. Mount GJ. Clinical performance of glass-ionomers. Biomaterials 1998

4;19(6):573-579.

56. Tyas MJ. Clinical evaluation of glass-ionomer cement restorations. Journal of Applied Oral Science} 2006 00;14:10.

57. Mickenautsch S, Yengopal V, Banerjee A. Retention of orthodontic brackets bonded with resin-modified GIC versus composite resin adhesives - a quantitative systematic review of clinical trials. Clin Oral Investig 2012 02/01;16(1):1-14.

58. Silva RM, Santos PHN, Souza LB, Dumont VC, Soares JA, Santos MH. Effects of cellulose fibers on the physical and chemical properties of glass ionomer dental restorative materials. Mater Res Bull 2013 1;48(1):118-126.

59. Moshaverinia A, Ansari S, Moshaverinia M, Roohpour N, Darr JA, Rehman I. Effects of incorporation of hydroxyapatite and fluoroapatite nanobioceramics into conventional glass ionomer cements (GIC). Acta Biomaterialia 2008 3;4(2):432-440.

60. Jevnikar P, Golobič M, Kocjan A, Kosmač T. The effect of nano-structured alumina coating on the bond strength of resin-modified glass ionomer cements to zirconia ceramics. Journal of the European Ceramic Society 2012 8;32(11):2641-2645.

61. Raggio DP, Calvo AFB, Branco EC, Bonifácio CC, Imparato JCP, Camargo LB. Knoop Hardness of Resin-modified Glass-ionomer Cements. IJD.International Journal of Dentistry 2009;8(3).

62. Basso M. Teeth restoration using a high-viscosity glass ionomer cement: the Equia® system. Journal of Minimum Intervention in Dentistry 2011;4(3):74-76.

63. Lee J, Lee Y, Choi B, Lee J, Choi H, Son H, et al. Physical properties of resin-reinforced glass ionomer cement modified with micro and nano-hydroxyapatite. Journal of Nanoscience and Nanotechnology 2010;10(8):5270-5276.

64. Khademolhosseini M, Barounian M, Eskandari A, Aminzare M, Zahedi A, Ghahremani D. Development of New Al2O3/TiO2 Reinforced Glass-Ionomer Cements (GICs) Nano-Composites. 2012.

65. u Y, Yap A, Cheang P, Koh Y, Khor K. Development of zirconia-glass ionomer cement composites. J Non Cryst Solids 2005;351(6):508-514.

66. Koch K, Brave D. A new day has dawned: the increased use of bioceramics in endodontics. Dentaltown April 2009;10(4):39-43.

67. Zoufan K, Jiang J, Komabayashi T, Wang Y, Safavi KE, Zhu Q. Cytotoxicity evaluation of Gutta Flow and Endo Sequence BC sealers. Oral Surgery, Oral Medicine, Oral Pathology, Oral Radiology, and Endodontology 2011 11;112(5):657-661.

68. Abramovitz I, Beyth N, Weinberg G, Borenstein A, Polak D, Kesler-Shvero D, et al. In Vitro Biocompatibility of Endodontic Sealers Incorporating Antibacterial Nanoparticles. Journal of Nanomaterials 2012;2012:12.

69. Beyth N, Houri-Haddad Y, Baraness-Hadar L, Yudovin-Farber I, Domb AJ, Weiss EI. Surface antimicrobial activity and biocompatibility of incorporated polyethylenimine nanoparticles. Biomaterials 2008 11;29(31):4157-4163.

70. Farea M, Masudi S, Bakar W, Zaripah

W. Apical microleakage evaluation of system B compared with cold lateral technique: In vitro study. Australian Endodontic Journal 2010;36(2):48-53.

71. Abdo SB, Al Darrat A, Luddin N, Husien A. Sealing ability of gutta-percha/Nano HA versus Resilon/ Epiphany after 20 months using an electrochemical model–an in vitro study. Brazilian Journal of Oral Sciences ;11(3):387-391.

72. Mortazavi V, Nahrkhalaji MM, Fathi MH, Mousavi SB, Esfahani BN. Antibacterial effects of sol-gel-derived bioactive glass nanoparticle on aerobic bacteria. Journal of Biomedical Materials Research Part A 2010;94A(1):160-168.

73. Waltimo T, Brunner TJ, Vollenweider M, Stark WJ, Zehnder M. Antimicrobial Effect of Nanometric Bioactive Glass 45S5. Journal of Dental Research 2007 August 01;86(8):754-757.

74. Venugopal J, Ramakrishna S. Applications of polymer nanofibers in biomedicine and biotechnology. Appl Biochem Biotechnol 2005;125(3):147-157.

75. Fukuda J, Khademhosseini A, Yeh J, Eng G, Cheng J, Farokhzad OC, et al. Micropatterned cell co-cultures using layer-by-layer deposition of extracellular matrix components. Biomaterials 2006;27(8):1479-1486.

76. Galler KM, Cavender A, Yuwono V, Dong H, Shi S, Schmalz G, et al. Self-assembling peptide amphiphile nanofibers as a scaffold for dental stem cells. Tissue Engineering Part A 2008;14(12):2051-2058.

77. Misawa H, Kobayashi N, Soto-Gutierrez A, Chen Y, Yoshida A, Rivas-Carrillo JD, et al. PuraMatrixTM facilitates bone regeneration in bone defects of calvaria in mice. Cell Transplant 2006;15(10):903-910.

78. Demarco FF, Conde M, Cavalcanti BN, Casagrande L, Sakai VT, Nör JE. Dental pulp tissue engineering. Braz Dent J 2011;22(1):3-14.

79. Wiesmann H, Meyer U, Plate U, Höhling H. Aspects of collagen mineralization in hard tissue formation. Int Rev Cytol 2004;242:121-156.

80. Kim NR, Lee DH, Chung P, Yang H. Distinct differentiation properties of human dental pulp cells on collagen, gelatin, and chitosan scaffolds. Oral Surgery, Oral Medicine, Oral Pathology, Oral Radiology, and Endodontology 2009;108(5):e94-e100.

81. Mizuno M, Miyamoto T, Wada K, Watatani S, Zhang GX. Type I collagen regulated dentin matrix protein-1 (Dmp-1) and osteocalcin (OCN) gene expression of rat dental pulp cells. J Cell Biochem 2003;88(6):1112-1119.

82. Hannig M, Hannig C. Nanomaterials in preventive dentistry. Nature nanotechnology 2010;5(8):565-569.

83. Hannig M, Kriener L, Hoth-Hannig W, Becker-Willinger C, Schmidt H. Influence of nanocomposite surface coating on biofilm formation in situ. Journal of nanoscience and nanotechnology 2007;7(12):4642-4648.

84. Reynolds E. Calcium phosphate-based remineralization systems: scientific evidence? Aust Dent J 2008;53(3):268-273.

85. Cross K, Huq N, Reynolds E. Casein phosphopeptides in oral health-chemistry and clinical applications. Curr Pharm Des 2007;13(8):793-800.

86. Rahiotis C, Vougiouklakis G, Eliades G. Characterization of oral films

formed in the presence of a CPP–ACP agent: An *in situ* study. J Dent 2008;36(4):272-280.

87. Morgan MV, Adams GG, Bailey DL, Tsao CE, Fischman SL, Reynolds EC. The anticariogenic effect of sugar-free gum containing CPP-ACP nanocomplexes on approximal caries determined using digital bitewing radiography. Caries Res 2008;42(3):171-184.

88. Roveri N, Battistella E, Bianchi CL, Foltran I, Foresti E, Iafisco M, et al. Surface enamel remineralization: biomimetic apatite nanocrystals and fluoride ions different effects. Journal of Nanomaterials 2009;2009:8.

89. Lv KL, Zhang JX, Meng XC, Li XY. Remineralization effect of the nano-HA toothpaste on artificial caries. Key Eng Mat 2007;330:267-270.

90. Piñón-Segundo E, Ganem-Quintanar A, Alonso-Pérez V, Quintanar-Guerrero D. Preparation and characterization of triclosan nanoparticles for periodontal treatment. Int J Pharm 2005;294(1):217-232.

91. Paquette D, Hanlon A, Lessem J, Williams R. Clinical relevance of adjunctive minocycline microspheres in patients with chronic periodontitis: secondary analysis of a phase 3 trial. J Periodontol 2004;75(4):531-536.

92. Brånemark P, Breine U, Adell R, Hansson B, Lindström J, Ohlsson Å. Intra-osseous anchorage of dental prostheses: I. experimental studies. Scandinavian Journal of Plastic and Reconstructive Surgery and Hand Surgery 1969;3(2):81-100.

93. Pye A, Lockhart D, Dawson M, Murray C, Smith A. A review of dental implants and infection. J Hosp Infect 2009;72(2):104-110.

94. Tomsia AP, Launey ME, Lee JS, Mankani MH, Wegst UG, Saiz E. Nanotechnology Approaches for Better Dental Implants. Int J Oral Maxillofac Implants 2011;26(Suppl):25.

95. Oh T, Yoon J, Misch CE, Wang H. The causes of early implant bone loss: myth or science? J Periodontol 2002;73(3):322-333.

96. Valiev RZ, Zehetbauer MJ, Estrin Y, Höppel HW, Ivanisenko Y, Hahn H, et al. The innovation potential of bulk nanostructured materials. Advanced Engineering Materials 2007;9(7):527-533.

97. Pecharroman C, Bartolomé JF, Requena J, Moya JS, Deville S, Chevalier J, et al. Percolative mechanism of aging in Zirconia containing ceramics for medical applications. Adv Mater 2003;15(6):507-511.

98. Deville S, Chevalier J, Fantozzi G, Bartolomé JF, Requena J, Moya JS, et al. Low-temperature ageing of zirconia-toughened alumina ceramics and its implication in biomedical implants. Journal of the European Ceramic Society 2003;23(15):2975-2982.

99. Cao W, Hench LL. Bioactive materials. Ceram Int 1996;22(6):493-507.

100. Jurczyk MU, Jurczyk K, Niespodziana K, Miklaszewski A, Jurczyk M. Titanium–SiO2 nanocomposites and their scaffolds for dental applications. Mater Charact 2013 3;77(0):99-108.

101. Mendonça G, Mendonça DBS, Aragão FJL, Cooper LF. Advancing dental implant surface technology – From micron- to nanotopography. Biomaterials 2008 10;29(28):3822-3835.

102. MendesVC,MoineddinR,DaviesJE.The effect of discrete calcium phosphate

nanocrystals on bone-bonding to titanium surfaces. Biomaterials 2007 11;28(32):4748-4755.

103. Mendes VC, Moineddin R, Davies JE. Discrete calcium phosphate nanocrystalline deposition enhances osteoconduction on titanium-based implant surfaces. Journal of Biomedical Materials Research Part A 2008;90(2):577-585.

104. Sato M, Sambito MA, Aslani A, Kalkhoran NM, Slamovich EB, Webster TJ. Increased osteoblast functions on undoped and yttrium-doped nanocrystalline hydroxyapatite coatings on titanium. Biomaterials 2006 4;27(11):2358-2369.

105. Galler KM, D'Souza RN, Hartgerink JD. Biomaterials and their potential applications for dental tissue engineering. J Mater Chem 2010;20(40):8730-8746.

106. Duncan L, Sprehe C. Mosby's dental dictionary. St. Louis, Mo.: Mosby; 2008.

107. Langer R, Vacanti J. Tissue engineering. Science 1993 May 14;260(5110):920-926.

108. Hargreaves KM. Cohen's pathways of the pulp. (10th ed.) Edinburgh: Mosby; 2010.

109. Greiner A, Wendorff JH. Electrospinning: A fascinating method for the preparation of ultrathin fibres. Angewandte Chemie-International (ed.) 2007;46(30):5670-5703.

110. Electrospinning for tissue regeneration. Oxford: Woodhead Publishing; 2011.

111. Li W, Laurencin CT, Caterson EJ, Tuan RS, Ko FK. Electrospun nanofibrous structure: A novel scaffold for tissue engineering. J Biomed Mater Res 2002;60(4):613-621.

112. Agarwal S, Wendorff JH, Greiner A. Use of electrospinning technique for biomedical applications. Polymer 2008 12/8;49(26):5603-5621.

113. Stevens MM, George JH. Exploring and Engineering the Cell Surface Interface. Science 2005 November 18;310(5751):1135-1138.

114. Liang D, Hsiao BS, Chu B. Functional electrospun nanofibrous scaffolds for biomedical applications. Adv Drug Deliv Rev 2007 12/10;59(14):1392-1412.

115. Amiraliyan N, Nouri M, Kish MH. Electrospinning of silk nanofibers. I. An investigation of nanofiber morphology and process optimization using response surface methodology. Fibers and Polymers 2009;10(2):167-176.

116. Cao H, Chen X, Huang L, Shao Z. Electrospinning of reconstituted silk fiber from aqueous silk fibroin solution. Materials Science and Engineering: C 2009 8/31;29(7):2270-2274.

117. Yeo I, Oh J, Jeong L, Lee TS, Lee SJ, Park WH, et al. Collagen-based biomimetic nanofibrous scaffolds: Preparation and characterization of collagen. Biomacromolecules 2008 APR;9(4):1106-1116.

118. A novel nanofiber scaffold by electrospinning and its utility in microvascular tissue engineering. MRS Proceedings: Cambridge Univ Press; 2004.

119. Linh NTB, Lee B. Electrospinning of polyvinyl alcohol/gelatin nanofiber composites and cross-linking for bone tissue engineering application. Journal of Biomaterials Applications 2012 September 01;27(3):255-266.

120. Foo CWP, Patwardhan SV, Belton DJ, Brandon Kitchel, Anastasiades D, Huang J, et al. Novel Nanocomposites

from Spider Silk-Silica Fusion (Chimeric) Proteins. Proc Natl Acad Sci U S A 2006 Jun. 20;103(25):pp. 9428-9433.

121. Vallés-Lluch A, Novella-Maestre E, Sancho-Tello M, Pradas MM, Ferrer GG, Batalla CC. Mimicking Natural Dentin Using Bioactive Nanohybrid Scaffolds for Dentinal Tissue Engineering. Tissue Engineering Part A 2010;16(9):2783-2793.

122. Cavalcanti BN, Zeitlin BD, Nör JE. A hydrogel scaffold that maintains viability and supports differentiation of dental pulp stem cells. Dental Materials 2013 1;29(1):97-102.

123. Peh RF, Suthikum V, Goh CH, Toh SL. Novel Electrospun-Knitted Silk Scaffolds for Ligament Tissue Engineering. World Congress on Medical Physics and Biomedical Engineering 2006, Vol 14, Pts 1-6 2007;14:3287-3290.

124. Park CH, Rios HF, Jin Q, Bland ME, Flanagan CL, Hollister SJ, et al. Biomimetic hybrid scaffolds for engineering human tooth-ligament interfaces. Biomaterials 2010 8;31(23):5945-5952.

125. Saiz E, Zimmermann EA, Lee JS, Wegst UGK, Tomsia AP. Perspectives on the role of nanotechnology in bone tissue engineering. Dental Materials 2013 1;29(1):103-115.

126. Lee Y, Livingston Arinzeh T. Electrospun Nanofibrous Materials for Neural Tissue Engineering. Polymers 2011;3(1):413-426.

127. Yang F. Fabrication of nano-structured porous PLLA scaffold intended for nerve tissue engineering. Biomaterials 2004;25(10):1891.

128. Honda MJ, Tsuchiya S, Shinohara Y, Shinmura Y, Sumita Y. Recent advances in engineering of tooth and tooth structures using postnatal dental cells. Japanese Dental Science Review 2010 2;46(1):54-66.

129. Bauer LA, Birenbaum NS, Meyer GJ. Biological applications of high aspect ratio nanoparticles. J.Mater.Chem. 2004;14(4):517-526.

Chapter 19

BONE REPLACEMENT GRAFT MATERIALS IN DENTISTRY

Dr. Zeeshan Sheikh, Dr. Mohamed-Nur Abdallah, Dr. Mohammad A. Javaid & Dr. Ahad S. Ahmed

PREAMBLE

Bone replacement is a highly complex and challenging task to accomplish. Bone grafts are the second most common transplanted tissue after blood. More than 2.2 million bone grafting procedures take place annually worldwide in order to repair bone defects in orthopaedics, dentistry and neurosurgery. The treatment of post-traumatic skeletal complications, such as delayed unions, non-unions, mal-unions along with spinal fusions, filling defects following removal of bone tumors and several congenital diseases, ridge augmentations prior to dental implant placement are some of the challenges that can be met successfully by grafting procedures. The exact mechanism of bone graft incorporation into host tissue still remains to be completely understood. There are a few theories which help to explain this phenomenon with the most important being probably the provision of the graft material working as a scaffold allowing deposition of bone and subsequent integration with the surrounding bone.

Periodontal therapy is directed not only at inflammation control but also at pocket reduction and correction of the associated bone defects. The ultimate goal in periodontal therapy is creation of an environment that is favorable towards maintaining patient's dentition in health, comfort, and function. Bone grafting procedures in periodontology are routinely carried out. Attention towards bone replacement grafts has emerged from the aspiration to pack furcations or fill intrabony defects rather than carrying out radical resection of the surrounding intact bone tissue. Osseous resection further compromises the support of the involved bone structure and adjacent teeth. When applicable, regeneration of the lost bone and periodontal attachment improves support of the teeth and potentially the long-term prognosis in cases with medium to extensive bone defects. Bone replacement grafts are not a contemporary treatment modality and have been used historically to meet this challenge. In the field of prosthodontics, bone augmentation is also often required because of the continuous resorption of the alveolar ridge following extraction/loss of all or few teeth. This ultimately results in an unfavourable denture bearing area and denture support with subsequent compromise in stability. Various ridge augmentation techniques are available using cancellous rib or cortico-cancellous iliac grafts for the extremely atrophic mandible. For single tooth replacement requirements, bone augmentation can be achieved by local bone graft tissue harvested from the symphysis area of the chin.

BONE: BIOLOGY AND CONSTITUTION

A basic understanding of bone biology and its constitutional elements is imperative in comprehending the many challenges that must be met when successful bone replacement by grafting is desired. Briefly, bone formation starts with the secretion of collagen molecules and ground substance (gelatinous medium which comprises of chondroitin sulfate and hyaluronic acid) by osteoblasts. The collagen molecules polymerize in order to create collagen fibers. Calcium salts then precipitate in the ground substance to form osteoid along the collagen fibers. The osteoblasts become trapped in the osteoid which are then referred to as osteocytes. Mature compact bone is composed of approximately 30% organic matrix and 70% calcium salts. In which 90 to 95% of the organic matrix is collagen fibers, and the remainder is ground substance. The collagen fibers are oriented along the lines of tensional force which provides mechanical reinforcement. The main crystalline salt, composed of calcium and phosphate, is hydroxyapatite $[Ca_{10}(P0_4)_6(OH)_2]$ (HA). Compact bone has HA crystals that are adjacent to and bound to the collagen fibers. The collagen fibers provide tensile strength, and the HA crystals are responsible for imparting compressional strength. Hence this natural composite we commonly refer to as bone is formed, comprised of organic and inorganic components. Bone formation is an elaborate process and it is beyond the scope of this chapter to cover all aspects in detail. Other text books may be referred for further understanding.

RATIONALE AND OBJECTIVES OF BONE REPLACEMENT GRAFTS

Bone replacement grafts serve as a structural framework for clot formation, maturation, and remodeling that ultimately leads to bone formation in bone defects. Bone graft materials may also demonstrate the ability (variable) to promote coordinated formation of bone, cementum, and periodontal ligament (PDL) when placed and retained in periodontal defects. Some bone graft materials may also possess the ability to promote greater clinical periodontal bone defect fill than flap debridement alone. Histological observations have confirmed the potential of bone replacement grafts to support new attachment in the apical portion of periodontal defects. Complete regeneration is not likely; however, some regeneration or new attachment can occur. After implantation, the hard and soft tissue host bed surrounding the graft must be viable and must have adequate blood supply. It is rare for grafts to survive when placed within nonvital host bone. In the weeks following the implantation, new blood vessels, interstitial cells and woven bone (by new osteoblasts) are produced by the host bed. All of these embed the graft to create the graft-woven bone complex.

The graft material and woven bone are fused together by cement lines to achieve the desired mechanical strength. Bone formation in grafting procedures involves one or more of the following biological mechanisms:

1. *Osteogenesis:* New bone formation by osteoblasts derived from the graft itself.
2. *Osteoinduction:* The ability of a material to induce the formation of osteoblasts from the surrounding tissue at the graft host site, resulting in new bone formation and growth.

3. *Osteoconduction:* The ability of a material to support the growth of bone over a graft surface.

From a periodontal viewpoint, an ideal bone replacement graft should be able to induce osteogenesis, cementogenesis and formation of PDL. Osteogenesis is achieved with autogenous grafts and the presence of cellular elements or progenitor cells in these autogenous grafts are thought to be responsible for this (Table: 19.3).

As will be discussed later in this chapter, other types of bone replacement grafts do not provide any cellular elements. The best case scenario for these non-autogenous grafts would be osteoinduction, which would stimulate phenotypic conversion of progenitor cells within the healing wound to those that can form osseous tissue (Table: 19.4). Demineralized freeze-dried human bone and bone morphogenetic proteins (BMPs) are known to be able to achieve this osteoinduction. However, some studies demonstrate that alloplastic graft materials based on acidic calcium phosphates such as dicalcium phosphate anhydrate (DCPA), commonly known as monetite does not only show impressive osteoconduction but also osteoinductive properties (Table: 19.5). Most bone replacement grafts are osteoconductive, relatively inert filling materials, and integrate with new bone without providing much histological evidence of extensive regeneration. These osteoconductive graft materials provide a scaffold allowing bone deposition and in-growth. Although osseointegration, which is the ability to chemically bind to surrounding bone, is not directly responsible for bone formation, is a desirable property as it aids in the incorporation of graft material at the host site. The most important aspect for the success of a bone graft is to be completely resorbed and remodeled, allowing the graft to not interfere with physiologic bone adaptation (Table 19.1).

Table: 19.1. Requirements of bone grafts for successful bone tissue replacement.

CHARACTERISTICS	COMMENTS
Biocompatibility	Should not provoke any graft rejection (immune response) and inflammation.
Bioactivity	Stimulate osteoconduction, osteoinduction and create biochemical bonding with host tissue (Osseointegration).
Biodegradability	Act as a temporary scaffold to be replaced with new bone formation at adequate pace (match degradation rate with bone formation rate).
Degradation modality	Surface and/or bulk erosion/biodegradation.
Osteoconductivity	Have intrinsic potential to support in-growing capillary network, perivascular mesenchymal tissues and the osteoprogenitor cells from the host.
Porosity within graft structure	To provide sufficient revascularization leading to adequate nutrition and oxygen supply. Also to maximize surface area for protein adsorption, cellular adhesion and extra cellular matrix secretion.

Three dimensional architecture	For support to the cellular in-growth and deep penetrative transport of nutrition and oxygen.
Vascular support	Channels for blood vessels ensuring adequate blood supply to maintain healthy bone growth.
Ease of manipulation	Should be easy to handle during surgical procedures.
Sufficient mechanical strength	Adequate structural integrity to bear the *in vivo* stresses during bone formation phase.
Sterilization compatible	Biologic and physico-chemical and mechanical properties should not be compromised.
Cost-effectiveness	Clinically affordable.

BONE REPLACEMENT GRAFTS

Bone replacement Grafts can generally be divided into natural and synthetic grafts according to origin. The natural sources of these grafts could be human or animal tissues (Table 19.2). The various options available for bone replacement with graft tissues will be discussed in detail in the subsequent sections of the chapter.

Table: 19.2. Bone replacement graft tissues and materials.

BONE REPLACEMENT GRAFTS
1. **Human bone sources** a. Autogenous grafts (autografts) ✦ Extra-oral (e.g. iliac crest) ✦ Intra-oral (e.g. tuberosity or chin) b. **Allogengc grafts (allografts)** ✦ Fresh frozen bone allografts (FFBA) ✦ Freeze-dried bone allografts (FDBA) ✦ Demineralized freeze-dried bone allografts (DFDBA)
2. **Bone substitutes (living non-human sources)** a. Xenogeneic grafts (xenografts) ✦ Bovine (derived) HA (porous, non-resorbahle) ✦ Coralline calcium carbonate
3. **Synthetic bone substitutes (alloplasts)** a. Polymeric materials (PGA, PLA, PGLA etc.) b. Bio-active glasses (Bio Glas) c. Bioceramics ✦ Hydroxyapatite a (dense, non-porous, non-resorbable HA) b (resorbable HA derived at low temperature) ✦ Other calcium phosphates (tricalcium phosphate, brushite, monetite)

PGA: Poly-glycolic acid ,PLA: Poly-lactic acid, PGLA: Poly-glycolic-lactic acid and HA Hydroxyapatite.

1. AUTOGENOUS BONE GRAFTS

Autogenous bone grafts, commonly referred to as autografts, are transferred from one site to another within the same individual. Autografts remain the gold standard to which all other graft materials are compared with. Being from the host itself, there is no risk of antigenicity and graft compliance is near ideal. Autografts provide optimal osteoconductive, osteoinductive and osteogenic properties (Table 19.3). The demerits of autografts include limited amount of bone available and morbidity associated with the harvesting procedure. Also a major concern is the increase in operating time leading to extensive hospitalization and procedural cost elevation. Moreover, residual pain and poor cosmetic outcomes are added disadvantages of autografts. It has also been noted that at times, it may fail in clinical practice as majority of cellular (osteogenic) elements do not survive the transplantation procedure.

Autogenous grafts can be of cancellous or cortical nature or a combination of both. Owing to their sponge like architecture, cancellous grafts have the ability to revascularize sooner than cortical grafts. This revascularization begins around the fifth day post transplantation. Prior to the revascularization, cellular survival in the graft tissues is heavily dependent upon the plasmatic diffusion for providing adequate nutrition and waste product removal. Osteocytes residing in their lacunae have been shown to survive if they are within 0.3 mm of the perfusion surface. In comparison, cortical autografts require considerable osteoclast mediated resorption before osteoblastic bone formation can commence. This process is termed as "creeping substitution" and can induce islands of necrotic bone. Due to the difference in biology and architecture of cancellous and cortical bone, graft characteristics vary greatly. The cortical grafts show initial high strength which weakens overtime before regaining strength again. Dynamic loading has been shown to be a critical factor for the preservation and increase in bone mass after implantation and on cellular level, for the modulation of osteoclastic and osteoblastic processes. After several weeks to 6 months post implantation, cortical autografts have

Table: 19.3. Merits and demerits of using autogenous bone graft (autografts).

ADVANTAGES OF AUTOGRAFTS	DISADVANTAGES OF AUTOGRAFTS
Biocompatible	Additional surgery to harvest bone and extensive hospitalization
High osteogeneic potential	Increase in operative time and cost
Osteoconductive	Post-operative pain and increased blood loss
Osteoinductive	Increased risk of fracture (donor site)
Adequate mechanical strength providing structural support	Dead bone is at potential risk for infection to set in
Easier incorporation into host site (none or minimal immune response)	High variability in quality of harvested bone tissue
Availability in cortical and cancellous forms	Limited amount of graft tissue can be harvested

been shown to be 40-50% weaker than normal bone. Conversely, cancellous autografts are weak initially after implantation because of their porous (open) architecture. Over a period of time they continue to gain strength and physiological stimulation is imperative for achieving adequate dimensional stability and strength.

There are case reports showing histological findings which demonstrate the potential for autogenous bone/bone marrow grafts to support periodontal regeneration in human beings. There is scarcity of literature reporting use of extra-oral autografts for periodontal use. Initially Iliac cancellous bone and marrow were highly sought after as they offered a high potential for osteogenesis, but their use lead to root resorption which has limited their clinical use. Intra-oral autografts are used widely and have shown to be more favorable for defect filling. Common harvestation sites for intra-oral autografts are the maxillary tuberosity and other edentulous alveolar areas (including healing sockets). Osseous coagulum harvested from surgical sites during osteoplasty procedures is also frequently utilized. Mental and mandibular retro-molar areas are other sites for cortical and cancellous autografts harvestation. Based on the size of the defect, autogenous bone may be grafted in combination with other tissues and materials.

2. ALLOGENOUS BONE GRAFTS

Allografts are taken from a genetically non identical member of same species. There has been a great interest in allografts due to their theoretical unlimited abundance and also because they match closely with the recipient in constitutional elements and architecture. Though allografts undergo various treatments prior to use, risk of disease transmission is still a possibility. It has been estimated that the risk of HIV transmission is 1 in 1.6 million with use of allografts. There have been some reports of cross-infection and incidences of disease transmission. Despite these risks, the recognition of the distinct advantages associated with allografts has resulted in an increase in bone grafting procedures with them. Allografts are mostly prepared as fresh, frozen, freeze-dried, mineralized and demineralized, and each of these are available as cortical chips, cortical granules, cortical wedges or cancellous powdered grafts.

A. Fresh or frozen iliac cancellous bone and marrow grafts

Fresh or frozen iliac cancellous bone and marrow tissues possess the highest osteoconductive and osteoinductive potential among all the available allografts. The risk of disease transmission, antigenicity and extensive cross-matching and treatment required has rendered the use of frozen iliac allografts unacceptable in modern periodontics.

B. Mineralized freeze-dried bone allografts (FDBA)

There has been an extensive use of FDBA in treatment of periodontal defects. This can be attributed to evidence that the health risks associated with fresh frozen bone is markedly reduced, and also due to the successful results of grafting procedures. Processing of FDBA involves placing the graft in antibiotic wash twice at 4°C for 1 hour. The material is then stored at -70 °C to dry up to 5% water. It is assumed that the process of freeze drying affects the immune recognition in the host by distorting the three dimensional presentation of the human leukocyte antigens on the surface of these allografts. FDBA possess inferior osteoinductive and mechanical properties as compared to fresh or frozen allografts. Cortical FDBA do not appear to elicit an immune response in non-human primates. The use of cortical FDBA is recommended in comparison with their cancellous counterparts because there is more bone matrix present and a higher inductive potential and also because the cortical bone is less antigenic.

FDBA are considered osteoconductive and studies have shown that mixing these with autografts enhances the osteogenic potential. FDBA are used successfully for osseous defect filling and in regenerative periodontal procedures covered with a polymeric membrane.

C. Demineralized freeze-dried bone allografts (DFDBA)

DFDBA are used frequently for maxillofacial and periodontal grafting procedures. Research has indicated that the removal of mineral component from grafts allows greater expression of osteoinductive proteins. This is because the mineral present blocks the effect of factors stimulating bone growth sequestered in bone matrix including BMPs. Animal studies have shown that DFDBA has osteogenic potential. However, Unlike FDBA, the addition of autograft materials to DFDBA does not increase the osteogenic potential to a significant degree. The bioactivity of DFDBA has been shown to be age dependent, with grafts harvested from the younger individuals having higher osteogenic potential in comparison to grafts from older individuals. In maxillary sinus augmentation procedures, DFDBA showed 29% new bone formation while autogenous grafts showed 40% in comparison. It has also been observed that DFDBA particles situated near pre-existing bone were enclosed by new bone, whereas particles located near the center of the graft showed no signs of remineralization or new bone formation.

Table: 19.4. Autografts versus Allografts.

BONE GRAFTS	STRUCTURAL STRENGTH	OSTEOGENESIS	OSTEOCONDUCTION	OSTEOINDUCTION
Autografts				
Cortical	3	2	2	2
Cancellous	0	3	3	3
Allografts				
Cortical				
Frozen	3	1	0	0
Freeze-dried	1	1	0	0
Cancellous				
Frozen	0	2	1	0
Freeze-dried	0	2	1	0

Scores: 0 (none), 1 (moderate), 2 (good) and 3 (excellent)

3. XENOGRAFTS

These are graft materials that are shared in between species. Currently, there are two kinds of xenografts available for bone replacement therapy and regenerative applications; bovine bone and natural coral. Both sources provide bone grafts that are biocompatible and structurally similar to human bone, however, their processing techniques are quite different. Xenografts are osteoconductive in nature and are readily available for clinical use.

A. Bovine-derived Xenografts

Commercially available bovine bone is processed to yield natural bone mineral without the organic component. Inorganic bone derived from bovine origin is the HA skeleton that retains the microporous and macroporous structure of cancellous and cortical bone following low-heat and chemical extraction of the organic component. Previously, bovine xenografts failed due to graft rejection, which was probably because the manufacturers employed chemical detergent extraction techniques which left residual proteins and hence produced adverse reactions. Xenografts of bovine origin carry a theoretical risk of disease transmission (bovine spongiform encephalopathy). Although evidence suggests that the risk is negligible yet concerns do exist. A given advantage of these grafts is the improved osteoconductive potential compared with synthetically derived materials. In summary bovine-derived HA bone replacement grafts increase the available surface area that can act as an osteoconductive scaffold owing to their higher level of porosity and have a mineral content that is comparable to human bone facilitating integration with host bone. Bovine-derived bone grafts have successfully been used for the treatment of intrabony defects and also in ridge augmentation procedures.

B. Calcium Carbonate Xenografts

Coralline calcium carbonate is obtained from natural coral, genus *Porites*, and is composed primarily of aragonite (>98% $CaCO_3$). It has a pore size of 100 to 200 μm which is quite similar to that seen in cancellous bone. The relative high porosity of ~45% provides a large surface area for graft resorption and replacement by new bone. Unlike HA, calcium carbonate is resorbable *in vivo* and can also be derived from the same coral by heat conversion. Calcium carbonate does not require surface transformation to carbonate like other grafts in order to induce bone formation; hence it can potentially initiate new bone deposition rapidly. Coralline calcium carbonate has also shown to have high levels of osteoconductivity because it does not undergo fibrous encapsulation. Coralline calcium carbonate has demonstrated a significant gain in PDL clinical attachment, reduction of probing depths and greater defect fill in periodontal applications.

C. Other Xenografts

Some other xenograft materials that are being researched upon include chitosan, red algae and gussuibu. Chitosan is a product of the exo-skeleton of crustaceans, and has shown the ability to stimulate and direct the mesenchymal stem cell differentiation into osteoblasts. When chitosan is combined with HA, the Osteoconductivity is markedly increased. Red Algae are one of the oldest and largest groups of eukaryotic algae with about 5,000–6,000 species of mostly multicellular, marine algae, including many notable seaweeds. Red algae can be chemically converted to HA, which can then be utilized for grafting bone defects. Gussuibu is a rhizome of perennial pteridophyte *Drynaria fortunei*. This herb has shown to have good osteoconductive properties and an increase in alkaline phosphatase expression that has a positive effect of promoting calcification.

4. ALLOPLASTIC BONE GRAFTS

Alloplastic bone grafts are synthetic materials that have been manufactured and investigated extensively for clinical use. Alloplasts include synthetic polymers, bioactive glasses, glass-ionomers and ceramics. The major advantage of using alloplastic materials are: their unlimited availability, no risk of disease transmission and the absence of antigenic response from host towards them. Alloplasts can be manufactured in various forms and with varying physico-chemical properties. They can be made available in both resorbable and non-resorbable forms and can be customized with varying levels of porosity and pore sizes. They can also be combined with bioactive proteins to provide osteoinduction.

A. Polymers

Polymers can be classified based on their origin: natural and synthetic. Natural polymers that have been utilized in the fabrication of bone grafts include polysaccharides (e.g. alginate, argose, chitosan and hyaluronic acid) and polypeptides (e.g. gelatin and collagen). Natural polymers possess weak mechanical properties and variable or negligible rates of degradation, hence their use is limited as bone grafting materials. However, natural polymers play an important role in composite graft production by serving as polymeric shell capsule which incorporate allograft particles. Synthetic polymers (e.g. poly-glycolic acid, poly-lactic acid, poly-orthoester and poly-anhydride) provide a platform for regulating and controlling the biomechanical properties of scaffolds and also serve as drug delivery carriers in tissue engineering applications.

HTR™ Synthetic Bone (Bioplant, Norwalk, CT) is a biocompatible microporous composite made up of poly-methylmethacrylate, poly-hydroxylethylmethacrylate, and calcium hydroxide. The acronym HTR stands for 'Hard Tissue Replacement' and acceptable clinical results have been achieved in treatment of intrabony and furcation defects with its use. Histologically, new bone growth has been observed on the particles of this material. This material has hydrophilicity that enhances clotting, and the negative particle charges on the surface allows adherence to bone. Clinically acceptable defect fill and resolution has been achieved and supports the use of HTR™ as a biocompatible alloplastic bone substitute. Polymers have also traditionally been used as barrier membranes in the periodontal guided tissue regeneration (GRT) and periodontal guided bone regeneration (GBR) procedures.

B. Bioactive glasses

Bioactive glasses were invented for use as bone substitutes more than 3 decades ago. The designation "bioactive" is in relation to their ability to bond to bone and enhance bone-tissue formation. This is attributed to their inherent similarity with the architecture of host bone. Bioactive glasses are non-porous and consist of silicon dioxide (SiO_2), calcium oxide (CaO), phosphorous pentaoxide (P_2O_5), and sodium oxide (Na_2O). Solubility of these grafts is directly dependant upon the proportion of sodium oxide found in the formulation. By alteration in the concentrations of sodium oxide, calcium oxide, and calcium oxide, glasses with different properties can be produced. Bioactive glasses are essentially non-resorbable bone graft materials and when exposed to tissue fluids, these bioactive glass particles are encompassed in a double layer composed of silica gel and a calcium-phosphorous rich (apatite) layer. The calcium-phosphorous rich layer attracts, promotes and concentrates the adsorption of proteins which are utilized by osteoblasts to form a mineralized extracellular matrix. It is thought that these bioactive properties guide and promote osteogenesis, allowing the rapid bone formation that is subsequently observed.

osteophillic and osteoconductive graft material which performs as a trellis for in-growth and deposition of new bone.

G. Other Calcium Phosphates

There are a number of calcium phosphate compounds that exist (Table: 19.6). DCPD or brushite and DCPA or monetite, are acidic calcium phosphates which are used for a variety of orthopaedic and dental applications. Although both these materials are chemically very similar, *in vivo* results tend to differ. A significant reduction in the rate of resorption is frequently reported due to the hydrolysis of brushite to octacalcium phosphate (OCP) (Fig: 19.1), which is a precursor for apatite formation and then ultimately to HA. Conversely it has been noted that monetite does not re-precipitate into HA *in vivo*, and studies have demonstrated its good osteoconductive and osteoinductive properties. The conversion of brushite to HA after implantation limits resorption and subsequently affects the replacement of graft material with new bone.

Table: 19.6. List of existing calcium phosphate compounds.

COMPOUND NAME	CHEMICAL FORMULA	SYMBOL	CA/P IONIC RATIO	MINERAL
Monocalcium phosphate monohydrate	$Ca(H_2PO_4)_2.H_2O$	MCPM	0.5	-
Monocalcium phosphate anhydrous	$Ca(H_2PO_4)_2$	MCPA	0.5	-
Dicalcium phosphate dihydrate	$CaHPO_4.2H_2O$	DCPD	1.0	Brushite
Dicalcium phosphate anhydrous	$CaHPO_4$	DCPA	1.0	Monetite
Octacalcium phosphate	$Ca_8(HPO_4)_2(PO_4)_4.5H_2O$	OCP	1.33	-
α-Tricalcium phosphate	$\alpha\text{-}Ca_3(PO_4)_2$	α-TCP	1.5	-
β-Tricalcium phosphate	$\beta\text{-}Ca_3(PO_4)_2$	B-TCP	1.5	-
Amorphous calcium phosphate	$Ca_xH_y(PO_4)_z.nH_2O$, n =3-4.5;15-20% H_2O	ACP	1.2 2.2	-
Precipitated hydroxyapatite	$Ca_{8-x}(HPO_4)_x(PO_4)_{6-x}(OH)_{2-x}$	PHA	1.33-1.67	-
Calcium-deficient hydroxyapatite	$Ca_{10-x}(HPO_4)_x(PO_4)_{6-x}(OH)_{2-x}$ [f] $(0<x<1)$	CDHA	1.5-1.67	-
Hydroxyapatite	$Ca_{10}(PO_4)_6(OH)_2$	HA	1.67	Hydroxyapatite
Oxyapatite	$Ca_{10}(PO_4)_6O$	OXA	1.67	-

Table: 19.5. Graft material bioactivity with bone.

TYPE	GRAFT	OSTEOGENESIS	OSTEOCONDUCTION	OSTEOINDUCTION
Bone tissue				
	Autograft	2	3	2
	Allograft	0	3	1
Biomaterials				
	Collagen	0	2	0
	DBM	0	1	2
Composites				
	β-TCP/BMA			
Composite	2	3	2	
	BMP/synthetic composite	N/A	N/A	3
Bioceramics				
	HA	0	1	0
	TCP	0	1	0
	Brushite	0	1	0
	Monetite	0	2	1

F. Hydroxyapatite

HA is the primary mineral component of bone. Synthetic HA have been marketed for use in variety of forms: porous non-resorbable, solid non-resorbable, and resorbable (non-ceramic, porous). Processing of the basic calcium phosphate parent mixture to form HA dictates which of the mentioned forms would ultimately exist. The resorbability of HA is dependent upon the temperature at which it is processed. When prepared at higher temperatures, the HA produced is dense, non-resorbable and has a larger crystal size. The dense HA grafts are osteoconductive, osteophillic and act primarily as inert biocompatible fillers. It has been shown that HA when used in conjugation with flap debridement results in greater defect fill in comparison to flap debridement alone in active treatment of intrabony periodontal defects. However, histological evaluation shows that new attachment is not achieved by using HA graft materials.

A resorbable HA, which is particulate and porous, processed at low temperatures is also available for clinical use. This type of HA is a non-sintered (not ceramic) precipitate with particles measuring 300 to 400 μm in size. It is believed that this non-sintered HA acts as a mineral reservoir inducing bone formation via osteoconductive mechanisms. This HA has slow resorption rate, yet it acts as a scaffold for bone replacement. Research has shown some indication towards the osteoinductive potential of porous HA.

In summary; there are three forms of HA, a dense particulate, non-resorbable form; a porous non-resorbable form derived from exoskeleton of coral (discussed in xenografts earlier); and a resorbable non-ceramic HA. HA is non-osteogenic, neither conclusively osteoinductive, but rather functions as an

CONCLUSION

Fresh autogenous cancellous bone, and to a lesser extent, cortical bone are gold standard graft materials, to which all other bone substitutes are compared with in terms of clinical performance. Periodontal bone defects are as diverse as the available treatment options. This creates a royal conundrum for the oral surgeon with respect to making the correct choice among the available graft materials. At times it is not one but a combination of graft materials that might be the correct choice. It would be sensible to assume that all grafts would not behave in the same manner and results would vary. This knowledge and its application in the treatment plan can make the difference between an acceptable and a near ideal clinical result.

Further advances in tissue engineering and gene therapy would ultimately allow us to construct new scaffolds (carrier constructs) which would enable us to obtain more predictable and clinically acceptable results. The newer constructs with time are expected to encompass additional families of growth factors, evolving biological scaffolds and incorporation of mesenchymal stem cells. The future is interesting and bears promise of rapid advancement in this fascinating field of research. It seems fitting to end this chapter with a quote which sums up entire efforts made up till now by modern science:

"This is not the end, this is not even the beginning of the end, but it is perhaps the end of the beginning" – Sir Winston Churchill

REFERENCES

1. Muschler GF, Negami S, Hyodo A, et al. Evaluation of collagen ceramic composite graft materials in a spinal fusion model. Clin Orthop 1996;328:250—60.
2. Lewandrowski K, Gresser JD, Wise DL, Trantolo DJ. Bioresorbable bone graft substitutes of different osteoconductivities: an istologic evaluation of osteointegration of poly (propylene glycol-co-fumaric acid) based cement implants in rats. Biomaterials 2000; 21(8):757—64.
3. Sauer HD, Schoettle H. The stability of osteosyntheses bridging defects. Arch Orthop Trauma Surg 1979;95:27—30.
4. Guyton AG, Hall JE. Textbook of medical physiology. Philadelphia: W.B. Saunders; 2000. p. 901–4.
5. Bowers GM, Chadroff B, Carnevale R, Mellonig J, Corio R, Emerson 7, Stevens M, Rosenherg E. Histologic evaluation of new attachment apparatus formation in humans. 111. J Periodontal 1989: 60: 683-693.
6. Dragoo MR, Sullivan HC. A clinical and histological evaluation of autogenous iliac bone grafts in humans. I. Wound healing 2 to 8 months. J Periodontol 1973: 44: 599-613.
7. Hiatt WH, Schallhorn RG. Intraoral transplants of cancellous bone and marrow in periodontal lesions. J Periodontol 1973: 44: 194-208.
8. Mellonig JT. Decalcified freeze-dried bone allograft as an implant material in human periodontal defects. Int J Periodontics Restorative Dent 1984: 4: 41-55.
9. Caton J, Nynian S, Zander H. Histometric evaluation of periodontal surgery. 11. Connective tissue attachment levels after four regenerative procedures. J Clin Periodontol 1980: 7: 224-231.
10. Dragoo MR, Sullivan HC. A clinical and histological evaluation of autogenous iliac bone grafts in humans. I. Wound healing 2 to 8 months. J Periodontol 1973: 44: 599-613.

Fluorapatite	$Ca_{10}(PO_4)_6F_2$	FA	1.67	-
Tetracalcium phosphate	$Ca_2(PO_4)_2O$	TTCP	2.0	Hilgenstockite

Brushite cements can be utilized as precursors to monetite. If provided with appropriate conditions DCP can react to form monetite. This can occur when the cements are set in water-deficient environments, at a very low pH, or in the presence of metallic ions that disrupt brushite crystals leading to monetite formation. Thermal hydrolysis of the set brushite cement can also lead to the conversion of brushite into monetite. Brushite crystals when heated above 60 °C have a tendency to degrade into monetite. If moisture is sufficiently maintained during the heating process then bulk shrinkage is prevented and the contraction that has been shown to be related with dry heating is replaced by an increase in the internal pore size. Both HA and DCPD demonstrate increased solubility at lower pH levels and a greater degree of local dissolution of the cement graft may take place. The increased resorption monetite cements (Fig: 19.2) compared to HA grafts is advantageous and attempts have been made to prevent brushite hydrolysis to HA.

H. Calcium Sulphate

Calcium sulphate, also known commonly as plaster of Paris, has been used for more than hundred years. The key features of this alloplastic material are: excellent biocompatibility, unique ability to stimulate osteogenesis, and rapid resorption rate. It has also been used as a binding and stabilizing agent in orthopaedic applications. Calcium sulphate has an osteoconductive matrix, which allows new blood vessels in-growing into the cement and also fibrous and osseous ingrowth, provided the material is in close proximity to viable periosteum or endosteum. After the graft has been placed, it resorbs over a period of 7 days through passive dissolution. It has also been reported that the calcium sulphate resorption is associated with new cancellous bone formation. In dentistry the clinical use of calcium sulfate remains rare in surgical periodontics, with its use mainly limited to prosthodontics in laboratory based procedures.

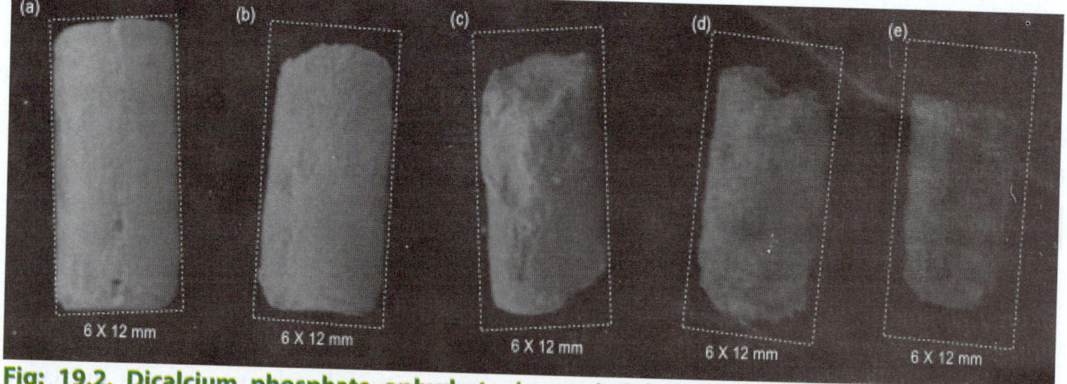

Fig: 19.2. Dicalcium phosphate anhydrate (monetite) bone graft cylinders at (a) before implantation, (b) 2 weeks in vivo, (c) 4 weeks in vivo, (d) 6 weeks in vivo, and (e) 8 weeks in vivo.

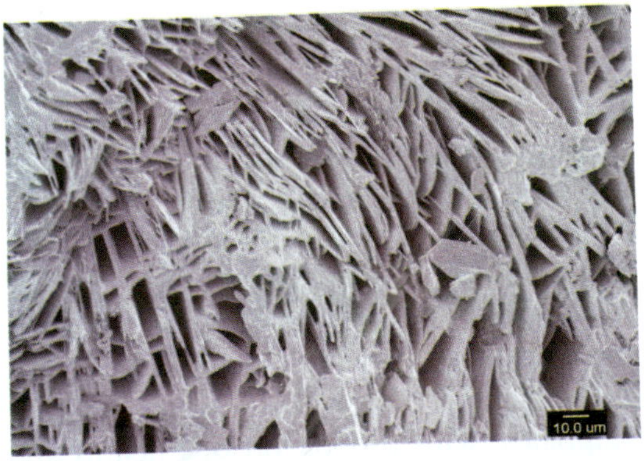

C

D

E

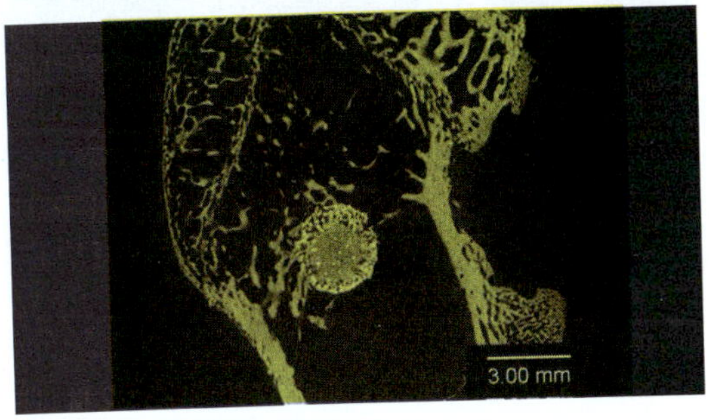

F

Fig: 19.1. Scanning electron microscope micrographs of (a) β-tricalcium phosphate granules, 50x magnification, (b) Hydroxyapatite, 5k X magnification, (c) Octacalcium phosphate, 5k X magnification, (d) Dicalcium phosphate dihydrate crystals, 5k X magnification, (e) Dicalcium phosphate anhydrous crystals, 5k X magnification; and micro-computed tomographic cross-sectional image of (f) Dicalcium phosphate anhydrous graft in cancellous bone (rabbit femural condyle).

E. Tricalcium phosphate (TCP)

TCP is a porous form of calcium phosphate. TCP has two crystallographic forms, β-tricalcium phosphate (β-TCP) and α-tricalcium phosphate (α-TCP). The most common type is β-TCP and it is used as filler that is partially resorbable and allows bone formation and replacement (Fig: 19.1). Over the years TCP has gained clinical acceptance as a bone filler material, however, results are not always predictable. When a direct comparison is made, the allogenic grafts appear to outperform TCP in terms of resorption and bone formation (Table: 19.5). There is evidence that TCP granules undergo fibrous tissue encapsulation and do not stimulate bone growth adequately. However there has been some evidence demonstrating bone deposition with TCP.

The currently available and commonly used bioactive glasses in dentistry include: PerioGlas® (Block Drug Co., Jersey City, NJ) and Biogran™ (Orthovita, Malvern, PA). It is thought that the more uniform particle size (less variability in size range) of Biogran™ would have a clinical advantage over the wider particle size range that is observed for PerioGlas®. Biogran™ has a narrower particle size range of 300 to 355 μm which has been reported to be advantages for promoting osteogenesis. Whereas, PerioGlas® has particle size ranging from 90 to 710 μm, facilitating handling and packing into osseous defects. A study has demonstrated that Biogran™ can be used successfully in the treatment of oral osseous defects. Also available are Unigraft (Unicare biomedical Inc, Laguna Hills, CA, USA) having a particle size of 200 to 320 μm and PerioGlas Plus (NovaBone products LLC) having a particle size of 90 to 700 μm (similar to PerioGlas®. Biogran™).

C. Glass ionomers

"Glass ionomer cements" were first used in dentistry as calcium/aluminium/fluorosilicate glass powder mixed with poly-carboxylic acid to produce a cement paste which hardens in approximately 5 minutes after which it is rendered water insoluble. Bone replacement grafts based on glass ionomer cements are porous, which leads to bone ingrowth via their osteoconductive nature. After 24h of setting glass ionomers have a compressive strength and modulus of elasticity (stiffness) that is comparable with cortical bone. Glass ionomers have been considered as a replacement for poly-methylmethacrylate based bone fillers which have an exothermic setting reaction (polymerization). A possible advantage of using glass ionomers could be their fluoride release mechanism which may be adapted for controlled drug delivery (e.g., antibiotics) in the local periodontal defect environment. A major disadvantage is the lack of resorbability, limiting the clinical use as a scaffold for bone regeneration application.

D. Ceramics

Ceramics or bioceramics (owing to their biological use) are alloplastic materials comprising mainly of calcium phosphate or sulphates, with proportion of calcium and phosphate similar to bone. The two most commonly used alloplastic (bioceramic) graft materials have been tricalcium phosphate and HA. Dicalcium phosphate dihydrate (DCPD or brushite) and dicalcium phosphate anhydrate (DCPA or monetite) are other calcium phosphates that have evoked interest from various researchers for bone augmentation and regeneration applications (Fig: 19.1).

A

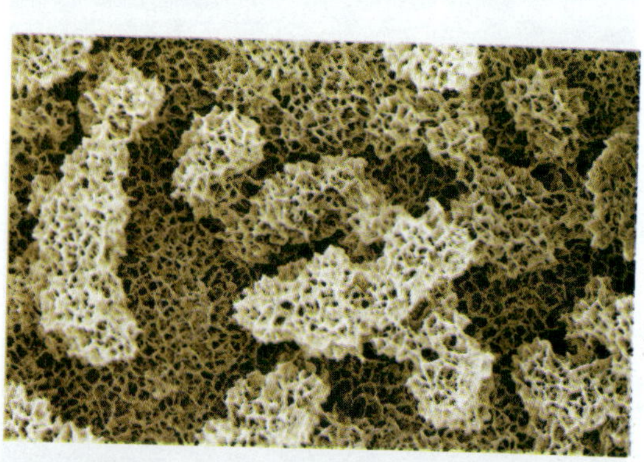

B

11. Nabers CL, Reed OM, Hamner JE. Gross and histologic evaluation of an autogenous bone graft 57 months postoperatively. J Periodontol 1972: 43: 702-704.

12. Bowers GM, Schallhorn RG, Mellonig JT. Histologic evaluation of new attachment in human intrabony defects. A literature review. J Periodontal 1982: *53:* 509-514.

13. Schallhorn RG, Hiatt WH, Boyce W. Iliac transplants in periodontal therapy. J Periodontol 1970: 41: 566-580.

14. Urist MR. Fundamental and clinical bone physiology. Philadelphia, PA: J.B. Lippincott Co., 1980: 348-353.

15. Urist MR, DeLange RJ, Finerman GAM. Bone cell differentiation and growth factors. Science 1983: 220: 680-686.

16. Tamimi F, Torres J, Kathan C, Baca R, Clemente C, Blanco L, et al. Bone regeneration in rabbit calvaria with novel monetite granules. Journal of Biomedical Materials Research Part A 2008;87A:980-5.

17. Tamimi F, Torres J, Bassett D, Barralet J, Cabarcos EL. Resorption of monetite granules in alveolar bone defects in human patients. Biomaterials 2010;31:2762-9.

18. Tamimi F, Torres J, Gbureck U, Lopez-Cabarcos E, Bassett DC, Alkhraisat MH, et al. Craniofacial vertical bone augmentation: A comparison between 3D printed monolithic monetite blocks and autologous onlay grafts in the rabbit. Biomaterials 2009;30:6318-26.

19. Tamimi F, Torres J, Lopez-Cabarcos E, Bassett DC, Habibovic P, Luceron E, et al. Minimally invasive maxillofacial vertical bone augmentation using brushite based cements. Biomaterials 2009;30:208-16.

20. Tamimi F, Nihouannen DL, Eimar H, Sheikh Z, Komarova S, Barralet J. The effect of autoclaving on the physical and biological properties of dicalcium phosphate dihydrate bioceramics: Brushite vs. monetite. Acta Biomaterialia 2012;8:3161-9.

21. Cypher TJ, Grossman JP. Biological principles of bone graft healing. J Foot Ankle Surg 1996;35:413—7.

22. Arrington ED, Smith WJ, Chambers HG, et al. Complications of iliac crest bone graft harvesting. Clin Orthop 1996;329:300—9.

23. Dodd CAF, Fergusson CM, Freedman L, et al. Allograft versus autograft bone in scoliosis surgery. J Bone Joint Surg Br 1988;70:431—4.

24. Summers BN, Eisenstein SM. Donor site pain from the ilium: a complication of lumbar spine fusion. J Bone Joint Surg Br 1989;71-B:677—80.

25. Younger EM, Chapman MW. Morbidity at bone graft donor sites. J Orthop Trauma 1989;3:192—5.

26. Sandhu HS, Grewal HS, Parvataneni H. Bone grafting for spinal fusion. Orthop Clin North Am 1999;30:685—98.

27. Wilk RM. Bony reconstruction of the jaws. In: Miloro M, editor. Peterson's principles of oral and maxillofacial surgery. (2nd edition). Hamilton (London): B C Decker; 2004. p. 785–7.

28. Heslop BK, Zeiss IM, Nisbet NW. Studies on transference of bone: a comparison of autologous and homologous transplants with reference to osteocyte survival osteogenesis and host reaction. Br J Exp Pathol 1960;41:269–72.

29. Enneking WF, Burcharot H, Puhl JJ, et al. Physical and biological aspects of

repair in dog cortical-bone transplants. J Bone Joint Surg 1975;57:237–52.

30. Oxlund H, Anderson NB, Ortoft G, et al. Growth hormone and mild exercise in combination markedly enhances cortical bone formation and strength in old rats. Endocrinology 1998;139(4):1899–904.

31. Duncan RL, Turner CH. Mechanotransduction and the functional of bone to mechanical strain. Calcif Tissue Int 1995;57(5):344–58.

32. Wilk RM. Bony reconstruction of the jaws. In: Miloro M, editor. Peterson's principles of oral and maxillofacial surgery. (2nd edition). Hamilton (London): B C Decker; 2004. p. 785–7.

33. Hiatt WH, Schallhorn RG, Aaronian AJ. The induction of new bone and cementum formation. IV. Microscopic examination of the periodontium following human bone and marrow allograft, autograft and nongraft periodontal regenerative procedures. J Periodontol 1978;49:495.

34. Ross SE, Cohen DW. The fate of a free osseous tissue autograft. A clinical and histologic case report. Periodontics 1968;6:145.

35. Sottosanti JS, Buerly JA, The storage of marrow and its relation to periodontal grafting procedures. J Periodontol1975: 46: 162-170.

36. Cushing M. Autogenous red marrow grafts: potential for induction of osteogenesis. J Periodontol 1969: 40: 492-497.

37. Hiatt WH, Schallhorn RG, Aaronian AJ. The induction of new bone and cementum formation. Microscopic examination of the periodontium following human allograft, autograft, and non-graft periodontal regenerative procedures. J Periodontol 1978: 49: 495-512.

38. Froum SJ, Ortiz M, Wilkin RT. Osseous autografts. 111. Comparison of osseous coagulum-bone blend implants with open curettage. J Periodontol 1983: 54: 325-328.

39. Garrett S, Bogle G. Periodontal regeneration with bone grafts. Curr Opin Periodontol 1994: 168-177.

40. Sanders JJ, Sepe W, Bowers GM, Lawrence JJ. Clinical evaluation of freeze-dried bone allografts in periodontal osseous defects. 111. Composite freeze-dried bone allografts with and without autogenous bone grafts. J Periodontol 1983: 54: 1-7.

41. Boyce T, Edwards J, Scarborough N. Allograft bone: the influence of processing on safety and performance. Orthop Clin North Am 1999;30(4):571–81.

42. CDC First Document, Center for Disease Control. Septic arthritis following anterior cruciateligament reconstruction using tendon allografts, Florida and Louisiana 2000. Morb Mortal Wkly Rep 2001;50(48):1081–3.

43. CDCSecond Document, Center for Disease Control. Update: allograft associated bacterial infections: United States, 2002. Morb Mortal Wkly Rep 2002;51(10):207–10.

44. Tomford WW. Transmission of disease through transplantation of musculoskeletal allografts. J Bone Joint Surg Am 1995;77–A(11):1742j–54j.

45. Bolander ME, Balian G. The use of demineralized bone matrix in the repair of segmental defects: augmentation with extracted matrix proteins and a comparison with autologous grafts. J Bone Joint Surg 1986;68–A:1264–74.

46. Oxlund H, Anderson NB, Ortoft G, et al. Growth hormone and mild exercise in combination markedly enhances cortical bone formation and strength in old rats. Endocrinology 1998;139(4):1899–904.
47. Friedlander G, Strong D, Sell K. Studies on the antigenicity of bone. Freeze-dried and deep frozen bone allografts in rabbits. J Bone Joint Surg 1976: 58A 854.
48. Mellonig JT. Freeze-dried bone allografts in periodontal reconstructive surgery. Dent Clin N Am 1991: 35: 505-520.
49. Quattlebaum J, Mellonig J, Hansel N. Antigenicity of freeze-dried cortical bone allograft in human periodontal osseous defects. J Periodontol 1988: 59: 394-397.
50. Friedlander GE, Strong DM, Sell Kw. Studies on the antigenicity of bone. 11. Donor-specific anti-HLA antibodies in human recipients of freeze-dried allografts. J Bone Joint Surg 1984: 66A 107-111.
51. Turner D, Mellonig JT. Antigenicity of freeze-dried bone allograft in periodontal asseaus defects. J Periodont Res 1981: 16: 89-99.
52. Goldberg VM, Stevenson S. Natural history of autografts and allografts. Clin Orthop 1987: 225: 7-16.
53. American Academy of Periodontology. Tissue banking and periodontal hone allografts. Chicago, IL: *AAE:* 1994.
54. Mellonig JT, Bowers GM, Levy RA, Branham G. Histologic evaluation of autograft-allograft composites. J Dent Res 1982: 61 (spec issue A): 1442.
55. Russel JL. Allografts and osteoinductivity. Presented at the European Federation of National Associations of Orthopaedics and Traumatology, Technical Symposium on "Demineralized Bone Allografts and Osteoinduction". Rhodes, June 4, 2001.
56. Bolander ME, Balian G. The use of demineralized bone matrix in the repair of segmental defects: augmentation with extracted matrix proteins and a comparison with autologous grafts. J Bone Joint Surg 1986;68–A:1264–74.
57. Hopp SG, Dahners LE, Gilbert JA. A study of mechanical strength of long bone defects treated with various bone autograft substitutes: an experimental investigation in the rabbit. J Orthop Res 1989;7(4):578–84.
58. Urist MR,Chang JJ, Leitze A, et al. Preparation and bioassay of bone morphogenic protein and polypetides fragments. Methods Enzymol 1987;146:294–312.
59. Urist MR, Strates B. Bone morphogenetic protein. J Dent Res 1971: 50: 1392-1406.
60. Mellonig J, Bowers G, Baily R. Comparison of bone graft materials. I. New bone formation with autografts and allografts determined by strontium 85. J Periodontol 1981:52:291-296.
61. Mellonig J, Bowers G, Baily R. Comparison of bone graft materials. 11. New bone formation with autografts and allografts: A histological evaluation. J Periodontol 1981: 52: 297-302.
62. Mellonig JT, Bowers GM, Levy RA, Branham G. Histologic evaluation of autograft-allograft composites. J Dent Res 1982: (spec issue A): 1442.
63. Dodson S, Bernard G, Kenney B, Carranza F. *In vitro* comparison of aged

and young osteogenic and hemopoietic bone marrow stem cells and their derivative colonies. J Periodontol 1996: 67: 184-196.

64. Jergesen H, Chua 1, Kao R, Kaban L. Age effects on bone induction by demineralized bone powder. Clin Orthop 1991: 268: 253-259.

65. Syftestad G, Urist M. Bone aging. Clin Orthop 1982: 162: 288-297.

66. Scarano A, Degidi M, Iezzi G, et al. Maxillary sinus augmentation with different biomaterials: a comparative histologic and histomorphometric study in man. Implant Dent 2006;15(2):197–207.

67. Jarcho M. Calcium phosphate ceramics as hard tissue prosthetics. Clin Orthop 1981: 157: 259-279.

68. Melcher AH. The use of heterogeneous anorganic bone as an implant material in oral procedures. Oral Surg Oral Med Oral Pathol Oral Radio1 Endod 1962: 15: 996-1000.

69. Emmings FG. Chemically modified osseous material for the restoration of bone defects. J Periodontol 1974: 45: 385-390.

70. Wenz B, Oesch B, Horst M. Analysis of the risk of transmitting bovine spongiform encephalopathy through bone grafts derived from bovine bone. Biomaterials 2001;22(12):1599–606.

71. Sogal A, Tofe AJ. Risk assessment of bovine spongiform encephalopathy transmission through bone graft material derived from bovine bone used for dental applications. J Periodontol 1999;70(9):1053–63.

72. Boyne PJ. Comparison of porous and non-porous hydroxyapatite and anorganic xenografts in the restoration of alveolar ridges. Special technical publication 953. Washington, DC: American Society for Testing and Materials, 1988.

73. Guillemin G, Patat JL, Fournie J, Chetail M. The use of coral as a bone graft substitute. J Biomed Mater Res 1987: 21: 557-567.

74. Yukna RA. Clinical evaluation of coralline calcium carbonate as a bone replacement graft material in human periodontal osseaus defects. J Periodontal 1994: 65: 177-185.

75. Guillemin G, Patat JL, Fournie J, Chetail M. The use of coral as a bone graft substitute. J Biomed Mater Res 1987: 21: 557-567.

76. Piatteli A, Podda G, Scorano A. Clinical and histological results in alveolar ridge enlargement using coralline calcium carbonate. Biomaterials 1997: 18: 623-627

77. Mora E Ouhayoun J. Clinical evaluation of natural coral and porous hydroxyapatite implants in periodontal bone lesions: results of a 1 year follow-up. J Clin Periodontol1995: 22: 877-884.

78. Kim C-K, Choi E-J, Cho K-S, Chai JK, Wikesjo UME. Periodontal repair in intrabony defects treated with a calcium carbonate implant and guided tissue regeneration. J Periodontol 1996: 67: 1301-1306.

79. Gao T-J, Tuominen TK, Lindholm TS, Kommanen B, Lindholm TC. Morphological and biomechanical difference in healing in segmental tibia1 defects implanted with Biocorale or tricalcium phosphate cylinders. Biomaterials 1997: 18: 219-223.

80. WongRWK, Rabie ABM. Effect of gusuibu graft on bone formation. J Oral Maxillofac Surg 2006;64: 770–7.

81. Cho BC, Chung HY, Lee DG, et al. The effect of chitosan bead encapsulating calcium sulfate as an injectable bone substitute on consolidation in the mandibular distraction osteogenesis of a dog model. J Oral Maxillofac Surg 2005;63:1753–64.
82. Ewers R. Maxilla sinus grafting with marine algae derived bone forming material: a clinical report of long-term results. J Oral Maxillofac Surg 2005;63: 1712–23.
83. Sokolsky-Papkov M, Agashi K, Olaye A, et al. Polymer carriers for drug delivery in tissue engineering. Adv Drug Deliv Rev 2007;59:187.
84. Yukna RA. Clinical evaluation of HTR polymer bone replacement grafts in human mandibular class I1 molar furcations. J Periodontal 1994: 65: 342-349.
85. Yukna RA. HTR polymer grafts in human periodontal osseous defects. I. 6 month clinical results. J Periodontal 1990: 61: 633-642.
86. Stahl *SS*, Froum SJ, Tarnow D. Human clinical and histologic responses to the placement of HTR polymer particles in 11 intrabony lesions. J Periodontal 1990: 61: 269-274.
87. Yukna RA, Greer Jr. RO. Human gingival tissue response to HTR polymer. J Biomed Mater Res 1992: 26: 517-527.
88. Froum SJ. Human histologic evaluation of HTR polymer and freeze-dried bone allograft. A case report. J Clin Periodontol 1996: 23: 615-620.
89. Murray VK. Clinical applications of HTR polymer in periodontal surgery. Compendium Contin Educ Dent 1988: 9(SUppl 10): 5342-5347.
90. Buck B, Malinin T, Brown M. Bone transplantation and human immunodeficiency virus: an estimate of risk for acquired immunodeficiency syndrome (AIDS). Clin Orthop 1989: 240: 129.
91. Murphy KG, Gunsolley JC. Guided tissue regeneration for the treatment of periodontal intrabony and furcation defects. A systematic review. Ann Periodontol 2003;8:266.
92. Hench LL, Wilson J. Surface active biomaterials. Science 1984;226:630–6.
93. El-Ghannam A, Ducheyne D, Shapiro IM. Formation of surface reaction products on bioactive glass and their effects on the expression of the osteoblastic phenotype and the deposition of mineralized extracellular matrix. Biomaterials 1997: 18: 295-303.
94. Kenney EB, Lekovic V, SaFerreira JC, Han T, Dimitrijevic B, Carranza FA. Bone formation within porous hydroxylapatite implants in human periodontal defects. J Periodontol 1986: 57: 76-83.
95. Kim C-K, Choi E-J, Cho K-S, Chai JK, Wikesjo UME. Periodontal repair in intrabony defects treated with a calcium carbonate implant and guided tissue regeneration. J Periodontol 1996: 67: 1301-1306.
96. Hench LL, Wilson J. Bioactive glasses and glass ceramics: a 25 year retrospective. Ceramic Trans 1995: 48: 11-21.
97. Schepers E, DeClercq M, Ducheyne D, Kempeneers R. Bioactive glass particles material as filler for bone lesions. J Oral Rehabil 1991: 18: 439-452.
98. Schepers E, Ducheyne P, Barbier L, Schepers S. Bioactive glass particles of narrow size range: a new material for the repair of bone defects. Implant Dent 1993: *2:* 151-156.

99. Jonck LM, Grobbelaar CJ. The biological compatibility of glass ionomer cement in joint replacement. Clin Mater 1989;4:85–107.

100. Denissen H, Van Beek E, Martinetti R, Klein C, van der Zee E, Ravagioli A. Net-shaped hydroxyapatite implants for release of agents modulating periodontal-like tissues. J Periodont Res 1997: 32: 40-46.

101. Shetty V, Han TJ. Alloplastic materials in reconstructive periodontal surgery. Dent Clin North Am 1991: 35: 521-530.

102. Hashimoto-Uoshima M, Ishikawa I, Kinoshita A, Weng HT, Odo S. Clinical and histologic observation of replacement of biphasic calcium phosphate by bone tissue in monkeys. Int J Periodontics Restorative Dent 1995: 15: 204-2 13.

103. Strub JR, Gaberthuel TW, Firestone AR. Comparison of tricalcium phosphate and frozen allogenic bone implants in man. J Periodontal 1979: 50: 624-628.

104. Baldock W, Hutchens LH, McFall WT, Simpson DM. An evaluation of tricalcium phosphate implants in human periodontal osseous defects of two patients. J Periodontol.

105. Amler MH. Osteogenic potential of nonvital tissues and synthetic implant materials. J Periodontol 1987: 58: 758-761.

106. Klein CP, Driessen AA, de Groot, van der Lubbe HB. Biodegradation behavior of various calcium phosphate materials in bone tissue. J Biomed Mater Res 1983: 17: 769-784.

107. Meffert RM, Thomas JR, Hamilton KM, Brownstein CN. Hydroxylapatite as an alloplastic graft in the treatment of human periodontal osseous defects. J Periodontol 1985: 56: 63-73.

108. Rabalais ML, Yukna RA, Mayer ET. Evaluation of Durapatite ceramic as an alloplastic implant in periodontal osseous defects. I. Initial six month results. J Periodontol 1981: 52: 680-689.

109. Froum SJ, Kushner L, Scopp W, Stahl SS. Human clinical and histologic responses to Durapatite implants in intraosseous lesions. Case reports. J Periodontol 1982: 53: 719-725.

110. Wagner JR. A clinical and histological case study using resorbable hydroxylapatite for the repair of asseaus defects prior to endosseous implant surgery. J Oral Implantol 1989: 15: 186-192.

111. Ricci JL, Blumenthal NC, Spivak JM. Evaluation of a low temperature calcium phosphate particulate implant material: physical-chemical properties and *in vivo* bone response. J Oral Maxillofac Surg 1992: *50:* 969-978.

112. Yamasaki H. Hetertopic bone formation around porous hydroxyapatite ceramic in the subcutis of dogs. Jpn J Oral Biol 1990: 32: 190-192.

113. Heughebaert M, LeGeros R, Gineste M, Guillhem A, Bone1 G. Physiochemical characterization of deposits associated with HA ceramics implanted in non-osseous sites. J Biomed Mater Res 1988: 22(suppl) 257-268.

114. Penel G, Leroy N, Van Landuyt P, Flautre B, Hardouin P, Lemaitre J, et al. Raman microspectrometry studies of brushite cement: In vivo evolution in a sheep model. Bone 1999;25:81S-4S.

115. Constantz BR, Barr BM, Ison IC, Fulmer MT, Baker J, McKinney LA, et al. Histological, chemical, and crystallographic analysis of four calcium phosphate cements in different rabbit

osseous sites. Journal of Biomedical Materials Research 1998;43:451-61.

116. Tamimi F, Sheikh Z, Barralet J. Dicalcium phosphate cements: Brushite and monetite. Acta Biomaterialia 2012;8:474-87.

117. Bohner M, Gbureck U. Thermal reactions of brushite cements. Journal of Biomedical Materials Research Part B-Applied Biomaterials 2008;84B:375-85.

118. Aberg J, Brisby H, Henriksson HB, Lindahl A, Thomsen P, Engqvist H. Premixed Acidic Calcium Phosphate Cement: Characterization of Strength and Microstructure. Journal of Biomedical Materials Research Part B-Applied Biomaterials 2010;93B:436-41.

119. Tamimi F, Torres J, Kathan C, Baca R, Clemente C, Blanco L, et al. Bone regeneration in rabbit calvaria with novel monetite granules. Journal of Biomedical Materials Research Part A 2008;87A:980-5.

120. Kosar-Grašić B, Purgarić B, Füredi-Milhofer H. Precipitation of calcium phosphates from electrolyte solutions—VI the precipitation diagram of calcium hydrogen phosphate. Journal of Inorganic and Nuclear Chemistry 1978;40:1877-80.

121. Martin RI, Brown PW. Phase Equilibria Among Acid Calcium Phosphates. Journal of the American Ceramic Society 1997;80:1263-6.

122. Bohner M, Merkle HP, Lemai, tre J. In vitro aging of a calcium phosphate cement. Journal of Materials Science: Materials in Medicine 2000;11:155-62.

123. Alshaaer M, Cuypers H, Rahier H, Wastiels J. Production of monetite-based Inorganic Phosphate Cement (M-IPC) using hydrothermal post curing (HTPC). Cement and Concrete Research 2011;41:30-7.

124. Brown PW, Chow LC. A calcium phosphate water setting cement. Biomaterials 1989;10:475-80.

125. Bohner M, Matter S. Brushite hydraulic cement stabilized with a magnesium salt. US patent 2004.

126. McKee JC, Bailey BJ. Calcium sulphate as a mandibular implant. Otolaryngol Head Neck Surg 1984;92: 277–86.

127. Snyders RV, Eppley BL, Krukowsky M. Enhancement of repair in experimental calvarial bone defects using calcium sulphate and dextran beads. J Oral Maxillofac Surg 1993;51:517–24.

128. Bell WH. Resorption rates of bone and bone substitutes. Oral Surgery 1964;17:650–7.

129. Beeson WH. Plaster of paris as an alloplastic implant in the frontal sinus. Arch Otolaryngol 1981; 107:664–9.

Chapter 20

INTRODUCTION TO PARTIAL DENTURE

Dr. Shujah A Khan

PROSTHODONTICS

Prosthodontics is the dental speciality pertaining to the diagnosis, treatment planning, rehabilitation and maintenance of the oral function, comfort, appearance and health of patients with clinical conditions associated with missing or deficient teeth and/or maxillofacial tissues using biocompatible substitutes.

PROSTHESIS

An artificial replacement of an absent part of the human body.

REMOVABLE PROSTHODONTICS

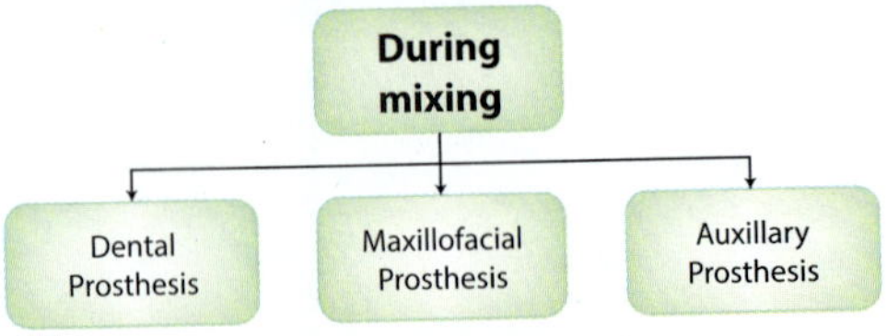

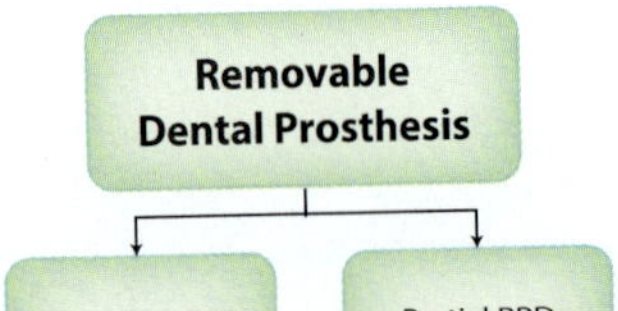

1. TREATMENT OBJECTIVES

a. Preserve remaining teeth.
b. Restore esthetics and phonetics.
c. Restore and/or improve mastication.
d. Restore health and quality of life.

2. INDICATIONS FOR RPDS

a. Lengthy edentulous span.
b. No posterior abutment for a fixed prosthesis.
c. Excessive alveolar bone loss.
d. Reduced periodontal support for a fixed prosthesis.
e. Cross-arch stabilization of teeth.
f. Need for immediate replacement of missing/extracted teeth.
g. Cost/patient desire.

3. ALTERNATIVE TO RPDS

a. Fixed partial denture.
b. Implant supported prosthesis.
c. Complete denture.
d. No treatment. (Shortened Dental Arch)

4. DEMERITS OF PARTIAL DENTURES

a. Stomatitis.

b. Poor access for oral hygiene.
c. Caries.
d. Periodontal and endodontic lesions.
e. Tooth mobility.
f. Poor speech and mastication.
g. Bone resorption.

COMMONLY USED TERMS

1. SADDLE

The part of a denture that rests on the oral mucosa and to which the teeth are attached.

2. CONNECTOR

The portion of a removable dental prosthesis that unites its components.

3. SUPPORT

The resistance to displacement away from the basal tissue or underlying structures.

4. RETAINER

That component of a partial removable dental prosthesis used to retain and prevent dislodgment, consisting of a clasp assembly or precision attachment.

5. INDIRECT RETENTION

The effect achieved by one or more indirect retainers of a partial removable denture prosthesis that reduces the tendency for a denture base to move in an occlusal direction or rotate about the fulcrum line.

6. FULCRUM

A theoretical line passing through the point around which a lever functions and at right angles to its path of movement.

7. BRACING

The resistance to horizontal components of masticatory force.

8. GUIDE PLANES

Vertically parallel surfaces on abutment teeth or/and dental implant abutments oriented so as to contribute to the direction of the path of placement and removal of a removable dental prosthesis.

9. SURVEY LINE

A line produced on a cast by a surveyor marking the greatest prominence of contour in relation to the planned path of placement of a restoration.

10. STRESS BREAKER

A device or system that relieves specific dental structures of part or all of the occlusal forces and redirects those forces to other bearing structures or regions.

11. GUM STRIPPER

A tissue borne partial denture which can sink into the gums.

CLASSIFICATION OF PARTIALLY EDENTULOUS ARCHES

Most commonly accepted and used classification system is the *Kennedy's Classification* for partially edentulous arches.

KENNEDY'S CLASSIFICATION

Class I – bilateral edentulous area located to all posterior teeth

Class II – unilateral edentulous area located to all posterior teeth.

Class III – Bilateral edentulous area bounded by anterior and posterior natural teeth.

Class IV – A single but bilateral (crossing the midline) edentulous area located anterior to the remaining teeth.

- Edentulous areas other than those that determinethe basic classes were designated as modification spaces except for Class IV.

For example

CLASS II MODIFICATION 1.

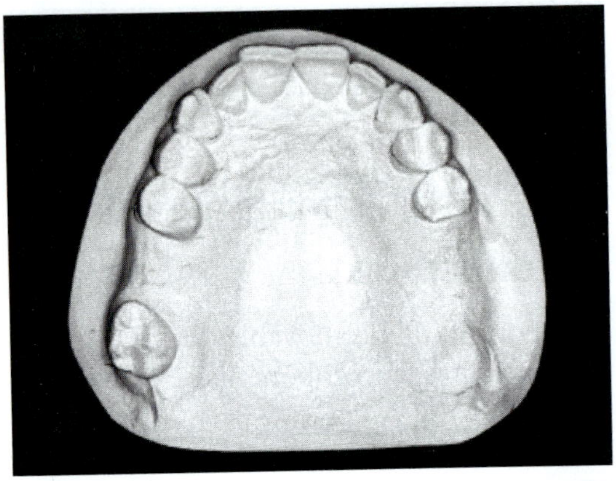

CLASS II MODIFICATION 2.

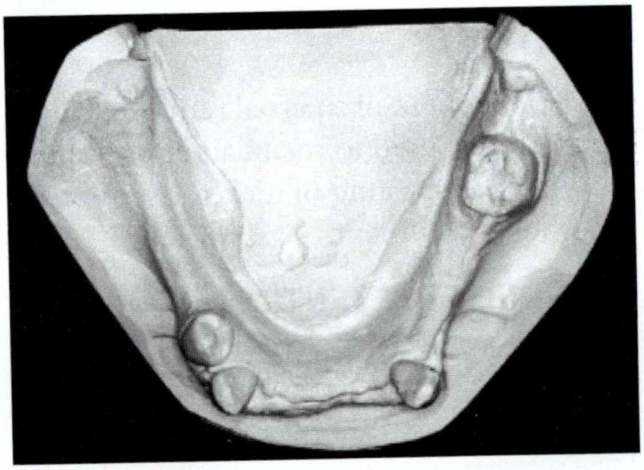

CLASS II MODIFICATION 3.

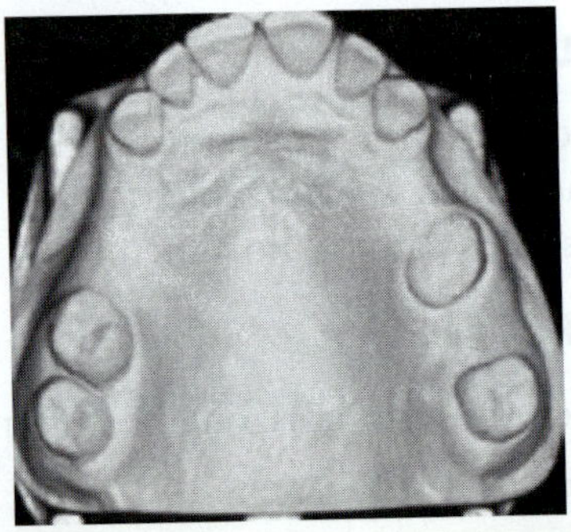

APPLEGATE – KENNEDY'S MODIFICATION SYSTEM

Applegate offers a system which is a modification of the Kennedy's system.

Rule 1: Classification should follow rather than precede extraction.

Rule 2: If the 3rd molar is missing and not to be replaced, it is not considered in the classification.

Rule 3: If the 3rd molar is present and to be used as an abutment, it is considered in the classification.

Rule 4: If the second molar is missing and not be replaced, it is not considered in the classification.

Rule 5: The most posterior edentulous area determines the classification.

Rule 6: Edentulous areas other than those determining classification are called modificationspaces.

Rule 7: The extent of the modification is not considered, only the number.

Rule 8: There is no modification space in Class IV.

CLASSIFICATION ACCORDING TO THE DENTURE TYPE

This classification is based on the type of support for dentures, also known as Support or Craddock classification.

1. TOOTH-BORNE.

All support for the partial denture comes from the teeth

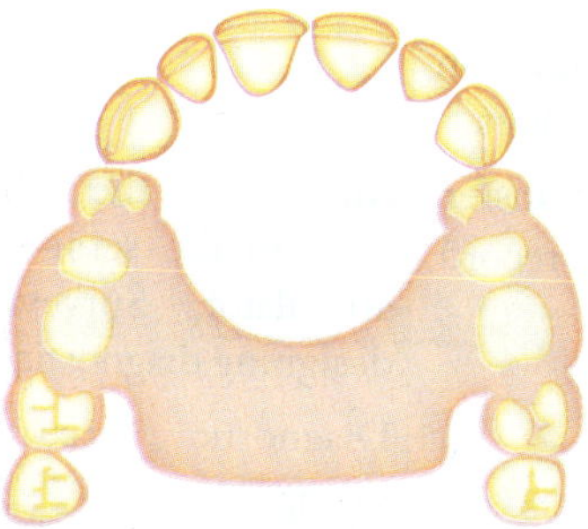

2. MUCOSA-BORNE.

The denture is entirely supported by the mucosa and underlying alveolar ridge

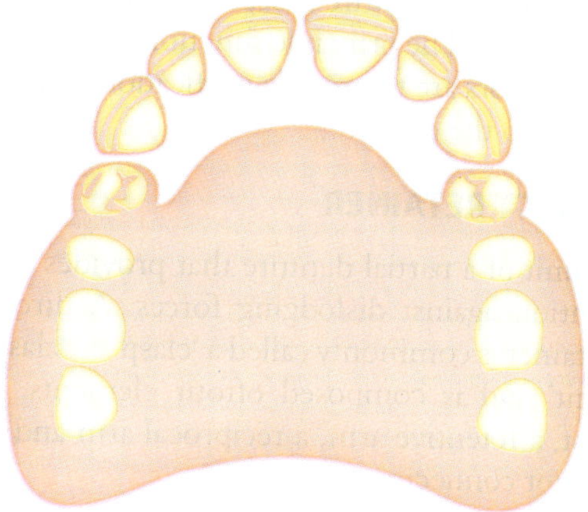

3. MUCOSA- AND TOOTH-BORNE.

Some parts of the denture are supported by teeth and some by the mucosa

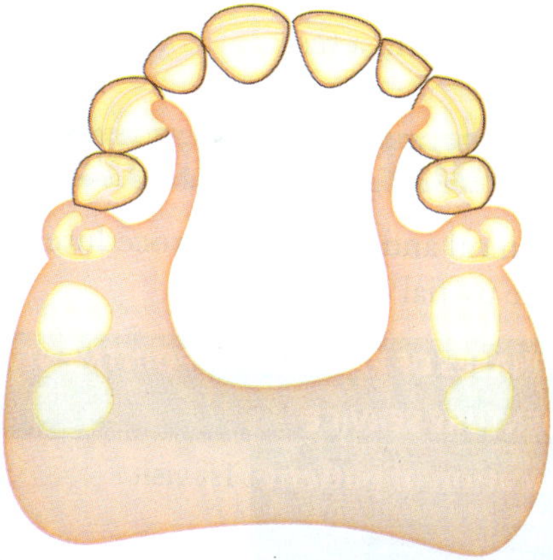

COMPONENTS OF PARTIAL DENTURES

MAJOR CONNECTOR

The unit of a removable partial denture that connects the parts of oneside of the dental arch to those of the other side. Its principal functions are to provide unification and rigidity to the denture.

MINOR CONNECTOR

A unit of a partial denture that connects other components (i.e. direct retainer, indirect retainer, denture base, etc.) to the major connector. The principle functions of minor connectors are to provide unification and rigidity to the denture.

DIRECT RETAINER

A unit of a partial denture that provides retention against dislodging forces. A direct retainer is commonly called a 'clasp' or 'clasp unit' and is composed offour elements, a rest, a retentive arm, a reciprocal arm and a minor connector.

INDIRECT RETAINER

A unit of a Class I or II partial denture that prevents or resists movement or rotation of the base(s) away from the residual ridge. The indirect retaineris usually composed of one component, a rest.

DENTURE BASE

The unit of a partial denture that covers the residual ridges and supports the denture teeth.

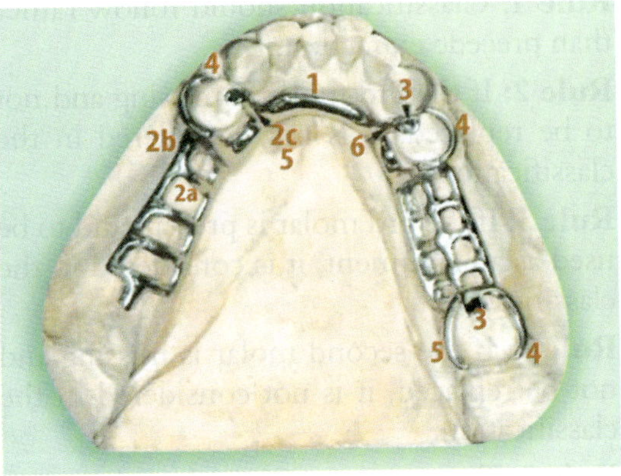

1. Major Connector
2. Minor Connector
3. Occlusal Rest
4. Direct Retainer
5. Reciprocal component of clasp
6. Indirect Retainer

STEPS OF FABRICATION OF REMOVABLE PARTIAL DENTURES

- Clinical and laboratory procedure to treat partially edentulous patients with the removable partial denture.

SIX PHASES OF PARTIAL DENTURE SERVICE	APPOINTMENT	CLINICAL PROCEDURE	LABORATORY PROCEDURE
Education of patient	1st visit	History taking, Extra- and Intra-oral examination, Radiographic examination, Preliminary impression with hydrocolloid, Consultation with other specialties.	Diagnostic cast fabrication with stone. Recording base if needed.
	2nd visit	Face-bow transfer, Centric relation record	Mounting the diagnostic casts to the semi-adjustable articulator, Surveying and designing diagnostic casts. Diagnostic wax-up and set-up.

Diagnosis, treatment planning, treatment sequencing, and mouth preparation	3rd visit	Diagnosis and Definitive Treatment Plan presented to the patients	Interim removable partial denture fabrication.
	4th visit	Preparation of mouth for removable partial denture(caries and plaque control, endodontic, periodontal, and oral surgery should be planned) Provisionalization	
	5th visit	Preparation of abutment teeth. Final impression for the metal framework.	Master cast fabrication Surveying and designing on the master cast. Block out and relief on the master cast. Duplicating the master cast to make the refractory (investment) cast. Preparing the refractory cast(Bees wax soaking). Waxing the partial denture framework. Spruing, investing, burnout, casting, and finishing of the partial denture framework.
Support for distal extension denture bases	6th visit	Try-in of the metal framework. Altered cast technique of impression making	Individual trays attached to the denture framework. Altered (corrected) master cast fabrication.
Establishment and verification of occlusal relations and teeth arrangements	7th visit	Maxillo-mandibular relationship. Selection of artificial teeth.	Mounting the casts and arranging the artificial (denture) teeth.
	8th visit	Try-in of partial denture.	Gingival festooning, investing the partial denture, Processing the denture. Laboratory remounting for selective grinding, Polishing the denture.

Initial placement procedures	9th visit	Initial placement, adjustment, and instructions to the patient.	
Periodic recall	10th visit	Recare and maintenance.	Relining and rebasing the removable partial denture if needed.

REFERENCES

1. Alan B.Carr & David T.brown (2010), *McCracken's Removable Partial Prosthodontics, 12th Edition,* Mosby.
2. Robert W. Loney (2008), *Removable Partial Denture Manual,* Dalhousie University.
3. David A. Mitchell & Laura Mitchell(2005), *Oxford Handbook of Clinical Dentistry,* (4th ed).
4. Irfan Ahmed (2012), *Prosthodontics at a Glance,* Wiley-Blackwell.
5. (2011), *Glossary of Prosthodontic Terms,* The Journal of Prosthetic Dentistry,Vol 94.

COMMON LAW AND COLONISED PEOPLES

Common Law and Colonised Peoples

Studies in Trinidad and Western Australia

JEANNINE M. PURDY

Routledge
Taylor & Francis Group
LONDON AND NEW YORK

First published 1997 by Dartmouth and Ashgate Publishing

Reissued 2018 by Routledge
2 Park Square, Milton Park, Abingdon, Oxon OX14 4RN
711 Third Avenue, New York, NY 10017, USA

Routledge is an imprint of the Taylor & Francis Group, an informa business

A Library of Congress record exists under LC control number: 96041978

ISBN 13: 978-1-138-61233-4 (hbk)
ISBN 13: 978-0-429-46347-1 (ebk)

Contents

PART III: LAW, VIOLENCE AND ECONOMICS

CONCLUSION

APPENDICES

List of Diagrams

List of Tables

Preface

Yeah, so I'm called a bastard
an animal, a trouble maker;
whilst my accusers watch my brothers
smashed,
thrown into dog-boxes drunk, crying for the
dreamtime.
My memory is still wet with my mother's tears,
flowing by, my father's grave.
Just another black family
alone and lost in the race for a dime.

As early as I remember,
I was made aware of the differences,
and slowly my pains educated me:
either fight or lose.
"One sided", I hear you say.
Then come erase the scars from my brain,
and show me the other side of your face:
the one with the smile painted on with the
colours of the sacred land you abuse.

Robert Walker [1]

In 1990, one of the Commissioners of the Royal Commission which had been appointed to investigate the high incidence of death amongst Australian Aboriginal people in police and prison custody, went to an informal meeting with Aboriginal fringe-dwellers.[2] On meeting one of the spokespeople, Robert Bropho, the Commissioner asked him if he thought it was important for police to study Aboriginal culture. Bropho replied that he thought it was important for police to study their own culture, saying that it was a very cruel culture. The Commissioner either did not hear or did not understand Bropho's reply, and agreed that police should have a better understanding of Aboriginal people (Robert Bropho, interview with the author, April 8, 1994; Margaret Jeffery, interview with the author, December 27, 1993).

This study is an attempt to understand my own, very cruel, culture. In saying that, it is clear that I am not seeking to understand that culture on its own terms. On these terms, the propagation of dominant white culture has been a "civilising mission" antithetical to the barbarity and violence of those whom it has sought to "civilise". In place of such a representation, I have attempted to understand dominant white culture as it might be perceived by those upon whom it has been imposed, the colonised. From such a perspective, it is often exploitation and violence which characterise the "civilising mission". And in such a context, the role of colonial law, as the focal site of "legitimised" violence within colonial societies, takes on a highly contested character.

In order to represent something of the nature of colonial law for those upon whom it has been imposed, it has been important to re-appraise a number of matters which are often taken for granted. How is the object of such a study, in this instance "the law", to be defined? Who has authority to speak on the subject? How are the issues which are relevant to such a project to be ascertained? The need to rethink these matters has had a number of implications for both the form and content of this work.

In conducting the research associated with this study, it has become apparent that the subject matter of scholarly works on law is often quite a different thing to "the law" that is known to the colonised. For this reason, the "experts" cited in this work are not usually those associated with examinations of racism and law. In this study, it is frequently the lives people have lived, more than what they have (or have not) read and written, which gives them authority to speak. And because many of these people's encounters with law are lived rather than contemplated, law is often known for what it does in daily practice rather than as an abstract discourse or ideological framework.

Emphasis has therefore been given to accounts and data which access the experience of law for colonised peoples, in some instances displacing discussion of legal theory or doctrine. It is the former influences which have also resulted in the adoption of some strikingly unfashionable positions in this work. Not only have I rejected the assertion that we now occupy a "post-colonial" world, but I have also found that Marxism remains influential or is at least resonant with many colonised peoples' understandings of contemporary legal relations.

That is not to say that the representations of law incorporated in this work are either unproblematic or comprehensive. Certainly this study has not been an attempt to provide an encompassing theoretical framework through which readers will be reassured of their own abilities to analyse and "know" the world in which they live. Rather, I have attempted to indicate that theoretical frameworks are not enough precisely because they reassure us of the adequacy of our own knowledge and therefore displace any serious and practical engagement with those people whose knowledges are not necessarily elaborated as theory or academic discourse.

This study has been shaped by such an engagement. It is important to note however that this engagement is not one which renders colonised peoples the objects of my study. Instead, it is an engagement which is essential if we are ever to move beyond comforting and self-legitimating understandings of ourselves, and to recognise something of the character of our culture and institutions, including law, for the peoples upon whom these have been imposed.

Notes

1. Robert Walker was an Aboriginal man who died in Fremantle Prison, Western Australia in 1984, at the age of twenty-five. His death was the result of being crushed to death by prison warders, after sustaining a battering with batons. Walker's death was one of ninety-nine Aboriginal deaths in custody examined, and legitimated, by the Royal Commission into Aboriginal Deaths in Custody (RCIADIC) (Aus, RCIADIC 1991a, 1991d; Purdy, 1992a). The poem is taken from the Royal Commission report of the inquiry into Walker's death (Aus RCIADIC 1991d, p.1).

2. I use the terminology of "Aboriginal" and "Aborigine" despite the problems associated with this usage given the construction and imposition of such an "identity" by the non-indigenous population of Australia. Although indigenous peoples' own identification is often more directly with one of the many distinct socio-linguistic groups which comprised the original population of Western Australia, the indigenous peoples of that state often use these "generic" terms to refer to the broad grouping of indigenous peoples of Australia. "Fringe-dweller" is another term which has been adopted by Aboriginal people to describe those who live on the fringes of towns, in camps and shanty towns; also known as "humpies". These Aboriginal peoples have few, if any, of the amenities regarded as basic for non-Aboriginal communities in Australia, and their living conditions are often described as "Third World".

Acknowledgments

This manuscript was originally submitted as a doctoral thesis through the School of Law and Legal Studies at La Trobe University, Victoria, Australia. I would like to acknowledge the assistance of the University in enabling me to complete the thesis, in particular through the award of a La Trobe Postgraduate Scholarship. I would also like to acknowledge the assistance of the University of the West Indies and Professor Maureen Cain in enabling me to study in Trinidad as a visiting research student throughout 1992, and the La Trobe University School of Social Sciences Research and Travel Grants Committee for contributing to the cost of my travel to Trinidad.

I also thank the administration and staff of the following institutions: the St Augustine Library of the University of the West Indies, the Central Statistical Office in Port of Spain, and the Alexander, Battye, Reid and Beasley Libraries of Western Australia.

Finally, I would like to acknowledge the contributions made by the following people towards this work. Their support, interest, criticisms or example have been much appreciated. Bilal Abdullah; the Aboriginal community of Iremugadu (Roebourne), Western Australia - especially Peter Coppin (now deceased); Kate Auty; Hayden Awai; Sharon Bartholomew; Greta Bird; Anand Birju; Sylvan Brooks; Robert Bropho; Maureen Cain; Martin Chanock; the Fitzroy Community & Youth Centre - especially the Marsdens; Lystra Hagley; Eric Hayward; Graham Holton; Margaret Jeffery; Margaret Jordan; Val Kerruish; Rob McQueen; Oliver Mendelsohn; Theo Michael; Tricia Moynihan; Abdullah Omowale; Darren Palmer; Uwe Petersen; Milton and Rose-Marie Purdy; Mary Sebalac; Raffique Shah; Lois "Rudy" Soloman; and the vendors of the Tunapuna markets, Trinidad.

INTRODUCTION

1 Introduction

Trinidad and Western Australia have a common history to the extent that both were, for many years, British colonies. Although neither jurisdiction retains the formal status of being a British colony, both share the legacies of that history. One such legacy is the existence of populations of colonised peoples: the descendants of African slaves and Indian indentured workers who today constitute the vast majority of the Trinidadian population, and the indigenous inhabitants of Western Australia who today constitute only a small proportion of the total population of that state.[1] Another legacy of British colonialism, amongst the many other British institutions which continue to operate in both jurisdictions today, is the existence of legal systems based upon common law.

The retention of the colonial legal system, although certainly not unusual, is to a degree surprising. The history of Trinidad is one of the almost complete obliteration of its indigenous peoples,[2] and the savage exploitation of African slaves, Indian indentured workers, and their descendants, for the purposes of European profit. The history of Western Australia is one marked by the devastation and continuing oppression of the indigenous Aboriginal population, the "convict stain" of a penal settlement and the on-going discrimination against non-British, particularly non-white, peoples. Much of these histories have been enacted under the auspices of British common law.

It may be that the retention of British common law systems in both Trinidad and Western Australia indicates something about the perception of the role of law in the production of such histories. It may also indicate something about our perceptions of who we think "we" are after a history of British colonialism. What is of particular interest to me, however, is the historical and continuing relationship between the common law and colonialism; specifically, the contribution of the criminal jurisdiction of such systems towards the manufacture of racist stereotypes imposed upon the colonised peoples of Trinidad and Western Australia.

In order to assess the contribution of common law towards the construction of unequal relations of ethnicity and race, I have studied how legal systems which are derived from the common law operate in the different social contexts of Trinidad and Western Australia. In place of those accounts which portray such legal systems as either an impetus towards equality or as merely reflective of broader social inequalities, the accounts which proclaim 'law's innocence',[3] I was to find that, in practice, the common law systems of both jurisdictions were actively constitutive of ethnic and racial inequality.

STUDIES IN TRINIDAD AND WESTERN AUSTRALIA[4]

Why?

> We fill their gaols all over the world.
>
> Tallman[5]

My focus on the colonised peoples of Trinidad and Aboriginal Western Australia for a study of the workings of the common law system met with very different, and sometimes strong, responses. Those activists who were seeking to improve the position of their people, whether Caribbean or Aboriginal, found the study a fairly obvious project to undertake. Others' reactions were quite different. Often people were surprised that I was undertaking such a study given the widely diverse societies concerned. In fact, one long-term (white) resident of Trinidad was of the opinion that my premise was racist, asserting that the only thing that the groups I was concerned with had in common was the colour of their skin.

As I was to find in both Trinidad and Western Australia, however, it does not necessarily constitute racism to recognise the significance of such physical markings as skin colour. Non-white peoples daily share the experience of the social reality of racially based, and derogatory, identities.[6] To quote an Aboriginal woman, Lila Watson (1993[1974], p.732), speaking of the oppression of non-white indigenous and non-indigenous peoples in white dominated societies, 'The common factor existing between us was the colour of our skin'.

What is of perhaps more interest, however, is that many people who were surprised by the study seemed not to recognise how very much more than skin colour Trinidadian and Aboriginal peoples have in common. As stated above, the legal system and many other inherited British institutions continue to be operative in both Trinidad and Western Australia. It seemed odd that people who were surprised by a study of what they asserted were such widely diverse societies were apparently in no way surprised - or even aware - that these societies should have come to have essentially the same legal system. The existence of a common law based legal system assumed an inevitability and invisibility that excised the nature of that system itself from contention and possibility. While the existence of such an institution in diverse societies may be symptomatic of what Edward Said (1993, p.401), describes as the 'homogenizing processes of modern life', what is striking is that people continue to assert the absolute incommensurability of such increasingly homogenised societies.

Other Trinidadians were shocked, if not offended, by my proposed study. There were those who resented the implication that racism may be institutionalised in Trinidad, and the Chief Magistrate of Trinidad and Tobago informed me that there was no 'policy of racism' in his courts, as there was in Australia (Melville Baird, interview with the author, January 29, 1992). Other Trinidadians considered that their position as subjects of a legal system derived from British common law was in no way comparable to that of Australian Aborigines. These people considered themselves to be, and no doubt were, much more Westernised than many Aboriginal people.

As indicated, however, the point of my research was precisely to see how legal systems which were derived from the common law operated in different social contexts. While I did assume that the existence of common law systems meant that there was a degree of commensurability between Trinidad and Western Australia, I did not know whether the legal system worked in a racist manner in Trinidad, as it does in Australia.[7] That was what I wanted to find out. Nor did I mean to altogether assimilate the position of Aboriginal peoples and Afro- and Indo-Trinidadians, although it seemed to me that these groups had more in common than the colour of their skin. And that was a history of British colonialism.

Moreover, "non-Englishness" marked the original ethnicities of these peoples in ways which made their colonial history distinct from others'. That is not to deny that the colonial history of convicts in Australia, for example, was also brutal and oppressive (Hughes, 1988). However, it seems to me that it would be wrong to underestimate the extent of destruction and dislocation resulting from the imposition of English institutions on groups whose original culture and language is not English.[8] Aborigines, Afro- and Indo-Trinidadians are not only often physically, but also ethnically, marked as being other than of English descent. The antagonism between these peoples' original culture and the imposed colonial culture frequently constituted their languages and ethnicities not only as "barbaric" and "uncivilised", but also as criminal. While there are no doubt very substantial and significant contrasts between Trinidadian and Aboriginal peoples, it was the particular character of the legal relations with their British colonisers, and not the nature of these peoples of themselves, which provided the basis for my study.

It became apparent to me, however, that to a degree my position had underestimated the extent to which some Trinidadians have come to regard their coloniser's culture as their own.[9] In the same way, it may be too that my reasons for comparing the position of Caribbean and Aboriginal peoples, and omitting white Australians, were in part a function of my own "blindness" as a white Australian to the impositions of British colonialism on a white Australian identity. As stated above, much seems to turn on who we think "we" are after a history of British colonialism.

An identification with British or Western culture and institutions is not, however, the only artefact of such colonialism. A quite different collective identity was adopted by "Tallman", a black Afro-Caribbean to whom I explained my intention to compare the position of Trinidadian and Aboriginal peoples under the common law system. He had been active in the Black Power Movement during the 1970s, and now walked with crutches as a result of injuries he sustained during the bombing of Grenada by the United States in 1983. He was neither surprised nor offended by my study, and his comment to me was simply, 'We fill their gaols throughout the world.' This identity, unlike those constituted by an identification with British or Western culture and values, was at least in part constituted by an identification with being *black* - and *imprisoned* in *someone else's gaols*.

I am not here seeking to explain colonised peoples' construction of their own ethnic/racial identities. Alternative identities, which sometimes appropriate elements of criminality as in the Caribbean "rude boy" persona,[10] may be actively constructed by colonised peoples as a result of their conscious resistance to Westernised values. What is of concern to me, however, is the construction and function of identities which are *imposed* upon colonised peoples by their colonisers. It is the criminal "other", as an imposed identity, that is the focus of my study.

My contention is that the practice of Western law, British common law in particular, is *actively* complicit in the constitution of colonised peoples as the criminal "other". The ethnic and racialised identities of the colonised provide ready, but mutable, constructions to which the label of criminal can adhere. In Trinidad and Western Australia today, people are often criminalised according to the degree to which they are perceived to be of non-Western culture or appearance. The interpolation of racialised and criminalised identities carries with it a signification of difference as inferiority and savagery. This, in turn, instils both superiority and fear in the Western, or Westernised, subject.

Although analysis of these processes in terms of ethnic/racial identity is significant; following Caribbean and other analyses, I hope to show how in the colonial context such criminalisation is not simply racist. The interpolation of criminality into racialised identities furthers the economic interests of dominant groups or classes.[11] Moreover, although British common law, particularly criminal law, has been effective in the oppression and exploitation of other groups, such as the white metropolitan working class, I hope to indicate that law continues to be effective in the exploitation of colonised peoples in a particularly unmediated way.

Before turning to the issue of how I conducted studies in Trinidad and Western Australia, it is perhaps important to further examine some of the assumptions - and objections - associated with this study. At one level, my choice of Trinidad and Western Australia as the sites for my research was a fairly prosaic matter. I am Western Australian, have studied law there, and worked for a Royal Commission investigating one of the most notorious Aboriginal deaths in police custody to have occurred in recent times.[12] Valerie Kerruish suggested the possibility of studying and researching in Trinidad, and this was made possible through the assistance of Maureen Cain, who was working at the University of the West Indies at that time.

Being able to conduct such a study, however, was not the reason I wanted to undertake it. Francis Snyder and Douglas Hay (1987, p.1), have stated,

> We have much to learn about the historical relationship of law to socio-economic change and about the nature of the state, power, and authority, as well as perhaps about the diverse roles of law in contemporary society, from a comparative, historical study of the inter-relationship of labour, law, and crime.

It was because I thought I had much to learn that I undertook a study of the common law of Trinidad and Western Australia.

It is of note that Snyder and Hay have also indicated that in order to undertake such a study a number of presuppositions must be made. Amongst these are included the notion that the law and the state in two different social contexts, despite differences in detail, are sufficiently similar to be worth comparing. Another presupposition is that either socio-economic processes or the forms, functions and role of law can be compared across time.

Such presuppositions run counter to academic distinctions between different categories of study. Snyder and Hay (1987, pp.3-5), characterise these distinctions as having led to two major divisions: between the First and the Third Worlds, and between the present and the past. Because my project was based upon the presuppositions identified by Snyder and Hay it also ran counter to the academic distinctions they identified.

I have set out above something of the similarities between Trinidad and Aboriginal Western Australia upon which I based my study. What is of perhaps more interest at a speculative level is the resistance with which my proposed study was so often met, and which has also been discussed. The *a priori* rejection of any comparison is of itself a phenomenon worthy of attention. On what basis can people object to a comparison that had not previously been undertaken? In the instance of a study of the common law as it applied to Trinidadians and Aboriginal Western Australians, there were a number of specific objections, but it seemed to me that these also fitted within a broader conceptual framework.

Part of that framework was alluded to above; that is, the "invisibility" of the common law system, and other inherited colonial institutions, in Trinidad and Western Australia. The invisibility of these shared institutions, in addition to the other objections to my study, seemed to me to relate to notions of "difference". Categorical "differences" were asserted to exist between Trinidad and Western Australia, between Trinidadians and Aborigines, between Trinidad's legal system and Western Australia's - all of which rendered the two societies incommensurable. With reference to Snyder and Hay's comments, the underlying objection seemed to be that there was no similarity upon which to conduct a comparative study of Trinidad and Western Australia.

To undertake a comparison of these incommensurables is therefore to question what is already "known": that Trinidad and Western Australia are *different*. It disturbs notions of who "we" know ourselves to be by unsettling the divisions that divide "us" from who we are not. White Western Australians did not think that their society shared anything with Trinidadian society; upper class non-white Trinidadians objected to being compared to Aboriginal people; Trinidadian legal officials objected to the comparison to a legal system which was evidently aberrant because it was racist; white Western Australians objected to the comparison because they regarded the legal system of Trinidad, but not their own, as corrupt.

These divisions tie in with those identified by Snyder and Hay, between First and Third Worlds, present and past. They also relate to the dualisms identified by Peter Fitzpatrick (1992) and Michael Taussig (1993); in particular the division between the "civilised" and the "savage". Moreover, as Fitzpatrick has shown, "the law", in the form of Western legal systems, is closely - and mythically - identified with what it means to be "civilised" (e.g. 1992, p.117). To blur the divisions between Third and First Worlds, between past and present, between a savage and a civilised "law", is therefore highly challenging.

It is perhaps because of these divisions that the histories of Aboriginal Australia and other indigenous peoples of the First World have so frequently been studied as if these were distinct from colonialism.[13] Nor would it seem merely coincidental that the application of colonial theory to Australian

Aboriginal history has only gained some currency amongst white academics at a time proclaimed to be "post-colonial". Even if the horrors of colonialism cannot be relegated altogether to the spatial dimensions of the Third World, the myth of "post-colonialism" at least confines such horror to a now distant and more barbaric past.

All of these asserted divisions however - between First and Third Worlds, present and past, civilisation and savagery - would seem to have more to do with the self-perception of colonisers than the perceptions or experiences of those peoples who were and who continue to be subjected to 'political domination, cultural oppression and economic exploitation' (Hartwig, 1978, p.121).[14] As indicated, the reactions of Caribbean and Aboriginal activists to my project were strikingly different to others'. To these people, the study of the common and imposed legal systems of Trinidad and Western Australia was a relatively obvious project; nor did it seem in any way unsettling of their self-perception or world view. From such perspectives, the existence of British common law systems in very different societies half way across the world from each other and from Britain itself, was not invisible, inevitable, nor necessarily good. It was because I also regarded this "common" law as a phenomenon worthy of attention that I undertook this project.

How?

Western academics often write in abstract terms, and their authority is often based precisely upon their ability to "move beyond" the concrete experience to obscured and obscure broader principles, and the debates and analyses of other Western academics. As Richard Delgardo points out in his 'The Imperial Scholar' (1984), it is in fact the work of white, usually male, academics which preoccupies other white academics even when examining issues such as racism. Caribbean writers, on the other hand, even when discussing theoretical issues, often write anecdotally, with obvious affinity and in concrete terms.

There can be no doubt that the supposed merit of the abstract nature of Western academic writing has been used to appropriate all claims to authority, and to exclude the expertise of those who do not share such an "academic" standpoint. However, rather than being reflective of differences in intellectual ability, the different style of discourse manufactured by many Western and Caribbean writers would instead appear to be reflective of the actual experiences of the authors themselves. For example, when many white middle class academics write about law in an abstract way, they are in fact no less writing of their actual experience of law than are the authors and activists of colonised groups who speak of the graphic violence of law. The direct impact of law upon white middle class academics' lives is likely to be precisely in the context of the theoretical: law as discourse and ideas.

There is a cultural, as well as class and other, specificity to how something is known. These specificities relate to the actual experiences of authors and include not just personal interactions, but also the more diffuse matters of the character of social relations in different social contexts and differences between inherited "cultural baggage". As indicated, the personal experience of law in a colonial context is likely to be far less ambiguous and remote than for white academics who are often middle class, relatively privileged and perceived as being "law-abiding". Even in a more general sense, there is a far more participatory and "dramatic" lifestyle in Trinidad compared to that of non-Aboriginal Western Australia.[15]

Moreover, the cultural baggage inherited about the legal system is itself likely to be different. The thorough-going cynicism in much of the Caribbean writing and discussion of the "civilising mission", particularly associated with the law and law reform, is often simply absent in many Western accounts.[16] Even Western accounts which are critical of law often deal with law's failings as aberrations (e.g. Eggleston, 1976; Aus RCIADIC, 1991a). Where there is a more systemic criticism, attention is still given to the positive or ambiguous aspects of the common law in the non-colonial context (e.g. Hall, Critcher, Jefferson, Clarke & Roberts, 1978; Hall et al [Boomer, Byrne, Coast, Dallos, Draper, Fitzgerald...], 1981).

The point of this discursion is simply that the abstract and theoretical bent of much Western discussion of law is culturally, class and often gender,[17] specific. Such an approach is neither more impersonal nor more intelligent than accounts based on the direct and unabstracted experience of law found in much Caribbean writing on the subject. Theoretical engagements may do no more than capture many Western academics' actual experience of law.

I am not here concerned to make any general claims about the validity or cogency of these different kinds of writing; it seems to me that much will depend upon the subject of research. That there is a material basis to these different approaches to law is not here at issue either. Caribbean authors such as William Calathes (1990) and Cynthia Mahabir (1980), for example, reject any assumption that contemporary criminalisation in the Caribbean can be equated to the processes associated with nineteenth century economic development in the industrialised countries. They assert a specificity to current uses of criminal law in the so-called developing countries, and associate this with relations to developed nations and decolonisation.

C.L.R. James (1980c[1964], p.154), Francis Snyder and Douglas Hay

(1987), Eboe Hutchful (1986) and Frantz Fanon (1990)[1961] also indicate that there is a specificity to colonised peoples' experiences of colonial legal systems in the Third World. The experiences of colonised peoples have not generally been affected by an ambiguous history of legal protections; by an ideology of "the rule of law"; by a mediating civil society; by a 'multitude of moral teachers, counsellors and "bewilderers" [who] separate the exploited from those in power' (Fanon, 1990[1961], p.29).[18] It does not require an extensive knowledge of Aboriginal history and social conditions since white intervention to recognise that their experiences of law fit within a similar category.[19] My point is, however, whatever its material basis, there is a specificity to the colonised's perceptions of law that cannot be subsumed under other peoples' accounts.

In this study therefore, precedence is given to accounts of law by those who have experienced the down-side of colonialism and racism. In addition, because the colonised are more likely to know law as a direct and often violent and exploitative force in their lives, it is these aspects of law which I have tried to capture in my work. To this end I have used data which indicate something of the graphic reality of life and law for colonised peoples, sometimes to the exclusion of more theoretical issues and debates.

It is of note that the alternative understanding of law which informs this work is far more profoundly the result of engaging with Caribbean accounts of the history of colonial law than any engagement with the issues of theory and methodology which preoccupy Western academics. Albert Memmi (1990[1957], p.171) has stated, 'The memory which is assigned him is certainly not that of his people. The history which is taught him is not his own.' Memmi is just one of many who have noted the significance of the absence of colonised peoples' histories from official and particularly educational institutions (see also Gilbert, 1977, pp.193,194; Huggins, 1990; Watson, 1988). Where the accounts of history by colonised peoples are documented, as in the Caribbean, the more conventional depiction of Western intervention as a civilising mission and colonised peoples as both passive and savage is radically displaced (refer e.g. Craig, 1988; James, 1963[1938]; Naipaul, 1969a; Singh, 1988; Trotman, 1986; Williams, 1961[1944]).

From such perspectives, far from resembling part of a civilising mission, colonial legal relations are shown to have been a mechanism which manufactured and legitimised the violent oppression and exploitation of colonised peoples. And far from being merely passive victims or "beneficiaries" of such oppression and exploitation, colonised peoples are shown to have been resilient in their resistances to colonial incursions. Moreover, in contrast to dominant notions of the nature of law, the "rules" are shown to have been highly malleable or ineffective in ways which blatantly corresponded to the interests of local or metropolitan elites. Law, as a *practice* of unmediated violence and multiple cruelties, transforms arguments concerning the imperatives of legal reasoning and the "good intentions" of the colonisers into, at best, irrelevancies.[20]

Caribbean accounts of the *practice of law* highlight the inadequacy of the *theories of law* which fail to reckon with both its inherent violence and its functioning within the politics of imperialism. More broadly, Susan Craig (1982a, p.170), a Tobagonian sociologist, notes that 'Sociological theorizing in the English-speaking Caribbean reached a "plateau" by the end of 1960s', and remains unable to explain contemporary social relations in the region. Given the limitations of contemporary theorisation, Caribbean accounts of history indicate the existence of an underlying pattern which (currently) can perhaps be best conveyed by Fanon's (1990[1961], p.31) term of a 'slightly stretched' Marxist analysis: 'The cause is the consequence; you are rich because you are white, you are white because you are rich.'[21] The form or effectivity of legal relations in the colonial context has consistently been associated with the economic or hegemonic interests of a metropolitan or local elite who, at the same time, maintain an ethnic or racial distance from those they exploit or oppress.

Perhaps the most sustained - and contentious - elaboration of such a relation is found in Eric Williams's (1961[1944]) analysis of the rise and fall of slavery, *Capitalism and Slavery*. Williams (1961[1944], p.7), sought to reconstruct a historical connection between metropolitan economic interests and colonial (legal) relations, in order to displace official historical accounts of the genesis of slavery in terms of race/racism, and its decline in terms of philanthropy. Indeed, Williams commented that such official accounts had been written 'almost as if Britain had introduced Negro slavery solely for the satisfaction of abolishing it'.[22]

It is of note that Williams, perhaps more than many other Caribbean authors, had attempted to elaborate his thesis within the disciplinary constraints of Western academic history. But not only did British publishers refuse to publish the text for some twenty years, his work has been subject to such sustained critique that '[i]t is fashionable nowadays to say that Williams's work is discredited' (Fryer, 1988, p.5). And yet while it is admitted that many details now require correction, Christopher Fyfe states, 'Still one wonders - has the edifice really fallen? Certainly it has not been replaced'.[23]

It seems to me that the edifice of economic interests and legal relations which are played out in the racialised context of the colonies is one which is substantiated through chronologies of the colonial histories of Trinidadian and Aboriginal peoples. That is, through the documentation of "just one damn thing after another": the changes in the economic interests of the metropolitan or local elite and the consequent changes in the form of the often violent and brutal repression of racially or ethnically distanced colonised peoples, either specifically through common law or in the absence of its censure.

It is of note that such chronologies have more to do with James Baldwin's politics of "bearing witness",[24] than with the disciplinary (and political) demands of Western academic history. It is for this reason that the chronologies of economics and law in a colonial context are absent from this work. Maureen Cain has indicated that Western academia often demands the primacy and privilege of epistemology over ontology. To exist, something must be knowable, known, named and analysed. She illustrates, however, that in the instance of sexual harassment, for example, women were aware of the pattern of the relationship before it was named (Cain, 1994, pp.20-22). In the same way, it seems to me that Caribbean accounts of colonial history indicate an underlying pattern of relationships, which, although they are not necessarily "named" or (currently) explicable in terms of causation, are nonetheless worthy of serious engagement.

But while the exclusion of such a treatment of history from my work seems to me to contribute to the profoundly conservative and ethnocentric character of Western academic texts, it is also the case that its inclusion in a work whose primary audience is academic can serve no purpose. For although one can take issue with epistemological primacy in theory, an attempt to put such theory into practice is considered simply inadequate on the basis of academic disciplinary standards.

In place of the chronologies of colonialism, economics, law and resistance which I found so useful in enabling me to engage with colonised peoples' knowledges of colonial law, I instead elaborate upon the theoretical and methodological issues which are of concern within a Western academic context. The issues and debates are discussed in Part I, Chapters 2 to 4, below, and are intended to sketch out a conceptual framework in which the project attempted in the following chapters will be accessible.

That project not only includes issues related to a study of law in a colonial context, but also raises issues related to the nature of academic study itself. As indicated above, Western academic discipline frequently demands what Cain (1994, p.21), refers to as 'this arrogant placing of human knowledge at the centre of the universe'. With reference to my own research, which was conducted in a cross-cultural context, the centrality of my own knowledge to any analysis would be particularly presumptuous.

Because I have wanted to "de-centre" my own interpretations, much of the data in Part II of the work is presented without specific analysis. Readers may well find this disconcerting, or worse, but it is not done simply because I am unaware of what is expected of academic discourse. My point has been to structure the discourse of this work in such a way that the contingency of my (or any) interpretation will be enmeshed within the work itself. More than this, however, I have sought to indicate that the significance of how colonised peoples are criminalised, live and die is not confined to my own interpretations. Such matters have a significance and gravity far beyond any gloss my interpretation may add to them.

Given that, Part II, consisting of chapters 5 and 6, is concerned with the contemporary conditions under which criminalisation takes place in Trinidad and Western Australia. Included in each chapter are statistical data on broader demographic and economic profiles as well as information on the operation of the criminal justice system in each jurisdiction. The demographic and economic data are included in order to create a context in which the operation of the legal system can be assessed. The information on the so-called "criminal justice system" indicates something of the continuity for many colonised people between the violent nature of law in their colonial past and its character in the contemporary context. The juxtaposition of data on the economic position of colonised peoples and the criminal justice system also suggests that economic influences continue to be profoundly connected to criminalisation.

Chapters 5 and 6 also include accounts of my field-work in the magistrates' courts of Trinidad and Western Australia. These are intended to indicate something of the mundane and personalised practice of law and to capture something of the complex tendencies that evolve out of this practice. However, these accounts also indicate that, despite the significant differences between the practice of law in the two jurisdictions, there is a consistency in the treatment of colonised peoples which contrasts with that of non-colonised peoples. This matter is developed further in the subsequent, final chapters.

In Part III, I return to the familiar themes of law, violence and economics. Unlike the previous two chapters however, this part of the work is more conspicuously concerned with the analysis and interpretation of data; although it is not concerned to present any comprehensive or intellectually reassuring theory of law. In dealing first with the issue of law, I discuss the ways in which law in the courts dominates perceptions of law for those not directly affected by its less public practices. This division not only coincides with the different relationship between the legal system and many colonised people as distinct from its interactions with non-colonised people, but also turns upon the direct exposure to law's violence.

In Chapter 8, I indicate that the problematic of violence is not confined to the legal system however, and that the violence of some colonised peoples cannot be simply characterised as resistance to oppression. This discussion engages with the contentious issue of internal violence amongst colonised peoples, and I explore this issue in terms of its relevance to the relationship between colonised peoples and colonial legal systems.

Following Caribbean analyses, however, I move beyond an analysis confined to an examination of either the ethnic/racial or racist content of contemporary legal relations. Instead, in Chapter 9, I explore the relationship between the stereotyped identities constituted for colonised peoples through the common law, and the colonial project. I hope to indicate how the interpolation of racialised and criminal identities continues to cohere with the economic exploitation of colonised peoples in the contemporary context.

COLONISED PEOPLES AND CULTURAL ORIGINALITY

Colonised Peoples

My usage of terms such as "colonial" and "colonised peoples" in the context of existing social and legal relations in Trinidad and Aboriginal Western Australia will not be an obvious choice to some. Current theory indicates that "post-colonial" is the appropriate category to describe the position of such peoples, in particular those of Trinidad who have attained political independence (see for example, Williams & Chrisman, 1994).

Clearly much will turn on one's definition of colonialism. Said (1993), for example, locates the current position of many non-Western nations and peoples as "post-colonial" because British and other European settlements are no longer "implanted" in these nations. Said distinguishes imperialism from colonialism and defines imperialism as 'the practice, the theory, and the attitudes of a dominating metropolitan centre ruling a distant territory', with colonialism being defined as 'almost always a consequence of imperialism, [and] is the implanting of settlements on distant territory'. Said (1993, p.8), concludes, 'In our time, direct colonialism has largely ended', but that imperialism lingers 'in a kind of general cultural sphere as well as in specific political, ideological, economic, and social practices'.

Even on his own usage of the term, Said's claim that direct colonialism has largely ended would seem to be inconsistent with the contemporary situations in such nations as the United States, Australia, (Northern) Ireland, New Zealand (Aotearoa) and Canada, amongst others. Said's claim can be reconciled to the current realities of these nations only if the definitive element of colonisation is taken to be coloniser perceptions. That is, on Said's terms colonialism exists where there is a physical presence of people who regard themselves as colonisers, that is, as representative of some *other* metropolitan centre. Therefore colonialism comes to an end either if the colonisers evacuate their settlements or if they decide to identify themselves with the "settlements" they implanted in other peoples' lands (see too McClintock's comments on 'break-away settler colonies': 1994, p.295).

Activists amongst the poor black peoples of Trinidad and Australia, and others, do not necessarily regard the issue of colonialism as being properly determined by colonisers' perceptions. Abdullah Omowale, an Afro-Trinidadian activist and journalist, stated in a series of articles entitled 'From Colonialism to Colonialism':

> The thing to understand, however, is that, although we have struggled, the system has not changed. We are still colonised. (*Sunday Mirror*, [commencing] November 29, 1992)

Robert Bropho (1992), a spokesman for a fringe-dwelling community of Nyungah (Aboriginal) people in Perth, Western Australia, writes of contemporary relations between white and black Australians as 'the fourth wave of destruction'. Although Bropho does not use the terminology of colonialism, it is implicit to his analysis that there has been no categorical shift in relations between his people and the white population. From Bropho's perspective these relations always have been and continue to be experienced by indigenous Australians as 'destruction'.[25]

Liam O'Dowd, an Irish academic, is also sceptical of the applicability of the term "post-colonial" to the existing situation in many parts of the world, including Ireland. He states that the failure to acknowledge and confront the resilience of colonialism into the late twentieth century 'promotes facile assertions of global interdependence and mutual interests in what is misleadingly termed a post-colonial and post-nationalist world' (O'Dowd, 1990, p.31). Roger Moody (1993, p.xxix) also comments that the differences between old-style colonialism, contemporary internal colonisation, neo-colonialism and neo-imperialism 'appear paper-thin and largely irrelevant to indigenous communities in their present struggles; ones of degree and motivation rather than kind'.

The impact of political decolonisation in Trinidad and changes to the regime of governance of Aboriginal people in Western Australia would not seem to have been experienced as fundamentally altering the nature of social relations by those who are not only committed to, but relevantly here, also share the lifestyle of those marginalised because of their ethnicity and/or race. In such a context, the writings of pre-political independence authors, such as Frantz Fanon (1968[1952]; 1990[1961]), Aimé Césaire (1972)[1955] and Albert Memmi (1990)[1957], have a contemporary relevance to the expression of current experiences both of and as colonialism. Although political changes in both

Trinidad and Western Australia cannot be dismissed as altogether irrelevant, it is important not to overstate their significance.

The tendency to overestimate the significance of political change is the result of both an underestimation of the degree of power exercised by (some) colonised peoples prior to independence or enfranchisement, and an overstatement of the power that they (all) now enjoy. The collaboration of some colonised peoples with the dominant culture has always been a part of colonial history. C.L.R. James recounted the story of a domestic slave who, during the earliest days of the slave era in Barbados, betrayed a planned slave uprising to his white master. James wrote,

> ...what I suspect, is that working in the house of a Justice of the Peace, he had acquired a certain respect, a subservience to the conceptions of law and order of the masters of the society which he had just entered.

James (1980d[1966], p.177), continues, 'And I say that because we shall see this type constantly reappearing, it is most prominent in West Indian society today: the house slave'.

In the same way, Geoff Clark, the deputy chairman of the Aboriginal Provisional Government, speaks of contemporary "Aboriginal representatives" in the following terms,

> This notion of naming someone King Billy and saying we'll negotiate with him has been around for donkey's years. You dress him up, put a suit on him, and pronounce him leader. (*The Australian Magazine*, April 12/13, 1994)

In James' opinion, the era of political decolonisation in the West Indies was the era of the prominence of the "house slave"; in Clark's opinion the "King Billys" of the past are the besuited Aboriginal representatives of today. In either instance the collaborations of the past are assimilable to those of the present. Other writers such as Michael Howard (1982a) and Ronald Robinson,[26] as well as the Royal Commission into Aboriginal Deaths in Custody (Aus RCIADIC, 1991a:10.5.18 - 10.5.22; 13.2.3; 13.2.8 - 13.2.11), have also examined the historical and contemporary collaborations of colonised peoples with their colonisers. (Although in the latter two instances I would think the degree of collaboration is overly emphasised and misleading.)

My point is that the exercise of power by colonised peoples within the institutional framework of the colony has *not* been a creation of their political independence and enfranchisement. What has been and remains significant, however, is how the exercise of such power is circumscribed by those institutions and the coercive force of colonising powers.

Noam Chomsky (1987) and Anne McClintock (1994) illustrate how the increasingly successful liberation struggles of colonised nations after World War II were not simply presaged by the declining power of Britain and other European governments and economies, but also by the growing strength of the United States. The era of so-called post-colonialism for many of the now politically independent ex-colonies has been coincidental with a growing dependence upon and domination by the United States. (The role of the U.S.S.R. as a colonial power in the "post-colonial" era has also been of much significance, but is not directly relevant to my discussion in this work.)

Eboe Hutchful (1986), concurring with Wallerstein and others, describes this era as being characterised by the internationalisation of capital in the form of transnational or multinational corporations. International economic relations no longer involved predominantly the export of commodities and capital by national producers and financiers, but the internationalisation of capitalist production. Capitalist relations of production and not just relations of exchange therefore became international. This had major ramifications for "the peripheral states".

Significantly here, this development has meant that accumulation in the periphery 'cannot occur autonomously, but must be conditioned and determined by the self-valorisation of international capital and must, moreover, occur as purely secondary results of this process' (Hutchful, 1986, p.155). In addition, the role of the Bretton Woods institutions, the International Monetary Fund and World Bank, have become increasingly important. Hutchful states that these institutions were 'intended to mediate and reconcile the contending interests of rival national capitals of the world market, consistent with the hegemony of U.S. capital as the most powerful national fraction' (Hutchful, 1986, p.170).[27]

In this context, it is difficult to regard changes since World War II as going to the substance of colonial relations, particularly for people occupying the lowest strata of the newly independent nations. To some extent colonialism has taken on a new form, but to consider this as signifying a post-colonial era would appear to require a restriction of analysis to the purely formal indicia of colonialism.

The Caribbean author W. Richard Jacobs noted that while contemporary Caribbean societies, like others, are essentially organised on a class basis they also continue to exhibit a distinctive colonial character. He states that these societies are characteristic of the classic model of the 'neo-colony',

> Independent by name, flying its own flag, promulgating laws from its own Parliament, but dependent in all material and metaphysical ways on the

> umbilical cord which ties it to the metropolitan centre.
>
> The neo-colonial status, while it might in the short-run satisfy the ruling class, is a most debilitating, humiliating and ultimately dehumanizing experience, for it facilitates the sucking of the economic blood of the neo-colony and the reciprocal fattening of the metropole in full view of all - the wretched of the earth as well as the metropolitan imperialist interests. (Jacobs, 1982, p.277)

To regard such societies as post-colonial is to rely upon obliviousness to the entrenched colonial institutions, the economic dependence and exploitation of these newly independent states, and the frequent and brutal military interventions into those countries when they fail to comply with "metropolitan" agendas. See, for example, studies on the histories of Haiti, Cuba, Panama, Guatemala, Chile, El Salvador, Nicaragua, Jamaica, Mexico, Dominica, Grenada and Guyana in the Latin American and Caribbean region alone (Barry, Wood & Preusch, 1984; Calathes, 1990; Casimir, 1982; Chomsky, 1987; Efremov, 1986; Harsch, 1981; Marable, 1987; McAfee, 1991; McClintock, 1994; Moreno, 1982).

In Western Australia, there have also been significant changes in the "style" of domination of Aboriginal peoples since the 1950s, as is documented in Chapter 9. The "post-colonisation" of Aboriginal peoples tends to be dated from legislative amendments of 1967, and particularly their enfranchisement. However, characterising the contemporary position of Aborigines in Western Australia as "post-colonial" is even less plausible than applying that term to West Indian nations. Quite apart from issues of economic dependency, Aboriginal peoples have yet to attain even the political status of decolonisation.[28] Moreover, Aboriginal law receives only scant and unformalised recognition within the common law system in both Western Australia, and Australia generally (refer Crawford, 1994; Dodson, 1991, pp.191-202; Eggleston, 1976; Payne, 1990).

Robert Bropho [1992] stated,

> Human rights is not just education, good health, and living in a white man's house in his cities. Human rights is the soles of Aboriginal people's feet. It is our Life, our Beliefs, our Culture, our Places of Worship, to be left alon[e] and respected.

It is the issue of autonomy - 'to be left alon[e] and respected' - which I consider to be a fundamental factor in the definition of colonised peoples; an autonomy that is not captured by political independence or enfranchisement as these terms are currently understood.

Cultural Originality

Frantz Fanon (1968[1952], p.18), the Afro-Caribbean author and anti-colonial activist, defined colonised people as

> every people in whose soul an inferiority complex has been created by the death and burial of its local cultural originality...[which] finds itself face to face with the language of the civilizing nation; that is, with the culture of the mother country. The colonized is elevated above his jungle status in proportion to his adoption of the mother country's cultural standards. He becomes whiter as he renounces his blackness, his jungle.

My usage of the term "colonised peoples" draws upon Fanon's, but with some important differences. Fanon writes of colonised peoples as those who have been defeated; people who have internalised inferiority, lost their local cultural originality, and renounced their colour.[29] My usage of the term is broader, incorporating those to whom Fanon refers, but extending it to also include those who struggle against such a fate.

I use neither the instilling of an inferiority complex nor the death of 'local cultural originality' as elements definitive of colonised peoples. Rather, I regard the tension or antagonism between this 'local cultural originality', including economic forms and values, and the imposed or even adopted culture of the 'mother country' as the defining characteristic of colonialism and colonised peoples.[30]

It is important to note, however, that the local cultural originality of colonised peoples is not, and cannot be, a return to the pre-colonial. Cultures are not static, and nor can contact with other cultures be erased. Cultural originality does not require the rejection of all aspects of the 'culture of the mother country'. This has been recognised by such fiercely anti-colonialist writers as C.L.R. James[31] and Aimé Césaire (1972[1955], p.31). Authors such as Frantz Fanon also emphasise the dangers of mythologising the nature of pre-colonial cultures (e.g. Fanon, 1990[1961], p.180).

Bilal Abdullah, a spokesman for the Trinidadian Jamaat al Muslimeen involved in the 1990 coup attempt, also recognised the fact of change and the desirability of appropriation of other cultural forms. An instance of this was when Abdullah spoke to me of the need to move away from a monarchical style of government which had become 'fetishised' in the Muslim religion, and towards a more democratic form (Bilal Abdullah, interview with the author, November 17, 1992).

A similar attitude can be seen in the comment of Harry Daphney

Kowanyama, an Aboriginal woman.

> We can't go back. The old law was for old problems. Now we got this new law - this whiteman's way. And we got these new problems. This law can't fix them either. It's no good. What we got to do is put them together - the old and the new. And they'll be hard and strong like cement. (Quoted in Atkinson, 1990, p.6)

A genuine cultural originality does not require a mythologising of the pre-colonial. And it is also clear that the attainment of (limited) autonomy will not result in some form of stasis in which the dynamics of oppression and power become irrelevant (see for example, Afshar, 1994; Das, 1994; Gilbert, 1977, pp.188-193; Helie-Lucas, 1994). At a minimum, however, cultural originality would seem to require the capacity for peoples to autonomously assess how far the imposed or adopted institutions and practices of 'the mother country' are imbricated with colonial values, and what if anything is worth salvaging from them. Such scrutiny may indicate, as did Said's assessment of Western literature, Abdullah's assessment of modern forms and ideals of government, and Kowanyama's of whiteman's law, that these institutions and practices contain elements that are of value to colonised peoples.

In the context of continuing colonial influences which include economic dependence and military/legal sanctions, however, there can be no genuine autonomy - no being left alone and respected - in deciding what to salvage out of the institutions and practices of 'the civilizing nation' (Fanon, 1968[1952], p.18). In this context, the only strategy may be one of the 'scandalous' exploitation of these colonial institutions and practices, as suggested by Valerie Kerruish's (1991, p.200), assessment of the common law. Such scandalous exploitation consists of the determination to use institutions but without reverencing them. It involves recognising these institutions for what they are: no more than human artefacts and in particular the 'products of the reason of empowered white men' (Kerruish, 1991, p.195).

The local cultural originality of colonised peoples is not dead and buried.[32] The cultural originality of all colonised groups, however, not only has been obviously altered by the colonial experience but is also often confined and limited by that history and what I would argue is colonialism's continuing presence. As indicated, I adopt the antagonism implied in Fanon's definition between local cultural originality and the imposed and dominating culture of the coloniser as the definitive characteristic of colonised peoples.

For some "colonised" people, however, this antagonism would have only a historical meaning, as they have come to adopt and identify with the coloniser's culture. As such, my use of the term "colonised peoples" would apply to people who now live a variety of lifestyles. Such peoples may be subjected to or may themselves be constitutive of a variety of political and social institutions; institutions which may be imposed, or alternatively may reflect a variety of accommodations, utilisations and rejections of what Fanon refers to as 'the culture of the mother country'.

There can be no doubt, I would think, that some individuals and classes amongst colonised populations do obtain substantial advantages from the perpetuation of colonial institutions, in one form or another, in their societies (for example, Jacobs, 1976, pp.9-26; Moran, 1993a; Morrison, 1992b; Unaipon, 1994). In some instances this benefit may be obtained through the exploitation of traditional forms within a colonial context (see, for example, Chanock, 1994a; Fitzpatrick, 1980; Scott, 1985). Others may enjoy the benefits of class privilege (see Fanon, 1990[1961]; Robinson, 1993).[33] But there are also many colonised people who suffer substantial disadvantage as a result of the perpetuation of colonial institutions and values in their societies. Moreover, Fanon's *Black Skin, White Masks* (1968)[1952] may also be read as portraying the high cost exacted from those elements of the colonised who would seek indiscriminately to appropriate colonial values.

I would add that, in any event, such accommodations, utilisations or rejections as do occur continue to take place within a framework which is dominated by colonial powers. While some movement within this overarching framework is tolerated, there is only limited autonomy. For nations, breaches of this framework may be met with economic sanction and military intervention, as indicated above. For individuals, there is also economic dependency and the punishing violence that may be enforced through a variety of disciplinary mechanisms, but most overtly through the retained colonial legal systems, as indicated in this work.

ETHNIC/RACIAL IDENTITY

Race and Ethnicity

It has been claimed that, as race is 'much more a social than a biological category differentiated by phenotypical characteristics', ethnicity, 'which incorporates factors of culture and awareness of common identity', is a more useful concept (Reddock & McCree, 1992, p.2). The social content of a category such as "race" can be seen in the manner in which notions of "race" in Trinidad differ considerably from those current in a country like Australia. In Trinidad, those of mixed African and white descent often tend to identify as "Trinidadian white", "red" or "mixed" and therefore as racially distinct from those who identify as being of African descent. Currently in Australia, people of mixed Aboriginal and white descent often identify as Aboriginal, whatever their phenotypical characteristics.

Moreover, as implied in the comments of Rhoda Reddock and Roy McCree above, the use of phenotypical and other biological characteristics as definitive of "race" has been used by dominant groups to deny a common identity to others. White colonisers have not only used "race" to distinguish themselves from blacks, but have also institutionalised divisions between "pure" and "mixed race", African and Asian peoples, and so on, in a strategy to divide and rule.

Nonetheless, I do not accept that ethnicity, with its reference to only social or cultural elements, is adequate. Like the sex/gender distinction, it seems to me that both variants - broadly the physical and the cultural - are significant.

Abandoning the word "race" as a strategy for dealing with racism assumes either that "race" exists only as a discourse or that the removal of the discourse will somehow remove the practices associated with it. The former view is inconsistent with empirical evidence of the effectivity of concepts of race, for example, in the persisting and disproportionate correlations between harassment/criminalisation and being black/dark-skinned (see, for example, Aus RCIADIC, 1989c, 1990a; Chambliss & Sbarbaro, 1993; Eggleston, 1976; Hall et al, 1978; Keith, 1993; Matthews & Young, 1992a; Trinidad & Tobago Central Statistical Office (T&T CSO), 1993 Prison census reproduced at Appendix II). If such evidence is accepted, it must also be acknowledged that race is a category of some material effectivity in contemporary social relations.

The strategy of abandoning "race" would then seem to be tied to the notion, mentioned above, that the removal of the discourse will somehow remove the practice.[34] Such a strategy, however, concentrates on the discourse to the exclusion of the practical functions it plays in the constitution of social relations. It assumes the primacy of the discourse over the material conditions out of which words, beliefs and ideologies develop and gain currency. This is part of what Cain (1994, pp.20,21), identifies as one version of the fallacy of epistemological primacy, according to which,

> since the world, including the social world, is not presentable in discourse it has no *potency* outside of discourse. Therefore all struggles for power can be interpreted as (and reduced to) discursive struggles. Because knowledge enters into the production and use of beliefs, the power of the bullet is the same as or arises from the power of its signifier.

Michael Rustin has described "race" as 'both an empty category and one of the most destructive and powerful forms of social categorisation'.[35] The problem with abandoning the category of "race" because it is used as an instrument of oppression and exploitation is that we are left only with the destruction, but no means of investigating how this powerful form of social categorisation works. Moreover, by confining ourselves to analyses based upon "ethnicity", we may actually contribute to the perpetuation of racism. By removing "race", in the sense of physical appearance, as a site of contemporary relevance to struggles against oppression we may well, for example, occlude recognition of the irreducible significance of physical appearance in the criminalisation process, as discussed further below.

Trinidad

Lloyd Braithwaite's pioneering study of Trinidad, first published in 1953, documented a system of social stratification which evolved out of the legislation and practice of the slave era. He concluded that the 'main common value' shared by the whole society remained 'the ascriptive one of "ethnicity" and colour' (Braithwaite, 1975[1953], p.138).[36] As such, one criterion which continued to determine one's place in the social hierarchy was skin colour (and other physical attributes such as hair texture and facial features), and stratification depended on the degree to which such physical characteristics resembled those of the white elite. Thus it was that, even after the dismantling of the institution of plantation slavery, the social stratification system tended to perpetuate a regime in which the lower and working classes were black, the middle class were of mixed descent and the upper class were white.

It is of note that, since Braithwaite conducted his research, there have been significant changes in Trinidad. The bureaucratic and political power of the local and expatriate white elite has been eroded (Ryan, 1991a, p.60), through political reform. Changes affecting the position of Indo-Trinidadians have also been important. Indo-Trinidadians previously held a position outside but to some extent at the bottom of the social hierarchy (e.g. Braithwaite, 1975[1953]; Camejo, 1972; Niehoff & Niehoff, 1960 and discussed further at Chapter 9). But although the traditional occupational and geographic division between Indo- and Afro-Trinidadians has been maintained to some degree,[37] Indo-Trinidadians are now regarded, and regard themselves, as a constitutive element of Trinidadian society.

But how have these changes affected the social stratification system of Trinidad? If Indo-Trinidadian incorporation had taken place according to the common value of ethnicity and colour identified by Braithwaite, one would expect them to now hold a relatively high position, attributable (at least in part), to their closer physical resemblance to "whites" than Afro-Trinidadians. Additionally one might expect an internal stratification within the Indo-Trinidadian community, according to which phenotypically blacker Indo-Trinidadians would generally hold a lower social position than other Indo-Trinidadians.

It is of note that Reddock and McCree (1992, p.26), have stated that Indo-Trinidadians 'as a group have historically resisted what they perceive as assimilation into some undefined national creole culture'. However, I would argue that the Hindu caste system, to the degree that it was based on colour stratification, could be absorbed and reconstituted into Trinidad's common value of ethnicity and colour, without the loss of a separate Indo-Trinidadian identity. Robert Ross (1982a, pp.5,6), cautions against assimilating social structures in existence after colonial intervention with those which existed prior to intervention; and certainly the "caste system" that exists in Trinidad is radically different to that which existed in India (Camejo, 1972, p.115; Niehoff & Niehoff, 1960). Nonetheless, if Indians were incorporated into the social stratification system of Trinidad, caste divisions would provide 'local' categories, in Fanon's (1968[1952], p.18) terms, which could accommodate stratification as it was traditionally constituted in Trinidad.

Recent commentary has suggested however, that the social stratification system described by Braithwaite 'has now largely disappeared' (Ryan, 1991a, p.60). But not all commentators agree on this point. Robin Cohen (1981) notes that, while several authors notice an increased social differentiation at the bottom and an increased diversity of recruits at the top of the class structure, the basic pattern has not altered fundamentally. He attributes the persistence of the old race/class hierarchy to dependency upon the metropole, 'whether it is formally or informally constituted, or mediated via multinational capital'. He writes, 'At the level of the transfer of tastes, values and cultural symbols alone, the texture of race relations cannot but maintain a strong pro-white bias' (Cohen, 1981, p.188).

Jacobs comments that the persisting colonial character of Caribbean societies has meant that the ruling elite has been 'made up of essentially white, near white or subjectively white elements who imbibe colonial character traits, institutional forms and behaviour patterns'. Jacobs (1982, p.277), following Fanon, refers to these managers who act on behalf of the capitalists, since they do not possess the means of production, as 'the black faces with white masks'. In this context, a comment by Pierre Bourdieu and Jean-Claude Passeron is worth noting. They state that the mobility of individuals from the lowest social stratum, far from being incompatible with the established order, can in effect help to conserve that order by legitimating the exclusions from "privilege" of the majority of those from the lowest stratum (Bourdieu & Passeron, 1977, p.167).

It seemed to me that aspects of the stratification system identified by Braithwaite were visible in the magistrates' courts that I observed in Trinidad in 1992 (refer Chapter 5). The predominance of Afro-Trinidadians and relative absence of Indo-Trinidadians in these courts was apparent and consistent with a stratification based upon phenotypical resemblance to whites. But more than this, the phenotypical blackness of those remanded to custody, whether Afro- or Indo-Trinidadian, was manifest and particularly obvious in contrast (generally) to the skin colour of lawyers and magistrates, and even other non-incarcerated defendants.

The widely documented discretionary powers of police and legal officials in common law systems allows the discriminatory application of laws against those whose appearance, and other characteristics, do not conform to dominant mores (see, for example, Brogden, 1982; Brown, Hogg, Phillips, Boehringer & Zdenkowski, 1984; Cunneen & Robb, 1987; McBarnet, 1981, and discussed further in Chapter 9). In a society which remains stratified according to phenotypical traits, criminalisation becomes at once an artefact and constitutive of a racism based on physical characteristics. Trinidad's law courts are one site in which the social stratification system identified by Braithwaite continues to be manifest.[38]

Social stratification according to race, of course, also has class, ethnic and other correlations; if Rustin is correct, race is nothing other than these imputed correlations. To quote Fanon (1968[1952], pp.51,52), 'One is white as one is rich, as one is beautiful, as one is intelligent'. In Trinidad, phenotypical stratification traditionally and contemporarily interpolates with class stratification.[39] Moreover, as indicated at note 38, a number of Trinidadians interpreted the stratification system that I observed in the courts in terms of economic stratification. I would not deny that there was an apparent class bias within the courts and legal system in Trinidad, as elsewhere; and that colour did often appear to correlate to class. The coincidence of class and colour, however, does not strike me as a very convincing rebuttal to allegations of racism.

It explains nothing of why or how it is that blacker people tend to be poorer, poorer people tend to be blacker. Indeed, as I develop further in Part III, it is precisely the coincidence of class and race/colour, and its ramifications, in multi-racial colonial societies, that is of crucial significance to the colonialist content of legal systems based upon British common law. For now, however, it is clear that race, even if only in the sense of physical characteristics which have meaning as a signifier of other things, whether wealth, beauty, intelligence or ethnicity, does remain significant in constituting personal and group identity in

Trinidad.

Western Australia

In Australia there are recognised correlations between criminalisation and class, with Aborigines, for example, being not only the most imprisoned but also one of the poorest groups in society (Dodson, 1991; Tatz, 1994; see too, Chapters 6 and 9). However, the prejudice against Aboriginal people is said by them not just to relate to their economic poverty but to their Aboriginality (Dodson, 1991, p.206). Research such as that conducted by Chris Cunneen (1988) and Kerry Carrington (1989, 1990) amongst many others shows the continuing relevance of Aboriginality to criminalisation and how discrimination is based upon cultural practice and other manifestations of ethnic identity.

However, visible physical characteristics associated with *race* also play a significant role in the differential treatment of Aboriginal people; particularly with respect to policing. Although a classificatory system based upon racial characteristics is no longer legally sanctioned in Western Australia, there has been a long history of the division of Aboriginal people according to their physical appearance. Legislation in effect until the 1960s enshrined distinctions according to degrees of Aboriginality and employed such terminology as "quadroon" and "full-blood" (for example, the Native Administration Act 1936 and the Native Welfare Act 1954).

One of the most significant aspects of stratification based upon physical characteristics was the removal of children who appeared to be of mixed descent from their Aboriginal families. The consequences of such practices are not confined to the past; many Aboriginal people today are attempting to relocate their families and reconstruct their lives after the devastation resulting from the implementation of these genocidal policies. Some individuals still bear the scars of being burnt as their parents attempted to blacken their skin with the soot from fires to prevent their abduction (see, too, Brock, 1992).

The on-going effects of these policies are not confined to Aboriginal people, and a stratification system based on physical characteristics remains operative in Western Australia today. (Although I would think it is less conscious than the one operative in Trinidad;[40] nor has it been elaborated in any study comparable to Braithwaite's.) This stratification does not relate simply to ethnicity; Patrick Dodson (1991, p.232), the only Aboriginal Commissioner to be appointed to the Royal Commission into Aboriginal Deaths in Custody, writes that, 'For Aboriginal people to be *black* and living in poor material conditions results in the widely held perception that they are "criminals"' (emphasis added). Such perceptions of who are the criminals are significant in the context of Aboriginal relations with law enforcers, and Aborigines claim that being Aboriginal constitutes the legal requirement of "suspicion" for the exercise of the discretion to interrogate by some police (Dodson, 1991, p.206; refer also to Chapter 9).

It should be noted that police do not perceive themselves as being racist; but then nor do some police regard the application of the term "nigger" to Aboriginal people as racist (Dodson, 1991, p.273). The submission of the West Australian Police Union of Workers (WAPUW) (1990) to the Royal Commission into Aboriginal Deaths in Custody provides further information on police attitudes towards Aboriginal people. The submission divided the Aboriginal population of the state into three groups, according to their 'blood-lines' ('pure and mixed') and lifestyles (WAPUW, 1990, p.5). It was also asserted that there is

> an increasing propensity for [agricultural and urban] Aboriginals to commit assaults of the most viscious [sic] nature on members from any section of society, not confined to [their own] domestic scene.

This was attributed to 'the watering down of the blood line and the loss of traditional life style laws and codes of conduct' (WAPUW, 1990, p.10). Whatever else the submission may show (and it would seem to be factually incorrect - refer Chapter 8), it is in any event indicative that, in direct opposition to many Aboriginal people's self-definitions of Aboriginality, 'blood lines' and hence physical appearance remain important to police.

Race as 'an empty category'?

> I ain't black, I ain't white
> If it comes to blows or fight
> I'll kill the black to save the white
> Hannibal[41]

Rustin claimed that race is an empty category. Its contents are undoubtedly an area of contestation, and will vary dramatically according to time and place. In Trinidad today, Jewish people fit within the racial category of "Syrian"; last century Portuguese people brought as indentured labour to that society were not considered to be white - because of the work they did (Brereton, 1979, p.34); the calypso sung by the mixed race Calypsonian, Hannibal, above, indicates that his allegiance was with 'the white'; Said (1993) states that the British considered white Australians to be an inferior *race*; Australian Aboriginal people of mixed descent today identify differently to how they might have in the past (Gilbert, 1977, pp.203,204).

But although "race" may be an empty category, it has been and remains a powerfully effective one in constituting social relations. To refuse to recognise its existence, because we do not like what it does, does not mean it will go away. More particularly, with reference to common law based legal systems, the "evolution" towards the use of ethnicity in place of "race" tends to understate and occlude the continuing significance of phenotypical differences in the manufacture of criminalised identities. It fails to engage with the issue of how police on the streets might go about identifying those who *appear* suspicious and who they believe require policing; it fails to engage with how judicial officials determine issues of credibility (in relation to the latter, refer, for example, to Ashforth, 1990, p.298). Such an "evolution", moreover, seems part of the denial of the physicality of human practices, including law, in contemporary societies (Taussig, 1993, pp.44,45; Sarat & Kearns, 1991). Hence it also contributes to the marginalisation of those knowledges which are learned other than through academic and discursive engagements, those knowledges which are gained through embodied experience, as has been discussed above.

Notes

1. An explanation of my use of terms such as "colonial" and "colonised" in the contemporary context follows, under the heading 'Colonised Peoples and Cultural Originality'.
2. I am unable here to explore the history of the indigenous peoples of Trinidad in any detail. For an account of the history of the indigenous peoples of the Caribbean, including references to the use of Western law in the oppression of these Amerindian populations, refer to the account of Chief Hilary Frederick, 'The Caribs and Their Colonizers: The Problem of Land' (Frederick, 1993[1981]).
3. Kerruish (1991) critiques the contemporary jurisprudence of (common) law exemplified through the work of Hart, Dworkin and Finnis, in terms of the thesis of "law's innocence", as propounded through their various jurisprudential frameworks. For an account based upon the notion of law as merely reflective of broader social inequality, refer to the *National Report of the Royal Commission into Aboriginal Deaths in Custody* (Aus RCIADIC, 1991a; Purdy, 1992a, 1993).
4. Although Trinidad is now a republic with Tobago, I have not attempted to include a study of Tobago within the framework of this work. The history of Tobago has been significantly different to that of Trinidad, and it continues to manifest a different

racial composition and economy. In the same way, although there are important similarities between the experiences of the Aboriginal peoples of Western Australia and elsewhere, there is also much which has been specific to the political economy of that state.

5. "Tallman" is an Afro-Caribbean man, and one of the many people who generously shared their time and thoughts with me while I worked on this project. The general policy adopted throughout this work with respect to the identification of sources is discussed in Chapter 3, 'An "Organic Intellectual"?'.

6. A discussion of the issues of race and ethnic/racial identity, as used in this work, follows, under the heading 'Ethnic/Racial Identity'.

7. Although by no means accepted by everyone, the contention that the Australian legal system has racist consequences is one for which there is ample evidence; see, for example, Aus RCIADIC (1989c, 1989d, 1990a, 1990b, 1991a); Australian Institute of Criminology (AIC) (1993a); Bird (1987); Bird & O'Malley (1989); Carrington (1989); Cunneen (1990, 1992a, 1992b); Cunneen & Robb (1987); Dodson (1991); Eggleston (1976); Fesl (1989); Kerruish (1991); Reynolds (1992). Although I elaborate on the issue of racism in the legal system of Australia in 'Racism and Law', its existence is essentially a starting point for my thesis. It is whether common law is merely reflective, actively counter to, or actively constitutive of, this racism which concerns me.

8. In this, I differ from Said, who in his *Culture and Imperialism* (1993), assimilates the experience of all colonised peoples, including that of Caribbeans and white Australians. Note, like Fanon (1968[1952], pp.17,18), Morrison (1992a, p.xxv), an African American, emphasises the significance of 'internalizing the master's tongue'.

9. The uncritical identification of colonised peoples with the coloniser and colonial values is illustrated in Fanon's *Black Skin, White Masks* (1968[1952]). Examples cited by Fanon (1968[1952], pp.146-147), include the identification of black Antillean children of African descent with the white explorers portrayed in Western novels, and their dissociation from the black "savages" of "uncivilised" Africa. For a more recent examination of domination by "Western" culture, see Reddock and McCree (1992, p.31; discussed also at note 32, below). Robinson (1993) indicates that such attitudes are more likely to be held by the black or mixed origin national petit-bourgeois of colonised countries. It is important to make clear, however, that not every appropriation of the coloniser's culture by colonised peoples is necessarily co-option. One of the hypocrisies of colonisers is that, unlike their own cultural appropriations and variations, "real" indigenous or colonised people must retain a pristine culture, "unpolluted" by contact with other peoples and changing circumstances. This matter is discussed more fully in the section on 'Colonised Peoples and Cultural Originality'.

10. The "rude boy", amongst a number of other identities including "badjohn" and

"ragamuffin", are part of a Caribbean tradition which extends back at least to the "jamets" and "jamettes" of the nineteenth century; jamet/te being patois and derived from the French "diametre" - an underworld type (Brereton, 1979, p.ix). All of these identities involve elements of being in trouble with the law and being proud of it. Similar influences can be seen in the attitudes of Aboriginal youths who sometimes regard imprisonment as 'almost prestigious' or as a 'status symbol' (Dodson, 1991, p.498; Hoddinott, 1985, p.31).

11. Chanock (1994a, p.299), notes that elites within oppressed groups prefer analysis in terms of ethnic/racial identity to Marxism, as the elites are 'not themselves oppressed in anything but a cultural sense'. Moreover, the Western world is also far more accepting of ethnic assertions than 'revolutionary rhetoric in Marxist terms [which] guaranteed the unacceptability and crushing of a political movement' (Chanock, 1994a, p.299). Note too the comments by Jacobs (1982, p.279), referred to in Chapter 2, note 9.

12. The inquiry I worked for investigated the death of sixteen-year-old John Pat.

13. In 1978, Hartwig (1978, p.105), identified one academic study which utilised a colonial analogy in the context of Aboriginal/white relations in Australia; C.D. Rowley's *Aboriginal Policy and Practice*. Another was Reece's (1974) *Aborigines and Colonists*. Refer to Williams and Chrisman's (1994, pp.3,4), introduction to *Colonial Discourse and Post-Colonial Theory* and Said's (1993) *Culture and Imperialism*, discussed in the section on 'Colonised Peoples and Cultural Originality', for examples of how colonialism in the First World continues to be ignored.

14. Divisions recognised within theories of colonialism themselves, including those between internal and external colonialism and between colonies of extraction and settlement, would also seem to focus principally upon perceptions and experiences of the non-colonised and are therefore not relevant to this study (see Moody, 1993, p.xxix, and 'Colonised Peoples and Cultural Originality').

    That is not to claim that all such distinctions are irrelevant to the colonised. Wolpe recognised three distinctions in his theory of internal colonialism which are likely to have been of profound significance to the colonised. He identifies these distinctions in terms of the relations between capitalist (colonist) and non-capitalist (colonised) modes of production, and states that these may involve the extraction of commodities or the extraction of labour power, in both of which cases the political policy is likely to turn on the domination and preservation of the non-capitalist society. A third instance of economic exploitation will be accompanied by a policy aimed at the destruction of the non-capitalist societies, "liberating" the work force from pre-capitalist modes of production (H. Wolpe, 'The Theory of Internal Colonialism - The South African Case', in I. Oxaal, T. Barnett and D. Booth (eds), *Beyond the Sociology of Development: Economy and Society in Latin America and Africa* (1975), pp.243,250, in Hartwig, 1978, p.129). For examples of the two forms of colonialism in Western Australia, refer to the accounts of Aboriginal workers on the pastoral stations of the north in Marshall (1988), in comparison to the settlement regimes of the south-west, described in Haebich (1992). In any event, however their experiences are classified, the colonised are likely to know colonialism as highly exploitative, violent and destructive.

15. This can be seen in the contrast between the field-work accounts in Chapters 5 and 6. The former, relating to the Trinidadian courts, indicates a far more unambiguous and intense experience than the latter, concerning my field-work in the courts of Western Australia.

16. See, for example, C.L.R. James's (1963[1938], p.51), comment about the abolition of slavery. He suggests that, as British colonies at that time had sufficient slaves for all the trade they were likely to do,

> With tears rolling down their cheeks for the poor suffering blacks, the British bourgeois who had no West Indian interests set up a great howl for the abolition of the slave-trade.

17. In relation to gender specific knowledges, refer to the collection of essays in Jaggar & Bordo (1989).

18. See too, Cain (1994), Fitzpatrick (1989), Sumner (1980a); and discussed further in Chapter 2, 'Marxism and Post-Modernism'.

19. See for example, extracts from that history in Davis' (1989) foreword to *Dying Inside*.

20. Despite the relative absence of published Aboriginal accounts of the history of relations between colonial law and Aboriginal peoples in Western Australia, if data are selected according to the model based upon Caribbean accounts, colonial legal relations are shown to have been as violent and exploitative as elsewhere. So too, the resistance of the colonised peoples of Western Australia has been equally tenacious and the imperatives of legal reasoning and the "good intentions" of colonists equally irrelevant. Note the different perspective available through those documentations of history in Western Australia where authors have been informed by Aboriginal accounts (e.g. Green, 1995; Haebich, 1992; Hawke & Gallagher, 1989).

21. Fanon's description is discussed further in Chapter 2, 'Race and Class'. If the present discussion evinces some slippage between past and present, the contemporary and the historical, that is because history is, to quote Benjamin, 'the subject of a structure whose site is not homogeneous, empty time, but time filled by the presence of the "now"' (Walter Benjamin, 'Theses on the Philosophy of History', *Illuminations* (1969), p. 261, in Taussig, 1993, p.39).

22. E. Williams, *British Historians and the West Indies* (1966), p.233, in Fryer (1988, p.5).
23. C. Fyfe, *Journal of African History*, XVII/1 (1976), p.141, in Fryer (1988, p.5).
24. J. Baldwin, 'No Name in the Street', in *The Price of a Ticket* (1985), p. 513, in Pemberton (1992, p.174).
25. See also Unaipon (1994), for an analysis indicating the continuity between the past and present as it is experienced by some Aboriginal people. Other Aboriginal people expressly adopt the terminology of colonialism; see for example Sam Watson, president of the Aboriginal Legal Service in Brisbane, 'We are Victims of the Legal System' (*Green Left Weekly*, March 16, 1994).
26. R. Robinson, 'Non-European Foundations of European Imperialism: Sketch for a Theory of Collaboration' (1977), in R. Owen and B. Sutcliffe (eds), *Studies in the Theory of Imperialism*, in Said (1993, p.316).
27. For a detailed analysis of the concrete implications of the internationalisation of capitalist production and U.S. economic domination in the Caribbean, refer to Barry, Wood & Preusch (1984), McAfee (1991) and Pantin (1989). This issue is pursued further in Chapter 9. More generally, see Efremov (1986), McClintock (1994) and Watkins (1992).
28. It is true that some Aboriginal communities are now permitted limited autonomy, but, even then, such autonomy as is available is largely conditional upon Aboriginal peoples' adoption of imposed legal forms and segregated lifestyles. The Aboriginal Communities Act 1979 (W.A.) permits Aboriginal peoples, who acquire a corporate identity, to make by-laws in respect to specified matters in relation to their community lands. Their powers do not extend to such matters as control over mining on their land, and therefore do not approach those of sovereignty. Moreover, the premise that Aboriginal autonomy must be conditional upon their segregation has unmistakable resonances with South African bantustanism. I am not here referring to Aboriginal peoples who choose to live in segregated communities, but the legal requirement that they must do so in order to exercise even limited autonomy over their relations internally, with their land or with others. See too Heilpern (1993, p.17), on the issue of the applicability of criminal law to Aboriginal people.
29. As referred to in note 9, Robinson (1993) shows that Fanon's definition was based upon the attitude of the black or mixed origin national petit-bourgeois of colonised countries. In Fanon's later works he clearly identifies these attitudes as belonging to a bourgeoisie which 'has totally assimilated colonialist thought in its most corrupt form' (Fanon, *The Wretched of the Earth* (1968), p.114, in Robinson, 1993, p.83).
30. It is for this reason too, that, in the context of this study, I do not adopt the distinction between indigenous and non-indigenous peoples. Although colonised peoples' ability to maintain links with their land may be of relevance to the experience

of colonialism, it is the imposition of a foreign culture and value systems that has been the focus of my research.

31. 'An Audience with C.L.R. James', in *Third World Book Review* 1, No.2 (1984), in Said (1993, p.300).

32. It does not seem that cultural influences need to be consciously retained in order to persist, and in 1971 James (1984b[1971], p.214), wrote that, as he became increasingly aware that Africa possessed a 'high civilisation',

> I begin to appreciate the civilisation that existed in the Caribbean among the people I knew. They brought it with them from where they came, because they had that civilisation in Africa. (See too, James, 1984c[1975], pp.218-235.)

The culture of Afro- and other Trinidadians continues to draw upon influences from Africa. This exists in overtly African traditions, such as the religious practices of some groups in Trinidad, including Obeah, and the cultural influences evident in Calypso, Steelpan and Carnival (Brereton, 1979; Herskovits & Herskovits, 1964[1947]; Lee, 1991; Liverpool, 1990; Tarradath, 1991). However, it also extends to less conscious retentions of African influence. Allsopp (1971) shows how Caribbean English, which is often considered "bad English", has an African grammatical context, with the format based on African grammar and translated into English (see too, Kurian, 1982, p.1778). Many Indo-Trinidadians now speak a similar African based English, but also draw upon Hindi influences, as well as contributing words and cadences to the whole of the society (see, for example, the dialogue in Ladoo's (1987) *No Pain Like This Body*). Reddock and McCree (1992, pp.30,31) note that it is in the areas of food; of creative arts, including Calypso, Reggae and Steelpan; of religion, including Shango, Pacomania and Rastafari; and of domestic family patterns, that Caribbean Africans have 'manifested adaption, (re)creation and survival most strikingly'.

However, they go on to note the concern in Trinidad and Tobago over the extent to which indigenous and ancestral African cultural forms are accepted generally, but especially amongst those of African descent 'when compared to the greater acceptance and affinity they display for Euro-American cultural forms'. Of particular concern is the apparent necessity for Afro-Caribbean popular culture to receive validation in North America for these cultural forms to 'gain more acceptance in the Caribbean'. Regis has referred to this process as 'cultural domination by re-exportation' (Regis, 'The Theoretical Framework for the Study of Cultural Domination by Re-exportation', in *Caribbean Affairs*, vol.4, no.1, 1991, in Reddock & McCree, 1992, p.31).

In relation to Indo-Trinidadians, Reddock and McCree (1992, p.26), note that Hindus have remained the majority grouping of the Trinidadian Indian population, and the 'core of the Indian intellectual and political leadership', as well as the predominant element of the Indian entrepreneurial class. 'The Indian problematic thus, more often than not, is a Hindu problematic', in spite of the number of Muslim and Christian Indians in Trinidad. Reddock and McCree state that Indo-Trinidadians generally have more successfully resisted assimilation because of 'the greater cultural baggage' that they were allowed to retain during indentureship (Reddock & McCree, 1992, p.26; contra Kurian 1982, p.1777). In relation to the cultural originality of Indo-Trinidadians, there is no doubt that the forms and practices of that culture are being deliberately maintained, in the teaching of Hindi, the maintenance of the Hindu religion (Camejo, 1972), and hybrid adaptions such as Chutney, and the Hosay and Divali festivals (Niehoff & Niehoff, 1960; Singh, 1988; and refer to Misra, 'Learning the Rules of a Culture', *Sunday Express*, September 20, 1992; Hodge, 'Cultural Douglarisation gets Stamp of Approval', *Sunday Mirror*, October 25, 1992) and the retention and dissemination of Indian cuisine.

Aboriginal peoples have maintained cultural originality in their system of kinship relations and obligations, their spirituality and relations with land, their artistic and musical forms; some have retained their own languages and others have reinvented these in the form of Kriol (e.g. Bropho, 1992; Dodson, 1991; Mudrooroo, 1992[1965]).

33. The issue of class stratification within colonised communities is discussed further in Chapter 2, 'Race and Class'.

34. This strategy is not one which is purely hypothetical; refer to Fryer (1988) and his suggestion that "clines" be used in place of "race", as if this will somehow resolve the problem of racism.

35. Quoted in Morrison (1992a, p.ix). Note that the articles in the Morrison collection, all of which were written by African American authors, consistently utilise race as a relevant category of differentiation, although with reservations.

36. I adopt the term "common value" not in the sense of being a value accepted by everyone, as it was used by Braithwaite, but instead as meaning that the value is accepted by some and imposed on others; a position shared with the pluralist interpretation of social "consensus" (Smith, 1991). As I hope to show, one institution which traditionally has imposed this "common value", through the legitimised use of force, has been the criminal justice system. See too the comments of LaGuerre (1988, pp.198,206).

37. For example, Omowale explains the differential impact of the economic policies of "structural adjustment" on Afro- and Indo-Trinidadians in terms of persisting occupational segregation of the Trinidadian working class along racial/ethnic lines (*Sunday Mirror*, September 6, 1992). See too, Kurian (1982, p.1777).

38. My experience of contemporary social stratification in Trinidad extended beyond that which was apparent in the courts. Although the issue of stratification on the

basis of phenotypical features was rarely discussed in the newspapers, for example, the language of stratification was incorporated into everyday speech, as is noted in Chapter 5. During the time I spent in Trinidad, I met people who were of African appearance who attributed their origins to other racial backgrounds; who stated that their dark skin was the result of a suntan; that they would be white if they lived in Australia. I was told of a woman who invited a friend to feel the skin texture of her baby, who was of a lighter complexion than herself, saying that the child's skin "was good"; that is, not like her own. Hair straightening was wide-spread amongst women of African descent, and skin bleaching was also common amongst both Afro- and Indo-Trinidadian women. One Indo-Trinidadian told me of an example of stratification amongst his own community, which he attributed to Hindu caste prejudice. It concerned the parents of a family who referred to one of their children, who was darker complexioned, as "Blackie", and favoured and spent money on the child's lighter coloured siblings. I was also told of a phenotypically black Indian who made derogatory comments about "blacks" to a white acquaintance.

I did raise the subject of phenotypical stratification with Trinidadians, generally only after I knew them well, given that I was white and foreign. I was told by some that there was no racism in Trinidad; and, by others, that stratification was complex and could occur on the basis of race, colour, money and social background as well as varying according to whether you knew someone in the relevant circles (i.e. in court matters, if you knew a police officer or lawyer). Still others confirmed my observations of phenotypical discrimination, although frequently such differentiation was interpreted in economic terms, it being asserted that blacker people were poorer. Generally in Trinidad, Afro/Indo discrimination dominated notions of what constituted racism (discussed further at Chapter 3, 'An "Organic Intellectual"?'); and although people were aware of stratification on the basis of colour, hair and skin texture, this often did not seem to be regarded as racism, but as some form of "classism". This is discussed further below. But in any event, it seemed to me that much of the Indo/Afro racialism of Trinidad was constituted within the framework of Braithwaite's (1975[1953], p.138), 'common value of "ethnicity" and colour'; that is, it was associated with notions of the superiority of phenotypical characteristics which resembled those of "whites".

39. Data on the relation between race/ethnicity and economic position in Trinidad are difficult to obtain, particularly since independence. Such statistics as I have been able to locate support the thesis of the relatively recent ascension of Indo-Trinidadians in the socioeconomic structure of Trinidad (Camejo, 1972, p.117; Craig, 1982, p.402; Harewood & Henry, 1985, pp.64,65,74,75). Omowale also points to working class Indo-Trinidadians' access to land as a major economic resource which has not been available to many working/under-class Afro-Trinidadians who tend to be urban (and ghetto) dwellers (*Sunday Mirror*, September 6, 1992).

40. As a white Australian, however, it may be that it is simply less apparent to me.

41. Hannibal, a Trinidadian Calypsonian of mixed background, lived during the second half of the nineteenth century. This quote is taken from Brereton (1979, p.104).

PART I
THEORY, METHODOLOGY AND ALL THAT

Outline of Part I

In an interview conducted in 1992, Edward Said commented,

> Theory has become a substitute. From my perspective, theory is really not interesting as a subject in and of itself - to write endlessly refined accounts of some theory or other. ... It has become an academic pursuit of its own. And I am totally impatient with it... The question of oppression, of racial oppression, the question of war, the question of human rights - all these issues ought to belong together with the study of literacy and other forms of texts; as opposed to the massive, intervening, institutionalised presence of theoretical discussion. (Quoted in Beezer & Osborne, 1993, p.26)

The problem with theory is that it seems impossible to give anything other than some endlessly refined account of it. Issues of theory, and related explanations, debates and justifications proliferate; once amongst the internecine debates found in "the literature" it becomes difficult to address anything else. This difficulty is compounded if, as in this work, it is the limits of theory itself which are at issue. Following Michael Taussig's (1993, p.45) discussion of Hegel, 'the present task [is] the very opposite of what he took to have been the task of the earliest epochs, namely "getting the individual clear of the stage of sensuous immediacy"'.

Reliance on theory for the acquisition of knowledge is not mandatory. To quote an Aboriginal man, Gary Murray,

> Some time ago we did a survey of our people. But it was not like an academic would do it. We actually lived the conditions that they were living in. (Quoted in Gilbert, 1977, p.66)

An alternative avenue for the acquisition of knowledge is "sensuous immediacy" - lived experience or practice. That is not to dismiss the importance of theoretical, methodological and other issues when conducting research. Certainly this work is very much the product of my own theoretical and methodological orientations, and these are elaborated upon below. Although based upon Marxism, feminist theory and "scientific realism"(Kerruish, 1991, pp.26-35), however, this work has also been significantly influenced by Caribbean and Aboriginal authors and activists as well as my practice while conducting research.

Part I is therefore concerned to elaborate upon the issues of theory and methodology raised by my research and thesis, so that the project attempted in the following chapters, if not uncontentious, will at least be accessible. More than this, however, Part I is also an attempt to bring to bear the issues raised by Caribbean and Aboriginal authors and activists, as well as my own practice, on matters of theory and methodology.

2 Theory

They got so much things to say right now
They got so much things to say...
So don't you forget no way
Who you are and where you stand in the struggle...
They got so very much to say
They sayin' everything
They say so much today.
Bob Marley[1]

REALISM

Realism, or at least the variety which I utilise in this work, draws upon the materialist philosophy of Marxism (Kerruish, 1991, p.29), was expanded upon in the context of feminist research (e.g. Cain, 1986b) and posits a basic ontology of inter-personal relations. These relations are defined by Maureen Cain (1986b, p.259), as intransitive; that is, as existing 'whether or not they are present to the minds of those involved'. In other words, we engage in these relations whether we know, intend or believe that we are or not. Kerruish (1991, pp.30-32), extends Cain's (1986b, p.259), 'enduring' relationships which configure around class and sex/gender structures, to include those of ethnicity/race. These structures are seen as being constituted by persisting patterns of relationships which are articulated but not reducible to each other. Moreover, although these structures and patterns appear always to have existed, this is not regarded as necessarily so (Cain, 1986b, p.260).

The realist ontology has certain implications for epistemology; what and how we can know about the social world. These implications principally turn on the historicity of knowledge. That is, not only are the relationships and knowledges one observes historical, but also the observer is her or himself involved in a historical process. The latter has two implications which are of particular importance for the researcher. The first is that researchers '*speak from a site* in the social structure' (Cain, 1986b, p.260); that is, the concepts and knowledge that are available to them will depend upon who (and when) they are.

Another epistemological implication is the requirement of reflexivity from the researcher, both in relation to theory as well as personally; a position long advocated amongst feminist methodologists (Cain, 1986b, p.260). Basically, reflexivity requires that researchers interrogate their own standpoint and the limitations consequent upon this; or as Bob Marley might have put it, researchers must seek to know who they are and where they stand in the struggle.

John Watson, an Aboriginal man and one-time chairman and executive officer of the Kimberley Land Council, commented in his introduction to the collection of Aboriginal drovers' stories in *Raparapa*,

> Someone read me a book once which had been written by a kartiya [white] drover. I don't know how many years he drove cattle for, but he had written the book to suit himself. Although he always had nine or ten Aboriginal drovers working with him, they didn't get much of a story, or much of a say, in his book. There were about 20 pages of Aboriginal story out of the 240 pages in the book. That made me very sad. (Watson, 1988, p.ix)

My adoption of realist theory means that criticisms such as that by Watson must be taken seriously. Assertions of objectivity do not negate, and in fact may compound, our tendency to write in ways which 'suit' ourselves. It is of note, therefore, that in the context of my research the application of realist theory is somewhat unusual. It is not utilised as a basis upon which to establish my authority to speak, as, for example, a woman might if she were conducting feminist research. In this project, situating myself on the basis of realist epistemology means that my work not only must be informed by those who are located so as to speak from a position on the down-side of racism and colonialism, but also indicates that I do not and cannot speak in place of such people.

The absence of a dogmatic and authoritative "voice" in this work is therefore a consequence of my theoretical position. It does not mean that I know less than other white academics who work in this area and write authoritatively of what colonised peoples think and do. As Said's (1991) *Orientalism* illustrates, the authority claimed by academics and others for their depictions of "other" peoples has often had little to do with their accuracy and more to do with their complicity in colonialist usurpation. See, for example, the following critique of Sania Hamaday's work.

> Verbs like "demonstrate", "reveal", "show" are used without an indirect object... This is another way of saying that these truths are self-evident only to a privileged or initiated observer...the Arabs have been totally transformed from people into no more than the putative subject of Hamaday's style. The Arabs exist only as an occasion for the tyrannical observer: "The world is *my*

idea". (Said, 1991, p.310)

Practice

The need for 'reflexivity', in relation to both my personal position and my theory, was reinforced in practice by both the reaction to my field-work and the differences between the locations in which I conducted research. To interpret and render my position in terms of a non-reflexive "observer" would be a blatant falsification of the research I conducted. Unlike Trinidad, however, where other factors were also relevant and which are discussed below, in Western Australia this seemed to relate significantly to my choice of methodology.

For reasons which I set out below, I intended to attend the magistrates' courts without notifying or seeking the permission of court officials. This is legitimate under common law doctrine because the courts are considered to be open to the public; and in fact common law systems greatly emphasise the virtues of their public nature. My intention was therefore to attend the courts as an "anonymous observer", partly because I did not wish to skew the proceedings through court officials' knowledge of the nature of my research. More crucially, however, I did not wish to view the legal proceedings from the position of these "insiders", the court officials, but was seeking to gain some understanding of the experience of court for "outsiders", defendants in particular. And defendants are rarely taken into the confidence of court officials or associate with them on a basis of equality.

Interestingly, it was precisely this attempt to neutralise any impact I may have had on the conduct of the proceedings, and my attempt to distance myself from court officials, which not only made me highly visible in the courts, but which also had a marked influence on the behaviour of officials. My interactions with these officials are documented below, but it is of note here that it was at least in part due to the fact that I did not clearly fit within the power structures of the courts that my role as "observer" proved unattainable. It seemed likely that, had I sought the permission of the officials prior to attending court, many of these interactions would have been avoided, and my own particular effectivity as a player in the court "drama" could more easily have been overlooked.

It is also of interest to note that the "invisibility" of the neutral observer of social relations, who is thereby enabled to avoid any reflexivity as to her or his own role in what is being observed, may in fact be associated with a willingness, or necessity, to conform to the power structures which the researcher is seeking to investigate. Even ignoring the biases inherent to one's own standpoint, the need to negotiate with those in control undermines the possibility of conducting "neutral" research.

In Trinidad, there were additional reasons for adopting a reflexive approach to my research; one being the nature of Trinidadian society itself or, perhaps more accurately, how that society appeared to be to me. That society, or at least the circles in which I moved, struck me as being far more participatory than (non-Aboriginal) Western Australian society. Perhaps oddly, it is a quote from a tract written by Friedrich Engels in 1844 that seems to me to capture the nature of Western Australian society in contrast to that of Trinidad.

> And still they crowd by one another as though they had nothing in common, nothing to do with one another, and their only agreement is the tacit one, that each keep to his own side of the pavement, so as not to delay the opposing streams of the crowd, while it occurs to no man to honour another with so much as a glance. The brutal indifference, the unfeeling isolation of each in his private interest becomes the more repellent and offensive, the more these individuals are crowded together, within a limited space... The dissolution of mankind into monads, of which each one has a separate principle and a separate purpose, the world of atoms, is here carried out to its utmost extreme. (Engels, 1973[1845], p.60)

In Trinidad, there was a general acknowledgment of people on the streets, strangers spoke, recognition and assistance were offered as a matter of course.[2] The differences between the Trinidadian and Western Australian societies were profound of themselves, but they also have implications for theory and methodology. The notion of being an "observer" in the sense that this term is used elsewhere is quite alien and strange in the context of Trinidadian social relations. Failing to acknowledge one's personal position and participation in that society would be overtly false.

The notion that someone *could be* a neutral observer of social relations is a concept that would seem to be more easily accepted in "Western" societies. That is not to say that the neutral observer is a reality in these societies, only that it may be easier to imagine that one is having no impact on the people who are the "objects" of one's study. Nor is it to say that the fictional nature of the neutral observer of social relations is unknown in such societies. Indeed, Condorcet, writing in 1782, stated that the study of the physical, organic and human worlds would be identical in principle only

> for a being who, as a stranger to our race, studied human society as we study the beaver and the bee... But here the observer is part of the society he observes, and truth can only be judged, imprisoned or bribed.[3]

My unfamiliarity with Trinidad also mandated that I adopt a reflexive approach to my theoretical framework. Much that is taken for granted about one's own society needs to be learnt in another society. It would require an inordinately closed mind, or extraordinary perspicacity, to live in a different society for an extensive period and not to have learned anything new. Moreover, rightly or wrongly, interpreting the behaviour of people who share a similar background to one's own is less contentious than interpreting the behaviour of peoples whose history and ethnicity is, in many ways, different.

As mentioned above, critiques such as Said's *Orientalism* (1991) indicate something of the arrogance of researchers who have imposed their interpretations upon "other" peoples, in addition to their usefulness to colonialist projects. Responsiveness to local understandings is required, as is restraint. This is not because other peoples are "inscrutable", "mysterious" or "alien", but because to do otherwise is to be guilty of the shamelessness of which Aboriginal people accuse their white "experts" (Dodson, 1991, p.355). It is also to take refuge in the mythology of value neutral knowledge.

Standpoint

The need for reflexivity and particularly consciousness of my own standpoint and the limitations that were consequent upon it were the result of both my theory and practice. Standpoint, however, need not be absolutely restrictive. Kerruish (1991, pp.31-33), notes that despite the intransitivity of relationships there is some choice as to one's place within these relationships. For example, a woman may choose to adopt the way of life of the white male elite, even while her position remains configured around the basic sex/gender structure. Adopting such a lifestyle, however, entails

> engaging in various social practices which, having a conventional and institutional character have a tendency or purpose which is characteristic of the practice itself. (Kerruish, 1991, p.32)

In this way individuals may become constituted as agents for one or other of the groups designated by basic social relations - even if they themselves are not members of that group and do not intend to further its interests. In this sense the non-white operatives within common law systems may reproduce a racism based on the superiority of white races and ethnicities, whatever their motivation in entering the legal system may have been. That is not to dismiss the efforts of such people; only to indicate something of the limitations by which they are constrained.

The possibility of becoming agents for groups other than one's own, however, is not restricted to acting in the interests of dominant groups and classes. Kerruish (1991, p.34), describes this as 'both the personal and the political challenge of standpoint...the ongoing process of finding ways of making and sharing standpoints with others'. Implicit to this challenge is the requirement of consciousness of standpoint and its ramifications; the most relevant here being that reason and knowledge are never value neutral, but are always relative to standpoint. This entails that others' knowledges and one's own research are not value free but will be effective in the interests of particular groups, whether intended or not. As James Duncan (1993, p.39) notes, no discourse reveals the naked truth, but 'operates in the service of power'. Because all knowledge is regarded as relative, this raises contention over the purpose of a social institution, such as the common law, the espoused objective of which is class, sex/gender and ethnic/racial "blindness". To be more precisely within the realist framework, the issue becomes one of ascertaining for whom such a "blindness" is useful (see Kerruish, 1991). Be that as it may, if the idea of value neutral or "blind" knowledge is rejected, it follows that research is conducted on the basis that it will be open in its commitment to the interests of a particular group, and that such research must be informed by the knowledges of members of that group.

It was because I am conscious of the limitations of my own and other white academics' standpoint that this work deliberately engages with the work of authors and activists other than those who are usually recognised in white academic circles as "authorities" in the area of racism and law. Moreover, as there is little black academic analysis of colonial institutions in Australia (given the very recent acceptance of Aboriginal peoples' entitlement to Western education; and see Huggins, 1990), my analysis tends to be influenced by Caribbean rather than Australian academic work. Although this may be interpreted as a lack of balance in my work, my theoretical framework would suggest that accounts of colonialism by Caribbean writers are likely to be more relevant to Aboriginal perspectives than those of white Western academics.

A Collective Understanding

As indicated in Chapter 1, the object of my research was the historical and continuing relationship between the common law and colonialism; specifically, the contribution of criminal law towards the manufacture of racist stereotypes in Trinidad and Western Australia. The object of my research therefore was the legal system and not so much people of colour; although I hoped that my research would be *for* such peoples, in the sense of being useful to them.

It is important to note, however, that the legal system does not exist in a vacuum, and is constituted by relations between people. Given that my concern was how these relationships affected people of colour in the colonial context, my work, of necessity, includes discussion with and about colonised peoples. It is therefore drawn, not only from their academic texts, but from more populist sources, including song lyrics and poetry, newspaper reports[4] and many personal discussions. While I have remained conscious of criticisms such as those of Aboriginal people referred to above, who say of non-Aboriginal "experts" on Aborigines, 'they no shame' (Dodson, 1991, p.355), I am also aware of the comment of Fanon (1968[1952], p.86),

> I sincerely believe that a subjective experience can be understood by others; and it would give me no pleasure to announce that the black problem is my problem and mine alone and that it is up to me to study it.

The attempt to reach a "common understanding" about law which is evinced in this research was based on a premise of learning from colonised people, rather than about them. Such learning included engaging with the theoretical frameworks which are the products of colonised communities; at least those frameworks which I was able to incorporate as part of '...the ongoing process of finding ways of making and sharing standpoints with others' (Kerruish, 1991, p.34). This has meant that my adoption of colonised peoples' interpretations has not been categorical. I discuss this matter further below, after I establish the framework which I have utilised in order to avoid the limitations consequent upon adopting any essentialist position on ethnicity/race.

RACE AND CLASS

A 'slightly stretched' Marxism

C.L.R. James (1963[1938], p.283), the Afro-Trinidadian activist and essayist, wrote,

> The race question is subsidiary to the class question in politics, and to think of imperialism in terms of race is disastrous. But to neglect the racial factor as merely incidental is an error only less grave than to make it fundamental.

I return to the practical application of this statement in Chapter 9; here I am concerned to discuss its theoretical implications. There are two matters raised by this statement with which contemporary theorists are likely to take issue. First is the use of the concept of "race", which has been addressed previously. The other issue likely to be taken is with the Marxian slant of James' assertion, which places primary significance on what he refers to as 'the class question'. One influential source of these latter objections is the critiques of structuralism - in particular post-modernist deconstruction.

The tendency of James' analysis of the politics of imperialism is towards economic reductionism; that is, race is regarded by James as being subsidiary to 'the class question' in this context. Robert Ross states, however, that not even hierarchical theories of race were 'merely some knee-jerk reaction to the needs of the capitalist world system'. Racism, although fundamentally flawed, was 'an intellectual formulation of some cogency and consistency', and had some degree of independent existence (Ross, 1982a, pp.2,3). (van Arkel's (1982) study, for example, indicates that European anti-Semitism, historically, was not invariably associated with the economic exploitation of Jewish people.)

Moreover, Rhoda Reddock and Roy McCree (1992, p.40), in their analysis of stratification in the Caribbean, write of

> the need for a proper overhaul or refashioning of the traditional theoretical and methodological approaches to explaining the nature, structure and dynamics of society... In this refashioning process, a primordial task is to recognise the independence and interdependence of race, class and gender as they articulate and disarticulate within and across differing historical conjunctures to shape/reshape human action and interaction.

In the inter-racial and ethnic imperial legal relations within Trinidad and Western Australia, however, I think that James' interpretation retains much cogency. The principal motivation of British colonisation of both Trinidad and Western Australia was economic; that is, the exploitation and appropriation of the labour, bodies and/or resources of the colonised.[5] And there is significant evidence that there remained an economic imperative to much (but not all) of the subsequent legal relations.

James is not alone amongst Caribbean writers in placing emphasis on the significance of economic relations in the colonial context. Like James, Frantz Fanon (1990)[1961], Aimé Césaire (1972)[1955], Eric Williams (1961)[1944], Susan Craig (1982a; 1988) and William Riviere (1971a), also utilise a strongly, albeit sophisticated,[6] Marxian framework in their analyses of inter-ethnic/racial relations between white and other peoples as mediated through colonial institutions.

That is not to reduce race to class, and beyond the influence of imperial politics the significance of economic relations may well be articulated differently. That ethnic/racial heritage and identity go far beyond economics can be seen in the spirituality and cultural values of many Trinidadian and Aboriginal peoples. One of the major conflicts affecting Aboriginal people today is precisely the dominant white class's inability to recognise the significance of (other peoples') land beyond its value as an economic commodity.

It is of note, however, that Aboriginal activists and writers also often interpret their oppression in terms of economic exploitation and marginalisation. Karen Moran (1993b), whose people, the Bundjalung, suffer the effects of labouring in and living near the asbestos mines of Baryulgil in New South Wales, is explicit in defining the struggle of her people for medical assistance and compensation as part of a class action. Helen Boyle, described as 'a leading Aboriginal activist', also identifies herself as a socialist and expressly analyses the position of Aboriginal people in terms of class structure, although she too notes the specificity of racist and sexist contexts in Aboriginal/white relations in Australia. Boyle cautions, however, that her approach is not common and that any 'Black person with socialist views, [is] still regarded with a lot of suspicion and [is] sometimes written off' by many Aboriginal people (quoted in Cole, 1986, p.28). Be that as it may, still other Aboriginal writers clearly interpret their relations with imperial nations and peoples, and the mediating colonial institutions, as being constructed in a context dominated by economic exploitation even if they do not utilise an explicit class analysis (Bropho, 1992; Dodson, 1991; Yunupingu, 1987).

Following the analysis of imperial politics by a number of colonised people, my position was also that 'the question of class' could not be ignored. Yet this coalescence of ethnicity/race and class would seem to be incompatible with the realist framework. Cain (1986b, p.261), writes that, 'One knows from a site in the social structure which is intransitive ... and it is *not possible to see or know from two quite different sites at once*.' However, Cain (1986b, p.256), also cautions that a researcher's subjective belief in the purpose of her or his study is not sufficient to define the character of that research.

> [N]ot anyone can do research which they subjectively believe will help women and that as a result it will be feminist. Women have suffered from men and non-feminist women "proving" that this, that or the other is for our good. So it is still necessary that the research should arise from an emerging collective understanding, achieved and disseminated by regular encounters and meetings with other women going in the same direction.

Although my methodology was significantly different to that recommended by Cain (discussed below), the aim of a 'collective understanding' was one to which I adhered. And it seems to me that Caribbean positions on theory often assert the possibility, indeed the necessity, of utilising the knowledges gained from all three structures at once but, particularly in the context with which I am dealing, from both the class and ethnic/race structures.

While Cain (1986b, p.261), allows that there can be alliances between disadvantaged people, for example women and the working class, she views such alliances as a matter of politics, and meaningless as epistemology. However, as Kerruish (1991, p.27) notes, realist and relational theory does not deny the being and significance of individuals, although it insists that individuals cannot be comprehended in abstraction from relations with nature and each other. Therefore, it seems to me that relational theory allows recognition that, although the sites of seeing and knowing may be in different social structures, the seer or knower is always the same: the embodied individual. And once the role of the embodied individual is acknowledged, the individual who always already occupies positions in structures of ethnicity/race, sex/gender and class, knowledges may be difficult to categorise.

To divide knowledges according to the three structures either ignores that some members of the working class are also women and/or of colour; that some people of colour are also women and/or upper class, and so on; or it assumes that people indefatigably define correctly the nature of the knowledge claimed. But the need to be cautious in making categorical distinctions between the sorts of knowledge being claimed is particularly significant if one accepts the intransitive nature of one's position in these relationships. As is indicated by Claudia Brodsky La Cour (1992) for example, *white middle class* women have often dominated feminist politics, as black *men* have dominated racial politics. The marginalisation of black women from the politics of feminism and race has been the result of a failure to concretise categories such as "woman" or "black" by the more dominant elements within these categories. In the same way, difficulties with essentialist politics have also been highlighted in Australia by Aboriginal and other women who have pointed to the exclusion of Aboriginal women because their specificity as black women has been omitted from the politics of race and feminism (Atkinson, 1990, 1991; Carrington, 1993; Payne, 1990; Pettmen, 1992; Scutt, 1990).

In this context it is important to move beyond the notion of people as seers and knowers, to one which also encompasses people as actors in a historical process. It is this, it seems to me, which relates to Caribbean theoretical positions which assert the necessity of amplification between sites in different social structures. In that society, the division between the seers/knowers and activists is not institutionalised as in other societies. Very often Caribbean theorists have been noted "activists"; refer, for example, to the biographical notes on James, Fanon and Césaire (James, 1984a, pp.1-4,221-236).

In any event, given the nature of Trinidadian society, theorists are less likely to perceive themselves and others as simply seers and knowers. This point relates to the issue raised earlier of the fallacy of the "neutral observer"; all, including "observers", are participants in human society. And from the perspective of the individual seer/knower/participant, from which truth can only be 'judged, imprisoned or bribed', the neat academic distinctions which would categorise to whom this truth belongs become artificial. When women contributed to the killing of the police officer, King, at the beginning of the Trinidad riots of 1937, were they acting on the knowledge learnt as women, as people of colour or as members of the working class?[7]

That is not to deny that the knowledges gained and practices pursued from all of these sites may be incompatible. Certainly, as Said notes, the womens' and union movements have not always sought to act in the interests of non-white peoples (Said, 1993, pp.62,268; with respect to unions, see also Russell, 1944). But it is equally the case that the notion that there is any 'necessary' connection between members who occupy the same site indicated by any one of the three identified social structures would appear to be persuasive only at a fairly abstract and unactualised level (contra Cain, 1986, p.261); a level at which the reality of the oppression of black women and/or the black working class is evaded.[8]

In the Caribbean, Craig has critiqued political movements and theoretical positions because of their exclusivism. She explains the inadequacy of the Black Power Movement in Trinidad during the 1970s, for example, as being the result of the need of a 'clearer analysis of the relationships between race and class... even though we accept... the irreducible fact of racial oppression in the society' (Craig, 1982a, p.168).[9] Craig (1982a, pp.169,170), notes that 'particularly for the Caribbean' the racial factor is not reducible to class; she also states that, 'Sexual oppression, as a major axis of social cleavage, and as an important component of the mode of production, must be brought into the analysis'. Craig (1982a, p.170) continues, however, that there is a need for a conception that poses the

> insertion of the Caribbean into the world capitalist system, the structure of production and of class formation, as well as the inter-relationship between all this and the systematic ways in which racial oppression/assertion is instituted in the process of production and distribution.

While acknowledging the irreducible significance of race and sex, Craig therefore also maintains the necessity of linking such factors to economic relations.

It is also the case that, in Caribbean literature, the hermeneutics of a

Marxian class based analysis has extended beyond the racial and ethnic relations between colonised peoples and their colonisers. It has also been applied to the internal relations between people of colour within the colonial context to fracture racial and ethnic identity along class lines (Cohen, 1981; Fanon, 1990[1961]; Jacobs, 1982; James, 1980b[1961]; Singh, 1988; Taddarath, 1991; and see too Robinson, 1993).

Such an analysis is rarely explicit amongst Aboriginal people. It is of note, however, that, although not always expressly in terms of class, similar divisions are recognised by a number of Aboriginal activists and writers. For example, Robert Bropho (1980, p.108), writes of the dangers of 'educated young blacks', and 'gift-of-the-gab brain-washed Aboriginal people who work for government departments'; Patrick Dodson (1991, pp.669,674,682,780,781), writes of the lack of representation of "grassroots" Aboriginal people by government appointed black spokesmen and women; Karen Moran speaks of the black bureaucrats who refuse to conduct meetings seated on the ground, according to Aboriginal customary practice, because they would dirty their suits (Moran, public lecture, December 4, 1993). Perhaps most acute of all is the following comment by 'A Ngarrindjeri Aboriginal Caring Woman', Amelia Stella Campbell "Unaipon" (1994),

> There is a secret war being run behind closed doors and against the uneducated and poor Ngarrindjeri Aboriginal People. This is not a war against ignorance, poverty, disease or neglect and want. It is the hidden killing of the harmless and defenceless by a hardened army of heartless Aboriginal hired hands, whose intentions may be good but whose actions are totally unacceptable. ...Australian governments are in the business of destroying all grass-roots Aboriginal people. The war plan is simple and cunning. Just get enough Aboriginal educated people to become black traitors to their own grassroots in killing off their own people by becoming the hard face and sharp edge of the new massacre policy of divide and bury.

In summary, a Marxian framework, albeit a 'slightly stretched' one (Fanon, 1990[1961], p.31) as indicated in Chapter 1, is often expressly adopted in Caribbean literature concerning both internal and external relations in the colonial context. Such a framework, although not always explicit amongst Aboriginal authors and activists, is consistent with much of their interpretation of Aboriginal history since white imperial intervention, with respect to both their relations with their colonisers and contemporary divisions within their own communities.[10]

Similarly, my utilisation of a (stretched) Marxian framework extends beyond my analysis of relations between the colonists and the colonised to my understanding of the internal relations within communities of colonised peoples. Therefore my research was not conducted on the basis of an undifferentiated essentialism revolving around the issue of ethnicity/race, and any 'collective understanding' I attained related to particular factions amongst colonised peoples.[11]

This 'collective understanding' was constituted by and a product of my own alignment, not with an undifferentiated "people of colour", but with the working and under-classes of Aboriginal and Trinidadian peoples. Moreover, it is of note that, in the colonial context, where ethnicity/race and class often coalesce, these classes tend to consist also of those who physically or ethnically least resemble their colonisers, those who are not the 'essentially white, near white or subjectively white elements who imbibe colonial character traits, institutional forms and behaviour patterns' (Jacobs, 1982, p.277).

Marxism and Post-Modernism

They think what we know,
is just what they teach us,
that we're so ignorant,
every time they can reach us...
Bob Marley

The strong structuralist and Marxian elements apparent or at least resonant with much of the Caribbean and Aboriginal analyses of historical and existing social relations do not easily conform to current Western trends towards deconstruction and particularly post-modernism. It should be pointed out, however, that the theoretical position of post-modernism is apparently one which is based upon the abandonment of the project of modernity. That is, post-modernism is a rejection of the notion of history as a serial development (Docherty, 1990). Given this premise it would be self-contradictory (perhaps post-modernists would prefer ironic?), to regard Caribbean and other peoples' understandings of their own society as "passé" or inadequate because it utilises what is regarded by many as an outdated theoretical framework (see, too, McClintock, 1994). Moreover, such an attitude would undoubtedly be complicit in the colonialist project of viewing Third World and other colonised peoples as somehow trapped by a retarded development in which they are *always* striving to reach the standards of the West, but *always* never attaining them.

Instead, it is my contention that there is a specificity to legal relations in colonial contexts which is not captured by others' analyses. It is not denied that colonised peoples do, for example, resort to the imposed legal system for their own purposes, much in the way metropolitan working class groups do and as has been documented by Stuart Hall et al (1978) (refer also to Chapters 5, 6 and 8). Moreover, Ivar Oxaal (1975) comments on the limitations of theories which posit the distinctiveness of colonial societies to the extent that class analysis is abandoned. Nevertheless, the character of relations between colonised peoples and the common law system would seem to be distinct from other working class peoples' relations with law.

James (1980c[1964], p.154) states that the expatriate character of the Caribbean has meant that all the 'old problems' seem posed in new terms which are easily grasped. These new terms relate to the way in which the 'old problems' are not dominated, as in the older countries, 'by long established growths and accretions'. Most West Indians had no part in the parliamentary political tradition until the 1940s (James, 1980b[1961], pp.132,133); only from the 1920s were West Indian peoples (mis)educated (to use James' term) by imperialist governments (James, 1980d[1966], p.189).

Eboe Hutchful (1986, pp.166,167), also comments that 'peripheral states' do not have the developed civil societies found in Western countries. With the 'absence of a hegemonic class capable of functions of cultural domination in relation to, but independently of, the state', the state assumes a role which is diametrically opposed to civil society. Accumulation in the colonies and former colonies, notes Hutchful, occurs under conditions of imperialism. The expansion of capital in these circumstances was said by Marx to be accompanied by a particular level of violence, unmediated by the claim of capital to "natural reason" (Hutchful, 1986, pp.156,157). Popular attempts to institute reform of these peripheral societies continue to be met with violence and oppression by internal elites, or overt economic and military intervention by Western powers, in ways which would not be tolerated in Western nations.

Specifically in terms of the legal system, Francis Snyder and Douglas Hay (1987, pp.12,30-32), state that differences in the legitimacy of law is 'one of the most striking contrasts between the First and the Third Worlds'. They note that, in its indigenous context, English law historically was either a useful or at least neutral institution for all classes; alternatively, it defused and confused class consciousness 'in a society with ancient traditions of juries, independent high court judges and even magistrates who refused for much of the early-modern period to be identified with capital'. In the colonial context, however, colonial law was perceived at least initially as wholly imposed. It not only lacked a basis in local culture, but also was comprised almost completely of authoritarian elements with provisions regarding social welfare, basic rights and other entitlements largely excised. The ideology of the rule of law in such a context plays only a limited role.

James, Hutchful, Snyder and Hay all indicate the specificity of the colonial experience in the Third World (see too the comments of Fanon, Mahabir and Calathes discussed in Chapter 1). It does not require an extensive knowledge of Aboriginal history since white intervention to realise that it could equally be described as posing old problems in new and easily graspable terms; as consisting of unmediated violence; as having little to do with an ideology of the rule of law. If colonised peoples assert that their historical and contemporary relations with their colonisers can be understood in terms of defined structures, and dominated by economic exploitation, they would seem to have good reason.

'They got so much things to say'

It may be, too, that the structures imposed upon colonial societies have not "dissolved" in the same way that has been the case in Western societies because of the attitudes of many colonised peoples. As is developed further below, there seems often to be a refusal to take seriously elite discourses. This attitude has no doubt been born of centuries of enslavement, indentureship, killing, torture, kidnapping, the decimation of families and kinship, attempted cultural obliteration, imprisonment, and institutionalisation - all *said* to be carried out in the best interests of its victims.

In assuming the same attitude towards elite discourses as such colonised peoples, my position may be seen as running contrary to 'what can be taken as read'. That is,

> of course, the sociologist must listen to everyone, because it is now a commonplace that *actors' understandings of and reasons for what they do are intrinsic to the action* and plainly it would not be possible to understand what lawyers do without taking account of what lawyers think, or of what police officers do without understanding their ideology. (Cain, 1986b, p.263; emphasis added)

It seems to me, however, that this privileging of actors' subjectivity as intrinsic to the action is mistaken; subjectivity may be intrinsic to understanding lawyers and police (or anyone else), but there is no reason why it should be regarded as intrinsic *to their actions*; that is, to what they do.

In terms of the previous discussion of realist theory, this issue is associated with the notion of a relational ontology and standpoint. Actions are interpersonal; police arrest, lawyers prosecute or defend and magistrates judge - *others*. And while these actors' motivations and understandings may well be relevant to their moral culpability, or how one can seek to work within their ideology to change or explain their position, the actor can provide only one of many interpretations of what she or he does. The researcher's decision regarding who to listen to when attempting to understand such actions will be dependent upon the nature of the project being undertaken.

My own project was one of attempting to understand something of the position of people who are subject to police and lawyers' actions.[12] And these people, the defendants, criminals and prisoners, are routinely denied knowledge of the actors' personal ideologies and motives. And yet can it be said that the rebellious slaves of Trinidad in 1809 had no understanding of what their gaolers were doing when they were whipped and tortured because they did not know their gaolers' ideology (Naipaul, 1969a); that the Muslim and other Indians of Trinidad taking part in the Muharram procession of 1884 had no understanding of what was happening when they were shot by police and naval forces because they did not know what the marksmen were thinking (Singh, 1988); that Aboriginal parents have no understanding of the removal of their children because police did not explain their motives? I would go further and claim that actors' understandings of and reasons for what they do may well be regarded as irrelevant to such peoples' understanding of what has taken place.

That is not to claim that the understanding of those who are subject to the actions of legal officials is necessarily accurate or adequate. Certainly there is reason not to romanticise the views of the oppressed; the sexism, racism and homophobia of large sections of the white male working class provides just one example of the reason why it is important to be careful about what I am advocating here. As stated above, there may well be reasons for wanting to engage with the motivations and understandings of the actors who are empowered by the legal system; much will depend on what one is trying to achieve and how one is trying to achieve it.

My point is, first, that I do not think such an engagement is *necessary* to understand what these actors are doing; an alternative understanding may be accessed through the interpretations of those who were subjected to these activities. Following from this, if one wants to take issue with the interpretations of those subject to such activities, it is not sufficient to claim that the actors meant well or that they thought that they were doing something quite different. Certainly the interpretations of those oppressed need not be accepted without qualification, but such qualifications need to be based on something other than arguments about the actors' intentions and what they thought they were doing.

The notion that we must consult with the powerful, as well as the disempowered, if we are to understand what is really happening in the world seems to me to have resulted in an increasing preoccupation with elite discourses in the West (see, too, Chapter 4, 'Discourse v. Coercion' below). It also seems to me that many colonised peoples' interpretations of events are often based upon a fairly sceptical attitude towards elite discourses. An Aboriginal person, identified only as I. J., stated, 'They've got a name for everything these white people and of course the police supports that... I just don't know where to look for that thing they call justice' (quoted in Ashforth, 1990, p.308).[13] The issue for colonised peoples is not so much what actors say and maybe even believe they are doing, but is one of whose material interests, as they perceive them, are being served.

In the context of the legal system, this attitude tends to an assessment of legal decisions that is result oriented, and there is little engagement with any justificatory discourse.[14] It is of note that such assessment tends to be the reverse of lawyers', which often takes the actual decision to be of secondary importance, while it is the "principles" enunciated in the judgement which are regarded as crucial. Sharing the former stance has meant that my treatment of the legal system is similarly result oriented and has little engagement with the discourses and motivations of legal officials.

SEX/GENDER

Before I conclude the discussion of theoretical issues, there is one other issue that needs to be addressed. My position has been strongly influenced by feminist theory and methodology, in its rejection of "objectivity" and dispassionate research. However, as can be seen in the chapters on field-work, the legal system most frequently and directly acts upon men. This has meant that my own work has similarly focused upon the position of men.

It should be noted that my work has thereby failed adequately to acknowledge the impact of the legal system upon women. For example, while I have provided numbers of the defendants and respondents appearing in court, which indicate a heavy concentration of men, I have not recorded the numbers of people who attended courts as relatives and friends of the defendants, and who were principally women.[15]

Nor have I fully investigated the extraordinary disproportion of imprisonments of Aboriginal women in comparison to non-Aboriginal women in Western Australia, where Aboriginal women constitute more than fifty per cent of the female prison population (WA Dept Corrective Services, 1992a). Moreover, I have not adequately acknowledged what is occurring in relation to the imprisonment of women in Trinidad, where there was an almost three-fold increase in just one year, between 1990 and 1991 (T&T CSO, 1993a, p.61).

Cheryl Buchanan (1993[1976], p.698), described as '[one] of Australia's leading Aboriginal campaigners', discussing issues of sexism and racism in the legal system, stated,

> Because of the chauvinism that exists within society, they [police] don't feel they can deal with you in the way they deal with black men. They frame the men on charges and get them put in gaol for three or five years or whatever, but with us they take you down to the watchhouse and get you to do a strip for them, line up four or five pigs and rape you there. They get their kicks that way.

And again,

> There's case after case of black women getting raped. You know if you're going to go to pigs that either they'll do nothing at all or keep you there and rape you themselves. I mean, this is just a known fact in the black community. (Buchanan, 1993[1976], p.699)

It seems to me that the issues relating to criminalisation and black women under common law systems deserve consideration on their own terms; something I have not attempted to address in this work.[16] I have however attempted to maintain an awareness of gender throughout my study which would be compatible with feminist research (Cain, 1986b, p.258). Moreover, in my discussion in Chapter 8, I hope to have paid sufficient regard to what is perhaps one of the most pressing concerns of colonised women in the context of issues relating to the legal system, and that is the escalation of violence in their societies.

Notes

1. Bob Marley was a Jamaican Reggae singer and Rastafari.
2. My own sense of my presence and the effect on those I "observed" was no doubt exaggerated in that I was not inured to the nature of Trinidadian society, as I would have been if I had been Trinidadian. My anomalous appearance also added to my visibility and the associated "commotion"; whites comprised something of the order of one per cent of the population and, as I discovered, were often expected to conduct themselves in accordance with their fairly privileged status. It was apparent to me, however, both from my observations and conversations, that the texture of social relations in Trinidad generally was of a different kind to that of Western

Australia.

3. Quoted in Mason (1962, p.296).
4. In relation to newspaper reporting in Trinidad, Kurian (1982, p.1788), in the *Encyclopedia of the Third World*, notes,

> The Trinidadian press has a long tradition of freedom. Its boldness and irreverence have occasionally alarmed the authorities, but few government efforts have been made to muzzle it or make it subservient to the ruling party's interests. Press censorship laws have been enforced only sporadically.

The popular and populist bi-weekly *Mirror* newspapers exemplify this boldness and irreverence. It is of note that Raffique Shah, who led the mutiny of the soldiers during the 1970s uprising, is now an editor; Abdullah Omowale, one-time member of the National United Freedom Fighters, and recent Muslimeen insurgent and death row prisoner, is one reporter amongst others, who, in an Australian context, would be regarded as having strikingly diverse and dissident backgrounds.

5. Although the British had initially intended to take possession of Trinidad only for the duration of the war against the French and Spanish, by 1802 the island was formally ceded to Britain by the Spanish. It is likely that the destruction of the sugar industry in Haiti and the great potential of Trinidad's sugar industry caused the British to revise their attitudes towards Trinidad (John, 1988, pp.1-19; James, 1963[1938]; Ottley, 1974) Western Australia was initially established expressly on the basis of an investment proposal according to which the Crown made grants of "its" land in Western Australia to those who invested in the colony, although owing to labour shortages it later became a penal settlement (Statham, 1987).
6. James (1984a, p.2), for example, was advocating a special and autonomous role for black working class people, women and youth in revolutionary politics during the 1940s; and see Cleaver (1979, pp.45-49).
7. King had attempted to arrest Butler, the Afro-Caribbean working-class leader, while he was addressing a public meeting. While Butler maintained his loyalty to the British Crown, his speeches were a mixture of class and race analysis; for example, he was prosecuted for (allegedly) saying,

> that damn bastard the Warden, who say there was no land, but he can give it to the white man. But that damn vagabond; he can give it to them but not the people, damn vagabond, he can give it to them to make a village in those places Vessigny and La Brea in their mad scramble for oil. It is the Fascist Imperialist Band that is sinking us into slavery. They are enemies of the British Constitution in

> Trinidad. Some of them have been Governors, some Colonial Secretaries. Some of the Judges, like Judge Gilchrist, like certain British Judges, trample justice under their foot. (Jacobs, 1976, p.27)

King himself was an unpopular policeman and had a reputation for framing the lovers of women he desired. Five women and four men were charged, and later acquitted by a jury, over King's murder. The killing of King marked the beginning of almost three weeks of national riots and strikes, which ended with the intervention of imperial reinforcements (Reddock, 1987).

8. The need for Australian white women to recognise their own complicity in the mistreatment of Aboriginal women (and men) is just one example (Pettmen, 1992). History indicates a similar lack of solidarity amongst the working class. In Western Australia the union movement was a major instigator of the White Australia policy, in order to exclude particularly Asian working peoples from the country (vanden Driesen, 1987, pp.374,375). Many unions also sought to have Aboriginal workers excluded from union membership (Haebich, 1992, pp.42,43,226, 227). A Labour government in Britain refused to allow the workers of Trinidad the same rights as were permitted British workers (Basdeo, 1987; Craig, 1988, pp.23,24; Great Britain Colonial Office (GB CO), 1938, p.48 [The Forster Report]; Hart, 1982, p.69).
9. Another Caribbean author, Jacobs (1982, p.279), critiques the Black Power Movement in Trinidad in 1970 for failing to translate racial hostilities into broader class principles, and giving people 'the hope only of changing a white capitalist oppressor for a black capitalist oppressor'. Refer also to the comments of Reddock and McCree (1992) quoted above, under the section 'Class and Race'.
10. Other categories are also relevant to internal divisions within the Aboriginal community, including sex/gender, as well as family and tribal affiliation, although I do not pursue these divisions in this thesis (but see Gilbert, 1977). With respect to Caribbean society, see Chapter 1, note 38.
11. One obvious example of this, as indicated above, was that I sought to avoid contact with court officials and police, although they too were sometimes people of colour.
12. I do not mean to imply that people who are subject to the activities of police and lawyers are merely passive. Certainly, as I hope to illustrate in the field-work accounts, colonised people are often actively engaged in pursuing lifestyles or deliberate resistance when they are apprehended by police, spoken for and about by lawyers and judged by magistrates. Their interpretation of what is happening, however, may be quite different to officials' interpretations, but is no less valid for that. For an example of this kind of divergence in interpretation between officers of the law and the criminalised, in the context of the "race riots" in Britain during the 1980s, see Keith (1993).
13. Note that this scepticism needs to be qualified in relation to at least some Aboriginal

people. Gilbert (1977, p.48), states that,

> Aborigines have swallowed a lot of indoctrination about how this is a just society - freedom, democracy, equality and all that stuff - so they assume the problem *must* be one of communication. How, then, do you point out to those who are seemingly blind the size of what to you is so yawning a chasm of injustice? And once you succeed, wouldn't well being follow, for don't whites profess all these things?

Something of this attitude can be seen in the journey across Australia, under extreme conditions, made by a group of Western Australian Aboriginal people in the hope of speaking to the federal minister for Aboriginal Affairs and described in Bropho's *Fringedweller* (1980). The lack of success of this and many other Aboriginal attempts to communicate 'so yawning a chasm of injustice' may well result in Aboriginal reappraisal of white professions of justice. The point I am making here, however, is that even Aboriginal people who are not dismissive of elite discourses tend to assess such discourses in terms of concrete and non-discursive results, as indicated by the examples cited in note 14, below.

14. Note, for example, the Aboriginal agenda for the Royal Commission into Aboriginal Deaths in Custody was simply that 'the culprits', those who they regarded as guilty for the killing of Aboriginal people in custody, 'be caught' (Aus RCIADIC, 1991a:10.4.1). Unfortunately, for Aboriginal people at least, the Commission did not regard its role in those terms, and produced many thousands of pages of words, but declined to recommend that anyone be prosecuted (Purdy, 1992a). Despite the Commission's elaborate justifications of its position, many Aboriginal people now regard it as simply a "white wash" (for example, see the debate between an Aboriginal commentator and one of the Royal Commissioners in *Aboriginal Perspectives on Criminal Justice*: Craigie, 1992, pp.13-17; Wootton, 1992, pp.49-52).

An example of this kind of attitude towards elite discourses in Trinidad concerned the reporting of the case involving the killing of a twelve-year-old child. Charges of manslaughter against the alleged killers were dismissed when it was found that the only witness to have identified the child's body was married to one of the defendants. According to the laws of Trinidad and Tobago, his evidence was therefore inadmissible against his spouse, and because she was jointly charged, his evidence was also inadmissible against the other defendant (*Express*, June 12, 1992). A comment on the case was published under the headline, '23 reasons to jail mother', a reference to the number of injuries sustained by the child before he died. The comment did not acknowledge the legal reasoning put forward to justify the decision in that case, and looked only to the result, which the article claimed had 'put the fight against child abuse a century backwards' (*Express*, June 20, 1992).

15. Refer also to the comments of Payne (1990) and Carrington (1993) on this issue.
16. Note that it is for similar reasons that I have not amended the use of masculine pronouns in the quotes that I have utilised in this manuscript. It seems to me that the applicability of the statements to colonised women should not simply be read into the text.

3 Methodology

AN "ORGANIC INTELLECTUAL"?

I have indicated above that I attempted to come to a "collective understanding" with (some) colonised peoples with respect to my research. A significant aspect of this understanding was arrived at by adopting local analyses of colonial history and social relations. I was criticised while in Trinidad, however, for not meeting the requirements of being an "organic intellectual" in Gramsci's terms. In fact, I was told that there was no agenda against the legal system in Trinidad; and that it was actually the system that 'they' (i.e. Trinidadian people) wanted. For me to come to Trinidad with "imported" criticisms of that system was nothing less than to repeat the incursions of white, arrogant colonisers of earlier times. Others, who did not use academic terminology, told me that I had come to Trinidad with a preconceived attitude towards the legal system, and that was what I had chosen to see while I was there. Both criticisms related to my being insufficiently responsive to the realities of Trinidad. I raise these criticisms here because they relate specifically to how I conducted my research in Trinidad.

Let me concede straight away that there was not the official monitoring of racism and the law in Trinidad, as exists in Australia. Also that I did not become a part of a structured political movement which involved 'regular encounters and meetings with other[s] .. going in the same direction' (Cain, 1986b, p.256). I would add, however, that there was an awareness of the issue of racism in the law in Trinidad, although this tended to be perceived in terms of the highly conscious Afro/Indo racialism of that country.[1] The official "acknowledgment" of this issue can be seen in the fact that I was informed by a Central Statistical Office employee in 1992 that the results of a prison census conducted in relation to prisoners' ethnic origins in 1990 were considered too sensitive to publish (although these were subsequently published in 1993; refer to Appendix II: T&T CSO, 1993b, Table 9).

Moreover, there was a more than evident dissatisfaction with the legal system. Allegations of police and prison corruption and violence were rampant. (Although many allegations included the harassment, and in some instances the killing, of honest police officers.)[2] One of the pieces of folk-lore of Trinidad is that "You never go to a police station to report a crime; you won't leave without being charged". There had also been a number of inquiries into the magistracy; allegations of both the complicity of and threats against judges, magistrates, police and others in relation to drug trafficking; a magistrate was released from prison pending his appeal on corruption charges while I was in Trinidad; a court case was lost by the Chief Justice over the suspension of another judge; there were allegations of bias by judges related to lodge membership; one judge was said to be involved in a hit and run car accident in which a child was killed; a finding was made that the coroner's inquiry into the shooting of the Muslimeen leader's stepson by police during the coup attempt was perverse and irrational.[3] Finally, as is discussed further in Chapter 5, there was a great deal of concern about the extreme backlog of cases awaiting hearing in the courts, which added significantly to the general dissatisfaction with the legal system of Trinidad and Tobago.

On my raising the issue of the alleged lack of political agitation in relation to the legal system of Trinidad in discussions with Abdullah Omowale, the Trinidadian activist and journalist, he was somewhat bewildered. Omowale stated that the National United Freedom Fighters, of which he had been a member and which had formed after the Black Power uprising in Trinidad, had been opposed to the law and the police as these were constituted in Trinidad.[4] Omowale also commented that the first act of the Muslimeen during their coup attempt had been the fire-bombing of Central Police Headquarters (Omowale, interview with the author, November 16, 1992).

Clearly any statement that the British common law based legal system of Trinidad was what "they" wanted fails to acknowledge that Trinidad, like any society, is comprised of people of different sexes and genders, classes, races and ethnicities, and there will be a variety of attitudes towards any issue. While no doubt some Trinidadians were satisfied with the legal system as it was, this view cannot be universalised on the basis of some categorical essentialism.[5]

Although my analysis of the legal system was not clearly one which was already current in Trinidad, at the same time it did take seriously issues that had already been raised: principally the over-representation of Afro-Trinidadians in the prisons,[6] and dissatisfaction with the legal system. Nor can there be any doubt that stratification according to skin colour was also well-known in the community; although, as noted, it seemed to be less consciously an issue than Afro/Indo racialism in the contemporary context.[7]

Being responsive to local conditions and views, however, does not entail that the "intellectual" should not contribute anything new to popular debates. Nor does it entail adopting local explanations without question, as discussed previously. In Trinidad, many social problems tend to be understood within the context of a highly conscious Afro/Indo racism. With reference to the current over-imprisonment of Afro-Trinidadians, popular explanations consisted of alleged Afro-Trinidadian racial deficiency or, alternatively, Indo-Trinidadian racist corruption. My research, however, indicated the inadequacy of such popular explanations.

Any assertion that imprisonment was simply a function of the racially "inherent" criminality of Afro-Trinidadians was confounded by the fact that during the last century it was those of *Indian* descent who were over-represented in the gaols of Trinidad (refer Chapter 9). Nor could the over-representation of Afro-Trinidadians in the prisons be simply attributed to Indo-Trinidadian racism. It was evident that the police, courts and parliament were in fact dominated by those of African descent (refer Chapter 5). It is a sad reflection on how entrenched is the Afro/Indo racism of Trinidad, however, that a number of responses by both Afro- and Indo-Trinidadians to newspaper coverage of my research findings were the same;[8] that is, they liked my work, but assumed that those of the "opposing" ethnic/racial group must not have. It seemed a number of people were unable to regard anything as beneficial to their own racially defined group unless it was at the same time detrimental to those they perceived as their opposite.

This then finally leads to my methodology. As indicated above, I read many of the texts produced by Caribbean authors and activists. In addition, I spoke with many people in Trinidad, although I rarely conducted formal interviews in the course of my research.[9] I regarded formal interviews in most instances as intrusive and my approach was fairly consistently informal.[10] In fact much that I have learnt has been from friends I have made both in Trinidad and amongst Aboriginal communities. I also met many people casually, and spoke to them at their own initiative. I have attempted not to use any of these people as "objects" exploitable by me for the purposes of my research. However, at the same time I have wanted to be informed by colonised peoples' attitudes and to incorporate what in both Trinidad and Aboriginal Australia is referred to, and respected as, "grass roots" knowledges within my work.

This has created difficulties in the presentation of the information that people have shared with me. As a rather unsatisfactory compromise, I have attempted to avoid direct references as much as possible, unless the person had agreed to a formal interview, to be quoted, or was taking part in the public processes of the court. In other instances, where I have used comments taken from informal discussions, I have left my source unidentified. Given the often sensitive nature of the issues referred to in this work and what people said to me, it seems fairer to preserve people's anonymity in these instances.[11]

More generally, I hope that my work reflects something of the attitudes, concerns and interests of (some) colonised peoples. Clearly, my work is only partial, and in some senses reinforces particularly negative stereotypes of colonised peoples, precisely because it is concerned with the issue of criminality.

As Dave Palmer and Len Collard (1993) indicate, the reality of being Aboriginal goes far beyond this narrow issue, and it is a negative marginalising of Aboriginality to focus on Aboriginal criminality. Such a criticism undoubtedly applies to the treatment of colonised peoples in my work, and my only response can be that I hope I have been clear in delineating the limited nature of my investigations and representations.

In addition, I have attempted to provide something of a broader perspective on Aboriginal and Trinidadian criminalisation, through the provision of some historical and broader statistical data. As a result, I hope to have indicated that criminalisation does not necessarily relate to the negative qualities of the criminalised. Criminalisation has often been used against the powerful and resilient resistances of colonised peoples. Moreover, such an interpretation is not confined to the overtly political uses of criminal law, but extends to the mundane processes of criminalisation.[12] I have attempted to indicate how, in the colonial context, the common law and particularly criminal law is fundamentally articulated to economic exploitation. As Snyder and Hay (1987:26) have commented, 'one of the prime purposes of criminal law is the delegitimation of acts by removing them from their contexts'. To recontextualise criminalisation can therefore be to reclaim, to some extent, the legitimacy of the "criminals".

CONTEXTUALISING

> Dear friend, theory is all grey,
> And the golden tree of life is green.
> Johann Wolfgang von Goethe[13]

The attempt to contextualise the criminalisation of colonised peoples in Trinidad and Western Australia has resulted in the inclusion of contemporary demographic, economic and criminal justice statistics as well as field-work accounts in this study. Each perspective is used to provide a context in which criminalisation can be understood, with particular emphasis on law as a lived experience. In this, my project has been an attempt to gain what Hegel described as, 'True scientific knowledge, [which] on the contrary, demands abandonment to the very life of the object' (Hegel, Preface to *The Phenomenology of Mind*, in Taussig, 1993, p.45).

One consequence of seeking abandonment to the very life of the object is the "undisciplined" character of this work. Not only does it range across a number of academic disciplines, but the information provided does not always conform to my own preferred interpretation based on the nexus of colonial economic relations and criminalisation. Indeed, information is often provided without overt interpretation. Moreover, there are both congruities and incongruities between the different perspectives utilised both in relation to each other and in relation to the different jurisdictions. My purpose has been not only to indicate that the greyness of theory cannot capture life, but to take issue with what Cain (1994, p.21), refers to as 'this arrogant placing of human knowledge at the centre of the universe', as discussed in Chapter 1.

I have been told that this approach tends to raise more questions than it answers. I do not know that this is a bad thing and, in any event, I prefer criticism of that nature rather than attempting to provide all the answers and holding myself out as an "expert" on colonised peoples.

Statistics

I have provided demographic, economic and criminal justice statistics on the colonised peoples of Trinidad and Western Australia, for the reasons set out in Chapter 1. Although the meaning of such statistical data is limited, I do not consider their significance to reside in their comparative ranking. The significance of the data does not lie in engaging in some calculus of deprivation; as Oliver Mendelsohn and Upendra Baxi (1994a, p.3) comment, the point is not to reinforce divisions between subordinated people through the manufacture of 'hierarchies of suffering'. How people live and die has a significance that should not be subsumed for the purposes of academic classification and analysis.

Nonetheless, if readers find the meaning of statistics concerning Trinidadian and Aboriginal peoples opaque, they may be better able to assess something of the significance of the demographic, economic and criminal profiles by considering these in relation to their own lives. Such a consideration will indicate the degree of hardship experienced by colonised peoples, and in particular, their economic marginalisation and dependency.

With respect to the statistical data provided, it should be noted that I have generally relied upon readily available official data.[14] To that extent, data provided on Aborigines and Trinidadians are not in any event strictly comparable, although I have attempted to provide similar statistics where these were available. In addition, I have included data which may be regarded as being of broadly similar effect, for example, information on religion (with respect to Trinidadians) and language (with respect to Aboriginal people) as indicia of assimilation.

More broadly, the use of official data raises the issue of the apparent "scientificity" of statistics. The data used are imbricated by an "official" genealogy on a number of levels. On a fairly obvious level, published data to some extent reflect the official agenda of what information should and should not be available to the public.[15] This issue is of particular significance in relation to data on the criminal justice system, and is discussed further below, in terms of my departure from official agendas through "impressionistic" field-work.

In relation to the demographic and economic data, however, it is also clear that the methodology of data collection will have implications for its outcome. Census methodology in both Trinidad and Western Australia is basically reliant upon information completed by "households". This creates difficulties for a highly mobile population, as noted by Dodson (1991, p.45). This form of data collection will also tend to exclude those who do not reside in a "household", particularly the homeless, and those with poor literacy skills. Another issue raised by Dodson is the unwillingness to identify amongst members of particular ethnic/racial groups (Dodson, 1991, p.45). Distrust or fear of government institutions may profoundly affect census results. Certainly, those whose children may have been taken from them because of their ethnic/racial origin were likely to have been reluctant to identify their origins correctly. More recently, it has also been noted that mistrust of government officials may still cause fears about including visitors on census forms (Aus RCIADIC, 1989b, p.9). Because the methodology of census taking reflects mainstream values, attitudes to government, and lifestyles, the marginalisation of such already peripheral groups is perpetuated and reproduced by their absence from census data.

The failure to acknowledge the nature of the limitations and biases associated with statistical data has other ramifications. It is particularly important that data relating to ethnic or racial identity are recognised for what they are; that is, by and large a reporting of people's self-identification. It seems that it was because of the failure to acknowledge the nature of these data that the 1986 census in Australia created such controversy. That census indicated a massive increase in the number of Aboriginal persons by over forty per cent since the previous census (Aus RCIADIC, 1989b).[16] A former demographic officer with the Central Statistical Office of Trinidad and Tobago told me of a similar phenomenon which occurred in that nation during the 1970s. The Black Power Movement resulted in different patterns of identification by a number of persons of mixed African and white descent who began to consider themselves to be of African rather than "mixed" racial origin (Linda Hewitt, interview with the author, August 25, 1992). Such shifts are disconcerting only if there is a failure to recognise that even apparently scientific data are influenced by the social context and the ideas of the participants involved in their manufacture (see Australian Bureau of Statistics (ABS), 1989, p.vii).

Field-Work

As I was interested in the perspective of those excluded from actively constituting legal processes, I wanted to conduct research at the sites where such people most frequently came into contact with the legal system. Statistics indicate that the magistrates' courts are by far the most frequent site of such interactions in the court system (refer Chapter 5, note 7; and Chapter 6, note 12). Although I would have liked also to pursue such interactions at the level of general policing, an area of even more significance in the context of the interface between the legal system and its "outsiders", this was not feasible. The magistrates' courts, however, are readily accessible as they are, at least in legal theory, open to public observation.[17]

The attempt to gain some insight into how a colonised person might perceive the legal system also informed the methodology I adopted while undertaking field-work in the courts. As indicated above, in addition to not wishing to skew the proceedings by advising legal operatives of the purpose of my research, I was also concerned not to "skew" my own research by observing the proceedings from the perspectives of the legal officials. Nonetheless, as I was a foreigner in Trinidad, and given the importance of recognition of others in that society, I regarded it as appropriate for me to advise the Chief Magistrate of Trinidad and Tobago of my intention to conduct a study of "his" courts.

Although, initially, the Chief Magistrate seemed in favour of my research and he offered to arrange a tour of the courts for me, his opinion of my study changed abruptly.[18] He became quite emphatic and reiterated a number of times that he wished to make it clear to me that he did not regard the relation between ethnic identity and sentencing as relevant in Trinidad. In any event, the Chief Magistrate stated that, as I was a member of the public and would be observing from the public gallery, I was 'entitled to attend and take notes as [you] so wish' (Baird, interview with the author, January 29, 1992).

In the event, however, I was not permitted to take notes during the court sessions.[19] The practice of taking notes or recording proceedings from the public gallery was also prohibited in the courts of Western Australian. My inability to keep a record of proceedings had clear implications for my methods and the accuracy of the data I collated. As is explained in Chapters 5 and 6, it meant that the results of my field-work are essentially impressionistic. The alternative was to work with legal officials in a way which I considered would compromise my research, as indicated above. Such are the unsatisfactory choices confronting the researcher, and I chose the former.[20]

Public Courts, Bacchanal and Self-Regulation

My research in the courts of Trinidad and Western Australia did not proceed at all according to what I had envisaged, but was no doubt all the more educative and useful for that. As stated above, my role as originally envisaged could perhaps be best described as a court "observer". This role is conceivable in terms of legal theory (if not in practice, as discussed above), as anyone is entitled to attend the courts without seeking approval and without introduction or explanation. As I was to find, however, the most basic legal rights are in any event of remarkably little meaning in practice, unless they also suit the interests of those empowered by the legal system.

Trinidad and Bacchanal

My presence in the magistrates' courts of Trinidad was controversial, to say the least, a matter which is documented below. For now I wish to make the point that, although my methods were perhaps inappropriate in the social context, they were essential to my research for the reasons given above. But more importantly in this context, my methods were also perfectly legitimate at law. And law was, after all, the power base of the very people who were disturbed by my presence.[21]

One factor which should not be omitted from my account, however, is the nature of the controversy about my presence in court. Although the reaction to my presence was important, particularly as to what it taught me about Trinidadian society and the practical effectivity of legal rights, that reaction needs to be contextualised by reference to the nature of the broader social relations of Trinidad.

It is difficult to render the nature of life in Trinidad for those unfamiliar with it. However, it seemed to me that elements of controversy and drama, what is there referred to as "bacchanal",[22] are not only embedded into everyday existence in a way that is not the case in the more restrained (and etiolated) existence I had known in Australia - but to a degree are also actively sought after and enjoyed. To some extent my intention of being an "observer" in any context in Trinidad was a product of my ignorance about that society; it has a participatory and "bacchanalian" culture that is quite distinct from the individualistic and disengaged culture with which I was more familiar.[23] Thus, although there was controversy ("bacchanal") over my attending the courts in Trinidad, it would be wrong to interpret the significance of this as if it meant the same that it would in Australia.

Whether because of my anomalous colour, because that colour was associated with wealth, or because of what I wore,[24] I was usually the subject of much attention when I attended the courts. On one occasion, a journalist who was covering another matter in the court, assuming that I had a case before the court, approached me about publishing details in the press, apparently because my appearance rendered any case newsworthy.

On another occasion, after I had attended one court for a number of days, it was closed to the public. I was told that only those who were appearing before the court were allowed to enter, although I was permitted access after explaining to the policeman guarding the entrance who I was and what I was doing. The stated reason for the closure of the court was overcrowding, and certainly it could not be denied that the court was extremely overcrowded. But it was also true that I was the only "disinterested" observer to attend the court; everyone else was either summonsed or related in some way to witnesses or defendants. It also seemed that no one else appeared to regard themselves as excluded from the court - or for that matter, to be excluded by the police officer at the door. Later a journalist advised me that all the journalists and court staff had earlier been discussing who I might be as people "like me" did not normally go to the magistrates' courts.

On yet another occasion, a police prosecutor whom I had met earlier observed me being accompanied from a courtroom by a police woman. Apparently the prosecutor, like myself, was unaware of the reason for which I was being removed from the court, and sent another officer after me. I was taken to a "police" office in the court building, and the police woman asked the three other officers who were present in the room to leave. The police woman then explained to me that the magistrate whose court I was attending wanted to know who I was. I was explaining this when the officer sent by the police prosecutor entered the office and advised the woman officer and myself that I was wanted in another court. I was then escorted by him to the police prosecutor's court, where I was invited to sit next to the prosecutor - much to the apparent surprise of the magistrate, prisoners and others in that court. The police woman entered the court a few minutes later and told the police prosecutor that the magistrate in the first court wanted me to return to his court. I returned to that court and the magistrate invited me to sit at the barrister's table at the front of the court.

It was not unusual for magistrates to send police to investigate who I was in both Trinidad and Western Australia, although it tended to occur more rapidly and frequently in Trinidad. This was due not only to understandable curiosity about who I was and what I was doing there, but no doubt was accentuated in Trinidad by my anomalous colour. It is of note that cultural factors may also have been relevant, as in Trinidad there was a lesser reticence in approaching "strangers" and talking to them, whether foreigners or not. Courtesies, particularly in acknowledging others, are also significant in that society, and my unintroduced and unexplained presence in the courts no doubt affronted those social conventions to some degree.

It is also of note that, once court officials ascertained who I was, I was not only shown much courtesy, but also offered assistance. I was sometimes allowed to observe hearings that were otherwise closed to the public, and invited to sit with the barristers, or in areas set aside for police witnesses. I was told by one police prosecutor that, if they had known who I was earlier, I would not have had to sit with "the people". (The notion that I should sit in a segregated part of the court seemed to me to have a resonance with the nineteenth century practice whereby the plantocracy (whites) had separate facilities when they attended the courts: Trotman, 1986, p.85.)

Certainly, almost all court officials, the police, magistrates and lawyers, whom I dealt with were undeniably kind and helpful to me, and if my project had been a different one their friendliness could have been accepted without reservation. As it was, however, their approaches risked biasing my field-work. It should be further noted that, although I in no way mean to doubt or denigrate the kindness that was shown to me, such attention and concern was not normally directed towards others in court.[25]

Western Australia and Self-Regulation

I have attempted to contextualise my court-work in Trinidad by briefly outlining my impressions of the broader society, and in particular the participatory and bacchanalian character of social relations. In Western and more thoroughly capitalistic societies (and classes), social being is of a different character. As described by Peter Fitzpatrick (1992) and Patricia Moynihan (1993), the emphasis in such societies is on self-regulation by the individual: the "sovereign" self. This creates the expectation of a personal space and sphere of control upon which others should not directly infringe. The Trinidadian practice of commenting to strangers on their appearance or walk, for example, would be regarded as infringing on this "personal space".

As Fitzpatrick notes, the sovereign self is subject to the law, and only the law. This creates the impression that one is free in all aspects of social life except when constrained by law. As Fitzpatrick (1992, pp.121-141), also indicates, however, the obsessive pursuit of self-constrained compliance with uncertain laws undermines any such "freedom"; it leads to anxiety and tends to social conformity and homogeneity. The corollary of the ideal of the sovereign self is a sense of "humiliation" or affront when what is regarded as one's "lawful" actions or decisions are publicly doubted or rebuked. Such treatment is associated with being treated like a child (Goffman, 1968, pp.43,47; Hall et al, 1978, pp.142-144).

In Trinidad, people often adopt a robust attitude to public comment and criticism; such comments are commonplace and one can choose to respond or to "not take it on". In the dominant culture of Western Australia, however, public comments and criticisms are rare; people scarcely acknowledge one another's presence, let alone express their opinion as to one's appearance or behaviour. Public questioning or criticism is therefore more likely to be unsettling to one's self-image and to be regarded as invasive. In the context of the character of broader social relations, it is not surprising that the approaches made to me in the courts of Western Australia and the treatment of defendants and others in the courts generally were restrained in comparison to what had occurred in Trinidad.

Nonetheless, I was questioned in Western Australia as to my attendance at the courts, as I had been in Trinidad, often by uniformed police officers. During my field-work in the former jurisdiction, I was specifically asked as to my identity and purpose in attending court on four occasions; three times by police.[26] On another occasion, the magistrate adjourned the court in the middle of a session, and a police orderly approached me and told me that the magistrate had ordered me to leave the court; I declined. When I attended that court the next day, I was told that the magistrate was going to "check my credentials". Later that day I was told by a police officer that I was wanted in the magistrate's chambers, in order to explain who I was and what I was doing in the court.[27]

As indicated, quite apart from the fact it was often uniformed police officers who were questioning me or relaying messages to me, public questioning and reproval may be considered an affront in the dominant social context of Western Australia. This was consistent with the behaviour of court officials. When I was approached in the courts it tended to be while the court was not in session, and usually by officers who would sit next to me or stand in close proximity to me and speak in quiet tones; one passed me a note written by the magistrate. This style of interaction tended to be very different to that of Trinidad where I might be called out of court by an officer or before the bench by a magistrate while the court was in session.[28] The manner in Western Australia could be described as "discreet" in comparison. Nonetheless, it is important to note that, while the manner adopted by court officials in the two jurisdictions was generally different, as were the social connotations, in neither jurisdiction was my lawful presence in the courts tolerated without deliberate and overt policing.

Field-Work Presentation

The information provided in relation to my court work in Part II is an attempt to render, as closely as possible, the actual experience of field-work. If such data appear unfocused, limited and to raise unanswered questions then that is what field-work is like. To excise aspects of my field-work observations which I found ambiguous or could not conclusively explain would be to falsify my observations and capacity as a researcher. Individuals who conduct field-work do not necessarily become omniscient as to why other people behave the way they do merely because they have adopted the role of a researcher.

This position is significantly influenced by feminist approaches to knowledge (Jaggar & Bordo, 1989) and particularly accentuated by a context of inter-racial and ethnic studies. To limit the account of my observations to those aspects which fortify my conclusions would also be to give the experience of field-work a singularity which is far from the reality. In including a broader dimension to my reporting of the field-work, I am deliberately seeking to provide an account of a more complex reality, of which my understandings and analysis can only, at best, be one, partial explanation (see, too, Cain, 1994).

In my comments on the field-work I emphasise that my data on race and/or colour with respect to defendants and respondents before the court are not exact. This is emphasised in particular because by presenting the data in table form it appears to imply a more formal data collection process than was actually the case. As explained, the method adopted for the collection of data was dictated by the circumstances under which I was allowed to attend court and, in Trinidad, by my unfamiliarity with the social and racial categories. My methods were therefore based more on impression than on conventional data collection.

I do not regard this as a weakness in my work; obtaining data through more conventional methods would of itself have undermined my research. I would have either had to resort to using existing statistical data (where they existed), or to working in collaboration with legal officials. As indicated above, available statistical data are collated on the basis of an already extant agenda and are imbued with the values and perspectives of the official agencies which collate them. The attempt to initiate alternative statistical collections with the approval of officials would of itself have compromised the project I was seeking to undertake by positioning myself in a radically different context to that of marginalised people before the court.

Of course it is arguable that I should have abandoned my project altogether; but conceding that a project should not proceed because conventional data collection methods are unavailable or not feasible is to concede too much. Such a position ignores issues of who it is who has collated official data, how they were able or empowered to do so, and why such data collection was undertaken. It is precisely the apparent scientificity of data such as statistics, which conceals the issues raised if one recognises that it is human agency which initiates and allows data collation. That is not to dispute that such data can be a very powerful resource, but it is to indicate something of the politics behind the apparent impartiality of the numbers.[29]

Moreover, impressionistic research may itself constitute a particularly valuable method if one is seeking to reach new understandings which allow a researcher to move beyond the limitations of received wisdom. In Trinidad, data as to colour stratification in the courts is nowhere collated. Without "impressionistic" research, I would not have been alerted to this important dimension of the imprisonment trends within that jurisdiction (refer Chapter 5). In Western Australia, where statistical data were readily available as to the ethnicity/race of defendants and prisoners, it was from impressions gained by observing the courts that I was alerted to the specificity of Aboriginal encounters with the law (refer Chapter 6). Abandoning research because more conventional methods of data collection are not feasible is to remain within the constraints of what is already documented and to conform to the demands of those already empowered (refer also to Bird, 1987, p.3).

Statutes and Case Law

I do not undertake a statutory or case law analysis of the magistrates' courts. This is in keeping with my theoretical framework and standpoint. As explained above, my project was one of attempting to render something of the nature of law from a position outside of that system. From that position, statutes and case law are not of primary significance.

There is little basis for those outside the legal system to view statutes and statutory changes as being of much relevance of themselves. For example, Mary Edmunds (1989, p.107), cites an account by a long-term resident of Roebourne of the granting of "drinking rights" to Aboriginal peoples in the north of Western Australia:

> they're all standin round down the town, the guys, and they're pushin each other to see who was goin to go into the hotel and get chucked out first. Eventually, after one man had gone in and been served without being 'chucked out', there was 'a mass exodus for the pub'.

What was important for these Aboriginal people was not that legislation had been changed, but whether or not they would be 'chucked out'. For them, written laws hold no magic; what mattered was the practice of law. In my view this is not some quaintly naive attitude for such people to hold. In the context of their history and current experience, their more pragmatic attitude may be characterised as a sophisticated response to the legal system.[30]

Of course, there are also those who regard themselves as bound by written laws, in the sense that they internalise those rules. It would be important to assess how this attitude affects operatives within the legal system, such as magistrates and police, if one was interested in presenting their view of the operation of the legal system. I am not. All that I will note here is that the actions of persons who consider themselves "bound by the law" may remain largely unpredictable. What "the law" is, is largely a matter of interpretation; and considering oneself bound by the law often disguises, even for the operatives themselves, how much discretion is permissible within such a framework.

It is also true that being "bound by the law" has a relational significance that goes beyond the psychology of individuals. That is, people who are perceived as breaking the law may be held to account by others; whether the law breakers be "criminals", police who exceed their powers or magistrates who make errors in law. The point I would make here, however, is that the mere existence of a written law - whether as a statute, a legal precedent or procedural guideline - does not of itself ensure that it will be enforced even when there is consensus as to what it means. To be effective it requires some agency to intervene, and in particular an agency that exercises power within the legal system.

It is this gap between what is written and the practice of law that makes it plausible to characterise the attitude of people outside the legal system as in some respects more sophisticated than those who sometimes view the delivering of judgements and enactment of statutes as being of themselves sufficient to change the actual practice of law and peoples' lives. This issue is taken up again in Chapter 4, in the discussion of 'Discourse v. Coercion'. My point here, as indicated above, is that the absence of any statutory or case law analysis of the magistrates' courts in my field-work is a consequence of my project of attempting to represent something of the nature of law for the marginalised.

Ethnographic Comment

I am not Aboriginal or Trinidadian. The "standard" I tend to assume in my work is that which relates to white Australians, and my textual comments tend to refer to issues and practices which "deviate" from this standard. Although the extensive time I spent in Trinidad meant that to a degree I was able to observe the conduct of Western Australian courts and society, on my return, as 'indeed counter, original, spare, strange' in accordance with Said's (1993, p.403) recommendation, there was also no doubt much that I neglected. Simply in terms of what is considered worth commenting on, the reporting of the field-work would have been quite different if the researcher had been Trinidadian or Aboriginal. White Australian practice is often the implicit norm I apply both to court procedure and more generally.

In reporting on the court work and other issues related to law I have sometimes expanded upon elements of Trinidadian society which go beyond the legal context, and which are based on my own experience or reading about that society. I have only done so when I felt it important to attempt to place the court or other legal practice in the context of the wider social practice in Trinidad, and where that was markedly different to the social practice of white Australia.

I am reluctant to expand too much upon my experience and understanding of Trinidadian society because I am a foreigner to it. While I am able to give an account of what it is like to be a white foreign female in that society, that was not the purpose of this study. But although I do not feel competent to comment too broadly on aspects that did not relate to me and my direct experiences and observations of that society, I would add the caveat that I do not feel so constrained about commenting on the Trinidadian legal system. That system is not Trinidadian but British; it is explicitly based upon British common law, principles and jurisprudence, as is the legal system of Western Australia. Indeed, my qualifications would enable me to practise law in both jurisdictions.

As to the manifestations of Aboriginal social practice in the courts, again my comments are limited and often reliant on other texts. In relation to Aboriginal people, in fact, my ability to comment more broadly than on the legal system is even more limited than with respect to Trinidadians, as I have not had the opportunity to live in an Aboriginal community.

My knowledge of both Trinidadian and Aboriginal society has been drawn from texts and my own relations with people in those communities. My knowledge of these communities is therefore a function of both the particular texts I have read and the particular people I have known, and is not systematic. As indicated above, I hope only to have reflected something of the concerns, attitudes and understandings of the marginalised towards the legal system in my work.

Notes

1. Certainly when I mentioned that I was doing a comparative study of race and law, court officials immediately interpreted this in terms of an allegation of partiality in the treatment of Afro- or Indo-Trinidadians. For an awareness of this issue beyond those working within the legal system, refer to a letter to the Editor, 'Claims of Discrimination Filled with Half-truths', *Express*, April 22, 1992, which disputes the allegation of 'Africans being responsible for all the crime'; and refer to Omowale's article, 'TnT Jails Full of Africans', *Sunday Mirror*, September 6, 1992.

   For just a few of the newspaper articles referring to the broader issue of Afro/Indo Trinidadian racialism, refer to 'Why We Should Keep Racial Passions Under Wraps', *Sunday Mirror*, April 26, 1992; 'TnT can Still be a Happy Melting

Pot', *Mirror*, May 29, 1992; 'Race is not the Issue', *Express*, June 2, 1992; 'Seapaul: Let's Sow the Seeds of Racial Unity', 'Focus on Ethnic Rivalry, Racial Unity', *Express*, June 16, 1992; ' "There's a Lot of Discrimination in Trinidad" - Prof. Ken Ramchand', *Mirror*, August 8, 1992; '12 Years of Licks for Frankie..."because I'm the only Indian squatter in Waterhole"', *Mirror*, September 6, 1992; 'Strangest Thing about Trinidad: One Nation but Still Two People', *Sunday Express*, September 20, 1992; 'Racism Alive', *Express*, September 22, 1992; 'Cultural Douglarisation gets Stamp of Approval', *Sunday Mirror*, October 25, 1992; 'Let's Stop this Race Talk', *Express*, May 15, 1992. See, too, letters to the Editor, 'Rise Above Past Discrimination', *Express*, April 23, 1992; 'Getting the Race Issue off our Chest', *Express*, April 28, 1992; 'We cannot Leave Ethnicity Out', *Express*, May 1, 1992; 'Leave Trinidadians Alone - Dougla', *Sunday Mirror*, May 3, 1992; 'Why the Racism?', *Express*, May 4, 1992; 'Let's not Split the Rainbow into Two', *Express*, May 26, 1992; 'All Members of the Black Race', *Express*, November 6, 1992.

There were occasional references to racialism involving other groups, such as Syrians and French Creoles (both groups being "white" or "near white" according to Trinidadian classifications), although these were significantly less frequent. See, for example, 'Where's the Syrian Mafia?', *Express*, May 25, 1992; 'Be Careful Race Monster does not Devour you, Panday', *Express*, June 2, 1992. Refer also to LaGuerre [1972], (1988).

2. Just a few examples of the official inquiries and popular allegations concerning police during the year I spent in Trinidad follow: 'Brutality in Cunupia..."Cops made me eat cow dung"', *Mirror*, January 31, 1992; 'Cop Fined for Beating Man'; 'Magistrate Probes Police Bullpistle Beating', *Sunday Mirror*, February 2, 1992; '"Probe Police Investigations Unit"', *Mirror*, February 7, 1992; 'Uniformed Cop carries out Oral Sex at Market', *Mirror*, February 14, 1992; 'Man Shot by Cops', *Express*, February 24, 1992; 'Row after Cop Refuses to "Set Up" Man with Drugs', *Mirror*, March 6, 1992; 'Muslim group Complain to U.N. about Police "Frame-Ups"', *Sunday Mirror*, March 22, 1992; 'Govt Probing Drug Charges among Cops', *Guardian*, April 4, 1992; 'Toddler Injured during Shootout', *Guardian*, April 21, 1992; 'The Rodwell Murray Affair: Commission to Meet in Private', *Express*, April 22, 1992; 'Man Rats and the Missing Cocaine Rocks (Another Strike by the Police "Drug Cartel"?)'; 'Maraval Man says he was Tortured by Cops: Blows and More Blows'; 'Cops go Wild in Residential Area', *Mirror*, April 24, 1992; 'Wrong Brother Beaten?...Battered teen vows to take cops to court over "mistaken identity" licking'; 'Suspended Cop seen as Mr. Clean', *Sunday Mirror*, May 10, 1992; 'Escaped Prisoner Shot by Cops', *Express*, May 14, 1992; 'Bernard Demands Drug Info from Cops'; 'Police Framed, Beat me - Prosecution Witness', *Mirror*, May 15, 1992; '3 Cops Freed of Brutality Charges... Malony residents threaten "L.A. riots"', *Mirror*, May 22, 1992; 'No Money to send Chris to School...He stays Home...Killed by Police Bullet: Mom "My Son was no Bandit"', *Mirror*, June 5, 1992; 'Who Killed Steve Niamath? Police Drug Cartel implicated in Two Murders'; 'Contract on Drug Prober's Life', *Sunday Mirror*, June 7, 1992; 'If you Report a Rogue Cop, Leave the

Country and Run... advice from Suspended Officer', *Mirror*, June 19, 1992; 'C.O.P. Summoned in "Weasel" Inquest: Crucial Bullet Photos Missing'; 'Fatal Blunder by Cops: Rasta "Bible Man" Gunned Down in case of Mistaken Identity', *Sunday Mirror*, July 5, 1992; 'Cop, Prisoner Shot during Struggle', *Express*, July 7, 1992; 'Two Killed in Police Shootout', *Express*, July 8, 1992; '"Police Kill Youths in Cold Blood"', *Express*, July 24, 1992; 'Cover-Up charge in St James Killing', *Express*, August 3, 1992; 'Family alleges Cover-Up after...Cop accused of Hit-and-Run Death'; 'Drug Cartel linked to Death of Vagrant Cop: Murder!', *Mirror*, August 7, 1992; 'Car Theft Racket... Top Cop Escapes Justice', *Mirror*, August 14, 1992; 'Man Shot by Cop', *Express*, August 15, 1992; 'Cops Shoot Vagrant in South', *Express*, August 18, 1992; 'Scotland Yard Probes Cops', *Mirror*, August 21, 1992; 'Making a Mockery of Justice', *Express*, September 4, 1992; 'La Tinta Cop on the Run in New York: "Cartel out to Wipe me Out"', *Sunday Mirror*, September 13, 1992; 'Cops Batter Man to Death', *Mirror*, September 25, 1992; 'Charge La Tinta "Outlaw" Cops: Lying on Oath, Conspiracy to Traffic "Coke", Misconduct Slammed by Probe Team'; 'Senior Officer Shirked Duty'; 'Top Man made False Report'; '"Buy and Bust" Team: Where are they now?'; 'Probers Slam La Tinta Cops'; 'La Tinta File long overdue for action'; 'Profile of an "Outlaw" Band'; 'Cops Grilled as Never Before', *Sunday Express*, September 27, 1992; 'Police Cover-Up in Bernadette James Affair: Constant efforts were made to lead woman investigator down wrong path'; 'Turn these Files over to Scotland Yard'; 'Drunk and Disorderly W.P.C. in Free Sex Show'; 'Guilty until Proven Innocent... a never-ending story for the poor', *Sunday Mirror*, September 27, 1992; '3 Sons Killed, one Kidnapped... "Time for Scotland Yard to move in"', *Mirror*, October 2, 1992; 'The W.P.C. Bernadette James Inquest... Mysterious object gave a ringing sound... unlike the blank found three days later at accident site', *Sunday Mirror*, October 4, 1992; 'Cops Cripple Man with Blows claims Attorney', *Mirror*, October 9, 1992; 'The W.P.C. Bernadette James Inquest... Pierre knew difference between blank and live ammo', *Sunday Mirror*, October 11, 1992; '5 Youths Battered and Forced to Sign Confession', *Mirror*, October 23, 1992; 'Who'll Guard the Guards?', *Express*, November 6, 1992; 'Police Nightmare! A Way of Life in TnT?', *Sunday Mirror*, November 22, 1992.

Reports in relation to the prisons were less common but nonetheless significant; some examples follow: 'Ex-Senior Magistrate Confronts Gays, Men he threw behind bars: Patrick Jagessar Tells All - My 3-Year Ordeal in Jail'; 'Save me from Prison Homos pleads Detainee', *Mirror*, May 22, 1992; 'Now, a Prison Cartel'; 'More Bail would help Jail', *Mirror*, May 29, 1992; 'Prisoners Dying on Death Row: Boochoon does not want to become Fatality No. 5', *Sunday Mirror*, June 7, 1992; 'Ensuring that our Prisons are Secure', *Express*, June 9, 1992; '"Prison Officers gave me Drugs to Push Off"', *Mirror*, June 19, 1992; '"How did Dave Roberts Die?"', *Express*, June 22, 1992; 'Danger Lurks in our Prisons', *Express*, June 25, 1992; 'Wanted: AIDS Education behind Bars', *Mirror*, June 26, 1992; '200 Prisoners Stricken with Food-Poisoning', *Express*, July 22, 1992; 'Jailbirds served Spoilt Rice, Fish, Meat, Peas:

Rotten Food for Prisoners!', *Mirror*, July 31, 1992; 'After 9 Year Legal Battle Innocent Prison Officers say... Give us back our jobs', *Mirror*, August 21, 1992; 'State explains Prison Transport Problems: No Money, No Court', *Express*, October 16, 1992; 'Drugs, Alcohol on Sale in Jail... Says Man Freed on Murder Charge', *Express*, October 17, 1992; 'Prison Officer Assaulted me', *Mirror*, October 23, 1992.

3. Refer for example, to the Statement concerning the Report of the Commission of Inquiry into the Working of the Magistracy, St George West (T&T House of Representatives, U/d); Scott Report (T&T Commission of Enquiry into the extent of drug abuse in Trinidad and Tobago, 1986), and newspaper articles, 'Abuse in our Courts', *Guardian*, January 16, 1992; 'Attorneys Threaten Action in Gramoxone Murder', *Mirror*, January 31, 1992; 'Now Death Threats for Magistrate Peters', *Mirror*, March 20, 1992; 'Law Body moves to Clean Bar', *Express*, March 20, 1992; 'The Judge's Car', *Express*, April 1, 1992; 'Angry Attorney Slams State: Men held for years without going to court', *Express*, April 15, 1992; 'Jagessar Pardoned - says man who put hex on him', *Mirror*, June 19, 1992; 'Death Threats for Couva Court Clerks'; 'Suspend C.J. too!', *Mirror*, July 24, 1992; 'J.P. linked to Central Bail Racket', *Mirror*, August 14, 1992; 'Ramesh calls for Commission of Inquiry into Judiciary: "The Question of Lodges could be raised"', *Sunday Mirror*, August 23, 1992; 'Judge for Witness Stand in "Hit and Run" Accident - "Police Never asked my Daughter what happened"', *Sunday Mirror*, October 4, 1992; 'Reign of Terror in Nation's Courts: Druglords target magistrates', *Mirror*, October 9, 1992; 'Judge orders New Inquest into Omowale's Death', *Express*, October 9, 1992; 'Attorney Slams: C.J. for the Guinness Book', *Mirror*, October 9, 1992; 'Justice in Distress'; 'Wills to Quit - Judge in fatal hit-and-run tangle enters the hotel business', *Sunday Mirror*, October 11, 1992; 'Khan's Perverse Ruling', *Mirror*, October 16, 1992; 'Justice Crane Wins Appeal', *Express*, November 21, 1992.

4. Omowale, who had himself trained as a police officer in the 1960s, was a member of the Freedom Fighters in the 1970s. Along with another Freedom Fighter, Kirklon Paul, he was sentenced to death in 1975 on charges of having murdered a policeman, and spent more than twelve years on death row. In 1987, a Trinidadian judge ruled that the incarceration of Omowale and Paul amounted to unconstitutional and illegal punishment, and the death penalty was revoked and a lesser punishment substituted. Two months later Omowale and Paul received a presidential pardon (Omowale, interview with the author, November 9, 1992; 'Deadlock on Death Row', *Sunday Mirror*, November 15, 1992).

5. Another issue that is relevant here is how far it can be assumed that people are satisfied with the legal system when data on how it operates are being withheld for significant periods of time, such as, in this case, the prison census. However, it is also of note that, in Trinidad, informal methods of obtaining and disseminating information would reduce the significance of this. On the point in issue, information provided in an article in one of the weekly newspapers, referred to elsewhere, meant

that information similar to that provided by the prison census was already in the public domain even prior to its official dissemination in 1993.

6. See particularly, 'TnT Jails Full of Africans', *Sunday Mirror*, September 6, 1992.
7. When I first broached my findings with Trinidadian people, it was often an issue with which they were uncomfortable. This was particularly true of Afro-Caribbeans who quite understandably were disturbed by research which apparently emphasised African criminality, particularly coming from a white researcher. It also disconcerted people of other racial/ethnic backgrounds who were striving to be part of a society which was not marked by racism; a long term debate in Trinidad, as elsewhere, being whether it is the acknowledgment or denial of race which is racist (Brereton, 1979, pp.199,200).
8. '37,000 prisoners, mostly Africans, in TnT Jails: "Legal system against Blacks"', *Sunday Mirror*, November 22, 1992.
9. The primary reason for this was a discussion I had a number of years prior to beginning my doctoral research with Dorothy Parker, an anthropologist who worked for many years with Aboriginal peoples in Western Australia. She told me that Aboriginal people were tired of white researchers who regularly made their name out of researching them, and then left these people in the same state of poverty and oppression as they had been.
10. Refer to Gorelick (1989) too, for a critique of formal attitudinal research methods.
11. References to discussions and other data concerning my field-work are based upon notes I recorded at the time of my doctoral research (Purdy 1992/3).
12. For examples of the uses of criminal law in overtly political contexts, see Calathes (1990), on Jamaican firearm legislation and the politicisation of the legal system, and Mahabir (1980), on the use of Emergency Powers during the 1970s uprising in Trinidad.
13. Goethe (1749-1832) was a German poet and philosopher.
14. An exception is the information relating to the issue of race/ethnicity and imprisonment in Trinidad which I referred to above, and which at the time was embargoed from publication in Trinidad.
15. An important example of this in Trinidad was my inability to obtain contemporary data relating to race/ethnicity and income. Given other data which were publicly available, it was apparent that this data could have been compiled. But despite my offer to pay for any work this may have involved for the Central Statistical Office, I still was unable to obtain data correlating race and income.
16. The author of the Royal Commission report attributes this result to differences in the wording of questions, the efficiency of data collection from Aboriginal communities and the adequacy of processing (Aus RCIADIC, 1989b, pp.6-9).
17. The confining of my field-work to the relatively public arena of the magistrates' courts itself had important consequences in relation to what I was able to observe of

the manufacture of unequal relations of ethnicity/race through law, and this is discussed in Chapter 7.

18. It is possible that the Chief Magistrate had not originally realised the purpose of my research, as he asked me to write him a letter subsequent to the interview stating more clearly the purpose of my work. Originally I had written a brief letter of introduction, stating only that I was doing a comparative study of the common law in Trinidad and Western Australia (January 16, 1992). I did write a clarifying letter to the Chief Magistrate (February 4, 1992), as he had requested, but received no reply with respect to his offer to arrange a tour of the courts.

19. On my first attendance at a magistrates' court in Trinidad, I was asked to leave by the Magistrate when a man waiting in the public gallery commenced speaking to me. The man advised the Magistrate that he had been the one speaking, but the Magistrate ordered me to leave anyway. I had the impression that the Magistrate did not like me taking notes in court, but had felt obliged to let me do so. I then attended a second court where I again began to keep a record of proceedings, until I was approached by a police officer and told I was not allowed to take notes (or record proceedings) unless I was a journalist. I ceased, and shortly after that when there was a brief recess, I advised the police officer that the Chief Magistrate had said that I was allowed to take notes. The officer stated that I required something in writing and suggested that other students had obtained written permission from a Justice of the Peace. I approached a Justice of the Peace, who advised me she would not issue such a written authorisation, but that I should see her supervisor, after she advised him of my position. When I did see the supervisor, presumably after he had contacted the Chief Magistrate, he told me to write directly to the Chief Magistrate and request written authority from him. Later the Justice of the Peace who I had originally spoken to said she was surprised at her supervisor's refusal, as he had given such authorities to students before. I wrote to the Chief Magistrate stating that I required his written authorisation to take notes from the public gallery (April 7, 1992), but received no reply.

20. In any event, even though I did not take notes of court proceedings, in almost all the courts I attended for any period of time, I was eventually approached by one or more court officials as to my presence. I replied to any initial inquiry as to the nature of my study that I was conducting a study of magistrates' courts in Trinidad and Western Australia. If I was questioned further, I would explain that the particular area of interest was racism and law. I did not mislead court officials as to the nature of my research.

21. In both jurisdictions, none of the defendants and others attending court seemed concerned about my presence, although many probably assumed I was also a witness, a defendant, or related to one. In the Trinidadian courts, particularly before I felt obliged to dress well or later when I wore black clothing, prisoners seemed to regard my presence favourably. Some defendants did seem disappointed when they discovered that I was not attending the court on the same basis as them. In any

event, unlike court officials, they were in no position to take any action about my presence. It is of note too, that, when I was given permission to attend proceedings that were otherwise closed to the public, defendants or applicants were not generally asked whether they consented; the decision as to my presence was fully appropriated by court officials.

22. "Bacchanal" does not carry overtones of drunken revelry as it is used in Trinidad. Brereton (1979, p.62) defines it as meaning 'scandal'. Conflict, controversy and discord are elements of the meaning of that term as it is used in Trinidad, although it is perhaps indicative of the values of that society that the meaning does have a resonance with the non-Trinidadian definitions of that word, in that it will also often have celebratory overtones as well.

23. Unlike more thoroughly capitalistic lifestyles, which are characterised by stability and certainty, many Trinidadians tend to reject the possibility of certainty and control over social life. For some, planning the future is regarded as inappropriate if not impertinent and the rejection of certainty and belief in human control is imbued with a spirituality, evidenced by the term "Please God" which often accompanies any statement as to future intentions. Nonetheless it is quite wrong to equate this with a belief in or love of anarchy; Trinidadians also have a strong (but as in any society, not necessarily uniform) sense of things being appropriate to their time and place, albeit a dynamic rather than static concept. Moreover, Trinidadian society is embedded with class, colour, race/ethnicity and sex/gender stratification and divisions, as well as other political and social constructions, associated with the configuration of social relations (Best, 1991). It is therefore a heavily structured society. Bacchanal seemed to me to be more an acknowledgment and celebration of the inconsistencies within and between social structures; it exists at the limits of social control and not in its absence, although it may be, too, that the participatory and bacchanalian elements of Trinidadian culture have contributed to the history of revolt and resistance in that country.

24. Originally I had attempted to dress like others attending the courts, rather than those who worked there: the magistrates and lawyers who dressed well and formally. After a few days, I was advised by a police officer not to enter court because the magistrate might object to what I was wearing. I was under the impression that, being white, I was expected to dress better than others in the court. Not wishing to jeopardise my access to the courts, nor to give offence, I dressed more formally. I was then approached by people who would say that I "stood out" in the court because I did not dress like the defendants and others who were attending.

25. The only exception of which I was aware was the treatment of students studying law at the Hugh Wooding Law School, who were invited to sit at the barristers' table and look through prosecution files.

26. On one occasion, the police orderly was inquiring apparently in order to determine whether I should be allowed to be present in court while a matter which would otherwise be closed to the public was being heard. Although he allowed me to stay,

shortly afterwards, two Department of Corrective Services employees entered the court room to observe the proceedings and told me that I had to leave.

27. The "interview" was conducted in the presence of another court official, and I was asked for my name and address, the university where I was studying and the name of my supervisor. The magistrate also said that court staff had advised that I was taking notes in court, justifying the blatant impropriety of demanding personal details from a member of the public observing the court. Later, court staff managed to pass me a hand-written note in court, explaining that no-one had told the magistrate that I was taking notes. In any event I was in full view of the magistrate, and certainly under close observation, while in court and it would have been obvious that I was not taking notes.
28. This was not always the case in Trinidad; note the example cited above of the closure of the court to the public, possibly as a device in order to ascertain who I was.
29. In an article aptly entitled, 'White Man's Magic makes Black Deaths Disappear', Broadhurst and Maller (1990) show how the apparently "objective" numerical data concerning the incidence of Aboriginal deaths in custody was manipulated in an attempt to remove the issue of Aboriginal deaths from the political agenda.
30. Refer also to Chapter 2, note 14.

4 Other Matters

RACISM, LAW AND CORRUPTION

Racism and Law

Given the amount of material available today which documents the relations between Australian Aboriginal peoples and the law, it is hard to credit that it was only with Elizabeth Eggleston's (1976, p.ix) pioneering research, conducted in the late 1960s, that this area of study opened up in Australia. Since that time research and writing on the subject have become prolific, culminating in a Royal Commission consisting of some ninety-nine reports of investigations into individual Aboriginal deaths in custody, various state reports, general research reports, criminology research papers, an interim report, a two volume report on underlying issues, and a five volume final report of over 1,500 pages and 339 recommendations.[1]

Much research documents racism in the practice of criminal law; some focusing on the statistical over-representation of Aboriginal people in the criminal courts and gaols; other research being on the overt racism of legal officials.[2] Such accounts illustrate the routine and massive criminalisation of Aboriginal peoples in Australia as well as the overt racism of legal officers including police, judges and justices of the peace. Still other research documents the criminalisation of Aboriginal people in the context of sex/gender relations or in terms of working class issues such as the use of public space (e.g. Carrington, 1989; Cunneen, 1988).

Research has also focused on the explanation of the phenomenon of Aboriginal criminalisation. Early research, such as Eggleston's (1976), advocated Aboriginal people's access to legal representation and the decriminalisation of drunkenness (neither of which strategy appears to have reduced the proportion of Aboriginal prisoners[3]). Other studies have been concerned with cultural differences which contribute to misunderstandings in the legal context (Foley, 1984; Kearins, 1990; Ligterwood, 1984). Another area of research has been that which follows from broadly based studies of the problems of policing, accountability and discretion in law (e.g. Brogden, 1982; Brown et al, 1984; Lustgarten, 1986). This research has indicated how institutional factors, such as the numbers of police and types of policing, as well as the discretionary exercise of power within the legal system have resulted in the over-representation of Aboriginal people in the courts and prisons (Bird, 1987; Carrington, 1989; Cunneen, 1990, 1992c; Cunneen & Robb, 1987).

The recognition of the level of violence involved in the contemporary criminalisation process, however, has only recently been apparent in Australian research (e.g. Wilson, 1982; Zdenkowski & Brown, 1982). If Douglas Hay (1922) is correct, this recognition of law's violence is itself a reflection of the increasingly violent nature of a society undergoing economic decline. In any event, focus on the graphic nature and consequences of legitimised violence against Aboriginal people has also been publicised by campaigns conducted by Aboriginal people and organisations, and consequent international pressure (Cowlishaw, 1991). It was these campaigns which resulted in the Royal Commission, referred to above, which was established specifically to investigate the incidence and causes of Aboriginal deaths in custody. The graphically violent nature of Aboriginal criminalisation in contemporary Australia is now a fertile area of academic and institutional studies (e.g. Amnesty International, 1993; Carrington, 1991; Cunneen, 1990; Moss, 1991).

My own understanding of the operation of the common law upon Aboriginal peoples was also significantly shaped by my experiences while working on the Royal Commission inquiry into the death of John Pat. Pat was sixteen years old when he died in custody, after being involved in a brawl with off-duty police officers outside a pub in Roebourne. Four white police officers and an Aboriginal police aid[4] were charged with manslaughter over his death. They were all acquitted by an all white jury. Subsequently the police officers, but not the Aboriginal police aid, were promoted. None were subject to internal disciplinary action over Pat's death.

The Royal Commission inquiry was held in Roebourne some seven years after Pat's death, and six years after the acquittal of those charged with his killing. During the hearing itself I witnessed the intimidation and harassment of Aboriginal witnesses and others attending the hearing; the refusal to acknowledge Aboriginal peoples' attempts to be heard; the refusal to acknowledge the validity of Aboriginal practices and ways of conducting meetings. Of even more concern, however, was the construction of stereotypes of Aboriginal peoples as violent through the legal processes both prior to and including the Commission. At the same time, the violence perpetrated by the *white* police officers in the name of the law was denied, diminished or legitimised (refer Purdy, 1992a). The outcome of the John Pat inquiry, and every one of the other ninety-eight inquiries into Aboriginal deaths in custody, was that no Aboriginal death in custody was 'the product of deliberate violence or brutality by police or prison officers' (Aus RCIADIC, 1991a:1.2.2).

My preliminary understanding of law was based upon current Australian academic analysis of the position of Aboriginal peoples subjected to the common law system and my own experience and interpretation of the Royal Commission into Aboriginal Deaths in Custody. This analysis indicated that many Aboriginal people had a different understanding of what law is than is taught as legal doctrine. It also indicated that violence, both actual and attributed, played a crucial role in the relations between Aboriginal people and the law. The processes of criminalisation of Aboriginal people were often, although also routine and commonplace, extremely violent. At the same time, the legal system manufactured an identity for Aboriginal people in which they were the ones who were associated with the perpetration of violence.

In Trinidad, I was wanting to establish whether the common law system operated in a similar fashion and carried similar consequences for the colonised peoples of that society. In comparison to Western Australia, however, there was little research available in Trinidad or the Caribbean specifically concerning law and racism. Indeed there was a marked resistance evident in much of the literature I read, and many of the discussions I had, to relegating the phenomenon of racism outside of an economic context (e.g. Abdullah, interview with the author, November 17, 1992; Craig, 1988; James, 1963[1938]; Omowale, 1992a; Williams, 1961[1944]). It was the incorporation of these views with my earlier position which resulted in the current manuscript.

Corruption and Racism

In this section I wish to deal with the issue of treating racism as a corruption of the legal system. This issue is of particular significance given that, in Trinidad at least, much is made of the ineptitude and corruption of public officials. I do not doubt that this exists in Trinidad as elsewhere; although I would not venture to say whether it is more widespread in Trinidad, of a different nature, or just that people are better informed.[5] In Western Australia, allegations of the corruption of public officials such as police and magistrates are nowhere near as widely published and discussed as in Trinidad.

I do not intend here to make any quantitative comparison of corruption within the two systems, even if that were possible. The relative wealth of the different economies may be relevant, but for now I just wish to note that the widespread knowledge of corruption in Trinidad is not necessarily indicative that corruption is more widespread. There is a strong oral tradition in Trinidad which entails a lesser reliance on official discourse. Moreover, although population sizes are roughly the same, a more informed local knowledge may in part be the result of the smaller geographical size of Trinidad. In any event, incidents of apparent corruption occurred while I conducted my field-work in the magistrates' courts of both Trinidad and Western Australia.

Corruption implies that the operatives within an institution are not complying with "the rules" of that institution for reasons which cannot be morally excused. When applied to the legal system, a study of corruption would focus on incidents in which operatives breached the law, as specified in statutes, standing orders, precedent, or more generally breached the perceived ethos of a common law system. Corruption is therefore analysed as an aberration. An obvious example of what would amount to (possible) corruption occurred during my field-work in Western Australia. I was told by a court official that there recently had been two complaints lodged over a magistrate's behaviour in court. In order to make out their complaints, however, complainants were required to obtain transcripts of the recorded proceedings. I was told that one of the relevant tapes could no longer be located. If the tape had in fact been taken or wiped clean, the conduct would clearly be illegal as amounting to theft or destruction of property.

Another, more abstract, notion of what amounts to corruption in the legal system may be adopted; one which relies on some notion of the ethos of common law systems. An example of what may be considered corruption in this second sense occurred in Trinidad. A black and obviously poor Afro-Trinidadian man had been arrested and charged with unlawful possession of a bag of green mangoes. The "unlawful possession" charge enables police to arrest individuals on suspicion that any item they have in their possession is not lawfully their own. Such individuals are then held in prison until they are brought before a magistrate and required to convince her or him of their innocence. (I was informed that bail is not available on this charge.)

It seems that the defendant in the particular case at issue was brought from prison to the magistrate on the day following his arrest. The arresting officer was called to give evidence explaining his suspicion as to the defendant's ownership of the mangoes. That evidence consisted of the defendant behaving in a suspicious manner, and the inability of 'some men' who were playing cricket nearby, and who were not called as witnesses, to verify the defendant's explanation. The defendant then testified, claiming that his employer had told him to take the mangoes. The magistrate found the defendant guilty, and then asked him whether he would be able to produce his employer as a witness if he were given the opportunity. The defendant said he would. The magistrate, however, then sentenced the defendant, saying that he had already been found guilty.

This instance raises issues of a more diffuse kind of corruption. The magistrate, by failing to ensure that the defendant had an opportunity to present his defence, would no doubt have breached procedural guidelines. But more generally the magistrate's actions could be regarded as inconsistent with the broader tenets of a common law system which require that defendants be given a fair trial. The case also raises issues related to the discriminatory application of widely discretionary laws within the legal system. Offences such as "unlawful possession" effectively amount to status offences as their application by police and determination by magistrates will ultimately depend on the sort of person involved. The corruption associated with these kinds of laws could therefore also be related to notions of the ethos of common law systems, and in particular the tenet of equality before the law.

In the same way, evidence of racism within the legal system may be viewed as a corruption of that system, perhaps infringing a specific law or procedural guideline, but in any event infringing the tenet of equality before the law. However, I do not regard this as a useful way of analysing the existence of racism within the legal system for the purposes of my research. The legality or otherwise of legal officials' conduct may often be of little relevance to those who have no ideological commitment to the system. For example, it would have been of no comfort to the many thousands of Australian Aborigines to know that their families were torn apart, not by corrupt officials, but by officials whose conduct carried the full imprimatur of the law.

Moreover when the notion of corruption is extended to include actual laws which fail to meet some presumed standard of the law's ethos, the distinction between what is law and what is corruption becomes something of an act of faith. It requires some sort of teleological view of law, exemplified by Ronald Dworkin's notion of law as 'working itself pure' (Dworkin, 1986). Those excluded from the legal system but subjected to its violence, such as Aboriginal Australians, have little reason to adopt such a justificatory view of what law is.

It is important to note that such peoples may well be able to use the legal system's distinctions and justificatory ideology strategically, as Kerruish (1991) indicates, and as is discussed more fully in Chapters 7 and 8. Such attempts to manipulate the legal system for their own ends, however, do not necessarily indicate such peoples' respect for or acceptance of the legal system rather than their recognition of its power.

But apart from their strategic uses, allegations of corruption tend toward an analysis in which the particular, in this instance individual court officials or specific laws, is judged against a general law or tenet. In the context of my study this approach is not useful for two reasons. C.L.R. James (1980a[1961], p.131) wrote,

> I set out to show that the blunders and deficiencies of which they are guilty are historically caused and therefore can be historically corrected. Otherwise we are left with the demoralising result: "That is the way West Indians are",

> and closely allied to this: "The man or men who have brought us into this mess are bad men. Let us search for some good men." As long as you remain on that level, you understand nothing and your apparently "good" men turn rapidly into men who are no good.

Like James I am interested in a broader historical analysis of individuals' 'blunders and deficiencies'. This is not only because 'the demoralising result' of failing to take a historical view can be very much a part of the project of colonialism, that is, locating the failings of imperial institutions in the apparent corruption and incompetence of the colonial operatives,[6] but also because focusing on the 'blunders and deficiencies' of 'bad men' and women, the corrupt officials, tends to occlude any broader perspective on an issue such as racism as it is perpetuated and constituted by legal systems based on British common law.

COMMON LAW, DISCOURSE AND COERCION

Common Law

It is true that the formal ties between the legal systems of Trinidad and Tobago, Australia and Britain have lessened; particularly in relation to Australia, and in recent years (Cross, 1988; Toohey, 1990). However, it is difficult to discern any change in the role or character of law in periods identified by the change in political relations between the colony and the metropole, or within the political relations of the jurisdictions, such as the obtaining of universal franchise.[7] Even on the level of purely formal connections to the "metropole", the common law systems of Trinidad and Australia cannot easily be periodised into colonial and post-colonial eras.

It was not until 1986 that the supervisory role of the British Privy Council over Australian state legal systems was removed from Australian national and state constitutions (Toohey, 1990); the British Privy Council to this day exercises that role over the legal system of Trinidad and Tobago. In any event, common law systems are administered by a minority who are the product of a particular elite education, as are lawyers and judges (Kerruish, 1987), or of an insular culture, as are police (Queensland Commission of Inquiry, 1989 [The Fitzgerald Report]). These legal operatives are therefore insulated from more broadly democratic influences and are trained to acquire a particular and peculiar ideology. As common law systems are based on precedent and statutes, they are also largely based upon the "received" wisdom of earlier, often overtly colonial, times.[8] Even allowing that the legal systems of Trinidad and Tobago and Australia have achieved increasing autonomy from the formal controls of British institutions and an increasing responsiveness to local conditions, these legal systems remain far more profoundly imbued with British influences than the law and values of their colonised populations.[9]

Moreover, such modifications as have been made have been effected through the same kinds of institutional sites and roles, discourses, practices and jurisprudence as originated in British common law. It is in this sense that the legal systems of nations such as the United States, Canada, India, New Zealand and South Africa, as well as those of Australia and Trinidad and Tobago, all remain part of the common law tradition.[10]

The jurisprudence and practice of law in common law based systems engenders certain attitudes towards law by its practitioners. Lawyers (and others) often perceive the resolution of problems as existing in the obtaining of a favourable judgment or the passing of relevant legislation or amendments. Should such remedies fail,[11] lawyers will often displace any blame onto the inadequacies of the individuals who enact, rule upon or enforce the law. Faults may be attributed to the racism of individual police officers or sexism of individual judges, and, particularly in colonial settings, the corruption and incompetence of officials or parliamentarians, as discussed above. Alternatively, as in the *National Report of the Royal Commission into Aboriginal Deaths in Custody* (Aus RCIADIC, 1991a), the failings of law in practice may be seen by lawyers to be reflective of the nature - and inequalities - of the broader society.

It is of note that these analyses of law depend upon the entrenched ideological divisions utilised in Western ontology, the individual and society. Allocating law's (aberrant) failures to either individuals or society allows "the law" to occupy the (conceptual) space between the individual and society and to exist as a (disembodied) body of rules and rights which are separable from the law in practice. Within the slippage between individuals and society, "the law", godlike, remains innocent and blame tends to be allocated elsewhere if that system is shown to be an instrument of injustice. And it is also in this context that law - understood as a system of rules - is thought to assume a purely discursive existence.

Kerruish's (1991) thesis of the fetishism of law dissects and rejects the adequacy of the view of law as an intangible system of rules; "the rule of law and not by men" is a *non sequitur*. As indicated above in the discussion on scientific realism, Kerruish's analysis is based upon a relational ontology, and she treats law, not as a system of rules, but as a specific institutional site which generates social practices which are both based upon and constitutive of the basic unequal social relations of class, sex/gender and ethnicity/race. But more particularly here, a relational ontology also takes issue with law as discourse.

"Discourse" itself has multiple meanings, and can refer simply to what is said or written, or it may also, at least in the context of academic work, include references to practices and institutions as well as language (e.g. Burton & Carlen, 1979 re the former; Foucault, 1979 re the latter). This confluence of meaning is of itself significant, in that it seems indicative of how it is that even institutional settings and practices, that is the concrete, tend to be perceived from an academic perspective. Like language, institutions and practices come to be *known* as discourse in its narrow sense. Indeed, the tendency towards discursive reductionism is such that one of the significant streams of contemporary legal scholarship is the "law as literature" genre (Weisberg, 1992).

As indicated previously, Cain (1994, p.20), asserts that it is assumed that what 'is not presentable as discourse... has no *potency* outside of discourse'. The assumption that knowledge is captured by discourse diminishes the importance of lived experience. It also fails to come to terms with how such an assumption as it is applied to the legal system may itself be specific to and further the interests of particular classes and groups, as indicated below.

Discourse v. Coercion[12]

In *Principles of Policing*, Sir Robert Peel stated,

> the extent to which the co-operation of the public can be secured, diminishes proportionately, the necessity of the use of physical force and compulsion for achieving police objectives.[13]

I would argue that as co-operation diminishes the experience and awareness of law as being constituted by 'physical force and compulsion', it likewise engenders a perception of law as something which is written or spoken.[14] For example, while a lawyer or academic is likely to know law as a verbal system of rules or discourse which exercises its own logic, others' knowledge of law may be principally derived from encounters with officials empowered to enforce the criminal law, and their experience of law will be in terms of the activities of police, court appearances, imprisonment, and often alienation and violence.

It is of note that such knowledges of law are likely to be correlative to class. It is also true, almost as a matter of definition, that colonised peoples' knowledge of law is more likely to be gained other than via discourse. Unless such people become acculturated into the language, practices and values of their colonisers, the colonial legal system will not be experienced by them as a verbalised system of rules, but in its most extreme form as an alien, repressive and often violent force. For the marginal elements of Trinidadian and Aboriginal peoples, the common law represents just such a legal system. Teresa Ashforth's (1990, p.308), work with the Nyungah fringe-dwellers of the Swan Valley revealed,

> When Aboriginal people speak of their social experience of law what they have to say comes closer to the Poulantzas evocation of law as violence than it does to any other sanitised and privileged interpretations within the self-referentiality of legal discourse itself. They also clearly recognise, like Poulantzas and others, that it is in the "white man's" capacity to "name" that the justification for the violence towards them resides.

Because what concerns me is the operation of law from the perspective of those who are not, or who are perceived as not being, "co-operative", I do not regard it as useful or accurate to conceptualise law as discourse. That is not to say that law cannot or should not be conceptualised in such terms, but that the utility of so doing will depend upon the context of the study undertaken. For example, to conceptualise law as a (verbalised) system of rules may be useful to understand lawyers, judges and legal reasoning (Kerruish, 1987, p.18).

It is also true that law is often thought of as constituted by the words and principles found in statutes and judgments, and I would not deny that one of the artefacts of legal processes is discourse, in its narrow sense. As such, law has been usefully analysed by theorists such as Frank Burton and Pat Carlen (1979). However, I do not think such an understanding is adequate to comprehend the operation of law in relation to those who do not conform to certain dominant social norms and behaviours (see also Bourdieu & Passeron, 1977, p.36). Such outsiders to the legal system are likely to be excluded from an understanding of law as rules or discourse because of factors such as language, jargon, lack of information and intimidation; alternatively such people may be simply disinterested or cynical about what operatives within the legal system *say* they are doing, as has been discussed elsewhere.[15]

It would only follow that law is not known to such outsiders, if one was prepared to acquiesce to the image of law projected through legal rhetoric. That is, an image of law as an essentially verbal practice; and an image that is employed by many legal practitioners. However, I would argue that there is no reason why an internalised perspective of law should be privileged as being the only correct view of law, or the only view worthy of attention. And although analysts such as Burton and Carlen do not share altogether in a lawyer's perspective of the law, their analysis does coincide in significant ways with what might be called law's image of itself.

Burton and Carlen postulate that delegitimised modes of experience can be accessed by deconstructing official discourse (Burton & Carlen, 1979, p.20). Therefore, like the authors of legal reports and judgments whom they criticise, Burton and Carlen themselves marginalise "officially" marginalised people by making them redundant; by failing to consult them. The assumption of theorists like Burton and Carlen is that what is suppressed by official discourses can be reconstituted through the analysis of that discourse. Taking the myth of the 'transparence and universality of language' one step further even than the 'Presiding Judge' who 'has obviously no scruples in exchanging words with [even] the old [and] "uneducated"' (Barthes, 1974[1957], p.44), these theorists presume that what the old, "uneducated" and other accused know may be accessed through the language of the judge. But as Roland Barthes (1974[1957], p.46), has also noted, 'To rob a man of his language in the very name of language: this is the first step in all legal murders'.

The position of such analysts coincides with a lawyer's view of law in that both engender the attitude that law is best (or only) known through its *own* words. By concentrating on the rhetoric of law largely to the exclusion of its practice, analysts and lawyers alike tend to exclude the standpoint and discourses of those upon whom 'the use of physical force and compulsion' is regarded as a 'necessity'. In this they are complicit with the 'spectacle of a terror which threatens us all [but perhaps some more than others], that of being judged by a power which wants to hear only the language it lends us' (Barthes, 1974[1957], p.46).

It is the physical practices and enforced rules of law which combine to create a space in which legal discourse in the form of judgments and reports can be constructed. This space is created by not only the determination of who will be allowed to speak and what they will be allowed to say in the public arena of court proceedings, but also who will be able and prepared to speak and what they will be able and prepared to say. I am not here just referring to the doctrinal rules of relevance and admissibility, although these are significant. I am also concerned with people's lived experience in the form of prior encounters with the law, and the standpoint sensitivity of legal processes and practitioners, including the police. I am talking about history, coercion, intimidation and fear (see also Hogg, 1991; Cowlishaw, 1991).

The end result of legal processes and rules is the curtailment or exclusion of knowledges gained from particular standpoints; that is, the absence of the actual perceptions, understandings and demands of marginalised groups from law. If one artefact of law is discourse, another is silence; or perhaps what is worse than silence, not 'deprived of language, ...[but instead] rigged out in that of our accusers, humiliated and condemned by it' (Barthes, 1974[1957], p.46). And it is this which enables the authors of legal discourse to construct the legal fictions which come to represent marginalised groups in law.

Moreover, if we as academics are content to study only legal discourse, we are complicit in the reproduction of such absences and fictions. It is in order to redress this emphasis on legal discourse that I have attempted to engage with the knowledges of colonised peoples and bring these to bear on the representations of law incorporated in this thesis.

Notes

1. Waller comments that the amount written about Aborigines and Aborigines within the criminal justice system over the last fifty years is such that the 'academic study of Aborigines and the law is an established enterprise' (L. Waller, 'Elizabeth Eggleston, Aborigines and the Law', Hanks & Keon-Cohen (eds), *Aborigines and the Law* (1984), p. 304, in Lincoln & Wilson, 1994, p.61).
2. With respect to statistically based studies of racism, refer to Aust RCIADIC (1989a, 1990a, 1990b); Behrendt & Behrendt (1992); Cunneen (1992a); Thomas (1987). For studies which also refer to the explicitly racist practices and discourses of legal officers, refer to Bird (1987); Cunneen (1992b); Cunneen & Robb (1987); Dodson (1991); Eggleston (1976); Foley (1984).
3. Although there is now widespread access to legal representation by Aboriginal people, Lyons (1984, p.137), commented that, 'The most important achievement of ALSs [Aboriginal Legal Services] has been their acceptance by Aboriginal people'. Bird's (1987) research indicated that legal representation of Aboriginal people had not resulted in a decline in their over-representation in court and prison statistics. Refer to Chapters 6 and 9 for a discussion of the effect (or lack of effect) of the decriminalisation of drunkenness.
4. Aboriginal police aids, who are authorised to arrest only Aboriginal people, have no avenues of promotion available within the Police Force. Refer to Grabosky (1988) for further details of the death of John Pat.
5. Note that corruption is often defined as the failure to comply with standards which may be regarded as "universal", "consensual" or "efficient" as opposed to self-interested or particularistic (in the Parsonian sense). Although I do not have the opportunity to pursue this issue here, it should be noted that standards, such as what will constitute "merit", are frequently defined by, and further the interests of, the white male elite. (For a discussion of this issue in the context of women and employment, refer to Purdy, 1989.) Failure to comply with these standards may be indicative only of a refusal to adopt the values of the white male elite rather than any retrogressive or immoral practice, particularly in the colonial context.
6. This attitude was exemplified when the government of Trinidad and Tobago requested that two Scotland Yard detectives investigate corruption in the Trinidad and Tobago Police Service in 1992 (refer to Chapter 3, note 2). This followed a government commissioned report by British officers in 1991 about how to restructure the Trinidad and Tobago police service (O'Dowd, 1991). The stance adopted by the government of Trinidad and Tobago seems oddly ignorant, if not deeply cynical, in the face of the widely-publicised and very serious claims about corruption and ineffectiveness directed at the "Metropolitan" Police Service and its

regulatory institutions, cited in McLaughlin and Muncie (1993), and dating from the early 1980s.

7. These changes have been significant for some individuals of all classes and races, who are now able to access political power and, to some extent, to distribute its benefits. By and large this has not affected many in their constituencies, whether poor Trinidadians or Aborigines.
8. Like many other "ex-colonies", in Trinidad and Tobago, the laws and legal system that applied under colonialism were simply adopted under the new Constitution of the Republic; and in fact, colonial laws over-ride any constitutional guarantee; refer to section 6. I am indebted to Bilal Abdullah for this point.
9. Although the continued role of the Privy Council as overseer of the legal system of Trinidad and Tobago also remains relevant. So too is the apparent practice of that country's legislature of modelling its laws upon those of the U.K. I was informed of this latter practice by a number of Trinidadian lawyers and magistrates, often with some degree of pride.
10. It should also be noted that in referring to the common law I am not using the term in the technical legal sense in which it is distinguished from statutory law. I use the term to refer to those legal systems which are based on British common law, and which are usually defined in opposition to other European legal systems, known as "civil law".
11. See Mendelsohn's (1991) case study for a striking example of the efforts taken through the legal system to improve working and living conditions for Indian stone quarry workers. Although actions at law were repeatedly successful, the working and living conditions of the workers did not change.
12. Note that the following discussion is in part based upon 'Royal Commissions and Omissions' (Purdy, 1991).
13. Quoted in Olive (1990, p.111).
14. Of course, if one considers "the law" to be the preserve of the judiciary, what I am arguing runs counter to the traditional Westminster separation of powers doctrine, as physical coercion is more commonly associated with police and prisons. I would not deny the utility of recognising the division between the three arms of state, particularly in so far as it denotes a power struggle between them. But to the extent that the doctrine occludes recognition of the very extensive commonality of interest which can exist between all arms of state, it may also be ideological in a negative sense.
15. The analysis by Hall et al (1978) of (metropolitan) working class attitudes towards the legal system indicates that their position may be more ambivalent than that of the colonised, for the reasons discussed in Chapter 1, and above, under the heading 'Marxism and Post-Modernism'.

PART II
CONTEMPORARY CRIMINALISATION

Outline of Part II

Part II is concerned with the criminalisation of colonised peoples in contemporary Trinidad and Western Australia. The aim is to provide alternative perspectives from which the operation of the common law system can be viewed, or perhaps more accurately, different contexts in which the operation of that law is lived in a contemporary setting.

Chapters 5 and 6 engage with issues associated with criminalisation in Trinidad and Western Australia respectively, and act as counterpoints illustrating similarities and differences between the two jurisdictions. Each chapter is divided into three sections, and includes statistical data on broader demographics and economics, statistics on the criminal justice system and finally, accounts of my field-work in the magistrates' courts. The different sections provide a variety of frameworks in which the operation of law in relation to colonised peoples can be understood. These perspectives range from the more general, in which criminal law processes are seen to be just one of many inhibiting forces to which colonised peoples are subjected, to the more particularistic, in which the operations of the criminal justice system are portrayed in terms of the relations between court officials and defendants.

The demographic and economic statistics provide a broad outline of the contemporary conditions under which Trinidadian and Aboriginal peoples live and die, and with which readers may be unfamiliar. These statistics are also used to provide the broader context within which the criminalisation of colonised populations takes place. As indicated in Chapter 1, that context is characterised by great hardship for many colonised peoples, and is particularly one of economic marginalisation and dependency. In such a context, the criminal justice system can appear to be merely incidental to the oppressive conditions in which many colonised peoples live and die. Moreover, with poverty, illness and dependency characterising much of their existence, the data also indicate that conditions for significant elements within colonised populations seem scarcely to have improved since earlier colonial times.

By going on to elaborate data on the criminal justice system itself, however, I hope to indicate that there is also a continuity between the colonial legal systems of the past and the present. Such data illustrate not only the very violent nature of relations constituted through the contemporary criminal justice systems in both jurisdictions, but also the extreme intervention of these systems into the lives of very large proportions of colonised populations. Just as the general conditions under which many colonised peoples live today indicate that Western "civilisation" has brought few benefits to them, so too, specific data on the criminalisation of these peoples indicate that the historical excesses of the colonial legal system have hardly diminished.

More than this, however, the juxtaposition of data on the economic position of colonised peoples and the criminal justice system also indicates that economic influences continue to be profoundly connected to contemporary criminalisation. If the brutality of contemporary legal relations with colonised peoples has not declined, nor has the stimulus for such violence changed. Together the data on the contemporary demography, economy and criminalisation of Trinidadian and Aboriginal peoples provide evidence of the persisting nature of social relations as these are lived by significant sections within colonised populations.

In order to understand something of how law contributes to the constitution of such social relations in the contemporary context, this Part also documents my field-work in the courts of Trinidad and Western Australia. Because of their "public" nature, the courts provided an accessible site in which to examine the interaction of those empowered by law and those subjected to its processes. The accounts of my field-work are therefore intended to indicate something of the mundane and personalised practice of law.

I have attempted to capture something of the complex tendencies that evolve out of the practice of law at this level. Such tendencies are apparent in the significant, albeit limited, ability of individuals who work within the legal system, such as magistrates, to have an impact upon the experience of court for those brought before them. More importantly, the contradictory uses of law can be seen in the ability of colonised and other oppressed groups to wrest important, albeit small, victories and uses from the legal system. It is from within the small scale lacunae - the conflicts between court officials, the sympathetic individual and the arrogation of legal procedures - that colonised peoples are able to occasionally extract what they want from what is an overarchingly antagonistic legal system.

For despite the complexities of law in practice there is also clear evidence that it is an overarchingly antagonistic system in relation to colonised peoples. Such antagonism is evident in the generally different treatment accorded defendants depending upon their ethnic/racial identity. For example, there is a marked difference between the impact and substance of the accounts of my experiences in the two jurisdictions, with the intensity and graphic quality of the court experience in Trinidad being absent from that of Western Australia. It seems to me that the differences are, at least in part, attributable to the different colonial status of the majority of defendants in the two jurisdictions. Even in

Western Australia, however, where there was only a small number of colonised people, it was evident that there was a marked variation between the treatment of Aboriginal as opposed to non-Aboriginal defendants.

It is important to note that much of my interpretation of the court experience and the other data presented in this Part is postponed until the subsequent, and final chapters of my manuscript. The lack of clear direction and analysis in this Part, if disconcerting, is also intentional. As is elaborated more fully in my discussion of theory and methodology in Part I, my approach has deliberately been one in which I situate myself in terms of the limitations consequent upon the available data and, more significantly, my standpoint as a non-colonised "observer".

As also mentioned previously, if data, particularly those documenting how colonised peoples live and die, are not sufficient of themselves to convey meaning to the reader without analysis and ranking, I would suggest that readers consider these statistics in relation to the conditions in which they themselves and those they know live and die. Matters which readers may wish to consider include the ethnic diversity of their own society; their own health status and that of those they know; their own access to education, housing, electricity, water, employment or government assistance; their own dealings with law - in particular whether they have ever been arrested, handcuffed, strip searched, imprisoned.

5 Criminalisation in Contemporary Trinidad

A DEMOGRAPHIC AND ECONOMIC PROFILE [1]

Trinidad and Tobago, covering a land mass of some 5,000 square kilometres, has one of the highest population densities in the world (Kurian, 1982). The most recent census of 1990 indicated that there were 1,184,106 people in Trinidad alone, with females comprising slightly less than fifty per cent of the population. Although the population had increased since the last census in 1980 (from 1,039,046), data also indicated declines in the total population of Trinidad and Tobago in 1988 and 1989 due to falling birth rates and negative net migration, and no net change in 1990. Net migration from Trinidad and Tobago in 1988 alone was almost 45,000 people, or five per cent of the population. It is of note that the policies of the International Monetary Fund (I.M.F.) were implemented at this time. It has been expressly acknowledged by I.M.F. personnel that such emigration is considered essential to the I.M.F. 'development strategy' for the Caribbean region (McAfee, 1991, p.11).

Although only 5.9% of the population were foreign born, the 1980 census indicated that of the population of Trinidad, 42.2% were of Indian origin, 38.8% were of African origin, 16.8% were of mixed origin, 1% were white, 0.5% were of Chinese origin and 0.1% were of Syrian/Lebanese origin. If the population of Tobago is included, the proportions become 40.8% African origin and 40.7% Indian origin.[2] More recent data, however, indicate that those of Indian origin now outnumber those of African origin in Trinidad and Tobago combined (Reddock & McCree, 1992, p.7). Like most other Caribbean nations, Trinidad and Tobago was traditionally dominated, at least numerically, by those of African descent. This change in the ethnic/racial identity of the majority population is therefore of considerable significance (LaGuerre, 1988).

The religious denominations indicated in the 1980 census were 25.9% Hindu, 6.2% Muslim, 4% Presbyterian, 3.4% Pentecostal, 2.4% Baptist, 13.6% Anglican, 33.8% Roman Catholic, as well as Seventh Day Adventists, Jehovah Witnesses and Methodists. These statistics are misleading, however, to the extent that they do not indicate the degree to which some religious groups, particularly within the Baptist and Pentecostal religions, are strongly influenced by African spirituality.

In 1991, the death rate in Trinidad and Tobago was 662.04 per 100,000. Of this total rate, the most common causes of death were heart disease and malignant neoplasms (259.98 and 83.40 per 100,000 respectively), although the death rate as a proportion of live births indicates that the perinatal period was high risk. At the same time, the homicide rate was 7.68 per 100,000; the suicide rate was 11.06 per 100,000; deaths from injury and poisoning were 51.4 per 100,000. Still births were 12.8 per 1,000 births and the neo-natal death rate was 7.2 per 1,000 live births. In 1980, male life expectancy was 66.88 years and life expectancy for females was 71.62 years. By 1990, almost sixty per cent of the population of Trinidad were below the age of thirty.

The 1980 census indicated that there was 4% illiteracy; 1.6% of the population had university qualifications; and 62.6% had primary education only. Also in 1980, 3.4% of the outer walls of dwellings in Trinidad were constructed out of wattle/adobe or tapia (a mixture of mud and cow-dung), but 86.4% were constructed out of brick and/or wood and on average there were 4.7 persons resident in each dwelling. In 1988, almost thirty per cent of households were without pipe-born water and almost ten per cent were without electricity.

In 1991, unemployment was officially 18.5% of the work-force; but for those seeking employment between the ages of fifteen to nineteen years, almost one in two (43.2%) were unemployed. For females of that age group unemployment was 56.6%. In 1992, it was reported that unemployment had risen to 20.6% (*Express*, October 7, 1992). Unemployment benefits were not available in Trinidad.

There is however, a scheme of employment on public works in Trinidad and Tobago.[3] Colloquially known as a "ten days", the schemes provided ten day periods of employment to some of the unemployed on public works projects. Unpublished Ministry of Works data indicate that by 1982, 50,000 people, or one-third of the work-force, received income under a similar scheme - which was largely funded by windfall gains made due to the "oil crisis" (Singh, 1989, p.26; Auty & Gelb, 1986). That scheme was radically reduced and reformed as a result of structural adjustment conducted in conjunction with I.M.F. intervention into the economy after 1986, and currently operates as L.I.D.P. (Labour Intensive Development Programme) (*Sunday Mirror*, September 6, 1992). In October 1992, the Works and Transport Minister announced plans to reduce salaries of persons employed under the programme (*Express*, October 24, 1992).

For those *with* jobs, the average income in 1991 was just TT$1,600 per month (US$384). Since 1988 the number of people in the top wage earning category had increased by more than sixty per cent, but the number of those in the lowest category, less than TT$250 per month (US$60), had also increased - by almost eighty per cent. Moreover, a Value Added Tax of fifteen per cent was instituted in 1990. While average income declined or remained static, retail prices increased so much between 1982 and 1991 that the value of the Trinidad and Tobago dollar declined to TT43c. The major causes of the decline were increases in the cost of basic necessities such as food, light and fuel, which were attributable in part to the devaluation of the currency of Trinidad and Tobago and the removal of subsidies as part of the policy of "structural adjustment".

The Gross Domestic Product (G.D.P.) of Trinidad and Tobago in 1991 was TT$20,516.1 million, although at constant prices this was lower than the value of G.D.P. in 1986. Also in 1991, Trinidad and Tobago was a net importer of almost all items except mineral fuel and chemicals, but had a net balance of trade to the value of TT$1,351,528.9. The balance of trade had declined to almost one-third of the 1990 balance, however, and this was associated with reduced value of oil exports after the 1990 Gulf War price increases, and the relaxation of the Negative List on imports, as part of structural adjustment (*South Survey*, 1992; *Sunday Mirror*, May 3, 1992).

The chief trading partner of Trinidad and Tobago in 1991 was the U.S., supplying thirty-nine per cent of imports and taking forty-nine per cent of exports. In that year, the U.S. had a trade balance in favour of Trinidad and Tobago to the value of TT$1,349 million, a balance which was less than half that for 1990. In 1991, Trinidad and Tobago also had a favourable trade balance with the other Caricom and Caribbean countries. Its export income was essentially dependant upon mineral fuels (oil and gas) and related products.

In 1990, public debt in Trinidad and Tobago totalled TT$11,920.6 million (Holton, 1994, p.375); more than half the G.D.P. of 1991. It was reported that in 1992, debt servicing was absorbing more than twenty per cent of Trinidad and Tobago's export earnings. This was in spite of there being an arrangement in place which had rescheduled debt repayment of US$736 million due between 1988 and 1992 (*Express* October 8, 1992).

In 1989, more than one in every five inhabitants of Trinidad and Tobago were living below the poverty line (Holton, 1994, p.366).

CRIME STATISTICS

Since 1935 the daily average rate of imprisonment in Trinidad and Tobago had peaked at 1.9 prisoners per 1,000 population in 1945 (during oil-fields strikes), and fallen as low as 0.7 prisoners per 1,000 population in 1981. However in 1989, the imprisonment rate increased by a factor of three, to 2.1 prisoners per 1,000 population, and again to 2.5 in 1990 (Hagley, 1993). The attempted coup of 1990, and associated looting, contributed to the latter figure, ironically just the year following the Caribbean economist, Dennis Pantin's (1989, p.19), warning about the impact of I.M.F. policies and 'I.M.F. riots and deaths'. Figures provided by the Trinidad and Tobago Central Statistical Office show that the daily average prison population was even higher in 1991, when the rate increased to 2.7 per 1,000 (T&T CSO, 1993a, pp.8,30,61).

Diagram 1 Trinidad and Tobago
Daily average prison population 1935 - 1991

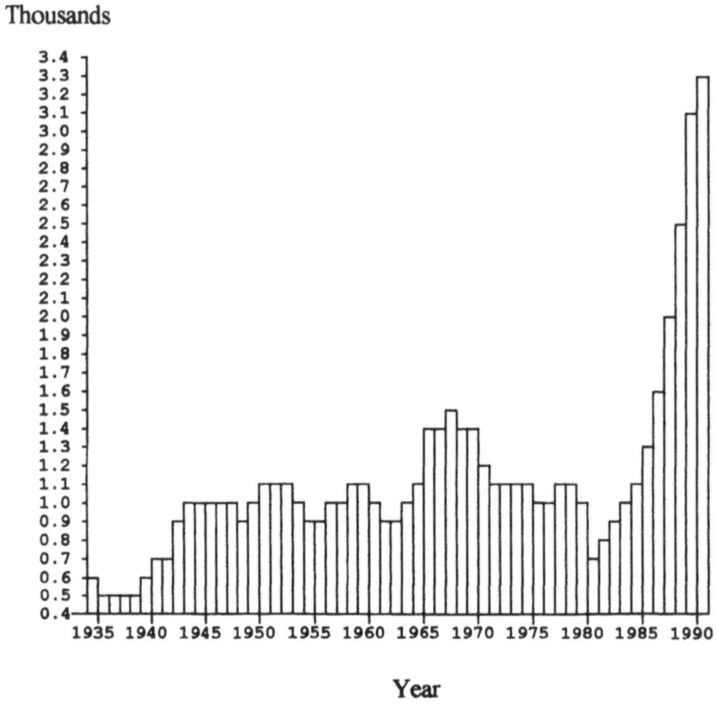

Sources: Hagley (1993); T.&T. C.S.O. (1993)

Maureen Cain and Anand Birju (1992) indicate that there was an increase in sentencing severity in the lower courts of Trinidad and Tobago after 1985, with imprisonment becoming a more likely outcome than previously had been the case. In 1985, 295 persons were committed to peremptory imprisonment; by 1990 this had risen by a factor of almost six, to 1,714. However, Lystra Hagley (1993) shows that an even more important factor in the spiralling imprisonment rate of Trinidad and Tobago had been the increasing number of defendants remanded to custody. In 1988, 2,843 persons were remanded to custody; by 1990 the number remanded had increased by a factor of more than eleven, to 33,486.

Diagram 2 Trinidad and Tobago
Total prisoners remanded into custody 1940 - 1991

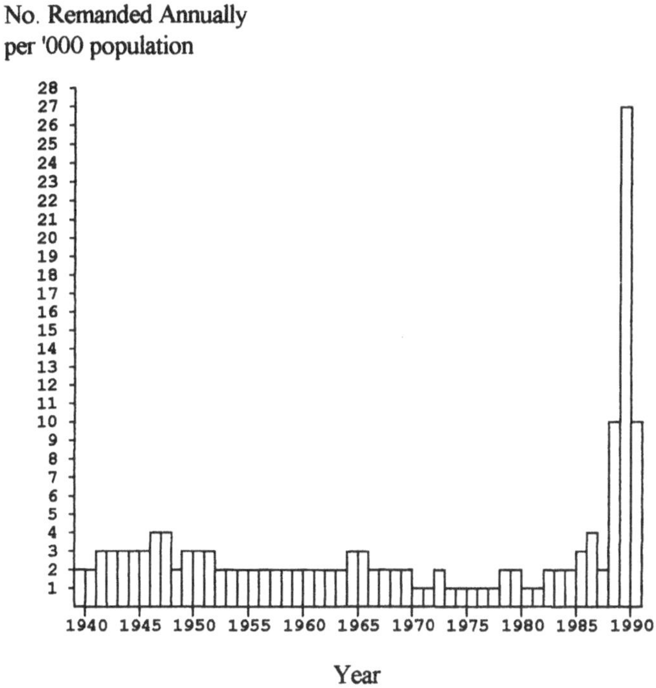

Sources: Hagley (1993); T.&T. C.S.O. (1993)

In 1991, there was a small decline in the number of peremptory imprisonments, to 1,495, but a dramatic fall in the number of people remanded to prison, to 12,858 (T&T CSO, 1993a, p.61). This no doubt was the result of the processing of cases related to the 1990 coup attempt, although remand figures remain extremely high and appear to have little relation to those prior to 1989. It is of note that many of the remands to custody which I observed while conducting field-work in the courts of Trinidad were the result of defendants being unable to raise the bail amounts required, and therefore were directly related to defendants' economic position. It is also of note that in 1991 there were almost as many committals to prison because of fine default and debt (1,230) as there were peremptory imprisonments (T&T CSO, 1993a, p.61). The circumstances of non-remand imprisonments again indicate the manifest significance of economic factors.

It is also of note that, although there had been a significant decline in the number of people being remanded to custody, the average daily prison population had actually increased in 1991, as indicated in Diagram 1. This would indicate that, although there were fewer people being committed to prison, those in prison were being held there for more extensive periods. Given that unconvicted prisoners still constituted up to seventy-four per cent of the prison population, this is a matter of particular concern, and is consistent with my observations in 1992 that the courts were unable to process cases for extensive periods of time, many of which involved defendants who were being held in custody on remand.

Hagley (1993) notes further that in 1990 prisons built to accommodate 1,342 prisoners were holding a daily average of 3,070. She reports a survey of Caribbean prisons, which stated that remand conditions in Trinidad and Tobago were such that cells built for one or two and measuring eight foot by twelve foot were holding up to ten prisoners. As Hagley notes, in the existing over-crowded conditions, there can be no separation of remand and convicted prisoners. Moreover, with ten prisoners to a cell, bodily functions such as excretion become public activities.

I was informed by one prison source that prisoners would have to sleep in rotation, as there was insufficient floor space for all of those held in a cell to sleep at one time. In relation to the Youth Training Centre, I was also informed that youths who were remanded so that reports could be obtained prior to sentencing were denied remission, weekend visits to their families and training. These "privileges" were all available to those who had been sentenced. Remanded youths could be incarcerated for years before the reports were obtained and, when these reports eventually became available, they could in any event recommend a non-custodial sentence. I am unsure whether similar restrictions affected adult remandees. However, Abdullah Omowale, one of the Muslimeen activists who had himself spent a considerable time in prison, stated that prisoners were only eligible for prison issue clothing on conviction; he had known of men to be incarcerated for extensive periods of time wearing only jockey shorts (Abdullah Omowale, interview with the author, November 16, 1992).

Because there have actually been increases in the daily average number of prisoners since 1990, prison conditions are likely to have deteriorated even further. Patrick Jagessar, who had been a magistrate in Trinidad, was interviewed in 1992 while out on release pending an appeal against conviction on corruption charges. He had spent a considerable period of time in prison, and reported of over-crowding, hunger, illness, rape, AIDS deaths, and of instances of rats and cockroaches nibbling at prisoners' flesh (*Mirror*, May 22, 1992; see too, Kirklon Paul, 'The Prison Sharks', *The Light*, May 1990). A brief excerpt from one report stated,

> Homosexuality and the killer AIDS are rampant, and violence is an everyday affair, with some getting pierced in their eyes with sharpened toothbrushes. Hygiene and comfort are virtually non-existent, since most sleep near to bucketfuls of human filth on bare floors. They survive on a couple of dried loaves of bread and the ill groan all day with no health care. ('Not just Prison anymore...It's Hell behind Bars', *Mirror*, May 29, 1992)

Although persons convicted of murder continued to be sentenced to death, the death penalty had not been carried out in Trinidad and Tobago since 1979. Those sentenced to death were incarcerated in cells for twenty-three out of every twenty-four hours that they served (*Mirror*, November 15, 1992). And even though prisoners were not being executed, many died in prison. Between 1982 and 1991, sixty-one prisoners died; eighteen in 1990 alone. Based on average mortality statistics and prison numbers, the 1990 figure indicated a rate of death in prison which was at least two and a-half times the ordinary mortality rate (T&T CSO, 1993a, pp.33,61).

During 1989 and 1990, and with the rapid escalation of prison numbers, expenditure on prisons actually declined significantly, and specifically in relation to staff funding (T&T CSO, 1993a, p.61). The effect on staff morale and attitudes towards prisoners can be imagined. In 1991, however, substantial increases in expenditure on prisons and staff were approved. A further response by the government to the deteriorating conditions in the prisons was to pass legislation authorising the arming of prison officers with automatic weapons and tear gas canisters. There was also an announcement made of plans to build a new prison - together with the granting of the loan required to finance it (*Express*, February 2, 1992; *Express*, July 15, 1992).

The problems associated with the criminalisation process in Trinidad were not confined to the prisons. For example, between mid-January and mid-November 1992, the local press reported one hundred killings in Trinidad and Tobago; nine of these deaths were attributed to shootings and beatings by on-duty police officers.[4] There were also extensive reports of police brutality and corruption (as indicated in Chapter 3, note 2). But it is clear that violence was not merely an adjunct to the legal system. In Trinidad and Tobago, perhaps more so than many other common law jurisdictions, violence was manifestly inherent to the legal system and not only associated with the corruption and impoverishment of that system and the individuals who operate within its framework.[5] Over the period cited above, there were twenty-one sentences of corporal punishment reported - these consisting of "strokes" of either the whip or cat-o'-nine-tails. Nine of the sentences related to robbery convictions; one for an offence involving only TT$500 (*Express*, March 25, 1993).

During the same period, it was reported that eight death sentences were handed down by the courts of Trinidad and Tobago, such sentences remaining mandatory for murder convictions. In November 1992, the government announced that, after a thirteen year moratorium, the execution of prisoners sentenced to death was to be resumed. Death warrants were issued authorising the execution of three long-serving prisoners in four days' time (*Express*, November 6, 1992).[6] In response to a successful appeal to the Privy Council by two death row prisoners in Jamaica, however, the government of Trinidad and Tobago announced, on December 10, 1993, that prisoners who had spent more than five years on death row would have their sentences commuted to life imprisonment (*Green Left Weekly* February 2, 1994).

Unless, like Michel Foucault (1979), one assumes that crisis and failure are standard products of the legal system, statistics reveal deficiencies in the operation of the legal system of Trinidad and Tobago which could be regarded as alarming. It was reported in the local press in 1992 that the legal system was then so overloaded that cases could take up to twenty years to be determined and hundreds of matters were on the waiting lists of the upper courts. Possibly thousands of cases in the magistrates' courts were being adjourned for hearing at later dates (*Express* May 16, 1992; *Sunday Guardian* May 17, 1992; *Sunday Express* August 9, 1992). The sense of crisis that permeates the courts is developed further below.

FIELD-WORK

Background

Originally, I had intended to observe the magistrates' courts only briefly, in order to gain some awareness of the personal interactions which take place within that institutional site. However, during a preliminary interview I conducted with the Chief Magistrate of Trinidad and Tobago, I was advised that statistics on ethnicity/race and imprisonment were not available (Baird, interview with the author, January 29, 1992). I therefore extended my work in these courts for a lengthier period in order to also collect data on the racial origins of defendants and prisoners. As it turned out, my inability to take notes in the courts, discussed in Chapter 3, meant that this aspect of my work did not result in a quantitative study, but nevertheless provides an impression of the racial composition of those going through the courts and particularly of the prison population of Trinidad.[7]

Social Stratification in the Courts

It was by undertaking field-work in the courts that I first became consciously aware of a Trinidadian system of social stratification based upon colour and other physical characteristics, in addition to the categorisation according to broadly defined racial origins.[8] Initially this awareness derived from the reaction to my own presence in the courts. Naively (perhaps putting it kindly), I had not realised that my presence would be so anomalous.[9] Although I had realised that whites made up only a small proportion of the population and were therefore likely to be rarely present in the courts, I had not been aware of the *significance* of being a white person in the courts. This related to the privileged status usually associated with being white, as well as the "disgrace" associated with attending particularly the lower court, for whatever reason.[10]

At the same time another aspect of stratification was being manifested in the courts "before my very eyes". In Trinidad there can often be very significant divisions between those of African and Indian descent, and there was an evident preponderance of those of African descent being processed through the courts. However, it also struck me that, whether of African or Indian descent, the general colour of prisoners as a group was visibly different to the colour of the others, as a group, who attended court. There was a concentration of people who were phenotypically *blacker* amongst the prisoners. It was therefore while I was doing field-work that I first came consciously to observe variety of skin tone, hair texture and facial features as being hierarchically stratified according to approximation to "whiteness" and correlative to social status. This matter was discussed in detail in Chapter 1, 'Ethnic/Racial Identity', where it was argued that one axis upon which social stratification continues to occur in Trinidad is on the basis of colour and other phenotypical characteristics.

In Trinidad, the variety of colour categories in that social stratification regime are named, and people are classified, in ascending order, as blue black; black; cocoa; brown; sapodilla; red; Trinidadian white; white. There are also Douglas (African and Indian mix), Spanish (Hispanic but often with some African background also); Mulattos (White and African); and Creoles (locally born but sometimes French and African). Meanings, however, were quite fluid, particularly, as Lloyd Braithwaite (1975)[1953] noted, in respect to self-description and identification. It may be too, that "white" as such is no longer the apex of the hierarchy. Possibly the highest social status is now bestowed upon those who are considered to be "red", that is, of mixed descent but (generally) without African hair or facial features, and most significantly having what in Trinidad is called a "high" complexion - light skin colour.

Sample

I attended courts in four jurisdictions during a three month period, my selection of jurisdiction being determined by a number of factors. I attempted to attend courts in a variety of areas and presiding over populations constituted by different ethnic/racial concentrations. Factors such as availability of transport and distance were also considerations.

I conducted field-work in five courts in the central N.I.P.D.E.C. House complex in Port of Spain, two suburban and one rural magistrates' court, on some thirty sitting days[11] during the period from April to June 1992. I observed eleven magistrates; two women and nine men. Two of the magistrates were of Indian descent, and the others were of African or mixed African and white descent, ranging across the stratification spectrum. I normally attended the courts for the morning sessions only. These were the busiest sessions, the afternoon sittings often being reserved for trials and inquests. Being unable to take notes meant that it was difficult for me to recall the details of court appearances as it was, it would have not been worthwhile to attempt to observe for longer periods.

Difficulties

I found the field-work difficult for a number of reasons. It required considerable concentration in demanding circumstances. On a personal level, I was disconcerted by the controversy I created and the attention I received. Moreover, as previously indicated, because I was attempting to approximate the position of defendants in the courts, I wanted to avoid personal contact with court officials. This created further dilemmas as officials often sought to be friendly, helpful or explain their position to me in ways which they would not have done for "ordinary" people in the courts. Moreover, for some time I was affected by what I believe was dengue fever while conducting the research. In addition, I often found the treatment of defendants and prisoners disturbing. While this was no doubt related to different cultural sensitivities, I think that this was only partly the cause. Certainly when I described some aspects of the court practice to Trinidadians who had no contact with the courts they were also angered.

On a more general level, courts were often over-crowded. In some courts there was insufficient room to be seated, and with defendants, witnesses, their relatives and friends, I would stand sometimes for hours in waiting rooms. Seating, when available, often consisted of uncomfortable wooden benches. Often there was no air conditioning, fans or ventilation; or these were insufficient or inoperative.[12] Along with defendants and others, I would sometimes have to wait for hours for magistrates - who could have responsibility for more than one court - to arrive. Of course, while such factors affected me as well as others, the full brunt of these difficult conditions would have been carried by those who themselves, or whose friends and relatives, were facing charges. And yet, although some expressed frustration and annoyance at delays, there was rarely anger. Such conditions would also have created a very difficult working environment for magistrates, court officers and police; although they too often dealt with the circumstances with a great deal of equability.

Law in Practice

No truth in justice,
No justice in the law,
The law works for the rich,
No hope for the poor...

Luta[13]

My initial response to court practice was surprise at the degree to which it resembled the functioning of courts in Western Australia. As in Western Australia, the pettiness of many of the matters dealt with was striking.[14] The dominating police presence in the courts and magistrates' tendency to accept police testimony was also evident and familiar. Finally, although the meaning of the term varied between the jurisdictions, the relative "blackness" of prisoners was all too familiar. These matters are discussed in Part III. In this section, I first want to establish the context of legal relations in the court by outlining court formalities and organisation. Later I go on to discuss aspects of the law in practice which exhibited marked differences between the courts of Trinidad and Western Australia.

Court Formalities and Organisation

The courts were organised along traditional British lines and, as in Western Australia, all magistrates were qualified at law. Legal qualifications from Britain, and knowledge of British case law, appeared to be particularly esteemed. Many of the formalities of the legal proceedings were also the same as those adopted in Western Australia. In all courts the magistrates were seated on a raised podium, sometimes shared by an officer of the court who recorded proceedings by hand. People attending the court were expected to stand when the magistrate entered or left the court.

The magistrates' courts in nearly all instances that I observed lived up to their traditional appellation of "Police Courts", with a large number of uniformed officers present. Usually the prosecutor was a uniformed officer, as was the orderly. There were also a number of other police officers present in the courts - usually on benches or in areas set aside for police - who were guarding prisoners or attending as witnesses. Almost all of the officers who were present would at times adopt a "policing" role in that they questioned me as to my presence in court, as well as reprimanding prisoners and others in the court, if they considered that they were behaving or clothed inappropriately.

Barristers were seated directly in front of the magistrates, with their backs to the prisoners and general "audience" in the courts. Police witnesses usually had seating on benches located along the side of the court rooms. In the central courts, prisoners sat at some distance behind the barristers. They would be under police escort and often handcuffed. Apparently handcuffing was supposed to be dependent on the nature of the charge, but in many of the courts it seemed to be standard practice. In these courts, prisoners who were "shackled", as it is there referred to, would be released when their matter was called. After their matter was heard, the prisoners would be returned to the benches where they were again shackled until they were removed to the cells, which I believe were located under the building.

In the rural court, prisoners were kept in a lock-up at the side of the court building; although when they were brought into the court they were often shackled in groups or singly. In both of the suburban courts there were large cages - "docks" - inside the court rooms in which prisoners were locked during the court hearing. Individual prisoners were removed from the cage when their matters were called and returned afterwards. Prisoners in these courts were also shackled when they entered or left before and after the court session; and occasionally when appearing before the magistrate. To my knowledge, female prisoners were not held in the docks or shackled for court appearances. Other defendants, applicants and the "public" were seated behind the rows of benches set aside for the prisoners.

When matters were called, defendants and applicants were required to stand at the front of the court. Testimony was normally delivered from a raised podium and evidence was required to be either sworn or affirmed, although the vast majority of the matters I observed did not involve the giving of evidence. One of the few concessions which were made in respect to the formalities adopted in the courts which might reflect any divergence between contemporary Trinidad and traditional British society was that it was not assumed that witnesses would be sworn on the Bible; they were generally given a choice of the Bible, the Koran or what was referred to as the Hindu Bible.[15]

Over-Crowding

One of the most important distinguishing features of the Trinidadian courts was the extreme over-crowding which particularly affected the suburban and rural courts. Hundreds of matters could be listed on any one day. Most cases would be called only to be given a later hearing date. These procedures also applied to many remand prisoners, whose return dates were regulated by statute. Such prisoners were therefore returned time and time again to the courts; and although many had not been found guilty of any offence, they might be brought into court in shackles and held in cages. Remand prisoners also often missed return dates because of a lack of police/prison vehicles to transfer them to the courts (see, too, 'State explains Prison Transport Problems: No Money, No Court', *Express*, October 16, 1992).

As indicated above, conditions in the courts were difficult; there was over-crowding, delays, frustration. The impression created was that the system was breaking down and, for those caught up in the system, there could be little confidence in its operations. Examples abounded, from a prisoner facing a murder charge, who was currently undergoing a third preliminary hearing and who had already spent seven years in prison,[16] to matters which had been listed on as many as twenty-seven previous occasions. On some occasions it was the defendants who requested adjournments, but much more frequently matters were adjourned because police witnesses were not available or prepared. On a number of occasions, after many police stations had their telephone services cut because accounts were not paid, court staff were unable to locate the police witnesses and prisoners listed to appear in court.

In other instances it was simply beyond the capacity of the court to hear the large numbers of matters which were listed. This was particularly so because infrequent guilty pleas meant that matters could take a considerable time to determine. The result was that the vast majority of cases were adjourned to a later date. The few cases where guilty pleas were entered, together with those cases which were eventually dismissed for want of prosecution, made up the majority of the small number of criminal cases which were disposed of in the magistrates' courts that I observed.

One consequence of delays was that defence witnesses would stop attending the courts. As a result, when cases were eventually tried they often involved the word of only the defendant against the police or police and other prosecution witnesses. And, as is found throughout the common law world, the evidence of police officers tended to carry more weight with magistrates. In relation to non-custodial defendants themselves, a factor which was frequently mentioned by those who had been required to repeatedly attend court was their fear of jeopardising their employment. When defendants failed to appear, bench warrants were usually issued for their arrest, thereby further adding to prison numbers. The scale of the problem of spiralling imprisonments has already been discussed in the preceding sections.

Social Distancing

In Trinidad, as elsewhere, court officials play little active role in the selection of people who are brought before them on charges. To a great degree, the race, ethnicity, colour, class, sex/gender and other characteristics of those brought before the courts is determined by authorities and practices which exist outside of the courts. The constituency of the courts therefore to some degree appears to be an "already given". If the personal characteristics of defendants are different to those of court officials, this is often a function of factors beyond the control of those officials.

However, there was also the overt creation of social distance between court officials and defendants in Trinidad, which was significantly different to that which I observed in Western Australian courts. By social distancing, I am referring to the construction of relations between people in terms of superiority and inferiority. While the creation of such distance (difference) is institutionalised to some extent in all courts through their physical arrangement for example, I have not witnessed anything similar to the degree of overt social distancing that was carried out in Trinidad.

Defendants, prisoners and others in the court were relentlessly reprimanded and corrected by magistrates, lawyers and police about how they dressed, stood, sat, spoke; they were often the object of laughter and ridicule. A list of criticisms made in the court as recorded by me (and therefore incomplete) are of interest, not only in respect to what they reveal about "policing" by police, lawyers and magistrates in the courts; but perhaps more importantly what is revealed about defendants' and others' attitudes towards the court.

> *Defendants and witnesses* There was a refusal to enter an appearance because a defendant's shirt was untucked; repeated enjoiners to witnesses to "just answer the questions"; grammatical errors in witnesses' testimony were corrected; one woman who was before the court was told to remove a mint from her mouth; a defendant was ordered out of court for tucking his shirt in while he was in court; at other times defendants and people in the public gallery were told not to laugh; defendants were not allowed to fold their arms, have their hands in their pockets, lean on the bench in front of them and were told to stand straight; others were told to dress better next time, to speak up while giving evidence, to only speak through their lawyers or when spoken to, not to suck their teeth in court (known as "stuepsing" in Trinidad - a sign of annoyance); to obtain legal representation; to move back from the magistrate's

bench; to thank the magistrate after being bailed; to refer to the magistrates as "M'am" or "Sir"; not to ask counsel to hand documents to the magistrate; asked if they were 'brought upsy or dragged upsy'; defendants were told to do up their shirts; to walk more quickly; one defendant was reprimanded for laughing when the prosecutor asked the magistrate if he wanted a magnifying glass to see the quantity of cocaine that the defendant was charged with possessing; another for not having anything to say by way of explanation or expiation after pleading guilty to an offence; yet another for insisting on his innocence at the same time as refusing to plead other than guilty (he said he did not want to 'hang around in gaol' on remand; he was sentenced to two months hard labour for the theft of two cans of motor oil); prisoners were removed from court when they became angry at further delays in their trials.

The "Public Gallery" Those in the gallery were (sometimes) told to sit up straight on the benches, not to read or chew gum and one man was told not to hold his head in his hands, others were told not to sleep; at other times people were reprimanded for trying to speak to each other or to prisoners or for attempting to sit near the prisoners; members of the public were forbidden to leave the court at the same time as prisoners; people were (sometimes) excluded from the courts for wearing short pants, singlet tops and told to tuck in their shirts; they were told to remove caps and hats; people were (sometimes) told to move from the front benches and side benches, to move further down benches (one man being called "Fat Boy" by the police officer), to sit down, to find a seat or leave; to be quiet in the court, in the corridors and outside; some were questioned as to what they were doing in the corridors; some were not allowed to bring bags into the courts.

There were frequent demands for silence in the court, and although many people were excluded by police for failing to be quiet, police officers often spoke loudly and volubly during hearings. It is also of note that the "rules" of court decorum often varied from magistrate to magistrate, and according to the police officers who were in charge or simply present. For example, one magistrate objected to men appearing before him with their shirts untucked; although he did not object to "short pants"; another magistrate did not object to untucked shirts but did object to short pants. Although somewhat arbitrarily applied, the significance of dress standards was accentuated by the standard of dress of many of the prisoners who were brought in wearing what they had on while arrested; many being in ragged and dirty clothing.

The degree of social distancing in Trinidad may be related to a number of factors. First, Trinidad has much more of an oral culture than Western Australia. It is normal for people to verbalise their opinions to each other - and to strangers.[17] In Western Australia, such comments may be regarded as infringing on personal liberty and to some extent as patronising. In Trinidad, however, such comments seemed to be more a mechanism which incorporated individuals into a community, perhaps relevantly in the context of colonised peoples, by informing individuals of community standards and conventions. Another aspect of the oral culture of Trinidad which is here relevant is what is referred to as "picong". That is, the development and pride in verbal skills - particularly of a sharp and humorous nature. I often witnessed lengthy exchanges between friends that were very funny and enjoyed by all. Humorous but sharp exchanges were also used in more hostile contexts, as an informal means of social control.

While both of these elements of the oral culture were present in the reprimanding and correcting which took place in the courts of Trinidad, the institutional location of these "interchanges" warped them to a degree.[18] One of the favourite sayings of Trinidadians is the advice "not to take it on"; people could tell you what to do or might express disapproval about your behaviour, but you were entitled and able to dismiss their opinion. Moreover, inherent to the normal verbal exchange is the ability of both parties to respond if they want. In the institutional setting of a court and legal system, however, one will almost certainly pay dearly if one chooses "not to take on" the comments of magistrates, lawyers and police. The opportunity to respond to criticisms also is severely curtailed. The inherently democratic nature of these aspects of the oral culture was transformed through its incorporation into the court setting.[19]

Some Positive Aspects

In determining what are the "positive aspects" of the court process, I am principally concerned with the extent to which the courts are a forum that can be accommodated or is accessible and exploitable by those who are subjected to it; that is, principally the poor and working - and black - classes of Trinidad. As can be seen in the example given below, the "crime control" function of the court does not necessarily fit these criteria.

Crime Control The left realist movement in criminology has done much to highlight the importance of "crime" control in the interests of the poor and marginalised. This issue is discussed more fully in Chapter 8. It is relevant to note here, however, that while the suffering of marginalised people through violence and other harmful activities should not be overlooked or dismissed, incorporating the response to such activities within the legal system can result in outcomes that are not perceived by such people as being in their interests.

One example I witnessed involved the theft of food from a vendor's stall. The defendant had pleaded guilty and the virtual complainant, an elderly and obviously poor man, told the magistrate that he forgave the thief, and in fact felt sorry for him. The complainant said that he believed that the thief and his family were hungry, and wanted the matter taken no further. (Given the highly conscious Afro/Indo racialism in Trinidad it is also worth noting that the defendant was of Indian descent and the complainant was of African descent.) The magistrate held that since theft was such a prevalent crime he would find the defendant guilty as charged, record a conviction against him and order him to compensate the complainant for the goods stolen.

Clearly, not all cases of complainants' decisions to withdraw complaints can be viewed in a positive light; it seemed that, in a number of cases, threats had in fact led to the alteration or withdrawal of complainants' evidence. In one such case that I witnessed, the complainant was further threatened by the magistrate with being charged with perjury. But in any event when the marginalised resort to the legal system by reporting crimes, they do so at the risk of losing control over outcomes.

Compensation payments The practice of ordering compensation to the victim at the time of making a finding of guilt, however, does often fit the criteria indicated above, by which the courts may become a forum that can be accommodated or is accessible and exploitable by poor and marginalised people. Often such people are not only the perpetrators of crimes which are tried at magistrates' court level, but are frequently also the victims. Ordering compensation at the time of determining the guilt of the defendant avoided the need for subsequent and protracted legal proceedings. It finalised matters as well as giving those found to be injured or harmed a sense of immediate involvement in and control over the criminal process, particularly when the magistrates consulted them as to what they considered a fair amount of compensation.[20]

However, it should also be noted that, if offenders were too poor to pay the compensation ordered, this benefit may well have proved illusory for the victims. As conversion of fines and compensation orders into community service was not available in Trinidad, the end result may well have only been prison, or more prison, for the offender.[21]

Private prosecutions Private prosecutions were popular and again appeared to be often initiated between parties of relatively equal and lowly socio-economic status. To this extent such people were using the courts and the power of the law to achieve their own ends. In order to do so however, it is necessary to formulate the controversy or problem in terms that are recognised by the legal system as conferring jurisdiction. An interesting development arising from this was a number of cases which appeared to be argued amongst the parties in terms which apparently did not go to the real matter at issue. (Of course, it is difficult to be certain whether or not this was the case, as parties obviously could not acknowledge that this was what they were doing.)

Such innovations were not confined to private prosecutions, and also affected public criminal prosecutions. One case in particular struck me as involving an issue which was not directly litigated. The case involved a bail tout, whose occupation was frowned upon by the courts. He was charged with attempting to pick the pocket of a man outside the court who appeared to be a potential client of the tout. The defendant denied knowing the man and attempting to take the money. The complainant stated that he not only knew the tout but had had dealings with him in the past. Unfortunately for the defendant, the magistrate not only found against him, but was so affronted by the man's behaviour on the, to quote, 'hallowed ground' of the court precinct, he sentenced him to eighteen months hard labour. The man was thirty-four years old and had one prior conviction for vending on a footpath.

Another form of "private prosecution" involved domestic violence and maintenance applications. Women were almost always the applicants in domestic violence cases and complainants in maintenance matters. As applicants and complainants they are not included in my statistics, below, although they constituted significant numbers of those who sought to make use of the courts. Interestingly, unlike Western Australia, there were few attempts to withdraw charges in relation to domestic violence matters. This may have been because the matters I observed were all private applicants seeking injunctions under domestic violence legislation. As such the women involved would have been entitled to withdraw their applications if they had wished to do so. (In Western Australia, nearly all the cases I observed were police prosecutions, and therefore control over proceedings was taken out of the complainant's hands.)

Individuals in the system It would be wrong to give the impression that there was absolute consistency between all courts. Magistrates' attitudes varied greatly and their courts were conducted with considerably different levels of formality, and hence the level of "policing" of behaviour in the courts also varied greatly. The relations between police and magistrates also varied: from one court where it was quite genial, others where there was a formal distance, to one in which the police seemed openly contemptuous of the magistrate, ignoring his requests and directives.

People's attitude towards magistrates also varied. One magistrate who was quite strict and formal in his approach was regarded as "fair" in his rulings. Another seemed to have not so much the respect of his community, but did have their approval.[22] I was told that his verdicts tended to be the same as "what was said on the streets". The court, despite being one of the more hectic ones, was run with the least degree of formality, and the magistrate himself seemed to have little time for the etiquette of law.

It seemed to me however that, while this magistrate did approach the views common on the streets, these were the views of "the man" on the street in particular. His views in cases involving domestic issues were not accommodative of women's concerns.[23] This did not seem to me unusual in a Trinidadian context, where men and women generally appear to accept that they have to some degree incompatible interests, but where each group exercises dynamic and interactive spheres of power. Again, it is the incorporation of this more organic culture into the institution of British common law - where there is a single and formal arbiter - which distorted and to a degree transformed the culture.

But life is hard, yes?
Junior

Attitudes In spite of their treatment in the courts, prisoners and defendants rarely seemed over-awed by the system, as can be seen from the kinds of behaviour for which they were reprimanded and which were detailed above. The large number of defendants in Trinidad who do not plead guilty may also be taken to indicate a resistance to official interpretations and authority, although it is also of note that this resistance was not necessarily hostile, and occasionally there seemed to be quite friendly relations between defendants and court officials.

In any event, defendants and others were apparently rarely intimidated by the court and the officious behaviour of its staff. Defendants and prisoners were tenacious in their attempts to speak, even when told repeatedly to keep quite or, where they had legal representation, to allow lawyers to speak on their behalf.

Certainly few showed any sign of the embarrassment or mortification at being publicly corrected and reprimanded that I had felt when subject to attention from police and magistrates in the courts. This may have been culture or class specific, or perhaps a combination of the two. As indicated above, it seemed common in Trinidad to be told what to do and how to behave, and did not carry with it the implication of being treated like a child as it does in more Westernised societies (refer also to Chapter 6, note 16 below). Moreover, Trinidadians, particularly those of African descent, rarely show either physical or emotional hurt in public, and it was often regarded as a matter of pride for both men and women to appear "strong". The determination to appear impervious is therefore likely to be to some extent related to ethnicity. It is also true that I was of a different class to most of the others before the courts. Perhaps among other indulgences that are denied the poor, one is that such people cannot afford to show their hurt and embarrassment.[24]

People whom I knew or observed in Trinidad were often in extremely difficult circumstances, but would rarely complain or spend time dwelling upon or analysing their personal problems. Such resilience and determination to "not take things on" is not easily come by. One theory used in Trinidad to explain the traditionally harsh treatment of children by their parents was that parents were seeking to prepare their children for the difficult life that lay before them (Brereton, 1979, pp.121,122; Trotman, 1986, pp.174). With reference to the legal system, I once commented to a young black unemployed Trinidadian man that I thought the legal system was too hard on people. He had himself just spent time in the courts, accompanying one on his friends who was charged with a criminal offence. He replied, 'But life is hard, yes?'

Resignation in the face of the overwhelming power of the courts appeared to mark the reactions of some defendants. In one instance a young black Afro-Trinidadian man waited throughout the sittings, at the end of which (a common practice in the courts), the magistrate or prosecutor would ask everyone still waiting what they wanted. The young man explained that he had attended the court some time earlier and been given a return date which he had forgotten. The magistrate, in what seemed light-natured banter, told the man he should not have let him out of prison; that if the man forgot again he would 'send him up the road'. The young man played along with the role of "fool" ascribed to him, and appeared to take these "threats" good-humouredly.

A few points can be made here. First there would have been good reason for the man to be angry; there could be hundreds of cases called every morning - often a matter was called and a new date issued before the defendant even got to the front of the court. There was no written notification of relisted hearings. And given the appalling conditions in the gaols, outlined above, being threatened with being returned to prison would hardly seem a matter to take lightly.

In discussing the reaction of slaves to the increasing brutality of their owners, C.L.R. James (1963[1938], p.15), stated that the slaves accommodated themselves by adopting 'a profound fatalism and a wooden stupidity before their masters'. Whether this was the case in what I witnessed in the courts, I do not know, but there seemed a certain resonance with the older strategy of accommodation. Moreover, it is of note that James interprets such behaviours as strategies for survival; this should not be confused with any internalising of the "master's" norms.

Race/Ethnicity and Law

As indicated above, the secondary aim of my field-work was to develop some impression of the race (and later colour) of people attending court, and particularly those held in custody. A table of these findings is included, below, for convenience, although it cannot be regarded as more than a basis for indicating general trends in the Trinidadian criminal justice system. Moreover, it should be noted that, although data concerning defendants/respondents in the majority concern those being prosecuted on criminal charges by the state, they also encompass a wider range of those appearing before the court. Individuals answering domestic violence, maintenance and private prosecutions - both criminal and civil - are included, although the only applicants included are those who applied for licences.[25]

Table 1 Trinidad
Defendants and others appearing in the magistrates' courts

	Central Courts		**Suburban Court (1)**		**Rural Court**		**Suburban Court (2)**	
	Total	**In Custody**	**Total**	**In Custody**	**Total**	**In Custody**	**Total**	**In Custody**
Male	114 (93%)	51 (94%)	357 (92%)	97 (97%)	312 (100%)	46 (100%)	199 (100%)	59 (98%)
Female	9 (7%)	3 (6%)	29 (8%)	3 (3%)	*	-	*	1 (2%)
African Origin	97 (79%)	45 (83%)	218 (56%)	64 (64%)	145 (46%)	31 (67%)	131 (66%)	41 (68%)
Indian Origin	19 (15%)	6 (11%)	134 (35%)	23 (23%)	160 (51%)	14 (30%)	43 (22%)	13 (22%)
Mixed/ Other	7 (6%)	3 (6%)	34 (9%)	13 (13%)	7 (2%)	1 (2%)	23 (12%)	6 (10%)
Black/Dark Colouring	81 (66%)	50 (93%)	220 (57%)	83 (83%)	133 (43%)	29 (63%)	81 (41%)	36 (60%)

* Data not available

The collection of data on defendants/respondents allowed me to compare the characteristics of those held in custody with the broader spectrum of people who were appearing before the courts. As there are no data available on the general colour constituency of Trinidad, this comparison was important. My research indicated that "black/dark"[26] complexioned people were a larger proportion of those held in custody than of those attending court generally, and provided some substantiation of my impression that there was an anomalous concentration of phenotypically blacker or darker people in prison; whether those people were of African or Indian origin. I was later able to confirm this impression with Omowale, who had been incarcerated for a total of fourteen years as a result of his activities following the 1970s Black Power insurgence and the 1990 Muslimeen coup (Omowale, interview with the author, November 16, 1992).

As can be seen, my research also indicated that those of African origin were more likely to be in custody than those of Indian origin. There are two general matters that should be noted here before I continue to a more detailed examination of my findings. First, as indicated previously in my discussion of the social stratification system, racial origin and colour are not independent categories. People of African descent are more often darker complexioned than those of Indian descent. In Trinidad there are, however, a number of descendants of phenotypically black Indians from the south of India, whose status in Hindu caste classification tended (and continues) to be low. Because of their colour, their status in the Trinidadian stratification system tends also to be low. Nonetheless such Indians often hold a higher position than black Afro-Trinidadians, as their hair and facial features more closely resemble those of Europeans. Although only a small proportion of the total Indo-Trinidadian population (De Verteuil, 1990), however, many of the Indo-Trinidadian prisoners whom I observed were black complexioned. This would indicate that there may be other factors relevant to the criminalisation of Afro-Trinidadians than comprehended by the highly conscious Afro/Indo racialism of Trinidad.

Following from this, it is important to reiterate that, in the context of this Afro/Indo racialism, if it is the case that the courts and prisons are dominated by Afro-Trinidadians, it is also true that that dominance is not confined to those who are defendants and prisoners. As indicated above, nine of the eleven magistrates I observed were to varying degrees of African descent. Most police I observed were also of African descent. I illustrate in Chapter 9 that the disproportionate criminalisation of Afro-Trinidadians under the legal system cannot be simply attributed to any inherent criminality on the part of those of African decent. However, it is important to note here that nor is it possible to simply attribute this disproportionate criminalisation to racist practices of Indo-Trinidadians. My field-work indicates that it is not Indo-Trinidadians who dominate the legal system of Trinidad.

Returning to my specific findings, census statistics indicate that the custodial population proportions of Afro- and Indo-Trinidadians reported above are inconsistent with general population statistics. Whereas the Indo-Trinidadian population is at least three per cent larger than the Afro-Trinidadian population, my field-work indicated that persons of African origin constituted approximately seventy per cent of the prison population and those of Indian origin constituted only twenty-two per cent of the prison population. While these figures, as noted, are field-work estimates, Omowale's assessment of the prison population was broadly comparable to my own. He estimated that there were three Afro-Trinidadians in prison to every Indo-Trinidadian (*Mirror*, September 9, 1992).

I was later able to verify, to a considerable degree, both my own and Omowale's estimates of the racial composition of the prison population against data compiled by the Central Statistical Office, which at the time I conducted my research were embargoed from publication within Trinidad and Tobago. Those data indicated that, in 1990, sixty-six per cent of the prison population of Trinidad and Tobago were of African descent and twenty-one per cent were of Indian descent.[27]

It is of note that according to Omowale, the imbalance between those of African and Indian origin in custody had worsened in recent years. He stated that, while he was incarcerated during the 1970s and early 1980s, there was a lesser imbalance between the two major racial/ethnic groups in prison (Omowale, interview with the author, November 9, 1992). The only statistical data that I have been able to locate relating to this period was a survey conducted during 1975 and 1976 as part of the Abdullah Report on prison conditions. That data indicated that, overall, fifty-seven per cent of the prison population was of African origin, and thirty-six per cent was of Indian origin.[28] According to the then most recent census, of 1970, the general population consisted of forty-eight per cent Afro-Trinidadians and forty per cent Indo-Trinidadians (T&T Commission of Enquiry appointed to enquire into the existing conditions at the prisons, 1980, pp.19,22).

The survey indicates that, at that time, the racial composition of the prisons was much more closely reflective of the racial composition of the total society. It seems, therefore, that, the current racial imbalance in the prisons, like the dramatic increases in prison numbers and the deteriorating prison conditions discussed previously, are of more recent origin.

Notes

1. The reference for data on the demographic profile of Trinidad is T&T CSO (1993a), unless otherwise indicated. I have attempted to use the most recent information available although this has meant that data are not synchronous. Where possible, I have used the figures relevant to Trinidad alone. For a table of comparative data on Trinidad and Western Australia, refer to Appendix I.
2. According to the 1980 census, the population of Tobago was 39,524, of whom 93.5% were of African descent.
3. These schemes grew out of the steelband warfare of the unemployed during the 1950s, which were pacified through the then Prime Minister, Williams's, institution of the "Crash Programme" of employment. In the early 1960s, unemployed youths who were excluded from the programme and were involved in the Sun Valley/Law Breakers riot threatened further "rope" (violence) if the government did not provide them with a drum set as well as funding enabling them to construct a community centre. The Special Works Project grew out of this (Howe & Rennie, 1982).
4. 'Vagrant Shot Dead by Cops', *Guardian*, February 26, 1992; 'Two Killed on Carnival Tuesday', *Guardian*, March 5, 1992; 'Mom: My Son was No Bandit', *Mirror*, June 5, 1992; 'Fatal Blunder by Cops', *Mirror*, July 5, 1992; 'Two Killed in Police Shootout', *Express*, July 8, 1992; 'Cops Batter Man to Death', *Mirror*, September 25, 1992; 'Bandit Killed', *Express*, October 23, 1992; 'Kidnapper Shot Dead by Police', *Express*, October 28, 1992. Note that there was also extensive reporting of the violence perpetrated by police officers while not on duty - and particularly relating to their domestic situations.
5. Conditions for prison officers were referred to above, and see also Chapter 7. With reference to police, newspaper reports indicated that working conditions were severely sub-standard; for example, 'Cops who Work in "Garbage Heap"', *Mirror*, February 7, 1992; 'No Room for the Robbery Squad', *Sunday Mirror*, March 22, 1992; 'Cops Without Phones', *Mirror*, April 17, 1992; 'Not Fit for Vagrants', *Mirror*, May 1, 1992; 'Leave Bias against Female Cops', *Mirror*, June 19, 1992; 'Police: We're Working under Primitive Conditions', *Express*, July 10, 1992; 'Hardly a Bed of Roses', *Express*, July 11, 1992; 'Testing the Cops', *Guardian*, July 11, 1992; 'Media Barred from Seeing Police Dog Kennel "Houses"', *Express*, July 17, 1992; 'Tunapuna Cops have Filthy Problem', *Mirror*, October 2, 1992.
6. The men who were to be executed had spent years on death row, and it seems that there had been no forewarning of the government's change of policy. Appeals in the courts had temporarily postponed the executions when I left Trinidad in early December 1992. By that time the four prisoners involved had had warrants authorising their execution read to them on two occasions.
7. In Trinidad, data on the courts are incomplete. However, documents that I was able to view at the Central Statistical Office indicated that over 35,000 cases

were tried in the Magistrates' Courts of Trinidad and Tobago in 1990. Statistics on the total number of completed prosecutions in 1990 indicate that a much smaller number of cases were determined in the higher courts (T&T CSO, 1993a, pp.58,60).

8. Coming from a white dominated society, the stratification system in Australia is markedly different to that of Trinidad. As noted in Chapter 1, colour stratification was endemic to the legal classification of Australian Aborigines until the 1960s, and so is therefore likely to have continued to be influential, although I do not think there is the degree of significance accorded subtle distinctions based upon skin tones, hair types and facial features.
9. The "official" policy is that Trinidad and Tobago is a "Rainbow Country"; that is, people of all colours and ethnicities are said to be accepted and equal (Reddock & McCree, 1992, p.31). Moreover, on a number of occasions I was told that there was no racism in Trinidad - admittedly by more privileged members of that society.
10. Braithwaite (1975[1953], p.122) notes in his study that, in Trinidad, merely attending the magistrates' courts, even as a witness, could be regarded as disgraceful.
11. On a few occasions I arrived at the courts, and with defendants and others, waited for a number of hours, only to be advised that all hearings were postponed.
12. On one occasion, the magistrate adjourned all matters listed for the day because the air conditioning was inoperative. The court was filled principally by sugar workers of Indian descent, who would normally spend their days doing physical labour in the heat and humidity of a tropical climate, and who would not have found the court room conditions particularly oppressive. It is not surprising that many were annoyed at the adjournment.
13. Luta is a Trinidadian Calypsonian. He performs this calypso while dressed in a judge's wig and gown.
14. By "pettiness" I am referring to the relative severity of offences as indicated by maximum sanctions available under criminal law. In Trinidad prosecution for vending on the footpath, unlawful possession, very minor thefts or possession of small quantities of drugs made up a significant part of court work.
15. Witnesses were also able to give evidence on affirmation if they requested to do so.
16. Bail was not available to those charged with murder. I was informed that the magistrate who had first heard the matter had been found guilty of corruption and been removed from office before handing down his finding. The second magistrate had simply had witnesses affirm the evidence given at the first hearing. This was taken to a higher court on appeal, and it was ordered that all evidence had to be heard again. In the meantime the defendant remained in

prison.

17. People on the street frequently commented to me on how I was dressed, how I walked, how my hair was done and what I was doing. (No doubt my conduct was often different to that of local people (Mauss, 1973[1934]), but the point that I am making is that people would comment on this.) Although friends told me that people often spoke to me because they were curious to find out where I was from, commenting to and upon strangers (whether foreign or not) was by no means unusual, as discussed previously.
18. Cole (1990, pp.306,307) notes that "public shaming" is also a part of magistrates' court processes in Nigeria, and Hoddinott (1985, p.31) makes a similar comment in respect to the court practice of Aboriginal justices of the peace in Western Australia, the latter stating that such a technique was a traditional Aboriginal law sanction. As Cole's analysis indicates, however, these techniques can be adopted in very contemporary projects, and in his own study he interprets this "ritual of degradation" as consolidating class stratification in the courts. See too Chanock (1994a) for an analysis of how the colonial context can warp the apparent perpetuation of traditional relations through law.
19. Crenshaw (1992, p.249), would dispute the characterisation of verbal exchanges between black men and women as essentially democratic. She states,

    > The humour or verbal competition that typifies the way some black women react to harassment probably results from the dearth of options available to non-elite black women within a society that has demonstrated manifest disregard for their sexual integrity.

    In any event, the court room context would further distort the "power dimensions" of any verbal exchange.
20. I was told of one magistrate who would also order the parties to shake hands or hug. I did not have the opportunity to witness this myself, and do not know how the parties reacted to this kind of resolution.
21. There were provisions for the extension of time to pay.
22. Trinidadians whom I met rarely had "respect" for the legal system as such, although they did recognise its power.
23. For example, one case I observed involved a domestic matter in which a woman was seeking a restraining order against her husband after he had been violent towards her on a number of occasions. The woman also complained about his treatment of their eleven-year-old son, stating that the child was treated like a slave, being made to fill the car radiator in the mornings, massage his father's feet and go to work with his father as a cashier. Afterwards the magistrate

commented informally that there was nothing wrong with the father's behaviour towards his son.

24. I am not claiming that, whether for cultural or class reasons, the people whom I observed in court were hardened to the oppressions to which they were subjected. The point I am making is that there were social conditions which made displays of emotional hurt inappropriate. A young man who wept in court, because he feared being returned to prison where he said he had been raped, was laughed at. Nor could there be any doubt about the distress of one woman I observed, who was speaking to a magistrate in an effort to have her young son spared incarceration, and was trying to restrain her tears.
25. At the rate at which matters were processed, it was difficult to distinguish licence applications from prosecutions; the parties involved in both kinds of action were generally an applicant and the police.
26. Note that during the field-work I refined the category of "black/dark" so that it became more in keeping with Trinidadian applications of those terms. That category is therefore not comparable for findings made with respect to Courts 1 and 2, and Courts 3 and 4. The significance of this category is therefore confined to what it reveals about the proportions of "black/dark" people as defendants/respondents and as prisoners in any one court.
27. For the complete prison census data, refer to Appendix II.
28. The survey indicated that sixty per cent of sentenced prisoners were of African origin and twenty-six per cent were of Indian origin; forty-three per cent of remand prisoners were of African origin and forty-three per cent were of Indian origin.

6 Criminalisation in Contemporary Western Australia

A DEMOGRAPHIC AND ECONOMIC PROFILE[1]

The more than two and a-half million square kilometres which make up the state of Western Australia are populated by only 1,586,825 people; a land mass which is some 500 times the size of Trinidad and Tobago with a population which is only some 1.25 times as large (Australian Bureau of Statistics (ABS), 1993a; 1993b). Aboriginal people comprised only 2.5% of the total population of Western Australia (39,080) and hence constituted a minority population of only slightly larger proportions than the white population of Trinidad (1%).

Between 1971 and 1986, census returns indicated that the Aboriginal population of Western Australia had increased by 72.5%. This rapid increase, however, seems to have been largely due to changing self-perceptions of Aboriginal identity during the 1970s and early 1980s; and between 1986 and 1991, the Aboriginal population of Western Australia increased by only 5.9%. Aboriginal women also attribute recent increases in the Aboriginal population to the lessening effects of older government policies en-couraging (-forcing) the sterilisation of Aboriginal women.[2] Note too that the total population of Western Australia increased significantly over the same era (ABS, 1989, p.1; Ghosh, 1987, p.287). Like the total population of Western Australia, Aboriginal females comprise slightly more than fifty per cent of that population.

The death rate of Aboriginal people in Western Australia during 1987/8 was approximately 1,610 per 100,000. The death rate of Aboriginal males in Western Australia in 1987/8 was 2.5 times that of the total Australian male population; for Aboriginal women it was 2.6 times that of all Australian females.[3] Aboriginal mortality was higher than that of the total Western Australian population at all ages, but particularly high in respect to young adults.

> While Aboriginal death rates in infancy and early childhood are much lower than for developing countries, beyond the teenage years the position is reversed, and death rates for young and middle aged adults,

particularly males, being higher. (Thomson & Briscoe, 1991, p.15)

Of particular concern are those illnesses which were most disproportionately fatal amongst the Aboriginal population of Western Australia. The mortality rate of Aboriginal males as a result of mental disorder was ten times the rate for non-Aboriginal men; the mortality rate of Aboriginal women from genitourinary disease was almost fifteen times the rate for other women (WA Health Department, 1992).

In 1986/8, the infant death rate per 1,000 live births was 24 for the Aboriginal population of Western Australia; for the total Australian population it was 8.7. The perinatal mortality rate (i.e. the number of still births plus neonatal deaths per 1,000 births) was 19.6; for the total Australian population it was 10.9.[4] The most common cause of Aboriginal deaths for both males and females was diseases of the circulatory system. Deaths due to motor vehicle accidents, homicide, suicide and other injuries, self-inflicted or otherwise ('External causes of injury and poisoning'), totalled approximately 125 per 100,000, and were the second highest cause of death for Aboriginal males. The life expectancy for Aboriginal males in Western Australia in 1987/8 was 58.3 years, which was almost sixteen years less than the general male population in Western Australia. For Aboriginal females the estimated life expectancy was 65.7 years; for females generally it was 79.7 years. According to the 1986 census 71.2% of the Aboriginal population of Western Australian were less than thirty years of age.

Although 73.4% of the dwellings occupied by Aborigines reported in the 1986 census were separate houses, 9.2% of Aboriginal dwellings were classified as 'improvised housing'. That is, almost one in ten Aboriginal people were accommodated in sheds or tents on a permanent or semi-permanent basis. Almost one-third of the improvised dwellings were without bedrooms and on average were occupied by four persons. The median number of occupants was 5.4 per Aboriginal dwelling and 3.3 for other Western Australians. Statistics on the supply of electricity and water are unavailable, although it is clear that in some areas, such as Kalgoorlie and others less remote, neither is available to Aboriginal communities. Patrick Dodson (1991, pp.83,84), reported Aborigines in communities near Kalgoorlie living in 'caves and holes'; in South Hedland, where they were known as "ditch warriors", and lived in the drainage ditches; those in Perth, who lived under bridges; and those who lived in the Aboriginal "village" in Roebourne where up to fifteen people would reside in one house. It was estimated that in 1987 over 70,000 Aborigines, Australia wide, or almost one-third of the Aboriginal population, were homeless or living in inadequate accommodation.

According to the 1986 census, 12.5% of the Western Australian Aboriginal population had not attended school, compared to 0.9% of the general population. Tertiary qualifications had been obtained by 0.9% of the Aboriginal population, compared to 9.5% of non-Aborigines; only 7.9% of Aborigines completed Year 12 (secondary education), compared to 49.9% of the total population. Seventy-three percent of the Aboriginal population aged five years and over spoke English only; twenty-three per cent also spoke an Aboriginal language and 1.4% spoke no English at all.

According to the same census, 40.6% of males aged fifteen and more were not in the labour force, compared to 22.8% of non-Aborigines. Of females, 68.8% of Aborigines were not in the labour force compared to 50.4% of other Western Australians. For males in the labour force, 40.2% of Aborigines were unemployed compared to 8.8% of non-Aboriginal males. For females, 36.9% were unemployed compared to 9.3% of non-Aboriginal women in Western Australia. Compared to 34.8% of other Western Australians, only 10.9% of Aborigines had incomes of more than A$15,000 p.a. Over half of the 59.8% of Aboriginal people receiving a gross weekly income of less than A$173 (A$9,000 p.a.) were women. Of employed Aboriginal males, 45.4% were employed in labouring and related low status occupations, compared to 15.6% of non-Aboriginal males in Western Australia. For females, the relevant figures were 28.9% Aboriginal and 13.9% non-Aboriginal women.

According to data published in 1988, fifty-three per cent of Aboriginal people received financial support from the Department of Social Security, compared to only eleven per cent of non-Aborigines (Dodson, 1991, p.479).

CRIME STATISTICS[5]

Have you ever been ordered to strip
Before half a dozen barking eyes,
Forcing you against a wall-
Ordering you to part your legs and bend over?
Have you ever had a door slammed
Locking you out of the world,
Propelling you into timeless space-
To the emptiness of silence?
Have you ever laid on a wooden bed
- In regulation pyjamas,
And tried to get the bucket to talk

- In all seriousness?
Have you ever begged for blankets
From an eye staring through a hole in the door,
Rubbing at the cold air digging into your flesh-
Biting down on your bottom lip, while mouthing
'Please, Sir?'
Have you ever heard screams in the middle of the night,
Or the sobbings of a stir-crazy prisoner,
Echo over and over again in the darkness
- Threatening to draw you into its madness?
Have you ever rolled up into a human ball
And prayed for sleep to come?
Have you ever laid awake for hours
Waiting for morning to mark yet another day of being alone?
If you've never experienced even one of these,
then bow your head and thank God.
For it's a strange thing indeed-
This rehabilitation system!

Robert Walker[6]

Contrary to assumptions that Aboriginal imprisonment rates have been relatively stable throughout this century (ABS, 1991b; Brock, 1992), it has only been since the 1950s that Aboriginal imprisonment in Western Australia increased to the extent that it approached what it had been at the beginning of this century. In 1950/1, there was a daily average of 394 persons in prison, and the prison census indicated that eleven per cent of prisoners were Aboriginal. By 1959/60, there was a daily average of 644 persons in prison, and the prison census showed that Aborigines comprised sixteen per cent of prisoners. By 1967/8, the daily average prison population was 1,196, of whom twenty-eight per cent were Aboriginal. The 1982 prison census indicated that there were 1,350 prisoners and 32.7% were Aboriginal (Aus RCIADIC, 1989c, p.4). In 1991/2, the daily average number of prisoners was 1,861, of whom 32.1% were Aboriginal (WA Department of Corrective Services, 1992a, p.1).

By the end of the 1980s, a Royal Commission was convened to investigate the high number of Aboriginal deaths occurring in custody. It attributed the incidence of these deaths to the disproportionately high rate at which Aboriginal people were taken into police and prison custody. The Commission found that, on the basis of adult population statistics, Aborigines in Western Australia were forty-three times more likely to be taken into police custody and twenty-six times more likely to be in prison than non-Aborigines (Aus RCIADIC, 1991a:9.2.5;9.3.3).

Table 2 Western Australia
Imprisonment trends, selected years 1946/7 - 1991/2[7]

		1946/ 1947	1954	1966/ 1967	1982	1991/ 1992
Population (in '000s)	**Non-Aboriginal**	502 (95.8%)	633 (96.8%)	840 (97.4%)	1,244 (97.5%)	1,547 (97.5%)
	Aboriginal	22 (4.2%)	21 (3.25)	22 (2.6%)	30 (2.5%)	40 (2.5%)
Prison Census Population	**Non-Aboriginal**	307 (91.1%)	378 (89.8%)	812 (71%)	909 (67.3%)	1,325 (69.6%)
	Aboriginal	30 (8.9%)	43 (10.3%)	333 (29%)	441 (32.7%)	578 (30.4%)
Imprisonment Rates per 100,000 Population	**Non-Aboriginal**	61	60	97	73	86
	Aboriginal	136	205	1,514	1,470	1,445

It is of note that police lock-ups have been highly significant sites of Aboriginal incarceration. Elizabeth Eggleston (1976, p.191), found that in 1966, thirty-six per cent of Aboriginal prisoners were held in police lock-ups as opposed to prisons; only sixteen per cent of non-Aboriginal prisoners were so confined. She attributed this to the high number of Aboriginal prisoners held in rural areas where prisons were not available. In a survey conducted during August 1988 it was found that 54.2% of people held in police custody were Aboriginal, and it was thought that incarceration because of drunkenness was a major factor leading to this result (Aus RCIADIC, 1990a).

Amnesty International reported that the decriminalisation of drunkenness in 1990 in Western Australia had resulted in significant changes to Aboriginal imprisonment. Amnesty reported a reduction in the number of arrests in Halls Creek, a north-western town, from between fifty and sixty Aboriginal people every night to two or three every second night (Amnesty International (AI), 1993). However, such a dramatic decline is not reflected in general statistics on police lock-ups. A survey conducted in August 1992, indicated that, despite the decriminalisation of drunkenness, there was little reduction in the number of Aboriginal persons being held in police custody in Western Australia. Fifty-seven per cent of those held in police custody were Aboriginal and twenty-six per cent of these were kept for "protective reasons" because they were drunk. The level of over-representation of Aboriginal people in police custody was in fact higher than it had been in 1988, and was 51.9 times the level of non-Aboriginal custody rates (Australian Institute of Criminology (AIC), 1993a).

Amnesty International reported in 1993 that the formal function of police lock-ups, to hold prisoners short-term until the next court sitting if police bail was denied, is 'nearly everywhere belied in practice by the absence of a clear demarcation between police and prison custody' (AI, 1993, p.3). Conditions in the lock-ups were often sub-standard. Amnesty attributed the high number of Aboriginal deaths in police custody to police attitudes to Aboriginal people, chronically bad physical conditions and the lack of adequate systems of protection for vulnerable prisoners.

While there was often a great deal of flexibility in the running of the police lock-ups which had a favourable impact on prisoners, there were also problems associated with the lock-ups being left unattended for considerable periods by custodial staff. In Halls Creek, for example, the station was attended only between 7 a.m. and midnight; there was no means by which prisoners could notify custodians of any emergency occurring in the night. There were also no mattresses or blankets for prisoners. Amnesty was also critical of prison conditions in the remote north of Western Australia (AI, 1993, p.8).[8]

In relation to prisons generally, Amnesty noted that the rate of incarceration for both Aboriginal and non-Aboriginal people had actually increased since the Royal Commission into Aboriginal Deaths in Custody was established in 1987. Dodson (1991, pp.749,751), explains the persisting high incarceration rates for Aboriginal people in Western Australia, in spite of decriminalisation of drunkenness, by reference to the police practice of using charges of drinking in public (which has remained an offence), or disorderly behaviour, as alternatives to charges of drunkenness. Moreover, for Aboriginal people, traffic related violations in 1987 were of a greater magnitude than drunkenness offences during the 1970s (Dodson, 1991, p.284).[9]

In 1991/2, the daily average number of prisoners in Western Australia, as indicated above, was 1,861; the highest figure for the past ten years. The total number of prisoners received during 1991/2, however, was significantly lower than it had been for the past two years. This would indicate that, while there were fewer people in prison, those who were detained tended to be incarcerated for longer periods. The reduction in short-term prisoners was due mainly to a reduction in the number of fine defaulters entering the prison system, a result of legislative changes implemented in 1991. Note that these changes only allowed offenders to reduce their fines through time spent in police lock-ups, in addition to time served in prisons (WA Department of Corrective Services, 1992b, p.16) and hence did not address the problem of holding people in custody in default of fine. In any event, in 1991/2 those held in default of fine only, whether Aboriginal and non-Aboriginal, continued to constitute almost one-third (32%) of all those held in prison (WA Department of Corrective Services, 1992a, p.6; excluding those held in police lock-ups). By 1993, the number of distinct persons committed to prison in lieu of fine had risen to 45.7% of the sentenced prison population (Broadhurst, Ferrante, Loh, Reidpath & Harding, 1994, p.75).

It is of note too that an additional twenty-nine per cent of all prisoners held in Western Australian prisons were unsentenced; and almost one-third (31%) of these were Aboriginal prisoners (WA Department of Corrective Services, 1992a, p.2). Unsentenced prisoners are those who have been remanded to custody to await conviction or sentence, or who have been unable to raise bail and sureties required. If the number of prisoners in 1991/2 who were unsentenced is added to those who were imprisoned for non-payment of fines, some sixty per cent of those held in Western Australian prisons had not been found guilty of a crime which was considered to warrant imprisonment. Their presence in prison would often seem to be related to their economic position, and their inability to pay fines or post bail, rather than directly to any "criminality".

In spite of constituting fewer than three in every hundred people in Western Australia, two in every five prisoners received into Western Australian prisons during 1991/2 were Aboriginal. Three in every five female prisoners received were Aboriginal women (WA Department of Corrective Services, 1992a, p.2). More than one in every five prisoners in Western Australia (23%) were Aboriginal people who could not pay fines or who had not been sentenced for any crime (WA Department of Corrective Services, 1992a, pp.2,6). Together with figures relating to the police lock-ups of Western Australia, where almost three in every five persons held in custody were Aboriginal (AIC, 1993a, p.3), these statistics show something of the magnitude of Aboriginal incarceration in the contemporary context.

It is of note that the experience of incarceration for Aboriginal people in Western Australia is not merely one of "sub-standard" conditions and lack of substantial justification. As the investigations of the Royal Commission into Aboriginal Deaths in Custody (Aus RCIADIC, 1990b) revealed, Aboriginal apprehension and imprisonment were also particularly violent. Such violence was found by the Royal Commission to be attributable to a variety of sources: self-inflicted injury, the actions of police and prison officers, and the activities of other prisoners. Some of the deaths occurring in Western Australia which were investigated by the Royal Commission included those of sixteen-year-old John Pat, discussed previously; the death of nineteen-year-old Ricci Vincentti, who was shot in the head attempting to escape custody while on remand for stealing food when he was hungry; and the deaths of two men who were suffering from psychotic conditions, Robert Walker, who had his life crushed out of him by four prison warders, and Charles Michael, who was hog-tied with a windlass arrangement used to tighten his bonds, until he died (Aus RCIADIC, 1989a, 1991c, 1991d, 1991e). The $30 million dollar Royal Commission reported in 1991 and, following a long tradition of such devices, found that no Aboriginal death in the custody of police and prison officers was the result of deliberate violence.

At the same time, however, it was this "unintentional" violence, together with death from "natural causes" (that is, the deaths which resulted from the critically poor health of many Aboriginal people in Australia), which meant that Aboriginal people were dying in Western Australian prisons at rates which exceeded even those of blacks in the custody of the notorious old South African regime.[10]

Blacks in South Africa are clumsy
they fall off balconies
out of windows
tumble down stairs
maybe they don't like tall buildings
They are earth people

Blacks in Australia
have strange habits also
Such as climbing up walls
with singlet or sock
Or perhaps they don't like the symmetrical
precision of iron bars
They too are earth people
Or perhaps the reason is
or could it possibly be
could be?
No no white man
You tell me

Jack Davis[11]

FIELD-WORK

Background

In Western Australia, wide-ranging statistics are published about the criminal justice system, particularly relating to the ethnicity/race of prisoners, as can be seen in the section above. The purpose of my field-work in that jurisdiction was therefore more limited than my work in Trinidad, and confined to gaining some insight into law in practice.[12] As a considerable amount of my field-work involved the observation of non-Aboriginal, as well as Aboriginal, defendants before the courts, however, I was also able to witness something of the specificity of Aboriginal criminalisation under the common law system in Western Australia.

Social Stratification in the Courts

Many Aboriginal people have rejected the white classificatory system by which they were divided into categories such as "full blood", "half caste", and "not a real Aborigine", according to the degree to which they physically resemble whites. The Aboriginal definition is fundamentally one of self-identity and acceptance by their own community (Dodson, 1991, p.328). Therefore the visual cues as to identity, such as skin colour and facial features, are not always useful criteria upon which to determine Aboriginality.

This meant that my ability to recognise Aboriginal defendants in court simply by observation was limited. This limitation was to some extent countered by my local knowledge of the family names of many local Aboriginal peoples. Another method by which I was able to identify Aboriginal defendants was their representation by lawyers from the Aboriginal Legal Service, although not all Aborigines were represented by the Service.

Sample

I attended six different courts at the Perth Central Law Courts complex as well as magistrates' courts in two suburban areas, one court attached to a city lock-up and one rural court. Statistics indicate that the largest concentration of Aboriginal people in Western Australia is in the Perth area (26.7%: Dodson, 1991, p.46) and my field-work also concentrated on that area. There were very few Aboriginal people in the suburban courts, however, and I was advised by one lawyer that the number of Aboriginal defendants in one of these courts had fallen dramatically since the decriminalisation of drunkenness. I was also advised by lawyers who worked with Aboriginal defendants that many Aboriginal people were going through the lock-up and country courts, and so I conducted further field-work at these venues.

I observed the courts for twenty-five days over a period of eight weeks from January to March 1993. My observation of the two suburban courts was very brief owing to the small number of Aboriginal defendants present in those courts. In the course of my field-work, I observed eleven magistrates, all of whom were white and three of whom were women. As in Trinidad, my observations were confined to the morning sessions of the court sittings.

Difficulties

The physical conditions of all the courts I attended were very different from those in Trinidad; nor was there the same extent of over-crowding. Although I was surprised that my presence in the courts generated the degree of interest amongst court officials that it did, I personally felt less ambivalent about my position, not only because I am Western Australian but also because I was of the same racial origins as almost all court officials. Again, however, it was difficult to attempt to maintain a distance from officials who were sometimes friendly to me, although generally this occurred less often than it did in Trinidad.

Law in Practice

Perhaps the most striking aspect of my field-work in Western Australia was the relative *absence* of Aboriginal people in many of the magistrates' courts. Certainly, the Aboriginal presence in the courts was dramatically over-representative of their number in relation to total population statistics. However, given data which indicate that more than one-third of the prison population and more than half those held in police lock-ups were Aboriginal, I had expected to observe a large number of charges being processed through the courts involving Aboriginal defendants. As the table below indicates, however, this was not the case, particularly in the central law courts. Fewer than seventeen per cent of the more than 450 court appearances I observed involved Aboriginal people. This has had a number of implications for my field-work account.

Unlike my account of field-work in the Trinidadian courts, I have relied more heavily upon external written sources. This was in part because my observations of Aboriginal interactions in the court were limited. More significantly, however, Aboriginal assessments of aspects of the legal system were available, equivalent information not being published in Trinidad.

Beyond these external sources, however, I have also included significant detail about non-Aboriginal people appearing before the courts. This serves two purposes. Given my contention that the criminalisation of Aboriginal people is not simply a function of their ethnicity/race, but that it is fundamentally a matter of economic relations (discussed further in Chapter 9), I regard data on non-Aboriginal but economically marginalised defendants as elucidative of aspects of the relations between law and Aboriginal people. It is partly for this reason that much of the commentary below refers to non-Aboriginal defendants.

It is important, however, not to misconstrue what can be learned about Aboriginal relations with the law from the observation of non-Aboriginal defendants before the court. The institutional biases in relation to class may be revealed, as will some of the strategies of resistance or accommodation of the marginalised. But I am not claiming that the treatment of Aboriginal people under the common law system can be simply subsumed under a broader analysis of relations with the working class. One very significant issue raised by my research is the specificity of relations between law and Aboriginal people. And this issue is raised crucially in the context of how Aboriginal people experience law. In spite of Aboriginal people being captured by the "impersonal" and more administrative character of the legal relations of white Australia, in other respects there were marked divergences between the treatment meted out to black and white defendants.

Most significantly, whereas a mere seventeen per cent of non-Aboriginal defendants appeared before magistrates while in custody, sixty per cent of the Aboriginal defendants who I observed were in custody at the time of their court appearance. Clearly, Aboriginal people's encounters with law are likely to be characterised by the far more intrusive and physically invasive experiences of incarceration than are whites'. This matter is developed further in Part III, but it is relevant here because it also explains why my field-work account extends beyond that directly concerning Aboriginal defendants. It is the reference to non-Aboriginal interactions with law which sets out the context in which the specificity of Aboriginal relations may be recognised.

Court Formalities and Organisation

As noted in Chapter 5, the court formalities and organisation of the Trinidadian magistrates' courts were in many respects similar to those of Western Australia, although, as was also indicated above, the physical conditions of the courts that I attended in the latter jurisdiction reflected the greater wealth of that society. One aspect of this was the relative "stateliness" of the court buildings and facilities. Another could be seen in the mechanical recording of all proceedings in Western

Australia, although associates to the magistrates still recorded some information by hand in addition to organising official documents.

There were also some formal differences between the courts of Trinidad and Western Australia, one being the assumption made in Western Australia that all defendants, whether Asian, Aboriginal or anything else, would be sworn before giving evidence using an evidently Christian form of oath. This I think attests to the greater homogeneity, and possibly the more dominant hegemony, in Western Australia.

The most striking difference between jurisdictions, however, was in the treatment of prisoners. In none of the courts that I attended did the docks resemble those of Trinidad. In Western Australia the docks were raised areas, fronted by a low partition from which those in custody gave evidence. There were no bars or wiring to separate prisoners from the court. The dock areas normally backed on to a door through which prisoners were brought from wherever they were incarcerated, which was out of view from the court. Prisoners whom I observed were never hand-cuffed on entering or leaving court and were normally accompanied by one or two police officers.

Usually there was only one prisoner and the accompanying officer(s) in the dock at any one time. This also meant that, although there was a noticeable police presence in the courts, the police numbers were much lower than in Trinidad where a large number of police would be in court guarding a large number of prisoners. As in Trinidad, however, women prisoners in some instances were permitted to sit in the public gallery, and were not confined to the holding cells and docks.

It should be noted that, whatever the differences in the treatment of male prisoners in the two jurisdictions, their status as prisoner was always clearly displayed in the court. In both jurisdictions, female prisoners' status as "prisoner" was less clearly marked. Also in the two jurisdictions the relative blackness of many prisoners remained noticeable, as did the pettiness of many of the charges.

Another contrast between the two jurisdictions, although less apparent, was of much significance in the construction of court relations. This was the formal role of corrective service officers and services in the courts of Western Australia. In Trinidad, apart from the occasional probation report, mainly for young offenders, there was little use made of officials and services other than those directly involved in law enforcement. In Western Australia magistrates frequently directed that pre-sentence reports be obtained in relation to defendants. This was a mandatory requirement when the magistrate was considering imposing prison sentences on defendants, but was also used in other instances. Reports would be obtained as to background, sentencing options, psychiatric profiles, drug use, chances of rehabilitation, and so on; and any recommended "treatment" was often incorporated as part of the sentence.[13]

The use of these kinds of extra-judicial services was often tied to the articulated attitude of court officials (magistrates and lawyers in particular) that the court was a "helping" agency.[14] A magistrate told a defendant that the court was there not just to punish but could also help her; a lawyer stated that his client needed to come under "the care" of the court; terms of parole and other non-custodial sentences were associated with drug treatment programmes; a magistrate assured unemployed defendants who could not afford to pay fines that '*We'll* get you work' when sentencing them to community service.

It did not seem, however, that defendants generally regarded the court as a "helping" agency, and this divergence in perspective is graphically illustrated by the following example. A middle-aged woman pleaded guilty to charges relating to receiving stolen property. The police "facts" indicated that the woman had discovered that her sixteen-year-old daughter had been involved in a theft and that the woman had taken the goods to a pawn shop to dispose of them. The (female) magistrate questioned the defendant's ability to be a mother and stated that the defendant should have notified the police of her daughter's behaviour as they then would have been able to get the daughter into 'the care of the court'. The defendant replied that she would not 'dob in' her daughter. The magistrate stated that the defendant's behaviour was so incomprehensible to her that she required the defendant to be psychiatrically assessed before she could feel competent to sentence her. The division between the magistrate's and the defendant's attitudes towards the role of the police and the courts clearly turned on the issue of the legal system as a "helping" institution.

The notion of the court as a "helping" agency was not apparent amongst anyone in Trinidad, including court officials, although magistrates would occasionally lecture defendants about the morality of their actions or recommend that they pray. The institutional link via corrective services between the courts and welfare or health related organisations in Western Australia seemed to me to be tied to perceptions about the formal function of the courts in that jurisdiction; just as the absence of such connections were relevant to perceptions about the function of the Trinidadian courts. This matter is taken up again below, in the discussion of the construction of social relations in the courts of Western Australia.

Over-Crowding

Rarely was anything like the over-crowding that occurred in Trinidadian courts manifest in the courts of Western Australia. Although there were considerable delays in getting matters heard, and some frustration and anger from defendants, this too was relatively rare. Unlike Trinidad, however, matters were likely to be determined when called, and defendants normally were only given a later date if they themselves requested an adjournment. This was no doubt associated with the relatively high number of guilty pleas made in the Western Australian courts, compared to Trinidad. In Western Australia, I observed very few cases which were adjourned at the request of the prosecution or which were dismissed for want of prosecution.

There was nothing like the feeling of chaos and crisis that pervaded the courts in Trinidad; proceedings in Western Australia could be said to be more orderly altogether. This no doubt was in part due to the different nature of social relations in the two jurisdictions, but I would think that the physical conditions and practices also were relevant. For example, in Western Australia, defendants who were given later hearing dates were given written notification of the new date. This avoided confusion. Also, as indicated above, most of the cases which I observed in Western Australia were determined by way of a guilty plea, which would have significantly reduced the number of outstanding matters in the courts. It is likely that Trinidadian defendants' determination to dispute the legal authorities added to the sense of crisis within the legal system in more ways than one.

Social Distancing

The most obvious form of social distance in many of the observed magistrates' courts of Western Australia, where the vast majority of defendants were white, was class-based.[15] In comparison to the active manufacture of social distance in the courts of Trinidad, however, there was little active participation in its manufacture by court officials in Western Australia. The social distance between defendants and magistrates and lawyers, as signified through employment, dress and speech (quite apart from the nature of the alleged crimes committed) simply appeared as if an "already given"; that is, independently of the cognisance and the control of the court and its officials.

There was little comment on how defendants and others stood, sat, spoke and dressed, in striking contrast to what occurred in the courts of Trinidad. The most common direction to defendants was to avoid walking across the front of the court, and magistrate, after collecting paperwork from the associate. There were occasional reprimands and comments as to dress and stance, particularly in relation to younger men and women.[16] However, this occurred relatively infrequently.

It is of note that Aboriginal people were often similarly positioned to other defendants. They frequently shared many of the social indicators with reference to dress, employment and speech of other lower class defendants, although Aboriginal people's physical appearance often consolidated the social distance between themselves and the white and generally higher class court officials. It was also the case that the interactions I witnessed between Aboriginal people and officials were similar to other interactions in the court; that is, basically impersonal.

Before I discuss the impersonal nature of court interactions in Western Australia, however, it is important to make clear what I do *not* mean by that term. I am not claiming that defendants' personal qualities were irrelevant to the legal processes; that is, that there was equal treatment in the courts. It was clear during my field-work that matters of wealth, for example, greatly affected the outcome of cases.[17] Aboriginal defendants, who would rarely have access to the employment, contacts or capital that privileged certain classes of defendants and criminals before the courts, would therefore be discriminated against in the same way as other lower class white defendants. When I refer to the interactions of Western Australian courts as "impersonal", therefore, I mean only that the distance between defendants and court officials is one which tends not to be overtly constructed by the officials.

The lesser emphasis on the overt manufacture of social distance in the courts of Western Australia cannot be explained on the basis that there was any greater reverencing of the court in that jurisdiction. The manner, dress and appearance of many of the defendants and others in the courts would not have been tolerated in Trinidad. Defendants, who were not in custody, appeared before magistrates in shorts, singlet-tops, sandals/thongs, few addressed the magistrates formally, some gave evidence while chewing gum. The degree to which such tolerance/indifference was extended is exemplified by a number of young (white) male defendants who appeared on charges wearing t-shirts that could have been considered highly disrespectful to the status of the court. These young men wore t-shirts with dog motifs on them, dogs with musical quavers or other dogs' heads emerging from their rear ends ("It's a dog eat dog world") - and without any comment being made by either police or magistrates.

The administration of criminal justice in the courts of Western Australia was so "impersonal" that the actual presence of the defendant had, in some instances, been dispensed with all together. On minor drug possession and implement charges, for example, defendants were allowed to plead guilty by way of summons which were returned to the court by mail.[18] In relation to the matter of pleas by way of summons, however, it should be noted that there are prior "non-public" processes which determine whether a defendant will be summonsed, taken into custody or bailed. Studies have shown that Aboriginal defendants are two times more likely than non-Aboriginal defendants to be arrested rather than summonsed (approximately equal proportions are granted bail) (Broadhurst, Ferrante & Susilo, 1992, p.30). Aboriginal defendants therefore tend to be excluded from this form of "de-personalisation" in the courts; it would seem that their physical presence - their bodies - are required in court.

Another example of the apparent de-personalisation of the legal process in the courts, was *magistrates'* insistence that defendants have legal representation. Although sometimes couched in terms indicating that this would be in the defendants' interest, it was often explicitly noted that representation was an aid to the magistrate as it allowed the hearings to proceed more quickly, and the magistrate to feel more confident that (legally) relevant material was brought before the court. This result is achieved because lawyers provide a standardised discourse concerning events and "facts" and, unlike the defendants, omit details that are considered irrelevant at law.

The provision of duty counsel[19] in the major courts in this context is difficult to view as being unambiguously in the defendant's interest. Certainly, one Aboriginal activist whom I observed seemed well aware of this ambiguity when she declined representation by an Aboriginal lawyer provided by the Aboriginal Legal Service. The defendant not only rejected the externalisation of her capacity to speak on her own behalf but to some degree diversified the otherwise homogenous discourse in the courts. It may also be relevant that this defendant did not plead guilty as charged.

Clearly it is institutions and practices which exist outside the court which result in the concentration of lower class and Aboriginal defendants before the courts. Moreover, it is often institutional biases within the legal system which privileged the relatively few wealthier defendants. However, court processes in Western Australia were not completely "de-personalised", nor was the manufacture of social distance between defendants and court officials altogether confined to pre-court processes and institutional bias. Although not a common feature of court practice in Western Australia, the active manufacture of distance was apparent in some instances. These are highlighted below, although it is important to note that these instances were much more the exception than the rule. They are, however, highly elucidative of the character of legal relations as these are constituted in the courts of Western Australia.

In one instance, a magistrate asked an Aboriginal lawyer to provide written proof of her authorisation to appear in the courts of Western Australia, stating that she had been told that the lawyer was from inter-state. The magistrate then went on to claim that the lawyer was in fact not a lawyer at all, but a field-officer; a non-professional position.[20] The magistrate refused to hear any other matters being defended by the lawyer until she provided documentary proof to the court of her authorisation to appear as a lawyer.

By requiring written proof in order to accept that an Aboriginal person could share the same professional qualifications as many of the court officials, the magistrate "betrayed" the fundamental dynamic behind such distancing in the courts. As in Trinidad, the dynamic establishes difference - relations of superiority and inferiority, frequently within a highly racialised context. What is of relevance in the context of the Western Australian courts, however, is the specific form in which these relations of superiority and inferiority were constructed.

As was discussed above, these relations frequently concern the construction of legal system as a "helping" agency, and court officials as knowing what is in (Aboriginal) defendants' best interests. Aboriginal people's, and others', recalcitrance in the face of the proffered "assistance" of the legal system was construed as irrational. Moreover, the discourse of assistance frequently eclipsed that of retribution and punishment in the magistrates' courts of Western Australia.

One case I observed involved a young Aboriginal girl who pleaded guilty to possession of 0.8 of a gram of marijuana. When asked by the magistrate, the girl indicated that she would prefer a fine to a community service order. The magistrate commented,

> Thank God for Captain Cook. We have a country now where people are on the dole, and would prefer a fine to working - and magistrates get criticised for too harsh sentences.

The magistrate's frustration can to some degree be understood, given that almost half of the sentenced prisoners in Western Australia are in custody because they have defaulted on fine payments. However, the reference to Captain Cook to an Aboriginal defendant being punished under a British legal system can at best be regarded as obtuse;[21] the pettiness and general circumstances of the offence only making the matter worse.[22] It should perhaps be noted that it was not common for magistrates to refer to Captain Cook in the course of their judgments. The magistrate's reference would seem to indicate that his irritation was with what he regarded as the subversion of a benign and "helpful" legal system by a specifically Aboriginal intractability.

A similar dispute arose in the case an Aboriginal man, who was being held in custody, and had been charged with failing to leave licensed premises and resisting arrest. The man pleaded guilty and his lawyer suggested that a bond or fine would be appropriate. The magistrate declined, stating that the man was an alcoholic. The man denied drinking on the night in question, and indeed for a number of years. Although the issue was completely irrelevant to the charges, the magistrate stated that the matter would have to go to trial if the defendant disputed the police facts as to his drinking. The refusal to allow a bond or fine would seem to be related to the magistrate's opinion that the defendant needed the court's "help". Thus, not only was the Aboriginal defendant represented in terms of being the stereotypical Aboriginal alcoholic, but the dispute was again constructed in a way which implied that the man was unco-operative with the court's preference to "help" - rather than punish - him.

One other case concerned an Aboriginal woman who had been charged with (a relatively minor) assault. The defendant claimed she had been provoked by a racist taunt, being called a "black nigger". The woman's own lawyer suggested that the woman have a psychiatric appraisal as she had a history of using violence. The magistrate, apparently so uncomprehending of the woman's behaviour, not only agreed to order psychiatric assessment, but committed the woman to Graylands Hospital (a mental institution) for what apparently was intended by the magistrate to be at least a two week period.

During the hearing I attended, the woman's lawyer was making a plea in mitigation of sentence. Discussing the racism that the woman continually confronted, the lawyer cited an example of what the woman had claimed to have witnessed while attending court on a previous occasion. She stated that a court worker had sprayed one of the lifts after a group of Aboriginal people got out, and had advised two police officers not to use the lift as it smelt. The (white) magistrate commented that this was totally irrelevant and that, 'Race has nothing to do with physical violence'.[23] The magistrate went on to quote from the report issued by Graylands Hospital which stated that the woman was not suffering from any mental illness, but was selfish, exaggerated the degree of racism in the community, over-reacted and blamed others.

This incident raises a number of issues; again the medicalisation of crime, as in the case, cited above, of the woman who refused to turn her daughter over to the police. (This aspect itself would appear to resonate with the specific treatment of women in the criminal justice system: Allen, 1987; see, too, note 15.) It is also consistent with the notion of the legal system as a "helping" agency. Through devices such as the medicalisation of crime, legal processes become translated into a discourse of treatment and care, rather than of punishment.

In this particular case, however, there was also a specifically racialised context in which there is the appropriation of expertise and knowledge by (white) court officials and psychiatric practitioners; again relating to notions of superiority and inferiority. In the instance discussed above, this appropriation goes so far as to manufacture the professional in Graylands Hospital as an "expert" witness on matters of racism. This person was somehow entitled to determine that the defendant exaggerated the degree of racism in society. Even more significant was the magistrate's assertion that race had nothing to do with physical violence. In all of this, the Aboriginal woman's personal knowledge of racism and violence is dismissed as simply irrelevant - if not, fortunately for the woman, as insane.

Oddly enough, the notion of the court as "helping" agency was not at all active in another instance of a young Aboriginal man who was obviously in need of assistance. The man had been held in custody for a number of days, and when he was brought into court, he was wearing shorts, bandages were visible on his thighs and he repeatedly wiped blood from his legs while he stood in the dock. The fact that this man was bleeding in court was ignored throughout the fairly lengthy proceedings, and it was decided that, as he had previously failed to meet bail conditions, he was not suitable for release before his trial.[24]

Before the defendant was removed from the court, the defence lawyer asked the magistrate to order that prison medical authorities treat the prisoner's apparently self-inflicted wounds. The magistrate's reaction was one of apparent embarrassment, and he commented that he was sure that the authorities would treat the injuries. The lawyer stated that the prisoner had been in custody for over a week and the wounds were yet to be stitched. Nothing further was said, and the prisoner was then removed from the court.

It is difficult to imagine another situation where it would be considered appropriate to speak to (or more accurately about) someone who was visibly injured and bleeding, without offering assistance. More so where the court is responsible for the person's inability to obtain assistance. In the context of a recent and high profile Royal Commission which highlighted the danger of the continued incarceration of Aboriginal prisoners, and the associated risks of self-mutilation and suicide, the conduct of the hearing was even more striking. Moreover, given the frequently avowed purpose of the courts to "help" rather than "punish" those brought before them, the failure to help in this instance is curious, to say the least.

It is difficult to account for the magistrate's behaviour in the instance outlined above. Perhaps it was because the defendant, in one sense, was a confronting and very physical embodiment of violence within the legal system; an embodiment which was totally inimical to court relations as they are frequently constructed in Western Australia. As indicated, these relations are often constructed in terms of the legal system as a benign institution. The presence of a bleeding Aboriginal man in the docks graphically portrayed such a construction of legal relations as mythical, at least in its applicability to Aboriginal peoples.

Some Positive Aspects

As indicated in Chapter 5, I am interested in the extent to which the courts are a forum that can be accommodated or is accessible and exploitable by those who are subjected to it. As also indicated, the "crime control" function of the court does not necessarily fit these criteria, but is discussed in more detail in the following chapters.

Private prosecutions Private prosecutions, *per se*, were not entered into by either Aboriginal or non-Aboriginal people in Western Australia to the extent that these were pursued in Trinidad, although similar court actions (in that they were privately initiated by individuals), were of some importance. There were a number of Aboriginal women who attended the courts seeking applications for restraining orders in domestic violence situations, although I was only able to observe one such case. Such proceedings allowed these women a degree of autonomy not available in criminal proceedings, but they too were fraught with difficulties. Dodson (1991, p.381), reported that Aboriginal women who resort to white institutions such as the police in situations of domestic violence may be regarded as betraying their community; they may be blamed for their partners' incarceration and subject to retaliation.

It should be noted again that in these situations applicants are forfeiting self-determination to some degree. In one instance I observed, a (non-Aboriginal) man was before the court on charges of having breached a restraining order. The man's defence was that his wife, in whose favour the order had been issued, had not lodged a complaint. The magistrate pointed out to him that he was in contempt of a court order, regardless of his wife's attitude.[25]

The results of pursuing domestic violence situations through the criminal justice system may be regarded as even more problematic. In another instance, also involving non-Aboriginal parties, a woman was involved in the prosecution of an assault charge against her son. (The woman was the victim of the alleged assault, but a neighbour had notified the police.) The woman had unsuccessfully sought to have the charges withdrawn. The prosecutor commented prior to the trial that the case would not succeed, given that the woman's attempt to withdraw the complaint could be used by defence counsel. In the event, the prosecution did not succeed, although the woman was first made to go through a process which she obviously found upsetting and humiliating.

Other proceedings akin to private prosecution were those actions taken by Aboriginal people to enforce the by-laws of Aboriginal communities, under the Aboriginal Communities Act. These actions are associated with segregated communities that are usually remote from the capital, and are largely confined to rural courts.[26] Dodson (1991, pp.455-471), reported that there have been problèms associated with the Aboriginal Communities Act, in particular in relation to the application of by-laws to family members, kinship obligations taking precedence over other obligations in traditional Aboriginal societies. There had also been criticism that, because this arrangement makes communities reliant on the courts, the underlying philosophy is essentially assimilationist in that it transplants into Aboriginal communities the values and authority system of white Australian law.

Dodson pointed out, however, that there was community support for the project. Judy Atkinson (1990, p.7), also writes that the by-laws of such communities can be developed beyond local government purposes,

> to facilitate development of new law at local level, enabling greater local social control and a public forum for making statements about appropriate behaviour.

Customary law To some degree there is accommodation of Aboriginal customary law in the white legal system of Western Australia. One traditional Aboriginal man whom I observed before the court explained that he had breached his bail conditions by failing to attend court because of "law business". The magistrate expounded, at some length, upon the court's recognition of the obligations imposed under Aboriginal law, and that breach of bail conditions in such circumstances were normally excused. However, in the instant case, the defendant had failed to attend the court for over a year, and the demands of customary law could not account for that total period. (Having missed the hearing date, however, it is not clear whether the defendant knew that he was under a continuing obligation to appear in court.)

Dodson (1991, pp.191,192), noted that, while it was true that the courts sometimes recognised traditional Aboriginal law, as indicated by Eggleston (1976), it was important to be aware of the nature of this recognition; that is, it was idiosyncratic, ad hoc, confusing, open to abuse and over-statement and over-simplification. Dodson expressed the concern that this type of recognition of customary law creates a kind of "folk-history" about giving Aboriginal people a "fair go" under the white legal system. He states that, without formal requirements, recognition of Aboriginal law remains precarious and dependent upon patronage by particular legal officers.

Attitudes There was a great deal of resilience in the attitudes to the courts adopted by many defendants. As indicated above, defendants' and others' dress and manner often did not indicate any great respect for the court; nor were they indicative of any attempt by defendants to ingratiate themselves with the court officials. Defendants refused to keep quiet when told to allow their lawyers to speak for them. Some maintained their innocence while pleading guilty, much to the chagrin of magistrates, saying that they did not wish to waste more time in the courts. This attitude displayed a significant degree of contempt for the legal proceedings and its punishments. One man swore loudly as he left the court, although he was brought back into court by a police officer at the request of the magistrate and made to deny that he had said anything.

Although many of the defendants behaving in the manner referred to above were non-Aboriginal, the same attitude was apparent amongst some Aboriginal defendants, although mainly in relation to the urban and younger defendants. The attitude of more traditional Aboriginal people was markedly different to other Aboriginal and non-Aboriginal urban defendants. They often stood with their heads bowed, spoke little and quietly. Dodson (1991, p.146), noted that Aboriginal people are in any event often more "respectful" in the courts than their white counterparts; some had long records, were "resigned" and frequently said nothing.

It is of note, however, that in contrast to Trinidad, in Western Australia, whether defendants were Aboriginal or non-Aboriginal, urban or traditional, most pleaded guilty. As indicated above, the guilty plea sometimes indicated the defendant's disdain for the court and its punishments. However, this was by no means always the case, and, to quote an Aboriginal perspective of court proceedings cited in Dodson's report, 'I've always pleaded guilty. That's what they get you to say. Not explained properly. Every time that's happened' (quoted in Dodson, 1991, p.101).

Individuals in the system As in Trinidad, individuals within the legal system could make the experience of law for defendants vary considerably. One example of which I was told by a court official was that, whereas a magistrate I observed was allowing defendants bail with sureties of thousands of dollars, in the same court the week before another magistrate was allowing bail at $5 and $10. While some magistrates ran the courts with a great deal of informality, others would be more insistent upon defendants addressing them correctly and adopting more formal stances while giving evidence. However, as indicated, where there was some officiousness shown to non-defendants attending court as to their demeanour and dress, it was, in my experience, directed mainly towards younger people.

Relations between magistrates, lawyers and police also varied markedly. As in Trinidad, these relations ranged from formal respect, to a more informal camaraderie, to outright hostility. One court I attended required police to unlock the entrance to the court by pressing a buzzer; one magistrate I observed was kept waiting outside the court for a considerable time, while police went about other business, such as talking on the telephone while in arm's reach of the buzzer. In another instance, involving the same magistrate, there was uproar coming from the cells attached to the court. I was told by a court official that the prisoners had been 'riled up' in order to 'upset' the magistrate.

Defendants' and other non-officials' attitudes towards individual magistrates was difficult to assess in Western Australia, as such people in the public gallery and outside the court rooms were generally less talkative. One Aboriginal man, however, indicated a fairly pragmatic attitude towards one magistrate, who had a reputation amongst court officials as being severe. The magistrate had recently been moved from another jurisdiction and the Aboriginal man had previously been imprisoned in that jurisdiction by the magistrate. He explained to me that 'they'd chucked out' the magistrate, as the magistrate was 'filling up their gaols there'.

Race/Ethnicity and Law

As indicated in Chapter 5, the inclusion of a table of my findings is only for reasons of convenience. It should be noted in respect to the following table that there were a number of defendants whose racial origin was difficult for me to categorise; they may have been Torres Strait Islanders, Maori or people of mixed Aboriginal and Asian background. I have included the small number of these people under the category of non-Aboriginal; in any event their presence was only evident in the central law courts. Note that even then the basis of my categorisation of Aboriginal people was imprecise for the reasons given previously. It is also of note that, again, those referred to in the table are not confined to defendants appearing in criminal matters. A small number of applicants for extraordinary licences, a few civil cases and domestic violence matters are also included.

Table 3, following, indicates something of the disproportion of Aboriginal people caught up in the legal system, but particularly amongst those who are held in custody in Western Australia. It is of note that, although the Aboriginal defendants in the central courts were relatively few in number, they constituted a much greater proportion of the defendants appearing before those courts while in custody. The number of Aboriginal defendants in the less accessible and less "public" rural and lock-up courts was massively disproportionate; and even more so in relation to those held in custody in those courts. As in Trinidad, the legal processes outside of the central courts exhibit a more "exaggerated" manifestation of what occurred in a more subtle form in the main courts of the jurisdiction.

Table 3 Western Australia
Defendants and others appearing in the magistrates' courts

	Central Courts		**Lock-up Court**		**Suburban Courts**		**Rural Court**	
	Total	**In Custody**	**Total**	**In Custody**	**Total**	**In Custody**	**Total**	**In Custody**
Male	231 (80%)	33 (92%)	57 (89%)	54 (89%)	55 (76%)	2 (67%)	43 (80%)	9 (60%)
Female	56 (20%)	3 (8%)	7 (11%)	7 (11%)	17 (24%)	1 (33%)	11 (20%)	6 (40%)
Non-Aboriginal	264 (92%)	27 (75%)	38 (59%)	35 (57%)	68 (94%)	3 (100%)	29 (54%)	3 (20%)
Aboriginal	23 (8%)	9 (25%)	26 (41%)	26 (43%)	4 (6%)	-	25 (46%)	12 (80%)

As is now very well known in Western Australia, Aboriginal people are highly over-represented within the legal system. It is also well known that Aborigines constitute a far greater proportion of the prison and lock-up populations than their numbers warrant. What is less known, however, is that Aboriginal people are not "merely" imprisoned at a high rate. With the majority of Aboriginal people who appear in court being held in custody, it is also the case that the whole framework of Aboriginal peoples' relationship with law is likely to be different to others'. In contrast to non-Aboriginal people, for whom law is often experienced as an administrative process, the Aboriginal experience of the criminal justice system is much more likely to be one of incarceration.

Notes

1. Unless otherwise indicated, data are taken from Aus RCIADIC (1989b); Australian Bureau of Statistics (ABS) (1989, 1992); Thomson & Briscoe (1991).

2. For discussion of the policies of sterilisation of indigenous women in Australia, refer to Moody (1993, pp.324-326).
3. The discrepancy was even greater in respect to the total Western Australian population where death rates were lower than those of the total Australian population.
4. Note that Briscoe (1993[1977], p.639), cautions about the uses and limitations of statistics such as infant mortality rates. He states,

> While I concede that infant mortality is a valid measure it cannot take precedence over the need of a more comprehensive indice that can put resources in the hands of black communities, rather than in the hands of whites who can use these misleading data for the creation of facilities such as the child health unit in Alice Springs that provides accommodation for white nurses, etc. Additionally, such a measure as infant mortality... can persuade white policy-makers to make on-the-spot assumptions about what they see Aboriginal societies need... Such models attract greater and greater resources and fundamentally are useless "white elephants" that have no impact on the status of Aboriginal social health profiles. The urban and rural black communities are equally vulnerable because as long as their babies are not dying they are assumed not only to have good health, but also the demand for better quality health delivery cannot be justified in the eyes of the white decision-makers.

5. Unless otherwise indicated, data are taken from Western Australian Annual Statistical Registers.
6. The poem is entitled 'Solitary Confinement', and taken from Graham (1989, pp.27,28).
7. I have used the Western Australian Statistical Register for the year 1945/46 to obtain the estimate of the Aboriginal population for 1947, although other data for that year are taken from the Register for 1950/51. For the data relating to 1954, I have used the Register for 1954/5. Population statistics for 1967 are taken from Eggleston (1976, p.6); other data are taken from the combined Register for 1966/7 and 1967/8. Data for 1982 are taken from Aus RCIADIC (1989c, p.4) and ABS (1983, 1989). Data for 1991/2 are taken from ABS (1992) and WA Department of Corrective Services (1992a). There is some uncertainty about the size of the Aboriginal population and number of prisoners, as not all sources are consistent. Moreover, it is not clear whether Aborigines

of less than "full blood" were counted in the census prior to 1967, and whether they appeared as "Aborigines" in the prison data. Obviously, then, this table can only be a rough guide to imprisonment trends.

8. At Wyndham prison there was cramped dormitory accommodation with virtually no privacy and no space for personal belongings, although, as it was a low security prison, prisoners were required to occupy the dormitory only at night and many were employed outside the prison during the day. Some prison authorities claimed that dormitory accommodation, which had been used heavily for catering for Aboriginal prisoners until recently, was preferred by Aborigines themselves. Amnesty noted that, whatever the validity of such cultural suppositions, they should not be used 'as an excuse to provide grossly inadequate, overcrowded or degrading communal accommodation specifically for Aboriginal people' (AI, 1993, p.8).

9. Traffic offences in the early 1960s accounted for eight per cent of Aboriginal committals; by 1978, this had grown to thirty-five per cent. And while it is common for traffic violations to be dealt with by fines, it should not be overlooked that conversion to work and development orders has not been available in relation to small fines. This has meant that those unable to pay small fines (i.e. the very poor) have no option but to go to prison.

10. See Purdy (1992a, p.1). More recent studies have indicated that the rate of death for Aboriginal people held in custody has declined (AIC, 1994a, 1994b). However, there has not to date been evidence of a sustained decline in the death rate. And refer to the 1994 report of the Aboriginal Justice Advisory Committee (WA Aboriginal Justice Advisory Committee, 1994).

11. Jack Davis (1992, p.3), is an Aboriginal poet, playwright and activist. This poem, 'Earth People', is taken from his collection, Black Life Poems.

12. As in Trinidad, the lower courts are far more typical of the nature of legal interactions than what occurs in the higher courts. In Western Australia in 1992/3, a total of 79,875 charges were determined in the Courts of Petty Sessions (magistrates' courts). In the same year, only 5,941 charges were determined in the higher courts (ABS, 1994, p.6).

13. Interestingly, for officials who often eschewed personalised interactions in the courts, it seemed that these reports were supposed to provide them with complete insight into the person they were sentencing, to a degree which would be unusual in the highly personalised courts of Trinidad. As one Western Australian magistrate commented to a defendant, 'I want to know all about your life so I can sentence you properly'. It seems that this sort of knowledge was not required, however, in order to properly determine a person's guilt.

14. The notion of the court as a "helping agency" in this sense is different to that which I adopt concerning people's ability to manipulate, accommodate or

control court processes for their own purposes. When magistrates and lawyers speak of the courts helping or caring they are generally not referring to directly empowering the people they claim to aid, but committing them to some kind of "treatment".

15. Other forms of stratification were also evident, but to a lesser degree, and unfortunately beyond the scope of this study. Amongst non-Aboriginal defendants there were many immigrants, particularly those of non-English backgrounds, and I suspect that they were also disproportionately represented in the courts, although this is not supported by other research. There was also an obvious sex/gender imbalance, with males far out-numbering females, but to a lesser degree than in Trinidad. Of interest with regard to stratification amongst women defendants was their sympathetic treatment, at least before some magistrates, if they wept or were prepared to medicalise their crimes.
16. Goffman (1968, p.47), notes that being considered "adult" in our society means being regarded as having the capacity to be self-determining, autonomous and have freedom of action. The particular concentration on young adults and youths in the courts for reprimanding by court officials would emphasise to them that they are not regarded as being fully adult.
17. Examples which I observed included the granting of extraordinary driving licences on the basis of employment requirements (unemployed people had to make do without a living wage, without employment and without transport); the granting of a dismissal as a first offender to a man who had 'exposed his person', but had obtained character references from powerful people and organisations; and the obvious example of the capacity of the rich to comply with security and bail requirements far beyond that of the poor.
18. In the courts, the officials went through the somewhat strange ritual of reading the charge out, followed by the sentence being announced by the magistrate. This ritual normally took place at the close of proceedings and I was often the only non-official in the court. I was therefore the only member of "the public" to literally hear the determination of the case. The purpose of the ritual, on one level, would seem to be in order to maintain the ideology of a public system of justice; but no doubt of more concern to court officials was having the determination recorded on official transcripts. As Kerr (1993) noted in relation to other legal proceedings, this constitutes yet another example of the written text inverting the ideological hierarchy of legal doctrine, and taking precedence over the oral discourse.
19. That is, free legal counsel who are provided for all unrepresented defendants, and who give defendants rudimentary advice and often speak on their behalf.
20. Field-officers work at the Aboriginal Legal Service in a para-legal capacity; they do not have qualifications to practise law as lawyers although they often

represent Aboriginal people in the courts. Field officers are usually Aboriginal and do not have the status (or income) of lawyers.

21. Note that one of the definitions of "Blackisms", as complied by Aboriginal students, was, '**Black is**, hating Captain Cook' (quoted in Moody 1993, p.290).
22. The police "facts" were that the girl had been speaking to two plain clothes police officers and told them about the marijuana in her possession. The girl, however, claimed that the police had chased two boys into a games parlour; when they lost track of the boys they grabbed and searched her. The magistrate made no comment on the girl's allegations.
23. The magistrate was equally dismissive of the issue of violence and sex/gender. When the lawyer attempted to plead in mitigation by reference to the numerous physical injuries inflicted upon the woman in the course of her violent domestic situation, the (female) magistrate commented, 'Well that's her choice; she could leave'.
24. The magistrate added that in any event the defendant did not appear to have any surety available as previously he could not meet bail and surety of "$500 by $500".
25. In fact, the (female) magistrate went on to advise the man to be wary if his wife ever rang and invited him over; the restraining order 'can be a weapon used against you'.
26. I observed one group of Aboriginal people in the rural court making an application under these provisions, although the matter was adjourned.

PART III
LAW, VIOLENCE AND ECONOMICS

Outline of Part III

> The violence which has ruled over the ordering of the colonial world, which has ceaselessly drummed the rhythm for the destruction of native social forms and broken up without reserve the systems of reference for the economy, the customs of dress and external life, that same violence will be claimed and taken over by the native, at the moment when, deciding to embody history in his own person, he surges into the forbidden quarters.
>
> Frantz Fanon[1]

The violence which continues to rule over the ordering of the colonial world is evident in Chapters 5 and 6. It is also clear that law is imbricated in the processes by which violence against the colonised is inflicted and, at least for the colonisers, legitimised.

In stark contrast to this violent law is the perception of law traditionally held by the colonisers. Colonial law is in many respects seen from this perspective as the very antithesis to violence. In Chapter 7, I examine the legal processes through which this antithesis is constructed. What is at issue here is the apparent dichotomy between how the law has been and continues to be perceived, at least by some, and its actual effectivity in relation to colonised peoples. Crucial to this apparent dichotomy are the separations between law in public and law away from the public gaze, with the latter being characterised by violence.

As will become evident, this dichotomy is treated essentially as one which is relevant only to non-colonised people, and my discussion is constructed in the broad terms of "coloniser" as opposed to "colonised" understandings of law. This, however, tends to a reductive treatment of these issues, as a variety of attitudes are adopted by people within these two categories. Of particular significance is the class segmentation of colonised peoples, referred to previously - and how this segmentation relates to their attitudes towards the colonial legal system.

It seems to me, however, that a specificity does characterise all colonised peoples' relations with law, and the attitudes of members of the elite classes amongst the colonised cannot simply be assimilated to those of the colonisers. For example, even if such people respect the legal system, they are likely to have a much greater awareness of its violent character, both historically and contemporarily, than many non-colonised peoples. Moreover, they are far more likely to be affected by the violence in their own societies than members of the elite in a non-colonised population.

Members of the colonial elite often occupy particular "hybrid" positions in relation to the colonial legal system. As such I would imagine that certain elements of the analysis presented in Chapter 7 would be relevant to their positions. However, whether such people can be characterised by the angst described in Frantz Fanon's *Black Skin, White Masks* (1968)[1952], the cynicism of V.S. Naipaul's *Mimic Men* (1967), as C.L.R. James' 'house slaves' (1980d[1966], p.177), or the 'gift-of-the gab brain washed Aboriginal people' of Robert Bropho's *Fringedweller* (1980) and the 'black traitors to their own grassroots' of Amelia Campbell "Unaipon's" 'A Ngarrindjeri Aboriginal Caring Woman' (1994), or whether they indeed occupy very different positions, I do not claim that their particular positions in relation to law are comprehensively addressed in this thesis. As indicated in Part I, my concern has been with those most marginalised by the colonial legal system and the culture of the coloniser.

It is these people who bear most acutely the colonial representations of themselves as debased and violent and, to quote Albert Memmi, 'It would have been too good if that mythical portrait had remained a pure illusion' (Memmi, 1990[1957], p.156). Following the discussion of the "hidden" nature of law's violence, particularly in the non-colonial context, is an analysis of the (overt) violence which has come to characterise some sectors within colonised communities. I argue that such violence cannot be simply characterised as resistance to oppression. The colonised have brought violence not only into Fanon's 'forbidden quarters', but more particularly into the homes and communities of colonised peoples themselves.

I seek to illustrate how this violence can itself engender desperate or violent responses. Significantly, such responses can include colonised peoples' attempts to appropriate what is known by them to be a brutal legal system. This violence which has come to characterise the internal relations of elements within colonised populations can be seen to be a consequence of the desperate circumstances in which they live, circumstances which are themselves, however, at least in part, a corollary of the colonial legal system. Moreover, as violence becomes embedded into colonised communities, such communities become more reliant upon legal interventions, and colonial domination gains legitimacy.

The third chapter of this Part is concerned to relate the analyses of law and violence with the economic substructure of colonialism. An interpolation of racial and criminal identities has been constructed out of the problematic of violence. However, as is noted in Chapter 7, the recognition of violence extends only to that which is apparent *through* the framework of colonial law - and which therefore largely excludes the violence of law itself.

By focusing on the violence of the "criminal" other, the coercion and devaluation of the colonised gains legitimacy, and the colonial myths concerning the nature of such peoples gain substance. Such mythology also masks the operation of law in the economic exploitation of colonised peoples. Moreover, it is this very exploitation which at the same time contributes to the desperate situations in which many colonised peoples continue to live and die.

Note

1. Fanon, *The Wretched of the Earth* (1990[1961], p.31).

7 Law

THE PUBLIC FACE OF LAW

At least the drunk looks happy:
Jutting belly, strutting stiff-legged,
But no-one notices, caught between the Acts.
Dapper lawyers dance through doorways,
Confiding legal loopholes to the unrehearsed;
Seasoned players entrance, exit
Expecting no bouquets.

A bikie giant, stuffed in overalls
Balances his helmet like a bomb;
Worn mothers juggling offspring
Seem about to drop the lot;
A fading lady plucks a falling hemline
(St. Vinnie handouts seem to come unstuck
At times like this.)

The stagey magistrate
Delivers lines of pompous rhetoric,
Encouraging no dialogue
With the unrepentant poor.
Bit players hang on syllables,
Waiting for breaks that never come.
In the dock, the black man acts his part,
Played out for centuries.
And so the session goes.

Cherie Imlah[1]

Cherie Imlah's poem focuses on the essentially theatrical nature of court proceedings and discourse. The interactions which take place in the courts are acted out before an audience and they occur within a context in which everyone has ascribed roles. The consciously staged nature of court interactions creates an interesting social context of itself. But what is of particular interest to me is how the public nature of these interactions means that what occurs in the courts cannot be taken to be the essence of "the law". What occurs in the courts is only the public face of law.[2]

The Criminal Courts

Like all courts involved in the administration of the criminal justice system, the magistrates' courts are a site in which the public inscription of an identity as "criminal" takes place. However, the particularity of the magistrates' courts in comparison to other courts needs to be emphasised. Magistrates' courts are by far the most common public arena in which people, particularly the marginalised, come into direct contact with the institutions of law.[3] It was because law in the magistrates' court was not only accessible to me as a researcher, but is also indeed "common", that I chose to conduct field-work at this level.

It is the higher courts, however, which assume a far greater significance in terms of legal doctrine and media coverage. Because of the nature of legal pedagogy, it is the rulings and discourse of the higher courts which are the focus of doctrinal studies (see, too, Sarat & Kearns, 1991, p.212). And because of the notoriety of higher court cases, and the media interest, it is frequently also these cases which colour broader public perceptions of who are the criminals and what is the nature of crime, particularly in a predominantly non-colonised context such as Western Australia (Bird, 1987, p.26).[4]

It is significant to note, however, that although lower courts may occasionally conduct preliminary inquiries into a number of serious offences, the criminal jurisdiction of the higher courts tends to be very different to that of the magistrates' courts. Therefore, the higher courts are not only statistically far less significant in terms of the number of cases tried, but the nature of the "criminals" they produce/identify cannot be taken to be representative of those in other courts.

In contrast to the higher courts and as indicated in the preceding chapters, much of the "crime" prosecuted in the magistrates' courts is of a very different nature, even if traffic offences are excluded.[5] In Trinidad, the crimes prosecuted in the magistrates' courts I observed often consisted of vending without a licence, unlawful possession of small items and possession of small quantities of illicit drugs. In Western Australia, petty shoplifting, vandalism and again the possession of small quantities of illicit drugs (or drug implements) constituted a significant proportion of the prosecutions I observed at magistrates' court level. The nature of the defendants was also significant. In both jurisdictions, defendants often were young and/or clearly very poor, many suffered from substance abuse and others were obviously suffering from mental disabilities.

The characteristics of the "crimes" and the "criminals" in the magistrates' courts were much less likely than those in the higher courts to invoke either fear or vehement condemnation amongst the "law-abiding" population. Indeed they frequently did not provoke such reactions amongst court officials, and in both jurisdictions more prisoners are imprisoned *almost* fortuitously, because they cannot afford bail or fines, than by way of deliberate (and public) judicial determination (T&T CSO, 1993a, p.61; WA Department of Corrective Services, 1992a, pp.2,6).

An examination of the connection between prison sentences imposed in the higher courts, or indeed any court, and actual imprisonment is highly revealing. In Western Australia, more than twice the number of prison penalties were imposed in the lower courts than in the higher courts during 1992/3 (ABS, 1994, p.7; declining from a factor of almost five to one in 1988/9: ABS, 1990, p.9; ABS, 1991a, p.13). Moreover, the large proportion of prisoners received for default of fine would almost all have been processed through the lower courts,[6] although it is also significant to note that the official court sentence of "fine" would not necessarily reflect the actual imprisonment outcome. In 1991, the sentences of the higher courts accounted for less than one in nine prisoners in Western Australia.[7] As indicated previously, fewer than one in two prisoners in that jurisdiction were in any event imprisoned on the basis of conviction and a judicial determination that their crimes warranted imprisonment.

Data on the courts in Trinidad and Tobago are less complete than those of Western Australia, but the situation would seem to be broadly similar. In 1991, the total number of peremptory imprisonments was some 1,500. As indicated previously, however, the total number of imprisonments for that year exceeded 16,000. The majority of these imprisonments were remands to prison with another 1,200 imprisonments being the result of fine default (T&T CSO, 1993a, p.61).

In both jurisdictions, concentration on the imprisonment penalties imposed by any court, but particularly the higher courts, not only distorts perceptions of the nature of law and official constructions of "crime", but also seriously distorts perceptions of who and why people are held as prisoners.

In order to move beyond the distortion inherent in relying upon the "official outcomes" of cases prosecuted through the criminal courts and towards an alternative understanding of the operations of the legal system, it is essential to move beyond the limits of judicial discourse, to the actual processes at work both outside and inside the courts. Outside of the magistrates' courts, many of those who appeared as defendants on criminal charges would resemble nothing so much as those on the down-side of an intolerant, iniquitous and harsh social structure. Inside these courts, however, legal processes frequently construct these same people as criminal.

This outcome is important on two levels. One is the manufacture of crime statistics for public consumption: statistics which complement the representations of law and crime manufactured through the higher courts and which justify the practices and costs of the legal system. This issue is discussed further in the Chapter 9. The construction of people as criminal also relates to the manufacture of personalised relations of domination and subordination within the magistrates' courts itself. These relations crucially involve the public manifestation and acknowledgment of the power of the legal system over and by those whom it deems to be "criminal". Given limited media interest, which in any event is generally concerned only with official outcomes, and few "public" observers, the power relations between court officials and defendants as they are played out in the magistrates' courts are essentially a matter of relevance to the "players" themselves, the magistrates, lawyers, police and, particularly, the defendants and their family and friends. It is this issue that I want to pursue here.

Inside the Magistrates' Courts

For defendants, and their family and friends, court appearances of themselves can indicate not only instances of interruption to employment, family life and self-determination. The courts are also a site in which defendants (and to a lesser degree others) come into face-to-face contact with those who, because of their institutional positions, exercise vast powers of domination over them. This is true of the operation of law in both the Trinidadian and Western Australian jurisdictions.

Nonetheless, the field-work accounts in Chapters 5 and 6 point to the evident differences between the lower court processes as they are acted out in different jurisdictions. Moreover, the Western Australian account of itself illustrates something of the differences in the general character of law as it impinges upon the lives of the colonised and non-colonised. One useful focus for a discussion of these variations is on the manufacture of social distance in the courts.[8] As indicated, by this term I am referring to the construction and imposition of characteristics in relation to defendants which mark them as different and inferior to the officials, and others, who are not subjected to these processes.

It may well be that it is through these processes that the attribution of criminality gains substance and legitimacy for court officials. But for the "criminals" and others present in the court, such processes, whether regarded as legitimate or not, are clear manifestations of the relative powerlessness of those deemed to be criminal to define themselves, their actions or their relations with others.

As indicated earlier, it is apparent that the active and overt manufacture of social distance by court officials was much less visible in Western Australia than in Trinidad. Cultural differences, also adverted to elsewhere, concerning the less impersonal nature of social relations in Trinidad and the strength of the oral tradition in that culture may be relevant here. It is of note, however, that without further comment such an explanation tends to correspond to a teleological framework, in which the more "modern" nature of social relations in Western Australia is seen as resulting in the adoption and application of impersonal and "universalised" norms.

Such an interpretation seems to me, however, to ignore a number of significant factors. Although I do not mean to simply "functionalise" the different ethnicities in which these factors find expression in the different social contexts, it remains the case that, on a fundamental level, there was no need for the deliberate manufacture of social distance in the courts of Western Australian as there was in those of Trinidad.

There was an air of almost complacent, albeit mundane, authority in the courts of Western Australia that was markedly absent in the Trinidadian courts. If defendants and others were not constantly being harassed into adopting "appropriately" submissive postures and decorum in Western Australian courts, it was because in a sense the (public) battle had already been won. The impermeability of "the law" was represented in the permanence, dimensions and substance of its court buildings, the routinised nature of proceedings and, most significantly in this context, the overwhelming acceptance by defendants of the official constructions of themselves as guilty and criminal.

In sharp contrast, Trinidadian courts were often old, makeshift and grossly inadequate for the numbers of people brought before them. They were often the sites, not of routine processing, but of overcrowding, heat, delays, contention. The court scene was populated by massive numbers of defendants, shackled and caged prisoners and a highly visible police presence. Coupled with this was defendants' overwhelmingly rejection of official constructions of themselves as guilty and criminal. In the Trinidadian context, there was a volatility in the courts which undermined any confidence that the exercise of law would take place without the direct coercion of the ruled. A tentativeness often characterised the public administration of (British) justice by consent that was not apparent in the public arena of the magistrates' courts in Western Australia.

A "Helping" Agency

To some extent, too, there was a positive constriction upon Western Australian court officials to move away from the form of court interaction that existed in Trinidad. The manufacture and display of authority through the badgering and humiliation of defendants is difficult to reconcile with the espoused aim of Western Australian magistrates' courts to be "helping" agencies for those brought before them. In this context, public humiliation, ridicule and the threatened violence of massed and often belligerent police officers will not be the preferred mode of public behaviour for court officials.

Fanon distinguishes the situation of colonised peoples from that of the non-colonised where

> expressions of respect for the established order serve to create around the exploited person an atmosphere of submission and inhibition which lightens the task of policing considerably. (Fanon, 1990[1961], p.29)

As indicated previously, Fanon asserted that colonised peoples were not subjected to a 'multitude of moral teachers, counsellors and "bewilderers" [who] separate the exploited from those in power' (Fanon, 1990[1961], p.29). In Western Australia the courts were structured so as to connect with "welfare" oriented services, and court officials frequently spoke of law in terms of its being a "helping" agency. Whether one dismisses such a structure and discourse as simple "bewilderment" or not, it remains true that these mute the construction of court relations of superiority and inferiority in a predominantly non-colonial context. In such a context, these relations are frequently formulated in terms of court officials assisting less able and less wise defendants, in place of the overtly punitive character they manifested in Trinidad.

It is of note, however, that where defendants publicly contested the nature of the legal system as a "helping" agency, court officials departed from the usual impersonal and administrative character of social relations in the courts of Western Australia. The failure of defendants to accept the courts' "assistance" rendered their positions publicly untenable. One woman was ordered to undergo psychiatric examination, another was subjected to a public criticism which carried a specific racial connotation, and an Aboriginal man was returned to prison until it was determined whether he was an alcoholic or not. Whether the posture of the legal system as a "helping" agency in a predominantly non-colonised context has substance or not, it is of evident concern to the court officials in such a jurisdiction. Disputing this attribute was one of the few incidents which would cause officials in Western Australian courts to deliberately manufacture a social distance between themselves and defendants; that is, they personally distanced themselves from the "mad", "black" and/or "alcoholic" defendants who did not want their "help".

Institutionalised Distancing

It is of note that in any event social distancing in the courts went further than individual interactions between court officials and defendants. The physical elevation of the magistrate and the traditional requirement that everyone stand when she or he enters or exits the court are perhaps just the more obvious and common examples of such institutionalised distancing.

Again it was in Trinidad that these processes were most explicitly manifest and the graphic inscription of criminality upon male prisoners was one striking instance of institutionalised distancing. Male prisoners' clothing was often markedly different to what was worn by others in the court (although the latter was frequently also under the overt compulsion of court officials). More significant, however, were the caging and shackling of prisoners. Such measures appeared as security precautions and hence implied a potential dangerousness or threat on the part of the prisoners. At the same time, however, the treatment of prisoners also inscribed upon them their relative powerlessness. Caged, shackled, guarded by armed police, ordered about, taunted, these prisoners also made manifest the dominance of those empowered by the legal system.

The "marking out" of the status of prisoners was also obviously signified in the courts of Western Australia. Prisoners' court appearances occurred in a physical context which distinguished them from other defendants. The presence of police guards again indicated something of their potential "dangerousness", but also the prisoners' simultaneous subordination. However, it is of note that, in contrast to Trinidad, the overt recognition of prisoners' dangerousness/subordination was minimal. As indicated above, there was a presumption of a certain inviolability and benevolence to the exercise of law in Western Australia which would have been compromised by too overt a display of coercive power; prisoners were neither a real threat, nor need their subordination be flaunted.[9] But it is also significant that, whatever the differences between the two jurisdictions, in both it was the law, its institutions and officers which publicly assumed the role of subduing prisoners' latent dangerousness and rendering them powerless for public exhibition in the courts.

Erving Goffman (1968, p.120), describes imprisonment as being perceived as the mark of the "real criminal". Be that as it may, the stigmatisation of imprisonment is not in fact correlative to the categories adopted in legal reasoning. As indicated above, the confinement of people to prison, according to statistics relating to both Trinidad and Western Australia, is *not* "as a rule" associated with conviction and committal to prison, but instead have a clear association with poverty. Whatever the reasons defendants find themselves in custody, however, imprisonment of itself has a highly evocative significance in terms of social distancing.

Imprisonment marks where legal officials determine that the social marginality of individuals is such that they must be kept at a physical distance from "society". And in the magistrates' courts of both Trinidad and Western Australia, it is also imprisonment which most clearly relates to race/ethnicity as it is signified in the courts. In both jurisdictions, the coincidence of race/ethnicity and imprisonment created a public nexus between being "black", according to its local meaning, and being "criminal", with its connotations of dangerousness.

It is perhaps also the case that the need to more deliberately inscribe the criminality of prisoners and defendants in Trinidad, through shackling or ridiculing for example, is to a degree connected to the lack of clearly defined racial categories which distinguish court officials from defendants. If Peter Fitzpatrick's (1992) thesis is accepted, the notion of the black, violent, primitive and un-lawed savage permeates British legal systems and jurisprudence. Should the black, mixed or other non-white operatives within this system come to be influenced by this mythology, there will be an imperative for them to distance themselves from the people of colour brought before them, in ways which are not pressing upon white court officials in their dealings with black defendants, whose "difference" is already inscribed upon their bodies.[10]

Colonised Peoples and Common Law

Be that as it may, the discussion of social distancing also raises the issue of the differences between legal relations as these bear upon colonised and non-colonised peoples under the common law. It is important to return here to a point made by James. He noted that the peoples of the Caribbean are not dominated as in the older countries by 'long established growths and accretions' (James, 1980c[1964], p.154). In this context, there is a much greater fluidity and sense of flux associated with social relations.

In colonial societies, therefore, there is a greater necessity deliberately to manufacture the imported social relations of dominance and subordination. Although white Australian social structures are not "older" than those of Trinidad, in terms of geographic location, this point returns to that which I made earlier, in Chapter 1, that the culture which was introduced by the colonists into Australia was predominantly British, as were the majority of convicts and "settlers".

The imposition of alien structures of domination and subordination upon colonised peoples requires more deliberate and violent processes than their imposition amongst peoples for whom such structures are already deeply imbricated into the social fabric. In Trinidad, many people continue to contest publicly the official construction of themselves as "criminal". The need aggressively to construct the relations of domination and subordination in the court arena finds expression in the extreme reinforcement of institutional positions of power through the humiliation, shackling and caging of those who are to be made subordinate.[11]

Aboriginal people, like others in contemporary Western Australia, rarely experience such treatment at the hands of court officials, but also rarely contest the relations of domination and subordination as these are enacted in the courts. Aboriginal people often appear to be acquiescent to the public role of "criminality" ascribed to them in the courts. It seems to me, however, that it would be quite wrong simply to attribute this "acquiescence" to the bewilderment (or otherwise) of Aboriginal people.

Although, as indicated above, the construction of relations of domination and subordination in the courts of Western Australia is often overlayed with a structure and discourse of "assistance", other factors need to be considered. And it is essential to be aware that any apparent acquiescence to an identity as criminal takes place in a context in which the majority of Aboriginal defendants make their court appearances while in custody.

As indicated, the courts provide only the public face of the legal system. Whatever "violence" the court processes do to people's self-image and public persona, actual violence is only threatened or incipient. Even the most directly violent jurisdictions and judicial determinations, as in the floggings or executions of Trinidad, are manifested in the court site only through discourse and ritual; for example, the breaking of the pencil used to sign the warrant of execution. It is usually away from the public gaze that the real violence of law is acted out.

Sites in which such violence is acted out include police lock-ups and prisons. And both groups of colonised peoples, but particularly Aborigines, are subjected to imprisonment in the lock-ups and gaols of the colonial legal system on a massive scale. Despite the smaller population, the number of prison receivals in Trinidad and Tobago in 1991 was four and a half times that for non-Aboriginal Western Australians. At the same time, and without even referring to custody in police lock-ups, Aboriginal people in Western Australia were imprisoned at something of the order of twenty-three times the rate of non-Aboriginal people.[12]

It seems to me that Aboriginal peoples' massive exposure to the violence of law is relevant to frequent Aboriginal acquiescence in the courts to the public construction of themselves as criminal.[13] It is my contention that imprisonment constitutes another and more violent dimension to the deliberate imposition of alien social structures upon colonised peoples. And it is this aspect of law - that which exists away from the public gaze - which I investigate in the following section.

LAW AWAY FROM THE PUBLIC GAZE

Colonised peoples often confront law away from its staged manifestation in the court room; they confront it on the streets, in police vans and cells, and in the prisons. And frequent claims of beatings and misuse of power by police and prison officers indicate that the behaviour of those empowered by the legal system can be even less restrained in these contexts.

Policing

Such an interpretation is borne out by many of the allegations made about police in the Trinidadian newspapers as well as by the numerous official enquiries which have been established to investigate police behaviour. The circumstances referred to in many of the Royal Commission reports on Aboriginal deaths in custody provide no reassurance that such abuse does not occur in Australia. The findings of the Australian Human Rights Commission investigation into racist violence is just one other example of official recognition of the existence of such abuse (Moss, 1991). Rather than here repeating the litany of violence which has characterised policing in the colonised context, however, I want very briefly to indicate something of the broader circumstances in which such brutality becomes comprehensible.

The Trinidadian context provides an extreme example of the situation in which police are located. As indicated in Chapter 5, police stations were critically sub-standard; police officers slept in barracks without mattresses or windows, sanitary facilities were grossly inadequate, stations were infested with rats and cockroaches; finances were so limited that telephones were disconnected and there could sometimes be only one police vehicle available per station. Additional to this was the great degree of contempt for officers exhibited by much of the population.[14]

That is not to ignore or excuse the indications of extreme brutality by police in Trinidad. There are large numbers of police killings and woundings, frequent claims that police have battered suspects, sexually harassed women, made one man eat cow dung and so on.[15] But in a context where police, for example, are stationed in kennels that were found to be unsuitable to accommodate police dogs, violence and corruption become more explicable. To quote the Secretary of the Police Social and Welfare Division,

> It is a fact that officers were neglected and treated less than human beings and yet they were expected to provide professional service to the public. (Quoted in 'Cops: We're being Treated like Dogs', *Express*, July 9, 1992)

In Western Australia, there are also indications of extreme police brutality, particularly in their dealings with Aboriginal people. Allegations of police violence and corruption are not as widespread as in Trinidad, but this does not preclude the specific dealings between police and Aboriginal people resembling those of Trinidad. Certainly in Western Australia it was the allegations of brutality and the incidence of Aboriginal deaths particularly while in the custody of police which led to widespread dissatisfaction with the legal system and the institution of a (palliative) Royal Commission.

It is also certainly the case that work conditions for many police in Australia are not comparable to those of Trinidad. A significant exception to this, however, can be found in relation to the Queensland Aboriginal communities' police forces. The Royal Commission into Aboriginal Deaths in Custody reported that these Aboriginal police officers had work conditions and pay which were unlikely to be tolerated by others. They wore second-hand Queensland police uniforms and boots, and received no training. It seems no coincidence that the same police officers were said to be notorious as 'virtually a law unto themselves', and had been known to lock away community residents if they were merely disrespectful to community police officers or councillors. It is also of note that eight of the Aboriginal deaths in custody in Queensland which were investigated by the Royal Commission occurred in Aboriginal communities which had their own Aboriginal police and prison officers (Aus RCIADIC, 1991a:3.2.12;29.7.21).

It is true too that other police, particularly in remoter country areas, do complain of having to put up with what they regard as sub-standard conditions.[16] But although Western Australian police have lobbied for improved facilities at police lock-ups, they do not cite work conditions as generally contributing to the nature of their dealings with Aboriginal people, or to the deaths of Aboriginal people which occur in their custody. Instead, the Western Australian Police Union of Workers (WAPUW) states,

> unless Aboriginal people are encouraged to embrace the society in which they live, and the rules and norms of that society, they will always be *at war* or at odds with that society, and it is a matter of inevitability that there will always be a social fall-out from that conflict. (WAPUW, 1990, p.18; emphasis added)[17]

Just as it has historically been the role of the police to fight the "war" against Aboriginal people, so it seems that police continue to perceive their position in similar terms. Given the number of official inquiries which have exonerated police treatment of Aboriginal people both historically and contemporarily, it is perhaps difficult to find fault - at least at law - with the Police Union's interpretation of the causes of Aboriginal deaths in their custody.

Prisons

As indicated above, the violence of the legal system in its dealings with colonised peoples is further illustrated by the massive imprisonment of such peoples. Something of the personal experience of the brutality of imprisonment is graphically portrayed in Jagessar's account of prison life in Trinidad and the poem by Walker, quoted in Chapters 5 and 6. The routine violence of the imprisonment process is discussed further below. But even beyond this mundane violence, extreme instances of brutality by prison officers and the brutalisation of prisoners in the prison context would also appear to be an almost inevitable consequence of prison policies.

As indicated previously, during the time prison admissions rose in Trinidad from 3,000 to 36,000 per annum, staff funding was significantly reduced. One Trinidadian prison officer advised me of his fear in taking up to fifteen prisoners on work detail, while "armed" with only a baton. The recent change in government legislation authorising the arming of prison officers with semi-automatic weapons and tear gas canisters may do something to alleviate the prison officers' fears, but is unlikely to be of much comfort to prisoners.

With reference to Western Australia, the Royal Commission report on the death of Robert Walker also provides an indication of the brutalising nature of the prison regime. The report details the arrangements at Fremantle prison, in Western Australia. The prison was opened in 1855 and remained the major gaol in Western Australia until its closure in 1991, after prison riots and arson in 1988. The nightly practice at Fremantle prison was to lock two unarmed prison officers into a division building which, on the night of Walker's death, held more than three hundred prisoners and exceeded the maximum accommodation capacity. The prison officers did not have access to keys to unlock the division and would have to telephone through to the main gate to have someone bring keys over from the other side of the prison compound before they could get out. A sense of terror permeates the accounts of the prison officers who worked in these conditions. As in the instance of Walker, prisoners might on occasion be delusional and mentally unbalanced, adding to officers' fear and tendency to over-react. Walker himself was battered and crushed to death by the prison officers who had come to his "aid" while he was in a psychotic state (Aus RCIADIC, 1991d).

Bad Men and Women?

James (1980b[1961], p.131) indicates something of the problem of limiting assessment to the condemnation of "bad" men and women (refer Chapter 4). The brief interludes above, concerning the conditions under which police and prison officers work, are neither systematic nor are they meant to excuse the brutality that many officers perpetrate. I am not advocating the sort of abstentionism which marked the reasoning of the Royal Commission into Aboriginal Deaths in Custody, and which denied the existence and unlawful nature of such brutality, or excused whatever failings it did acknowledge as the fault of the whole of society (refer also to Brown, 1987, p.101). Although, as advocated by James, it is important to recognise the historical causes which make our "good" men and women turn "bad", it is also important not to pretend that our "bad" men and women are in fact good. Recognition and condemnation of the brutality perpetrated by individual police and prison officers is neither unwarranted nor inappropriate; what is inappropriate is the demonising of such people.

Such caution is particularly important in the instance of colonised peoples, as indicated by James. It is not only demoralising for colonised peoples, but also often convenient for others, to present the colonised as corrupting the inherited and "civilised" institutions bequeathed them by their colonisers. Although this issue is not so pressing in Australia, what Paul Havemann (1988) refers to as the 'indigenization of social control' makes it increasingly an issue to be confronted. Certainly, part of the strategy of the Royal Commission into Aboriginal Deaths in Custody was to deflect criticism of police brutality onto the Aboriginal police aides of the past and present (Purdy, 1992a).

In any event, the class issue is relevant when discussing the brutality of police and prison officers. Those on the "front line" of policing and in the prisons are likely to be men and women from lower social strata. As Goffman wryly noted, people in these "front line" positions are also much less able to exercise "clemency" and "justice" than those who occupy more privileged institutional positions. Goffman posits that it is precisely because those in supervisory positions rarely deal with the imperatives of control at a direct level that they are enabled to deal with inmates' and others demands more equitably (Goffman, 1968, p.107). If understood in terms of a class analysis, the elite are able to maintain positions of moral superiority precisely because it is the lower classes who work under conditions in which brutality becomes directly entrenched as the institutional culture.[18]

This also relates to the issue of court practice. As indicated, the courts are institutional sites highly charged with the symbolic roles which are ascribed to the players. These sites, despite (or perhaps because of?) their effectiveness in constructing identities of inferiority and criminality for the marginalised, rarely operate on an overtly violent level. This has reference not only to the public occasion of court processes, but also has reference to the status of the officials, particularly the magistrates and lawyers, who are operative at this level.

It is of note that, at this level, the violent interactions of policing or imprisonment are rarely adverted to, and generally ignored. But on occasion, when those who complain are considered "credible", the higher status officials who operate from within the courts are enabled to maintain a position of moral superiority over those (lower class) operatives whom they supervise, and be suitably outraged by the behaviour of their underlings.

There is another dimension, too, in the dichotomy between the attitudes of court officials and police or prison officers. This relates once more to the division between law in public and law away from the public gaze. It is precisely because law's violence is not overt in its public manifestations, particularly in a non-colonial context, that the public image of law assumes a non-violent aspect. As I hope to show below, law indeed comes to appropriate a position as the antithesis to violence.

Disaggregating Law and Violence

The public face of law, what occurs in (particularly the higher) courts and is represented in published judgments, has come to dominate the perceptions of what law is for those not subject to its other manifestations. As discussed in Chapter 3, for Western academics law is often known simply as discourse; even the experience of law is something which is read about rather than lived. For many other non-colonised people, law is also unlikely to be known in the same character it presents to colonised groups, such as Aboriginal people. Extreme instances of violence which are perpetrated by officers of the law, such as police killings, are occasionally acknowledged amongst broader sections of the public, but tend to be understood as aberrations. These incidents are often interpreted as being the fault of the "bad" men or women who either provoke the officers or, less often (particularly in a non-colonised context), as the fault of officers who abuse their power.

Although the extreme violence of law is very well known to the non-colonised under-classes, such people constitute only a relatively small proportion of non-colonised populations. The inverse is more likely to characterise colonised peoples' knowledges of the legal system. Because the violent nature of legal interventions is obscured from those who do not directly experience them, the specific relationship between colonised peoples and the law is often unrecognised by others.

It is this point which significantly distinguishes my analysis from that of Austin Sarat and Thomas Kearns (1991). These authors' concern is with the 'disturbing disparity between the importance and ubiquity of law's violence and the vanishingly small attention paid it in legal theory and jurisprudential thought' (Sarat & Kearns, 1991, p.211). Although clearly their work intersects with my own, this agreement does not extend to the assertion made by Sarat and Kearns that the violence of law is ubiquitous. As I develop further below, my analysis indicates that the violence of law is by no means ubiquitous, but tends to be highly class and ethnic/race specific.

In this context, the absence of recognition of law's violence in legal theory and jurisprudential thought is not so puzzling, given the class and ethnicity/race of most legal theorists. Moreover, if it is accepted that law's violence is not ubiquitous, it is those who are actually subjected to it who occupy "privileged" positions in terms of their knowledge of this aspect of law. "We" others, therefore, cannot appropriate expertise in this area to ourselves by asserting the ubiquity of law's violence.

It is of note too, that the lack of recognition of the specific relations between colonised peoples and the law is also related to other factors. Certainly historical representations and education are important influences in this area. To again quote Memmi, 'The history which is taught him is not his own' (Memmi, (1990)[1957], p.171). However, confining the discussion to a specifically legal context, the same obfuscation takes place. Just as the history of colonialism has for a long time been written (or discredited) from the perspective of the coloniser, so too the story of colonial law was, and continues to be, written by the colonisers. From this perspective, law is represented as the antithesis of violence, its function as preventing or punishing violence. In opposition to a civilising and pacifying law stands a violence which comes to be constructed as if it were an attribute of criminality (e.g. Weisburg, 1992, pp.175-178). Moreover, as indicated above, this antithesis is frequently made to resonate with racialised identities.

The Courts

As discussed, in the lower courts the antithesis between law and violence is played out essentially in a physical rather than discursive context. The division between the law and violence, however, is amplified through legal discourse.[19] And it is not only in the higher courts that law assumes an essentially discursive form but it is also at this level that the most notorious and violent criminal cases are tried - the murders, sexual assaults and armed robberies. Because it is the practices of the higher courts which are often taken to be representative of "the law", as discussed above, it is chiefly through this public arena that law is specifically and deliberately dis-*articulated* from physical violence and articulated to and through a discourse of "civilised" reason.

The elaborateness of such reasoning is discussed further below, but a rather crude example of the kind of reasoning I am referring to can be found in one of the instances I witnessed in the magistrates' courts of Western Australia. As indicated in Chapter 6, an Aboriginal woman had been committed to an asylum for reacting violently to racist taunts. The magistrate's posture was that the woman's violence was so incomprehensible and dangerous that she required psychiatric assessment and institutionalisation. After all, according to the magistrate's (public) posture, 'Race has nothing to do with physical violence'.

However, as I hope is becoming evident, it is precisely the processes of the law which are crucially effective in the manufacture of social relations inextricably constitutive of and by race and physical violence. On the one hand, (white) law comes to be perceived as non-violent, while the "criminals", particularly black people, come to be associated with violence. On the other hand, the actual - but denied - violence of (white) law is largely used against black "criminals". It is perhaps this refusal to publicly recognise the connection between violence and race, *as it is constructed by and through law*, which explains another instance I observed in the courts; the silence and embarrassment of white court officials when confronted by a bleeding Aboriginal prisoner in the docks.[20]

Colonised Peoples' Appropriations

It would nonetheless be simplistic to present colonised peoples as simply victims of law's violence. The constructed antithesis between law and violence can be and is exploited by colonised peoples in some instances. As I hope to show in the following chapter, the utilisation of the legal system in disputes arising between colonised peoples themselves can enable such people to obtain highly punitive forms of vengeance; a retributiveness which would be regarded as "uncivilised" if it were exacted outside the asserted legitimacy and temperance of the legal system. Sarat and Kearns in fact describe law's 'crowning achievement' as being 'its reputation as the only alternative to general, barbaric violence when its own violence is a numbing commonplace of everyday life' (Sarat & Kearns, 1991, p.211) - or at least a commonplace in the everyday life of the oppressed.

However, I am interested here to examine legal actions which are initiated by colonised people against colonialist practices and institutions. The legal discourse which presents law's practice as "civilised" and non-violent provides an avenue which can be exploited by colonised people against at least factions of the dominant elite.

Following Marx's analysis of the reforms effected through the Factory Acts (U.K.), what I am claiming here is that gains for the marginalised which have been effected through law can often be interpreted as coinciding with divisions between individual as opposed to collective interests of the elite, or divisions between other configurations of elite groups and classes (Hunt, 1993, pp.33,34). The latter is illustrated in the interpretation of the abolition of slavery found in the work of Eric Williams (1961)[1944] and others, as was discussed in Chapter 1, and according to which industrialists supported the abolition of slavery in order to undermine the plantocracy and mercantilism.

Perhaps an even more striking example of such an interpretation of legal reform is an Aboriginal woman's interpretation of the legal prohibition against "blackbirding" practices in Western Australia during the 1870s. The woman who related this account stated that it was what she had been told by her mother, who had lived in the north of the state at the time the legislation was enacted.[21] The interpretation is unequivocal in constructing the apparently ameliorating prohibition against pearlers' exploitation of Aboriginal people in terms of pastoralist demands to keep the indigenous work force, and particularly Aboriginal women, available for their own exploitations. (It is possible that a similar analysis in terms of the interests of the miners as opposed to those of the pastoralists may also be relevant to the implementation of assimilationist policies in Western Australia during the 1950s and '60s, although this interpretation seems to remain unexplored. But see Edmunds, 1989, p.7.[22])

Two of the activists whose work I have referred to in this thesis, Robert Bropho and Abdullah Omowale, have both on occasion sought to utilise the colonial legal system. Bropho and his people, for example, have initiated a series of court battles over the development of a sacred site in Perth, Western Australia (Churches, 1990; 1992). Within the legal framework, the many issues in dispute turned critically on power relations between government and legal officials. Any "victory" won by Aboriginal people would be dependent upon their ability to exploit the divisions between the institutions of law and parliament.

Omowale and the other members of the Jamaat al Muslimeen have also been involved in a series of legal actions, both preceding and following their coup attempt in Trinidad. Actions initiated have concerned the army occupation of the Jamaat grounds, the threatened and eventual demolition of Jamaat property and the Presidential pardon granting an amnesty to those involved in the attempted overthrow (Omowale, 'The Muslimeen Fight for Survival', *Sunday Mirror*, July 28, 1992; August 2, 1992; August 9, 1992; August 16, 1992; August 23, 1992; August 30, 1992; September 6, 1992).

Such engagements with law do not necessarily constitute evidence of law's hegemony rather than a 'scandalous' exploitation of law by colonised peoples, as described and advocated in Valerie Kerruish's *The Ideology of Jurisprudence* (1991, p.200). Whatever the motivations of those who resort to law as a means of asserting their identity and existence, it may also evidence a certain pragmatic recognition of law as an avenue through which divisions between ruling elites can be exploited.

The decision of the British Privy Council concerning the Presidential amnesty granted the Muslimeen provides an illustration of how such divisions can be exploited to the benefit of those most marginalised, but also why the marginalised would have reason to be sceptical of any such legal "victory".[23] Significantly here, the Privy Council ruling created a powerful legal precedent which not only benefited the Muslimeen but at the same time entrenched (and revealed) something of the racist logic of law.

A Case Study

The attempted coup of 1990 was brought to an end by the granting of a Presidential amnesty to the Muslimeen involved. The amnesty stated, amongst other things, that the Muslimeen had been granted a pardon for any criminal offences associated with the coup attempt. On surrendering the Red House (Parliament House) and the television station that they had commandeered, the Muslimeen were rounded up and eventually taken to prison, with the leaders being held on death row. It was decided to prosecute the Muslimeen on criminal charges of treason, murder and assault.

Lawyers for the Muslimeen commenced proceedings under the Constitution and also sought a writ of *habeas corpus*. The local courts held that the validity of the Presidential pardon could only be determined at the same time as the criminal prosecutions. On appeal, the Privy Council held that imprisonment of the Muslimeen was *prima facie* unlawful, and returned the matter to the courts of Trinidad and Tobago.[24] In a very telling comment, which was published in the Trinidadian media, Lord Ackner of the Privy Council, stated,

> No civilised system of law should tolerate the years of delay contemplated by the courts below, before the lawfulness of this imprisonment could be effectively challenged. (*Phillip v. DPP* [1992] 1 AC 545, at 560 and quoted in the *Trinidad Guardian*, December 11, 1991)

Given the very large number of unsentenced prisoners who are incarcerated and unable to effectively challenge the lawfulness of their imprisonment in Trinidad (and, for that matter, in Britain[25]), many for no better reason than that they are unable to pay bail, the Privy Council's concern over the delay before the lawfulness of imprisonment could be challenged seems somewhat disingenuous. Moreover, the treatment of Irish Republican Army (I.R.A.) suspects as sanctioned under British law itself would make the condemnation of the legal system of Trinidad and Tobago more than disingenuous. (One can only speculate over the attitudes of the Law Lords had the pardon concerned I.R.A. members who had taken over 10 Downing Street by armed insurrection and shot and humiliated a British Prime Minister, while thousands rioted in the streets.) But more to the point here is the Privy Council's reference to the legal system of Trinidad and Tobago as one lacking 'civilised' standards.

Such a comment clearly resonates with Fitzpatrick's (1992) thesis, that the mythology of British civilisation permeates British "justice". Moreover, as also asserted by Fitzpatrick, this sense of civilisation and superiority would seem to be largely nebulous, and essentially characterised only by its asserted opposition to what the "uncivilised" and "inferior" do. As indicated above, there would seem to be nothing inherently "uncivilised" about delay before the lawfulness of imprisonment can be determined; apparently it is not uncivilised when the British do it. Nor does it seem that arguments that the Presidential pardon was void due to duress were obviously unsound. As Fitzpatrick indicated, what is at the heart of the myth of British (legal) superiority is the mere appearance of difference and the representation of this difference as "civilised".

Nonetheless, it remains true that this posture of being "civilised" is not altogether arbitrary and is often effected through British legal (and other) institutions adopting a less punitive position than the colonial courts. In the contemporary context, this can be seen in the Muslimeen case itself, or in the Privy Council decision banning the death penalty for those imprisoned on death row for more than five years and referred to in Chapter 5. In contemporary Australia, the same opposition revolves around notions of the relative benevolence of white law as opposed to the harshness of traditional Aboriginal law (Ashforth, 1990, p.2; Bolger, 1991, p.52).

This opposition seems often to relate to Goffman's analysis, referred to above, and according to which those who occupy privileged institutional sites are exempted from dealing with the imperatives raised by the daily interactions of more direct control. In any event, as Edward Said has indicated, condemnation of the depredations of others is facile - and does not necessarily reflect upon how such critics conduct or assess their own affairs (Said, 1993, pp.250,291).[26]

But it is also of note that such constructed oppositions are not *necessarily* confined to dualisms of British (Western)/ civilised/ benign and non-British/

uncivilised/ violent. Legal interventions into the lives of Aboriginal juveniles, for example, are often legitimised precisely in terms of the "failure" of Aboriginal families to be sufficiently punitive or disciplinary in dealings with their children (O'Malley, 1992). This would indicate that to some degree such constructions are essentially arbitrary (Bourdieu & Passeron, 1977) and provide those who exercise institutional power with significant scope to manoeuvre.

In the Muslimeen case itself there were potentially different ways in which this kind of reasoning could be effective. In the context of an independent nation which has retained a British legal system, the colonial courts become at once hybrids of British justice and the meniality of the colonial peoples. In the context of the colonial myth, these courts may be constructed as outposts of (British) civilisation or, alternatively, as exemplars of the inadequacies of the colonies and the colonised.

Influencing the attitudes of the Privy Council will be the degree to which the interests of the British (elite) coincide with those of the local elite. In the Muslimeen case, it seems relevant that Britain no longer had the financial interests in Trinidad which had seen British warships unloading their marines at Port of Spain and San Fernando in order to re-impose public order - through gunfire - during earlier mass uprisings, and which had also seen the Privy Council as a party to the appalling treatment of the working class leader, Uriah "Buzz" Butler, during the 1930s (Craig, 1988; Jacobs, 1976; Singh, 1987). Issues of political stability in Trinidad and Tobago are not, for the British at least, as significant as they once were.[27]

Moreover, the stirrings amongst the local elite to create a West Indian Court of Appeal in place of the Privy Council may have been of particular relevance to the Privy Council.[28] In such a context, there are factors which would predispose the Privy Council to take an oppositional stance to any adopted by the local elite, and thereby undermine the local elite's attempts to claim legitimacy ("civilisation") for themselves. In the instance of the Muslimeen appeal, the members of the Jamaat obtained their freedom from prison and death row, but the Privy Council consolidated its position as the overseer and protector of "civilisation" in the colonies.

In doing so, the Privy Council employed the dominant cultural construction of the opposition between (British) law and colonised peoples: between civilisation and savagery. The potency of such a construction has two major catalysts. One, which is discussed below, is the degree of violence apparent amongst particularly the most marginalised factions of communities of colonised peoples. The other, which has been the principal subject of the preceding chapters, is the denial, legitimation and concealment of the inherent violence of Western "civilisations", particularly the legal systems of such societies, in their dealings with those whom they colonise.

Notes

1. Cherie Imlah is an Aboriginal poet. Her poem, 'Between the Acts', is taken from Cunneen (1992d, p.18).
2. For a discussion of the deliberate organisation of verbal interactions in the courts, see Atkinson & Drew (1979). Possibly the difficulties I encountered with my own field-work arose because I did not fit within any of the categories of people who normally are part of the court drama. Other works which have noted the "dramatic" nature of court interactions and official discourse include Worrall (1990, p.14) and Cole (1990, p.302). McBarnet's (1981) study of the magistrates' courts, in particular, moves beyond the equation of law in the courts with 'law'.
3. Refer to notes Chapter 5, note 7; and Chapter 6, note 12.
4. Although there is disproportionate reporting of higher court cases in Trinidad with reference to the number of matters heard in the different courts, there was significantly more coverage of magistrates' court cases than in Western Australia. Such reporting tended to focus on the harsh sentences handed down at that level, a matter which is taken up again later. Apart from initial bail applications and determinations in the magistrates' courts of Trinidad, however, the hundreds of cases which, daily, were merely remanded to another date were generally not considered newsworthy.
5. In the Port of Spain magistrates' courts in 1990, for example, the highest number of prosecutions were for what is there classified as 'Minor Offences', and which included predominantly charges of assault and battery and obscene language; or 'Class iii' offences, which were predominantly embezzlement. In Western Australia, the highest number of convictions in 1992/3 in the magistrates' courts were for 'Fraud, forgery and false pretences', 'Possess and/or use cannabis', and 'Offences against good order', including predominantly breach of probation and resist/hinder police. In both jurisdictions, the highest number of prison sentences imposed in these lower courts, and therefore excluding remands to custody, were for crimes such as fraud and larceny (T&T CSO, unpublished data; ABS, 1994).
6. In 1993, 1,791 persons were imprisoned for default of fine (Broadhurst et al, 1994, p.76). In the lower courts in 1992/3, 54,825 fines were imposed; compared to only 596 fines imposed by the higher courts (ABS, 1994, p.7).
7. In 1991, 1,099 distinct persons received penalties of imprisonment in the higher courts of Western Australia. In that same year, almost 5,000 distinct persons were received into Western Australian prisons. Another 5,000 sentenced prisoners served their sentences at police lock-ups (Broadhurst et al, 1992, pp.53,54,94,100). No data are available on unsentenced lock-up prisoners.
8. My analysis is influenced by Goffman's work on the social dynamics of total institutions. He states that one of the main accomplishments of total institutions

is 'staging a difference between two constructed categories of persons', staff and inmates. He also applies the analysis to relations between different levels of staff within the institutions (Goffman, 1968, pp.104-108).

9. In interesting contrast to this construction of a highly visible "criminal" identity for male prisoners was the absence of such constructed identities in respect to female prisoners in both jurisdictions. In both jurisdictions, not only were few women held in custody, but even those who were prisoners were rarely distinguishable from other female defendants, in terms of their treatment in the courts. It is perhaps because the constructed (male) identities connote not only subordination but dangerousness that there is a less concerted effort to maintain these identities in relation to female prisoners. Of particular interest here is that this common theme of women's "innocuousness" is apparent in both jurisdictions despite the different ethnically specific gendered identities which exist outside of the courts. As adverted to earlier, in relation to Afro-Trinidadian culture at least, it appeared to me that a great deal of value was placed on the notion of the physical and emotional strength of both women and men. In contrast to this, the manufacture of gendered identities in common law courts generally did not recognise the possibility of female "dangerousness".

10. While no such difference is inscribed on the bodies of white court officials and white defendants, it is of note that other techniques applied; and if these were not as blatant as in Trinidad it is also the case that such a context is not one in which racism and colonialism feature. It is also of note that in a context in which adults in Western societies are regarded as being self-regulating (Goffman, 1968, p.43; Hall et al, 1978, pp.142-144; Fitzpatrick, 1992, pp.121-123), subjection to external control and reprimand is likely to be far more "self-mortifying" than in cultures which do not have such an individualised sense of social regulation. Again it may be that there is less reason for any overt display of domination in Westernised cultures, as the mere fact of being in a position in which one is not considered to have satisfactorily discharged one's mature duty to self-regulate may be incompatible with defendants' self-perceptions (Goffman, 1968, p.31). I do not mean to overstate this factor, however, as I suspect that the notion of self-regulation as adult and Foucault's 'stifling anguish of responsibility' to which Fitzpatrick refers (1992, p.123), are also to some degree class specific, and the emphasis is far stronger amongst those other than the lower classes.

11. For an even more extreme example of the construction of these relations through a British-based court system in a colonial context, refer to Cole's (1990) 'Rough Justice: Criminal Proceedings in Nigerian Magistrates' Courts'. Note that Cole (1990, p.300) also found that pleas of guilty were comparatively rare.

12. Refer to T&T CSO, 1993a, pp.27,61; Broadhurst et al, 1994, pp.74,79. In 1990, the year of the attempted coup, the disproportion of imprisonment rates

between Trinidad and Tobago and non-Aboriginal Western Australia increased to a ratio of ten to one.

13. Refer to Ashforth (1990, pp.300,301), for an Aboriginal account of the relevance of the threat of violence to Aboriginal acquiescence to constructions of themselves as criminal. Of course, other factors are also highly relevant; note the comment extracted in Chapter 6, according to which guilty pleas were on occasion a consequence of the continuingly alien nature of white legal proceedings for Aboriginal people. Ethnic differences are also significant (e.g. Kearins, 1990; Ligterwood, 1984). In addition, Hoddinott (1985) refers to some defendants' lack of concern about the outcome.
14. One indication of how widespread is the disdain for police in Trinidad was an instance I witnessed when a visiting (white) British academic was lecturing a class of students at the University of the West Indies. The academic spoke of his good relations with his "local bobby", and the sense of reassurance he felt at the police officer's presence. The students laughed loudly at such a proposition, and made comments about the stupidity of police officers, and how they would cross the street rather than walk near a police officer who was just as likely to shoot them. As elsewhere, the university students of the West Indies were generally of relatively privileged backgrounds, and were not particularly radical.
15. Refer to Chapter 3, note 2, for an extensive list of newspaper articles reporting police brutality in Trinidad.
16. Refer to the testimony of P.C. Armitt in the Royal Commission Inquiry into the death of John Pat, transcript, pp.3757-4335 (Aus RCIADIC, 1990c). In the course of his evidence, Armitt complained of having to live in departmental housing which was located in close proximity to Aboriginal people's housing, and to the verbal abuse of his wife and children.
17. Clearly such a statement can only be taken as a general declaration of police attitudes. However, the insular culture of policing (Queensland Commission of Inquiry [Fitzgerald Report], 1989) together with the measures taken against those who do not conform (e.g. Purdy, 1992a, p.20), ensure that most officers do, or are made to, comply with such dominant understandings of their relationship with Aboriginal people.
18. Such an analysis also has a resonance with relations between the Privy Council and the colonial courts, discussed below.
19. Sarat and Kearns (1991, p.212), write,

> Leviathan, it seems, is an insubstantial (if deadly) monster, alternately operating through disembodied choices, the manipulation of texts, and mere mindless, mechanical motions: the full-fledged, pain-imposing, responsible agent eludes our grasp. Indeed, thanks to the rhetorical ingenuity of those who

> interpret legal texts, the complex chains of bureaucratic connection, and legal theory's complicitous silence, the awful acts almost seem to have no cause. Even the pain and suffering come to have but a shadowy status, hidden from view, recorded in the barely audible testimony of those who endure them or buried in the recesses of unspeakable fears.

20. To similar effect is Sarat and Kearns's discussion of a U.S. case in which the Supreme Court upheld the legitimacy of attempting to execute a convicted murderer twice (*Francis v. Resweber*, 329 US 459 (1947)). They state, 'It is difficult to imagine how law's violence could be more painfully present and, ironically, more absent, that is, invisible...' (Sarat & Kearns, 1991, p.213).
21. I have not identified this woman because she is now deceased and I have been requested not to use her name, according to Aboriginal custom.
22. It is important to emphasise that such interpretations do not preclude the significance of resistance and struggle by marginalised groups. As Fryer noted, the significance of slave revolt to the profitability of the slavery enterprise should not be underestimated (Fryer, 1988, pp.86,92). Note too the killing of pearlers and police by Aboriginal people in 1872 (or 1868) may well have been relevant to the enactment of legislation prohibiting "blackbirding" in 1873 (Green, 1987, p.102; Edmunds, 1989, p.6). In terms of the decline of pastoralism, the Aboriginal strikes in the north-west from the 1940s on would also seem relevant (Bolton, 1987, p.152; Hawke & Gallagher, 1989, p.68).
23. Kerruish points out that, even when Bropho "won" a court action, he in fact regarded it as a defeat; a token of respect due to the goodwill of 'a white liberal judge' rather than any mutuality of understanding (Kerruish, 1991, p.17).
24. I was told by a Trinidadian lawyer that the Privy Council indicated its preference for making an outright finding that the amnesty was valid. As a measure of the cynicism common in Trinidad about the legal system, the lawyer added that the leading Queens Counsel for the Muslimeen declined the Privy Council's offer to make a determination on the validity of the amnesty because he wanted the opportunity to be paid to argue another case before the courts in Trinidad.
25. Note that in 1992/3, twenty-two per cent of all prisoners in England and Wales were unsentenced (GB HM Prison Service, N/d). During 1991 in England and Wales, police made 117,000 arrests in which people were held in custody without trial (GB Home Office, 1992). Neither the Prison Service nor the Home Office published data on the length of imprisonment of unsentenced prisoners.
26. An example of this concerns the much-vaunted benevolence of the British in their concern for Australian Aboriginal people (refer, for example, Reynolds,

1992). Reece (1974, pp.209-215) notes, however, that early colonists in New South Wales were cynical of British efforts to ameliorate conditions for Aboriginal people - claiming that the only measures which were put into practice were those for which the colonists paid themselves. Moreover, in the very year that the British Colonial Office refused to allow the newly formed Western Australian government jurisdiction over Aboriginal welfare because of the notorious mistreatment of Aboriginal people in that state, the Privy Council handed down a judgment confirming the doctrine of *terra nullius* in Australia, and therefore confirming the somewhat less than human status accorded Aboriginal people under British law (Constitution Act 1889; *Cooper v. Stuart* (1889) 4 & 5 Will., IV C.95). See, too, the recent British stance on the issue of cleaning the nuclear waste from the Maralinga test site, and Aboriginal land, contaminated by British nuclear testing in Australia during the 1950s. Also refer to Russell's (1944) trenchant criticisms of British colonial rule in *Colour, Race and Empire*.

27. That is not to say that the Privy Council has allowed the local courts and legislature complete autonomy in matters of finance. The ruling of the Privy Council concerning the Retrenchment and Severance Benefits Act was that debenture holders had prior claim to the assets of companies in receivership over workers' entitlement to severance benefits (*Express*, August 8, 1992). Given the high degree of foreign ownership of companies in Trinidad, it seems that the Privy Council decision would mean that company holdings could be claimed by foreign shareholders in preference to local workers; further depleting national assets and income.

28. Cross (1988, p.279) and see 'Call for West Indian Appeal Court', *Express*, January 29, 1992; 'West Indian Court of Appeal a Must Says Former Attorney General', *Express*, February 12, 1992; '$$ Woes Hamper Caribbean Court of Appeal Being a Reality', *Guardian*, February 15, 1992; 'Sir Lionel Wants Caribbean Court of Appeal', *Express*, April 15, 1992.

8 Violence

THE VIOLENCE OF COLONISED PEOPLES

> The colonized man will first manifest this aggressiveness which has been deposited in his bones against his own people. This is the period when the niggers beat each other up, and the police and magistrates do not know which way to turn when faced with the astonishing waves of crime...
>
> Frantz Fanon[1]

A review was conducted of national murder rates for twenty-three countries, including Australia, Mexico, Sudan, the Philippines and Trinidad and Tobago. In the pre-oil boom days from 1966 to 1970, Trinidad and Tobago had the highest per capita murder rate, more than ten times the national rate for Australia (Beirne & Messerschmidt, 1991, p.650). The murder rate in Trinidad and Tobago has declined since that time, but the number of homicides has remained significantly higher than the total number for Western Australia, despite the latter's larger population (T&T CSO, 1993a, pp.39,40; WA Police Department, 1993, p.30). And although the kinds of homicides and crimes of Trinidad which are described below also occur elsewhere, it is the prevalence of such extreme instances of violence amongst a relatively small population, during just one year, which is striking.

The drug trade was a major factor contributing to the contemporary levels of violence experienced in Trinidad, with addicts, dealers and gangs being involved in violent confrontations between themselves and with others. Local newspapers reported cases of areas which were over-run by armed gangs involved in violent warfare, and drug addicts who continually robbed and harassed residents.[2] Many of the murders in Trinidad were linked to the drug trade and often involved execution style shootings. However, such executions on occasion were also accompanied by mutilation, as in the case of two middle-level dealers and alleged hit-men, "Tooks" and "Bulls", one had reportedly been castrated, had his penis stuffed into his mouth and had his eyes removed. Both had been disembowelled.[3]

Even a greater number of reported deaths were committed by family members. Women and children were frequently stabbed, poisoned, bludgeoned or chopped to death by male members of their families. Although suicide rates in Trinidad and Tobago were similar to those in Australia, of particular concern were the number which were associated with the murder of other family members (T&T CSO, 1993a, pp.39,40; Bennett et al, 1992, pp.274-277). Of one hundred reported murders the details of which I recorded during 1992, more than one-tenth were associated with the suicide or attempted suicide of the perpetrator.

Murders and suicides often bore direct testimony to the violence and despair that inhabits family life - parents aged eighteen and twenty, who poisoned their five-month old daughter and then attempted to kill themselves; two boys, aged thirteen and eleven, whose father first poisoned and then slashed them before killing himself - the younger child also dying but the thirteen-year-old surviving to require psychiatric as well as medical treatment; the strangling and chopping to death of two women who had both previously sought injunction orders against their violent partners - in one case the court rejecting the woman's application; the killing of a forty-three-day-old child by his mother, who stated that she 'didn't want him to be like her'.[4]

Still other murders and crimes indicate the oppressive conditions that characterise the life of the poor in Trinidad - the stabbing to death of a man over TT$3; a seven-months pregnant prostitute 'who was stabbed in her womb, buttocks and has a right breast almost severed by a man who wanted free sex'; the suicide of an eighteen-year-old after losing his job; a man who stabbed his wife and drank poison before setting himself alight; three prostitutes, aged between fifteen and sixteen years, one of whom was five months pregnant, who were alleged to have stabbed a woman to death; the robbery of two brothers, aged nine and two, of their sneakers and a school bag by armed bandits; the suicide of a ten-year-old after he was accused of stealing money from his family; the murders of at least two women, aged seventy-eight and eighty, allegedly by a seventeen-year-old boy.[5]

Other examples included an unemployed man who was savagely bashed by two men because he collected two empty bottles outside a bar. Refunds on the bottles were worth fifty cents each. The man was reported as saying to his assailants, 'Like allyuh want to kill me for nothing, or what?' It seems they did, and he died from his injuries twenty-four days later.[6] Another reported case involved an elderly woman who had obtained a court injunction against her son, a crack cocaine addict. It was reported that the police failed to act on the injunction and that the son had verbally and physically abused his family, as well as stabbing his father with a screwdriver. He had stolen

> foodstuff, gold bracelets, tools, gas cylinders, wheel barrow, cutlass, spade and even medicine for the family dog. He stole plants, then the baskets and

when that was depleted, he dug up what was in the ground and sold those too.

He sold his brothers' cutting board (needed for his work), all the buckets in the garden, the garden hose, two teddy bears and, one day, hearing the water flowing downstairs, the family discovered that the connection to the water pump had also been stolen.[7] Trinidadian Harold Sonny Ladoo's evocatively titled *No Pain Like This Body* (1987), taken from the Hindu *Dhammapada*, provides another graphic account of the violence that can inhabit the life of the poverty stricken farmers of Trinidad. Ladoo himself was murdered in Trinidad at the age of twenty-eight.

Data from Australia indicate that conditions for many Aboriginal people are similarly bleak. In the Kimberley region of Western Australia, it was found that an indigenous woman was thirty-three times more likely to die as a result of domestic violence than any other person in Australia (Judy Atkinson, quoted in *The Weekend Australian*, June 18-19, 1994). A study carried out in the Northern Territory found that Aboriginal women were twenty-eight times more likely to be victims of homicide than other Australians. The list of their assailants included their spouses, sons, grandsons, uncles and other male relatives (Payne, 1990, p.10). In some communities more Aboriginal women died as a result of violent assault than there had been Aboriginal deaths in custody for the whole of the state concerned (Atkinson, 1990, p.6). A study of one community in Queensland revealed that not one Aboriginal girl over the age of ten had not been raped (Atkinson, 1990, p.6).

Sharon Payne quoted Paul Wilson's description of Aboriginal communities in northern Australia in 1982,

> Murder, self-mutilation and alcoholism are rife... People of differing tribes and from various areas mix with each other in an atmosphere of tension and violence.[8]

She notes in 1990, 'The situation has not improved since then' (Payne, 1990, p.10). Even ameliorating reforms such as the decriminalisation of public drunkenness were seen as adding 'another burden for Aboriginal women'. Although not objecting to the reforms of themselves, which were described as 'commendable', Payne points to the failure to provide sobering-up centres or detoxification units as meaning that a greater number of drunken men are taken home. It is 'the wives, mothers and grandmothers who are left to deal with the violent mental and physical problems associated with alcohol abuse' (Payne, 1990, p.10).[9]

Dodson (1991, pp.359,369), reports a study of fifty Aboriginal men in a desert community in Western Australia. Ninety-eight per cent of these men had spent at least one occasion in a police lock-up and sixty-four per cent had spent time in prison. But it is also of note that sixteen per cent of the men had been imprisoned for violent crimes; still others were reportedly violent to their wives. One man had had two wives who had both died after histories of violent abuse. A number of men carried permanent scars as a result of violence accompanying alcohol use, injuries which were both self-inflicted and resulting from the acts of others. At least four per cent of the men had been hospitalised because of serious sickness related to alcohol over the past year. The average age of the group was twenty-six.

Dodson (1991, pp.415,416), also describes the social and cultural circumstances of a number of Aboriginal people who died in custody. He states,

> This is not done to blame anyone, but to highlight that there is much to be done about tension, violence and neglect within those sections of Aboriginal society where alcohol use has created its own alien environment that exhibits no respect for anyone.

One death in custody occurred while the Aboriginal prisoner was being held for allegedly bashing her cousin/sister (according to Aboriginal kinship classifications); another concerned a man who was taken into custody after being left on a railway bridge by his drinking mates. Yet another death involved an Aboriginal man who had been excluded from his community as a "trouble maker" and one man died after allegedly being assaulted by another Aboriginal prisoner. Another death in custody concerned an Aboriginal prisoner who had been imprisoned many times for assaulting his wife (Dodson, 1991, p.416). It is also of note that Robert Walker, whose poetry and death in custody have been referred to previously, died in custody while serving a sentence for having raped a nine-year-old girl (Aus RCIADIC, 1991d, p.1).

A recent study of reported crime has documented a grim statistical profile of Aboriginal victimisation and violence in Western Australia. It found that Aboriginal people were 6.5 times more likely than other Western Australians to be the victims of violent crime and almost 15 times more likely to be the victims of homicide. This disproportion is even more stark in relation to Aboriginal women, who are 10.7 times more likely to be the victims of violent crime than are non-Aboriginal women, 37.5 times more likely to be the victims of spousal violence, 11.9 times to be the victims of violence as children. Aboriginal people were also found to be far more likely to be the perpetrator of crimes against their own people and, as has been found elsewhere and indicated above, specifically against their own families (Broadhurst et al, 1994, pp.17,21,22,24-26).

Colin Tatz, who had conducted field-work in more than seventy Aboriginal communities during 1989 and 1990, comments,

> When I see a gambling mother pour petrol on a blanket and then suffuse her crying infant's face to quieten it while she deals the cards, I know that calamity is taking place. (Tatz, 1994, p.177)[10]

Such data provide only one facet of the extreme violence and hardship under which many colonised people live. Aboriginal activist Kevin Gilbert, who himself served fourteen and a half years in prison on a charge of murder, notes, however, that there is a reticence amongst Aboriginal people to publicly acknowledge the nature of their community and domestic relations (Gilbert, 1977, pp.1,2). Aboriginal women who have highlighted the immense terror that infuses their own and their children's lives have faced criticism from other Aboriginal groups (Payne, 1990; Atkinson, 1990, 1991; and refer 'Domestic Violence Divides Black Women', *The Weekend Australian*, June 18-19, 1994).[11] The public silences on the issue of internal violence within oppressed groups is understandable given the devaluation of these peoples by dominant cultures. Moreover, Isabell Coe expressed the concern that establishing separate legal representation for Aboriginal women who were victims of internal violence within their communities, for example, was 'just another way of dividing our people' (quoted in *The Weekend Australian*, June 18-19, 1994).

It is of note, however, that silence on the issue of internal violence has also enabled others, who themselves are unaffected by that violence, and even though they might be sympathetic to those who are oppressed, to imagine comfortable and inane explanations of what is happening in these communities. For example, it has been claimed that 'any acts of deviance must be taken to be acts of resistance however inarticulately expressed or formulated' (I. Taylor, P. Walton & J. Young, *The New Criminology*, (1972), p. 252, in Hunt, 1993, p.98).

The inadequacy of such an explanation becomes evident if one has any regard for those who are likely to be the victims of such "resistance". As the left realist movement in criminology has since acknowledged, the victims of most violence and theft are the poor and marginalised (e.g. Matthews & Young, 1992a). In his study, Wilson cites research which indicated that the victims of homicide in Australia were far more likely to be of the lowest occupational status (Wilson, 1982, p.116). The findings of the recent study of Aboriginal violence in Western Australia, referred to above, indicate that such analyses are relevant to Aboriginal people (Broadhurst et al, 1994, pp.14-28).

> The overwhelming nature of Aboriginal victimisation is that it involves Aboriginal perpetrators. In particular, women and children are especially

> vulnerable to victimisation at the hands of their own people. (Broadhurst et al, 1994, p.27)

Silence on the issue of violence within marginalised groups has meant that those who suffer from it most are abandoned to deal with it as best they can. For those not caught within the dynamics of this violence, it is transformed into myths of savages or freedom fighters.

The alternatives confronting people who live in conditions of extreme violence are very limited, particularly so for people who occupy the most marginal of social positions and who therefore lack access to avenues which may be available to others. Perhaps the most significant constraint upon such marginalised peoples is the urgency with which *something has to be done*. In the context of internal violence, such alternatives as are accessible by the colonised consist of either supplanting the colonial legal system ("informal justice") or trying to appropriate it ("formal justice").

Informal Justice[12]

In Trinidad people frequently do not resort to the colonial legal system when facing what is perceived by them to be criminal conduct. This may be because of the under-resourcing of the legal system or because of public alienation from that system, but probably both elements are influential. Certainly there is much that is positive in a strategy of autonomy which in many ways has an affinity with the historical position of members of slave and indentured labourer societies. In these societies, indigenous social structures continued to control relations *inter se* during the plantation era.[13] Moreover there is a degree of communal self-reliance and empowerment associated with autonomy from official law enforcers.

On occasion such an autonomous sense of communal justice can be active in limiting what is perceived to be unjustified official interference. For example, two reported instances of public intervention while I was residing in Trinidad occurred when the police were physically forced to cease beating and harassing suspects by massed and active members of "the public".[14] Moreover, this autonomous sense of justice may play a significant role in mobilising the frequent massed uprisings against the formal and imposed authority structures which have characterised much of the history of Trinidad.

However, it is important not to romanticise such "informal justice". Other reported instances of "informal justice" included the death of a man who was battered by a mob while (allegedly) attempting to steal a car from the Sunnydale Estate compound; the scalping of a "piper" (a user of crack cocaine, many of whom beg, borrow or steal anything to supply their addiction); the throwing of acid into the face of another; the "planassing" to death (beating with the broad side of a cutlass) of an addict who had stolen a pair of sneakers, a gold watch and other valuables; another thief was beaten with 'pieces of wood, iron and cutlasses [and received] 50 stiches after his battering'.[15] One woman was charged with having cut off her husband's penis,[16] and, in another instance I observed, a woman who was appearing in court had poured boiling oil over her husband during a domestic dispute. Another instance of which I was aware was the beating of an obviously ill black man who would occasionally call by my apartment seeking money. Once when he called and I was out, he was accused of being a thief by a group of the landlord's workers and was taken away in a car and beaten. Such an instance indicates that the racist social structure of Trinidad is not simply an artifice of the legal system, and is also constituted within broader communal perceptions of who are the "criminals".

Pat O'Malley's (1992) study of the problem of petrol-sniffing youths in remote Aboriginal communities raises similar issues of violent retribution in the context of contemporary colonised Australia. Responses to the offences committed by affected youths, which include crimes against not only white law but also Aboriginal law, often involved the infliction of physical violence. O'Malley states,

> One such form of reaction occurs where a group of men is finally goaded into action and, wielding nullahs, storm the petrol sniffers' camp or house and lay waste to all around them.

Another use of physical violence noted in O'Malley's (1992) study concerned "strict liability" offences involving kinship obligations, and he cites the case of a woman who was beaten for failing to attend a funeral, although she had not been able to attend.

Formal Justice

The alternative to "taking the law into their own hands" for colonised peoples is to attempt to appropriate the mechanisms of the formal legal system for their own purposes. There is historical evidence of such appropriations. For example, in Trinidad there are references to both Afro- and Indo-Trinidadians utilising Obeah to affect the outcomes of cases fought through courts of law. Indeed David Trotman notes these practices went so far as to pose a threat to any hegemony of law - reducing the "rule of law" to mere actions by human beings which could be manipulated by others through the use of Obeah (Niehoff &

Niehoff, 1960, pp.171,173; Trotman, 1986, pp.228,229). A form of appropriation is also evidenced in accounts of the early "Native Police" in Australia. It is claimed that Aboriginal police used their position in the white legal system to give effect to traditional tribal enmities (Aus RCIADIC, 1991a:10.5.18-10.5.20; Reece, 1974, p.214).

As was indicated in the accounts of my field-work, it is evident that members of marginalised groups continue to seek to utilise the legal system against members of their own communities. Examples of such attempted appropriations can be seen in the prevalence of private prosecutions in Trinidad and the attempts of Aboriginal communities in Western Australia to enforce their by-laws through the white legal system. I have discussed previously, in Chapters 5 and 6, the limitations placed on people when seeking to resort to the legal system in these circumstances. Such limitations can include a need to redefine disputes in terms acceptable to the legal system and the loss of control over the outcomes.

As also indicated, however, commentators have criticised such attempted appropriations as the use of by-laws by Aboriginal communities. Critics claim that such appropriations are inherently assimilationist because implicit to them is a reliance upon white authority structures. Dodson (1991, pp.455-470) noted however, that the communities involved were relatively happy with the system, and Atkinson (1990, p.7) also notes the great potential of such schemes. I repeat this debate here because it brings together a number of important issues.

First is the notion that colonised peoples should not or can not appropriate elements of colonial society for their own purposes. This attitude seems to me to be tied to an erroneous dogma which demands the "purity" of colonised peoples' cultures - but no-one else's - and which is discussed in some detail in Chapter 1. Related to this is the notion that "we" know better than colonised peoples what is in their interest.[17] Finally, such a debate appears to take place in a context which ignores a critical characteristic of the legal system in modern societies: with its enforcement mechanisms, its institutions, its personnel and its very significant capacity to attract funding, the power of law can be tangible in the here and now.

One area of particular significance in this context is the attempts by colonised peoples to utilise law to deal with criminal matters, including violence, within their communities. The following discussion concerns only these matters, and in other contexts, the imperatives, aims and gains of colonised peoples' utilisation of the legal system may be different (see too, the discussion at 'Colonised Peoples' Appropriations', above).

In Trinidad, resort to the criminal law can result in the highly punitive treatment of offenders.

> A case involving the larceny of fifty-six bars of chocolate resulted in a sentence of two years hard labour. Another larceny involving the theft of fifteen packets of carrots resulted in a fine of TT$1,000 or six months gaol; since the guilty party had no money he was sent to gaol. The theft of TT$30 resulted in a sentence of two years hard labour. A robbery with aggravation of over TT$9,000 resulted in eight years hard labour. An attempted rape resulted in a sentence of twenty years hard labour with fifteen strokes of the cat-o'-nine-tails. A man who raped his twelve-year-old daughter received a sentence of fifteen years hard labour with fifteen strokes of the cat-o'-nine-tails. Four counts of robbery resulted in a sentence of twenty-three years hard labour plus ten strokes. Robbing a soft drink seller of TT$500 at gun point resulted in a sentence of twenty years gaol and ten strokes of the cat-o'-nine-tails. A man charged with purse snatching from a seventy-one-year-old pensioner was sentenced to two years hard labour. The theft of three ducks resulted in three months hard labour. The charge of raping a woman while armed with a broken bottle resulted in a sixty year fixed sentence, the judge commenting that he would order castration if he were able to, also that 'the law is an ass' because he could not sentence the guilty party to be whipped as he had a previously been whipped for another offence. The theft of a car resulted in five years hard labour. Possession of two grams of marijuana resulted in TT$2,000 fine or nine months gaol in default. One man was fined TT$300 for the theft of three paint brushes, but as he had no money he was taken to gaol. The theft of eight soursops and one bag of plums resulted in a sentence of fourteen days gaol on each offence. A woman was sentenced to two years prison for the possession of one rock of cocaine. Possession of a "five piece" of marijuana resulted in TT$1000 fine or four months prison. On charges of the theft of two coconuts, thirty avocados and two bunches of coconuts, a man received six months gaol on each count. For being asleep on the street a man was fined TT$120 or ordered to spend twenty-four days in prison in default. Four men who were charged with rape, buggery and two counts of robbery while armed with meat cleavers were each sentenced to fifteen years and ten strokes, ten years and seven strokes, ten years and seven strokes and ten years and seven strokes on the charges respectively. A man was gaoled for twenty-one days gaol when he was unable to pay a fine of TT$150 after he was charged under the Litter Act for refusing to pick up peanut shells in the waiting room outside a magistrates' court.[18]

A judge who quashed the twenty year/twenty stroke sentence of a rapist criticised the length of gaol sentences for rape in Trinidad, in comparison to those of England. There was an outcry amongst women's groups condemning his comments.[19] As stated previously, the death sentence was mandatory for all persons found guilty of murder. When the thirteen year moratorium was lifted on the carrying out of the death sentence, there was much - but not absolute - public support for the executions.[20]

There can be no doubt that the legal system in Trinidad and Tobago is highly punitive, as indicated by the sentences highlighted above. Some of the cases illustrate the perpetuation of class relations through law, as in the instances of praedial larceny and sleeping on the streets. However, it is also true that not all cases fit within this category. The punishment of rapists and those who rob old age pensioners or street vendors is not readily explained in terms of the perpetuation of exploitative relations of class.[21] And even if it can be shown that the legal system itself is implicated in the subordination of people of colour, women, children and the poor, this of itself provides no answer to what such people are to do when they have been further brutalised or further impoverished by individuals in their community.[22] Support for the death penalty and harsh sentences in Trinidad indicates that punitiveness in the legal system is to a degree a calibration of that system to the demands of significant sectors of "the public" in a colonised society.[23]

The situation in Aboriginal Australia would appear to be different in a number of ways. One significant difference lies in the frequently reported attitude of Aboriginal people towards imprisonment, that it is a minor penalty. In Wilson's study of Queensland's remote Aboriginal communities, this attitude related to the extreme harshness of community life outside the gaols (Wilson, 1982, p.78), an attitude which is reinforced by the fact that few Aboriginal people from remote areas die from self-inflicted injuries in custody (Aus RCIADIC, 1991a:11.9.55). To some extent the perception of imprisonment as non-threatening is also borne out by the appalling statistic that, although many Aboriginal people die in prison, their risk of death from natural causes is actually higher *outside* prison (Aus RCIADIC, 1991a:22.1.2). Moreover, in some communities, Aboriginal peoples' risk of dying from violence is such that they 'are considerably safer in ... gaols than they are in their own communities' (Bolger, 1991, p.24).

Similarly, Dodson (1991, p.498) states that for some Aboriginal juveniles being sent to a detention centre is 'almost prestigious', and they often consider going to gaol to be 'a big joke'. He comments,

> It seems that a simple but tragic matter of poverty and deprivation at home and in the community, with little hope of improvements being made, means that detention centres might present as the best option. (Dodson, 1991, p.499)

Annie Hoddinott's (1985, pp.31,35), study of remote communities in Western Australia reveals similar attitudes towards imprisonment, with young Aboriginal men claiming that it is 'the holiday camp', and elders stating that imprisonment is not a sufficiently severe penalty. Her findings indicate that, while communal violence in these communities is markedly less than was found in the communities studied by Wilson, gaol remains 'a means of escape from poverty, family disputes and/or tribal sanctions' (Hoddinott, 1985, pp.24,25,31; Wilson, 1982, p.4).

Aboriginal attitudes towards imprisonment would therefore appear to be influenced by factors such as the harshness of life outside the gaols and, in more traditional societies, the severity of traditional punishments. And it is also certainly the case that prisons in Australia are not what they are in Trinidad. At the same time, however, it is also evidently true that imprisonment and other legal interventions can have a devastating effect on Aboriginal people (and others); their deaths in custody are just the most obvious indication of the destruction that can be wrought by arrest and imprisonment. Moreover, there is also evidence that Aboriginal people do, on occasion, utilise the white legal system, and sometimes in relatively punitive ways.

The excesses of some Aboriginal police forces have already been discussed above. Another scheme, which was established in Western Australia in 1980, led to the appointment of Aboriginal justices of the peace to administer community by-laws enacted by remote Aboriginal communities. The by-laws generally dealt with what on contemporary white standards are considered only comparatively minor offences, and generally involved alcohol consumption or supply. It was expected that the scheme would result in a reduction in the very high rates of Aboriginal imprisonment. In fact the already high imprisonment rates almost doubled in the first year after the scheme was implemented. Although it was not possible to conclude that this was directly because of the Aboriginal justices scheme, it was evident that the scheme by no means reduced the rate of Aboriginal imprisonment (Hoddinott, 1985).

There were a variety of reasons put forward to explain this phenomenon, not least being the corrosive effect of the scheme on traditional social controls. And although a number of issues were canvassed in relation to the scheme with the Aboriginal justices, these all related to issues which would *reduce* sentences, such as family affiliations, time lapses between offences and processing, and "payback" in terms of victims who themselves had offended before (Hoddinott, 1985, pp.29,36,37). There was little reference to why it was that imprisonment and other penalties should be utilised so extensively by Aboriginal justices of the peace.

It seems to me that the high rates of imprisonment are indicative of a certain punitiveness amongst sectors of Aboriginal society. In fact, the complaint made by the Aboriginal justices of the peace interviewed was that the penalties available to them under the scheme, including imprisonment, were not *sufficiently* severe.

> What is a fine? It is paper only. Does it teach a lesson? No. There is no discipline in white law - no lessons to be learned. If a man commits a serious crime in the white man's law. The Court makes him "sit down" in a room for a while [prison]. (Meeting with Council and community members at La Grange on November 16, 1984, in Hoddinott, 1985, p.35.)

Teresa Ashforth, in her study of communication between Aboriginal people and the representatives of white law, discussed one case in which she was involved, and in which an Aboriginal woman reported an assault to the police. The woman had her jaw broken by an Aboriginal man. Ashforth (1990, p.344) noted that the woman's 'interests and needs are immediate ones and have nothing to do with the criminal constructions of a man...'; she was seeking both to punish the defendant and to protect herself from further injury.

O'Malley's (1992) study adds further evidence of the elements of punitiveness in Aboriginal people's appropriations of white law. He states that many people in the remote Aboriginal community he studied, particularly the older people, wanted police not only to remove petrol sniffers but to keep them incarcerated away from the community for long periods of time. Indeed, O'Malley comments, 'To spend a few days in a community with a serious petrol sniffing episode is to understand immediately why this course of action is preferred by many'.

If one can gain an understanding of these attitudes after a few days' exposure to the sorts of conditions under which such people are forced to live, it is conceivable that a lifetime's exposure may well result in the adopting of such attitudes. In these circumstances, punitiveness or retributiveness are functions of neither ignorance nor savagery. A similar sense of the desperation which can imbue the attitudes of people confined in circumstances of marginality and desolation is indicated by Raffique Shah's editorial on the death sentence in Trinidad. Shah, who led the mutiny of the Army officers during the 1970s Black Power uprising in Trinidad when directed to "restore order" on the streets, comments, 'Today, gun-and-cutlass-crazed criminals out there have made the entire country mad as hell, crying out for blood'.[24]

Desperation and Retribution

It is of note that many of the penalties ordered by the courts of Trinidad and Tobago, adverted to above, were handed down to people who had long histories of similar offences. It would seem evident that the rationale for such sentencing was not deterrence, at least deterrence of the individuals concerned. As can be seen in the instance of the judge who complained of not being able to sentence a man to be flogged for raping a woman because he had previously been flogged, the case itself is illustrative of the failure of the punishment as an individual deterrence. It is also of note that the view of the Aboriginal justices of the peace, involved in the scheme outlined above, was that the punishments they handed down served no deterrent purpose (Hoddinott, 1985, pp.34,35).[25]

Moreover, instances of "informal" justice were no more effective as a deterrent. It was reported that the week following the battering to death of the (alleged) car thief at Sunnydale Estate, referred to above, vehicles were again being stolen from the same compound.[26] Violent incidents in Aboriginal communities did not resolve the problem of petrol sniffing. It would seem that there was no strong expectation that these punishments would deter crime; rather a sense of retribution often characterised the sentiments associated with punishment both under, and outside, the legal system.

Although there is no simple answer to such an issue, there can be no question that there is support (although it is by no means unanimous) for the punitive treatment of "criminals" in colonised societies. The legal system has been notorious in empowering groups within colonised societies in ways which distort traditional power relations,[27] and may well be instrumental in the dissemination of violence throughout society (Hay, 1992), although it seems to me quite wrong simply to attribute the punitiveness found in the appropriations of the legal system by (members of) colonised populations to corruption or ignorance. This punitiveness can also on occasion be seen in the attitudes of those who themselves suffer most from the vicissitudes of an unequal society, and who moreover know better than anyone the nature of the society in which they live.

Alan Hunt notes that theorists of the Left have abandoned their "constituency" by failing to engage with particular legal issues and strategies which directly oppress the subordinate (Hunt, 1993, pp.90-116). I would argue that the Left has also failed to recognise that retributiveness is not only acceptable to those of the political Right and the privileged. It seems to me that Left analyses which attribute the causes of crime to structural inequality, as if this were somehow a resolution to the problem of crime, fail to engage with the demands of those who bear the consequences of that crime. These people have often been regarded as being ignorant of the causes of crime (attributing it to the moral failings of individuals) or as being the "dupes" of conservative media reporting and ideologies. While I would not deny that such readings have a specific relevance to particular elements within the working class, as discussed by Stuart Hall et al (1978) in *Policing the Crisis*, such an interpretation cannot be generalised to apply to all of those who demand retribution.

Colonised peoples are often well aware of the problems associated with seeking to utilise the colonial legal system. Atkinson (1990, p.7) refers to the need for Aboriginal women to resort to non-Aboriginal law as rupturing and subordinating internal mechanisms of social control. Urban Aboriginal women were reported as stating, 'How can we call the police in? They come with their guns drawn and an innocent person gets killed' (quoted in Atkinson, 1990, p.6). The interface with other modes of justice can create further dilemmas for those caught within the cycles of internal violence. As indicated previously, Dodson (1991, p.381) reports that, when Aboriginal women turn to the police in cases of domestic violence, they are sometimes held accountable for any injury or death inflicted upon the men while in custody.

It is clear that such people do not resort to the colonial legal system in ignorance; they known better than anyone else that it is alien and brutalising. Moreover, they are also often more aware than anyone else of the structural causes of crime - the crushing racism and poverty. Resort is made to colonial legal systems in a context where there are few alternatives and also because, despite its dangers, it is an avenue which can sometimes yield benefits to them, a short-term respite from a violent situation; a degree of retribution.

It would seem that, whether one examines the nature of violence in colonised communities, or as it is expressed through informal or formal "justice", brutality and harshness often characterise relations between colonised peoples themselves. As indicated in Chapter 5, when I criticised the legal system as being too harsh, I was told, 'But life is hard, yes?'

THE "UNCIVILISED"

> All these patterns of conduct are those of the death reflex when faced with danger, a suicidal behaviour which proves to the settler (whose existence and domination is by them all the more justified) that these men are not reasonable human beings.
>
> Frantz Fanon[28]

Although the kinds of behaviour discussed above are easily interpreted by Western or Westernised observers as evidence of the savagery of colonised and "uncivilised" peoples, such a perspective fails to take into account a number of factors. First is the issue of the cultural relativity by which people become immune or insensitive to the violence of their own cultures. No matter what horror was inflicted upon the colonised, it was said - and often believed - to be 'for their own good'.[29]

James Duncan, discussing nineteenth century representations of Africa, comments that it is precisely because such representations 'seem so false, so preposterous so despicable to us today' that they need to be examined.

> Only when we seriously explore those representations which we find self-evidently false can we begin to question the representations which we find self-evidently true. (Duncan, 1993, p.55)

The representations I want to examine here are those which I consider to be the concretisation of the myth identified by Fitzpatrick (1992); that is, the representations of Western law as non-violent, and its "antithesis", the criminal, as black (or non-Western) and violent.[30]

Clearly violence is resorted to in the administration of justice, although this is, particularly in a non-colonised context, often seen as subsidiary or in fact aberrant to the normal course of the legal processes. Such instances of violence, involving the use of extreme physical force by police and prison officers, have been discussed above. Here I am more concerned to examine those processes which are less likely to be perceived in terms of violence: that is, processes which because of their "routine" nature come to be seen as unexceptionable to the coloniser; processes such as imprisonment.

It is of note that both forms of violence - extreme force used by police or prison officers and imprisonment - are used disproportionately against colonised peoples. In order to appreciate the degree of violence inherent to these latter processes for many colonised peoples, however, it is first necessary to remove the veneer of legitimacy from their commission; that is, to attempt to perceive such processes as a colonised person might. If one does not assume that imprisonment is imposed with the best interests of the prisoner in mind, or that such treatment is deserved, the nature of such incarceration and its attendant cruelties alters dramatically.[31]

One aspect of the processes through which this antithesis between violence and imprisonment is constructed is captured by Kerry Carrington's (1991) term, 'normalising racial horror'. To illustrate this process, Carrington cites the death of a young Aboriginal man, Mark Quayle, who was taken by members of his family to a local hospital for treatment. He was hallucinating and suffering from alcohol withdrawal. When he was left unattended by the nursing staff, he wandered away from the hospital. The nurse reported him to the police. Although she later phoned to state that Quayle had returned, the police were already on their way and when they arrived at the hospital they took Quayle to the lock-up. Quayle was not intoxicated, threatening or in any way abusive. He was unlawfully detained in the cell, and left unattended overnight. Some five hours later, Quayle was found dead, hanging in the cell. One of the police officers involved in the incident conducted the police investigation into the death and cleared himself of any responsibility.

Carrington (1991) notes that it is through the sheer historicity of racial divisions and their daily re-enactment that racial 'horror' in Australian communities becomes transformed into the simply routine. In the case of Mark Quayle, imprisonment is so routine a response to Aboriginal people that it occurs almost as a matter of course. The solitary confinement in a police cell of an obviously ill man struck none of those officially responsible for his care as being in any way exceptionable, let alone "horrifying".

The graphic trauma of imprisonment described in Walker's poem, quoted in Chapter 6, provides another dimension to the sort of degradation and hardship that Western communities inflict in the name of "humane" treatment - or rather, as Walker refers to it, in the name of rehabilitation.[32] Other cases, concerning the suicide of Aboriginal prisoners, provide little reason to be assured of the virtuousness of Western ways of dealing with "crime". One Aboriginal man committed suicide after being denied permission to attend his brother's funeral (Aus RCIADIC, 1991a:25.3.13). Quite apart from ordinary feelings for our kin, funeral obligations are extremely important under Aboriginal kinship relations, as evidenced by the beating of the Aboriginal woman referred to above. The lack of basic empathy and cultural sensitivity within imprisonment regimes, however, is just one dimension of the cruelty of the legal system.

A twenty-four-year-old Aboriginal man was found hanging in his cell two weeks after he had been sentenced to six months' imprisonment for destroying a blanket in a police watch-house. He had torn that blanket into strips in an attempt to hang himself (Aus RCIADIC, 1991a:24.5.28). Another young Aboriginal prisoner did not have a shirt button done up on the morning prison "parade". In response to the prison officer's query as to why the button was not done up, the prisoner is alleged to have smiled. For this "offence", he was told that he would have three days "early bed" as a punishment; this meant no television or socialising. The prisoner was escorted back to his cell, and while there had another "confrontation" with a prison officer. The prisoner was advised that he would be charged with using obscene words, and was left alone, locked into his cell. The prisoner was found dead some time later, leaving a note which said, 'This is to say that if I die it is because of the fucked up chief of this place' (Aus RCIADIC, 1991a:25.7.2; 25.7.3).

The propensity of Western cultures to transform the violence inflicted in their own interests into a "civilising mission" adds a further dimension to the mere absence of self-awareness. It is important, however, not to allow scepticism of Western notions of "civilised" behaviour to lead to complete abstentionism in respect to the violence of other peoples. It remains important not to simply dismiss the violence within colonised groups as either "traditional" or necessarily "libratory". What is important is to remain alert to what is being said by people within these groups.[33]

Aboriginal women state that the claim that internal violence and oppression within contemporary Aboriginal communities is acceptable is neither white man's law nor traditional law. Instead they state that it falls within a third category, 'bullshit law'.

> [T]he latter being used to describe a distortion of traditional law used as a justification for rape and assault of women ("it's Aboriginal law you don't interfere"), or for spending all the family income on alcohol and sharing it with his cousins, justifying the action as an expression of cultural identity and fulfilling familial obligations. (Payne, 1990, p.10)

Payne is also critical of studies which portray Aboriginal men as simply 'freedom fighters'. She states that such studies tend to be both andro- and eurocentric. To perceive the internal violence of colonised groups in such terms would indicate a degree of callousness about its victims which is hard to reconcile with any view of colonised peoples other than one which renders them 'anonymous and stereotyped' (Payne, 1990, p.9).

Commentators from within colonised's groups assert that current levels of violence are a distortion of traditional cultural practice. Dodson notes that, although traditional Aboriginal methods of dispute resolution often involved overt physical violence, such violence was highly ritualised. Violence was used according to established patterns regarding the degree of violence, and punishments normally were of a public nature with "on-lookers" playing defined roles.

Dodson notes, however, that many of the traditional mechanisms of control are now unknown, and concludes that the use of physical force in many Aboriginal communities has increased, and has become 'almost uncontrollable and mindlessly violent' (Dodson, 1991, pp.371,762,763). O'Malley (1992) also notes that the retaliatory violence inflicted by Aboriginal people reacting against petrol sniffers is often itself associated with alcohol use: a far from traditional stimulus.

As indicated above, Fanon writes of the first manifestation of the aggressiveness 'which has been deposited in the bones' of the colonised as being against their own people. Such violence is clearly regarded as an accretion or deformation which has evolved out of a history of colonial oppression. If there is consensus amongst many colonised peoples that the degree of violence within their communities is a matter of grave concern, there is also consensus as to its derivation.

In order to comprehend such violence, one need only have an awareness of the extreme conditions under which many poor or working class Aborigines and Trinidadians live (refer Chapters 5 and 6). In 1982, Wilson (1982, p.7), described these conditions as 'violence-provoking', and Atkinson (1990, p.6) has more recently adopted his assessment. Shah, writing of contemporary Trinidad, states,

> Murderers, after all, don't drop from trees. They come out of wombs, from homes, schools.
>
> And having created this uncivilized wasteland, we have reverted to animal instincts, much like the very murders and rapists we seek to condemn and put to death. (Shah, 'Hang 'em All, Russell...', *Sunday Mirror*, November 22, 1992)

In a similar vein, and as cited above, Fanon writes of the 'death reflex' of the colonised to the situation in which they now live as 'a suicidal behaviour'.

Significantly, Fanon goes on to note that it is this same behaviour which comes to justify the coloniser's domination. As some groups within the colonised community come to resemble the violent and ungoverned peoples that they have been made out to be in white colonial myth, they give credibility to the racist stereotypes created for them by their colonisers.

One concrete example of these processes can be seen in the extraordinarily high homicide rates involving Indian women in the indentured labourer communities of Trinidad during the latter part of the nineteenth century. There is no denying the brutality of the killings, a contemporary description of which was the following:

> There is but one serious crime prevalent in the colony, and that is committed by the East Indian who with one sweep of his machete beheads his wife if she proves unfaithful to him. (James H. Starke, *Guidebook and History of Trinidad* (1892), pp.81,82, in Niehoff & Niehoff, 1960, p.101)

Notwithstanding the brutality, there are also significant factors which can contribute to our understanding of how these murders occurred. Principal amongst these were the segregated lifestyle of the labourers, who were expressly confined to the plantations, the extremely harsh conditions of these plantations, and imbalance in the male:female ratio of imported labourers. Added to this were the frequent absences of husbands, in the gaols or hospitals, and the new-found independence of the women, who received their own income under indentured labour contracts. The lack of formal recognition of traditional Indian marriage rites in Trinidad both aggravated the situation by undermining the legitimacy of Indian custom and also led to violent confrontations over inheritances (Brereton, 1979, pp.182,183; Niehoff & Niehoff, 1960, pp.99,100; Samaroo, 1982; Trotman, 1986, pp.169-174).

It was at this time that the Indian indentured labourers of Trinidad acquired a reputation for being violent, untrustworthy and dishonest (Brereton, 1979, pp.186,187). Although discredited as an accurate account (refer Thomas, 1969[1889]), Froude's *The English in the West Indies*, first published in 1888, does provide an indication of the racist attitudes held by colonists in the Caribbean at that time. He wrote, 'Coolies [Indians] do not have a good reputation with police. Negroes quarrel with their tongue but the coolies kill' (quoted in Niehoff & Niehoff, 1960, p.100). It is also of particular note that it was at this time that the indentured labourers were being imprisoned in massive numbers. And although the murder of Indian women gave notoriety to the indentured population, by far the most significant number of criminal prosecutions and imprisonments related to breaches of the Immigration Ordinance regulations which governed the working lives of the indentured labourers (Trotman, 1986).

The "criminal" of this era had strong associations with the "coolie" - the highly derogatory term used in the plantation society for those of Indian descent. And it cannot be denied that there was a worrying degree of internal violence within the indentured community which gave some substance to this association. However, this violence was itself largely the product of the conditions under which the indentured workers were forced to live. The legal powers vested in the plantocracy enabled them to confine workers to male dominated dormitories and to force them to labour in conditions which resulted in great suffering, frequent physical and mental illness, and death.

But much more than this, the legal system itself was also instrumental in the creation of Indian "criminality" in a more direct way. And that was through the criminalisation of the labourers' resistance to colonialist oppression, and in particular, economic exploitation. It is worth noting here that I am not claiming that the notoriety of the internal violence amongst the indentured community was merely a front for the massive criminalisation of the labourers as an aid to their economic exploitation. Rather, it seems to me that internal violence is a very real problem for colonised peoples, but that it is also largely the result of 'violence-provoking' conditions, to adopt Wilson's phrase, which are themselves a necessary consequence of extreme exploitation.

Memmi, who experienced colonialism under the French in Tunisia, wrote,

> It would have been too good if that mythical portrait had remained pure illusion... However, impelled by the same needs which created it, it cannot fail to be expressed in actual conduct, in active and constructive behaviour.
>
> This conduct, which is common to colonizers as a group, thus becomes what can be called a social institution. In other words, it defines and establishes concrete situations which close in on the colonised, weigh on him

> until they bend his conduct and leave their marks on his face... That myth is furthermore supported by a very solid organization; a government and a judicial system fed and renewed by the colonizer's historic, economic and cultural needs. Even if he were insensitive to calumny and scorn, even if he shrugged his shoulders at insults and jostling, how could the colonized escape the low wages, the agony of his culture, the law which rules him from birth until death? (Memmi, 1990[1957], pp.156,157)

Memmi adds a particular dimension to the understanding of how it is that the myth of the colonised comes to acquire substance. He acknowledges that colonial social institutions do create concrete situations which 'bend' the conduct of the colonised and leave their 'marks' on his or her face. As indicated above, an extreme violence can characterise relations between colonised peoples; relations which are constituted both through and beyond the legal system.

But more than this, there is the 'very solid organisation' of a government and judicial system which is shaped by the colonisers' historic, economic and cultural needs, and which gives substance to the myths about the colonised. It is the economic dimension of colonial legal relations that I pursue in the next chapter.

Notes

1. Fanon, *The Wretched of the Earth* (1990[1961], p.40).
2. *Mirror*, March 29, 1993; *Sunday Mirror*, April 5, 1992; *Express*, April 24, 1992; *Express*, June 16, 1992; *Guardian*, August 14, 1992.
3. *Express*, June 16, 1992; *Sunday Mirror*, June 28, 1992. See, too, the report of the killing of Earl "Roxanne" Fortune in 'Forced to eat his penis', *Mirror*, October 23, 1992.
4. *Guardian*, June 7, 1992; *Mirror*, October 9, 1992; *Mirror*, October 16, 1992; *Mirror*, August 14, 1992; *Guardian*, July 19, 1992.
5. *Mirror*, March 6, 1992; *Mirror*, May 8, 1992; *Mirror*, April 10, 1992 ; *Express*, June 16, 1992 ; *Mirror*, June 5, 1992; *Express*, July 3, 1992; *Express*, March 27, 1992; *Express*, June 11, 1992.
6. 'Cover-up Charge in St James Killing', *Express*, August 3, 1992; 'Killed over 50 cents Bottles', *Sunday Mirror*, August 9, 1992.
7. 'Coke Man gives Mom Hell', *Mirror*, June 12, 1994.
8. P. Wilson, *Black Death, White Hands* (1982), in Payne (1990, p.10).
9. This is not the only instance of Aboriginal people adopting oppositional positions to those advocated by civil libertarians and others who believe they have the best interest of Aboriginal people at heart. A number of Aboriginal

people to whom I have spoken have been critical of the granting of "drinking rights" as part of the assimilationist policies of the 1960s and '70s, although to many legal reformers this was a victory of equality over racism. See too Bropho (1980) and Shandley (1988, p.38). Note that prior to "drinking rights" Aboriginal people were frequently imprisoned for alcohol consumption and supply offences; afterwards they were frequently imprisoned for drunkenness (WA Government Statistician, 1953, 1969; Aus RCIADIC, 1990a). With another victory over "racism" and the decriminalisation of drunkenness, Aboriginal imprisonment rates have not declined. Instead Aboriginal people are arrested on other "public order" offences or taken into the "safe custody" - of the lock-ups (Dodson, 1991; AIC, 1993a). In fact, studies have found that Aboriginal imprisonment rates in some areas actually rose after the decriminalisation of drunkenness (Aus RCIADIC, 1991a:21.1.3). There would seem to be good reason for Aboriginal people to be sceptical of our legal reforms.

10. For other studies relating to the internal violence of Aboriginal communities, refer to Wilson (1982) and Bolger (1991).
11. The position of white social researchers who investigate and publicise these issues is even more contentious; refer Bell (1994).
12. The "informal justice" to which I refer should be distinguished from the 'collective justice' of the extra-legal but conscious and cohesive "institutions" such as barrio and trade union courts identified by Cain (1985).
13. See, for example, Bush (1990, pp.6,7) and Niehoff & Niehoff (1960). Note, however, exposure to other and dominant social structures could also erode indigenous mechanisms, as in the *panchayat* and *jajmani* systems brought by the Indian indentured labourers to Trinidad (Haraksingh, 1991).
14. Refer 'Public Cries Stop Arrest of City Vendor' and 'Mob Beats Inspector', *Mirror*, February 14, 1992. A similar sense of autonomous "justice" can be seen in the up-risings of Aboriginal people against official agents of law and order, as when the Roebourne Aboriginal community rioted two days after the killing of John Pat, after an Aboriginal women had been taken into police custody. The police were forced to release their prisoner (Purdy, 1992a).
15. Refer to 'Prowler Beaten to Death', *Express*, July 15, 1992; 'Addict Scalped by Vigilantes', *Mirror*, July 10, 1992; 'Coke Addict, Doused with Acid, Gives Up Drugs... "I feel I'm going mad!"', *Mirror*, June 28, 1992; 'Coke Addict Chopped to Death', *Mirror*, November 27, 1992; 'Malabar Vigilantes Beat Man', *Mirror*, August 7, 1992.
16. Refer 'Penis Paradise Lost: wife Sita Mohammed to answer wounding charge on July 6', *The Bomb*, July 3, 1992.
17. I am not here ignoring that there can be divisions amongst colonised peoples themselves about what is in their own good; rather I am concerned with

commentators who have no direct contact with the people concerned, such as those in Aboriginal communities, making judgments about the worth of projects which are apparently accepted by the groups involved.

18. *Express*, January 17, 1992; *Express*, February 17, 1992; *Express*, January 17, 1992; *Express*, January 10, 1992; *Express*, January 11, 1992; Express, February 22, 1992; *Express*, January 30, 1992; *Express*, March 25, 1992; *Guardian*, April 4, 1992; *Mirror*, April 10, 1992; *Express*, June 26, 1992; *Express*, June 26, 1992; *Mirror*, July 3, 1992; *Mirror*, July 31, 1992; *Mirror*, July 31, 1992; *Mirror*, June 19, 1992; *Mirror*, June 12, 1992; *Express*, August 10, 1992; *Mirror*, August 14, 1992; *Express*, November 6, 1992; *Mirror*, November 6, 1992.
19. Refer *Express*, April 12, 1992; *Mirror*, April 17, 1992. Note that the male judge had singled out rape sentences for comparison with those of England; he did not take issue with sentences for praedial larceny or the myriad other offences for which the "tariff" is significantly higher in Trinidad and Tobago than it is in England.
20. Note that of the more than one hundred men on death row, the decision was made to first execute a man who had raped a four-year-old child to death, another who had kidnapped a two-year-old child and then slit his throat, and another man who had chopped his girlfriend to death. For discussions about the death penalty and the various positions adopted in public debates, refer *Express*, November 10, 1992; *Express*, November 11, 1992; *Mirror*, November 13, 1992; *Express*, November 14, 1992; *Sunday Mirror*, November 15, 1992; *Sunday Mirror*, November 22, 1992.
21. Hunt notes that by treating the capital of the employer and the personal property of others as if they were the same the law asserts and reinforces an ideology in which there is a unity of interest between classes (Hunt, 1993, p.29). This may be true, but it seems to me that empirical research would need to be conducted to ascertain upon whom such an ideology is effective, a point noted later by Hunt himself (1993, p.149). My own impression from working amongst marginalised groups is that many make very clear distinctions between the property of the poor and the property of the rich.
22. The frustration and anger directed against individuals within the community does not necessarily indicate lack of understanding as to the causes of such "crime". As Hunt points out, crimes of the powerful are often diffuse, while working class crime is immediate and inflicted on individuals (Hunt 1993, p.100).
23. Note too that there are other circumstances which dictate the particular brutality of the "peripheral" state: see, for example, Hutchful (1986), discussed further in Chapter 9. Hay (1992) argues that overt violence in the legal system in fact *precedes* more general levels of violence in society. I am not here making any claims in terms of causation; rather I am claiming only that, in Trinidad, the

legal system is overtly violent and there is widespread support for it.

24. Shah, 'Hang 'em All, Russell... but you pull the lever first', *Sunday Mirror*, November 22, 1992. Shah points out in his article that he spent several months in prison, next to the gallows and where the body of the executed would hang for forty-five minutes before being cut down. Shah states he has no problems with individuals, or their families, being allowed to act out retribution; but that the state should not be 'allowed the luxury of revenge'.
25. I am not unaware that similar impulses to punish and seek vengeance motivate particularly right wing law and order campaigns. My point is that these impulses are not the monopoly of the Right. Automatic dismissal of the validity of these claims on the basis that they are based upon ignorance or lack of humanity is a significant failure to engage with the circumstances in which many people live. Particularly in relation to colonised peoples, such interpretations of demands for punishment and retribution feed directly into colonial myths as to the nature of such peoples. This issue is discussed further below.
26. *Express*, July 24, 1992.
27. See, for example, Chanock (1994a); Hoddinott (1985); Fitzpatrick (1980); Scott (1985).
28. Fanon, *The Wretched of the Earth* (1990[1961], p.42).
29. The quote is taken from the title to Haebich's (1992) account of the appalling treatment of Aboriginal peoples in the south-west of Australia during the height of the segregationist era.
30. Any text book used in the teaching of legal doctrine is illustrative of the mythology that Western law is a non-violent process, so too, socio-legal studies such as Burton and Carlen's (1979) which treat law as a discourse. Sarat and Kearns (1991), referred to previously, provide a more overt exposure of the mythology of Western law as non-violent. For references relating to the criminal/violent identities of colonised peoples refer to Dodson (1991, pp.232,242,244,401-408,703-730) (Aboriginal people); Hall et al (1978) and Keith (1993, p.3) (West Indians in Britain); Havemann (1993, pp.18,19) (the Maori); Chambliss and Sbarbaro (1993, pp.10,11) (African Americans); Matthews and Young (1992a, p.5) (black people in Western countries); and generally on the antithesis of Western "civilisation" and non-Western "barbarism", see Said (1993) and Taussig (1993).
31. The analogy would be to kidnappers subjecting their captives to the sorts of treatment described below; the analogy being particularly apt given that imprisonment is frequently on the basis of "captives'" inability to pay the ransom demanded - bail or fines.
32. Because the notoriously violent nature of the prisons of Trinidad is in any event likely to be viewed in terms of a corruption of the Western ideal of the "civilised" treatment of prisoners, I do not refer to them in the following

argument.

33. Of course, normally, there will be a variety of responses from the different members and factions within colonised groups. It is then the researcher's responsibility to determine which, if any, will be listened to. My own position on this issue is discussed at some length in Chapters 2 and 3.

9 Economics

ETHNIC/RACIAL IDENTITY IN AN IMPERIAL CONTEXT

There are a variety of theories which are used to explain the association of criminality with specific ethnic/racial groups, including theories based upon genetic and cultural inferiority or difference. I am not here concerned to directly engage with any of these particular theoretical elaborations, but rather to discount the underlying premise on which many are based; that is, that there is any constant or necessary association between particular ethnic/racial groups and criminality.[1]

This approach is concerned to undermine the stability and power of identities noted in works such as those by Stuart Hall et al (1978), Michael Keith (1993), Paul Havemann (1993), William Chambliss & Edward Sbarbaro (1993) and Michael Taussig (1993), and which are based upon the nexus of criminalisation (alterity) and colonised peoples of colour (refer also to Matthews & Young, 1992a, p.5). Something of the significance and power of contemporary constructions of this identity as the criminal "other" for the Aboriginal people of Western Australia is discussed by Dodson (1991, pp.726-729). Although there has not to my knowledge been any contemporary academic study in the Caribbean which examines the correlation of African descent and/or relative "blackness" with criminality, such an association was one of which people were aware and upon which they sometimes acted.[2]

The examination of historical records of criminalisation in Western Australia and Trinidad indicates that the correlation between criminality and specific ethnic/racial groups is more contingent than current "criminal identities" tend to suggest. The official indices of criminality of the past counter any claims that it is any qualities inherent to either Aboriginal or Afro-Trinidadian peoples which have resulted in their criminalisation. The first example concerns the significant variation in the rates of Aboriginal criminalisation in Western Australia throughout this century. The second concerns the transposition of the "criminal" identity of Afro-Trinidadians and Indo-Trinidadians since last century.

Historical Constructions of Criminality

Criminality and Aboriginal Peoples

During much of the first decade of this century, Aboriginal people in Western Australia constituted between thirty and fifty per cent of the prison population. By the 1930s, however, the average rate of Aboriginal imprisonment over the decade was just six and a half per cent of the prison population. Aboriginal imprisonment rates started to rise again during the late 1950s and, by 1967, Aboriginal people again constituted some thirty per cent of the prison population. The proportion of Aboriginal prisoners has remained consistently high since that time (Aus RCIADIC, 1990a, 1991a; AIC, 1993a; *Annual Statistical Registers*; Bird, 1987; Eggleston, 1976; WA Department of Corrective Services, 1992a).

It is clear that any assumption that official "recognition" of criminality is simply reflective of inherent ethnic or racial characteristics cannot coexist with these dramatically fluctuating imprisonment rates. Account must be taken of broader social factors which have a direct impact upon the relationships between different ethnic/racial groups and their criminalisation according to the institutions of law; factors which have made such criminalisation contingent. In the episode described above, a number of factors were relevant to the changing rates of Aboriginal imprisonment.

The massive rates of Aboriginal criminalisation during the first decade of this century were the result of the continuing dispossession of Aboriginal people, which had two key impetuses during this era. One was the on-going dispossession of Aboriginal people through colonial expansion in the north-west of the state. Aboriginal peoples strongly resisted this expansion and the destruction of their traditional lifestyles and food sources, attacking "settler" livestock both in retaliation and as a source of food (Thomas, 1987; Hawke & Gallagher, 1989).

The other key impetus during this era was the end of the gold rush and the resulting unemployment of miners and prospectors. As whites were given preference in employment and provided with government grants to establish farms, Aboriginal people, particularly those in the south-west, were forced from the lands they had occupied and worked. Many moved to the towns (Haebich, 1992).

Much Aboriginal imprisonment at this time was the result of highly discretionary charges of loitering and cattle killing and, in particular, large numbers of Aboriginal people were being arrested on the latter charge if they were merely in the vicinity of dead or missing cattle. The decrease in Aboriginal imprisonment after its peak of fifty per cent in 1908 was the result of directions to police to reduce the number of arrests on these two charges. The directions were issued expressly because of the high costs associated with the massive incarceration of Aboriginal people which had been the result of these policing practices (Bolton, 1987, p.126; Haebich, 1992, p.11; Thomas, 1987, p.486).

At about this time, a policy of enforced segregation of Aboriginal people on missions, reserves, settlements and stations began to be implemented (Haebich, 1992, pp.30,42,43,71). It was shown during the 1930s that it was significantly cheaper to confine Aboriginal people to reserves than to incarcerate them in prison (Haebich, 1992, p.310). More than this, however, Aboriginal people were in competition with white workers during a time of severe unemployment. The confinement of Aboriginal people to reserves, missions and settlements was not only condoned by many unions, but was a policy for which they had actively agitated (see, for example, Haebich, 1992, pp.42,43).

From the 1920s to the mid-50s, Aboriginal people were in practice generally subjected to a regime of governance distinct from that which ruled others in Western Australia. Specifically they were subject to the Aborigines and Native Administration Acts, in addition to other criminal laws which applied more generally. Despite the proliferation of laws which criminalised the conduct of Aboriginal people, however, rates of criminalisation declined significantly. This was largely due to Aboriginal people being governed by the internal discipline and punishments of the segregated institutions to which they were confined. Within these total institutions, although the jurisdiction of the criminal law remained applicable (contra O'Malley, 1993), it was rarely invoked.

Anna Haebich's (1992) study of the south-west between 1900 and 1940 indicated that Aboriginal people in the settlements were beaten, tortured and confined to solitary confinement by managers and overseers within the regimes established by law, but without the adoption of the usual forms and procedures of law. Comments by Aboriginal drovers and white pastoralists in the north indicate that the pastoralists shared a similar position of domination over their Aboriginal labourers (refer, for example, to the stories of the Fitzroy River drovers documented in *Raparapa* (Marshall, 1988)). One pastoralist complained in 1955 that the appointment of S.G. Middleton as Commissioner of Native Affairs, and the move towards assimilation,

> had taken away from us our means of discipline. Before he took over we could physically chastise any native who was cheeky or lazy, now we can't. (*Annual Report of the Department of Aborigines* 1955, p. 44, in Bolton, 1987, p.127)

The activities of police and courts were of only marginal importance and were used in the relatively rare instances of serious crime, or to control those relatively few Aboriginal people who lived beyond the confines of the reserves, stations, missions and settlements.[3] Another area which remained heavily criminalised for Aboriginal people was the consumption and supply of alcohol. Perhaps the most significant function adopted by the criminal law over this period, however, was its mobilisation to control the movement of Aboriginal people to and from the segregated institutions, forcing such people into these 'concentration camps' (Bropho, 1992), capturing them when they sought to escape and ensuring that they did not breach curfew (WA Government Statistician, 1931, 1942, 1953). Like the Africans during the era of slavery in Trinidad, therefore, Aboriginal people during this period were largely ruled by the internal and non-legal mechanisms of the institutions to which they were confined by law.

Following World War II, however, the economy of Western Australia began to boom, with the wool and wheat industries expanding at rapid rates. In 1948, concessions were offered for the first time to foster the search for oil in Western Australia (Black, 1987c, p.442) and in the same year an (other) investigation into Aboriginal policy was conducted. Bateman's recommendations, implemented in the following year, are described by Dodson as assimilationist in policy and concentrated on the removal of children and their education in missions, where they were to be removed form the influence of 'adult full-bloods, parents and otherwise' (*Annual Report Department of Native Affairs* (1950), in Dodson, 1991, p.31).

In 1951, a policy advocating the assimilation of Aboriginal peoples was officially adopted throughout Australia (Bolton, 1987, p.155). It was at this time that the closure of the government run segregated institutions of Western Australia commenced. By 1967, assimilationist policy had resulted in the dismantling of much of the discriminatory legislation which had controlled Aboriginal peoples; they were to be encouraged - and allowed - to seek to live like anyone else in Australian society. It was also at this time of "equality" and "assimilation" that Aboriginal criminalisation again became a massive phenomenon.

The above outline is just the most basic step in the process through which the nexus between official constructions of criminality and ethnicity/race can be broken. Even those who would assert an inherent Aboriginal criminality are forced to concede that such (assumed) criminality is not *necessarily* reflected in official crime statistics. The point, if a relatively simple one, is also one which needs emphasis in a context in which official constructions of criminality are seen as simply correlative to peoples' inherent moral worth and/or ethnic/racial character.

When writing of mental health, Goffman (1968, pp.124-126) has argued that those who are institutionalised suffer not so much from mental illness as from contingencies. The same, at one level, is true of criminalisation. The history of Aboriginal criminalisation in Western Australia during this century indicates that official constructions of criminality more directly reflect economic conditions, government concerns over imprisonment costs, white unemployment, and policies of segregation and assimilation, than it has any direct reference to Aboriginal peoples' ethnicity or race or, for that matter, conduct.

Trinidadians and Criminality

Historical records indicate that Afro-Trinidadians' ethnicity/race no more predicated their criminalisation than did Aboriginal peoples'. As discussed in Chapter 7, during the latter part of the nineteenth century it was those of Indian descent who were disproportionately imprisoned in Trinidad (T&T Commission of Enquiry [The Abdullah Report], 1982, p.12; Trotman, 1986, p.98). At that time, those of Indian descent acquired reputations for violence, dishonesty and untrustworthiness. At the same time, those of African descent constituted a smaller proportion of the prison population than they did of the total population.

It has also been indicated that the rate of criminalisation of those of Indian descent in Trinidad during the nineteenth century was largely associated with their status as indentured labourers. Thirty per cent of indentured labourers were charged annually with criminal offences relating to their indentureship (Brereton, 1979; Trotman, 1986). With the end of indentureship and the declining significance of the sugar industry, however, the rates of Indo-Trinidadian criminalisation declined (Basdeo, 1982; GB CO [Forster Report], 1938, p.22; Rothenberg & Wishner, 1976; T&T Superintendent Prisons, 1946). Today, Indo-Trinidadians have a relatively low rate of imprisonment, and it is now Afro-Trinidadians who are over-represented in the prisons of Trinidad (refer to Appendix II). It is also Afro-Trinidadians who are now assumed to have a racially or ethnically based propensity to commit crime - or alternatively, to be criminalised.

Once again the historical context creates difficulties for those who would assume that criminality is directly related to ethnicity or race - whether such a connection is seen to reside in the ethnic/racial inferiority of those criminalised or in the racism of the colonial legal system. The transformation of the identity of the "criminal" in this century, from those of Indian descent to those of African descent, is difficult to reconcile with constructions of criminality which are seen as simply correlative to ethnicity/race or racism. Instead, these changes point not only to the political process through which criminality is manufactured but to the specifically economic context of these processes.

The relationship between criminalisation and economic conditions is not simple, and a number of factors may have contributed to the decline of Indian criminalisation. The campaign of the Presbyterian missionaries to establish missions 'for special benefit of the coolies' after 1868 (John Morton, the founder of Presbyterian missions in Trinidad, quoted in Premdas & Sitahal, 1991, p.341), the granting of land to indentured immigrants at the end of their contracts after 1869, and the end of Indian indentured immigration in 1916 would all have contributed to the decline in Indian criminalisation.[4] But it is also true that, while Indo-Trinidadians constituted the majority workforce in the most important industry in Trinidad, they were subjected to pervasive attention from the criminal law. Once that industry declined in significance, the levels of criminalisation of Indo-Trinidadians also declined.

The Timeliness of Crime

As in the episode of Aboriginal criminalisation described above, the history of Indo-Trinidadian criminalisation is illustrative of a relatively simple and obvious point. The rates of criminalisation of specific ethnic/racial groups fluctuate over time. At least historically, criminalisation cannot be seen simply as a function of the ethnic or racial characteristics of the criminalised, or simply of the racism of colonialist institutions. Even the Aboriginal peoples of Western Australia, who have probably been subjected to one of the most sustained campaigns of criminalisation, and currently experience one of the highest, if not the highest rate of imprisonment in the world (Moody, 1993, p.435), do not have a constant association with official indices of criminality.

Robert Hughes' (1988) study of the era of convict transportation to Australia, *The Fatal Shore*, provides a graphic account of the non-transcendent nature of official constructions of crime; not in terms of fluctuating criminalisation rates but instead in relation to the substance of what is criminalised. He situates the promulgation of British laws enacting capital punishments for what 'seemed a limitless variety of human deeds, from infanticide to "impersonating an Egyptian" (posing as a gypsy)', during eighteenth century England, a time of severe social disorder.

Hughes also notes that, between 1660 and 1819, 187 new capital offences became law, more than six times the number enacted over the previous three hundred years. Nearly all were concerned with the protection of property. Forgers were to be hanged, as were those found guilty for 'steal[ing] an heiress'.

Other capital offences included burning a house, poaching a rabbit, cutting down an ornamental shrub, or appearing on the highway with a sooty face. Attempted murder, however, was classed as only a "misdemeanour" until 1803 (Hughes, 1988, p.29). Arthur Koestler's *Reflections on Hanging* (1970)[1956] provides another and more contemporary critique of capital punishment under British common law or, as it was known, the 'Bloody Code'; and Douglas Hay's 'Time, Inequality and Law's Violence' (1992) elaborates upon the relationship between law's violence and changing economic conditions.

Again, it may be an obvious point to assert that official constructions of what is criminal change over time, as does the nature of law enforcement. But such changes also have a more immediate relevance to the criminalisation of colonised peoples. A significant number of offences which constituted Aboriginal people and Indo-Trinidadians as criminal during the periods referred to above would not now be classified as criminal behaviour. For an Aboriginal man or woman, criminal offences included being in the metropolitan area or getting married without permission.[5] For the Indian indentured labourer, criminal offences included leaving the plantation without a pass or having more than one pound of sugar in his or her possession.[6] Such offences clearly situate the formulation of criminal law within a context of contemporary politics, rather than as being denotative of any enduring ethnic or racial characteristics of colonised peoples.

Contemporary Constructions of Criminality

> Since the colonized is a presumed thief, he must in fact be guarded against (being suspect by definition, why should he not be guilty?).
>
> Albert Memmi[7]

Now and Then

The meaning of any past iniquity or exploitation on the part of British or other Western societies in their dealings with other peoples will vary according to the different theoretical frameworks through which the nature of these societies are interpreted. For some, such iniquity or exploitation may indicate something of the inherent character of the processes of colonisation. For others, who hold the firm conviction that these societies are inevitably progressing, such a demonstration may do no more than validate reassuring notions of how far "we" have progressed since earlier and less "civilised" times.

It may be possible to show that in the past the criminal justice system of

British colonies did not always criminalise the same peoples to the same degree, and in fact frequently criminalised peoples for reasons and in ways which would now appear absurd or patently unjust. But this will not necessarily encroach upon the validity of contemporary criminalisation for people convinced by the notion of progress. For such people the 'self-evidently false' criminalisation of the past does not detract from the 'self-evidently true' criminalisation of today (contra Duncan, 1993, p.55). Even if criminalisation of the past was racist and exploitative, this does not indicate that contemporary processes share the same character.

Part of the legitimacy of contemporary criminalisation for non-colonised peoples and others not directly subject to legal interventions, particularly in its more violent manifestations, I think, derives from the matters discussed in Chapter 7. Crucial to any such legitimacy is the distortion of who and why people are criminalised. As indicated, the high profile of criminal cases tried in the upper courts creates images of criminals as convicted murderers, rapists and robbers.

It is true that even the construction of such criminals, both in law and in actuality, raises significant matters relating to class and racial bias in the legal system, its abuses, and broader issues relating to the social conditions of violence, which were discussed above. But even if one makes allowances for all of these matters, such crimes and criminals would seem to fall into a different category to others. The murderers, rapists and robbers are not generally representative of the nature of crime and criminals as they are constituted in and through the criminal justice system of the common law.[8]

Poverty

> According to the length of the purse they give justice. The magistrate only gives justice to the rich; and to the poor man he will say "Go there; to gaol."
>
> Uriah Tubal "Buzz" Butler[9]

In order to recognise the character of the relations between common law systems and colonised peoples, there is a need to disaggregate the minority of offences, with their connotations of physical brutality, threat and degradation, and the majority of acts which are criminalised. Consisting of behaviours such as "offences against good order", the latter are likely to be regarded as far less personally threatening. But not only does such disaggregation fail to take place; common law systems actively manufacture a category under which such a diverse range of behaviours and interactions as rape and swearing are aggregated; and that is the category of "crime".

As Francis Snyder and Douglas Hay have noted, the criminal law delegitimises acts by removing them from their contexts (Snyder & Hay, 1987, p.26). Such decontextualising is not surreptitious, however, but instead comes to be linked to notions which imply that it indeed means equality; that is, that all are entitled to equal treatment under British law.[10] Depending upon who one is, however, there is reason to be sceptical of such equality. To quote the often repeated aphorism by Anatole France,

> the law, in its majestic equality, forbids both the rich as well as the poor to sleep under bridges, to beg in the streets and to steal bread. (Quoted in Eggleston, 1976, p.318)

But more than this, the law, in its majestic equality, also categorises both stealing bread and murder as crimes, and makes both "criminals" liable to imprisonment.

This majestic equality not only has repercussions for how non-criminalised people imagine the "criminal". As the death of Ricci Vincenti illustrates, it also has very concrete results. The fact that Vincenti had stolen food because he was hungry was not at all relevant to the legitimacy of his being shot to death while attempting to escape custody. Indeed nor was it relevant that, at the time he was killed, he was only being held on remand. Because Vincenti was a "criminal", the guard who shot him in the head was only "doing his job" in "protecting society"; the actual specificities of Vincenti's "crime" and imprisonment were irrelevant. In the eyes of the law, Ricci may as well have been a murderer as a hungry nineteen-year-old who had taken some food (Aus RCIADIC, 1991e).[11]

A point returned to repeatedly throughout the preceding chapters is the nature of the majority of contemporary imprisonments in both Trinidad and Western Australia. It needs to be emphasised that the bulk of the criminalisation of colonised peoples (and others) is *not* on the basis of the commission of violent offences. Even those (few) who are imprisoned on the basis of express judicial sentence have most often been found guilty of minor public order, embezzlement or fraud charges (refer Chapter 7, note 5). But in any event, the majority of imprisonments in both Trinidad and Western Australia, relating to default of fine and remands, in fact have a clear association with poverty.

As was discussed in Chapter 8, it is also true that violence within colonised communities is an undoubted reality. It is in this context that - at least some of - the interventions of the legal system become, if not legitimate, at least imperative for individuals amongst colonised populations (e.g. Bolger, 1991, p.99). It is not always the case that demands for such intervention and punitive punishments are the result of ignorance as to the social causes of crime. Rather it is because explanations of the causes of such crime will be of only limited significance to those people, usually people of colour, the poor, women and the marginalised, who often bear its consequences. And while there is good reason to be cautious of the demands for harsh responses to crime, it is important not to dismiss automatically its proponents as either ignorant or savage.

But although the explanations of violent crime may not be of much consolation to its victims, such explanations remain important for others who are part of the genesis of this violence. It is important for Western peoples to be aware of who it is who benefits from the violence inflicted both through and beyond the retained colonial legal systems. It is important for Western peoples not to construe the continuing oppression and exploitation of colonised peoples as self-imposed; to construe the contemporary world as if it were a "post-colonial" one.

Fanon (1990[1961], p.31), wrote, 'In the colonies the economic substructure is also a superstructure. The cause is the consequence; you are rich because you are white, you are white because you are rich'. Colonisation, as a violent process in which racism justifies economic exploitation, and economic exploitation justifies racism, cannot now be relegated to the past and to the Third World.[12] As is indicated below, the same dynamic remains conspicuous in the contemporary impoverishment and criminalisation of Afro-Trinidadian and Aboriginal peoples. Even though today many Afro-Trinidadian and Aboriginal peoples constitute the poorest factions in their societies,[13] the specific ethnic/racial dimension to their contemporary impoverishment and criminalisation cannot now be dismissed.

CONTEMPORARY COLONISATION

> The race question is subsidiary to the class question in politics, and to think of imperialism in terms of race is disastrous. But to neglect the racial factor as merely incidental is an error only less grave than to make it fundamental.
>
> C.L.R. James[14]

As indicated in Chapters 5 and 6, the economic exploitation and marginalisation of colonised groups continues to be fundamental to much of their criminalisation. It is of note, however, that the ethnic and racial identities of such groups have not been merely incidental to these processes. Although there is a fluidity between criminalisation and ethnic/racial categories, as indicated above, the ethnicity/race of Afro-Trinidadians and Aboriginal peoples has come to be integral to "criminality" as it is currently constituted. That is, there is a degree to which the contemporary criminalisation of Afro-Trinidadian and Aboriginal peoples occurs because of who they are, and not just because of their poverty.

Pierre Bourdieu and Jean-Claude Passeron note,

> physical repression ... can continue to have an effect once it has ceased to be applied only in as much as it always tends to exert an additional symbolic effect (the emperor is never naked). (Bourdieu & Passeron, 1977, p.36)

Today, in the prisons of Trinidad and Western Australia there is a preponderance of those who are not only poor, but who are also "black" according to the local meaning of that term. Because imprisonment implies dangerousness, the ethnic/racial identity of criminalised populations itself becomes infused with the same elements apparent in colonial mythology. Notions of the savagery, lawlessness and barbarity of colonised peoples acquire substance. At the same time, the economic, and other, exploitations of the colonised are obscured.

Imprisonment, therefore, not only involves the application of physical repression to those who are exploited, it also serves a symbolic purpose through the manufacture of an identity as the criminal "other" for those who are repressed. Indeed, the emperor is never naked - at least for the colonisers, who as Jean-Paul Sartre (1990[1961], p.7) notes, prefer the truth 'with clothes on: the native had to love them, something in the way mothers are loved'.

Trinidad and the I.M.F.

> Then he opened the pages of the IMF Doomsday Book putting the entire country into social, political, economic and moral reverse gear.
>
> Twenty-eight years of national independence was swept aside as the cast-off garment of colonialism was rebuttoned tightly around us.
>
> Abdullah Omowale[15]

Rates of Afro-Trinidadian imprisonment would seem to have been high relative to those of the Indo-Trinidadian population throughout much of this century (T&T Superintendent of Prisons, 1946, 1957; T&T Commission of Enquiry [The Abdullah Report], 1982, pp.19,22). However, as discussed in Chapter 5, there are indications that the current level of Afro-Trinidadian over-representation in the prisons of Trinidad is of relatively recent origin. Moreover, total imprisonment rates have also escalated dramatically since 1985 (Diagrams 1 & 2). These increases do not correspond to any equally dramatic increase in the reporting of offences to police. In fact over the relevant period, reports of serious offences declined (T&T CSO, 1993a, pp.48,53).

Nor does the rapid increase in imprisonment rates in Trinidad and Tobago coincide with specific legislative changes, as in the instance of the effects of Jamaica's firearm legislation (Calathes, 1990, pp.270,271). It is also clear that imprisonment rates were not initially associated with massed public protest, as in the 1970 Black Power uprising in Trinidad (Mahabir, 1980), although looting associated with the coup attempt no doubt contributed to the statistics for 1990. Finally, the escalation of imprisonment rates did not directly coincide with any particular decline in the economy (Cain & Birju, 1992).[16]

It is unclear whether the dramatic changes in imprisonment trends in Trinidad are attributable to express judicial and police policies to increase arrests, sentencing severity and remands to custody. The escalation of imprisonment rates is, however, associated with the implementation of "structural adjustment" and the "conditionalities" of the International Monetary Fund and other multilateral lending agencies in Trinidad and Tobago, and which adjustment included express economic policies.[17]

In a country with an official rate of about twenty per cent unemployment and no unemployment benefit, these policies included reductions to the government labour programmes which had provided at least occasional income to as many as one-third of the work force (Singh, 1989, p.26). As indicated previously, other policies were aimed at public servants (reducing salaries and abolishing cost of living allowances), reduced subsidies on essential commodities and services, imposed flat taxes and devalued the local currency (Chapter 5).

Omowale points to the historical access of Indo-Trinidadians to land as being significant during such times of severe financial constraint, when land at least enables subsistence. Afro-Trinidadians, unlike those of Indian descent, were never granted land (or anything else) in return for their enforced labour on the plantations, and the majority continue to live in urban ghettos. Omowale states that, given the persisting racial occupational segregation of the Trinidadian working (and unemployed) class, the policies of "structural adjustment" have had unequal impact on the two major ethnic/racial groups of Trinidad. The differential impact of the policies of structural adjustment have in turn aggravated the racial imbalance between prisoners since 1987 (Omowale, 1992a). John Gaffer LaGuerre (1988) supports Omowale's contention as to the segregated workforce of Trinidad, and in particular notes the traditional domination of the public sector by Afro-Trinidadians. As indicated, this sector was the specific target of stringent measures as part of "structural adjustment".

Bilal Abdullah, another of the Muslimeen, indicates that, moreover, access to land had enabled those of Indian descent to retain a greater degree of autonomy and traditional culture, but also had meant they were positioned to capitalise more easily on the oil boom, through the mortgaging of property and establishment of businesses. Abdullah cites the destruction of the African family as another significant factor in denying those of African descent access to the economic resources available through the kinship networks which were available to those of Indian descent (Bilal Abdullah, interview with the author, November 17, 1992).

Although there is therefore an economic context which is directly relevant to the specific criminalisation of those of African descent in Trinidad, it is clear that issues of ethnicity/culture have also been significant. The cultural practices of those of Indian descent in Trinidad were never subjected to the sustained campaign of criminalisation which was used to undermine African culture and particularly the traditional role of African men (Cain, 1994; Herskovits & Herskovits, 1964[1947]; Reddock & McCree, 1992). This is likely not to have been due to any particular liking for Indian culture, as can be seen in the dominant attitudes towards Indian people during the latter half of the nineteenth century, discussed above. Instead, it is likely to have been associated with the attitude held for many years in Trinidad that those of Indian descent were merely a transitory labour force (Brereton, 1979).

Nonetheless, the relevance of ethnicity/race to contemporary criminalisation in Trinidad should not be confined solely to how these feature in the constitution of poverty. For there is reason to be cautious in attributing criminality directly to poverty. It is not denied that poverty may well cause people to commit the sorts of crimes which criminal justice systems actually criminalise, offences such as unauthorised vending, praedial larceny and unlawful possession - as opposed to child sexual abuse or white collar crime, for example. But Maureen Cain and Anand Birju point to the relatively low rates of imprisonment of women in Trinidad and Tobago as indicative that there is no direct link between criminality and poverty. Although women were more likely to be unemployed than men, they constituted only a fraction of the prison population. Cain and Birju postulate that, with the rich becoming richer and the poor becoming poorer in Trinidad and Tobago, criminality was instead associated with relative deprivation, a deprivation felt most keenly by young men (Cain & Birju, 1992, pp.144,145).

Certainly the dramatic decline since 1982 from being a country with one of the highest per capita incomes in the world (*Sunday Mirror*, March 22, 1994), the continuing prosperity of the local elite and the direct telecast into people's homes of the U.S. C.N.N. (Cable News Network) - complete with U.S. advertisements - are all likely to foster a keen sense of relative deprivation. It is of note, too, that during the looting which occurred during the Muslimeen coup attempt, it was the expensive, imported sports shoes, the Reeboks and Nikes, and brand name jeans which were a prime target of the young men engaged in the "rioting".[18]

Commentary in local newspapers concerning the attitudes of the unemployed and ghetto dwelling young men canvass something of the complex factors which have contributed to the growing criminality in Trinidad - the drug culture, racism, poverty, unemployment and alienation. One article dates "the vibe" as being 'first frighteningly apparent' in 1988, continuing to build through the curfew parties (which many Trinidadians used to while away the hours of curfew imposed during the State of Emergency after the coup attempt) and into the present. Citing the attractions of 'a meal, a gun, a pair of swanky sneakers, rock, cocaine or maybe just rank', and unlawfulness 'just for the heck of it', the commentator writes,

> But I daresay we have reached the point of no return with these youths. For all of the 1992 Carnival season, they milled around ... moving restlessly in numbers, showing they have outgrown our politicians, institutions and most of the fundamental, moral values. ...In fact, the lawlessness shown by youths on Carnival Sunday night is more frightening, taken in the context of who have been perpetrating most of the crimes in recent times. ('Do You Know Where Your Children Are?', *Mirror*, March 20, 1992)

Another commentary on Port of Spain, two days after the Los Angeles riots, states,

> Thousands of youths who think nothing (and have no choice in some instances) about committing crimes need no motivation. It may take next to nothing to spark the flame, especially since the problem of unemployment remains unsolved, and has, in fact, exacerbated. ...Our urban youth are in tune with the radical rap music, have identified with Malcolm X's rationalisation, "By any means necessary", and have experienced days of lawlessness during the July '90 insurrection. Our leaders, on the other hand, have shown no foresight in dealing with the youth. Instead, men who once walked amongst the crowds and showed passion in their desire for change, are now clogging the corridors of power. Surely, American leaders felt they could have stifled the cry for justice in their own yard, by focusing on, and interfering in other people's lives. But it is all an indication of the level of arrogance and how sure is the disgrace of the mighty. ..."Everywhere, there will be war", Haile Selassie told the League of Nations more than 30 years ago. Obviously nothing has changed... no one has progressed. ('Port of Spain on the Boil', *Mirror*, May 9, 1992)

Rather than simply attributing criminality to poverty, it is the processes of pauperisation, material and social, which seem relevant to contemporary

Trinidad. But if there is reason to be cautious about simply attributing crime to poverty, there is also reason to be cautious about attributing the increase in criminalisation to increased criminality. To do so is to take the mythological view of law as purely reflexive, and as not actively constitutive of social relations. And it is particularly in this aspect of law that the ethnic/racial identity of black Afro- and Indo-Trinidadians would seem to feature.

The processes resulting in the active manufacture of criminality *through law* may be understood as being the result of either deliberate or structural causes. The first, which often tends to be dismissed as simplistic, would postulate that legal officials, for example, receive specific directions to deliberately criminalise different classes or groups of people. It is of note, however, that such a view is not so readily dismissed in Trinidad.

For example, Omowale states that police in Trinidad are from the working class and expressly trained to exercise their "discretion" in ways which police only the working class. He cites the example of when he trained as a police officer during the early 1960s, and he and the other trainees were instructed to now exercise care when approaching Indo-Trinidadians in Indian clothing, as it could no longer be assumed that they were 'just cane-cutters' (Omowale, interview with the author, November 16, 1992). Another example of this reasoning concerns the Chief Magistrate's reaction when I raised the issue of race in the courts of Trinidad. As indicated in Chapter 1, he advised me that there was no 'policy of racism' in his courts as there was in Australia. The implication was that racism existed only as a deliberately formulated policy (Baird, interview with the author, January 29, 1992).

The attitude towards the construction of social relations of class and race through law, evident in the comments of both Omowale and the Chief Magistrate, indicate that such relations are more overt and deliberate in their construction than is often accepted elsewhere. A similar attitude is implicit to Lystra Hagley's analysis of the recent dramatic increase in the number of remand prisoners, which she relates to 'the exercise of judicial discretion' (Hagley, 1993). Again, it would be quite wrong and typically arrogant for non-colonised peoples to dismiss these attitudes as lacking in subtlety and substance. If it is true, as Sarat and Kearns (1991, p.212) note, that the law in Western societies 'alternately [operates] through disembodied choices, the manipulation of texts, and mere mindless, mechanical motions: the full-fledged, pain-imposing, responsible agent eludes our grasp', this should not automatically be thought to apply elsewhere.[19] Instead, the attitudes expressed by Omowale, the Chief Magistrate and Hagley would seem to me to be consistent with the nature of colonised societies in which imposed social relations do not come into existence as a "matter of course" but, as has been discussed previously, are deliberately manufactured.

It remains unclear, however, whether express policies relating to judicial practice were issued in conjunction with the implementation of the economic policies of structural adjustment. It is of interest to note that one source informed me that the increase in prison numbers over recent years was in fact the direct result of instructions which had been issued by a senior judicial officer to increase the number of people imprisoned and remanded to custody. Such a possibility should not be dismissed out of hand. For while it is the case that the machinations of the judiciary remain largely hidden from public scrutiny, in the area of policing it is clear that in Trinidad, as elsewhere, deliberate policies are implemented which require police to concentrate on particular crimes and areas (see, for example, Hall et al, 1978; Cunneen, 1990; Keith, 1993).

For example, just prior to the looting associated with the coup attempt in 1990, there had been a sustained campaign against street vending (Trinidad Express Newspaper, 1990, p.45). In Trinidad, making street vendors the targets of police surveillance will not only have predictable results in terms of the class of those scrutinised, but will also be of particular significance in criminalising alternative economies during a time of I.M.F. fostered "structural adjustment". Trotman (1986) has examined how the criminalisation of social economy "offences" has been used traditionally in Trinidad to marginalise the alternative economies of subordinate ethnic groups and to force them into compliance with the dominant wage-labour economy.

But more than this, in a society which tends to be racially segregated in terms not only of occupation, but also of residence, decisions as to where to locate police will be relevant. In Trinidad, those of African descent tend to be concentrated in areas along the northern corridor and it is the same area in which the highest concentration of police is located. Directions to police to concentrate on specific offences and areas, such as street vending and the northern corridor, will therefore tend to have a specific and predictable impact not only in terms of class but also on the ethnic and racial composition of those being processed through the legal system (Omowale, 1992a).

The second manner in which law can be actively constitutive in the criminalisation of different peoples relates to the embedding of racist and other stereotypes into "popular" consciousness or, more particularly, the consciousness of legal officials. Overlaying the economic stratification in Trinidad is a social stratification based upon colour. As legal officials, knowingly or unknowingly, act upon representations of black people as poor, inferior and powerless, they directly manufacture the criminality of such peoples.

One example of this can be seen in offences such as unlawful possession. These offences turn crucially on whether the alleged perpetrator appears to be suspicious; a matter which is "coloured" by notions of who is likely to be criminal, by who is likely to have lawfully acquired the items in their possession. Once charged with such an offence, the onus of proof is on the defendant to convince the magistrate that he or she lawfully came into possession of the property in his or her custody when arrested. A person's ability to convince the court of the lawfulness of possession will be influenced by highly discretionary notions of credibility, which once again will be coloured by notions of who is likely to be criminal.

Although connected to economic conditions and relations, criminalisation is therefore not merely *reflective* of pauperisation and marginalisation, but is also actively *constitutive* of them. Such processes mean that in addition to any actual crimes they may commit, particular ethnic/racial groups can also be targeted for, or the targets of, "criminalisation". And yet, as the fluctuating rates of official crime indices attest, it remains inadequate to explain such phenomena solely in terms of the ethnic/racial characteristics of the criminalised - or, for that matter, the racism of the "criminalisers". And so I return to James's fundamental 'class question'. It is in this context that an awareness of the contemporary economic relations between Trinidad and the United States becomes crucial.

The gradual lessening of British presence and influence in Trinidad consequent upon World War II was matched by the growing influence and presence of the United States, particularly in its association with the oil industry. The exploitative nature of that relationship, in terms of the oil industry and more recent efforts to industrialise, are documented by Trevor Farrell (1983), Graham Holton (1994), Jane Rothenberg and Amy Wishner (1976) and others.[20]

Between 1976 and 1981, transnational corporations in a number of Caribbean nations, including Trinidad, withdrew four times more as profits than they invested (Barry, Wood & Preusch, 1984, p.23).[21] Despite the massive profits which were made by the multinationals in Trinidad during the oil boom years, however, it is also true that government revenue increased by more than fourteen times over the same period. And although much of this money was invested in what Tom Barry, Beth Wood and Deb Preusch (1984, p.115) describe as 'capital-intensive industries that provide neither a large number of jobs nor essential products', in comparison to many other nations in the region, Trinidad and Tobago was able to maintain a relatively affluent level of existence for many of its people.

Significantly, however, much of the social amelioration was effected through government subsidies and allowances. Distribution of income in Trinidad remained unaltered, with ten per cent of households receiving one-third of total income while the bottom forty per cent of households earned only ten per cent of the total (Barry, Wood & Preusch, 1984, p.364). As noted by Oliver Mendelsohn and Marika Vicziany (1994, pp.100-101), the treatment of social inequality as a "welfare problem" results in benefits which are 'at once monumental in terms of the human number affected and utterly benign towards the holders of power and privilege'.

With the end of the influx of oil money, the I.M.F. and other multilateral lending agencies intervened in Trinidad and Tobago. Subsidies on food, fuel, electricity, education, allowances for cost of living and public works funding were reduced or discontinued. In the five years between 1983 and 1988, per capita income declined by fifty per cent and unemployment doubled. By 1988, the Republic's external debt totalled US$2.4 billion, equivalent to fifty-seven per cent of the nation's gross domestic product. Annual repayments on debt reached one-quarter of export earnings (McAfee, 1991, p.17).

Although institutions such as the International Monetary Fund and the Inter-American Development Bank had intervened in Trinidad at a much later date than in other Caribbean nations, Trinidad, despite its oil and gas resources, is now in a position of severe economic dependency. Both of the institutions referred to above subject recipient countries to economic interventions in the form of "conditionalities" which receiver governments are obliged to implement as a condition of these institutions' beneficence. Studies such as Kathy McAfee's (1991), Barry, Wood and Preusch's (1984) and others indicate how current relations between these institutions and the Caribbean are used by nations such as the U.S. to control and drain resource development in the so-called "developing nations". The parallels with earlier, formally "colonial" economic policies, as described in A.G. Russell's *Colour, Race and Empire* (1944), are striking.

In 1987, for example, US$207 million more flowed from the Caribbean to foreign governments, banks and multilateral lending agencies, than was received as "aid". Jamaica, the Dominican Republic and Trinidad and Tobago alone paid US$1.3 billion more as debts and interest payments between 1986 to 1988, than these countries received as loans and grants (McAfee, 1991, p.13). This money is being redirected from the programmes and services which governments, such as that of Trinidad and Tobago, had previously maintained (see, too, Hutchful, 1986).

In return, Caribbean nations have become targets for international money laundering and tax avoidance schemes, environmental damage and depletion, debased currencies, devalued commodities, and export oriented production. Caribbean people face under- and unemployment, emigration, or labour in Free Trade Zones where normal union, health and welfare, and any other government regulations do not apply. Moreover, there is keen competition between Caribbean governments to provide government built facilities as well as the most "attractive", and therefore unregulated and untaxed, locations for such foreign "investments" (Barry, Wood & Preusch, 1984; McAfee, 1991).

Eboe Hutchful states that,

> The adoption of "adjustment" programmes directed from the outside by more and more underdeveloped countries as a condition of their "recovery" from the present crisis in capitalism has been a crucial factor in the generalisation of the brutal forms of internal repression as well as popular violence throughout these countries. (Hutchful, 1986, p.171)

The problems of Trinidad, and other so-called "peripheral states", are constructed in terms of "adjustment", as if a purely internal solution can be found to current crisis conditions. Hutchful notes,

> To the extent that the real objective in this "solution" is to mobilise within these formations counterbalancing effects to the falling rate of profits in the advanced capitalist economies... it can only aggravate the crisis. (Hutchful, 1986, pp.173,174)

Economic policies now in place in the Caribbean mean that industries and governments which pander to foreign markets receive preferential treatment. The policies encouraged through foreign agencies have resulted in the pauperisation of substantial elements of local populations, massive emigration, escalating violence and drug abuse, and environmental degradation.[22] Moreover, the direct dominance of the economy of Trinidad by the U.S. ensures its continuing influence[23] - quite apart from the frequent U.S. military and other interventions into the Caribbean and Latin American region. (Between 1895 and 1965, the U.S. military intervened in the Caribbean region alone fifteen times; between 1979 and 1983, the U.S. conducted nine "mock invasions", war games and exercises in that region in addition to the real invasion of Grenada in 1983 (Barry, Wood & Preusch, 1984, pp.196,197); most recent was its (re-) intervention in Haiti. See also William Calathes (1990) and Ernest Harsch (1981) on Jamaica; Jean Casimir (1982) on Haiti; Jose Moreno (1982) on the Dominican Republic; Kathy McAfee (1991) on the Caribbean; and Noam Chomsky (1987) on the Latin American region.)

It is my contention that it is the criminal justice system which is used to ensure internal compliance with these conditions. The recent rapid escalation of imprisonment rates in Trinidad and the amplification of racial imbalance in the prison population has been associated with the implementation of "Western" economic theory and the direct intervention of "Western" international economic organisations into the Trinidadian economy. It has also coincided with the consolidation of highly exploitative economic relations with Western nations, particularly the U.S.[24]

In practice, the legal system in Trinidad has served to manufacture and perpetuate a stratification system that privileges not only according to wealth but, as has been indicated previously, also according to approximation to "whiteness" - both somatically and culturally. It is the coincidence of criminality, pauperisation and ethnicity/race which is crucial to these processes, just as it has been in the oppression and exploitation of colonised peoples in the past.

These processes have a number of different repercussions. One is the continuing degradation and oppression of peoples who come to be confined in circumstances which may be regarded as violence-provoking (refer Chapter 8). The construction of criminalised racial identities which characterise specific ethnic/racial groups in terms of inferiority and savagery also involves the forced submission of those criminalised to their own pauperisation and marginalisation. Such an identity as "criminal" in turn legitimises their impoverishment and coercion in others' eyes. For the "coloured" elite, constructions of racialised and criminalised identities lead to self-doubt and submissiveness to what are perceived to be "white" and "civilised" mores. Finally, in terms of Afro/Indo Trinidadian racialism, these constructions contribute to the continued division of particularly the poorest sectors of these groups, and perpetuates the agenda so clearly manifest in earlier colonial and "post-colonial" interventions - to divide and rule.[25]

Western Australia and the Mining Companies

> The settler and the native are old acquaintances. In fact, the settler is right when he speaks of knowing "them" well. For it is the settler who has brought the native into existence and who perpetuates his existence. The settler owes the fact of his very existence, that is to say his property, to the colonial system.
>
> Frantz Fanon[26]

There were a number of major shifts in the Australian economy following World War II. One was the movement out of recession and into boom conditions, which resulted in a growing demand for labour. A number of new technologies had also resulted from military/industrial developments associated with World War II which meant new markets and extraction processes for minerals found in Australia. The graph of the value of Australian mineral production between 1860 and 1953 (Diagram 3 below) indicates an exponential increase in the value of mineral production from approximately 1947. It also sets the context for the changing attitudes in Australia towards land which was previously regarded as being of little value. It was at this time that policies of assimilation began to gain acceptance in Australia.

Diagram 3 Australia
Recorded value Australian mineral production 1860 - 1953

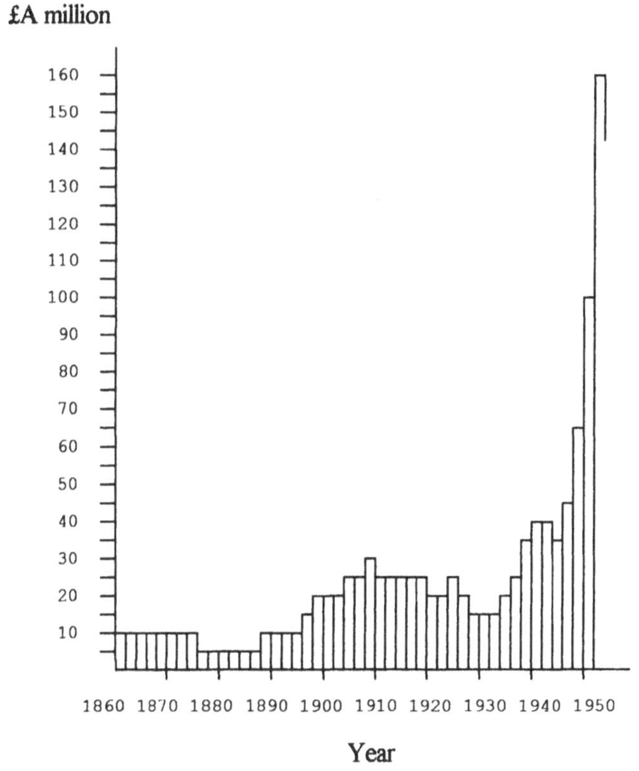

Source: Adapted from 'Australian Mineral Quarterly Review', Aug. 1954, Vol.7, #1, p.2[27]

The current phase of mineral development in Western Australia appears to have occurred somewhat later than in the rest of Australia and, in the immediate post-war years, it was the wool and wheat industries which expanded rapidly (Ghosh, 1987, pp.271,273). This meant however, that there was also an increasing demand for labour in that state as there was throughout Australia at this time. Moreover there was a growing demand for land and, while there were only 1.8 million acres under wheat in 1945/6, this had increased to 3.2 million acres by 1950/1 (Ghosh, 1987, p.273). Aboriginal people continued to work the pastoral stations of the north, and rural expansion provided job opportunities for Aboriginal people in the south-west, although they found it harder than others to obtain secure and well-paid employment (Bolton, 1987, p.160).

From 1948, the state government also encouraged mineral exploration, in addition to other appropriations of land which Aboriginal peoples had previously occupied.[28] And although mineral exploitation occurred somewhat later in Western Australia than is indicated by Diagram 3, in the twelve years from 1955/6 to 1968/9 the value of mineral production in the state increased by a factor of more than seven (Ghosh, 1987, p.282; and see Diagram 4).

Diagram 4 Western Australia
Net value mineral production in Western Australia, selected years 1938/9 - 1974/5

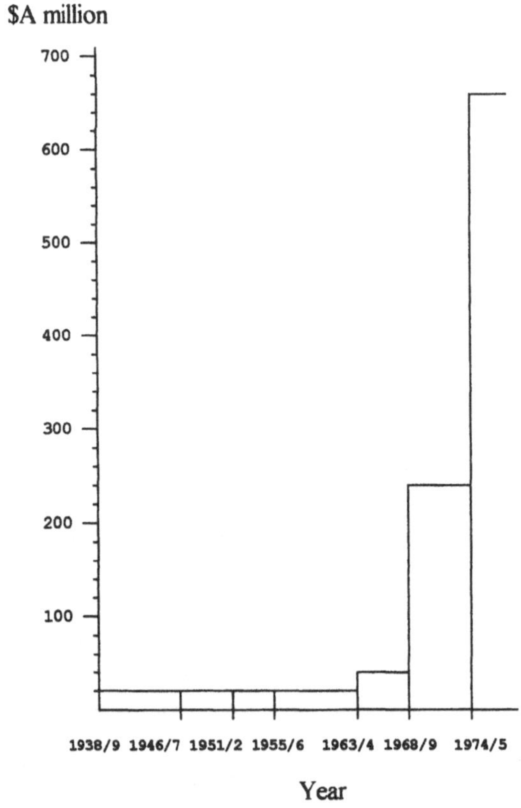

Source: Adapted from Ghosh, 1987, p.282

These economic developments in the rural and mining industries in Western Australia coincided with the gradual removal of the legal restrictions on the Aboriginal peoples of the state, and the adoption of assimilationist policies. Settlements and reserves were closed and Aboriginal people moved or were moved off the pastoral stations (Dodson, 1991; Haebich, 1992; Hawke & Gallagher, 1989; Marshall, 1988; and see Wilson, 1982 with reference to Queensland; Yunupingu, 1987 re the Northern Territory; and Brock, 1992 re South Australia). At the same time, the proportion of Aboriginal people in Western Australian prisons began to rise (refer Table 2).

Part of the assimilationist policy included the extension of the Pastoral Award to Aboriginal workers in 1968. This was a radically different position to that which had been adopted by the Court of Conciliation and Arbitration in 1924, when Award wages were calculated on the basis that two Aborigines counted as one white person; and in 1944, when the Court stated that it would be 'inadvisable and even cruel' to pay Aboriginal people the same wages as received by 'civilised "whites"' (quoted in Dodson, 1991, p.89). In 1968, the Court ruled that Aboriginal pastoral workers were entitled at law to the same pay as whites.

For many Aboriginal people of the north, this time was one of a new wave of dispossession as they were forced from land and lifestyles which had retained a traditional orientation (Marshall, 1988).[29] Although this dispossession is often associated with the implementation of the Pastoral Award and pastoralists' inability to pay (e.g. Green, 1987, p.109), Steve Hawke indicates that some managers reduced the effect of the award by invoking 'the slow workers provision' (Hawke & Gallagher, 1989, p.73). Mary Edmunds also points out that wages paid prior to the award were often almost equivalent, and that in any event most of the money was spent in the station stores. She states that it was the downturn in the pastoral industry which was more relevant to the second wave of Aboriginal dispossession (Edmunds, 1989, pp.26,27; see too Ghosh, 1987, p.273). Fitzroy River drovers, however, indicate that they received no wages until the implementation of the Award, and are quite specific in relating their dispossession to that Award (e.g. Eric Lawford (Yiji), 1988, pp.24,25). It is therefore likely that the Award had a different impact in the Kimberley as opposed to the Pilbara, where Edmunds conducted her research, and where, she indicates, conditions may have been generally better for Aboriginal workers.

In any event, it is of note that it was the pastoral regions of the Kimberley and the Pilbara which were the site of much of the mineral exploration and exploitation associated with the state's "mineral boom". Edmunds (1989, p.7) comments that it was the lifting of the embargo on the export of iron ore in 1960 which signalled the end of pastoral dominance in the north Western Australia. Since that time, iron ore has been of particular significance to Western Australian mineral production. Currently it accounts for twenty-four per cent of the state's $A12 billion annual mineral production.

Western Australia also currently produces more gold than does the rest of Australia combined. The magnitude of gold production is itself of note, and state production in 1990 was three times the amount produced at the peak of the gold rush around the turn of last century. Alumina production is another important mineral industry in the Western Australian economy. Production on a significant scale commenced only from 1964, and throughout the thirty years since then, Western Australia has almost consistently produced more than the rest of Australia combined. The production of petroleum in Western Australia only commenced after 1967, but it now accounts for twenty-one per cent of the value of the state's mineral production. While only something of the order of three per cent of the value of total mineral production was paid to the state government as royalties and lease payments, this nonetheless constituted the second highest source of revenue to government (WA Department of Minerals and Energy, 1993).

Accounts of the dispossession of Aboriginal peoples in the north of the state as a result of this phase of mineral exploitation can be found in Edmunds' *They Get Heaps* (1989), and Hawke and Gallagher's *Nookanbah* (1989). The dispossession of Aboriginal groups in the Kimberley as a result of the Pastoral Award is described in the *Raparapa* collection of drovers' stories (Marshall, 1988). In the south of the state, Aboriginal people were also moved out of the reserves and settlements, often into existence on the fringes of the towns, and seasonal and low-paid work, as part of the processes of "assimilation". It was at this same time that Aboriginal imprisonments increased at a rate which almost mirrors that of the exponential increase in the value of mineral exports from Western Australia. (See Diagram 5.)

Robert Bropho (1980, p.153), states,

> The white man came. He did not conquer. He invaded. He broke all the ten commandments in the Bible. He stole, he committed adultery, he killed, he raped and he plundered. He destroyed Aboriginal people. He used him up. And he made him what he is today, a fringedweller on the fringes of town. He's turned him into a dole bludger by kicking him off stations and shutting down reserves. He's forcing him to be something that he doesn't want to be. He's trying to brainwash him with white ideas. The only thing he hasn't done yet and that is to get a can of white paint and paint him white.

The assimilationist ideology not only justified the about-turn on the policy of segregation of Aboriginal people, but legitimised their removal from the tracts of land to which they had previously been confined and, initially at least, made them available as labour for low status positions. More recently, with another down-turn in the economy, Aboriginal employment has once again declined (refer Chapter 6). Official unemployment rates indicate that some forty per cent of Aboriginal people are currently unemployed (ABS, 1989, p.xii). As also indicated, many Aboriginal people remain dependent upon Social Security payments, and are subject to a form of colonialism which is in part effected through welfare dependency.[30]

Diagram 5 Western Australia
Aboriginal imprisonment rates as a proportion of total imprisonments 1931 - 1967

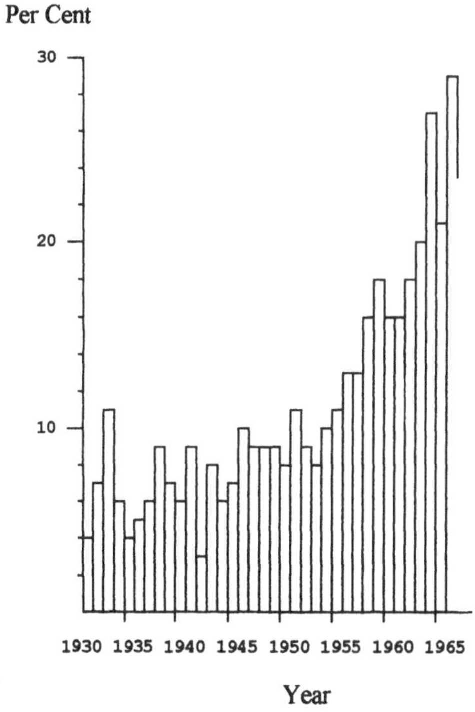

Sources: Statistical Registers of Western Australia for 1929/30, 1939/40, 1941/42, 1950/1, 1959/60, 1961/62, 1966/8

Moreover, the assimilationist policy provided a form of reasoning which continues to lend legitimacy to those who argue that any recognition of Aboriginal entitlement to land is unjust. Assimilation directly counters notions of any distinctive Aboriginality, particularly a distinctive ethnic/racial identity which is defined by way of connection to specific geographic areas; an identity which is exemplified in the comments of the Nyungah Elders (1993) and Aboriginal Provisional Government (1993) on the Native Title Act.

The burgeoning imprisonment of Aboriginal peoples throughout this period was in part a reflection of the continuing destruction of traditional culture and social structures, and increasing problems associated with substance abuse (see, for example, Edmunds, 1989; Bird, 1987). As discussed in Chapter 8, there has been (and remains) a level at which this criminalisation was also associated with violence which offends against both white and Aboriginal law.

Criminalisation is also a reflection, however, of the interplay of the highly discretionary elements of criminalisation in the common law system and a highly racist society (refer Lustgarten, 1986; Brogden, 1982; Cunneen & Robb, 1987; Eggleston, 1976; Dodson, 1991; Carrington, 1989). Images of Aboriginal peoples as inferior and savage were given substance through the practices of a dominant society which confined Aboriginal people to the margins of that society and impoverishment.

As indicated, default in fine payments and remands into custody because of inability to pay bail are substantial causes of contemporary Aboriginal imprisonment. But while this is significant in terms of what is revealed about the relation between imprisonment and poverty, it does not explain the primary processes through which Aboriginal people encounter legal officials. Chris Cunneen (1990) has shown how changes to the strength and nature of policing, coupled with legislative amendments, can result in Aboriginal criminalisation. With Tony Robb, Cunneen has also shown that Aboriginal over-representation in the criminal justice system is often associated with public order offences (Cunneen & Robb, 1987). For example, one study found that ninety per cent of street offences in towns with significant Aboriginal populations were laid against Aboriginal people. In three-quarters of the complaints which related to language, the language complained of was directed against police (Cunneen, 1990, p.42).

Teresa Ashforth (1990, pp.201-204), cites a number of individual instances which exemplify one aspect of relations between police and Aboriginal people. Cases included one in which a group of Aboriginal men were told to "piss off" by police outside a pub. When one Aboriginal man responded by telling police to "piss off", he was grabbed by police, and struggling with them, was charged with resisting arrest. In another instance, an Aboriginal man was driving a Volvo and was stopped by police who wanted to know who the car belonged to. He commented that it was not the first time he had been asked and stated,

> Then before you know where I am I could be up for abusive language and

things like that. Now that's just another way of opening a trap for you to put your foot in it. Now a lot of White people don't go through these things. It's only Aboriginal people. (Quoted in Ashforth, 1990, p.202)

Other instances included an Aboriginal man who was questioned by police while seated in a public park. He was told they wanted to 'clean up the park', and that he had to leave. When the man refused to leave and to give his name and address, he was taken to the lock-up and later found guilty of a criminal offence for refusing to give his name and address. Aboriginal youths were ordered by police not to walk in groups of more than three; an Aboriginal woman was almost arrested for soliciting because she was seated in a public park. In both of the latter two instances white people, behaving in the same way and in the same vicinity, were not subject to police harassment.

Moreover, Aboriginal people assert that, once they are in the courts, their version of what has happened is dismissed because they are black.

The magistrates don't listen to them because they're black, because they're Nyungars. They think they're no good, think their liars. (Quoted in Ashforth, 1990, p.298)

Other studies, such as those by Bird (1987), Cunneen (1992), Dodson (1991, pp.113-152) and Eggleston (1976), give ample substance to the claims of judicial racism. Moreover, because of their familiarity with police brutality, Aboriginal people in any event frequently admit to crimes they have not committed (Ashforth, 1990, pp.161,300).

Aboriginal imprisonment rates commenced rising with the implementation of assimilationist policies in the 1950s and have remained consistently high since 1967. Aboriginal people have also remained consistently poor, despite the extensive and expensive welfare programmes which have been initiated (Dodson, 1991; Tatz, 1994; ABS, 1989); what Bropho (1980, p.131) dismisses as 'a black bread and butter ticket' for the white people who work in these programmes. Bropho (1980, p.108), comments,

Black ideas mean that land comes first. Land is the only thing that is going to solve the Aboriginal problem. Without land the white advisers' ideas on how to solve the Aboriginal problem in the continent of Australia today will be as weak as yesterday's piss.[31]

The furore over the Australian High Court decision, *Mabo v. Queensland [No. 2]* (1992) 175 CLR 1, which, for the first time, recognised limited Aboriginal rights to land has been spearheaded by groups such as the Chamber of Commerce, which claimed that such rights jeopardise the exploitation of the mineral resources of Western Australia (*The Age*, May 1, 1993). The Chamber of Commerce further claimed that, in 1990/1, seventy-four per cent of the state's merchandise exports and fifty-three per cent of the nation's were minerals. The voluble protests of such groups have also tended to divert attention away from the fact that at the same time that the High Court recognised "native title" to limited land in Australia, it not only validated, but also denied any compensation for, the alienation of all Aboriginal land prior to 1975 when the Racial Discrimination Act was enacted. The majority of Aboriginal peoples in Australia, therefore, gain nothing under the *Mabo* decision, apart from the *purely* formal rejection of the *terra nullius* doctrine and a much belated recognition of their humanity.

The limited potential to accord (some) Aboriginal peoples access to land under the subsequent Commonwealth Native Title Act (1993) does not entitle Aboriginal people to compensation for mining on their lands, nor does it give them the right to veto mining. Moreover, that legislation enables any current mining lease to be renewed without limitation, thereby indefinitely postponing any occupation of "Native Title" land by Aboriginal people.[32] Currently Aboriginal groups receive little if anything in return for the exploitation of what many regard as Aboriginal land. As indicated in Chapter 6, more than fifty per cent of Aboriginal people in Western Australia remain so economically marginalised they remain dependent upon Social Security payments (Dodson, 1991, p.479).

As in Trinidad, the massive scale of Aboriginal criminalisation has contributed to an ethnic/racial identity infused with notions of savagery and inferiority; again the concretisation of the myth of "black" as "bad" and the instilling of fear and division. Also as in Trinidad, such an identity adds legitimacy to the pauperisation and coercion of these peoples in the eyes of others. For Aboriginal people themselves, they are often relegated to live in conditions which provoke violence, and they are made to learn a sense of frustration and powerlessness as a result of their massive criminalisation (Dodson, 1991).

Memmi was sceptical of colonialist proponents of assimilationist policies. He stated that the colonist never planned 'to remake the colonised in his own image! He cannot allow such an equation - it would destroy the principle of his privileges' (Memmi, 1990[1957], p.135). Aboriginal people must remain subordinate and "other" if the "settlers" are to continue to reap the profits of the land they appropriated and to keep the colonised economically dependent. In contemporary Western Australia, the "otherness" of Aboriginal peoples is largely institutionalised through the imposition of a racialised identity as criminal under the common law.

Notes

1. Note too that I am concerned only with official constructions of criminality; that is, with data concerning those who are arrested, summonsed, tried, fined or imprisoned. Of course it is possible to argue that particular groups are "criminal" but that this is not reflected in official crime statistics, as is often the case with reference to allegations about white-collar "criminals" for example. However, such arguments are beyond the scope of this thesis and I am seeking only to undermine those notions of criminality substantiated by reference to official indices.
2. Refer Chapter 1, 'Ethnic/Racial Identity'; Chapter 3, note 1; and see above, 'Informal Justice'.
3. Even then, after 1936 a special regime to try serious offences under the criminal law was established and operated in Western Australia as the "Native Courts".
4. Refer to Brereton (1979, pp.180,181) and Premdas & Sitahal (1991). Note both Samaroo (1982) and Basdeo (1982) indicate the Indo-Trinidadian resistance to "pacification" through Christianity and liberation from indentureship was more tenacious than is often assumed.
5. Refer to Jack Davis's play *No Sugar* (1986); also to the account of Elizabeth Pearce whose husband could have been subjected to imprisonment under similar legislation in the Northern Territory because he married her while she was subject to 'The Act' (quoted in Gilbert 1977, pp.9,10).
6. Refer to Ottley (1975, p.44), and Trotman (1986, pp.116,187).
7. Memmi, *The Colonizer and the Colonized* (1990[1957], p.156).
8. It is of interest to note that discussion of the alleged leniency of the legal system also tends to be preoccupied with issues related to the treatment of violent offenders.
9. As indicated, Butler was a working class leader in Trinidad. The quote is taken from a speech Butler was alleged to have delivered to a public meeting in 1937, events at which sparked massive strikes and subsequent brutal repression; and for which Butler was to spend years in prison (Indictment *Butler v. The King*, May 9, 1937, in Jacobs, 1976, p.28).
10. This notion of equal treatment can, in the legal context, result in the notion that extravagantly diverse occurrences bear upon the determination of legal issues. In the Privy Council judgment in the Muslimeen case discussed previously, the effect of granting of a pardon in 1990 to armed insurgents in Trinidad, who had taken over the house of government and were holding its representatives

hostage, was determined on the basis of a 1615 case which concerned a man who had been called a thief, and another of 1890 which concerned a man who had applied for a licence to sell liquor, amongst others of a surprisingly diverse and strange array (*Phillip v. DPP* [1992] 1 A.C. 545).

11. Perhaps one of the most extreme expressions of some presumed commonality between all forms of social "deviance" is the aetiology from "incivility" to "criminality" found in the work of James Q. Wilson and George Kelling, critiqued by Matthews (1992).
12. Note that in Western Australia, there is continuing contention as to even the colonial nature of white and black relations in the past. A recent attempt to deny this violence can be seen in the article on the Omelmari or Forrest River Massacre, 'Massacre Myth', published in the *West Australian* on October 8, 1994.
13. See, for example, Harewood & Henry (1985, p.65); Craig (1982, p.402); Camejo (1972); Dodson (1991); Tatz (1994).
14. James was an Afro-Trinidadian activist and author. The quote is taken from his *The Black Jacobins* (1963[1938], p.283). The theoretical implications of James's position were discussed previously, in Chapter 3.
15. Omowale, 'Robinson Pulls the Doomsday Coup', *Sunday Mirror*, August 9, 1992.
16. The decline in the economy of Trinidad and Tobago actually dates from 1982, and the end of the oil boom (Barry, Wood & Preusch, 1984; McAfee, 1991).
17. Although other studies may indicate that there is a lack of correlation between criminality and poverty, I again emphasise the specificity of the colonial context. It seems to me that the history of the direct intervention of criminal law in aid of colonial economic exploitation, as well as the analyses of those who have some familiarity with the operation of law in the colonial context, such as Calathes (1990), Fitzpatrick (1989), Guha (1994), Mahabir (1980), Sumner (1982a) and Snyder & Hay (1987), indicate that this context deserves analysis on its own terms.
18. Also in direct contrast to the notion of riots and lootings as "mindless" destruction and theft is the reporting that, amidst what appeared to be a war-torn Port of Spain, the "People's Mall", a shopping complex established by the government for street vendors, did not even have broken windows. Other businesses which had security guards or were owner occupied were also undamaged. The Muslimeen had specifically been against the looting and arson associated with the coup attempt. Nonetheless, it was reported that after the coup attempt young men in Trinidad who were seen wearing new clothes and odd size shoes would comment to each other, 'A Bakr ent [isn't it]? A Bakr!', referring to the leader of the Muslimeen (Trinidad Express Newspaper, 1990,

pp.45,49; Searle, 1991, p.29; refer also to Keith, 1993).

19. Refer to Chapter 7. In any event, my own work with the Royal Commission into Aboriginal Deaths in Custody evidenced that the processes through which politically expedient results are achieved in Australia can also be the result of both subtle and unsubtle pressures (Purdy, 1992a).
20. See also Barry, Wood & Preusch (1984); Singh (1989).
21. One stark example of the relationship between Trinidad and such corporations concerns the Tesoro dealings. Tesoro was virtually an unknown U.S. company, without contacts, markets or experience. In partnership with the government of Trinidad and Tobago, Tesoro provided only US$50,000 towards the purchase of the B.P. petroleum assets, the purchase price of which was US$20 million. (Other moneys were apparently paid as bribes to government officials in Trinidad.) What Tesoro did facilitate was a "foreign government's" access to U.S. loans and markets. On the basis of its oil concession in Trinidad, Tesoro's annual revenue was to eventually top US$3 billion p.a. (Rothenberg & Wishner, 1976; Sunday Mirror, March 22, 1992). The government of Trinidad and Tobago bought out Tesoro's interest in Trinidad in 1985 for US$64 million (Holton, 1994, p.242). The need to access U.S. funds and markets has remained a significant factor in "negotiating" the very high prices paid upon the nationalisation of petroleum and other assets with major U.S. based multinationals when these have decided that they no longer wish to maintain their interests in Trinidad (Barry, Wood & Preusch, 1984; Holton, 1994; Singh, 1989).
22. The mechanisms and impact of these interventions are discussed in some detail in works such as McAfee (1991); Barry, Wood & Preusch (1984); Chomsky (1987).
23. In 1990, forty per cent of imports into Trinidad and Tobago were supplied by the U.S.; fifty-five per cent of Trinidad and Tobago's exports were received by the U.S. (T&T CSO, 1992, pp.168,169).
24. It is of note that the nature of the relations instituted through the intervention of the I.M.F. and other agencies are both known and resented by many Trinidadians. When the Muslimeen took over the Red House, one of the insurgents shot the Minister of Finance (who had arranged the loan through the I.M.F.) in the leg, saying,'This is for you, Mr I.M.F.'.
25. Refer, for example, to the comments of the Commission of Enquiry into the Carnival riots of 1881, discussed by Singh (1988, p.15); and those of the first Afro-Trinidadian Prime Minister, Eric Williams, discussed in Craig (1982b, p.395).
26. Fanon, *The Wretched of the Earth* (1990[1961], p.28).

27. I am indebted to Graham Holton for locating the table upon which this diagram is based.
28. In 1955, a missile experimentation centre was established at Talgarno, and an Aboriginal sacred site was included in the military restricted area. In the Warburton Ranges region, Aboriginal people were denied access to the only good land and water by the establishment of the Maralinga bomb site and a Commonwealth weather station (Bolton, 1987, pp.163-165).
29. The form of colonialism to which these people were subjected required them to live according to their traditional lifestyles during the wet season. Refer to a discussion of the different forms of colonialism in Wolpe (1975).
30. For a discussion of the historical significance of welfarist policies for Aboriginal peoples, see Rowse (1990).
31. Refer also to the comments of Fanon (1990[1961], p.34), 'For a colonized people the most essential value, because the most concrete, is first and foremost the land: the land will bring them bread and, above all, dignity.' See too Said (1993, p.252).
32. This particular provision was effected through the most remarkably obscure piece of legislative drafting, by which "past act" is defined to include acts which occurred in the past as well as (some of) those occurring in the future (Native Title Act, ss. 228(1)-(10),231). In fact there is evidence that the Native Title Act was enacted to appease mining interests which were concerned by the disruption and uncertainty associated with the absence of clearly defined and speedy legal procedures to determine land ownership ('Keating's Mabo Bill: Real Land Rights?', *Green Left Weekly*, December 1, 1993).

CONCLUSION

10 Conclusion

If we, dear, know we know no more
Than they about the law,
If I no more than you
Know what we should and should not do
Except that all agree
Gladly or miserably
That the law is
W.H. Auden[1]

Gladly or miserably, we agree that the law is. What we may not agree, however, is what the law is. As I have indicated, *what* law is will often depend upon *who* one is, the position one occupies in dominant social relations. For an academic or lawyer, law may be a specific form of discourse. For a colonised person, law may be a systemic violence which intrudes into her or his life and the lives of other colonised peoples. It is of note that Gramsci, when he wrote of hegemony from his prison cell, did not include law as one of the civil institutions (Hunt, 1993, p.49).[2] In the same way, the practice of law for the colonised is not likely to be perceived as either legitimate or moral; that is, it is unlikely to exercise any hegemonic force.

The perspective of law held by many colonised peoples has much in common with earlier Marxist accounts of the nature of law in capitalist societies, as has been noted by Ashforth (1990, p.308). According to these accounts, law was seen as simply a repressive force which functioned in the interests of the dominant classes, or factions within these classes. More recent analyses, however, have emphasised the hegemonic effectivity of law and the necessity to 'take it seriously' (Hunt, 1993, p.91). According to these analyses, law is seen as not "merely" instrumental in the interests of the ruling classes and factions, but as being an avenue through which significant benefits can be gained by the working and other oppressed and exploited classes and groups. Whether formulated in terms of the 'relative autonomy' of law or post-structural/postmodern analyses of disarticulation and fluidity, law is seen as a site in which it is possible to gain significant advantages for the disadvantaged (see e.g. Hunt, 1993, p.17; Frug, 1992).

The enjoiner to Left academics to take law seriously is indicative of the gulf which separates the lives of such academics from the lives of the constituency on whose behalf they purport to work (see, too, Hunt, 1993, pp.93,97). Returning to the point raised above, it is precisely because law is not a discourse to marginalised groups, but a powerful and damaging practice, that such people will inevitably take law seriously. Engagement with the practice of law is one aspect of everyday experience; such people, their family and friends, are harassed by police, required to attend court, arrested and incarcerated at massive rates, and die in significant numbers in custody. Their engagement with law is not one of choice and it has concrete ramifications; as concrete as the floor of the police cell on which John Pat was dragged and left to die, alone, at the age of sixteen.

The continuing massive and intervening presence of law in the lives of the colonised is indicated by the criminal justice statistics in Chapters 5 and 6. Something of what those statistics mean for the people whose lives constitute the numbers is indicated by Patrick Jagessar's account of prison conditions and Robert Walker's poem. But if it is colonised peoples, particularly those who are least assimilated either physically or culturally, who are largely the victims of colonial law's violence, it is not sufficient to portray them purely as law's victims.

As was also indicated in Chapters 5 and 6, many people in the courts do not appear overawed by the power of that system. The courts are filled with resistance: the refusals to keep quite, to dress well, to stand in appropriately submissive stances, to accept the court's "help", to accept the identity of criminal. If the proponents of law's hegemony spent more time in the courts and amongst the marginalised, they might be better able to distinguish recognition of law's coercive force from respect for the legal system amongst those who do not share their privileged viewpoints.

Significantly, it is the coercive force of law which colonised peoples often seek to appropriate for themselves. Whether threatened with personal abuse or cultural obliteration, law is one of the very few avenues available to such people through which to seek redress. Attempts to utilise law do not mean that "supplicants" view law as either benign or "helpful". It does not mean that such people accept law's discourse as to its nature, law's hegemony. Instead it may be that such people seek to utilise law for what they know it to be - a powerful and brutal force.

Instead of cautioning colonised peoples against the dangers of resorting to the legal system, and being appalled by the violence that such peoples on occasion resort to both through and outside that legal system, those who identify with colonising societies may do well to heed Robert Bropho's advice and to seek to understand the cruelties of their own culture. A historical analysis indicates that underlying the "civilising mission" was the economic exploitation of colonised peoples. Such analysis also indicates how that exploitation remained indivisible from its highly racialised manifestation. Far from being a mediating influence in all this, the colonial legal system, and in particular the criminal law, was one facet of the violence through which colonialism was sustained.

In this thesis I have sought to indicate how economic exploitation and racism continue to characterise contemporary social relations as these are experienced by many colonised peoples. Moreover, I have sought to show how such unequal and oppressive social relations continue to be enforced through the violence of common law systems. Perhaps more cruel than any of this, however, is how such legal systems are effective in creating environments in which violence becomes so endemic that it is colonised peoples themselves who become advocates of law's violence.

Even those who seek to go beyond inherited institutional forms of their colonisers remain trapped within the dialectics of colonial violence. In 1985, Imam Yasim Abu Bakr stated,

> As long as people continue to feed their dogs with steak and people have mansions and others have nowhere to sleep, as long as people have fast speedboats and others do not have their basic needs like food and shelter, this rule [for Muslims to 'stand out firmly for justice, as witness of God'] must be enforced.
>
> When we live in a society like this we are operating in total contradiction. Our courts are there to protect a system that guarantees the oppression of the weak by the strong and we can't stand for that. (Quoted in Searle, 1991, p.36; and Trinidad Express Newspaper, 1990, pp.11,12)

Less than five years after making this statement, Bakr led a violent coup attempt against the government of Trinidad and Tobago which commenced with the fire-bombing of the Central Police Headquarters of the Republic. While a U.S. nuclear carrier and two cruise ships headed towards Port of Spain (Searle, 1991, p.41), C.N.N. falsely telecast that Libyan ships were anchored off Trinidad and Tobago (Trinidad Express Newspaper, 1990, p.42).

During the coup attempt, hundreds of people engaged in riot, looting and arson. Omowale writes,

> Seizing the opportunity, droves of people swarmed into the streets unable to restrain themselves from looting the business storehouses.
>
> Many whose only meals had been from garbage bins and the city-dump, now filled their bellies for the first time with milk, butter, cheese and meat.
>
> Many put shoes on their feet and clothes on their backs.
>
> But some looted for greed.

> The looting and burning of business houses, however, was not part of the Muslimeen agenda.
>
> It was the reaction of an oppressed and impoverished people to the IMF-inspired fascist programme that had taken the cost of living high above their heads and ground them into the dust without mercy. (Omowale, 'The Betrayal of the Truce', *Sunday Mirror*, August 30, 1992)

The Prime Minister and Finance Minister of Trinidad and Tobago were shot, thirty-eight people were killed, more than three hundred people were injured and an estimated TT$300 million was lost through damage and fires, mainly in the central business district of the capital (*Express*, July 3, 1992).

"We" - who gain not only a material advantage but also a sense of superiority from the economic exploitation and other oppressions of colonised peoples - may do well to seek to understand how it is that we are able to maintain the privileged positions from which colonised peoples continue to resemble the fictions of colonial myth.

Notes

1. W.H. Auden's 'Law Like Love', quoted in Hunt (1993, p.139).
2. Nor would it seem merely coincidental that Robert M. Cover, the author of 'Violence and the Word' (*Yale Law Journal*, 95 (1986) 1601), had himself experienced imprisonment as a result of his civil rights activism (Hay 1992, p.142).

APPENDICES

I Comparative Demographic Statistics

Table 4 Trinidad and Western Australia
Comparative demographic and economic data[1]

	Trinidadians	Aboriginal Western Australians	Non-Aboriginal Western Australians
Neo-Natal Deaths	20.0 per 1,000 (1991)	19.6 per 1,000 (1986/8)	10.9 per 1,000 (1986/8)
Most Common Causes of Death	Heart disease and Neoplasm (1991)	Heart disease and Injury (M)/ Neoplasm (F) (1987/8)	Heart disease and Neoplasm (1987/8)
Deaths from Injury etc.	51.4 per 100,000 (1991)	180(M)/60(F) per 100,000 (1987/8)	71(M)/28(F) per 100,000* (1987/8)
Male Life Expectancy	66.88 years (1980)	58.3 years (1987/8)	73.7 years (1987/8)
Female Life Expectancy	71.62 years (1980)	65.7 years (1987/8)	79.7 years (1987/8)
Population below 30 yrs	60% (1991)	71.2% (1986)	49.8% (1986)
Illiteracy	4% (1980)	12.5% (1986)	0.9% (1986)
University Educated	1.6% (1980)	0.9% (1986)	9.5% (1986)

(continued over page)

Table 4 Trinidad and Western Australia
Comparative demographic and economic data
(continued)

	Trinidadians	Aboriginal Western Australians	Non-Aboriginal Western Australians
Primary School Only	62.6% (1980)	1.9% (1986)	1.8%* (1986)
Unemployment	20.6% (1992)	40.2% (M) 36.9% (F) (1986)	8.8% (M) 9.3% (F) (1986)
Imprisonment Rate	2.7 per 1,000 (1991)	14.45 per 1,000 (1991/2)	0.86 per 1,000 (1991/2)

* Denotes statistical data based on total Australian population

Note

1. References for these data are taken from a variety of sources: T&T CSO (1993a) and Express, October 7, 1992 with respect to Trinidad, and ABS (1989, 1992a); Thomson & Briscoe (1991); and WA Department of Corrective Services (1992a) with respect to Western Australia.

II Prison Census 1990: Trinidad and Tobago

Table 5 Trinidad and Tobago
Prison population by ethnic origin and type of prison 1990[1]

	African Origin	Indian Origin	Other	Not Stated	TOTAL
Royal Gaol	208	72	29	4	313
Carrera	340	82	42	27	491
Golden Grove	556	192	124	2	874
TOTAL ADULTS	**1,104** **(65.8%)**	**346** **(20.6%)**	**195** **(11.6%)**	**33** **(2.0%)**	**1,678** **(100%)**
Youth Training Centre	151 (75.5%)	31 (15.5%)	18 (9.0%)	-	200 (100%)
TOTAL	**1,255** **(66.8%)**	**377** **(20.1%)**	**213** **(11.3%)**	**33** **(1.8%)**	**1,878** **(100%)**

Note

1. Data are taken from a census conducted by the Central Statistical Office of Trinidad and Tobago in 1990 (T&T CSO 1993b).

Bibliography

Aboriginal Provisional Government (1993), The Commonwealth's Native Title Bill 1993, Aboriginal Provisional Government, Hobart (December 1, 1993).

Achéen, René V. & Rifaux, Francis R. (1981), 'The French West-Indies: A Socio-Historical Interpretation', tr. S. Cohen, in S. Craig (ed.), *Contemporary Caribbean: A Sociological Reader*, S. Craig, Trinidad and Tobago, vol. 1, pp. 191-212.

Afshar, Haleh (1994), 'Fundamentalism and Women in Iran', in O. Mendelsohn & U. Baxi (eds), *The Rights of Subordinated Peoples*, Oxford University Press, Oxford, pp. 276-294.

Alcazar, H.A. (1928), 'The Evolution of English Law in Trinidad', *Minutes of the Canadian Bar Association*, 12:159-167.

Allen, Hilary (1987), *Justice Unbalanced: Gender, Psychiatry, and Judicial Decisions*, Open University Press, Milton Keynes, England.

Allen, Judith (1988), 'The "Masculinity" of Criminality and Criminology: Interrogating some Impasses', in M. Findlay & R. Hogg (eds), *Understanding Crime and Criminal Justice*, Law Book Co., Sydney, pp. 1-23.

Allsopp, S.R.R. (1971), 'Caribbean English and the Problem of Communication', in Caribbean Background, 3rd, Centre for Multi-Racial Studies, Barbados, 12-18 September 1971, *Report on the Short Course Caribbean Background III*, University of the West Indies and University of Sussex, pp. 100-121.

Amnesty International (1993), *Australia: A Criminal Justice System Weighted Against Aboriginal People*, Amnesty International, International Secretariat, London (February 1993).

Anderson, Patricia (1989), 'Protection and Oppression: A Case-Study of Domestic Service in Jamaica', paper presented at Women and Development Studies, 2nd Disciplinary Seminar, Social Sciences, University of the West Indies, Barbados, April 3-7, 1989.

Appleyard, R.T. (1987), 'Western Australia: Economic and Demographic Growth, 1850-1914' in C.T. Stannage (ed.), *A New History of Western Australia*, University of Western Australia Press, Nedlands, Western Australia, pp. 211-236.

Arnold, John & Attwood, Bain (eds) (1992), *Power, Knowledge and Aborigines*, La Trobe University Press in association with the National Centre for Australian Studies, Monash University, Victoria.

Arthur, Chris & McCarney, Joseph (1992), 'Marxism Today: An Interview with István Mészáros', *Radical Philosophy* (Autumn 1992), 62:27-34.

Ashforth, Teresa (1990), 'Aspects of Communication between Aboriginal People and Representatives of White Law', unpublished Phd thesis, Murdoch University, Western Australia.

Atkinson, Judy (1990), 'Violence Against Aboriginal Women: Reconstitution of Community Law - The Way Forward', *Aboriginal Law Bulletin*, Vol. 2 (October 1990), 46:6-9.

__________ (1991), '"Stinkin Thinkin" - Alcohol, Violence and Government Responses', *Aboriginal Law Bulletin*, Vol. 2 (August 1991), 51:4-6.

Atkinson, J. Maxwell & Drew, Paul (1979), *Order in Court: The Organisation of Verbal Interaction in Judicial Settings*, Macmillan, London.

Australia. Royal Commission into Aboriginal Deaths in Custody (RCIADIC) (1989a), *Report of the Inquiry into the Death of Charles Sydney Michael*, A.G.P.S. [Australian Government Printing Service], Canberra.

__________ Royal Commission into Aboriginal Deaths in Custody (1989b), *Research Paper No. 4. The Aboriginal and Torres Strait Islander Population*, R.C.I.A.D.I.C., Parkes, A.C.T.

__________ Royal Commission into Aboriginal Deaths in Custody (1989c), *Research Paper No. 6. Aboriginal Imprisonments - A Statistical Analysis*, R.C.I.A.D.I.C., Parkes, A.C.T.

__________ Royal Commission into Aboriginal Deaths in Custody (1989d), *Research Paper No. 7. Australian Deaths in Prison 1980-1988: An Analysis of Aboriginal and Non-Aboriginal Deaths*, R.C.I.A.D.I.C., Parkes, A.C.T.

__________ Royal Commission into Aboriginal Deaths in Custody (1990a), *Research Paper No. 13. National Police Custody Survey August 1988*, R.C.I.A.D.I.C., Parkes,

A.C.T.

_________ Royal Commission into Aboriginal Deaths in Custody (1990b), *Research Paper No. 15. International Review of Deaths in Custody*, R.C.I.A.D.I.C., Parkes, A.C.T.

_________ Royal Commission into Aboriginal Deaths in Custody (1990c), *Transcript of the Inquiry into the Death of John Pat*, March 6, 1990 - June 8, 1990, Commonwealth Reporting Service, Perth.

_________ Royal Commission into Aboriginal Deaths in Custody (1991a), *National Report of the Royal Commission into Aboriginal Deaths in Custody*, vols 1 - 5, A.G.P.S., Canberra.

_________ Royal Commission into Aboriginal Deaths in Custody (1991b), *Regional Report of the Inquiry into Individual Deaths in Custody in Western Australia*, vols 1 and 2, A.G.P.S., Canberra.

_________ Royal Commission into Aboriginal Deaths in Custody (1991c), *Report of the Inquiry into the Death of John Pat*, A.G.P.S., Canberra.

_________ Royal Commission into Aboriginal Deaths in Custody (1991d), *Report of the Inquiry into the Death of Robert John Walker*, A.G.P.S., Canberra.

_________ Royal Commission into Aboriginal Deaths in Custody (1991e), *Report of the Inquiry into the Death of Ricci John Vincenti*, A.G.P.S., Canberra.

_________ Royal Commission into Aboriginal Deaths in Custody (1991f), *Regional Report of Inquiry into Underlying Issues in Western Australia*, 2 vols, Australian Government Publishing Service, Canberra. (Also listed under Dodson, P.L. (1991) below.)

Australian Bureau of Statistics (ABS) (1983), *Census of Population and Housing: 30 June 1981, Western Australia*, Commonwealth Printer.

__________ (1989), *1986 Census of Population and Housing: Aboriginals in Western Australia*, Commonwealth of Australia.

_________ (1990) *Court Statistics: Higher Criminal Courts Western Australia 1988-89*, Commonwealth of Australia (November 27, 1990).

_________ (1991a), *Court Statistics: Courts of Petty Sessions Western Australia 1988-89*, Commonwealth of Australia (December 23, 1991).

_________ (1991b), *Compendium of Demographic and Social Statistics: Western Australia*. [No publisher listed.]

_________ (1992), *First Counts: National Summary 1991 Census of Population and Housing*, Commonwealth of Australia.

_________ (1993a), *Census Counts for Small Areas: Western Australia 1991 Census of Population and Housing*, Commonwealth of Australia.

_________ (1993b), *1993 Western Australian Year Book*, Commonwealth of Australia.

_________ (1994), *Court Statistics: Summary of Criminal Court Proceedings Western Australia 1992-93*, Commonwealth of Australia (October 5, 1994).

Australian Institute of Criminology (AIC) (1992), *Australian Deaths in Custody 1990 and 1991*, Australian Institute of Criminology, Canberra.

_________ (1993a), *National Police Custody Survey 1992: Preliminary Report*, Australian Institute of Criminology, Canberra.

_________ (1993b), *Australian Deaths in Custody 1992*, Australian Institute of Criminology, Canberra.

_________ (1994a), *Australian Deaths in Custody 1992-93*, Australian Institute of Criminology, Canberra.

_________ (1994b), *Australian Deaths in Custody 1993*, Australian Institute of Criminology, Canberra.

Australian National University Public Affairs Conference, Kununurra, May 11-13 (1987), *Aborigines and Development in the East Kimberley*, Centre for Continuing Education, Australian National University, Canberra, A.C.T.

Auty, Richard & Gelb, Alan (1986), 'Oil Windfalls in a Small Parliamentary Democracy: Their Impact on Trinidad and Tobago', *World Development*, 14(9):1161-1175.

Aveling, M. (1987), 'Western Australian Society: The Religious Aspect (1829-1895)', in C.T. Stannage (ed.), *A New History of Western Australia*, University of Western Australia Press, Nedlands, Western Australia, pp. 574-598.

Bakhtin, M.M. (1986), 'The Problem of Speech Genres', in *Speech Genres and Other Late Essays*, tr. V.W. McGee, C. Emerson & M. Holquist (eds), University of Texas Press, Austin, pp. 60-102.

Baptiste, O. (ed.) (1976), *CRISIS*, Imprint Caribbean Ltd, Trinidad.

Barry, Tom, Wood, Beth & Preusch, Deb (1984), *The Other Side of Paradise: Foreign Control in the Caribbean*, The Resource Center, Grove Press Inc., New York.

Barthes, Roland (1974)[1957], 'Dominici, or the Triumph of Literature', in R. Barthes, *Mythologies*, tr. Annette Lavers, Jonathan Cape, London, pp. 43-46.

Basdeo, Sahadeo (1982), 'The 1934 Indian Labour Disturbances in Trinidad: A Case Study in Colonial Labour Relations', in Symposium on East Indians in the Caribbean, the University of the West Indies, June, 1975, *East Indians in the Caribbean: Colonialism and the Struggle for Identity*, Kraus International Publications, Millwood, New York, pp. 49-70.

_________ (1987), 'British Labour and the Rise of Labour Organisation in Trinidad, 1929-1938', in R. Thomas (ed.), *The Trinidad Labour Riots of 1937: Perspectives 50 Years Later*, Extra-Mural Studies Unit, University of the West Indies, St Augustine, Trinidad (June 1987), pp. 305-339.

Beezer, Anne & Osborne, Peter (1993), 'Orientalism and After: An Interview with Edward Said', *Radical Philosophy* (Spring 1993), 63:22-32.

Behrendt, Jason & Behrendt, Larissa (1992), 'Aboriginal Custodial Deaths since May 1989', *Aboriginal Law Bulletin*, Vol. 2 (December 1992), 59:5-7.

Beirne, Piers & Messerschmidt, James (1991), *Criminology*, Harcourt Brace Jovanovich, Publishers, New York.

Bell, Diane (1988), 'Aboriginal Women and the Recognition of Customary Law in Australia', in B.W. Morse & G.R. Woodman (eds), *Indigenous Law and the State*, Foris Publications, Dordrecht, Holland, pp. 297-313.

_________ (1994), 'Representing Aboriginal Women: Who Speaks for Whom?', in O. Mendelsohn & U. Baxi (eds), *The Rights of Subordinated Peoples*, Oxford University Press, Delhi, pp. 221-250.

Bennett, Stan et al (1992), *Mortality Surveillance, Australia 1979-1990*, Australian Government Printing Service, Canberra.

Berman, Ruth (1989), 'From Aristotle's Dualism to Materialist Dialectics: Feminist Transformation of Science and Society', in A.M. Jaggar & S.R. Bordo (eds), *Gender/Body/Knowledge: Feminist Reconstructions of Being and Knowing*, Rutgers University Press, New Brunswick, pp. 224-255.

Best, Lloyd (1971), 'Possible Solutions to Political Problems', in Caribbean Background, 3rd, Centre for Multi-Racial Studies, Barbados, 12-18 September 1971, *Report on the Short Course Caribbean Background III*, University of the West Indies and University of Sussex, pp. 158-168.

_________ (1991), 'The Nine Political Tribes of Trinidad and Tobago', in S. Ryan (ed.), *Social and Occupational Stratification in Contemporary Trinidad and Tobago*, Institute of Social and Economic Research, St Augustine, Trinidad, pp. 145-146.

Bird, Greta (1987), *The 'Civilizing Mission': Race and the Construction of Crime*, Faculty of Law, Monash University, Victoria.

_________ & O'Malley, Pat (1989), 'Kooris, Internal Colonialism and Social Justice', *Social Justice* (Fall 1989), 16(3):35-50.

Black, David (1987a), 'Party Politics in Turmoil 1911-1924', in C.T. Stannage (ed.), *A New History of Western Australia*, University of Western Australia Press, Nedlands, Western Australia, pp. 381-405.

_________ (1987b), 'The Era of Labor Ascendancy 1924-1947', in C.T. Stannage (ed.), *A New History of Western Australia*, University of Western Australia Press, Nedlands, Western Australia, pp. 406-440.

_________ (1987c), 'Liberals Triumphant - The Politics of Development 1947-1980', in C.T. Stannage (ed.), *A New History of Western Australia*, University of Western Australia Press, Nedlands, Western Australia, pp. 441-470.

Bolger, Audrey (1991), *Aboriginal Women and Violence: A Report for the Criminology Regional Council and the Northern Territory Commissioner of Police*, Australian National University North Australian Research Unit, Darwin, Northern Territory.

Bolton, G.C. (1987), 'Black and White after 1897', in C.T. Stannage (ed.), *A New History of Western Australia*, University of Western Australia Press, Nedlands, Western Australia, pp. 124-178.

Bourdieu, Pierre (1977), *Outline of a Theory of Practice*, tr. R. Nice, Cambridge University Press, Cambridge.

_________ & Passeron, Jean-Claude (1977), *Reproduction in Education, Society and Culture*, tr. R. Nice, Sage Publications, London.

Braithwaite, Lloyd (1971), 'Problems of Race and Colour in the Caribbean', in Caribbean Background, 3rd, Centre for Multi-Racial Studies, Barbados, 12-18 September 1971,

Report on the Short Course Caribbean Background III, University of the West Indies and University of Sussex, pp. 90-99.

_________ (1975)[1953], *Social Stratification in Trinidad: A Preliminary Analysis*, Institute of Social and Economic Research, University of the West Indies, Mona, Jamaica.

_________ (1987), 'Introduction: The Trinidad Labour Riots of 1937', in R. Thomas (ed.), *The Trinidad Labour Riots of 1937: Perspectives 50 Years Later*, Extra-Mural Studies Unit, University of the West Indies, St Augustine, Trinidad (June 1987), pp. 1-20.

Brereton, Bridget (1979), *Race Relations in Colonial Trinidad, 1870-1900*, Cambridge University Press, Cambridge.

Briscoe, Gordon (1993)[1977], 'The Contemporary Extension of Historical Resistance', in R. Moody (ed.), *The Indigenous Voice: Visions and Realities*, 2nd edn, International Books, Utrecht, pp. 637-641.

Broadhurst, R.G. & Maller, R.A. (1990), 'White Man's Magic makes Black Deaths Disappear', *Australian Journal of Social Issues* (November 1990), 25(4):279-289.

Broadhurst, R.G., Ferrante, A.M. & Susilo, N.P. (1992), *Crime and Justice Statistics for Western Australia: 1991*, Crime Research Centre, University of Western Australia, Nedlands, Western Australia.

Broadhurst, R.G., Ferrante, A., Loh, N., Reidpath, D. & Harding R.W. (1994), *Royal Commission into Aboriginal Deaths in Custody. Aboriginal Contact with the Criminal Justice System: A Statistical Survey*, Crime Research Centre, University of Western Australia; W.A. Aboriginal Affairs Department, Nedlands, Western Australia.

Brock, Peggy (1992), 'Aboriginal Assimilation and Incarceration', paper delivered to the T.A.S.A. Conference, Adelaide, 1992.

Brodsky La Cour, Claudia (1992), 'Doing Things with Words: "Racism" as Speech Act and the Undoing of Justice', in T. Morrison (ed.), *Race-ing Justice, En-Gendering Power*, Pantheon Books, New York, pp. 127-155.

Brogden, Michael (1982), *The Police: Autonomy and Consent*, Academic Press, London.

Bropho, Robert (1980), *Fringedweller*, Alternative Publishing Co-operative Ltd with the assistance of the Aboriginal Arts Board, Australia Council, Chippendale [N.S.W.].

_________ [1992], 'Always Was - Always Will Be Our Sacred Land', pamphlet, Fringedwellers of the Swan Valley, Guildford, Western Australia.

Brown, David (1984), 'Policing the "Riots": A Commentary', in Brown, D. et al (eds), 'Policing: Practices, Strategies, Accountability', *Alternative Criminology Journal* [Kensington, N.S.W.], pp. 65-68.

_________ (1987), 'Some Preconditions for Sentencing and Legal Reform', in G. Wickham (ed.), *Social Theory and Legal Politics*, Local Consumption Publications, Sydney, pp. 94-119.

_________ & Hogg, Russell (1992), 'Law and Order Politics, Left Realism and Radical Criminology: A View from Down Under', in R. Matthews and J. Young (eds), *Issues in Realist Criminology*, Sage Publications, London, pp. 136-176.

_________, Hogg, Russell, Phillips, Richard, Boehringer, Gil & Zdenkowski, George (1984), 'Policing: Practices, Strategies, Accountability', *Alternative Criminology Journal* [Kensington, N.S.W.].

Buchanan, Cheryl (1993)[1976], 'Sexism and Racism', in R. Moody (ed.), *The Indigenous Voice: Visions and Realities*, 2nd edn, International Books, Utrecht, pp. 697-702.

Burton, Frank & Carlen, Pat (1979), *Official Discourse: On Discourse Analysis, Government Publications, Ideology and the State*, Routledge & Kegan Paul, London.

Bush, Barbara (1990), *Slave Women in Caribbean Society 1650-1838*, Heinemann Publishers (Caribbean), Kingston, Jamaica.

Cain, Maureen (1985), 'Beyond Informal Justice', *Contemporary Crises*, 9:335-373.

_________ (1986a), 'Who Loses Out on Paradise Island?: The Case of Defendant Debtors in County Court', in I. Ramsay (ed.), *Debtors and Creditors: A Socio-Legal Perspective*, Professional Books Ltd, Abingdon, pp. 101-146.

_________ (1986b), 'Realism, Feminism, Methodology, and Law', *International Journal of the Sociology of Law*, 14(3):255-267.

_________ (1994), 'The Policing of Culture in Trinidad and Tobago and the Caribbean: Transcending the "Modern" vs "Post-Modern" Divide', paper presented at the Annual Conference of the Law and Society Association, Arizona, June, 1994.

_________ & Birju, Anand (1992), 'Crime and Structural Adjustment in Trinidad and Tobago', in *Caribbean Affairs* (April-June 1992), 5(2):141-153.

Calathes, William (1990), 'Jamaican Firearm Legislation: Crime Control, Politicization and Social Control in a Developing Nation', *International Journal of the Sociology of Law* (August 1990), 18(3):259-285.

Camejo, Acton (1972), 'Race Relations in the West Indies', in Caribbean Background, 4th, Centre for Multi-Racial Studies, Bridgetown, Barbados, 17-24 September 1972, *Transcripts of Lectures: Caribbean Background IV*, University of the West Indies, pp. 102-121.

Carrington, Kerry (1989), 'Manufacturing Female Delinquency: a Study of Juvenile Justice', unpublished Phd thesis, Macquarie University, 1989.

_________ (1990), 'Feminist Readings of Female Delinquency', *Law in Context: A Socio-Legal Journal*, 8(2):5-31.

_________ (1991), 'The Death of Mark Quayle: Normalising Racial Horror in Country Towns and Hospitals', *Journal for Social Justice Studies*, 4:161-187.

_________ (1993), 'Essentialism and Feminist Criminologies: Relevant to All - Specific to None', *Critical Criminologist* (Winter 1993), 5(4):4-20.

_________ & Morris, Barry (1991), 'Politics, Prisons and Punishment - Royal Commissions and "Reforms"', *Journal for Social Justice Studies*, 4: viii-xiv.

Carty, Anthony (1991), 'English Constitutional Law from a Postmodernist Perspective', in P. Fitzpatrick (ed.), *Dangerous Supplements: Resistance and Renewal in Jurisprudence*, Pluto Press, London, pp. 182-206.

Casimir, Jean (1982), 'Two Classes and Two Cultures in Contemporary Haiti', in S. Craig (ed.), *Contemporary Caribbean: A Sociological Perspective*, S. Craig, Trinidad and Tobago, vol. 2, pp. 181-210.

Cassidy, Brendan (1987), 'Whose Law, Which Discourse?', in G. Wickham (ed.), *Social Theory and Legal Politics*, Local Consumption Publications, Sydney, pp. 24-39.

Césaire, Aimé (1972)[1955], *Discourse on Colonialism*, tr. J. Pinkham, Monthly Review Press, New York.

Chamber of Mines and Energy of Western Australia Inc. (1993), *Minerals in Western Australia: Bedrock of the Economy.* [No publisher listed.]

Chambliss, William J. & Sbarbaro, Edward (1993), 'Creating Moral Panic, Legitimizing Repression and Institutionalizing Racism through Law', *Socio-Legal Bulletin*

(September 1993), 8: 4-12.

Chanock, Martin (1994a), 'The South African Native Administration Act of 1927: Reflections on a Pathological Case of Legal Pluralism', in O. Mendelsohn & U. Baxi (eds), *The Rights of Subordinated Peoples*, Oxford University Press, Delhi, pp. 295-323.

__________ (1994b), 'The Science of Coercion. Creating Criminology and Criminal Law in a New State. South Africa 1902-1930', unpublished MS, La Trobe University, Victoria.

Chomsky, Noam (1987), *Turning the Tide: The U.S. in Latin America*, 2nd edn, Black Rose Books, Montreal.

Churches, Steven (1990), 'Aboriginal People and Government Responsibility and Accountability', *Aboriginal Law Bulletin*, vol. 2 (December 1990), 47:6-9.

__________ (1992) 'Aboriginal Heritage in the Wild West: Robert Bropho and the Swan Brewery Site', *Aboriginal Law Bulletin*, vol. 2 (June 1992), 56:9-13.

Cleaver, Harry (1979), *Reading Capital Politically*, The Harvester Press Limited, Sussex.

Cohen, Robin (1981), 'Class and Race: Introduction', in S. Craig (ed.), *Contemporary Caribbean: A Sociological Reader*, S. Craig, Trinidad and Tobago, vol. 1, pp. 187-189.

Cole, Bankole A. (1990), 'Rough Justice: Criminal Proceedings in Nigerian Magistrates' Courts', *International Journal of the Sociology of Law*, 18:299-316.

Cole, Mike (1986), 'The Aboriginal Struggle: An Interview with Helen Boyle', *Race & Class*, xxvii, 4:21-43.

Connell, John (1971), 'The Law and the Solution of Sociological Problems', in Caribbean Background, 3rd, Centre for Multi-Racial Studies, Barbados, September 12-18, 1971, *Report on the Short Course Caribbean Background III*, University of the West Indies and University of Sussex, pp. 148-157.

Connell, R.W. & Irving, T.H. (1980), *Class Structure in Australian History: Documents, Narrative and Argument*, Longman Cheshire, Melbourne.

Cowlishaw, Gillian (1991), 'Inquiring into Aboriginal Deaths in Custody: The Limits of a Royal Commission', *Journal for Social Justice Studies*, 4: 101-115.

Craig, Susan (1982a), 'Sociological Theorizing in the English-Speaking Caribbean: A Review', in S. Craig (ed.), *Contemporary Caribbean: A Sociological Reader*, S. Craig, Trinidad and Tobago, vol. 2, pp. 143-180.

_________ (1982b), 'Background to the 1970 Confrontation in Trinidad and Tobago', in S. Craig (ed.), *Contemporary Caribbean: A Sociological Reader*, S. Craig, Trinidad and Tobago, vol. 2, pp. 385-423.

_________ (1988), *Smiles and Blood: The Ruling Class Response to the Workers' Rebellion of 1937 in Trinidad and Tobago*, New Beacon Books, London.

_________ (ed.) (1981 and 1982c), *Contemporary Caribbean: A Sociological Reader*, S. Craig, Trinidad and Tobago, vols 1 and 2.

Craig-James, Susan (1987), 'Smiles and Blood: The Ruling Class Response to the Workers' Rebellion in 1937 in Trinidad and Tobago', in R. Thomas (ed.), *The Trinidad Labour Riots of 1937: Perspectives 50 Years Later*, Extra-Mural Studies Unit, University of the West Indies, St Augustine, Trinidad (June 1987), pp. 81-139.

Craigie, Bill (1992), 'Aboriginal People and the Criminal Justice System in the 1990s', in C. Cunneen (ed.), *Aboriginal Perspectives on Criminal Justice*, Institute of Criminology, Sydney, Monograph Series, no. 1, pp. 13-17.

Crawford, I.M. (1987), 'Aboriginal Cultures in Western Australia', in C.T. Stannage (ed.), *A New History of Western Australia*, University of Western Australia Press, Nedlands, Western Australia, pp. 3-34.

Crawford, James (1994), 'Legal Pluralism and the Indigenous Peoples of Australia', in O. Mendelsohn & U. Baxi (eds), *The Rights of Subordinated Peoples*, Oxford University Press, Delhi, pp. 178-220.

Crawfurd, John (1971)[1837], 'A Sketch of the Commercial Resources and Monetary and Mercantile System of British India, with Suggestions for their Improvement, by means of Banking Establishments', in K.N. Chaudhuri (ed.), *The Economic Development of India under the East India Company 1814-58: A Selection of Contemporary Writings*, Cambridge University Press, Cambridge, pp. 217-316.

Crenshaw, Kimberlé (1992), 'Whose Story is it, Anyway? Feminist and Anti-Racist Appropriations of Anita Hill', in T. Morrison (ed.), *Race-ing Justice, En-Gendering Power*, Pantheon Books, New York, pp. 402-440.

Cross, Ulric (1988), 'The Law, the Judiciary and the Development Process', in S. Ryan (ed.), *Trinidad and Tobago: The Independence Experience 1962 - 1987*, Institute of

Social and Economic Research, University of the West Indies, St Augustine, pp. 269-279.

Cunneen, Chris (1988), 'The Policing of Public Order: Some Thoughts on Culture, Space and Political Economy', in M. Findlay & R. Hogg (eds), *Understanding Crime and Criminal Justice*, Lawbook Co., New South Wales, pp. 189-208.

_________ (1990), 'Aborigines and Law and Order Regimes', *Journal for Social Justice Studies*, 3:37-50.

_________ (1992a), 'Aboriginal Imprisonment: During and Since the Royal Commission into Aboriginal Deaths in Custody', *Aboriginal Law Bulletin*, vol. 2 (April 1992), 55:13-14.

_________ (1992b), 'Judicial Racism', *Aboriginal Law Bulletin*, vol. 2 (October 1992), 58:9-11.

_________ (1992c), 'Policing and Aboriginal Communities: Is the Concept of Over-Policing Useful?', in C. Cunneen (ed.), *Aboriginal Perspectives on Criminal Justice*, Institute of Criminology, Sydney, Monograph Series, no. 1, pp. 76-93.

_________ (ed.) (1992d), *Aboriginal Perspectives on Criminal Justice*, Institute of Criminology, Sydney, Monograph Series, no. 1.

Cunneen, Chris & Robb, Tom (1987), *Criminal Justice in North-West New South Wales*, N.S.W. Bureau of Crime Statistics and Research, Sydney.

Das, Veena (1994), 'Cultural Rights and the Definition of Community', in O. Mendelsohn & U. Baxi (eds), *The Rights of Subordinated Peoples*, Oxford University Press, Delhi, pp. 117-158.

Davis, Jack (1986), *No Sugar*, Currency Press, Sydney.

_________ (1989), 'Foreword', to D. Graham, *Dying Inside*, Allen & Unwin, Sydney, pp. vii-x.

_________ (1992), *Black Life Poems*, University of Queensland Press, St Lucia, Queensland.

de Garis, B.K. (1987a), 'Political Tutelage 1829-1879', in C.T. Stannage (ed.), *A New History of Western Australia*, University of Western Australia Press, Nedlands, Western Australia, pp. 297-325.

_________ (1987b), 'Self-Government and the Evolution of Party Politics 1871-1911', in C.T. Stannage (ed.), *A New History of Western Australia*, University of Western Australia Press, Nedlands, Western Australia, pp. 326-351.

Delgardo, Richard (1984), 'The Imperial Scholar: Reflections on a Review of Civil Rights Literature', *University of Pennsylvania Review*, 132:561-578.

de Suze, Joseph A. [Original author] (1965), *The New Trinidad and Tobago: A Descriptive Account of the Geography and History of Trinidad and Tobago* [formerly *Little Folks' Trinidad*], 14th edn, Collins, London.

De Verteuil, A. (1990), 'Madrasi Emigration to Trinidad, 1846-1916', paper presented at 22nd Annual Conference of the Association of Caribbean Historians, University of the West Indies, St Augustine, April 1-6, 1990.

Dickie, Phil (1988), *The Road to Fitzgerald*, Queensland University Press, St Lucia, Queensland.

Docherty, Thomas (1990), *After Theory: Postmodernism/Postmarxism*, Routledge, London.

Dodson, P. L. (1991), *Regional Report of Inquiry into Underlying Issues in Western Australia*, 2 vols, Australian Government Publishing Service, Canberra.

Duncan, James (1993), 'Sites of Representation: Place, Time and the Discourse of the Other', in J. Duncan & D. Ley (eds), *Place/Culture/Representation*, Routledge, London, pp. 39-57.

Dutt, Romesh (1956)[1906], *The Economic History of India under Early British Rule*, 2nd edn, Routledge & Kegan Paul, London, pp. 280-281, 293-294.

Dworkin, Ronald (1986), *Law's Empire*, Fontana, London.

Edmunds, Mary (1989), *They Get Heaps: A Study of Attitudes in Roebourne Western Australia*, Aboriginal Studies Press, Canberra.

Efremov, Alexsandr (1986), *Neo-Colonialism on the Warpath*, tr. J. Shapiro, Progress Publishers, Moscow.

Eggleston, Elizabeth (1976), *Fear, Favour or Affection: Aborigines and the Criminal Law in Victoria, South Australia and Western Australia*, Australian National University Press, Canberra.

Elder, Bruce (1992), *Blood on the Wattle: Massacres and Maltreatment of Australian Aborigines since 1788*, National Book Distributors, New South Wales.

Engels, Friedrich (1973)[1845], *The Condition of the Working Class in England: From Personal Observation and Authentic Sources*, Progress Publishers, Moscow.

Fanon, Frantz (1968)[1952], *Black Skin, White Masks*, tr. C.L. Markmann, MacGibbon & Kee, London.

_________ (1990)[1961], *The Wretched of the Earth*, tr. C. Farrington, Penguin Books, London.

Farganis, Sondra (1989), 'Feminism and the Reconstruction of Social Science', in A.M. Jaggar & S.R. Bordo (eds), *Gender/Body/Knowledge: Feminist Reconstructions of Being and Knowing*, Rutgers University Press, New Brunswick, pp. 207-223.

Farrell, Trevor (1983), 'In Whose Interest? Nationalization and Bargaining with the Petroleum Multinationals: The Trinidad and Tobago Experience', in B. A. Ince et al (eds), *Issues in Caribbean International Relations*, University of the West Indies, pp. 171-208.

Fesl, Eve Mungwa D. (1989), 'White Manoeuvres and Koori Oppression', *Social Justice* (Fall 1989), 16(3):30-34.

Findlay, Mark & Hogg, Russell (1988), *Understanding Crime and Criminal Justice*, Lawbook Co. Ltd, New South Wales.

Fitzpatrick, Peter (1978), '"Really Rather like Slavery": Law and Labour in the Colonial Economy in Papua New Guinea', in E.L. Wheelwright & K. Buckley (eds), *Essays in the Political Economy of Australian Capitalism*, vol. 3, Australia & New Zealand Book Co., Sydney, pp. 102-118.

_________ (1980), *Law and State in Papua New Guinea*, Academic Press, London.

_________ (1983), 'Marxism and Legal Pluralism', *Australian Journal of Law and Society*, 1(2):45-59.

_________ (1989), 'Crime as Resistance: The Colonial Situation', *The Howard Journal of Criminal Justice* (November 1989), 28(4):272-281.

_________ (1992), *The Mythology of Modern Law*, Routledge, London.

Fletcher, Laadan (1987), 'Education of the People', in C.T Stannage (ed.), *A New History of Western Australia*, University of Western Australia Press, Nedlands, Western Australia, pp. 551-573.

Foley, Matthew (1984), 'Aborigines and the Police', in P. Hanks, & B. Keon-Cohen, (eds), *Aborigines and the Law: Essays in Memory of Elizabeth Eggleston*, George Allen & Unwin, Sydney, pp. 160-190.

Foucault, Michel (1979), *Discipline and Punish: The Birth of the Prison*, tr. A. Sheridan, Penguin Books, London.

Franklin, E.M. (1990), 'Comment on the Mining Act 1978 of Western Australia', *Australian Mining and Petroleum Law Journal*, 1(2):24-28.

Fraser, Nancy & Nicholson, Linda (1988), 'Social Criticism Without Philosophy: An Encounter between Feminism and Postmodernism', in *Theory, Culture and Society* (June 1988), 5(2-3): pp. 373-394.

Frederick, Hilary (1993)[1981], 'The Caribs and their Colonizers: The Problem of Land', in R. Moody (ed.), *The Indigenous Voice: Visions and Realities*, 2nd edn, International Books, Utrecht, pp. 398-409.

Frow, John (1987), 'The Subject of Law', in G. Wickham (ed.), *Social Theory and Legal Politics*, Local Consumption Publications, Sydney, pp. 56-67.

Frug, Mary Joe (1992), *Postmodern Legal Feminism*, Routledge, New York.

Fryer, Peter (1988), *Black People in the British Empire: An Introduction*, Pluto Press, London.

Fudge, Judy (1992), 'Review of Social Theory after Post-Modernism: Rethinking Production, Law and Class', in *C.J.L.S./R.C.D.S.* (Fall/Automne 1992), 7(2):312-317.

Ghosh, R.N. (1987), 'Economic Development and Population Growth in Western Australia since 1945', in C.T. Stannage (ed.), *A New History of Western Australia*, University of Western Australia Press, Nedlands, Western Australia, pp. 267-296.

Giddens, Anthony (1971), *Capitalism and Modern Social Theory: An Analysis of the Writings of Marx, Durkheim and Max Weber*, Cambridge University Press, Cambridge.

Giddings, Paula (1992), 'The Last Taboo', in T. Morrison (ed.), *Race-ing Justice, En-Gendering Power*, Pantheon Books, New York, pp. 441-465.

Gilbert, Kevin (1977), *Living Black: Blacks Talk to Kevin Gilbert*, Allen Lane, Melbourne.

Goffman, Erving (1968), *Asylums: Essays on the Social Situation of Mental Patients and other Inmates*, Penguin, Harmondsworth.

Gorelick, Sherry (1989), 'The Changer and the Changed: Methodological Reflections on Studying Jewish Feminists', in A.M. Jaggar & S.R. Bordo (eds), *Gender/Body/Knowledge: Feminist Reconstructions of Being and Knowing*, Rutgers University Press, New Brunswick, pp. 336-358.

Goveia, Elsa V. (1970), *The West Indian Slave Laws of the Eighteenth Century*, Caribbean University Press, Barbados.

Grabosky, Peter (1988), 'Aboriginal Deaths in Custody: The Case of John Pat', *Race & Class* (Winter 1988), xxix(3):87-95.

Graham, Duncan (1989), *Dying Inside*, Allen & Unwin, Sydney.

Great Britain (GB) Colonial Office (CO) (1903), *Trinidad: Papers Relating to the Recent Disturbances at Port of Spain, Trinidad*, HMSO, London.

_________ Colonial Office (1938), *Trinidad and Tobago Disturbances 1937: Report of the Commission*, HMSO, London. [The Forster Report.]

_________ HM Prison Service (not dated), *Prison Service Annual Report and Accounts: April 1992 - March 1993*, HMSO, London.

_________ Home Office (1992), *Criminal Statistics England and Wales 1991*, HMSO, London.

Green, Neville (1987), 'Aborigines and White Settlers in the Nineteenth Century', in C.T. Stannage (ed.), *A New History of Western Australia*, University of Western Australia Press, Nedlands, Western Australia, pp. 72-123.

_________ (1995), *The Forrest River Massacres*, Fremantle Arts Centre Press, South Fremantle, Western Australia.

Greenberg, David F. (ed.) (1981), *Crime and Capitalism: Readings in Marxist Criminology*, Mayfield Publishing Company, California.

Gribble, J.B. (1987)[1905], *Dark Deeds in a Sunny Land or Blacks and Whites in North-West Australia*, University of Western Australia Press with Institute of Applied

Aboriginal Studies (W.A.C.A.E.), Western Australia.

Guha, Ramachandra (1994), 'Fighting for the Forest: State Forestry and Social Change in Tribal India', in O. Mendelsohn & U. Baxi (eds), *The Rights of Subordinated Peoples*, Oxford University Press, Delhi, pp. 20-37.

Haebich, Anna (1992), *For Their Own Good: Aborigines and Government in the Southwest of Western Australia, 1900-1940*, 2nd edn, University of Western Australia Press, Nedlands, Western Australia.

Hagley, Lystra (1993), 'Crime and Structural Adjustment in Trinidad and Tobago: On the Exercise of Judicial Discretion', *Caribbean Affairs* (January-March 1993), 6(1):147-154.

Hall, Stuart, Critcher, Chas, Jefferson, Tony, Clarke, John & Roberts, Brian (1978), *Policing the Crisis: Mugging, the State, and Law and Order*, Macmillan, London.

Hall, Stuart et al [Boomer, Ann, Byrne, Val, Coast, Debbie, Dallos, Rudi, Draper, Nigel, Fitzgerald, Mike] (1981), *Law and Disorder: Histories of Crime and Justice*, Open University Press, Milton Keynes.

Hammond, J.E. (1980)[1933], *Winjan's People: The Story of the South-West Australian Aborigines*, Hesperian Press, Western Australia.

Hanks, Peter & Keon-Cohen, Bryan (eds) (1984), *Aborigines and the Law: Essays in Memory of Elizabeth Eggleston*, Allen & Unwin, Sydney.

Haraksingh, Kusha (1991), 'English Law and Indians in Trinidad', paper presented at International Institute for the Sociology of Law Workshop: Sociology of Law in non-Western Countries, Onati, July 1991.

Harewood, Jack (1981), 'Unemployment and Under-Employment in the Commonwealth Caribbean', in S. Craig (ed.), *Contemporary Caribbean: A Sociological Reader*, S. Craig, Trinidad and Tobago, vol. 1, pp. 143-166.

_________ & Henry, Ralph (1985), *Inequality in a Post-Colonial Society: Trinidad and Tobago 1956-1981*, Institute of Social and Economic Research, University of the West Indies, St Augustine, Trinidad.

Harsch, Ernest (1981), *U.S. Intervention in Jamaica: How Washington Toppled the Manley Government*, Pathfinder Press, New York.

Hart, Richard (1982), 'Trade Unionism in the English-speaking Caribbean: The Formative

Years and the Caribbean Labour Congress', in S. Craig (ed.), *Contemporary Caribbean: A Sociological Reader*, S. Craig, Trinidad and Tobago, vol. 2, pp. 59-96.

Hartwig, Mervyn (1978), 'Capitalism and Aborigines: The Theory of Internal Colonialism and its Rivals', in E. Wheelwright & K. Buckley (eds), *Essays in the Political Economy of Australian Capitalism*, Australia & New Zealand Book Co., Sydney, vol. 3, pp. 119-141.

Havemann, Paul (1988), 'The Indigenization of Social Control in Canada', in B.W. Morse & G.R. Woodman (eds), *Indigenous Law and the State*, Foris Publications, Dordrecht, Holland, pp. 71-100.

__________ (1989), 'Social Justice in the Corporatist Welfare State', *Social Justice* (Fall 1989), 16(3):167-180.

__________ (1993), 'Postfordism, Social Democracy, and the Rise of the Repressive State in Aotearoa/New Zealand 1984-1993', in *Critical Criminologist* (Winter 1993), 5(4):7-20.

Hawke, Steve & Gallagher, Michael (1989), *Noonkanbah: Whose Land, Whose Law*, Fremantle Arts Centre Press, Western Australia.

Hay, Douglas (1992), 'Time, Inequality, and Law's Violence' in A. Sarat & T. Kearns (eds), *Law's Violence*, University of Michigan, Ann Arbor, pp.141-173.

Hazelhurst, Kaylene (1992), 'The Context and Future of Aboriginal and Police Relations', in P. Moir & H. Eijkman (eds), *Policing Australia: Old Issues New Perspectives*, Macmillan, South Melbourne, pp. 236-265.

Heilpern, David (1993), 'The Mabo case - Black Law, White Order', *Critical Criminologist* (Winter 1993), 5(4):7-17.

Helie-Lucas, Marie-Aimee (1994), 'Strategies of Women and Women's Movements in the Muslim World *vis-à-vis* Fundamentalism: From Entryism to Internationalism', in O. Mendelsohn & U. Baxi (eds), *The Rights of Subordinated Peoples*, Oxford University Press, Delhi, pp. 251-275.

Henry, Paget (1981), 'De-Colonization, Tourism and Class/Race Structure in Antigua', in S. Craig (ed.), *Contemporary Caribbean: A Sociological Reader*, S. Craig, Trinidad and Tobago, vol. 1, pp. 243-263.

Herskovits, Melville J. & Herskovits, Frances S. (1964)[1947], *Trinidad Village*, Octagon Books, New York.

Heuman, Gad (ed.) (1986), *Out of the House of Bondage: Runaways, Resistance and Marronage in Africa and the New World*, Cass, London.

Hirst, Paul Q. (1975), 'Marx & Engels on Law, Crime and Morality', in I. Taylor, P. Walton & J. Young (eds), *Critical Criminology*, Routledge & Kegan Paul, London, pp. 203-232.

Hoddinott, Annie (1985), *That's "Gurdia" Business: An Evaluation of the Aboriginal Justice of the Peace Scheme in Western Australia*, Criminology Research Council, Perth.

Hodge, Merle (1970), *Crick Crack, Monkey*, Deutsch, London.

__________ (1992), 'Cultural Douglarisation gets Stamp of Approval', *Sunday Mirror*, October 25, 1992.

Hogg, Russell (1984), 'Policing the 1981 British Riots', in D. Brown et al (eds), 'Policing: Practices, Strategies, Accountability', *Alternative Criminology Journal* [Kensington, N.S.W.].

__________ (1987), 'The Politics of Criminal Investigation', in G. Wickham (ed.), *Social Theory and Legal Politics*, Local Consumption Publications, Sydney, pp. 120-140.

__________ (1991), 'Policing and Penalty', *Journal for Social Justice Studies*, 4:1-26.

Hohnen, Murray (1987), 'The Rainbow Serpent and the Crock of Gold', in Australian National University Public Affairs Conference Kununurra, May 11-13, 1987, *Aborigines and Development in the East Kimberley*, Centre for Continuing Education, Australian National University, Canberra, A.C.T.

Hollows, Fred (1987/8), 'An Analysis of the Situation of Aboriginal Society in Australia and Some Suggestions for Change', *The Australian Journal of Forensic Science*, 20(2/3):235-240.

Holton, G.E.L. (1993), 'The 1956 British Parliamentary Debate on the Texas Oil Co. and the Hegemony of U.S. Oil Companies', paper presented at the History Institute of Victoria 9th Post-Graduate Conference, Melbourne, November 6, 1993.

__________ (1994), 'State Petroleum Enterprises and the International Oil Industry: The Case of Trinidad and Tobago', unpublished Phd thesis, La Trobe University, Victoria (August 1994).

Howard, Michael C. (1982a), 'Aboriginal Brokerage and Political Development in South-

Western Australia', in M.C. Howard (ed.), *Aboriginal Power in Australian Society*, University of Queensland Press, St Lucia, Queensland, pp. 159-183.

_________ (ed.) (1982b), *Aboriginal Power in Australian Society*, University of Queensland Press, St Lucia, Queensland.

Howe, Darcus & Rennie, Bukka (1982), 'The Unemployed and the Special Works', in S. Craig (ed.), *Contemporary Caribbean: A Sociological Reader*, S. Craig, Trinidad and Tobago, vol. 2, pp. 127-136.

Howitt, Richie & Douglas, John (1983), *Aborigines and Mining Companies in Northern Australia*, Alternative Publishing Cooperative, Chippendale, N.S.W.

Huggins, Jackie (1990), 'Response', in S. Janson & S. Macintyre (eds), *Through White Eyes*, Allen & Unwin in conjunction with Australian Historical Studies, Sydney, pp. 168-171.

Hughes, Robert (1988), *The Fatal Shore: A History of Transportation of Convicts to Australia 1787-1868*, Pan Books, London.

Hunt, Alan (1993), *Explorations in Law and Society: Toward a Constitutive Theory of Law*, Routledge, New York.

Hunt, M. (1979), 'The Mining Act of 1978 of Western Australia', *Australian Mining and Petroleum Law Journal*, 1(2):1-23.

Hunter, Ernest (1990), 'Images of Violence in Aboriginal Australia', *Aboriginal Law Bulletin*, vol. 2 (October 1990), 46:12-14.

Hutchful, Eboe (1986), 'The Modern State and Violence: The Peripheral State', *International Journal of the Sociology of Law*, 14:153-178.

Irvin, George & Gorostiaga, Xabier (eds) (1985), *Towards an Alternative for Central America and the Caribbean*, Allen & Unwin, London.

Jacobs, W. Richard (ed.) (1976), *Butler versus the King: Riots and Sedition in 1937*, Key Caribbean Publications, Port of Spain, Trinidad.

_________ (1982), 'Societies in Crisis: Introduction', in S. Craig (ed.), *Contemporary Caribbean: A Sociological Reader*, S. Craig, Trinidad and Tobago, vol. 2, pp. 277-280.

_________ (1987), 'The 1937 Sedition Charge Against Tubal Uriah Butler', in R.

Thomas (ed.), *The Trinidad Labour Riots of 1937: Perspectives 50 Years Later*, Extra-Mural Studies Unit, University of the West Indies, St Augustine, Trinidad (June 1987), pp. 367-390.

Jaggar, Alison M. & Bordo, Susan R. (eds) (1989), *Gender/Body/Knowledge: Feminist Reconstructions of Being and Knowing*, Rutgers University Press, New Brunswick.

James, C.L.R. (1963)[1938], *The Black Jacobins: Toussaint L'Ouverture and the San Domingo Revolution*, 2nd edn, Vintage Books, New York.

_________ (1971)[1936], *Minty Alley*, New Beacon Books Ltd, London.

_________ (1980a), *Spheres of Existence: Selected Writings*, Allison & Busby, London.

_________ (1980b)[1961], 'The West Indian Middle Class', in *Spheres of Existence: Selected Writings*, Allison & Busby, London, pp. 131-140.

_________ (1980c)[1964], 'Parties, Politics and Economics in the Caribbean', in *Spheres of Existence: Selected Writings*, Allison & Busby, London, pp. 151-156.

_________ (1980d)[1966], 'The Making of the Caribbean People', in *Spheres of Existence: Selected Writings*, Allison & Busby, London, pp. 173-189.

_________ (1981), 'The Birth of a Nation', in S. Craig (ed.), *Contemporary Caribbean: A Sociological Reader*, S. Craig, Trinidad and Tobago, vol. 1, pp. 3-35.

_________ (1984a), *At the Rendezvous of Victory: Selected Writings*, Allison & Busby, London.

_________ (1984b)[1971], 'The Old World and the New', in *At the Rendezvous of Victory: Selected Writings*, Allison & Busby, London, pp. 202-217.

_________ (1984c)[1975], 'Presence of Blacks in the Caribbean and its Impact on Culture', in *At the Rendezvous of Victory: Selected Writings*, Allison & Busby, London, pp. 218-235.

John, A. Meredith (1988), *The Plantation Slaves of Trinidad, 1783-1816: A Mathematical and Demographic Enquiry*, Cambridge University Press, Cambridge.

Johnson, Howard (1987a), 'Oil, Imperial Policy and the Trinidad Disturbances, 1937', in R. Thomas (ed.), *The Trinidad Labour Riots of 1937: Perspectives 50 Years Later*, Extra-Mural Studies Unit, University of the West Indies, St Augustine, Trinidad (June

1987), pp. 141-181.

__________ (1987b), 'The Political Uses of Commissions of Enquiry: The Forster and Moyne Commissions', in R. Thomas (ed.), *The Trinidad Labour Riots of 1937: Perspectives 50 Years Later*, Extra-Mural Studies Unit, University of the West Indies, St Augustine, Trinidad (June 1987), pp. 265-304.

Karch, Cecilia A. (1981), 'The Growth of the Corporate Economy in Barbados: Class/Race Factors, 1890-1977', in S. Craig (ed.), *Contemporary Caribbean: A Sociological Reader*, S. Craig, Trinidad and Tobago, vol. 1, pp. 213-241.

Kearins, Judith (1985), 'Cross-Cultural Misunderstandings in Education', in J.B. Pride (ed.), *Cross-Cultural Encounters: Communication and Mis-Communication*, River Seine Publications, Melbourne.

__________ (1990), 'Factors Affecting Aboriginal Testimony', paper exhibited by the Royal Commission into Aboriginal Deaths in Custody, General Exhibit:G/W/6.

Keith, Michael (1993), *Race, Riots and Policing: Lore and Disorder in a Multi-Racist Society*, UCL Press, London.

Kelsey, Jane (1993), 'Globalisation of the Trade and the Sovereignty of the Nation-State', paper presented at the Australian Law and Society Conference, Sydney, December 10-12, 1993.

Kerr, Paul [1984], 'Street offences by Aborigines: A.B.D. Report 1982: A review', in Brown et al (eds), 'Policing: Practices, Strategies, Accountability', *Alternative Criminology Journal* [Kensington, N.S.W.].

Kerr, Peter (1993), 'The Black Deaths Inquiry: A Question of Truth', *Antithesis*, 6(2):43-51.

Kerruish, Valerie (1987), 'Epistemology and General Legal Theory', in G. Wickham (ed.), *Social Theory and Legal Politics*, Local Consumption Publications, Sydney, pp. 5-24.

__________ (1991), *Jurisprudence as Ideology*, Routledge, London.

Koestler, Arthur (1970)[1956], *Reflections on Hanging*, Hutchinson & Co Ltd, London.

Kurian, George Thomas (1982), *Encyclopedia of the Third World*, 2nd edn, Mansell, New York, vol. III, pp. 1775-1788.

Ladoo, Harold Sonny (1987), *No Pain Like This Body*, Caribbean Writers Series,

Heinemann, London.

LaGuerre, John Gaffer (1972), 'Africa and East Indians in Trinidad and Tobago', unpublished MS, held at University of the West Indies, St Augustine.

__________ (1988), 'Race Relations in Trinidad and Tobago', in S. Ryan (ed.), *Trinidad and Tobago: The Independence Experience 1962 - 1987*, Institute of Social and Economic Research, University of the West Indies, St Augustine, pp. 193-206.

Lattas, A. (1992), 'Primitivism, Nationalism and Individualism in Australian Popular Culture', in B. Attwood & J. Arnold (eds), *Power, Knowledge and Aborigines*, La Trobe University Press and Australian Studies Monash University, Victoria, pp. 45-58.

Lawford, Eric (Yiji) (1988), 'Crowbar Saved My Life', in P. Marshall (ed.), *Raparapa Kularr Martuwarra: All right, now we go 'side the river, along that sundown way*, Magabala Books, Broome, pp. 1-31.

Lee, Ann (1991), 'Class, Race, Colour and the Trinidad Carnival', in S. Ryan (ed.), *Social and Occupational Stratification in Contemporary Trinidad and Tobago*, Institute of Social and Economic Research, St Augustine, Trinidad, pp. 417-433.

Ligterwood, Andrew (1984), 'Aborigines in the Criminal Courts', in P. Hanks & B. Keon-Cohen (eds), *Aborigines and the Law: Essays in Memory of Elizabeth Eggleston*, George Allen & Unwin, Sydney, pp. 191-211.

Lincoln, Robyn & Wilson, Paul (1994), 'Aboriginal Offending: Patterns and Causes', in D. Chappell & P. Wilson (eds), *The Australian Criminal Justice System: The Mid 1990s*, Butterworths, Sydney, pp. 61-86.

Liverpool, Hollis Urban Lester (1990), *Kaiso and Society*, Juba Publishers, Trinidad.

Lustgarten, Laurence (1986), *The Governance of Police*, Sweet & Maxwell, London.

Lyons, G. (1984), 'Aboriginal Legal Services', in P. Hanks & B. Keon-Cohen (eds), *Aborigines and the Law: Essays in Memory of Elizabeth Eggleston*, George Allen & Unwin, Sydney, pp. 137-159.

Mahabir, Cynthia (1980), 'Crime and Nation-Building: The Emergency Powers Act, 1970, Trinidad and Tobago', in *International Journal of the Sociology of Law* (May 1980), 8(2):129-148.

Mandel, Ernest (1969), *An Introduction to Marxist Economic Theory*, Merit Publishers,

New York.

Marable, Manning (1987), *African and Caribbean Politics from Kwame Nkrumah to the Grenada Revolution*, Verso, London.

Marcus, Julie (1991), 'Under the Eye of Law', *Journal for Social Justice Studies*, 4:117-132.

Marshall, Paul (ed.) (1988), *Raparapa Kularr Martuwarra: All right, now we go 'side the river, along that sundown way: Stories from the Fitzroy River Drovers*, Magabala Books, Broome.

Mason, Stephen F. (1962), *A History of the Sciences*, rev. edn, Collier Books, New York, p. 296.

Matthews, Roger (1992), 'Replacing "Broken Windows"; Crime, Incivilities and Urban Change', in R. Matthews & J. Young (eds), *Issues in Realist Criminology*, Sage Publications, London, pp. 19-50.

Matthews, Roger & Young, Jock (1992a), 'Questioning Left Realism', in *Issues in Realist Criminology*, Sage Publications, London, pp. 1-18.

__________ (eds) (1992b), *Issues in Realist Criminology*, Sage Publications, London.

Mauss, Marcel (1973)[1934], 'Techniques of the Body', tr. B. Brewster, *Economy and Society* (February 1973), 2(1):70-88.

McAfee, Kathy (1991), *Storm Signals: Structural Adjustment and Development Alternatives in the Caribbean*, South End Press in association with Oxfam America, Boston.

McBarnet, Doreen J. (1981), *Conviction: Law, the State and the Construction of Justice*, Macmillan Press Ltd, London.

McClintock, Anne (1994), 'The Angel of Progress: Pitfalls of the Term "Post-Colonialism"', in P. Williams & L. Chrisman (eds), *Colonial Discourse and Post-Colonial Theory: A Reader*, Columbia University Press, New York, pp. 291-304.

McIntyre, Greg (1990), 'Bropho v. The State of W.A. and The W.A. Development Corporation', *Aboriginal Law Bulletin*, vol. 2 (December 1990), 47:8.

McLaughlin, Eugene & Muncie, John (1993), 'The Silent Revolution - Market-Based Criminal Justice in England', *Socio-Legal Bulletin* (Autumn 1993), 9:4-12.

Memmi, Albert (1990)[1957], *The Colonizer and the Colonized*, Earthscan Publishers, London.

Mendelsohn, Oliver (1991), 'Life and Struggles in the Stone Quarries of India: A Case Study', *The Journal of Commonwealth and Comparative Politics* (March 1991), 29(1):44-71.

_________ & Baxi, Upendra (1994a), 'Introduction', in O. Mendelsohn & U. Baxi (eds), *The Rights of Subordinated Peoples*, Oxford University Press, Delhi, pp. 1-19.

_________ (eds) (1994b), *The Rights of Subordinated Peoples*, Oxford University Press, Delhi.

Mendelsohn, Oliver & Vicziany, Marika (1994), 'The Untouchables', in O. Mendelsohn & U. Baxi (eds), *The Rights of Subordinated Peoples*, Oxford University Press, Delhi, pp. 64-116.

Milovanovic, Dragan (1989), *Weberian and Marxian Analysis of Law: Development and Functions of Law in a Capitalist Mode of Production*, Avebury, Aldershot.

Minson, Jeffrey (1985), *Genealogies of Morals: Nietzsche, Foucault, Donzelot and the Eccentricity of Ethics*, Macmillan, London.

Misra, P.K. (1992), 'Learning the Rules of a Culture', *Sunday Express*, September 20, 1992.

Mitford, Jessica (1977), *The American Prison Business*, Penguin Books, Harmondsworth.

Moody, Roger (ed.) (1993), *The Indigenous Voice: Visions and Realities*, 2nd edn, International Books, Utrecht.

Moran, Karen (1993a), 'Government Tells Aborigines, "We're Sorry for the Genocide"', *The Freedom Socialist* (July-September 1993), 14(3):3,6.

_________ (1993b), 'Baryulgil Atrocity', pamphlet, Radical Women, Melbourne.

Moreno, Jose A. (1982), 'The Dominican Republic Revolution Revisited', in S. Craig (ed.), *Contemporary Caribbean: A Sociological Reader*, S. Craig, Trinidad and Tobago, vol. 2, pp. 311-336.

Morrison, Toni (1992a), 'Friday on the Potomac', in T. Morrison (ed.), *Race-ing Justice, En-Gendering Power*, Pantheon Books, New York, pp. vii-xxx.

_________ (ed.) (1992b), *Race-ing Justice, En-Gendering Power: Essays on Anita Hill, Clarence Thomas, and the Construction of Social Reality*, Pantheon Books, New York.

Morse, Bradford W. (1988), 'Indigenous Law and State Legal Systems: Conflict and Compatibility', in B.W. Morse & G.R. Woodman (eds), *Indigenous Law and the State*, Foris Publications, Dordrecht, Holland, pp. 101-120.

_________ & Woodman, Gordon R. (eds) (1988), *Indigenous Law and the State*, Foris Publications, Dordrecht, Holland.

Moss, Irene (1991), 'The Report of the National Inquiry into Racist Violence', *Aboriginal Law Bulletin* (April 1991), 49:4-5.

Moynihan, Patricia (1993), 'The De-Colonisation of Modern Law: Dismantling the Relation between Race and Liberal Law', in *Canadian Journal of Law and Society* (Fall/Automne 1993), 8(2):191-203.

Mudrooroo [formerly Colin Johnson] (1992)[1965], *Wild Cat Falling*, Angus & Robertson, Pymble, N.S.W.

Muecke, S. (1992), 'Lonely Representations: Aboriginality and Cultural Studies', in B. Attwood & J. Arnold (eds), *Power, Knowledge and Aborigines*, La Trobe University Press and Australian Studies Monash University, Victoria, pp. 32-44.

Naipaul, V.S. (1964), *A House for Mr Biswas*, Deutsch, London.

_________ (1967), *The Mimic Men*, Andre Deutsch, London.

_________ (1969a), *The Loss of El Dorado: A History*, Andre Deutsch, London.

_________ (1969b), *The Suffrage of Elvira*, Penguin Books, Harmondsworth.

_________ (1974), 'The Killings in Trinidad', *Sunday Times Magazine* (England, May 19 and 26, 1974).

_________ (1982), 'Introduction', in Symposium on East Indians in the Caribbean, the University of the West Indies, June, 1975, *East Indians in the Caribbean: Colonialism and the Struggle for Identity*, Kraus International Publications, Millwood, New York, pp. 1-9.

Narayan, Uma (1989), 'The Project of Feminist Epistemology: Perspectives from a Non-Western Feminist', in A.M. Jaggar & S.R. Bordo (eds), *Gender/Body/Knowledge:*

Feminist Reconstructions of Being and Knowing, Rutgers University Press, New Brunswick, pp. 256-269.

Niehoff, Arthur & Niehoff, Juanita (1960), *East Indians in the West Indies*, Milwaukee Public Museum, U.S.A.

Nyungah Circle of Elders (1993), 'The First Law of the Land - and the Second: Comments on Mr Keating's proposed Native Title legislation', R. Bropho for the Nyungah Circle of Elders (November 23, 1993).

O'Dowd, D.J., Moss, D.C., Love, D.W. & Saunders, J.E. (1991), *Review of the Trinidad and Tobago Police Service: Summary Report.* [No publisher listed: Trinidad.] [The O'Dowd Report.]

O'Dowd, Liam (1990), 'Introduction' to A. Memmi, *The Colonizer and the Colonized*, Earthscan Publishers, London, pp. 29-66.

Olive, Noel [Counsel for the Committee to Defend Black Rights] (1990), 'Royal Commission into Aboriginal Deaths in Custody. Pilbara studies: Submission on underlying issues into Aboriginal deaths in custody in the Pilbara: Based principally on the death of a "young boy" at Roebourne in 1983', P.O. Box 8048 Stirling St. Perth.

O'Malley, Pat (1983), *Law, Capitalism and Democracy: A Sociology of Australian Legal Order*, George Allen & Unwin, Sydney.

_________ (1992), 'Empowerment, Liberalism and Post-Colonial Policy. Managing Petrol-Sniffing among Young People in Remote Aboriginal Communities', unpublished MS, La Trobe University, Victoria.

_________ (1993), 'Aboriginal Criminalisation and Colonialism in Australia', *Critical Criminologist* (Winter 1993), 5(4):9-21.

_________ (1995), 'Gentle Genocide: The Government of Aboriginal Peoples in Central Australia', *Social Justice* (Fall 1995), 20:911-939.

Omowale, Abdullah Bilal [formerly Andy Thomas] (undated), *The Soul of the World.* [No publisher listed.]

_________ (1992a), 'TnT Jails Full of Africans', *Sunday Mirror*, September 6, 1992.

_________ (1992b), 'From Colonialism to Colonialism', *Sunday Mirror*, November 29, 1992.

_________ (1992c), 'The Muslimeen Fight for Survival', *Sunday Mirror*, July 26, 1992; August 2, 1992; August 9, 1992; August 16, 1992; August 23, 1992; August 30, 1992; September 6, 1992.

Ottley, Carlton Robert (1964), *A Historical Account of the Trinidad and Tobago Police Force from the Earliest Times*, C.R. Ottley, Trinidad.

_________ (1974), *Slavery Days in Trinidad: A Social History of the Island from 1797-1838*, C.R. Ottley, Trinidad.

_________ (1975), *East and West Indians Rescue Trinidad*, Crusoe Publishing House, Diego Martin, Trinidad.

Oxaal, Ivar (1975), 'The Dependency Economist as a Grassroots Politician', in I. Oxaal, T. Barnett & D. Booth (eds), *Beyond the Sociology of Development: Economy and Society in Latin America and Africa*, Routledge & Kegan Paul, London, pp. 28-49.

Palmer, Darren (1990), 'The Making of the Victorian Colonial Police: From Colonisation to the New Police', unpublished masters thesis, La Trobe University, Victoria.

Palmer, Dave & Collard, Len (1993), 'Noonook Nyidiyand Bula Koorling Ye Yer Bulup Nginning Nulla Un Dwangk Nyungar Wonki Ngacung Koorlongka [Nyungar young people, youth policy and problems of theory]', paper presented at Rethinking Youth Policies Conference: Towards a National Perspective, April 14-16, 1993, Melbourne.

Palmer, Ian (1989), 'Restoring the Past? Kooris, Land Purchases and Australian Capitalism', *Social Justice* (Fall 1989), 16(3):51-68.

Pantin, Dennis (1989), *Into the Valley of Debt... An Alternative Road to the IMF/World Bank Path*, Gloria V. Ferguson Ltd, Trinidad and Tobago.

Paul, Kirklon (1990), 'The Prison Sharks: Nothing Escapes his Gaze when he looks about', *The Light*, May 1990.

Payne, Sharon (1990), 'Aboriginal Women and the Criminal Justice System', *Aboriginal Law Bulletin*, vol. 2 (October 1990), 46:9-11.

_________ (1992), 'Aboriginal Women and the Law', in C. Cunneen (ed.), *Aboriginal Perspectives on Criminal Justice*, Institute of Criminology, Monograph Series, no. 1, Sydney, pp. 31-40.

Pearce, Frank & Tombs, Steve (1992), 'Realism and Corporate Crime', in R. Matthews & J. Young (eds), *Issues in Realist Criminology*, Sage Publications, London, pp. 71-

101.

Pemberton, Gayle (1992), 'The Sentimental Journey: James Baldwin and the Thomas-Hill Hearings', in T. Morrison (ed.), *Race-ing Justice, En-Gendering Power*, Pantheon Books, New York, pp. 172-199.

Pettman, Jan (1992), 'Gendered Knowledges: Aboriginal Women and the Policies of Feminism', in B. Attwood & J. Arnold (eds), *Power, Knowledge and Aborigines*, La Trobe University Press and Australian Studies Monash University, Victoria, pp. 120-131.

Phillips, Richard (1984), 'A Note on Police Practice and the Law', in D. Brown et al (eds), 'Policing: Practices, Strategies, Accountability', *Alternative Criminology Journal* [Kensington, N.S.W.], pp. 70-72.

Pierluigi, Claudio (1991), 'Aboriginal Land Rights History: Western Australia', *Aboriginal Law Bulletin*, vol. 2 (October 1991), 52:24-26.

Pilger, John (1990), *A Secret Country*, Vintage, London.

Polan, A.J. (1984), *Lenin and the End of Politics*, Methuen & Co. Ltd, London.

Poliakov, Leon (1982), 'Racism from the Enlightenment to the Age of Imperialism', in R. Ross (ed.), *Racism and Colonialism: Essays on Ideology and Social Structure*, Nijhoff Publishers for Leiden University Press, The Hague, pp. 55-64.

Premdas, R.R. & Sitahal, R.H. (1991), 'Religion and Culture: The Case of the Presbyterians in Trinidad's Stratified Society', in S. Ryan (ed.), *Social and Occupational Stratification in Contemporary Trinidad and Tobago*, Institute of Social and Economic Research, University of the West Indies, St Augustine, pp. 337-349.

Purdy, Jeannine (1989), 'Women, Work and Equality: The Commonwealth Legislation', *University of Western Australia Law Review*, 19(2):352-378.

_________ (1991), 'Royal Commissions and Omissions', *Socio-Legal Bulletin* (Spring 1991), 4:2-4; *Alternative Law Journal*, 17(1):32-33.

_________ (1992a), 'Royal Commissions and Omissions: What was Left Out of the Report on the Death of John Pat', tabled in the Senate, Canberra, March 31, 1992; (1994) *Australian Journal of Law and Society*, 10:37-66.

_________ (1992b), 'Racism and the Law in Australia and Trinidad', *Sunday Mirror*, [commencing] November 29, 1992.

_________ (1992/3), 'Fieldnotes: Trinidad, January 6 to December 2, 1992; Trinidad Magistrates' Courts, January 29 to June 27, 1992; Western Australia Magistrates' Courts, January 18 to March 2, 1993'.

_________ (1993), 'Valerie Kerruish: *Jurisprudence as Ideology*' [review], *International Journal of the Sociology of Law*, 21(1):101-103.

_________ (1996), 'Common Law and Colonised Peoples: Studies in Trinidad and Western Australia', in G. Bird, G. Martin & J. Nielsen (eds), *Majah: Indigenous Peoples and the Law*, Federation Press Pty Ltd and Southern Cross University.

Queensland. Commission of Inquiry pursuant to Orders in Council (1989), *Report of a Commission of Inquiry pursuant to Orders in Council [into possible illegal activities and associated police misconduct]*, Government Printer [Brisbane]. [The Fitzgerald Report.]

Quintero Rivera, Angel (1982), 'The Socio-Political Background to the Emergence of the "Puerto Rican Model" as a Strategy for Development', in S. Craig (ed.), *Contemporary Caribbean: A Sociological Reader*, S. Craig, Trinidad and Tobago, vol. 2, pp. 9-57.

Ranger, T.O. (1982), 'Race and Tribe in Southern Africa: European Ideas and African Acceptance', in R. Ross (ed.), *Racism and Colonialism: Essays on Ideology and Social Structure*, Nijhoff Publishers for Leiden University Press, The Hague, pp. 121-142.

Reddock, Rhoda (1987), 'Women in Revolt: Women and the Radical Workers' Movement in Trinidad', in R. Thomas (ed.), *The Trinidad Labour Riots of 1937: Perspectives 50 Years Later*, Extra-Mural Studies Unit, University of the West Indies, St Augustine, Trinidad (June 1987), pp. 233-263.

_________ & McCree, Roy (1992), *The Future of the Caribbean: Race, Class and Gender in the Caribbean*, Institute of Social and Economic Research, University of the West Indies, St Augustine.

Reece, R.H.W. (1974), *Aborigines and Colonists: Aborigines and Colonial Society in New South Wales in the 1830s and 1840s*, Sydney University Press, Sydney.

Rex, John (1982), 'Racism and the Structure of Colonial Societies', in R. Ross (ed.), *Racism and Colonialism: Essays on Ideology and Social Structure*, Nijhoff Publishers for University of Leiden Press, The Hague, pp. 199-218.

Reynolds, Henry (1990), *The Other Side of the Frontier: Aboriginal Resistance to the European Invasion of Australia*, Penguin Books, Ringwood.

_________ (1992), *The Law of the Land*, 2nd edn, Penguin Books, Ringwood.

Riviere, William E. (1971a), 'The Origins and Development of African Slavery in the British Caribbean', unpublished MS, University of the West Indies, St Augustine.

_________ (1971b), 'Social Stratification during the Slave Age in the Caribbean', unpublished MS, University of the West Indies, St Augustine.

Robinson, Cedric (1993), 'The Appropriation of Frantz Fanon', *Race and Class*, 35(1):79-91.

Ross, Robert (1982a), 'Reflections on a Theme', in R. Ross (ed.), *Racism and Colonialism: Essays on Ideology and Social Structure*, Nijhoff Publishers for Leiden University Press, The Hague, pp. 1-9.

_________ (1982b), 'Pre-Industrial and Industrial Racial Stratification in South Africa', in R. Ross (ed.), *Racism and Colonialism: Essays on Ideology and Social Structure*, Nijhoff Publishers for Leiden University Press, The Hague, pp. 79-91.

_________ (ed.) (1982c), *Racism and Colonialism: Essays on Ideology and Social Structure by D. van Arkel...*, Nijhoff Publishers for Leiden University Press, The Hague.

Rothenberg, Jane & Wishner, Amy (1976), 'Focus on Trinidad', *N.A.C.L.A.* (October 1976), x(8):14-30.

Rowse, Tim (1990), 'Aboriginal as Historical Actors: Evidence and Inference', in S. Janson & S. Macintyre (eds), *Through White Eyes*, Allen & Unwin in conjunction with Australian Historical Studies, Sydney, pp. 132-154.

Russell, A.G. (1944), *Colour, Race and Empire*, Victor Gollancz Ltd, London.

Ryan, Selwyn (1991a), 'Social Stratification in Trinidad and Tobago: Lloyd Braithwaite Revisited', in S. Ryan (ed.), *Social and Occupational Stratification in Contemporary Trinidad and Tobago*, Institute of Social and Economic Research, University of the West Indies, St Augustine, pp. 58-79.

_________ (ed.) (1991b), *Social and Occupational Stratification in Contemporary Trinidad and Tobago*, Institute of Social and Economic Research, University of the West Indies, St Augustine.

Said, Edward W. (1991), *Orientalism*, Penguin Books, England.

__________(1993), *Culture and Imperialism*, Chatto & Windus, London.

Salloom, Sue, Biles, David & Walker, John (1993), *Australian Prison Trends No. 1 to No. 200: May 1976 to January 1993*, Australian Institute of Criminology, Canberra.

Samaroo, Brinsley (1982), 'Missionary Methods and Local Responses: The Canadian Presbyterians and the East Indians in the Caribbean', in Symposium on East Indians in the Caribbean, the University of the West Indies, June, 1975, *East Indians in the Caribbean: Colonialism and the Struggle for Identity*, Kraus International Publications, Millwood, New York, pp. 93-115.

__________ (1987), 'The Trinidad Disturbances of 1917-20: Precursor to 1937', in R. Thomas (ed.), *The Trinidad Labour Riots of 1937: Perspectives 50 Years Later*, Extra-Mural Studies Unit, University of the West Indies, St Augustine, Trinidad (June 1987), pp. 21-56.

Sandoval, José Migual (1983), 'State Capitalism in a Petroleum-Based Economy: The Case of Trinidad and Tobago', in F. Ambursely & R. Cohen (eds), *Crisis in the Caribbean*, Heinemann, Kingston, pp. 247-268.

Sarat, Austin & Kearns, Thomas R. (1991) 'A Journey through Forgetting: Toward a Jurisprudence of Violence', in A. Sarat & T.R. Kearns (eds), *The Fate of Law*, University of Michigan, Ann Arbor, pp. 209-273.

__________ (1992a), 'Making Peace with Violence: Robert Cover on Law and Legal Theory', in A. Sarat & T. Kearns (eds), *Law's Violence*, University of Michigan, Ann Arbor, pp. 211-250.

__________ (eds) (1992b), *Law's Violence*, University of Michigan, Ann Arbor.

Sartre, Jean-Paul (1990)[1961], 'Preface' to F. Fanon, *The Wretched of the Earth*, Penguin Books, London, pp. 7-26.

Sarup, Madan (1988), *An Introductory Guide to Post-Structuralism and Post-Modernism*, Harvester Wheatsheaf, Hemel Hempstead.

Schwendinger, Herman & Schwendinger, Julia (1975), 'Defenders of Order or Guardians of Human Rights?', in I. Taylor, P. Walton & J. Young (eds), *Critical Criminology*, Routledge & Kegan Paul, London, pp. 113-146.

Scott, James C. (1985), *Weapons of the Weak: Everyday Forms of Peasant Resistance*,

Yale University Press, New Haven.

Sculthorpe, Heather (1990), 'Review of Domestic Violence Resource Materials', *Aboriginal Law Bulletin*, vol. 2 (October 1990), 46:15-16.

Scutt, Jocelynne A. (1990), 'Invisible Women? Projecting White Cultural Invisibility on Black Australian Women', *Aboriginal Law Bulletin*, vol. 2 (October 1990), 46:4-5.

Searle, Chris (1991), 'The Muslimeen Insurrection in Trinidad', *Race and Class*, 33(2):29-43.

Shah, Raffique (1992), 'Hang 'em All, Russell... but you pull the lever first', *Sunday Mirror*, November 22, 1992.

Shandley, Jock (Puluku) (1988), 'In those Days you couldn't Cry', in P. Marshall (ed.), *Raparapa Kularr Martuwarra: All right, now we go 'side the river, along that sundown way*, Magabala Books, Broome, pp. 32-87.

Sharp, James (1981), *The Life and Death of Michael X*, Uni Books, Waterford.

Singh, Chaitram (1989), *Multinationals, the State and the Management of Economic Nationalism: the Case of Trinidad*, Praeger Publishers, New York.

Singh, Kelvin (1987), 'The June 1937 Disturbances in Trinidad', in R. Thomas (ed.), *The Trinidad Labour Riots of 1937: Perspectives 50 Years Later*, Extra-Mural Studies Unit, University of the West Indies, St Augustine, Trinidad (June 1987), pp. 57-80.

__________ (1988), *Bloodstained Tombs: The Muharram Massacre 1884*, Macmillan Caribbean, London.

Skinner, Quentin (ed.) (1985), *The Return of Grand Theory in the Human Sciences*, Cambridge University Press, Cambridge.

Smith, M.G. (1991), 'Pluralism and Social Stratification', in S. Ryan (ed.), *Social and Occupational Stratification in Contemporary Trinidad and Tobago*, Institute of Social and Economic Research, University of the West Indies, St Augustine, pp. 3-35.

Smith, Raymond T. (1982), 'Race and Class in the Post-Emancipation Caribbean', in R. Ross (ed.), *Racism and Colonialism: Essays on Ideology and Social Structure*, Nijhoff Publishers for Leiden University Press, The Hague, pp. 93-119.

Snooks, G.D. (1987), 'Development in Adversity 1913 to 1946', in C.T. Stannage (ed.), *A New History of Western Australia*, University of Western Australia Press, Nedlands,

Western Australia, pp. 237-265.

Snyder, Francis & Hay, Douglas (1987), 'Comparisons in the Social History of Law: Labour and Crime', in F. Snyder & D. Hay (eds), *Labour, Law and Crime: An Historical Perspective*, Tavistock Publications, London, pp. 1-41.

Stannage, C.T. (ed.) (1987), *A New History of Western Australia*, University of Western Australia Press, Nedlands, Western Australia.

Statham, Pamela (1987), 'Swan River Colony 1829-1850', in C.T. Stannage (ed.), *A New History of Western Australia*, University of Western Australia Press, Nedlands, Western Australia, pp. 181-210.

St. Pierre, Maurice (1982), 'The 1962-1964 Disturbances in Guyana', in S.Craig (ed.), *Contemporary Caribbean: A Sociological Reader*, S. Craig, Trinidad and Tobago, vol. 2, pp. 281-309.

Sturrock, John (ed.) (1979), *Structuralism and Since: From Levi-Strauss to Derrida*, Oxford University Press, Oxford.

Sumner, Colin (1982a), 'Crime, Justice and Underdevelopment: Beyond Modernisation Theory', in C. Sumner (ed.), *Crime, Justice and Underdevelopment*, Heinemann, London, pp. 1-39.

__________ (ed.) (1982b), *Crime, Justice and Underdevelopment*, Heinemann, London.

Tarradath, Selwyn (1991), 'Race, Class, Politics and Gender in Steelband', in S. Ryan (ed.), *Social and Occupational Stratification in Contemporary Trinidad and Tobago*, Institute of Social and Economic Research, University of the West Indies, St Augustine, pp. 377-398.

Tatz, Colin (1994), 'A Question of Rights and Wrongs', in O. Mendelsohn & U. Baxi (eds), *The Rights of Subordinated Peoples*, Oxford University Press, Delhi, pp. 159-177.

Taussig, Michael (1993), *Mimesis and Alterity: A Particular History of the Senses*, Routledge, New York.

Taylor, Ian & Walton, Paul (1975), 'Radical Deviancy Theory and Marxism: A Reply to Paul Q. Hirst's "Marx and Engels on Law, Crime and Morality"', in I. Taylor, P. Walton & J. Young (eds), *Critical Criminology*, Routledge & Kegan Paul, London, pp. 233-237.

Taylor, Ian, Walton, Paul & Young, Jock (eds) (1975), *Critical Criminology*, Routledge & Kegan Paul, London.

Therborn, Göran (1976), *Science, Class and Society: On the Formation of Sociology and Historical Materialism*, NLB, London.

Thomas, J.E. (1987), 'Crime and Society', in C.T. Stannage (ed.), *A New History of Western Australia*, University of Western Australia Press, Nedlands, Western Australia, pp. 636-651.

Thomas, J.J. (1969)[1889], *Froudacity: West Indian Fables by James Anthony Froude*, New Beacon Books Ltd, London.

Thomas, Roy (1987a), 'The Profit Situation in the Oil Industry around 1937', in R. Thomas (ed.), *The Trinidad Labour Riots of 1937: Perspectives 50 Years Later*, Extra-Mural Studies Unit, University of the West Indies, St Augustine, Trinidad (June 1987), pp. 183-223.

__________ (ed.) (1987b), *The Trinidad Labour Riots of 1937: Perspectives 50 Years Later*, Extra-Mural Studies Unit, University of the West Indies, St Augustine, Trinidad (June 1987).

Thompson, E.P. (1978), *The Poverty of Theory, and Other Essays*, Merlin Press, London.

Thomson, Neil & Briscoe, Norma (1991), *Overview of Aboriginal Health Status in Western Australia*, A.G.P.S., Canberra.

Thoorrbiliny, Ruby (1987), 'The Effect of White Land Use on the Miriwoong People', in Australian National University Public Affairs Conference Kununurra, May 11-13, 1987, *Aborigines and Development in the East Kimberley*, Centre for Continuing Education, Australian National University, Canberra, A.C.T.

Toohey, John (1990), 'Towards an Australian Common Law', *Australian Bar Review* (September 1990), 6(3):185-198.

Trinidad and Tobago. Central Statistical Office (1952), *Annual Statistical Digest*, Volume 1, 1935-1951, Central Statistical Office.

__________ Central Statistical Office (1991), *Population and Vital Statistics Report 1988/1989*, Ministry of the Economy, Port of Spain.

__________ Central Statistical Office (1992) (1993a), *Annual Statistical Digest*, Ministry of the Economy, Port of Spain.

_________ Central Statistical Office (1993b), *Population and Housing Census*, Ministry of the Economy, Port of Spain.

_________ Commission of Enquiry into the Organisation, Administration and Discipline of the Police Force and Procedures on the Investigation of Crime and Allied Matters (1964), *Report of the Commission of Enquiry into the Organisation, Administration and Discipline of the Police Force and Procedures on the Investigation of Crime and Allied Matters*, Government Printery, Trinidad and Tobago. [The Darby Report.]

_________ Commission of Enquiry into Subversive Activities in Trinidad and Tobago (1965), *Report of the Commission of Enquiry into Subversive Activities in Trinidad and Tobago*, Government Printery, Trinidad and Tobago. [The Mbanefo Report.]

_________ Commission of Enquiry appointed to Enquire into the Existing Conditions at the Prisons and to make Recommendations for Reform in the Light of Modern Concepts of Penal Practice and Rehabilitation Measures (1980), *Final Report of the Commission of Enquiry appointed to Enquire into the Existing Conditions at the Prisons and to make Recommendations for Reform in the Light of Modern Concepts of Penal Practice and Rehabilitation Measures*, Government Printery, Trinidad and Tobago. [The Abdullah Report.]

_________ Commission of Enquiry into the Extent of Drug Abuse in Trinidad and Tobago (1986), *Report of the Commission of Enquiry into the Extent of Drug Abuse in Trinidad and Tobago*, Government Printery, Port of Spain. [The Scott Report.]

_________ House of Representatives [undated], Statement concerning the Report of the Commission of Inquiry into the working of the Magistracy, St George West.

_________ Prisons Department (1951), *Administrative Report of the Superintendent for the year 1949*, Government Printery, Trinidad and Tobago.

_________ Prisons Department (1957), *Annual Administrative Report 1956*, Trinidad and Tobago.

_________ Superintendent of Prisons (1946) (1947) (1948) (1950), *Trinidad and Tobago Report of the Superintendent of Prisons*, Trinidad and Tobago Government Printery.

_________ Superintendent of Prisons (1952) (1953) (1955) (1956), *Administrative Report*, Trinidad and Tobago.

_________ Working Party on the Police Service Trinidad and Tobago (1964), *Working Party Report: the Role of and Status of the Police Service in the Age of Independence*, Government Printery, Trinidad and Tobago.

Trinidad Express Newspaper (1990), *Daily Express: Trinidad Under Siege: The Muslimeen Uprising: 6 Days of Terror*, Trinidad Express Newspapers, Trinidad.

Trotman, David Vincent (1986), *Crime in Trinidad: Conflict and Control in a Plantation Society 1838-1900*, University of Tennessee Press, Knoxville.

"Unaipon", Amelia Stella Campbell (1994), 'A Ngarrindjeri Aboriginal Caring Woman Speaks Out', Poste Restante Box 205 G.P.O. Adelaide S.A. 5001 (April 7, 1994).

van Arkel, D. (1982), 'Racism in Europe', in R. Ross (ed.), *Racism and Colonialism: Essays on Ideology and Social Structure*, Nijhoff Publishers for Leiden University Press, The Hague, pp. 11-31.

van den Boogaart, Ernst (1982), 'Colour Prejudice and the Yardstick of Civility: The Initial Dutch Confrontation with Black Africans, 1590-1635', in R. Ross (ed.), *Racism and Colonialism: Essays on Ideology and Social Structure*, Nijhoff Publishers for Leiden University Press, The Hague, pp. 33-54.

vanden Driesen, I.H. (1987), 'The Evolution of the Trade Union Movement in Western Australia', in C.T. Stannage (ed.), *A New History of Western Australia*, University of Western Australia Press, Nedlands, Western Australia, pp. 352-380.

van Onselen, Charles (1976), *Chibaro: African Mine Labour in Southern Rhodesia, 1900-1933*, Pluto Press, London.

Warner, I.K. (1990), 'Comment on the 1978 Mining Act of Western Australia', *Australian Mining and Petroleum Journal*, 1(2):29-32.

Watkins, Kevin (1992), 'GATT and the Third World: Fixing the Rules', in *Race and Class*, 34(1):23-40.

Watson, John (1988), 'Introduction', in P. Marshall (ed.), *Raparapa Kularr Martuwarra: All right, now we go 'side the river, along that sundown way*, Magabala Books, Broome, pp. vii-xi.

Watson, Lila (1993)[1974], 'Minority Groups in America: Their Struggle and Ours', in R. Moody (ed.), *The Indigenous Voice: Visions and Realities*, 2nd edn, International Books, Utrecht, p. 732.

Weisberg, Robert (1992), 'Private Violence as Moral Action: The Law as Inspiration and Example', in A. Sarat & T. Kearns (eds), *Law's Violence*, University of Michigan, Ann Arbor, pp. 175-210.

West Australian Police Union of Workers (WAPUW) (1990), 'Royal Commission into Aboriginal Deaths in Custody: Overview Submission of Members of the West Australian Police Union of Workers to Royal Commissioner Dodson'.

Western Australia. *Census of October 1848*, Government Gazette of Western Australia, Perth, No. 163 (December 19, 1848).

_________ Aboriginal Justice Advisory Committee on the Implementation of the Recommendations of the Royal Commission into Aboriginal Deaths in Custody (1994), *Getting Strong on Justice: 1994 Report of the Aboriginal Advisory Council Reference Group on the Royal Commission into Aboriginal Deaths in Custody - Aboriginal Justice Advisory Committee* (December 1994). [No publisher listed.]

_________ Department of Corrective Services (1992a), *Statistical Report of the W.A. Department of Corrective Services July 1, 1991 - June 30, 1992*. [No publisher listed.]

_________ Department of Corrective Services (1992b), *Annual Report of the W.A. Department of Corrective Services July 1, 1991 - June 30, 1992*. [No publisher listed.]

_________ Department of Minerals and Energy (1993), *Statistical Digest of Mineral and Petroleum Production 1992-3* (December 1993). [No publisher listed.]

_________ Government Statistician (1912) (1922) (1931) (1934) (1942) (1944) (1948) (1953) (1957) (1963) (1969), *Statistical Register of Western Australia*, Government Printery, Perth.

_________ Health Department (1992), *Mortality in Western Australia 1983-1989, with Particular Reference to the Aboriginal Population*, Health Department of W.A., Perth.

_________ Police Department (1992), *Annual Report of the Commissioner of Police for the Year ended 30 June 1992*. In house publication.

_________ Police Department (1993), *Western Australian Police Department Annual Report 1993*. [No publisher listed.]

_________ Protector of Natives (1841), 'Report of the Protector of Natives', *Government Gazette* No. 261, July 9, 1841.

_________ Registrar General (1854), *Statistics of Western Australia*, Registrar General's Office, Perth.

_________ Registrar General (1870), (1899), *Statistical Register for the Colony of Western Australia*, Government Printer, Perth.

Wickham, Gary (1987a), 'Turning the Law into Laws for Political Analysis', in G. Wickham (ed.), *Social Theory and Legal Politics*, Local Consumption Publications, Sydney, pp. 40-54.

_________ (ed.) (1987b), *Social Theory and Legal Politics*, Local Consumption Publications, Sydney.

Wilkie, Meredith (1991), *Aboriginal Justice Programs in Western Australia*, Crime Research Centre, University of Western Australia, Nedlands (July 1991).

_________ (1992), 'W.A.'s Draconian New Juvenile Offender Sentencing Laws', *Aboriginal Law Bulletin*, vol. 2 (April 1992), 55:15-17.

Williams, Eric Eustace (1961)[1944], *Capitalism and Slavery*, Russell & Russell, New York.

Williams, Patrick & Chrisman, Laura (1994), 'Colonial Discourse and Post-Colonial Theory: An Introduction', in P. Williams & L. Chrisman (eds), *Colonial Discourse and Post-Colonial Theory: A Reader*, Columbia University Press, New York, pp. 1-20.

Wilson, Paul R. (1982), *Black Death, White Hands*, Allen & Unwin, Sydney.

Wolpe, Harold (1975), 'The Theory of Internal Colonialism: the South African Case', in I. Oxaal et al (eds), *Beyond the Sociology of Development*, Routledge & Kegan Paul, London, pp. 229-252.

Wood, Donald (1986)[1968], *Trinidad in Transition: The Years after Slavery*, Oxford University Press, Oxford.

Wootton, Hal (1992), 'Aboriginal People and the Criminal Justice System', in C. Cunneen (ed.), *Aboriginal Perspectives on Criminal Justice*, Institute of Criminology, Sydney, Monograph Series, no. 1, pp. 49-52.

Worrall, Anne (1990), *Offending Women: Female Law Breakers and the Criminal Justice System*, Routledge, London.

Wylie, J.C.W. (1986), *The Land Laws of Trinidad and Tobago*, Government of Trinidad and Tobago, Port of Spain.

X, Malcolm & Haley, Alex (1968), *The Autobiography of Malcolm X*, Penguin, Harmondsworth.

Young, Alison (1990), *Femininity in Dissent*, Routledge, London.

Young, Jock (1975), 'Working-Class Criminology', in I. Taylor, P. Walton & J. Young (eds), *Critical Criminology*, Routledge & Kegan Paul, London, pp. 63-94.

Yunupingu, Galarrwuy (1987), 'Mining and Aborigines in the Northern Territory', in Australian National University Public Affairs Conference, Kununurra, May 11-13, 1987, *Aborigines and Development in the East Kimberley*, Centre for Continuing Education, Australian National University, Canberra, A.C.T.

Zdenkowski, George & Brown, David (1982), *The Prison Struggle: Changing Australia's Penal System*, Penguin Books, Ringwood.

Index

References from Notes indicated by 'n' after page reference